EYEWITNESS HANDBOOKS

AQUARIUM FISH

EYEWITNESS HANDBOOKS

AQUARIUM FISH

DICK MILLS

Photography by
JERRY YOUNG

Editorial Consultant
DR. ROBERT GOLDSTEIN

DORLING KINDERSLEY

London • New York • Stuttgart

A DORLING KINDERSLEY BOOK

Important Notice

The publisher has made every effort to ensure that the coloration of each fish has been reproduced precisely, but because the color of some species changes under the stress of photography, this may not have been achieved in every case.

Project Editor Jane Cooke
Project Art Editor Louise Bruce
Assistant Editor Lesley Malkin
Series Editor Jonathan Metcalf
Series Art Editor Spencer Holbrook
Production Controller Adrian Gathercole
U.S. Consultant Dr. Robert Goldstein
U.S. Editor Charles A. Wills

First American Edition, 1993
2 4 6 8 10 9 7 5 3

Published in the United States by Dorling Kindersley, Inc.,
232 Madison Avenue, New York 10016

Library of Congress Cataloging-in-Publication Data

Mills, Dick.
Aquarium Fish / Dick Mills.--1st American ed.
p. cm.-- (Eyewitness handbooks)
Includes index.
ISBN 1-56458-293-0 (flexibinding) ISBN 1-56458-294-9 (hardcover)
1. Aquarium Fishes--Identification. 2. Aquarium fishes--Pictorial works.
I. Title. II. Series
SF467.M55 1993
639.3'4--dc20 93-3155 CIP

Computer page makeup by Adam Moore
Text film output by The Right Type, Great Britain
Reproduced by Colourscan, Singapore
Printed and bound by Kyodo Printing Co., Singapore

CONTENTS

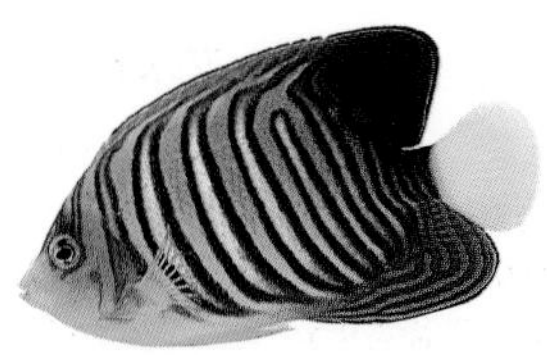

AUTHOR'S INTRODUCTION

There are now hundreds of strangely shaped and wonderfully colored fish to choose for the aquarium. Caring for them makes only modest demands on time and requires little technical knowledge. Dramatic improvements in aquarium equipment, collecting, breeding, and shipping have made the intriguing hobby of fish-keeping easier than ever before.

KOI
The result of dedicated fish cultivation spanning many centuries.

THE WIDE RANGE of fish that can be kept in an aquarium fall into one of four distinct areas, listed here in order of popularity: tropical freshwater species, tropical marine species, coldwater freshwater species, and, to a lesser extent, coldwater marine species. Fish are presented in this book within these divisions. Although many cold-loving freshwater fishes, such as Koi and Goldfish, are kept in garden ponds, it is the freshwater tropical species that are the most popular, because they are easy to keep.

ORIGINS OF FISH-KEEPING

Modern fish-keeping developed gradually from the basic need for food. Food fish were formerly the exclusive privilege of people living by the sea or rivers, as storing live fish was impractical. Keeping fish in captivity, therefore, became a rare luxury for inland dwellers. The first captive fishes are likely to have been members of the carp family. Over the years, fish-keepers may have learned to recognize individuals and then become attached to their charges, and it is likely that an occasional genetic sport, or non-standard colored fish, would appear and draw greater attention. Such fish would be segregated and kept for their appearance rather than their meat, and so the fish-keeping hobby was born.

THE HOBBY DEVELOPS

It is thought that the Ancient Egyptians were among the very first aquarists. Frescoes in their tombs indicate that fish were regarded by them as sacred. The Romans kept both freshwater and marine species in public aquariums, the former to sell as food, and the latter as decorative status symbols. But it was in China and Japan that fish-keeping really became a

ROMAN FOUNTAIN DETAIL
The Romans kept fish for food and for decoration; this mosaic dates from the 4th century AD.

PARIS EXHIBITION 1867
Fish-fanciers gather to admire the spectacular tropical marine aquarium.

culture. In the Sung Dynasty (AD 970–1279), the keeping of red carp was a common practice, and once regular exports of these fish arrived in Japan in the 1500s, their formal recognition and appreciation was established. The hobby reached Europe in the 17th century, and Goldfish were introduced to America a century later. The first major public aquarium was erected in the Zoological Gardens of London, England, in 1853.

FISH FOLLIES
Enthusiam for fish-keeping led to exotic inventions, such as this combined aquarium and terrarium.

NEW DISCOVERIES
Until recent years, new species were still being recorded with colorful drawings.

Modern Fish-keeping

The most realistic contribution that modern fish-keepers can make toward conservation is to observe the requirements and breeding of fish in their care and to write about what they've seen. With clearer understanding, fishes could be bred in commercial quantities, leaving natural populations untouched. Indeed, many freshwater fishes are already bred in captivity. However, aquarists should be aware of the current reality of collecting fish. Cyanide, for example, may be used to capture coral reef fish, and transportation conditions can be unconscionably crowded. Furthermore, there is little sense buying fish that cannot adjust to aquarium living, especially certain marine fishes with specialized feeding habits. Many countries are now limiting, or even banning, certain aquarium exports until habitats and fish stocks have recovered.

Club Regalia
National fish-keeping federations work to promote the hobby.

Aims and Limitations

This book illustrates all of the fish commonly available to the aquarist, plus some of the more unusual species for the specialist breeder. Some juveniles (often the most popular) have been photographed for this book, and this, together with the stress of photography, means that coloration and markings may differ from those of adult specimens, or from fish in their natural environments. The mix of photography and definitive text nevertheless provides everything the aquarist needs to start and stock a rewarding aquarium.

Home Sweet Home
Aquariums are available in many forms, including the high-tech model shown above. The hobbyist should always try to include features of the fish's natural habitat (left).

How This Book Works

THIS BOOK is arranged in four parts: tropical freshwater fishes, coldwater freshwater fishes, tropical marine fishes, and coldwater marine fishes. These are not scientific groupings, but are recognized and widely used by fish-keepers. Each section is further divided into fish families or groups, in which the species appear in alphabetical order by their scientific names. The page below explains a typical species entry.

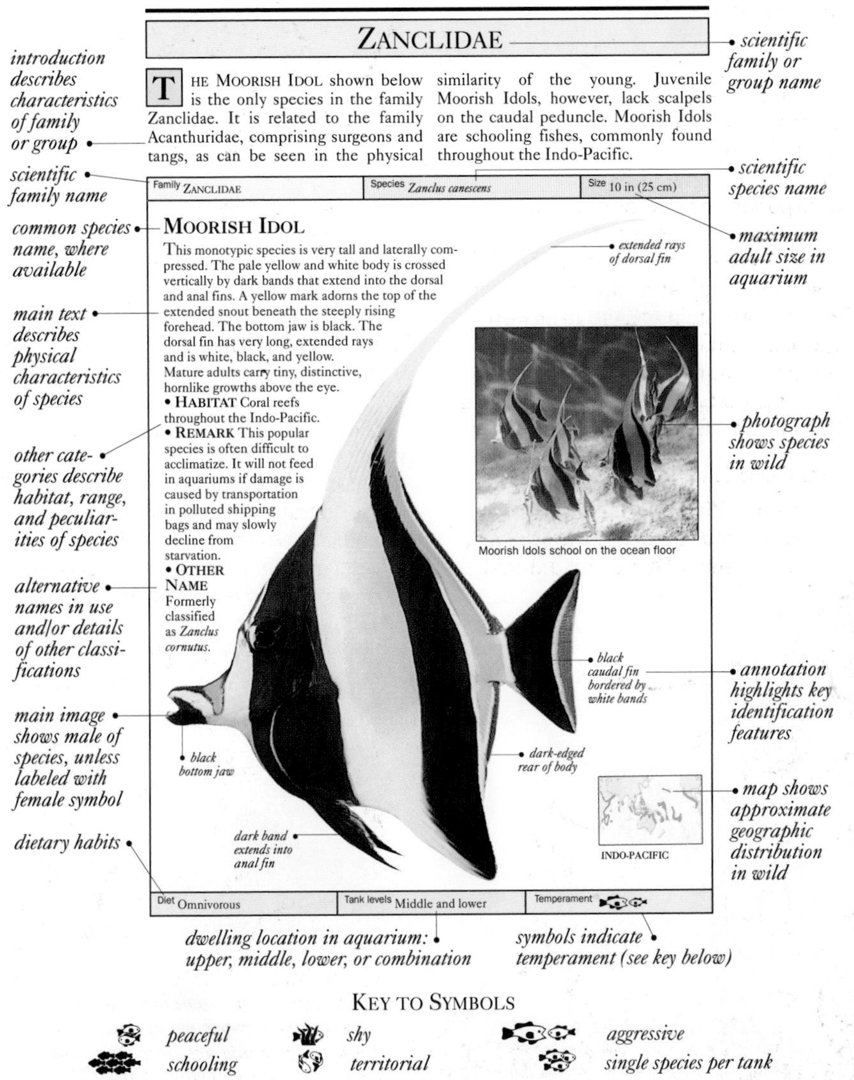

ZANCLIDAE

THE MOORISH IDOL shown below is the only species in the family Zanclidae. It is related to the family Acanthuridae, comprising surgeons and tangs, as can be seen in the physical similarity of the young. Juvenile Moorish Idols, however, lack scalpels on the caudal peduncle. Moorish Idols are schooling fishes, commonly found throughout the Indo-Pacific.

Family ZANCLIDAE	Species *Zanclus canescens*	Size 10 in (25 cm)

MOORISH IDOL

This monotypic species is very tall and laterally compressed. The pale yellow and white body is crossed vertically by dark bands that extend into the dorsal and anal fins. A yellow mark adorns the top of the extended snout beneath the steeply rising forehead. The bottom jaw is black. The dorsal fin has very long, extended rays and is white, black, and yellow. Mature adults carry tiny, distinctive, hornlike growths above the eye.

• HABITAT Coral reefs throughout the Indo-Pacific.

• REMARK This popular species is often difficult to acclimatize. It will not feed in aquariums if damage is caused by transportation in polluted shipping bags and may slowly decline from starvation.

• OTHER NAME Formerly classified as *Zanclus cornutus*.

Moorish Idols school on the ocean floor

INDO-PACIFIC

Diet Omnivorous	Tank levels Middle and lower	Temperament

KEY TO SYMBOLS

peaceful · shy · aggressive

schooling · territorial · single species per tank

WHAT IS A FISH?

CERTAIN PARALLELS can be drawn between the structure of a fish and a human: both have a skeleton supporting muscles and a heart that supplies blood to all parts of the body. A human's five senses are also present in the fish but are modified as required. However, the similarities end here, as fundamental changes occurred when life forms adapted to living on land. The greatest difference is in the fish's means of motion and maneuverability: fish are usually propelled by movements of the tail stem (caudal peduncle), with the fins acting as stabilizers. Nostrils are used normally only for smelling and play no part in respiration. Generally, a fish's skin is protected by scales that reduce friction and protect the soft tissues from predators, parasites, and even sunburn. The position and shape of a fish's mouth depends on its feeding habit and dwelling level in the water.

FISH MOUTHS

Fish with upturned (superior) mouths are surface feeders; a downturned (inferior) mouth facilitates feeding from the streambed; and a mouth situated at the tip of the snout (terminal) often indicates a midwater feeder.

SUPERIOR

INFERIOR

TERMINAL

dorsal fin

eye

mouth

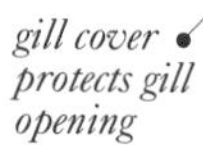

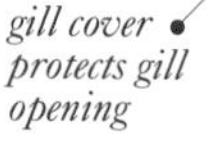

gill cover protects gill opening

pectoral fin

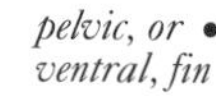

pelvic, or ventral, fin

FISH COVERINGS

The majority of scale types fall into two categories: ctenoid, with small teeth on the rear edge; and cycloid, with smooth edges. Scutes are bony plates found on many catfishes.

CTENOID SCALES

CYCLOID SCALES

Eye Structure

As fish eyes are carried on the sides of the head, fish do not have binocular vision, and judgment of distances is often inaccurate. Colors, however, are perceived well. Focusing is achieved by movements of a fixed-shape lens, while in humans, it is the lens shape itself that is adjusted.

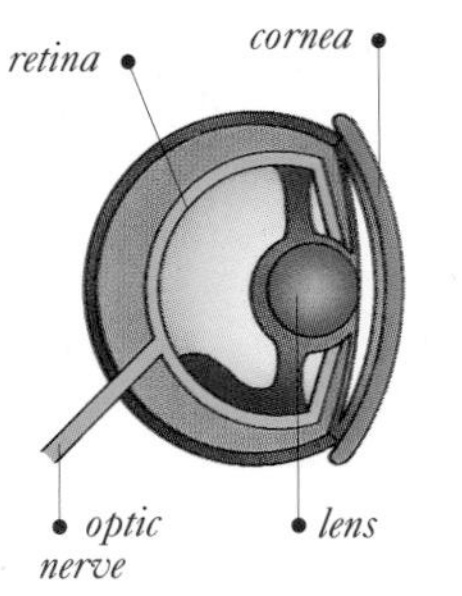

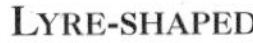

LYRE-SHAPED

BROAD

CRESCENT

ROUND

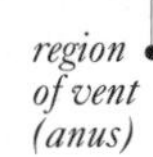

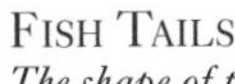

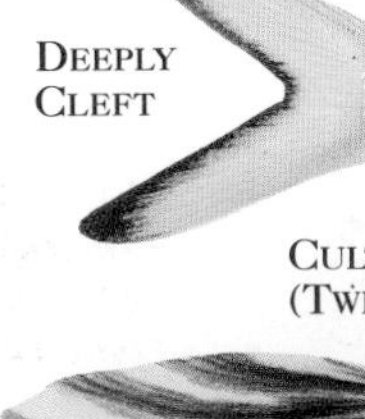

DEEPLY CLEFT

Fish Tails

The shape of the caudal fin affects swimming performance, and its colors may aid identification between species or provide camouflage. The lyre-shaped and deeply cleft tails shown here facilitate speed. Bright patterns assist identification on the broad and crescent tails, and sex differentiation on the round tail. Fins are cultivated for decoration only, and do not enhance function.

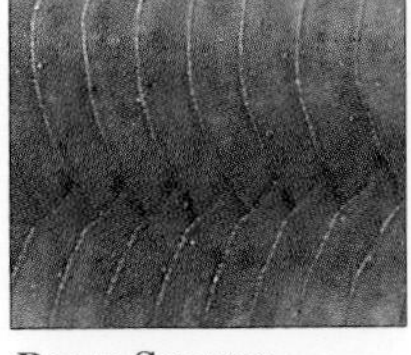

BONY SCUTES

CULTIVATED (TWINTAIL)

HOW FISH FUNCTION

FISH HAVE CERTAIN specialized functions that enable them to survive in water: gills instead of lungs, swim bladders to maintain buoyancy, and the "lateral line system" to detect changes in the fish's surroundings by a form of echo location.

BREATHING

Fish "breathe" by drawing water in through the mouth and passing it over the gills. Oxygen in the water is absorbed by the gill filaments and then passed into the blood. Meanwhile, carbon dioxide and other wastes are expelled. Some species have developed extra breathing organs for collecting oxygen in stagnating waters or in waters with decaying plants, where oxygen levels are low. Members of the anabantid family, for example, have an auxiliary organ near the gills that holds atmospheric air gulped from the surface and extracts oxygen from it. This mazelike organ has prompted the popular name of "labyrinth" fishes. Some catfishes also gulp air and extract oxygen in a capillary-rich offshoot of the gut.

SWIM BLADDER

Most fish have a gas-filled bladder that acts as a buoyancy compensation device, enabling them to maintain position anywhere in the water. The bladder automatically inflates or deflates to give the fish neutral buoyancy, equalizing the fish's weight with that of the surrounding water. Some species use their swim bladder to make or to amplify sounds.

SIXTH SENSE

Fish can navigate by detecting external vibrations through tiny scale openings along the "lateral line."

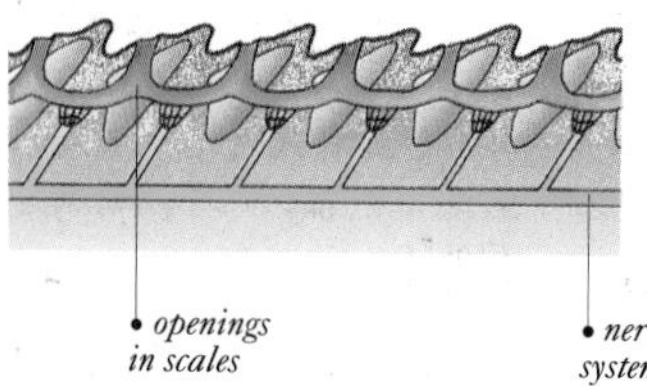

THE GILLS

Gills absorb oxygen from water as it passes into the mouth and out through the gill cavity.

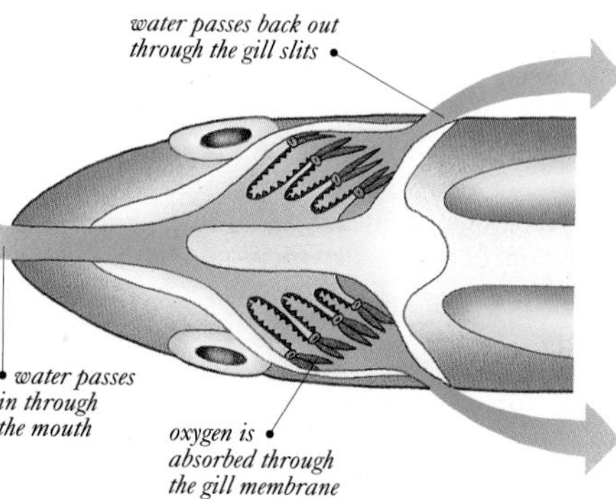

SIGHT AND SMELL

Sight is not as important to fish as it is to humans, as many fish can navigate and locate food in the darkest and murkiest waters by using their lateral line system (see below) to detect objects. A fish's eyes do not need eyelids because they are permanently lubricated by the surrounding water (see p.11). A fish's sense of smell is much more sensitive than a humans', and a fish has extra taste buds, usually on barbels and fins.

LATERAL LINE SYSTEM

A fish's nervous system is linked to the outside world through tiny perforations in a single row of scales known as the lateral line. The row runs horizontally along the length of

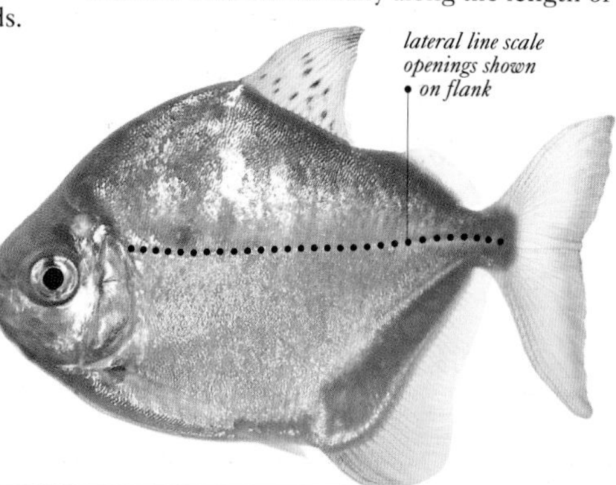

the fish. Vibrations caused by the fish's own movements are reflected back from obstacles or by other fish and are then detected by nerve endings deep inside the "portholes" in the lateral line scales.

Osmosis

A fish's skin acts as a semipermeable membrane, or a one-way transfer system for water. Osmosis causes fluid to diffuse through this membrane until there is an equal concentration on both sides of the membrane. The fluid of a freshwater fish's body is more concentrated than the liquid in which it lives. Thus, water constantly passes into the fish. To avoid bursting, freshwater fishes excrete as much water as possible and drink little. Conversely, marine fishes lose water to the more concentrated sea water outside, and must drink constantly but excrete little. Few fish can pass from one type of water to the other without distress.

FRESHWATER FISH

water passes through skin, diluting more concentrated fluid within

excess water is passed out

MARINE FISH

water is drunk to replenish fluids

water passes out to dilute more concentrated fluid outside

WATER BALANCE
Freshwater fishes absorb outside water, while marine fishes lose it to the outside.

Food-Finding Organs

A fish's ability to sense food is aided by taste buds on the ends of barbels, such as those of the catfishes, and on the hairlike cirri carried by blennies. Other fish, notably the gouramies, carry sensory cells on the tips of their pelvic fins.

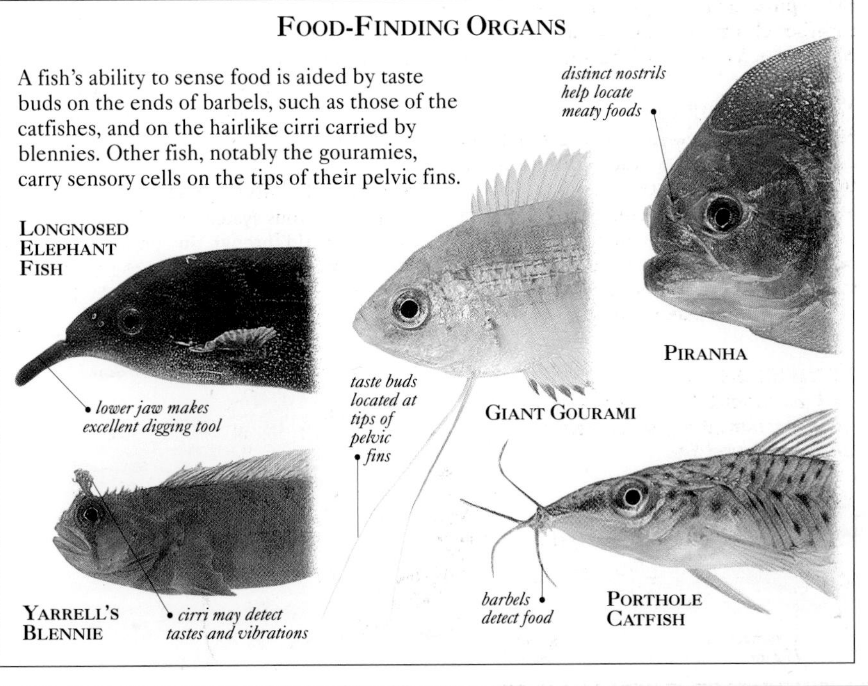

ADAPTING TO THE ENVIRONMENT

THE MOST DIVERSE adaptations to the shape and appearance of fish occur in fresh waters, where fish must cope with high or low water levels, fast or slow water flow, wide temperature ranges, and sparse or dense vegetation. Marine fishes adapt principally for species recognition, camouflage, and defense.

BODY SHAPE

The shape of a fish is the direct result of its environment. Fish that inhabit fast-flowing rivers, for example, are often more streamlined than the disk-shaped fish of shallow backwaters. Freshwater fishes may be flat-bottomed to hug the riverbed; thus avoiding being swept away by strong currents. Species with tall, thin (laterally compressed) bodies are often found living among plant stems in lakes, while fish with flat dorsal profiles swim just below the water's surface.

FUSIFORM
Basic shape for fast swimming in open waters.

TALL AND THIN
Its shape allows this fish to move easily between plants.

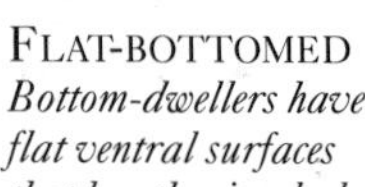

FLAT-BOTTOMED
Bottom-dwellers have flat ventral surfaces that hug the riverbed.

DEEP-SECTIONED
Deep, keel-like bodies house powerful muscles that enable the fish to leave the water, using their pelvic fins.

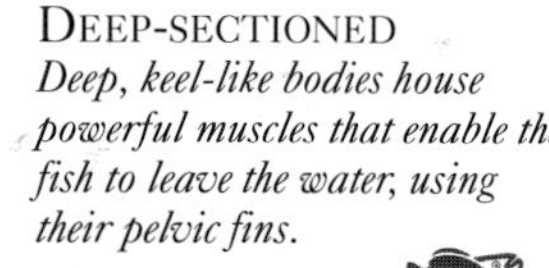

FLAT-TOPPED
Fish of this shape swim just beneath the surface.

CYLINDRICAL
Fish with slim, sinuous bodies can hide easily among plant roots and rocks.

Self-preservation

Fish have evolved defenses to deal with the dangers posed by predators. Sharp, erectile fins, for example, prevent the hunted from being pried from a safe crevice or swallowed, and some species excrete poison when danger threatens. Some fish generate electricity (which is used by other species as a navigational aid) to stun their enemies.

Surprise Size
The Porcupinefish can inflate its body to intimidate predators.

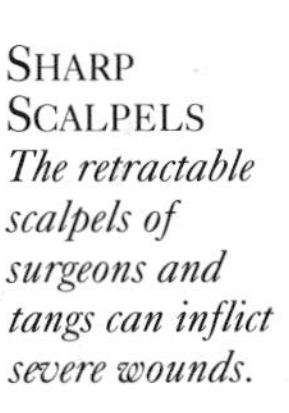

Venomous Spines
Lionfish fin rays contain powerful poison.

Sharp Scalpels
The retractable scalpels of surgeons and tangs can inflict severe wounds.

Coloration

The dazzling colors of fish, so admired by aquarists, have very practical purposes: recognizing fellow species and camouflage in the face of danger are priorities, but some fish mimic the colors of other fish for predatory ends. Colors intensify at breeding times to warn off others, and patterns may also help young fish recognize their parents.

Eye Protection
False eyes on tails or flanks confound predatory observers, while stripes hide real eyes.

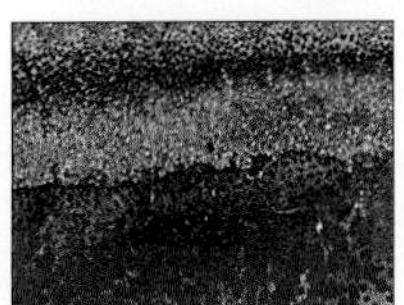

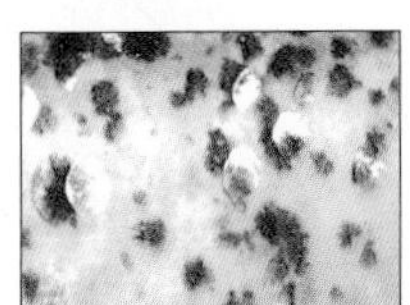

Making Color
Color is produced by light-reflecting crystals of guanin under the skin or by skin pigmentation.

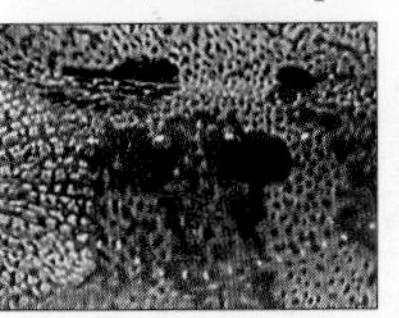

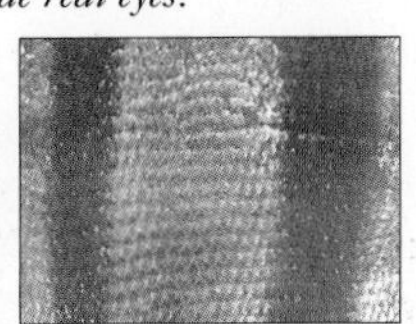

Hide and Seek
Vertical stripes and blotches may conceal the outline of fish among corals and plants.

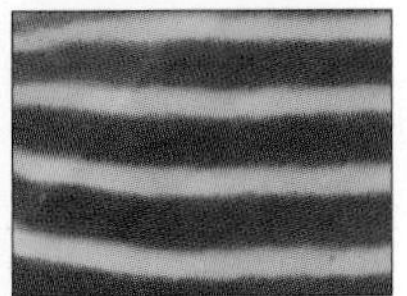

Young and Old
The colors of juvenile marine angelfish (left) alter dramatically in adulthood (right).

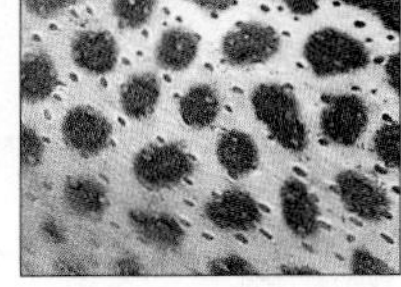

Who's Who?
Color patterns are vital for identification among the crowds of fish on coral reefs.

How Fish Breed

A HOST OF SUBTLE ADAPTATIONS distinguish the breeding methods of different fish families, although there are two general breeding categories. Most fishes (the "egg-layers") lay and fertilize their eggs externally; the eggs of others (the "livebearers") are fertilized and developed inside the female body. The ways in which eggs are fertilized, and young are protected and provided for, differ dramatically in the aquatic world, where predation and cannibalism are rife.

STICKLEBACK EGGS
The eggs of the Stickleback develop externally, with the eyes and backbone appearing first. The tiny fry emerge after 10–14 days.

Livebearers

The anal fin of a male livebearer is often modified to form a reproductive organ called the gonopodium. It is used to inject sperm into the female fish. Gestation takes about a month at average tropical aquarium temperatures, after which the young fry are ejected into the water, ready to fend for themselves. Females of the more popular cultivated livebearers, like guppies and swordtails, are able to store sperm internally and can produce successive broods of fry without remating. These are known as ovoviviparous breeders. For species that cannot store sperm internally (viviparous breeders), mating is necessary for each brood. All developing fry receive nourishment through a type of placenta.

LIVE BIRTH
The Green Goodeid, a wild, viviparous livebearer, gives birth to multiple live young.

Egg-scattering

This is the simplest form of egg-laying (or oviparous) reproduction. The eggs (ova) are ejected by the female into the water, usually after a hectic pursuit by a male, which stimulates egg release. They are fertilized by the male's liquid sperm, but only the eggs that float away on currents or fall among plants or pebbles survive; the rest are soon eaten by other fish and even the parents. Many eggs are laid to increase the chances of survival.

Egg-burying

The waters in which egg-buryers live dry up completely once a year. Species survival relies on the fertilized eggs withstanding dehydration, often for months, and then hatching once they are reimmersed in water during the rainy season. In captivity, the eggs from these fish must be collected and stored, nearly dry, for a period before rehydration.

Egg-depositing

Egg-depositing fishes protect their eggs to some degree after they are laid (see bottom right). The fish deposit the eggs carefully on the underside of leaves, inside rocky caves, or on the leaves of over-hanging plants above the water's surface. Some species use flat surfaces far out in the open water, or even a special pouch carried by the male. Egg-guarding and fry-herding are also practiced by this group. Fish that exhibit parental care will often pair off naturally.

MOUTH-BROODING

Mouth-brooding females store fertilized eggs in their throats until they hatch weeks later. They may abstain from feeding until the fry are free-swimming and, at any hint of danger, the fry seek refuge back in their mother's mouth. Mouth-brooders have no special breeding requirements apart from a separate tank. Male mouth-brooders of the Rift Valley cichlids have egg-spots on their anal fins. The female nudges these and so stimulates the release of sperm.

HIGH SECURITY
Mother's mouth is the safest place for these fry.

NEST-BUILDING

Tropical fishes build a variety of nests: some dig pits in the sand, while others build bubble nests. Males make a nest of saliva-coated bubbles and coax the female beneath them (see below), where eggs are laid, fertilized, and then placed in the nest. Depending on the species, bubble nests may be floating masses or collections of bubbles underneath plant leaves.

BREEDING IN CAPTIVITY

To produce high-quality fry, healthy parents with excellent color, finnage, and size must be chosen for breeding. The best specimens have been carefully conditioned, with close attention being paid to water quality and to the feeding of live foods and sometimes vegetables. Some fish may require special water conditions to breed, and you may need to prevent parent fish from eating their own eggs or young. The sheer numbers of fry that may arise from a successful spawning should also be anticipated and provided for.

SEPARATING BREEDERS

It is advisable to establish a separate breeding aquarium where water conditions can be adjusted and where fish can mate undisturbed. The risk of egg-eating is increased in the aquarium because of the small volume of water, but furnishing the breeding tank with dense, bushy plants or covering the floor with pebbles or marbles to hide the eggs, are ways of avoiding this behavior. Floating plants also provide retreats for newly hatched or free-swimmimg fry. Separating the sexes (especially the egg-scatterers) before breeding improves the chances of spawning once pairs are reunited. Male egg-scatterers generally have brighter colors, longer fins, and slimmer bodies than those of females.

COURTING BEHAVIOR
The male must coax the female beneath the bubble nest under the leaf before she lays and he fertilizes the eggs.

PATERNAL CARE
This male South American cichlid guards a carpet of newly hatched eggs that have been deposited on a flat rock.

Choosing Your Fish

Choosing fish for a collection involves more than simply going to the pet shop and buying the most attractive species. You should decide in advance which fish will suit your aquarium and equipment, and consider whether any species will require special care (such as being fed live foods). Tank size and water quality requirements vary from species to species. Once you are sure you have the right equipment, the criteria for purchase should be aquarium suitability, ease of care, compatibility, and physical health.

Aquarium Suitability

Not all fish sold in shops are suitable for the aquarium. Some grow too large too quickly, for example, while others, primarily marine fishes, never adapt to aquarium life. Fish are usually sold as juveniles, and it is wise to check that they will not grow too large – either for your aquarium or for smaller tank-mates that they may be tempted to eat.

Compatibility

Fish from different parts of the world cannot necessarily be expected to live in harmony in a community tank. Those that school in nature, for example, should be kept in numbers in captivity, but a solitary individual may pine away, even in a crowded tank. Sparring between adult males is another common aquarium problem, for example with the Siamese Fighting Fish, and marine fishes can be particularly territorial, even picking on similarly colored fishes of other species.

HUMBLE BEGINNINGS
It is important to check that your fish will not outgrow your tank. These examples show how similar-sized juveniles grow into different adult sizes.

BEWARE OF THE FISH
Smaller fish should not be kept with predators, such as the Moray Eel (above).

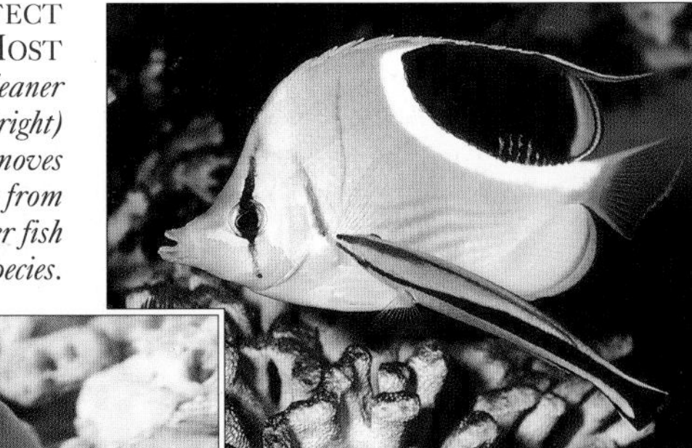

PERFECT HOST
A Cleaner Wrasse (right) removes parasites from other fish species.

AQUARIUM SANCTUARY
A nearby "hiding hole" among rocks or in the substrate, is reassuring for many fish of a nervous disposition, such as this Yellow Jawfish (left).

Health Checkpoints

A fish may have traveled thousands of miles before reaching the aquarium dealer, or it may have been collected using harmful methods. Either of these factors may leave it debilitated or may even prove fatal. Before purchasing a fish, check that it swims effortlessly and that it easily maintains its position in the water. Look also for sores, pimples, wounds, and split or folded fins. Make sure, particularly with marine fishes, that they are eating food readily, and try to personally witness them feeding. You should never buy a fish from a tank containing dead specimens.

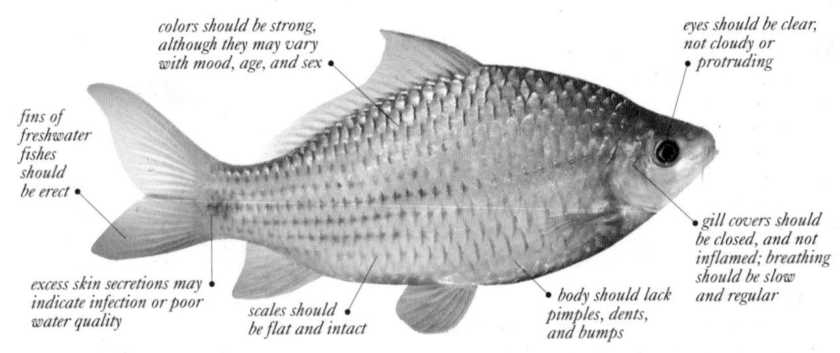

Signs of Ill Health

A fish hiding in the corner of an aquarium may not necessarily be sick; it may simply be nocturnal and unwilling to show itself in the glare of lights. Fishes with labored swimming actions should be avoided, but allowances can be made for extravagantly finned cultivated specimens. Folded fins on marine fishes are not always signs of ill health.

Creative Fish-keeping

It would be wrong to stipulate exactly which species to buy, as personal tastes differ and the availability of certain species may be restricted in local areas. Stocking an aquarium is a creative process involving the purchase of fish that you admire and can adequately care for. To get maximum benefit from the space in your aquarium, buy fish that will occupy all levels and spaces in the tank. Top, middle, and bottom-dwelling species can be included for a fuller representation of the underwater world. Your aquarium may house fish from all over the world or from one particular continent or area. Specialization often evolves over a period of years as experience is gained and as the fish-keeper's tastes change.

Top to Bottom

Stock the aquarium with a range of species so that all water levels are occupied.

Starting an Aquarium

EVERYTHING that is placed inside an aquarium alters its balance, so every action of the fish-keeper should be carefully considered. Fish need plenty of space and oxygen, as well as carefully monitored feeding and water conditions. The modern aquarium should be geared to help meet these requirements. Only the basic aquarium system is discussed here, as specialized fish may require certain modifications, which your aquarium dealer should advise you of.

Choosing a Dealer

A local aquarium shop is likely to share your water supply (and any related problems), so there should be less stress involved in establishing the fish in your tank. Try to monitor the shop's fish stocks over a period. Consider whether it has a fast turnover because of brisk trade or because the stock is dying. Find out whether new imports are quarantined before being sold. Good dealers will be interested in what you buy, not just how much you buy, and will know the requirements of every fish in their stock. They should get to know what fish you already have, and advise you against unsuitable purchases, or tell you about new species that may be of interest to you. Buy from a reputable source; cheap fish are never the bargains they appear to be.

NEWCOMERS
Transport new fish home in bags. To avoid a sudden temperature change, float a new fish's bag in the tank for 10–15 minutes.

MODERN OUTLETS
Choose an aquarium dealer who can offer sound advice on his range of fish and fish supplies.

Buying Checklist

- Do not buy fish that have recently arrived at the shop; wait until they have been quarantined and observed.
- Do not consider keeping rare, expensive, or delicate fish if you are in the early stages of fish-keeping.
- Do not be tempted to buy a sickly looking fish. It will probably not respond to any treatment offered.
- Do buy several specimens of a community species that is gregarious, or that is naturally schooling.
- Do ascertain the dietary needs of your new fish; if they are herbivorous, they may eat your aquarium plants.
- Do find out, before purchase, what adult size a fish will reach, and whether it requires special water conditions.

STOCKING LEVELS

A fish needs enough space to swim freely, but the size of the aquarium and the temperature of the water also affect oxygen content and will determine the number of fish that can be held. The oxygen consumption of the four main fish groups differs, partly because warmer waters carry less oxygen, so the recommended minimum sizes of tanks will differ accordingly. An aquarium measuring 24 in (60 cm) long and 12 in (30 cm) wide, with a surface area of 288 in^2 (1,800 cm^2), is roughly adequate for tropical freshwater fishes. But an aquarium of at least 36 in (90 cm) by 12 in (30 cm) is better for coldwater freshwater and all marine fishes, which consume proportionally more oxygen.

TROPICAL MARINE
Water with a surface area of 288 in^2 (1,800 cm^2) can support one 6 in (15 cm) marine angelfish.

COLDWATER FRESHWATER
A surface area of 288 in^2 (1,800 cm^2) supports two 4½ in (11.5 cm) Goldfish, or one of 9 in (23 cm).

SURFACE AREA

The depth of the tank is not relevant to the oxygen content calculations; it is the surface area of the water that is important. Tropical marine species require 48 in^2 (300 cm^2) of water per inch (2.5 cm) of body length; coldwater freshwater fishes require 30 in^2 (190 cm^2); and tropical freshwater fishes require 12 in^2(75 cm^2). The 24 x 12 in (60 x 30 cm) aquariums shown here, therefore, will hold approximately 6 in (15 cm) of tropical marine fishes (measured from snout to caudal peduncle), 9 in (23 cm) of coldwater freshwater fishes, and 24 in (60 cm) of tropical freshwater fishes.

TROPICAL FRESHWATER
A surface area of 288 in^2 (1,800 cm^2) supports four 6 in (15 cm) catfish, or one of 24 in (60 cm).

UPRIGHT TANK

UPRIGHT VERSUS HORIZONTAL
These two tanks contain the same volume of water and provide the same amount of swimming space but, because the upright tank has a smaller surface area of water compared with the horizontal tank, it will support far fewer fish.

greater surface area than upright tank

higher oxygen levels support many more fish

HORIZONTAL TANK

AQUARIUM EQUIPMENT

MODERN AQUARIUM TANKS are made of glass or of one-piece molded acrylic. They do not rust, which is a vital advantage if you intend to keep marine fishes. Tanks come in standard sizes, described either by dimension or water capacity. They should be positioned on a firm, level surface before any water is added. Any wood trim or cabinetry around the tank should be checked for strength and for resistance to condensation.

CLEAN EQUIPMENT

The aquarium must be kept clean using filters and aerated using air pumps. Many filters work in conjunction with an air pump, which drives aquarium water through the filter. The filter rids the tank of the fish's waste products, consisting of ammonia and other toxic chemicals, and general debris. Waste is also removed by regular partial water changes. Plants can further help to adsorb metals, nitrates, and carbon dioxide. Filtration equipment varies from simple foam filters to sophisticated "total" filter systems. Suspended matter in the water is mechanically strained out by the filter, and dissolved wastes are adsorbed within it by a special medium, such as activated carbon.

power head drives water under gravel

covering of pea gravel

water is drawn through slotted plastic plates

PREPARING UNDER-GRAVEL FILTRATION

UNDER-GRAVEL FILTRATION

This system of filtration (see above) works without a filter medium. The power head drives water through the gravel, where it comes into contact with a bacterial colony living on the gravel surface. These bacteria feed on the fish's waste.

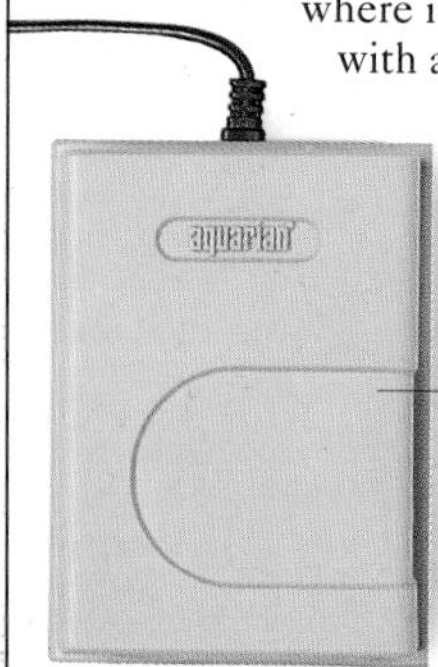

this device pumps compressed air through the water to aerate it

AIR PUMP

DWARF SWORD-PLANT

FURNISHINGS

Freshwater aquariums look best when furnished with clusters of rocks, sunken logs, and green plants. Herbivorous fishes, however, will quickly denude a tank of plants, and some fish uproot plants and furnishings when breeding. Plastic plants can be substituted, and molded resin replicas of logs, branches, and ornaments that do not leach chemicals or dyes are available. Enhance marine tanks with synthetic corals and colorful algae.

Water

Most aquarium fishes adjust well to domestic water supplies, provided that precautions are taken to remove or neutralize the effect of heavy metals, chlorine, and chloramines that are added. It is necessary to alter the composition of water further only when attempting to breed or to keep more delicate freshwater species. Water for marine aquariums should be made up using commercial synthetic salt mixes.

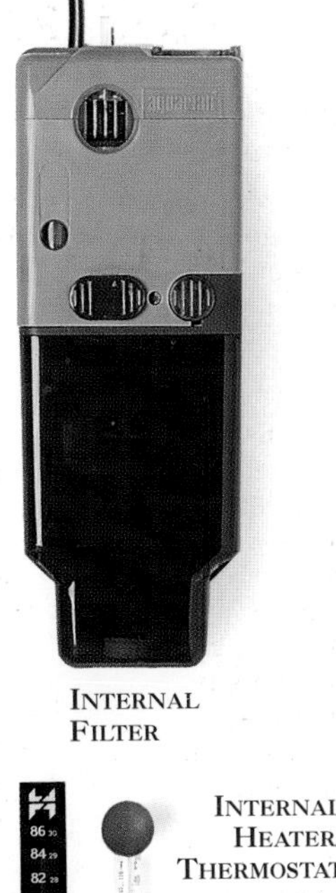

Internal Filter

Heating

Keep aquarium water for tropical freshwater and marine fishes constant at around 77°F (25°C). A thermostatically controlled heater will maintain this temperature level reliably. Two units can be used in large tanks to distribute heat quickly and evenly. Modern thermostats have microchip circuits for more accurate control, and some external thermostatic controls even have memories for recording temperatures, with alarms to warn of extreme changes.

Internal Heater/ Thermostat

Internal Thermometer

External Thermometer

Lighting

Light illuminates the aquarium and provides energy for photosynthesizing aquatic plants. Tanks deeper than 15 in (38 cm) and those with lush plantlife will need more lighting than is generally supplied with an aquarium. Aquariums are best lit by fluorescent tubes inside the hood; marine reef tanks require high-intensity halide or mercury vapor lamps. Tungsten lamps generate excessive heat but may be used to grow plants.

Fish Net

Amazon Swordplant

specimen plants may be planted complete with pot or container

safety device for connecting and switching electricity

Cable Organizer

Fluorescent tube Lighting

Caring for Your Fish

One advantage of fish-keeping is the small amount of time required for maintenance: a few minutes each day for feeding and perhaps an hour or so a week for cleaning. Periodic tests for water quality are advisable, especially with marine tanks, delicate fish, or when breeding, but water hardness need not unduly worry the average keeper.

Maintenance Chart		
	FRESHWATER	MARINE
Water Check temperature	daily	daily
Top up water level	weekly	weekly
Check specific gravity (using hydrometer)	not applicable	weekly
Check ammonia, nitrite, and nitrate levels (using test kit)	not applicable	before stocking tank, then periodically
Check pH (using test kit)	when breeding or specializing	weekly
Check hardness (using test kit)	when breeding or specializing	not applicable
Make partial water changes	monthly, more if required	monthly
Filters Clean or renew filter floss; replace carbon	as required	as required
Clean biological materials	partially every 2–3 months	partially every 2–3 months
Plants Trim excessive growth; remove decayed leaves	as required	not applicable
General Check health of fish	daily	daily
Scrape algae; clean light fittings; siphon out debris	as required	as required

Fish diseases are usually initiated by stress, often caused by a change in the aquarium environment or by pollution from over feeding or the decay of the carcasses of dead fish. Fortunately, most ailments can be diagnosed, and many respond to medication or treatments.

Treating Common Ailments

- **White Spot** (*Ichthyophthirius*) Small white spots appear on the body and fins. It can be remedied with a commercial water treatment. The marine equivalent is *Cryptocaryon.*
- **Velvet** Similar to White Spot, but spots are smaller. All forms are caused by *Oodinium* parasites, which respond to treatment.
- **Fungus** (*Saprolegnia*) The body has "woolly" growths; remedy with a salt bath, or, for freshwater fishes, a swab with a proprietary treatment.
- **Mouth "Fungus"** This usually responds only to antibiotics, which are available from a veterinarian.
- **Skin and Gill Flukes** Fish scratch against objects to relieve the irritation of skin flukes (*Gyrodactylus*). Gill flukes (*Dactylogyrus*) cause fish to hang, with gills inflamed, at the surface. Commercial treatments are effective.
- **Fin-Rot** Often a secondary ailment due to acidic water; tissue between the fin rays is gradually eroded by bacteria. Changing the water may prompt a recovery.
- **Dropsy** Scales stand out from the body and the fish becomes bloated; no cures are reliable, and fish are best destroyed.

Hospital Tank

A separate tank is useful both for treating sick fishes and as quarantine quarters.

Feeding

The types and amounts of food offered to fish are crucial, as uneaten food will rot, upsetting tank conditions. Fish should never be fed more than they can consume within a few minutes. Any food that is not eaten will simply be left to waste, depleting the aquarium of vital oxygen. Fish will not starve if left for a week or so during vacations, providing they have been well fed beforehand. Fish foods fall into two groups: dried or prepared foods and natural foods in the form of living creatures, seeds, or fruit. Aim to match the wild diet of a fish as closely as possible.

Dry Foods

Multimillion-dollar businesses have been established to provide nutritionally balanced diets for all types of captive fish. Modern fish foods aim to closely match fish's natural diets. Whether fish are carnivorous, herbivorous, or omnivorous, adult or fry, there are convenient foods available in several forms, including flakes, pellets, tablets, and liquids. In addition to proteins, carbohydrates, and fats, fish require vitamins and minerals just as humans do, and many manufacturers now add these during the production process.

Natural Live Foods

Freezing and freeze-drying also mean that live aquatic foods can be preserved. These are ideal, as living creatures, either water-borne or terrestrial, naturally contain all the nutrients that fish need. They also make a welcome treat, if offered only occasionally. Mosquito larvae can be collected from standing water, and bloodworms and water fleas are usually available from aquatic dealers.

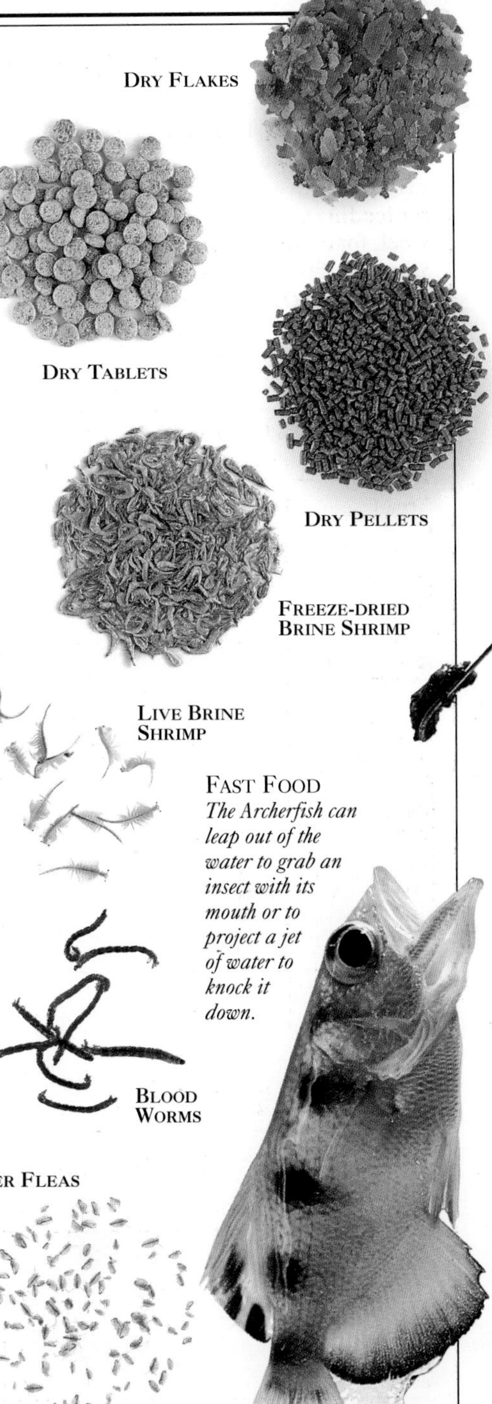

Dry Flakes

Dry Tablets

Dry Pellets

Freeze-dried Brine Shrimp

Live Brine Shrimp

Blood Worms

Water Fleas

Mosquito Larvae

Fast Food

The Archerfish can leap out of the water to grab an insect with its mouth or to project a jet of water to knock it down.

Freshwater Habitats

The proportion of fresh water in the world is very small – around two percent. Most of the world's water is in the oceans. But because of the diverse location, accessibility, and differing qualities of fresh water, the variety of freshwater fishes is vast. Freshwater fishes can cope with a wide range of water locations, qualities, and temperatures, and this adaptability and resilience has made them hardy and very suitable for life in the aquarium.

Types of Fresh Water

When water falls from clouds as rain, it is conditioned by the earth upon which it lands. This, in turn, affects the local fishes' tolerance of their water conditions. If water falls on granitic rock, its composition is altered very little, and it remains soft. But when it permeates limestone, it absorbs calcium, which makes it alkaline and hard. Peaty soil will acidify water, as will the rotting vegetation typically found in slow-moving streams. Fishes from such streams, including most aquarium fishes, such as barbs and rasboras, will, therefore, tolerate acidity in their aquarium water. Lakes with no inflow or outflow of water from rivers, as in the Rift Valley of Africa, have a high mineral

Asian Rain Forest
Although they contain many aquarium fish species, waters in southeast Asian jungles (below) usually contain much oxygen-consuming decaying vegetation. Waterfalls help boost oxygen levels.

Life on the Riverbed
The anostomus (above) searches for food on the riverbeds of Amazonia, home to a great many tropical aquarium favorites. The stripes help it blend in with its surroundings.

RIFT VALLEY
A vantage point by Lake Malawi in the Rift Valley of East Africa. Several of these hard-water valley lakes are home to the "Rift Valley cichlids." There are more than 250 cichlid species in this lake alone.

content that must be emulated in captivity using commercial mixes. Estuarine waters are regularly altered by tidal additions of sea water, and fish from these environments, such as the Mono and the Scat, appreciate a small addition of salt in their water. By the time rain water reaches the sea, it is of an entirely different composition. Once there, it evaporates and begins its journey back through the water cycle.

FRESH WATERS OF MEXICO
Lake Catemaco in Mexico has a tropical climate at an altitude of 1,212 ft (370 m). It contains cichlids, livebearers, and killifishes.

EFFECTS OF TEMPERATURE

Changes in temperature may also significantly alter the freshwater habitat: where the volume of water is small, the differences between day and night temperatures are greater. More drastic fluctuations include the melting of mountain snows, which add cool water to rivers.

CHINESE SAILFIN SUCKER
This sturdy species inhabits the temperate waters of China.

FRESHWATER AQUARIUMS

THERE ARE MANY MORE options open to the freshwater fish-keeper than to the marine aquarist. The freshwater keeper can recreate the conditions of a tropical river or lake, a backwater pond, a hard-water Rift Valley lake, or a coldwater stream. Whichever aquatic habitat you choose to create, water quality will be of great importance. Simulating the water chemistry of a location can be achieved using resins, minerals, and sometimes peat in the mechanical filter system. These will soften, harden, make alkaline, or acidify the water. Dilution by adding rain-water is one way to reduce water hardness, while soft water can be

ROCKS AND PEBBLES

WATER WISTERIA

high bank of sandy gravel

heavy vegetation

Goldie River Rainbowfish

SPECIALIZED TANK
Unlike the community aquarium (above), the specialized tank aims to accommodate fish and plants from a specific environment. The tank shown here emulates a sandy, upland river in Papua New Guinea, home to three species of rainbowfish.

THE COMMUNITY COLLECTION
A range of fishes from different worldwide habitats can be mixed together in a community tank.

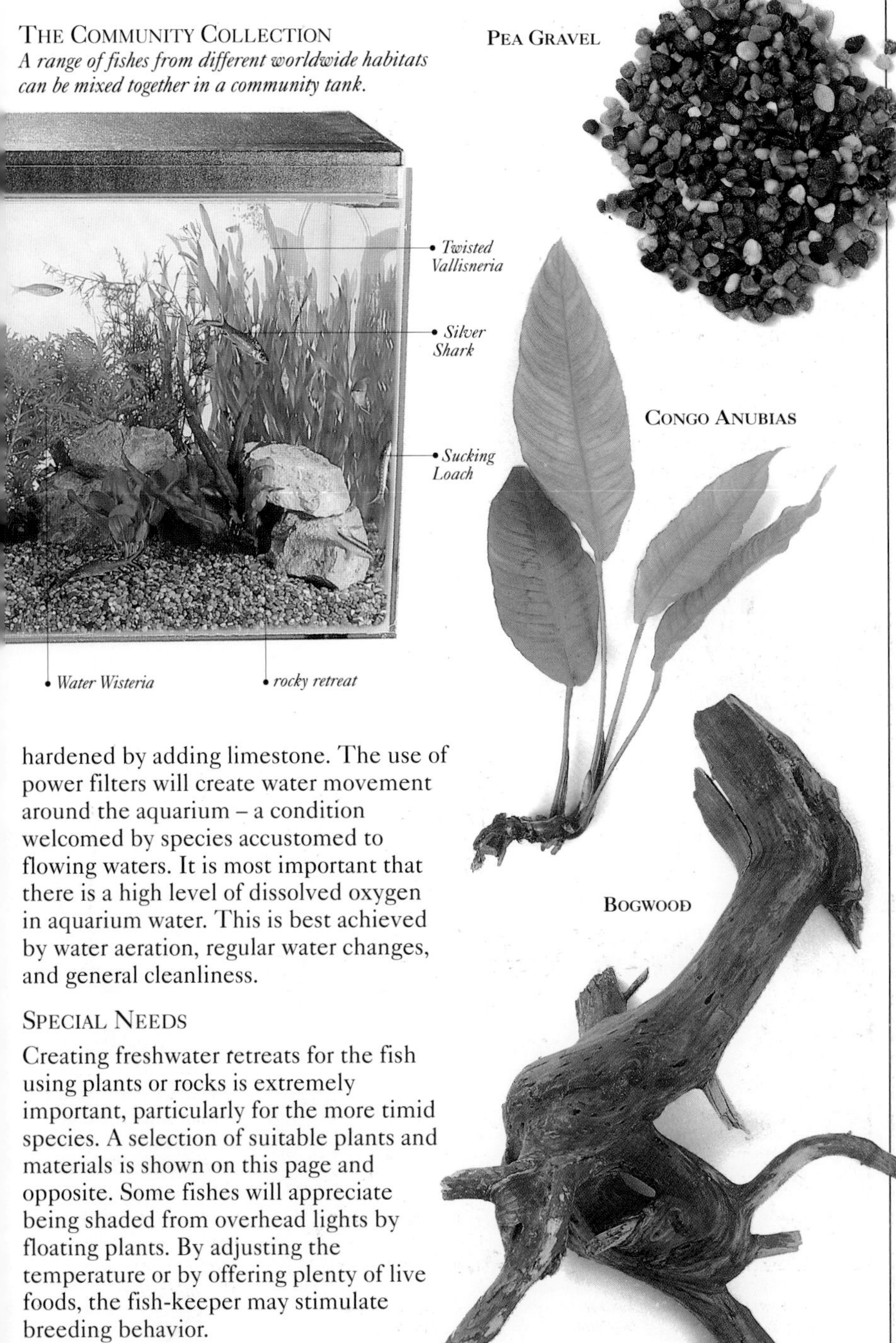

hardened by adding limestone. The use of power filters will create water movement around the aquarium – a condition welcomed by species accustomed to flowing waters. It is most important that there is a high level of dissolved oxygen in aquarium water. This is best achieved by water aeration, regular water changes, and general cleanliness.

SPECIAL NEEDS

Creating freshwater retreats for the fish using plants or rocks is extremely important, particularly for the more timid species. A selection of suitable plants and materials is shown on this page and opposite. Some fishes will appreciate being shaded from overhead lights by floating plants. By adjusting the temperature or by offering plenty of live foods, the fish-keeper may stimulate breeding behavior.

Marine Habitats

Covering approximately 77 percent of the Earth's surface, the saltwater oceans are regarded as a highly stable environment with only minor fluctuations in salinity. The problem that this brings to the keeper of marine fish is that these species have little tolerance to even the slightest change in water conditions, unlike their freshwater relatives. In addition, the vast ocean waters soon dilute the pollution of fish wastes and decaying organic matter. Even the largest marine aquarium cannot reproduce these self-cleansing conditions, and the water in marine tanks needs assistance if it is to support life.

Underwater Traffic
Despite the apparent crowding on this Fijian reef, there is plenty of food for all.

Supply of Species

Most marine species available for the marine aquarium come from shallow coastal waters near coral reefs, where fish can be captured easily. Unlike many freshwater fishes, most marine species are still caught from the wild. Despite the attraction and commercial value of their fantastic colors and unusual shapes, marine fishes have proved difficult to breed cost-effectively in captivity, and certainly not in the numbers required for commercial supply.

Coral Dwellers
Shy sea horses use corals and seaweeds to anchor themselves.

Fish Paradise
Coral reefs, such as these off tropical islands in the South Pacific, teem with fish life.

POOLS OF LIFE

On seashores in all temperate zones, receding tides leave behind tidal pools. These are ecosystems in their own right, containing easily caught schooling fishes, colorful seaweeds and algae, and unusual invertebrates. Although tidal pool dwellers are not as brightly colored as their tropical counterparts, their diverse sheltering and feeding techniques provide a special fascination.

SPECIALIZED FEEDING

Some marine fishes have specialized feeding habits that can cause problems for aquarists. Many species eat specific foods, such as sponges, algae, and even the coral itself. Providing these foods in captivity is difficult, and many marine fishes refuse to accept substitutes. Parrotfishes, for example, are beautiful and easy to collect, but they feed only on algae growing on coral rubble. Fortunately, commercial foods are now incorporating more of these natural foods. Other fishes with specialized feeding habits, such as the sponge-eating Atlantic angelfishes and the polyp-eating butterflyfishes, can adapt to aquarium life if captured very young. They will accept live brine shrimp and adapt to frozen food and flakes. Algae-eating pygmy angelfishes will adapt to meats supplemented with blanched vegetables.

SAFETY IN SEAWEED

Long, tapering pipefishes hide heads up, in grasses and slim seaweeds near the shore.

MARINE AQUARIUMS

PROVIDING FISH with the equivalent of the natural conditions found on coral reefs is the secret of successful marine fish-keeping. Controlling water quality within very specific parameters is first on the list of priorities. The marine aquarium should be as large as possible for maximum water quality stability – a minimum of 36 in (90 cm) in length and 12 in (30 cm) in depth. At least one fourth of the water should be changed every month. The replacement water must be mixed to the correct specific gravity (tested using a hydrometer) and aerated before being added: your aquarium dealer will advise you. An efficient filtration system is also vital to control dangerous toxins. Each aquarium has an optimum fish-holding capacity, but this should be reached gradually to allow the filtration system to

SEASHELL

TUFA ROCK

SPECIALIZED TANK
A coldwater marine tank is an interesting, if more demanding, alternative to tropical reef aquariums. A larger tank is needed to support fishes that grow to considerable sizes. Temperature, pH, specific gravity, and salinity must all be monitored. These aquariums should be kept cool in summer.

THE COMMUNITY TANK

Choose fish for their color, shape, or unusual behavior and for their utilization of swimming space. Add invertebrates such as anemones, marine worms, and crabs for further interest.

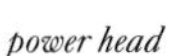

POWER FILTER

HYDROMETER

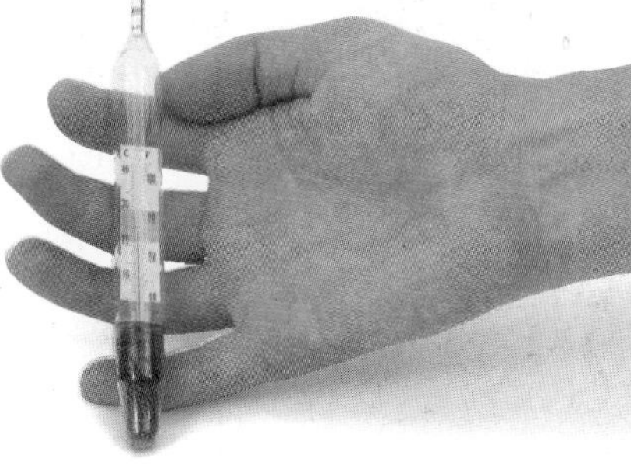

cope with the increasing waste load. You can achieve additional water purification using equipment such as protein skimmers, ultraviolet lamps, and ozone, an oxidizing agent.

OTHER NEEDS

Light intensity on the reef top is high, and intense lighting in the aquarium will encourage the algae required by herbivorous species. Reef aquariums should have more hideaways than fish, and the substrate should be fairly fine for certain burrowing species. Suggested materials and furnishings are illustrated on this page and opposite.

SEA SALT MIX

CRUSHED CORAL

HOW FISH ARE GROUPED

ALL FISH ARE DEFINED by their scientific species name, which is recognized worldwide. Similar species are grouped into "genera," which in turn are grouped into families, as shown below. Characteristics of the groups used in this book are set out on the following pages (pp.35–45).

FISH FOSSIL
Fossils help us trace the development of the common characteristics of a family, genus, or species.

FAMILY

A family usually contains several related genera, but sometimes only a single genus. The family name always appears in Roman type, e.g., Belontiidae.

GENUS/GENERA

A genus usually contains several related species, but sometimes only one. The scientific genus name always appears in italic type, e.g., *Sphaerichthys*.

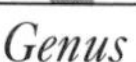

SPECIES

Members of a species share similar features and can breed together. The full scientific name consists of the genus name and species name, e.g., *Betta bellica*.

VARIETIES AND SUBSPECIES

Varieties (var.) are cultivated divisions within a species; subspecies (denoted by a second name on the scientific name) are usually geographically separate.

Subspecies (e.g. Trichogaster trichopterus sumatranus)

CYPRINIDS

TIGER BARB
A diamond-shaped body and high dorsal fin are typical of the barbs, the most common tropical cyprinids.

"SHARK"
Several family members have dorsal fins and flattened profiles similar to the true marine sharks.

GROUP CHARACTERISTICS

The cyprinid family contains around 1,300 species, widely distributed on most continents of the world. They inhabit all types of waters and adapt readily to various water conditions provided by the keeper.

The body shape is conventional, with symmetrical contours, but it may be slender or quite deep, depending on habitat. Cyprinids have seven fins: two sets of paired fins and three single ones. Pharyngeal teeth in the throat grind food before it reaches the intestine. The arrangement of these teeth provides positive identification between similar species.

Coldwater cyprinids (see pp.213–233) include the most popular aquarium fishes of all, the Goldfishes and Koi. Tropical cyprinids (see pp.46–73) are divided into three main aquarium groups: barbs, which are like miniature carp, inhabit the middle and lower water levels; danios are faster swimming and prefer the upper levels; and rasboras use all water levels. All cyprinids spawn using egg-scattering methods and do not usually exercise parental care.

RASBORA
Midwater-swimming rasboras can be either slim- or deep-bodied, brightly colored, or plain silver.

DANIO
These characins spawn easily. They are constantly active just below the water's surface.

CHARACINS

NATURAL DISTRIBUTION

BEACON FISH

The body shape of this fish is typical of the popular tetra group within the characin family. Upper and lower profiles are equally curved.

equally curved profiles

adipose fin

deeply cleft caudal fin

long-based anal fin

DISTICHODUS

This heavily built African characin requires plenty of room.

GROUP CHARACTERISTICS

The characin family includes around 1,300 species, distributed across Central and South America, and Africa. Most of these fishes school in lakes and rivers.

Body shapes and sizes vary considerably, from the 2-in- (5-cm-) long pencilfishes to the stocky African distichodus species, which measure 16 in (40 cm). Piranhas and pacus are muscular and heavily built to facilitate the tearing of flesh or fruits. Other characins, in contrast, may persistently eat aquarium plants. Characins have sharp teeth in the jaws and most have an extra fin, known as the adipose fin, on the back. The family contains many popular fishes, including the tetras, of which the brilliant Neon and Cardinal Tetras are prime examples.

Most characins spawn using egg-scattering methods. The male may have tiny hooks on the anal fin to hold the female against him during spawning. The eggs are adhesive and usually lodge among plants. One exception is the Splashing Tetra, which deposits eggs on a firm surface out of the water, to protect them from the attentions of aquatic predators.

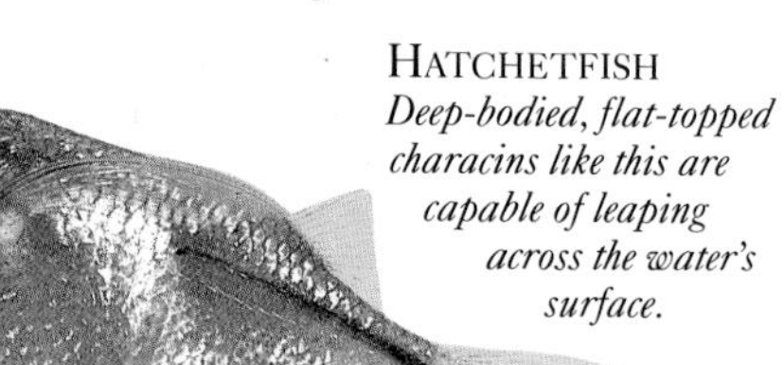

HATCHETFISH

Deep-bodied, flat-topped characins like this are capable of leaping across the water's surface.

PENCILFISH

The coloration patterns of these spindle-shaped characins alter at nighttime.

CICHLIDS

NATURAL DISTRIBUTION

GOLDEN-EYED DWARF CICHLID
Although modest in size, the stocky body of this fish is typical of the cichlid family.

long-based dorsal fin

rounded caudal fin

stocky body

pointed anal fin on male

ANGELFISH
This aquarium favorite has a very different body shape to most cichlids.

GROUP CHARACTERISTICS

The 1,000 or more members of the cichlid family are native to Central and South America, Africa, Asia, and parts of the USA. Most will acclimatize well to domestic tap water, although some species, such as the Discus Fish, need carefully controlled water.

The colors, shapes, and sizes of cichlids vary enormously, although they tend to be heavily built. Some grow too large for the average community tank, while others breed readily among other fishes in any aquarium. Male cichlids from the Americas may have longer, more pointed dorsal and anal fins, while male African Rift Valley cichlids often have yellow or orange spots on the anal fin. There is plenty of opportunity for specialization within this family: Rift Valley cichlids, for example, prefer hard water and rocky furnishings. Many are herbivorous, requiring vegetable foods. Cichlids are hearty eaters and produce a lot of waste, which calls for frequent water changes. Generally these fishes reproduce by egg-depositing, but they display diverse methods of breeding, all of which involve a high degree of parental care.

LARGER CICHLID
Some cichlids, like this Oscar, may outgrow the average aquarium. Although large, it can become hand-tame.

DISCUS
This graceful, colorful cichlid requires soft, acidic water conditions.

ANABANTIDS

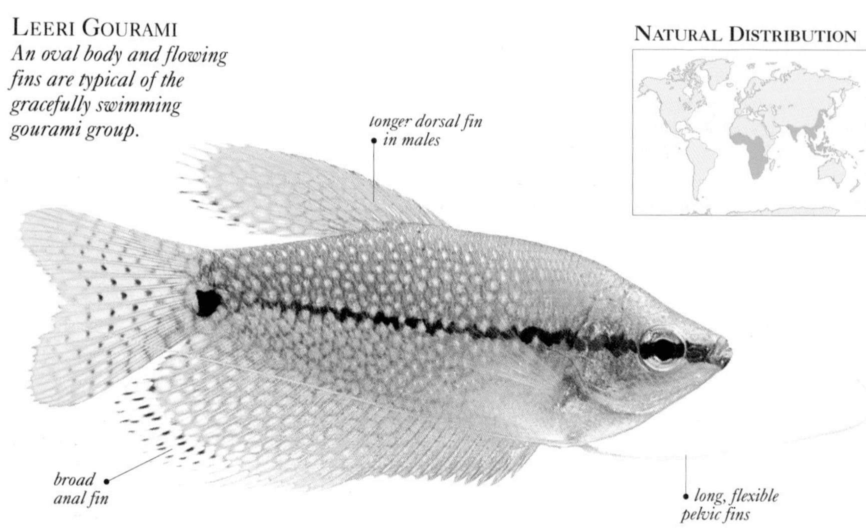

LEERI GOURAMI
An oval body and flowing fins are typical of the gracefully swimming gourami group.

NATURAL DISTRIBUTION

GROUP CHARACTERISTICS

Fishes within this group of families often inhabit oxygen-depleted waters of Africa and Asia. They possess an auxiliary breathing organ that enables them to use atmospheric air gulped at the surface. This "labyrinth organ" is a folded mass of bone and capillary-rich tissue, situated internally near the gills. Its function is to store air and extract oxygen.

The Asiatic anabantids are usually peaceful and swim gracefully. Gouramies have threadlike pelvic fins with taste cells at the tips. A few other Asian species make croaking noises when they are breeding or when removed from the water. African species are larger and are stealthy predators, often with spectacular colors and patterns.

Most anabantids build floating bubble nests in which the eggs are deposited. The male spurns the female once spawning is completed. He may even kill her as he takes on responsibility for guarding the eggs in the nest. An exception is the mouth-brooding Chocolate Gourami.

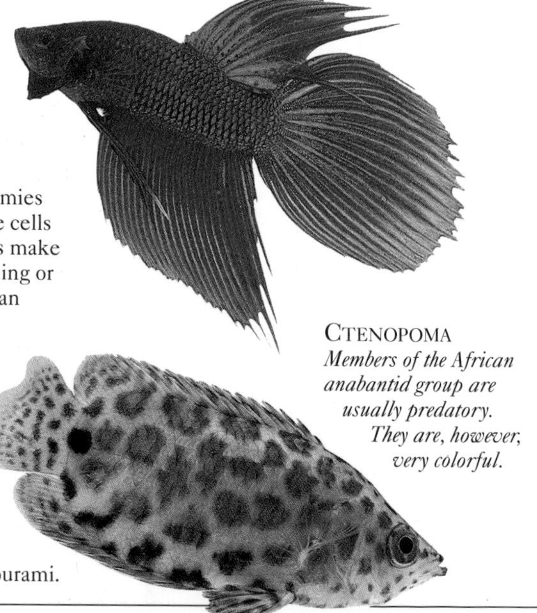

BETTA
The Siamese Fighting Fish, an aquarium-bred Betta *species, has a brighter coloration than its wild counterpart.*

CTENOPOMA
Members of the African anabantid group are usually predatory. They are, however, very colorful.

KILLIFISHES

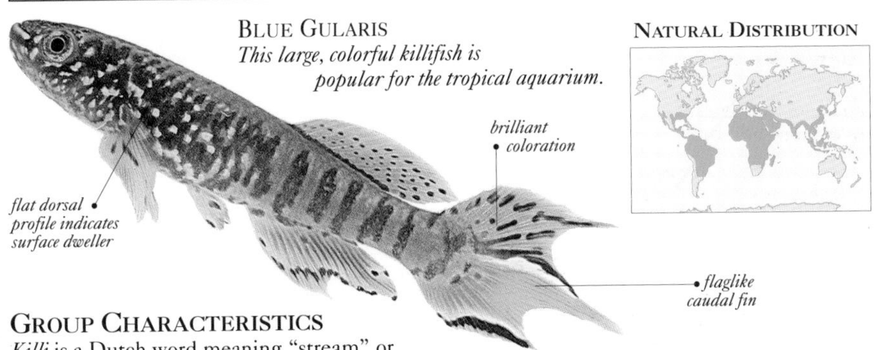

GROUP CHARACTERISTICS

Killi is a Dutch word meaning "stream" or "brook", but the 300 killifish members of the family Cyprinodontidae in fact inhabit a great variety of waters. These include ephemeral ponds, brackish marshes, lakes, and rivers of the Americas, Africa, Asia, and warmer parts of Europe. Their small, cylindrical bodies have upturned mouths for surface feeding. Males are usually more brilliantly colored. In captivity, killifishes accept most types of food. They lay eggs in plants or in the substrate. In both cases, eggs may take weeks or months to hatch and they can survive periods of almost total dehydration. Many subspecies of various coloration have led to confusion with identification.

CATFISHES

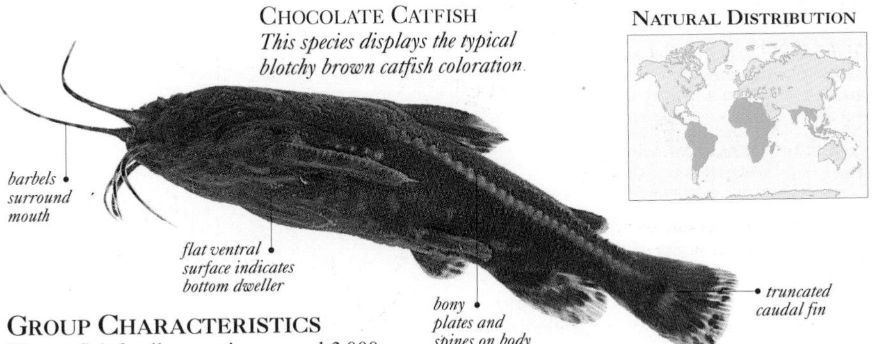

GROUP CHARACTERISTICS

The catfish family contains around 2,000 members, which include some of the more unusual aquarium attractions: certain species swim upside down; some can maneuver on land; and others can emit sound or use electricity to kill. All are from the Americas, Africa, and Asia and share the common characteristic of bottom-dwelling. Many are surprisingly gregarious and enjoy being kept in numbers, but some catfish are nocturnal, and their regular activities often go unnoticed. Catfishes are identifiable by the barbels around their mouths, which allow them to locate food in the dark. Instead of scales, the skin may be naked or covered with bony plates, or scutes. They often use oxygen that is gulped at the surface and extracted in the gut. Usually omnivorous, some species are herbivorous and are useful in controlling algae. Catfishes spawn in several ways, including egg-depositing and bubble nest building.

LOACHES

NATURAL DISTRIBUTION

COOLIE LOACH

The elongate body of the loach allows easy access to hiding places.

dark, camouflaging stripes

erectile spine beneath eye

pale ventral surface

GROUP CHARACTERISTICS

The various species of loach that are available to the aquarist come from India and Asia. They spend most of their time on the bottom of rivers and streambeds, hence their flat-bottomed bodies. A distinctive characteristic of this family is the erectile spine beneath the eye. It acts as a deterrent to predators, but it also tends to catch in the fish-keeper's net. The mouths of loaches are downturned and have barbels for detecting food.

Like anabantids and some catfishes, loaches can gulp atmospheric air at the water's surface and extract oxygen from it as it passes through the gut. Many species are nocturnal and hide among plants and rocks by day, emerging as darkness falls or when food appears at close range. Their natural diet includes worms and insects, but most loaches will accept prepared foods in captivity, especially tablets and other quick-sinking forms.

Little is known of their reproductive behavior, but loaches have been induced to spawn in captivity by using hormone injections. Loaches in the *Botia* genus are long-established aquarium favorites.

CLOWN LOACH

The flat-bottomed body and downturned mouth of this loach facilitate substrate feeding.

ZEBRA LOACH

Distinctive dark stripes provide camouflage for this loach.

HORSEFACED LOACH

The head of this species is longer than those of other loaches. It may become more active during stormy weather.

Other Tropical Egg-laying Species

Natural Distribution

Siamese Tigerfish
A slim body enables this predatory egg-laying species to lurk in plants.

second dorsal fin contains softer rays

spiny front to dorsal fin

powerful caudal fin

large, predatory mouth

Group Characteristics

Many egg-laying fishes are monotypic – occurring as a single species within their genus. Some genera contain very few species and other species do not fit conveniently into the major fish groups. These miscellaneous fishes are grouped together in this book in alphabetical order by scientific species name (see pp.180–196).

There is an extraordinary variety of fishes to choose for the aquarium within this category, from both brackish and fresh waters. Their physical characteristics are too varied to describe in general terms. These species are sometimes kept by hobbyists as interim choices before graduating to more the demanding field of marine fish-keeping.

They have been chosen to demonstrate the range of fishes available to enliven even the smallest aquarium. Commercial availability of some of these species may be limited.

Elephant Fish
The extended lower jaw makes this unusual tropical egg-layer easily recognizable.

Rainbowfish
Two separate dorsal fins are a distinctive feature of the rainbowfishes.

Leaf Fish
Mimicking a dead leaf, this predator may drift up to its prey unnoticed.

TROPICAL LIVEBEARERS

RED VEILTAIL GUPPY
Guppies, mollies, swordtails, and platys are a related group of extremely popular livebearers. The males are smaller but more colorful than the females.

NATURAL DISTRIBUTION

GROUP CHARACTERISTICS

Livebearing fishes are native to the Americas, from New Jersey down to Brazil, and in east Asia. They have been introduced into other tropical areas to combat malaria, as livebearers eat the waterborne larvae of disease-carrying mosquitoes.

Females are usually longer than males, but the latter have more striking colors and patterns, and often have longer fins. Most livebearers adapt well to the aquarium and will thrive in hard water. Feeding is uncomplicated, but these fishes appreciate the addition of vegetable matter.

A main attraction of these fishes is their propensity to breed in captivity, especially the brilliantly colored, aquarium-developed strains of guppies, mollies, platys, and swordtails. It is advisable to move a gravid female into a separate nursery tank for birthing. This should be heavily planted to shield the young from their hungry mother.

SAILFIN MOLLY
Plenty of green matter is appreciated in the diet of this livebearer.

SWORDTAIL
The swordlike extension on the tail distinguishes this species.

GOODEID
Males of the family Goodeidae lack the rodlike, fertilizing anal fin of other male livebearers.

COLDWATER FRESHWATER FISHES

SARASA COMET
The Goldfish is the most popular aquarium fish of all. Red and white patches are typical of this slim-bodied cultivated strain.

GROUP CHARACTERISTICS

The popularity of ornamental coldwater fishes sustained the aquarium hobby for hundreds of years until the tropical varieties were introduced in the 19th century. Coldwater aquarium species are mostly cultivated varieties of the Common Goldfish (*Carassius auratus*), a member of the cyprinid family originating in Asia. A near relative in the same family, the Koi (*Cyprinus carpio*) has been developed in Japan, although it is generally kept in the outdoor pond rather than the aquarium. Koi are traditionally viewed and judged from above and their colors are developed accordingly. Goldfishes and Koi are long-lived and adapt well to aquarium and pond culture. No standard size descriptions are offered in this book, as they generally grow to the limits of their environment, and no habitat is given, as they are aquarium-developed.

A number of species from temperate regions of North America, Europe, and Japan have recently become popular as aquarium fish. There may be local laws against selling some species or removing them from their habitat.

TWINTAIL GOLDFISH
A strain with divided anal and caudal fins.

SUNFISH
All sunfishes have a distinctive ear flap.

SHINER
Members of this fish group develop head tubercles when breeding.

TROPICAL MARINE FISHES

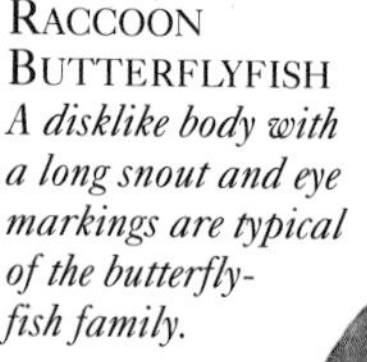

RACCOON BUTTERFLYFISH
A disklike body with a long snout and eye markings are typical of the butterfly-fish family.

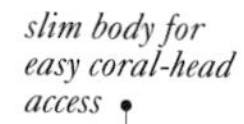

NATURAL DISTRIBUTION

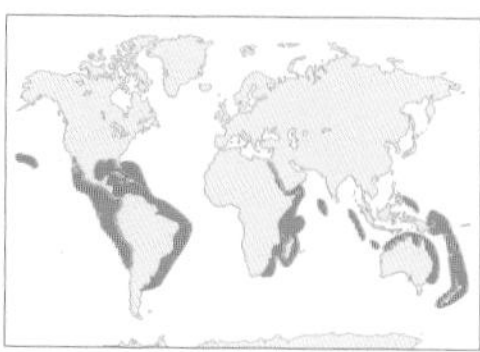

WRASSE
Although spectacularly patterned when young, adult wrasses soon outgrow aquariums and lose color.

GROUP CHARACTERISTICS

Marine fishes are the most beautiful candidates for the aquarium, but they are also the most intolerant of changes in water quality. Keeping them is a specialization that should be approached gradually and informatively. Beginning with the more hardy species is less expensive and is educational.

Tropical marine fishes generally come from coral reefs and coastal areas throughout the tropical oceans of the world. The choice of shapes, sizes, and colors is extensive, and the question of compatibility must be considered during selection. Many marine fishes are territorial, and they may be intolerant of other members of the same species. Hiding places should always be provided. Some species form natural relationships with other fishes or invertebrates, and these may be kept together: anemone-fishes, for example, appreciate the addition of sea anemones.

The breeding of these fishes is often restricted to anemonefishes and gobies. The more popular tropical marine groups are described in this book first, then genera with fewer species members.

ANGELFISH
Body shape is similar to that of the butterflyfishes, but a spine is present on the gill cover.

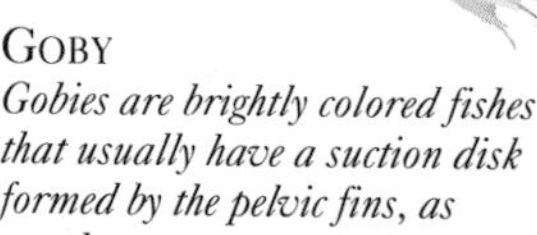

GOBY
Gobies are brightly colored fishes that usually have a suction disk formed by the pelvic fins, as seen here.

COLDWATER MARINE FISHES

LONG-SPINED SEA SCORPION
The spines of this magnificent fish are poisonous to other fish and to unwary fish collectors.

NATURAL DISTRIBUTION

decorative dorsal spines

bony ridges on head

flat ventral surface

GROUP CHARACTERISTICS

Fish-keepers who live near the seashore may be able to collect local species from pools that are isolated by receding tides. If these species outgrow the aquarium, they can easily be returned to the shore. The selection of species described in this section does not represent all temperate coastal regions but is offered as an indication of the variety of species that can be collected by the fish-keeper. Generally speaking, it is likely that coldwater fishes will be rather subdued in color compared with their tropical relatives. A mottled brown coloration is generally the norm.

Most coldwater marine fishes depend on rocky retreats, so these should be provided in the aquarium. A fine, deep substrate will enable burrowing fishes, like the wrasse, to feel secure. As with tropical aquariums, you can add invertebrates for interest: sea anemones, shrimps, starfish, and small crabs can all be included to enliven a coldwater marine scene. Native marine fishes can be kept fairly cheaply in a medium to large tank. Coldwater marine aquariums must be checked for overheating during the summer.

STICKLEBACK
These fish are easily identified by the spines and bony plates on their flanks.

LUMPSUCKER
A concealed first dorsal fin and a spiny skin characterize this unusual coldwater marine species.

CLINGFISH
Like the gobies, this fish adheres to surfaces using a special suction disk.

TROPICAL FRESHWATER FISHES

CYPRINIDS
BARBS, DANIOS, AND RASBORAS

THE FAMILY CYPRINIDAE is widespread and contains about 1,250 hardy, active species, of which barbs, danios, and rasboras are the most common. These attractive smaller cyprinids from both tropical and subtropical waters are undemanding in the aquarium and easy to feed.

Family CYPRINIDAE	Species *Barbus arulius*	Size 4 in (10 cm)

ARULIUS BARB

The brown-gray body is covered with three irregular and incomplete vertical black bands, reaching halfway down the flanks. A small black smudge appears at the dorsal fin's base. The dark-edged scales are marked with tiny iridescent dots, accentuated when the fish is viewed under side-lighting.

• **HABITAT** Rivers in southern India.

• **REMARK** This barb generally tolerates and breeds at any concentration of water hardness, producing an average of 100 fry.

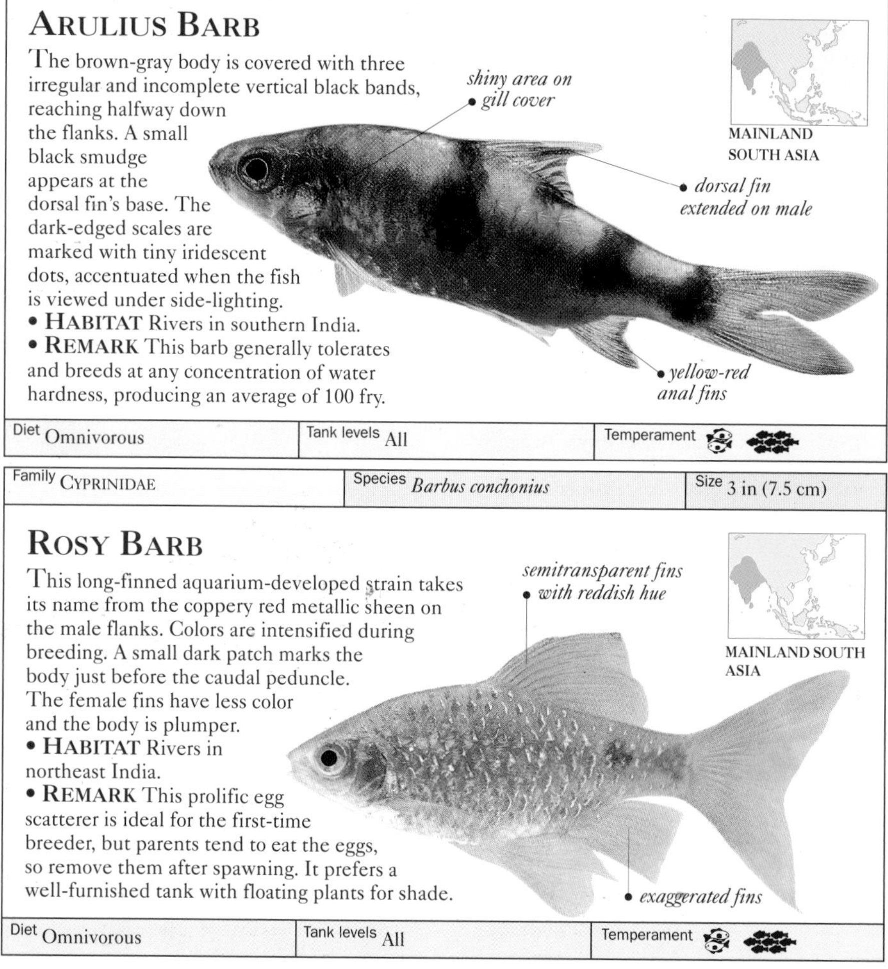

Diet Omnivorous	Tank levels All	Temperament

Family CYPRINIDAE	Species *Barbus conchonius*	Size 3 in (7.5 cm)

ROSY BARB

This long-finned aquarium-developed strain takes its name from the coppery red metallic sheen on the male flanks. Colors are intensified during breeding. A small dark patch marks the body just before the caudal peduncle. The female fins have less color and the body is plumper.

• **HABITAT** Rivers in northeast India.

• **REMARK** This prolific egg scatterer is ideal for the first-time breeder, but parents tend to eat the eggs, so remove them after spawning. It prefers a well-furnished tank with floating plants for shade.

Diet Omnivorous	Tank levels All	Temperament

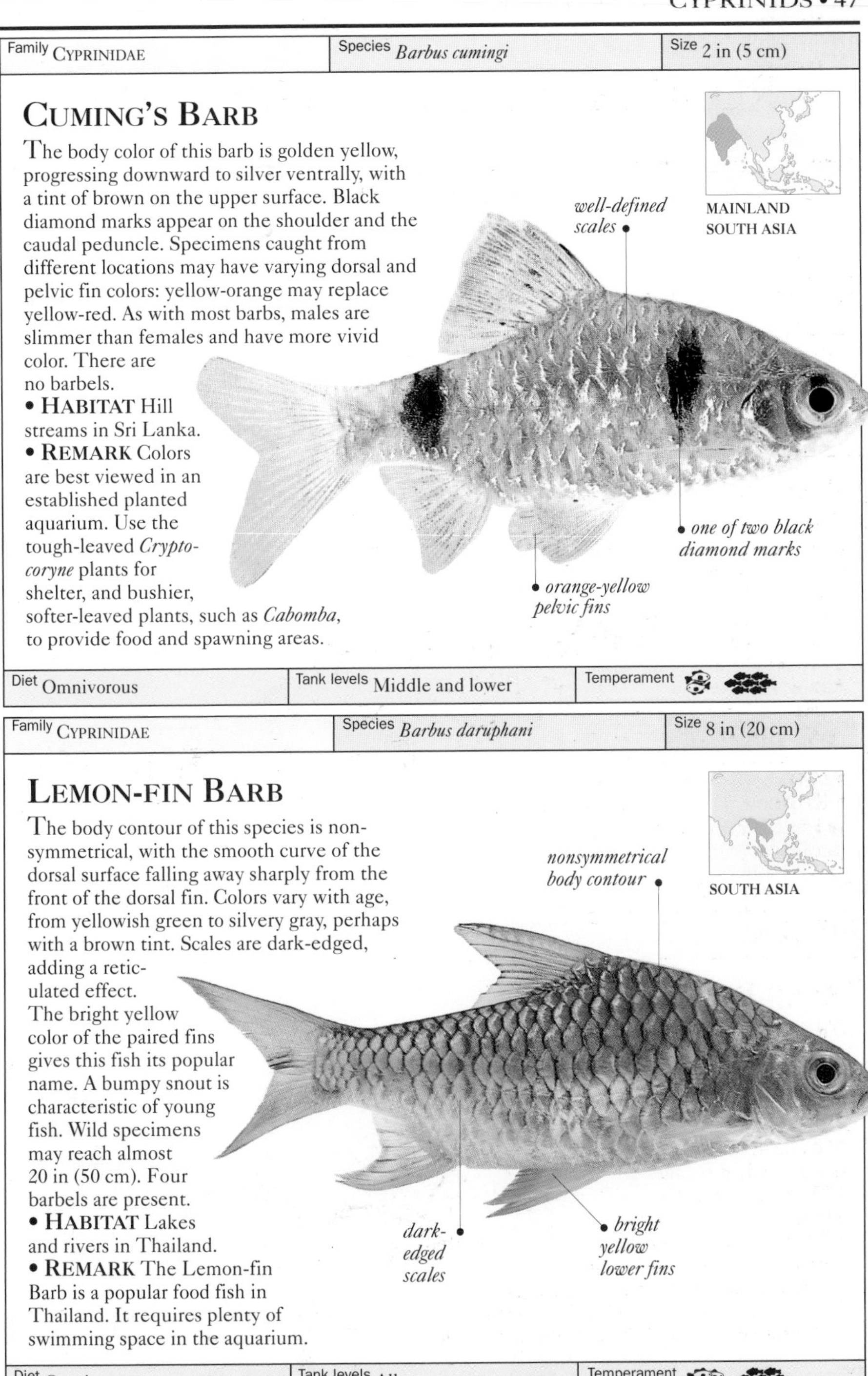

Family CYPRINIDAE	Species *Barbus cumingi*	Size 2 in (5 cm)

CUMING'S BARB

The body color of this barb is golden yellow, progressing downward to silver ventrally, with a tint of brown on the upper surface. Black diamond marks appear on the shoulder and the caudal peduncle. Specimens caught from different locations may have varying dorsal and pelvic fin colors: yellow-orange may replace yellow-red. As with most barbs, males are slimmer than females and have more vivid color. There are no barbels.

• **HABITAT** Hill streams in Sri Lanka.

• **REMARK** Colors are best viewed in an established planted aquarium. Use the tough-leaved *Cryptocoryne* plants for shelter, and bushier, softer-leaved plants, such as *Cabomba*, to provide food and spawning areas.

Diet Omnivorous	Tank levels Middle and lower	Temperament

Family CYPRINIDAE	Species *Barbus daruphani*	Size 8 in (20 cm)

LEMON-FIN BARB

The body contour of this species is nonsymmetrical, with the smooth curve of the dorsal surface falling away sharply from the front of the dorsal fin. Colors vary with age, from yellowish green to silvery gray, perhaps with a brown tint. Scales are dark-edged, adding a reticulated effect. The bright yellow color of the paired fins gives this fish its popular name. A bumpy snout is characteristic of young fish. Wild specimens may reach almost 20 in (50 cm). Four barbels are present.

• **HABITAT** Lakes and rivers in Thailand.

• **REMARK** The Lemon-fin Barb is a popular food fish in Thailand. It requires plenty of swimming space in the aquarium.

Diet Omnivorous	Tank levels All	Temperament

Family CYPRINIDAE	Species *Barbus dorsalis*	Size 5 in (13 cm)

DORSALIS BARB

This fish's body is symmetrical and generally more elongate than that of most barbs. Colors vary from metallic bronze to blushing red, and the brown-green dorsal surface shades down to silver on the ventral region. The dark apex at the front of each scale is distinct.

• **HABITAT** Streams and rivers in Sri Lanka.

• **REMARK** This active species needs an efficient filtration system to keep the water clear of suspended waste matter.

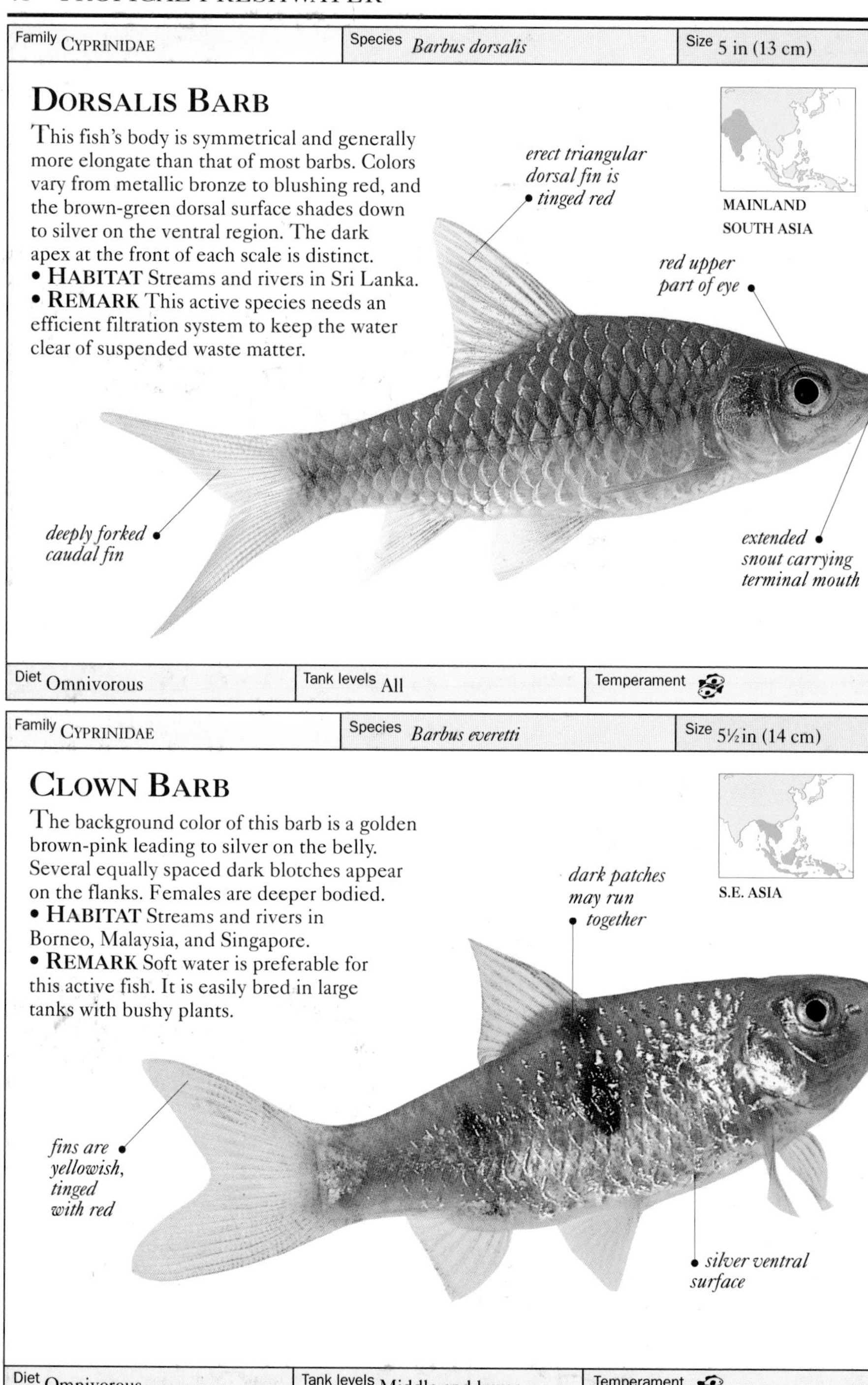

Diet Omnivorous	Tank levels All	Temperament

Family CYPRINIDAE	Species *Barbus everetti*	Size 5½ in (14 cm)

CLOWN BARB

The background color of this barb is a golden brown-pink leading to silver on the belly. Several equally spaced dark blotches appear on the flanks. Females are deeper bodied.

• **HABITAT** Streams and rivers in Borneo, Malaysia, and Singapore.

• **REMARK** Soft water is preferable for this active fish. It is easily bred in large tanks with bushy plants.

Diet Omnivorous	Tank levels Middle and lower	Temperament

Family CYPRINIDAE	Species *Barbus fasciatus*	Size 4¼ in (11 cm)

BANDED OR LINED BARB

The Banded or Lined Barb's pale golden body is crossed horizontally by a number of equally spaced dark stripes. The thickest stripe runs along the mid-line of the body, with three thinner stripes above it and one or two below. The plumper female has a higher arched back, and her stripes are not as bold.

• **HABITAT** Streams and rivers in Malaysia, Sumatra, and Borneo.

• **REMARK** Except for the barbels, this fish exactly resembles *Barbus lineatus*.

• **OTHER NAME** Recently re-classified as *B. eugrammus* or Striped Barb.

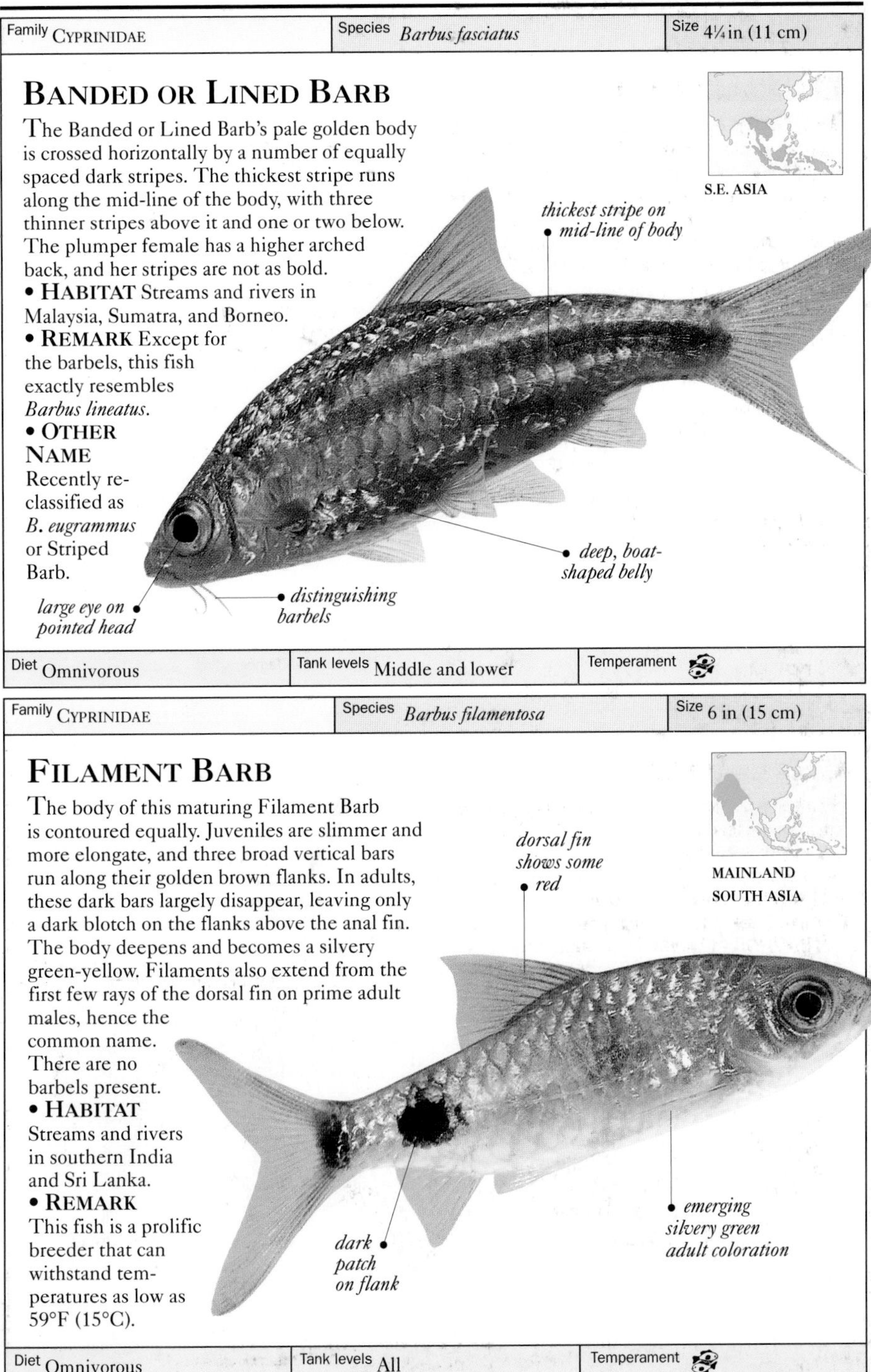

Diet Omnivorous	Tank levels Middle and lower	Temperament

Family CYPRINIDAE	Species *Barbus filamentosa*	Size 6 in (15 cm)

FILAMENT BARB

The body of this maturing Filament Barb is contoured equally. Juveniles are slimmer and more elongate, and three broad vertical bars run along their golden brown flanks. In adults, these dark bars largely disappear, leaving only a dark blotch on the flanks above the anal fin. The body deepens and becomes a silvery green-yellow. Filaments also extend from the first few rays of the dorsal fin on prime adult males, hence the common name. There are no barbels present.

• **HABITAT** Streams and rivers in southern India and Sri Lanka.

• **REMARK** This fish is a prolific breeder that can withstand temperatures as low as 59°F (15°C).

Diet Omnivorous	Tank levels All	Temperament

Family CYPRINIDAE	Species *Barbus gelius*	Size 1½ in (4 cm)

GOLDEN DWARF BARB

Dark irregular patches appear on the golden brown body of this small active fish. The high-backed shape is rounded by a deep belly, and it tapers toward a slender caudal peduncle in which there may be some red-gold coloring, especially in a well-fed male. Fins are held erect and are generally transparent.

• **HABITAT** Streams and rivers in northeast India and Bengal.

• **REMARK** This modestly sized fish is highly active and prefers to shoal. It is an excellent subject for the species or small fish community tank and can withstand fairly low temperatures.

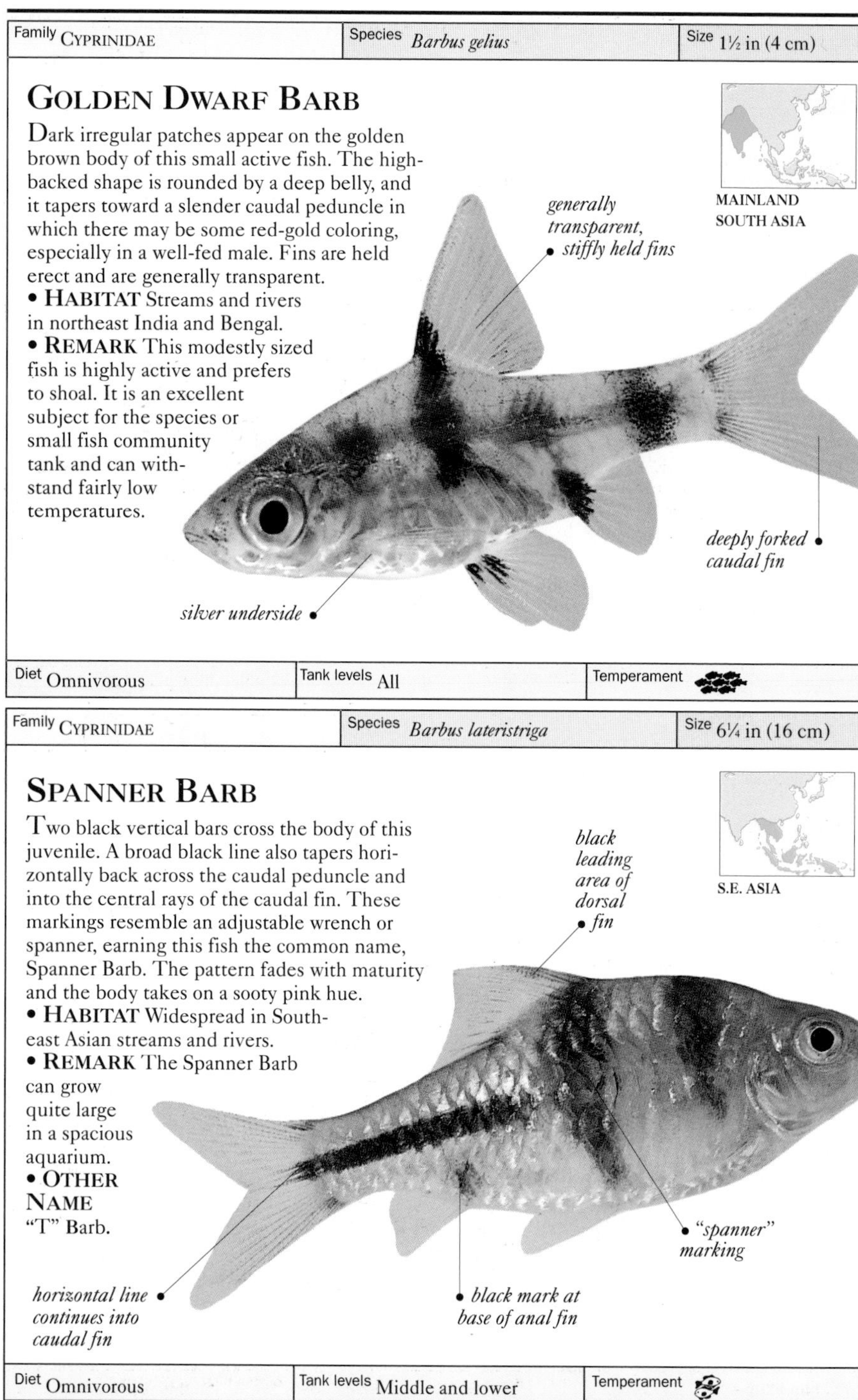

Diet Omnivorous	Tank levels All	Temperament

Family CYPRINIDAE	Species *Barbus lateristriga*	Size 6¼ in (16 cm)

SPANNER BARB

Two black vertical bars cross the body of this juvenile. A broad black line also tapers horizontally back across the caudal peduncle and into the central rays of the caudal fin. These markings resemble an adjustable wrench or spanner, earning this fish the common name, Spanner Barb. The pattern fades with maturity and the body takes on a sooty pink hue.

• **HABITAT** Widespread in Southeast Asian streams and rivers.

• **REMARK** The Spanner Barb can grow quite large in a spacious aquarium.

• **OTHER NAME** "T" Barb.

Diet Omnivorous	Tank levels Middle and lower	Temperament

Family CYPRINIDAE	Species *Barbus melanympyx*	Size 4 in (10 cm)

EMBER BARB

Four broad, incomplete black bars cross the body of the Ember Barb. A thin black line also crosses the end of the caudal peduncle. The general hue of the male is sooty pink which, when breeding, becomes a vivid pink-red, with black bars that almost merge.

• **HABITAT** Flowing waters of Malaysia and parts of Indonesia.

• **REMARK** The appearance is similar to that of *Barbus arulius*, but the male does not develop dorsal extensions.

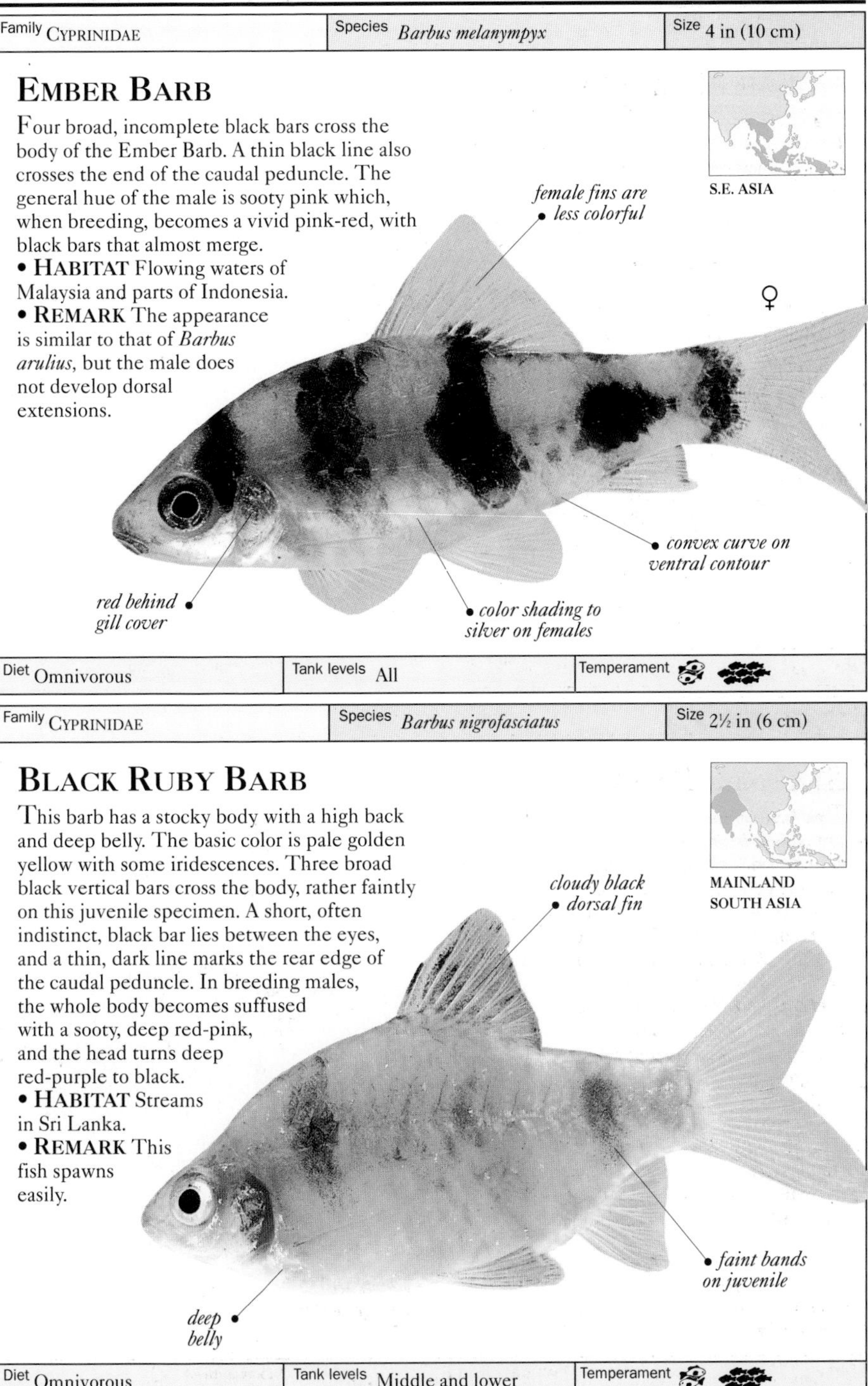

Diet Omnivorous	Tank levels All	Temperament

Family CYPRINIDAE	Species *Barbus nigrofasciatus*	Size 2½ in (6 cm)

BLACK RUBY BARB

This barb has a stocky body with a high back and deep belly. The basic color is pale golden yellow with some iridescences. Three broad black vertical bars cross the body, rather faintly on this juvenile specimen. A short, often indistinct, black bar lies between the eyes, and a thin, dark line marks the rear edge of the caudal peduncle. In breeding males, the whole body becomes suffused with a sooty, deep red-pink, and the head turns deep red-purple to black.

• **HABITAT** Streams in Sri Lanka.

• **REMARK** This fish spawns easily.

Diet Omnivorous	Tank levels Middle and lower	Temperament

Family CYPRINIDAE	Species *Barbus "odessa"*	Size 2½ in (6 cm)

ODESSA BARB

SOUTH ASIA

Two dark blotches mark the flanks of this pale greenish brown barb. Sexual differences are obvious, especially at breeding times, as the male has a broad band of red on the side and dark speckling in the dorsal fin. Like most egg-laying species, the female is generally plumper and less colorful.

• **HABITAT** This fish does not occur naturally. It is named after the Ukrainian town where it is reported to have first been bred for the aquarium.

• **REMARK** This species may be closely related to, or a variety of, the Ticto Barb (see p.57) from south Asia.

red intensifies during breeding

clear caudal fin

well-defined scales

Diet Omnivorous	Tank levels Middle and lower	Temperament

Family CYPRINIDAE	Species *Barbus oligolepis*	Size 2 in (5 cm)

CHECKER BARB

S.E. ASIAN ISLANDS

The most distinctive feature of this yellow-brown fish is the scale pattern. On prime specimens, each scale has a dark edge and front portion, which together account for the "checkered" effect. A dark line marks the flanks, and the area below it is often less speckled on the male. Male fins are usually edged with black, while the rays of the female are generally tinted yellow.

• **HABITAT** Streams and rivers in Indonesia and Sumatra.

• **REMARK** Males display to each other.

high triangular dorsal fin

dark line on flanks

male fins edged with black

Diet Omnivorous	Tank levels Middle and lower	Temperament  

Family CYPRINIDAE	Species *Barbus pentazona johorensis*	Size 2 in (5 cm)

FIVE-BANDED BARB

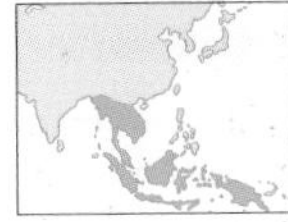

Five prominent, vertical dark bands cross the body of this subspecies. The first passes through the eye, not quite meeting at the ventral surface. Most fins have red shading, usually at the base; this is less evident in the caudal fin and on this juvenile. Females are plumper and less intensely colored.

• **HABITAT** Streams in Borneo, Malaysia, and Sumatra.

• **REMARK** There are several other subspecies of *Barbus pentazona*, which can be identified by differences in the bands.

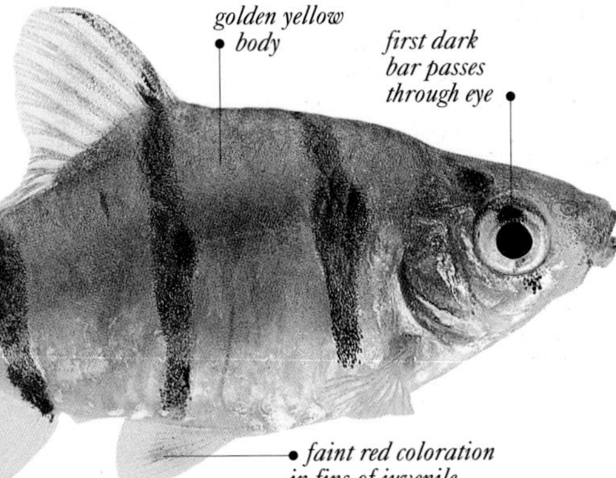

Diet Omnivorous	Tank levels Middle and lower	Temperament 

Family CYPRINIDAE	Species *Barbus roloffi*	Size 2 in (5 cm)

ROLOFF'S BARB

The dorsal surface of this barb is creamy, shading down to silver on the flanks. An indistinct line runs along the flanks, composed of dark streaks on the scales. Dorsal fins carry a prominent black tip. The head is pointed, and the eye is especially large. Females are plumper and duller.

• **HABITAT** Streams in Thailand.

• **REMARK** This rarely imported species may be the same fish as *Oreichthys cosuatis*, that was classified first, and is widespread in India.

• **OTHER NAME** Streak-scaled Barb.

Diet Omnivorous	Tank levels Middle and lower	Temperament  

Family CYPRINIDAE	Species *Barbus sachsi*	Size 4 in (10 cm)

GOLDEN BARB

SOUTH ASIA

This slightly elongate fish has a narrow caudal peduncle and plump sides. The general body coloration is yellow, with silver on the ventral surface. There may be some short, dark vertical streaks or marks randomly distributed over the body, especially on juveniles (like this specimen); but the marks usually fade with age. Female Golden Barbs are plumper.

- **HABITAT** Streams in Singapore.
- **REMARK** Differences between this species and the Schuberti Barb (below) are slight. It is thought that they might be related.

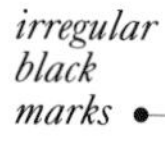

Diet Omnivorous	Tank levels Middle and lower	Temperament  

Family CYPRINIDAE	Species *Barbus "schuberti"*	Size 3 in (7.5 cm)

SCHUBERTI BARB

Barbs look their best in schools

A number of dark speckles appear on the dorsal surface of this species. Larger blotches run above the lateral line, and a dark blotch crosses the end of the caudal peduncle. The main color is yellow, with metallic green along the top. On prime specimens, fins are bright red and streaked with yellow, while the base of the caudal fin and the two tail lobes have bright red portions. Females are fuller.

- **HABITAT** Streams and rivers in south Asia.
- **REMARK** This fish has not been scientifically classified. It bears the name of the American aquarist who discovered it, Thomas Schubert. Some suggest that it is a color strain of the Golden Barb (above).

reddish eye

metallic green on flanks

SOUTH ASIA

dark blotch on caudal peduncle

Diet Omnivorous	Tank levels Middle and lower	Temperament 

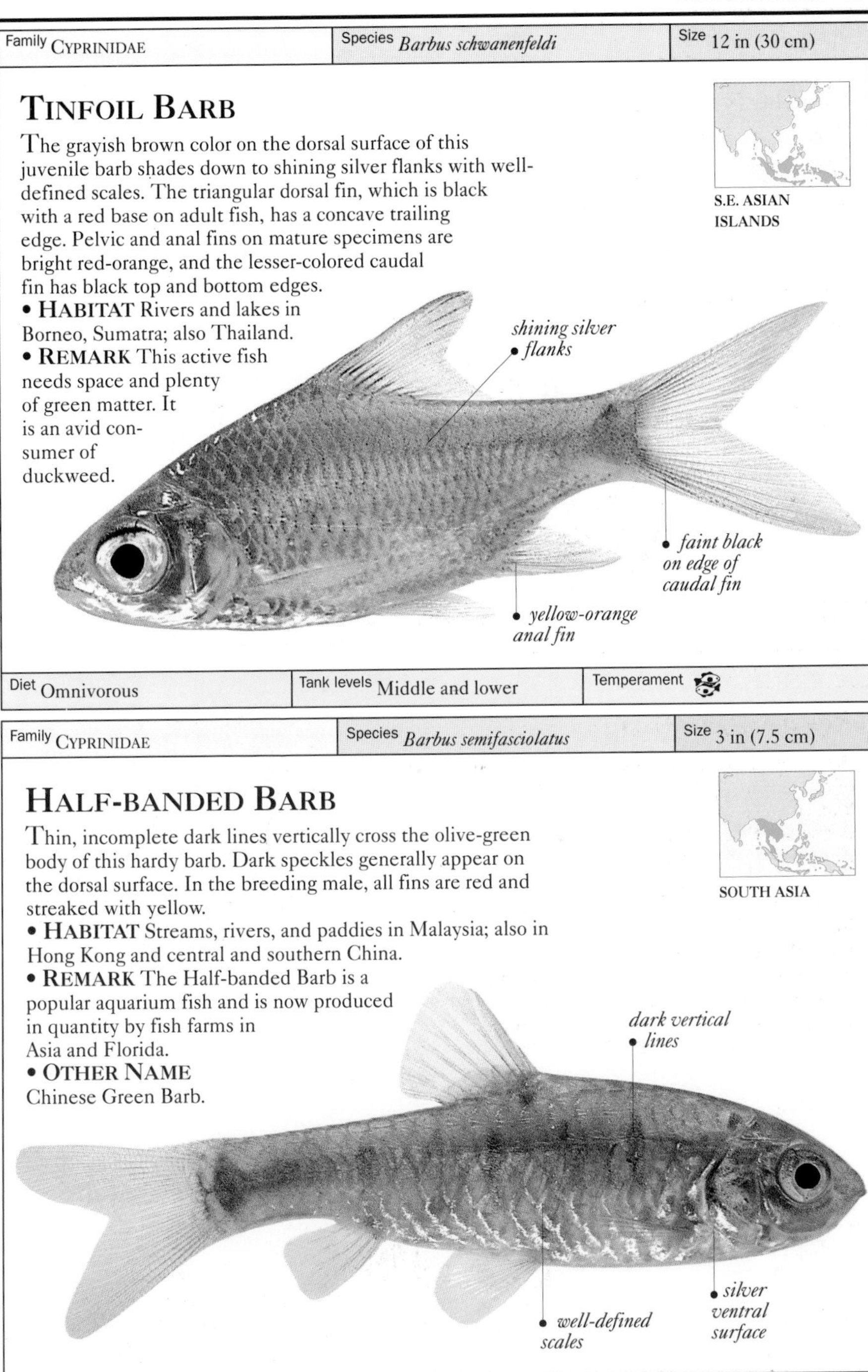

Family CYPRINIDAE	Species *Barbus schwanenfeldi*	Size 12 in (30 cm)

TINFOIL BARB

The grayish brown color on the dorsal surface of this juvenile barb shades down to shining silver flanks with well-defined scales. The triangular dorsal fin, which is black with a red base on adult fish, has a concave trailing edge. Pelvic and anal fins on mature specimens are bright red-orange, and the lesser-colored caudal fin has black top and bottom edges.

• **HABITAT** Rivers and lakes in Borneo, Sumatra; also Thailand.

• **REMARK** This active fish needs space and plenty of green matter. It is an avid consumer of duckweed.

Diet Omnivorous	Tank levels Middle and lower	Temperament

Family CYPRINIDAE	Species *Barbus semifasciolatus*	Size 3 in (7.5 cm)

HALF-BANDED BARB

Thin, incomplete dark lines vertically cross the olive-green body of this hardy barb. Dark speckles generally appear on the dorsal surface. In the breeding male, all fins are red and streaked with yellow.

• **HABITAT** Streams, rivers, and paddies in Malaysia; also in Hong Kong and central and southern China.

• **REMARK** The Half-banded Barb is a popular aquarium fish and is now produced in quantity by fish farms in Asia and Florida.

• **OTHER NAME** Chinese Green Barb.

Diet Omnivorous	Tank levels Middle and lower	Temperament

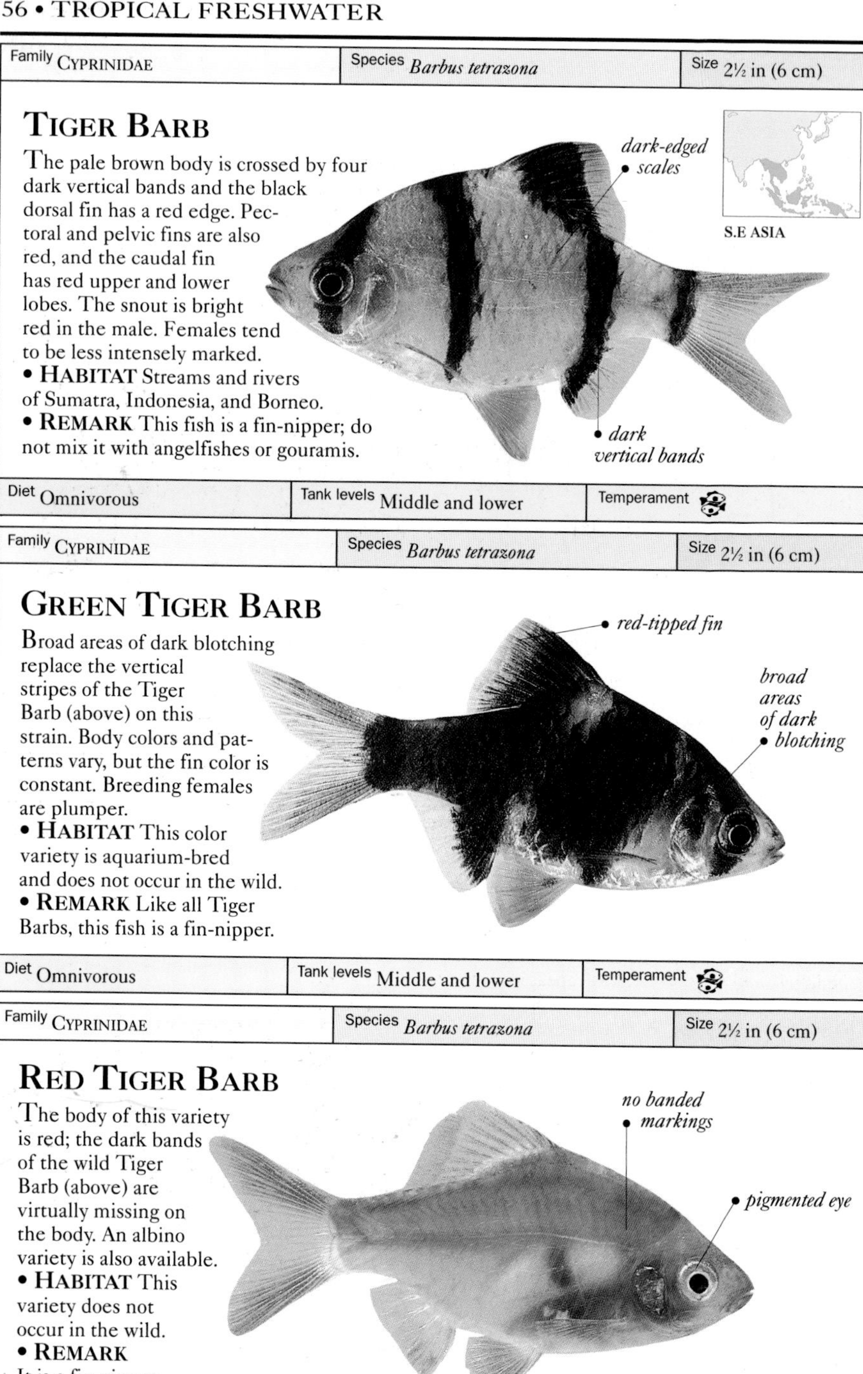

Family CYPRINIDAE	Species *Barbus tetrazona*	Size 2½ in (6 cm)

TIGER BARB

The pale brown body is crossed by four dark vertical bands and the black dorsal fin has a red edge. Pectoral and pelvic fins are also red, and the caudal fin has red upper and lower lobes. The snout is bright red in the male. Females tend to be less intensely marked.

• **HABITAT** Streams and rivers of Sumatra, Indonesia, and Borneo.

• **REMARK** This fish is a fin-nipper; do not mix it with angelfishes or gouramis.

Diet Omnivorous	Tank levels Middle and lower	Temperament

Family CYPRINIDAE	Species *Barbus tetrazona*	Size 2½ in (6 cm)

GREEN TIGER BARB

Broad areas of dark blotching replace the vertical stripes of the Tiger Barb (above) on this strain. Body colors and patterns vary, but the fin color is constant. Breeding females are plumper.

• **HABITAT** This color variety is aquarium-bred and does not occur in the wild.

• **REMARK** Like all Tiger Barbs, this fish is a fin-nipper.

Diet Omnivorous	Tank levels Middle and lower	Temperament

Family CYPRINIDAE	Species *Barbus tetrazona*	Size 2½ in (6 cm)

RED TIGER BARB

The body of this variety is red; the dark bands of the wild Tiger Barb (above) are virtually missing on the body. An albino variety is also available.

• **HABITAT** This variety does not occur in the wild.

• **REMARK** It is a fin-nipper.

Diet Omnivorous	Tank levels Middle and lower	Temperament

Family CYPRINIDAE	Species *Barbus ticto stoliczkae*	Size 2½ in (6 cm)

TICTO BARB

MAINLAND SOUTH ASIA

The pale brown-silver body of this fish is covered by dark-edged scales. It is marked by two small black patches – on the caudal peduncle and behind the gill cover. The dorsal fin is red and black and is brighter in the male. The other fins are yellowish. Females are plumper, particularly before breeding.

• **HABITAT** Streams and rivers in India and Sri Lanka; also Burma.

• **REMARK** The classification of this subspecies, along with *Barbus ticto ticto*, has caused confusion. This fish may be the ancestral stock that produced the Odessa Barb (see p.52). It is easily bred.

• **OTHER NAME** *Barbus stoliczkanus*.

red and black in male dorsal fin

black patch on flanks

red above eye

Diet Omnivorous	Tank levels Middle and lower	Temperament

Family CYPRINIDAE	Species *Barbus titteya*	Size 2 in (5 cm)

CHERRY BARB

MAINLAND SOUTH ASIA

The Cherry Barb's slim body is less carplike than most barbs. It is reddish brown and bright red in the breeding male. A dark longitudinal band runs from the snout to the end of the caudal peduncle and may be partially repeated on the row of scales beneath. A gold line appears above these bands. A pair of barbels is present on the upper lip and the plain fins match the body color. The female fins may lack color.

• **HABITAT** Streams thoughout Sri Lanka.

• **REMARK** The Cherry Barb is suitable for small aquariums and should be kept with other small fishes. It breeds readily in captivity. Subdued lighting conditions complement the fish's coloring.

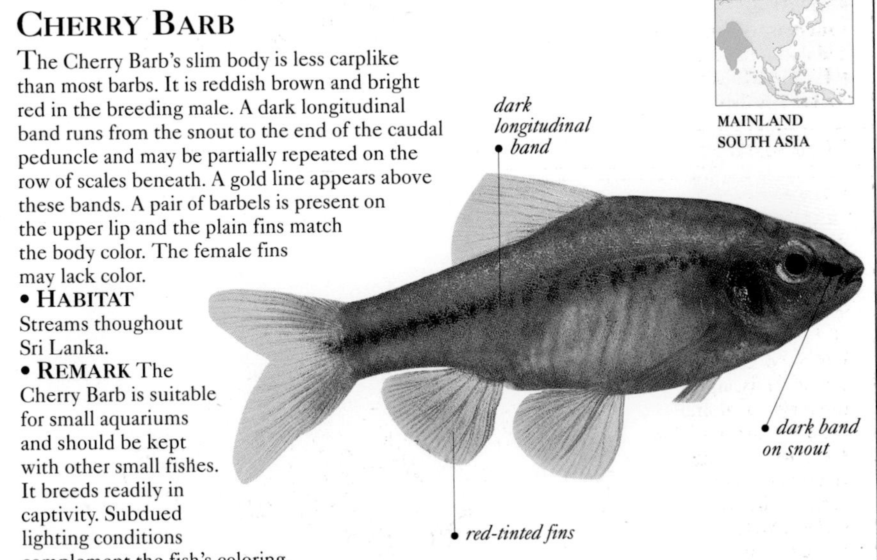

Diet Omnivorous	Tank levels Middle and lower	Temperament

Family CYPRINIDAE	Species *Barbus vittatus*	Size 2½ in (6 cm)

BANDED BARB

MAINLAND SOUTH ASIA

The shape of the Banded Barb is typical of the genus. An olive-green dorsal surface shades down to a greenish silver belly. Large scales may show iridescences under favorable lighting conditions. A dark spot appears at the base of the caudal peduncle. All fins are faintly greenish yellow, but the dorsal fin has an oblique black band passing through it from which the common name is derived.

• **HABITAT** Streams and rivers throughout India and Sri Lanka.

• **REMARK** This species is not common, as the aquarium market tends to favor more colorful barbs.

band through dorsal fin

scales may show iridescences

dark spot on caudal peduncle

Diet Omnivorous	Tank levels Middle and lower	Temperament

Family CYPRINIDAE	Species *Barbus walkeri*	Size 4 in (10 cm)

WALKER'S BARB

TROPICAL AFRICA

The body of this African barb is not as deep as those of the Asian barbs and is slightly more elongated. It is golden brown with well-defined scales. Three equally spaced dark spots appear on the flanks with a further indistinct spot just below the dorsal fin. The front two spots are connected by a dark zigzag line. Mouth and eyes are large. There are dark speckles in the dorsal fin, and the gill cover is reddish gold.

• **HABITAT** Coastal rivers in Ghana.

• **REMARK** Walker's Barb is similar in appearance to the Three-spot Barb, another African species.

dark zigzag line

reddish gold gill cover

three spots on flanks

Diet Omnivorous	Tank levels Middle and lower	Temperament 

Family CYPRINIDAE	Species *Brachydanio albolineatus*	Size 2 in (5 cm)

PEARL DANIO

S.E. ASIA

Mature specimens of the Pearl Danio are gray-green, with iridescences. Body coloration varies depending upon lighting conditions: under sidelighting, and especially when spawning, the fish takes on an attractive pearly, blue-violet luster. A thin gold line runs along the rear of the body. Fins are generally translucent green, but some may show red or yellow shading at their bases. The female has a deeper body.

- **HABITAT** Reasonably fast-flowing streams in Myanmar (Burma), Sumatra, and Thailand.
- **REMARK** This fish is an excellent jumper and needs a large tank fitted with a secure hood.

blue-violet gill cover

gold central line

yellow shading on translucent fins

Diet Omnivorous	Tank levels Upper and middle	Temperament

Family CYPRINIDAE	Species *Brachydanio kerri*	Size 2 in (5 cm)

BLUE DANIO

SOUTH ASIA

Normally gray-blue with iridescences, the variable colors of this fish take on a delicate pastel blue luster under side-lighting and especially when spawning. Two thin gold lines run back from the dark-centered, gold-rimmed eye to the end of the caudal peduncle. Fins are generally translucent green, but some may show yellowish shading. Sexual differences in this species include more intense colors in the male and a deeper female body.

- **HABITAT** Streams on islands in the Bay of Bengal off the west coast of Thailand.
- **REMARK** The Blue Danio shares the aquarium requirements of the similarly formed Pearl Danio (above).

gray-blue body with iridescences

dark, gold-rimmed eye

thin gold lines extend from eye to caudal fin

yellow shading on fin

Diet Omnivorous	Tank levels Upper and middle	Temperament 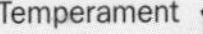 

Family CYPRINIDAE	Species *Brachydanio frankei*	Size 1¾ in (4.5 cm)

LEOPARD DANIO

Leopardlike spots on a gold background give these fish their popular name. Of the two fish shown here, the long-finned variety has been aquarium-developed. Spots on both are smaller and closer together on the upper body, giving a darker appearance; the spots may also group together to form interrupted "lines," particularly on the caudal peduncle. Faint patterning is apparent in the yellowish anal fin and the center of the caudal fin. The female is usually larger than the male, even outside the breeding season, with a more convex body outline.

• **HABITAT** The wild species is from southern and central India; also ranging into the Malay peninsula.

• **REMARK** The classification of this species has been argued over since its introduction to the aquarium, a process further complicated by its ready hybridization with *Brachydanio rerio* and *B. albolineatus*. Some authorities assume it to be an offspring of one of these two species.

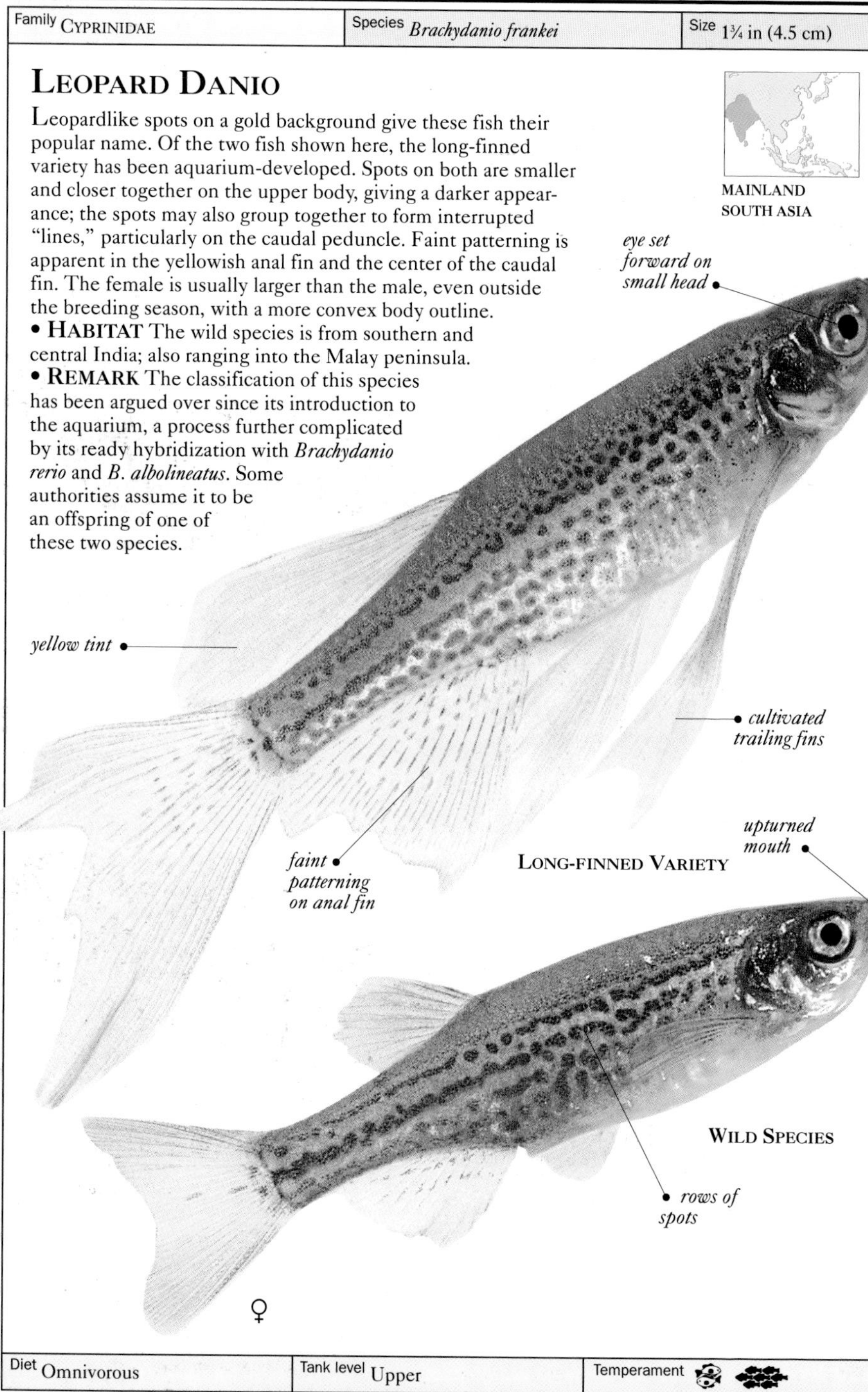

Diet Omnivorous	Tank level Upper	Temperament

Family CYPRINIDAE	Species *Brachydanio rerio*	Size 1¾ in (4.5 cm)

ZEBRA DANIO

This fish has a base color of silver or gold, strikingly marked by a number of bright blue or purple horizontal lines running from the head to the rear edge of the caudal fin. This pattern is repeated in the anal and caudal fins; the dorsal area is yellowish olive. The long-finned variety has been aquarium-developed. All males are slimmer and slightly smaller than the females.

- **HABITAT** The wild species is from east India.
- **REMARK** This is a very active species, constantly on the move in the upper levels of the water; a group is recommended. It is a prolific spawner, which makes it a good choice for first breeding attempts, but precautions should be taken to prevent the adults from eating the eggs, even though the eggs may be lodged in densely leaved plants provided for the purpose. Selective breeding has produced both long-finned and veil-tailed strains.

MAINLAND SOUTH ASIA

upturned mouth

slimmer body of male

LONG-FINNED VARIETY

unpatterned pelvic fins

pattern continues on anal fin

dorsal fin set well back

horizontal lines run length of body

WILD SPECIES

♀

pattern continues on caudal fin

Diet Omnivorous	Tank level Upper	Temperament

Family CYPRINIDAE	Species *Danio aequipinnatus*	Size 4 in (10 cm)

GIANT DANIO

The Giant Danio's body is pale blue, with three or four vertical yellow lines from the gill cover to the caudal peduncle. Females have bodies of greater depth and their yellow lines turn up at the beginning of the caudal fin.

- **HABITAT** Hill streams of southwest India and Sri Lanka.
- **REMARK** This fish is extremely active and requires plenty of space. It looks best when kept in a school.
- **OTHER NAME** Formerly known as *Danio malarbaricus*.

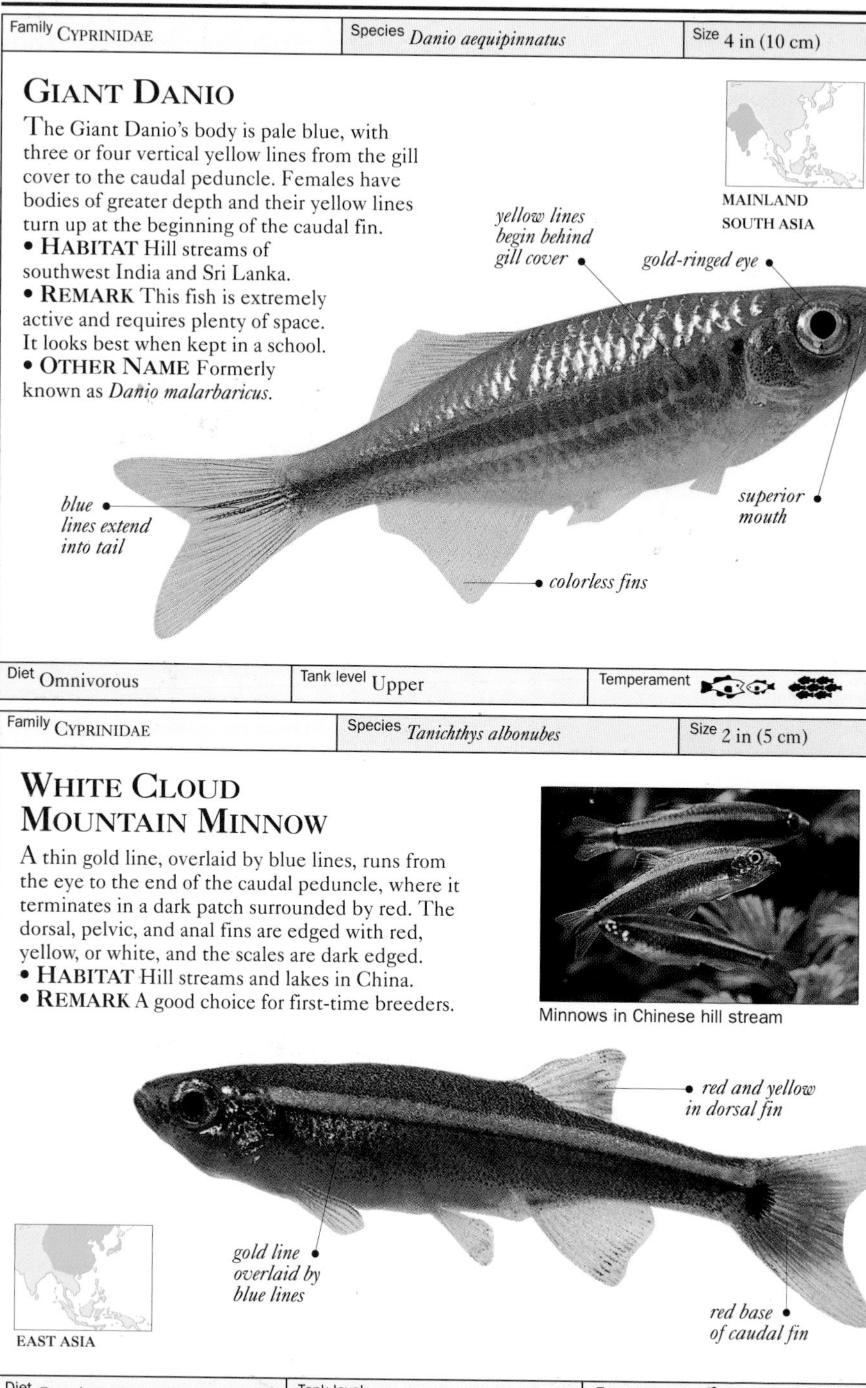

Diet Omnivorous	Tank level Upper	Temperament

Family CYPRINIDAE	Species *Tanichthys albonubes*	Size 2 in (5 cm)

WHITE CLOUD MOUNTAIN MINNOW

A thin gold line, overlaid by blue lines, runs from the eye to the end of the caudal peduncle, where it terminates in a dark patch surrounded by red. The dorsal, pelvic, and anal fins are edged with red, yellow, or white, and the scales are dark edged.

- **HABITAT** Hill streams and lakes in China.
- **REMARK** A good choice for first-time breeders.

Diet Omnivorous	Tank level Upper	Temperament

Family CYPRINIDAE	Species *Rasbora borapetensis*	Size 2 in (5 cm)

RED-TAILED RASBORA

The slim pale yellow body has a distinctive dark band from the gill cover to the end of the caudal peduncle, accentuated by a thin gold band above it. A dark line also runs along the base of the anal fin. The caudal fin is red on prime, mature specimens, giving the fish its common name. Males are the slimmer sex.

- **HABITAT** Streams in Thailand.
- **REMARK** These fish are prolific breeders but eat their eggs. A well-filtered medium-size aquarium with plenty of space suits this active species.

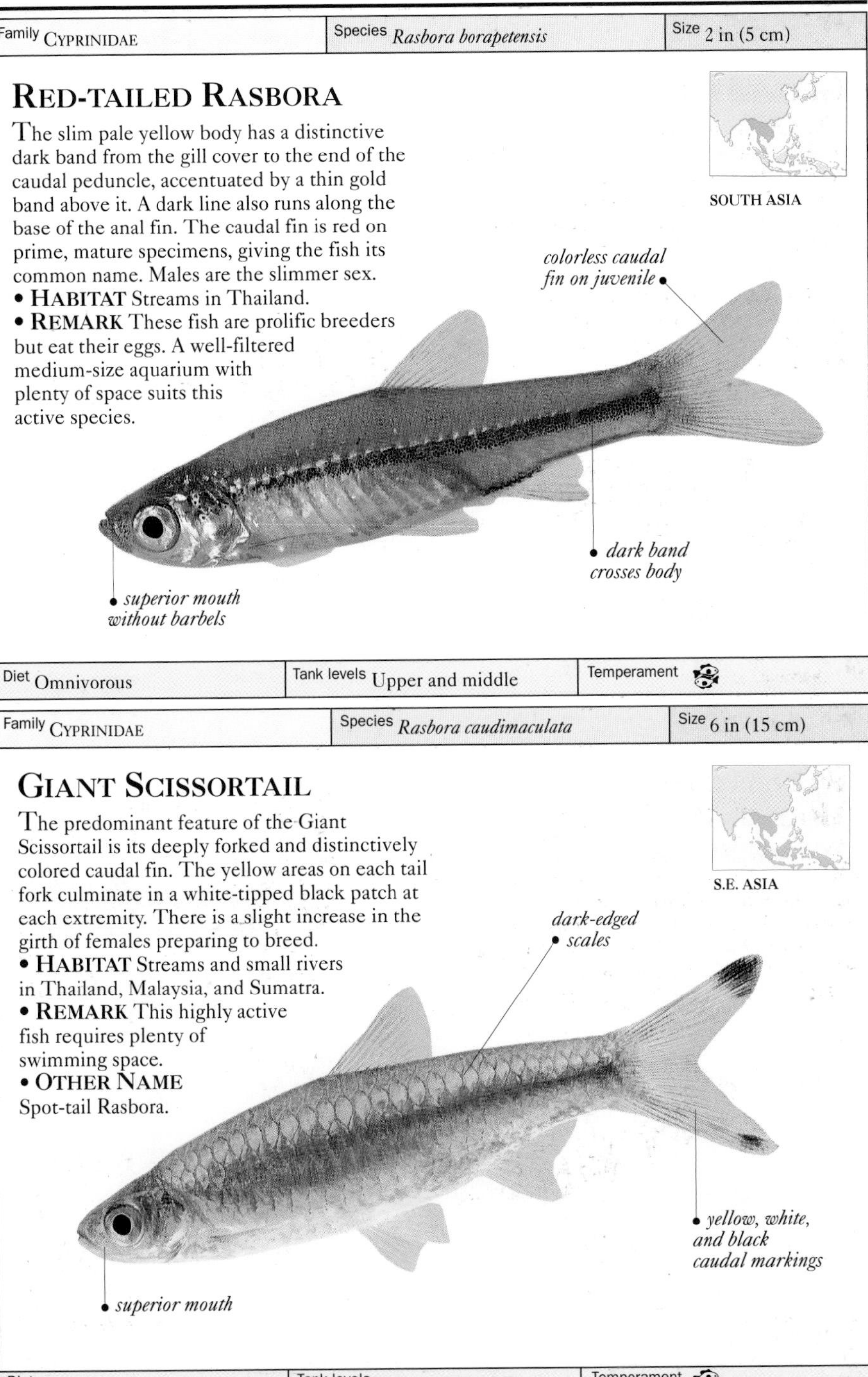

Diet Omnivorous	Tank levels Upper and middle	Temperament

Family CYPRINIDAE	Species *Rasbora caudimaculata*	Size 6 in (15 cm)

GIANT SCISSORTAIL

The predominant feature of the Giant Scissortail is its deeply forked and distinctively colored caudal fin. The yellow areas on each tail fork culminate in a white-tipped black patch at each extremity. There is a slight increase in the girth of females preparing to breed.

- **HABITAT** Streams and small rivers in Thailand, Malaysia, and Sumatra.
- **REMARK** This highly active fish requires plenty of swimming space.
- **OTHER NAME** Spot-tail Rasbora.

Diet Omnivorous	Tank levels Upper and middle	Temperament

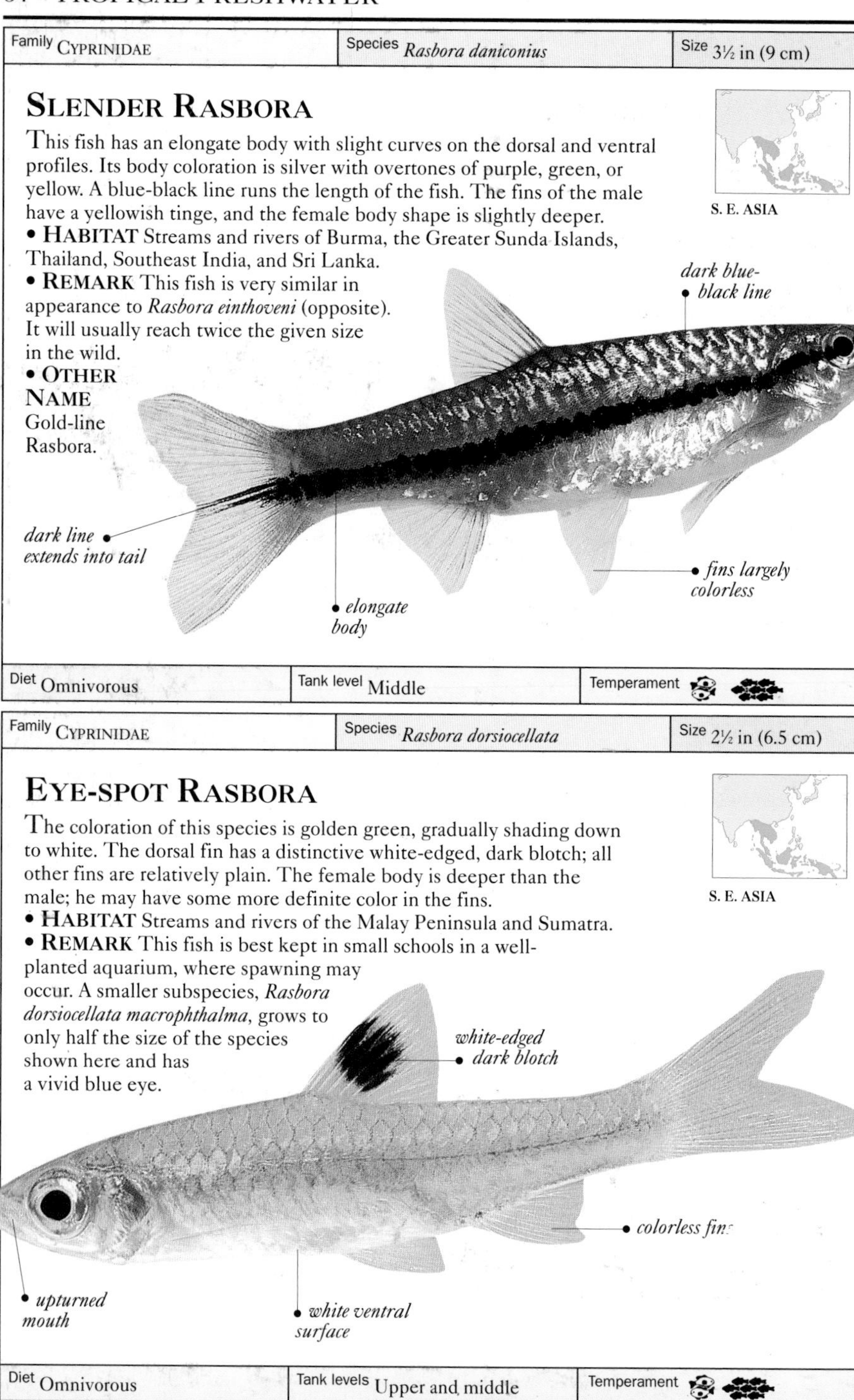

Family CYPRINIDAE	Species *Rasbora daniconius*	Size 3½ in (9 cm)

SLENDER RASBORA

This fish has an elongate body with slight curves on the dorsal and ventral profiles. Its body coloration is silver with overtones of purple, green, or yellow. A blue-black line runs the length of the fish. The fins of the male have a yellowish tinge, and the female body shape is slightly deeper.

• **HABITAT** Streams and rivers of Burma, the Greater Sunda Islands, Thailand, Southeast India, and Sri Lanka.

• **REMARK** This fish is very similar in appearance to *Rasbora einthoveni* (opposite). It will usually reach twice the given size in the wild.

• **OTHER NAME** Gold-line Rasbora.

Diet Omnivorous	Tank level Middle	Temperament

Family CYPRINIDAE	Species *Rasbora dorsiocellata*	Size 2½ in (6.5 cm)

EYE-SPOT RASBORA

The coloration of this species is golden green, gradually shading down to white. The dorsal fin has a distinctive white-edged, dark blotch; all other fins are relatively plain. The female body is deeper than the male; he may have some more definite color in the fins.

• **HABITAT** Streams and rivers of the Malay Peninsula and Sumatra.

• **REMARK** This fish is best kept in small schools in a well-planted aquarium, where spawning may occur. A smaller subspecies, *Rasbora dorsiocellata macrophthalma*, grows to only half the size of the species shown here and has a vivid blue eye.

Diet Omnivorous	Tank levels Upper and middle	Temperament

Family CYPRINIDAE	Species *Rasbora einthoveni*	Size 3½ in (9 cm)

BRILLIANT RASBORA

S. E. ASIA

The body of this pinkish brown fish may carry violet overtones, depending on lighting conditions. A blue-black line runs from the tip of the snout to the rear edge of the caudal fin. Females are plumper and more deep-set than males.

• **HABITAT** Flowing and stationary waters of Borneo, Malaysia, Sumatra, and Thailand.

• **REMARK** A hardy and active shoaling species, this fish can tolerate temperatures as low as 65°F (18°C).

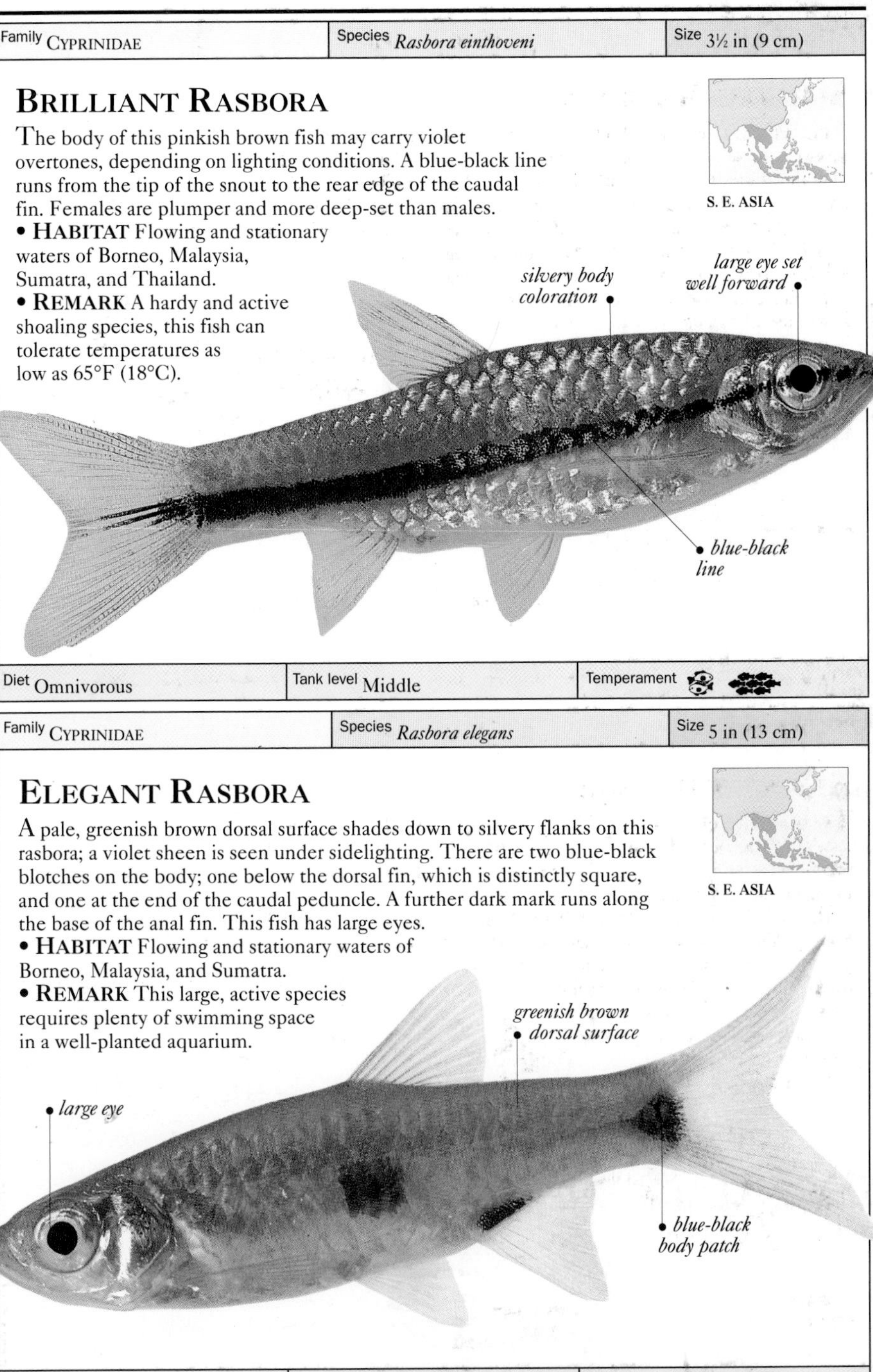

Diet Omnivorous	Tank level Middle	Temperament

Family CYPRINIDAE	Species *Rasbora elegans*	Size 5 in (13 cm)

ELEGANT RASBORA

S. E. ASIA

A pale, greenish brown dorsal surface shades down to silvery flanks on this rasbora; a violet sheen is seen under sidelighting. There are two blue-black blotches on the body; one below the dorsal fin, which is distinctly square, and one at the end of the caudal peduncle. A further dark mark runs along the base of the anal fin. This fish has large eyes.

• **HABITAT** Flowing and stationary waters of Borneo, Malaysia, and Sumatra.

• **REMARK** This large, active species requires plenty of swimming space in a well-planted aquarium.

Diet Omnivorous	Tank level Middle	Temperament

Family CYPRINIDAE	Species *Rasbora heteromorpha*	Size 1½ in (4 cm)

HARLEQUIN RASBORA

The distinguishing mark of the Harlequin Rasbora is a blue-black triangular patch on the flank, tapering back to the caudal peduncle. Coloration is olive-green on the dorsal surface, shading down to silver. Mature males have a straighter front edge and a more pointed lower corner to the triangle; the female body is considerably plumper.

- **HABITAT** Forest streams and rivers in Thailand, Malaysia, and Sumatra.
- **REMARK** After a courtship ritual by the male, eggs are laid and fertilized on the underside of a broad leaf.

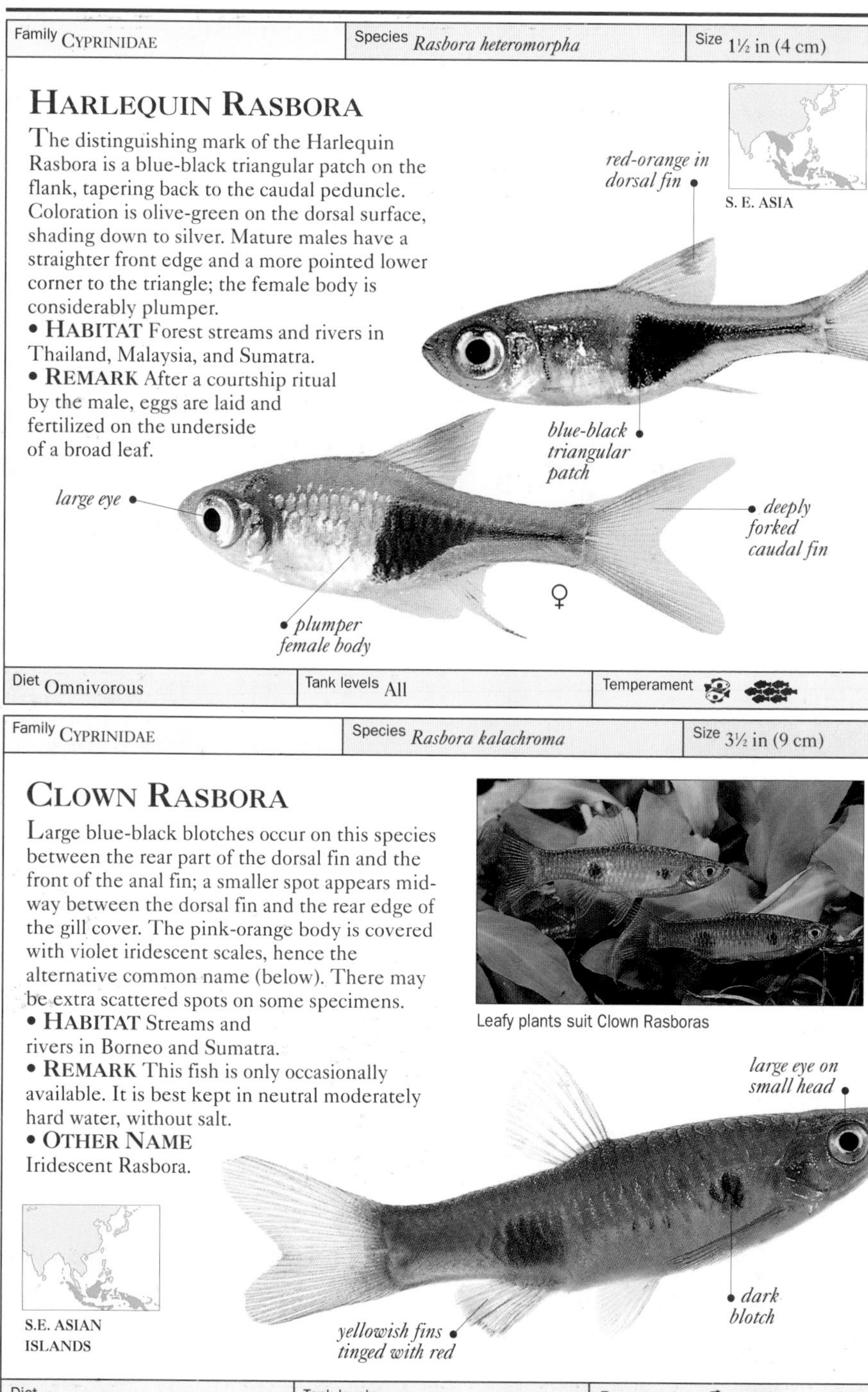

Diet Omnivorous	Tank levels All	Temperament

Family CYPRINIDAE	Species *Rasbora kalachroma*	Size 3½ in (9 cm)

CLOWN RASBORA

Large blue-black blotches occur on this species between the rear part of the dorsal fin and the front of the anal fin; a smaller spot appears midway between the dorsal fin and the rear edge of the gill cover. The pink-orange body is covered with violet iridescent scales, hence the alternative common name (below). There may be extra scattered spots on some specimens.

- **HABITAT** Streams and rivers in Borneo and Sumatra.
- **REMARK** This fish is only occasionally available. It is best kept in neutral moderately hard water, without salt.
- **OTHER NAME** Iridescent Rasbora.

Diet Omnivorous	Tank levels All	Temperament

Family CYPRINIDAE	Species *Rasbora maculata*	Size 1 in (2.5 cm)

SPOTTED RASBORA

The Spotted Rasbora is not uniform in shape compared with the Clown Rasbora (opposite); the caudal peduncle, in particular, is longer and narrower. Similarity is found in the dark spots along the flanks. The fins of this species may be reddish, and the dorsal fin has black and pink front rays. The ventral profile of the male is flat.

- **HABITAT** Streams and rivers in Sumatra, Malaysia, and Singapore.
- **REMARK** Small aquariums will suffice if tankmates are small.
- **OTHER NAMES** Pygmy Rasbora, Dwarf Rasbora.

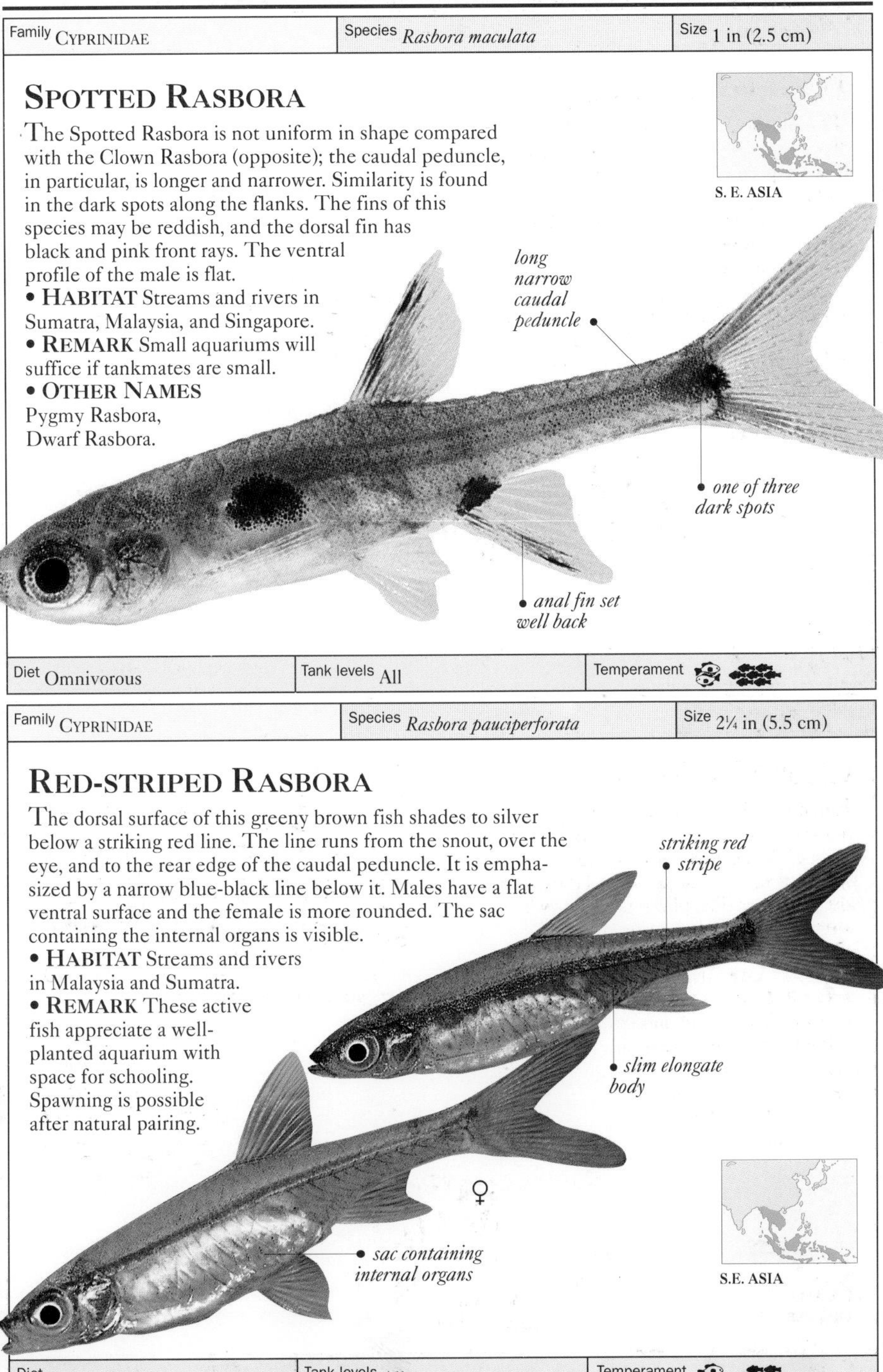

Diet Omnivorous	Tank levels All	Temperament

Family CYPRINIDAE	Species *Rasbora pauciperforata*	Size 2¼ in (5.5 cm)

RED-STRIPED RASBORA

The dorsal surface of this greeny brown fish shades to silver below a striking red line. The line runs from the snout, over the eye, and to the rear edge of the caudal peduncle. It is emphasized by a narrow blue-black line below it. Males have a flat ventral surface and the female is more rounded. The sac containing the internal organs is visible.

- **HABITAT** Streams and rivers in Malaysia and Sumatra.
- **REMARK** These active fish appreciate a well-planted aquarium with space for schooling. Spawning is possible after natural pairing.

Diet Omnivorous	Tank levels All	Temperament

Family CYPRINIDAE	Species *Rasbora trilineata*	Size 3½ in (8 cm)

SCISSORTAIL

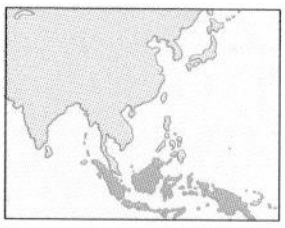

The caudal fin of the Scissortail is deeply forked, and on prime specimens it is marked with bold black and white areas; other fins are colorless. Body color is grayish green with a shiny, silvery belly. Sexual differences include the larger girth of females and the more intense colors of breeding males.

- **HABITAT** Streams in Borneo and Sumatra; also Malaysia.
- **REMARK** This fish twitches its caudal fin in a characteristic scissor action when at rest.
- **OTHER NAME** Spot-tail Rasbora.

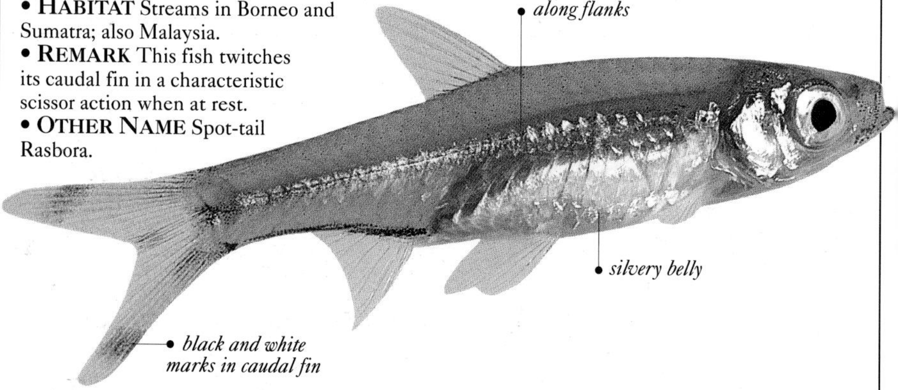

S.E. ASIAN ISLANDS

thin dark band along flanks

silvery belly

black and white marks in caudal fin

Diet Omnivorous	Tank levels Upper and middle	Temperament 

Family CYPRINIDAE	Species *Rasbora vaterifloris*	Size 1½ in (4 cm)

FIRE RASBORA

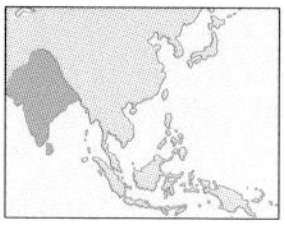

The body shape of this species is much deeper than the majority of rasboras, tapering rapidly behind the dorsal fin to a narrow caudal peduncle. Body color may be fiery orange, pink, or blue, but fins are always pinkish red. It has the same shape as the Harlequin Rasbora (see p.66) but lacks the dark triangular flank marking.

- **HABITAT** Mountain streams in Sri Lanka.
- **REMARK** A gray strain called the Pearly Rasbora is available.

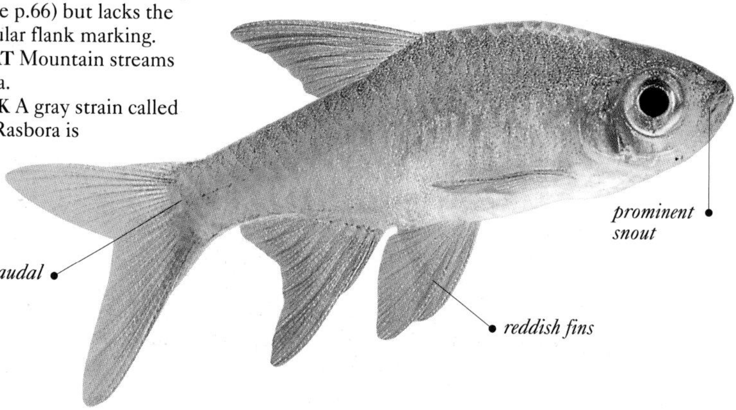

MAINLAND SOUTH ASIA

prominent snout

narrow caudal peduncle

reddish fins

Diet Omnivorous	Tank level Middle	Temperament  

OTHER CYPRINIDS

THERE ARE OVER 1,500 species in the family Cyprinidae, distributed on every continent except South America and Australia. Barbs, danios, and rasboras form the largest groups of tropical cyprinids; the smaller groups, including the sharks and flying foxes, appear in this section. These fishes are from a variety of climes, and each requires special water conditions.

Family CYPRINIDAE	Species *Balantiocheilus melanopterus*	Size 12 in (30 cm)

SILVER SHARK

The coloration of this "shark" is metallic silver with gleaming, well-defined scales. The triangular dorsal fin is held erect and, like the anal, caudal, and pelvic fins, is edged with a thick black margin.

- **HABITAT** Streams in Borneo, Sumatra, and Thailand.
- **REMARK** The active Silver Shark is capable of jumping out of an uncovered aquarium.
- **OTHER NAME** Bala Shark.

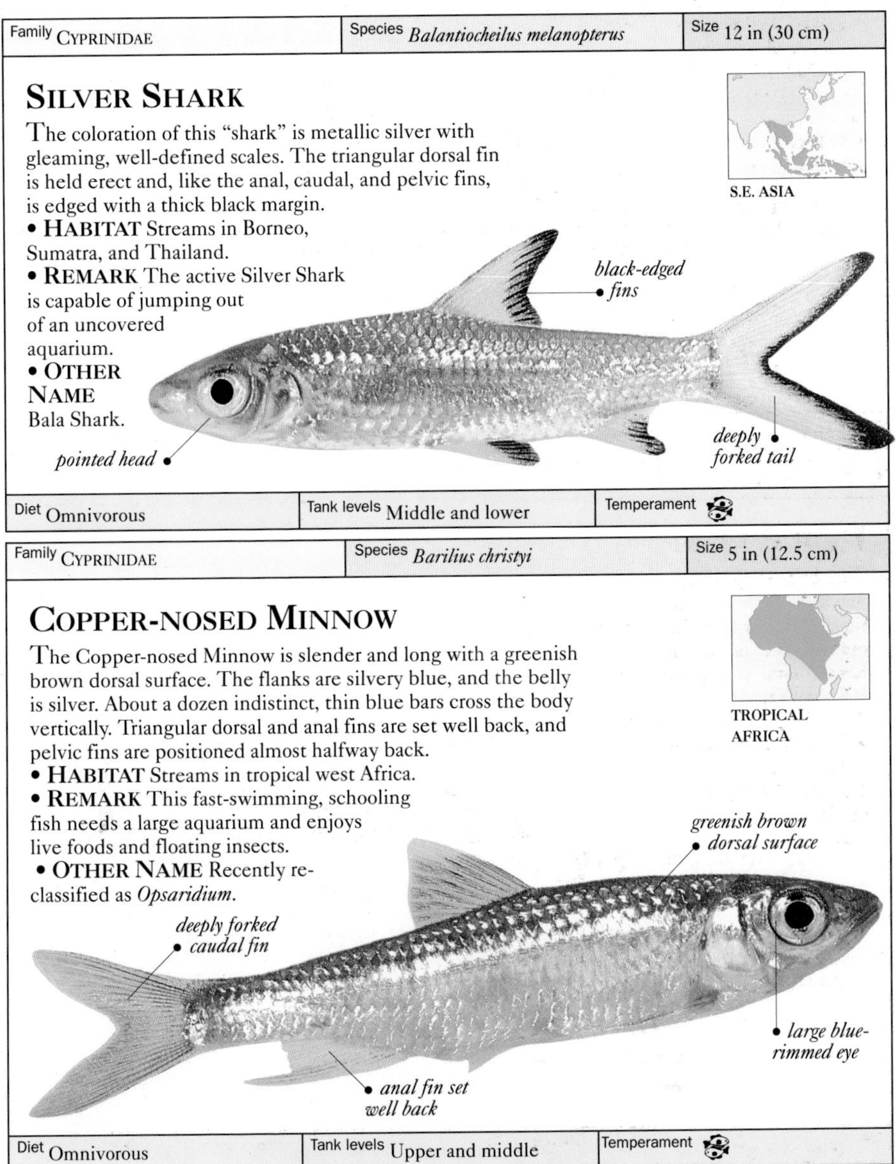

Diet Omnivorous	Tank levels Middle and lower	Temperament

Family CYPRINIDAE	Species *Barilius christyi*	Size 5 in (12.5 cm)

COPPER-NOSED MINNOW

The Copper-nosed Minnow is slender and long with a greenish brown dorsal surface. The flanks are silvery blue, and the belly is silver. About a dozen indistinct, thin blue bars cross the body vertically. Triangular dorsal and anal fins are set well back, and pelvic fins are positioned almost halfway back.

- **HABITAT** Streams in tropical west Africa.
- **REMARK** This fast-swimming, schooling fish needs a large aquarium and enjoys live foods and floating insects.
- **OTHER NAME** Recently reclassified as *Opsaridium*.

Diet Omnivorous	Tank levels Upper and middle	Temperament

Family CYPRINIDAE	Species *Crossocheilus oblongus*	Size 6¼ in (16 cm)

CROSSOCHEILUS OBLONGUS

The body is torpedo shaped and divided into distinct color sections. The top is brown-green and is separated by a pale yellow band from a thick dark band which runs the length of the body. The ventral surface is silvery yellow. All fins carry traces of yellow, and the dorsal fin has a black base. The down-turned mouth is used to browse upon algae-covered rocks, but live foods are also eagerly taken.

• **HABITAT** Running waters of Sumatra, Java, and Malaysia; also Borneo and Thailand.

• **REMARK** This species has not yet been bred in the aquarium, but males develop head tubercles when in breeding condition. It is easily confused with the Flying Fox (*Epalzeorhyncus kallopterus*) which has more intense colors.

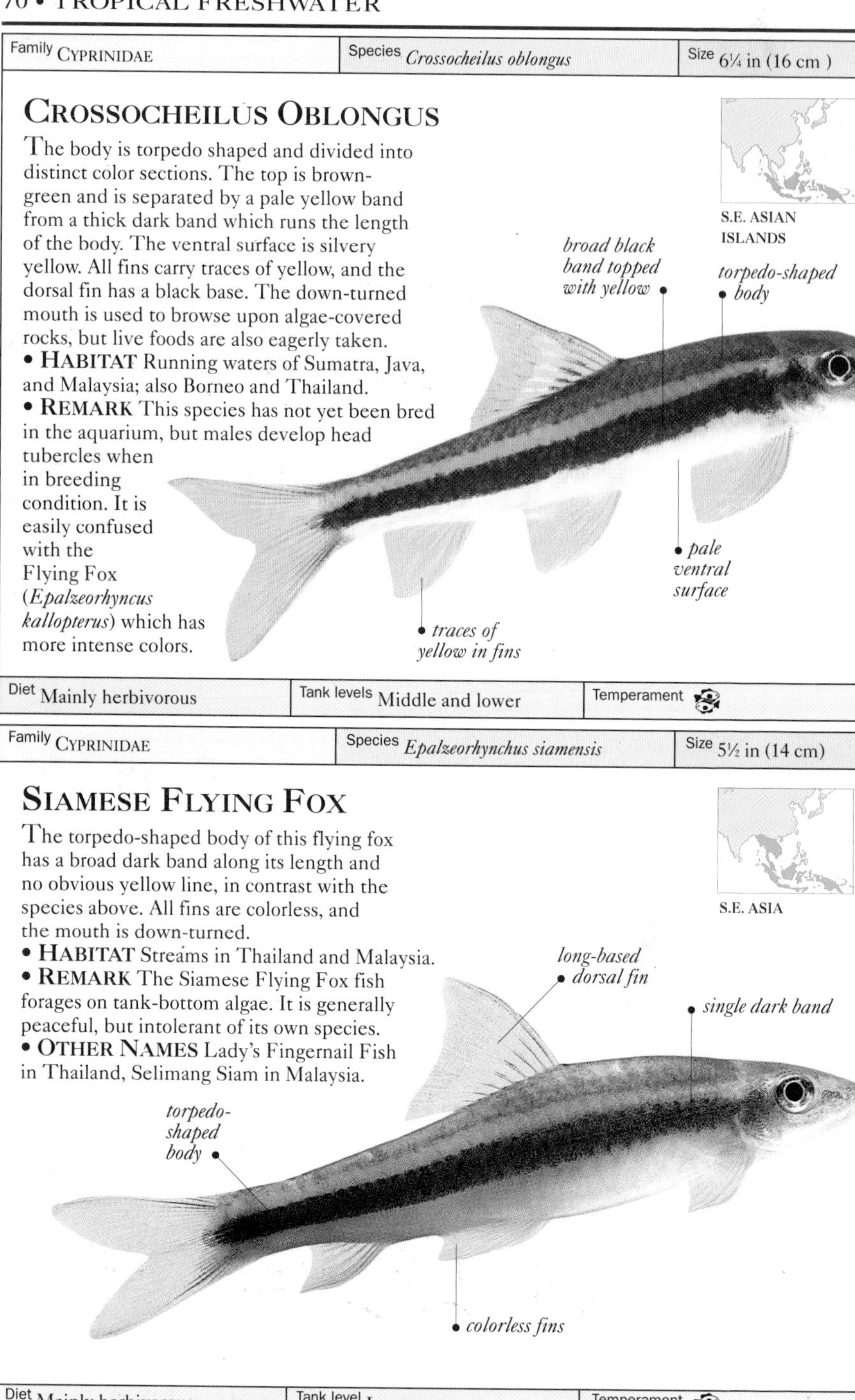

Diet Mainly herbivorous	Tank levels Middle and lower	Temperament

Family CYPRINIDAE	Species *Epalzeorhynchus siamensis*	Size 5½ in (14 cm)

SIAMESE FLYING FOX

The torpedo-shaped body of this flying fox has a broad dark band along its length and no obvious yellow line, in contrast with the species above. All fins are colorless, and the mouth is down-turned.

• **HABITAT** Streams in Thailand and Malaysia.

• **REMARK** The Siamese Flying Fox fish forages on tank-bottom algae. It is generally peaceful, but intolerant of its own species.

• **OTHER NAMES** Lady's Fingernail Fish in Thailand, Selimang Siam in Malaysia.

Diet Mainly herbivorous	Tank level Lower	Temperament

Family CYPRINIDAE	Species *Labeo bicolor*	Size 6 in (15 cm)

RED-TAILED BLACK SHARK

The flattened ventral contour, the underslung mouth, and the high, triangular dorsal fin give this fish its distinctive, shark-like shape. It also has the habit of patrolling the aquarium. The body is jet black, while the tail is bright red. Pectoral fins may be yellow-orange.

• **HABITAT** Streams in Thailand.

• **REMARK** It is quarrelsome with its own kind and others if there are no hiding places.

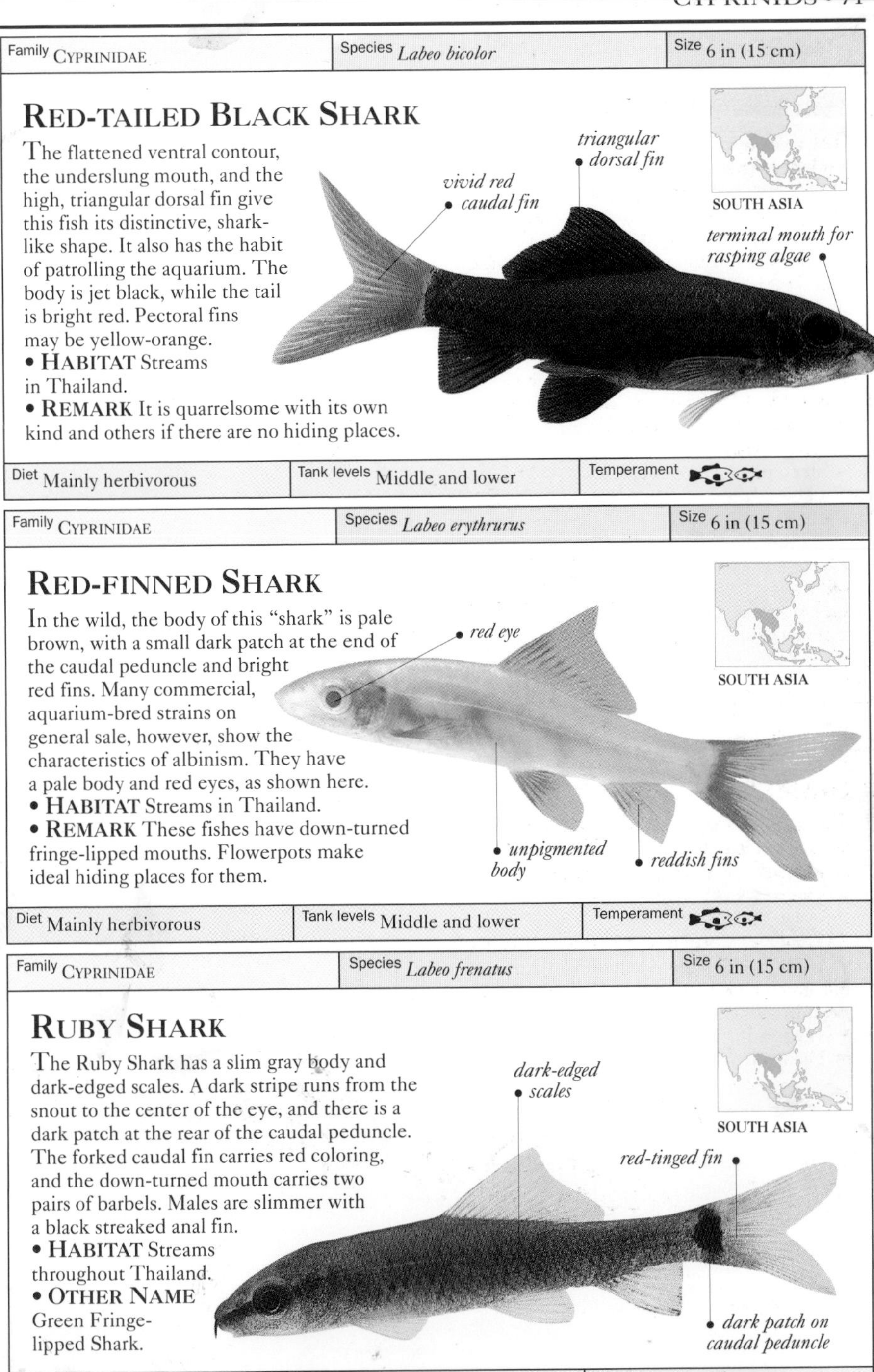

Diet Mainly herbivorous	Tank levels Middle and lower	Temperament

Family CYPRINIDAE	Species *Labeo erythrurus*	Size 6 in (15 cm)

RED-FINNED SHARK

In the wild, the body of this "shark" is pale brown, with a small dark patch at the end of the caudal peduncle and bright red fins. Many commercial, aquarium-bred strains on general sale, however, show the characteristics of albinism. They have a pale body and red eyes, as shown here.

• **HABITAT** Streams in Thailand.

• **REMARK** These fishes have down-turned fringe-lipped mouths. Flowerpots make ideal hiding places for them.

Diet Mainly herbivorous	Tank levels Middle and lower	Temperament

Family CYPRINIDAE	Species *Labeo frenatus*	Size 6 in (15 cm)

RUBY SHARK

The Ruby Shark has a slim gray body and dark-edged scales. A dark stripe runs from the snout to the center of the eye, and there is a dark patch at the rear of the caudal peduncle. The forked caudal fin carries red coloring, and the down-turned mouth carries two pairs of barbels. Males are slimmer with a black streaked anal fin.

• **HABITAT** Streams throughout Thailand.

• **OTHER NAME** Green Fringe-lipped Shark.

Diet Mainly herbivorous	Tank levels Middle and lower	Temperament

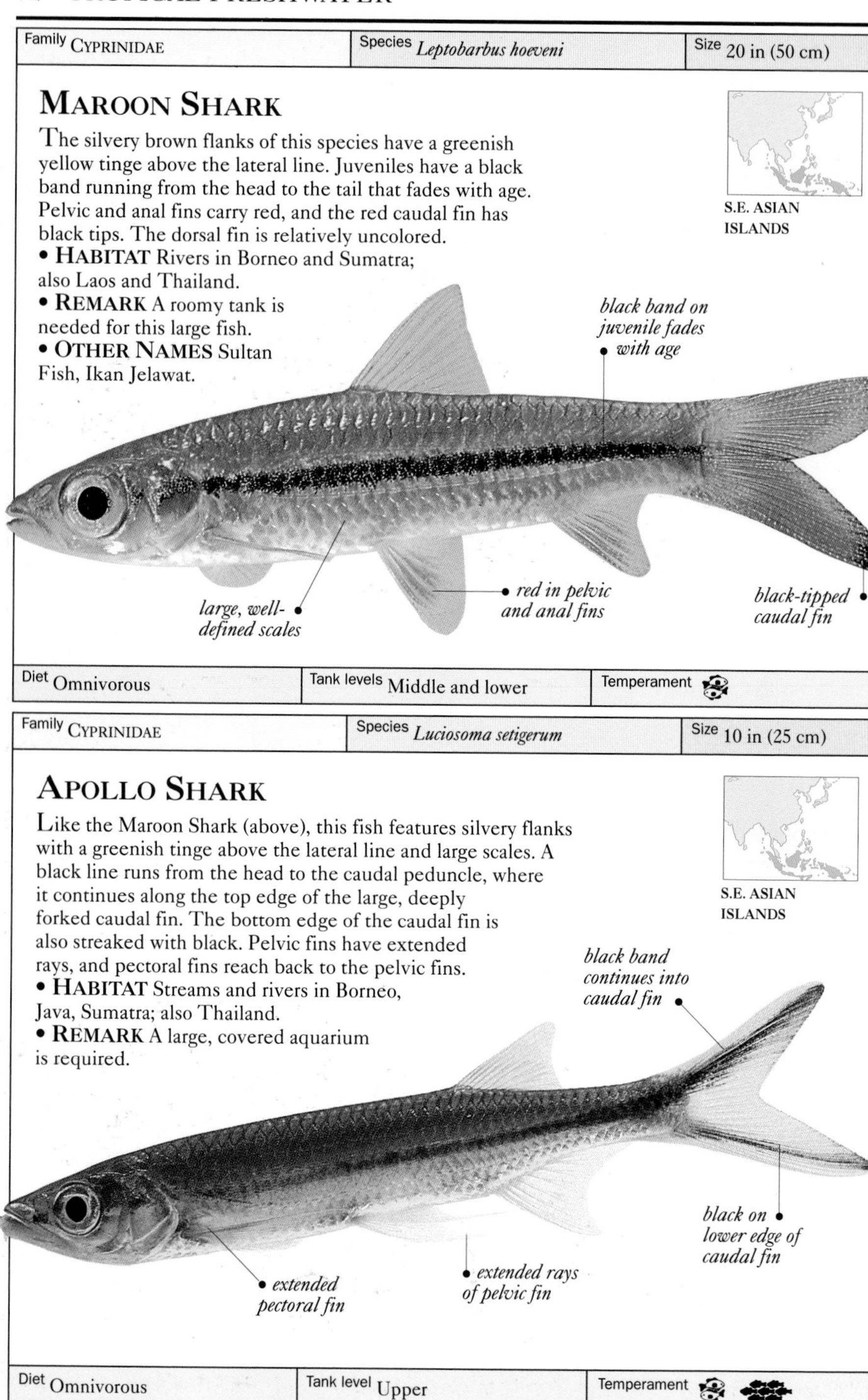

Family CYPRINIDAE	Species *Leptobarbus hoeveni*	Size 20 in (50 cm)

MAROON SHARK

The silvery brown flanks of this species have a greenish yellow tinge above the lateral line. Juveniles have a black band running from the head to the tail that fades with age. Pelvic and anal fins carry red, and the red caudal fin has black tips. The dorsal fin is relatively uncolored.

• **HABITAT** Rivers in Borneo and Sumatra; also Laos and Thailand.

• **REMARK** A roomy tank is needed for this large fish.

• **OTHER NAMES** Sultan Fish, Ikan Jelawat.

Diet Omnivorous	Tank levels Middle and lower	Temperament

Family CYPRINIDAE	Species *Luciosoma setigerum*	Size 10 in (25 cm)

APOLLO SHARK

Like the Maroon Shark (above), this fish features silvery flanks with a greenish tinge above the lateral line and large scales. A black line runs from the head to the caudal peduncle, where it continues along the top edge of the large, deeply forked caudal fin. The bottom edge of the caudal fin is also streaked with black. Pelvic fins have extended rays, and pectoral fins reach back to the pelvic fins.

• **HABITAT** Streams and rivers in Borneo, Java, Sumatra; also Thailand.

• **REMARK** A large, covered aquarium is required.

Diet Omnivorous	Tank level Upper	Temperament

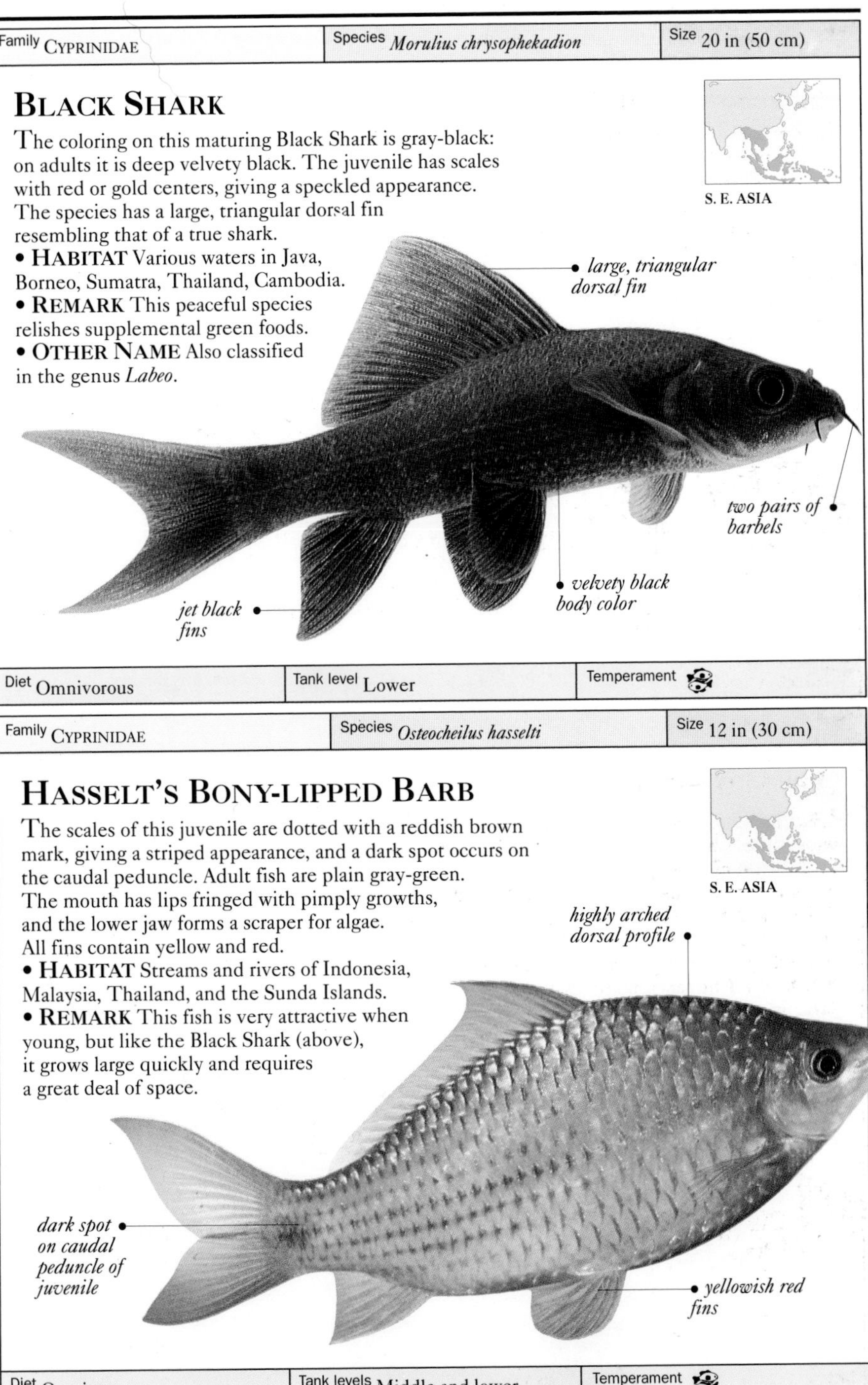

Family CYPRINIDAE	Species *Morulius chrysophekadion*	Size 20 in (50 cm)

BLACK SHARK

The coloring on this maturing Black Shark is gray-black: on adults it is deep velvety black. The juvenile has scales with red or gold centers, giving a speckled appearance. The species has a large, triangular dorsal fin resembling that of a true shark.

- **HABITAT** Various waters in Java, Borneo, Sumatra, Thailand, Cambodia.
- **REMARK** This peaceful species relishes supplemental green foods.
- **OTHER NAME** Also classified in the genus *Labeo*.

Diet Omnivorous	Tank level Lower	Temperament

Family CYPRINIDAE	Species *Osteocheilus hasselti*	Size 12 in (30 cm)

HASSELT'S BONY-LIPPED BARB

The scales of this juvenile are dotted with a reddish brown mark, giving a striped appearance, and a dark spot occurs on the caudal peduncle. Adult fish are plain gray-green. The mouth has lips fringed with pimply growths, and the lower jaw forms a scraper for algae. All fins contain yellow and red.

- **HABITAT** Streams and rivers of Indonesia, Malaysia, Thailand, and the Sunda Islands.
- **REMARK** This fish is very attractive when young, but like the Black Shark (above), it grows large quickly and requires a great deal of space.

Diet Omnivorous	Tank levels Middle and lower	Temperament

CHARACINS
SMALLER TETRAS

WHEN COMPARED WITH larger characins, such as the Pacu, the diminutive size of the smaller tetras illustrates the great range within the family Characidae. Temperaments, likewise, vary in the extreme, from the tranquility of the Neon Tetra to the ferocity of the Piranha. Native to South America and Africa, all characins make decorative additions to the aquarium – there are about 1,200 species in the wild. They have teeth in their jaws, unlike cyprinids. Many carry an additional small adipose fin behind the dorsal fin, although this is not an exclusive feature of characins (some other genera have it too, e.g., *Corydoras* catfish). Many smaller tetras are readily bred in soft waters, but very often the eggs are light sensitive.

Family CHARACIDAE	Species *Gymnocorymbus ternetzi*	Size 2 in (5 cm)

BLACK WIDOW

The Black Widow's oval body is marked by three dark vertical bars: through the eye, just behind the gill cover, and at the base of the dorsal fin. Sex is generally distinguished by the more pointed dorsal fins and broader fronted anal fins on males, and by the plumper bodies of females.

• **HABITAT** Among tall plants in rivers in the Mato Grosso area, South America.

• **REMARK** This is an ideal starter fish. A long-finned cultivated variety is shown here.

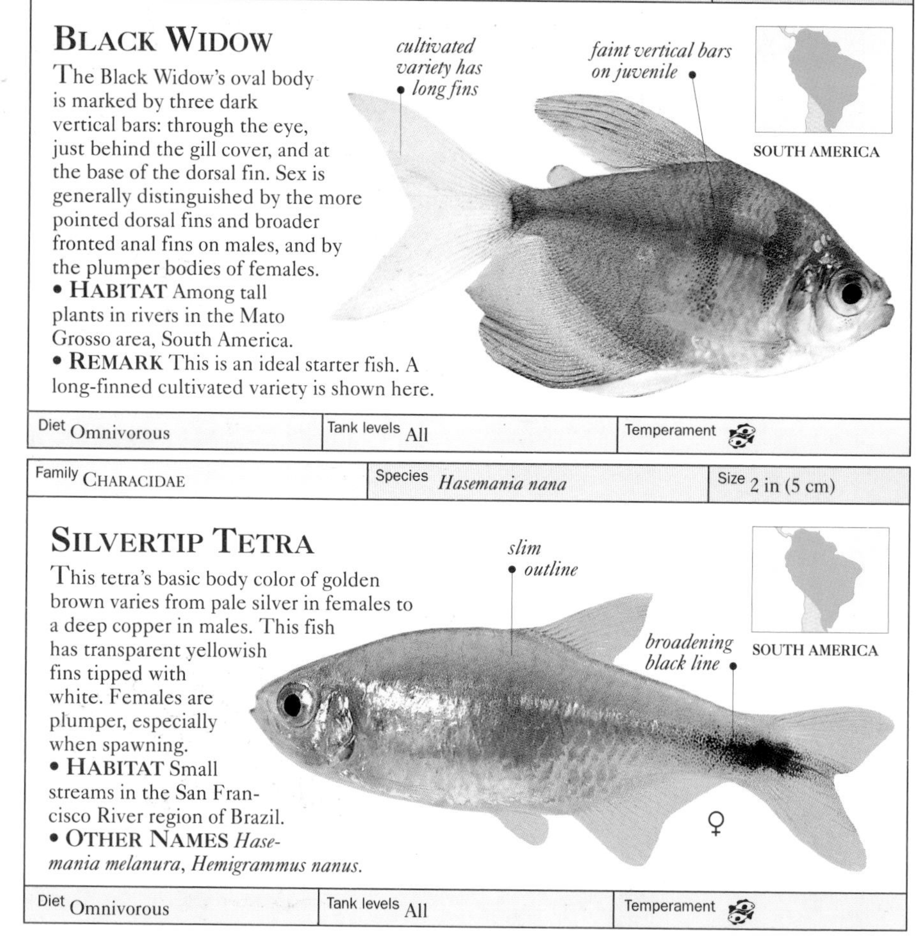

Diet Omnivorous	Tank levels All	Temperament

Family CHARACIDAE	Species *Hasemania nana*	Size 2 in (5 cm)

SILVERTIP TETRA

This tetra's basic body color of golden brown varies from pale silver in females to a deep copper in males. This fish has transparent yellowish fins tipped with white. Females are plumper, especially when spawning.

• **HABITAT** Small streams in the San Francisco River region of Brazil.

• **OTHER NAMES** *Hasemania melanura, Hemigrammus nanus.*

Diet Omnivorous	Tank levels All	Temperament

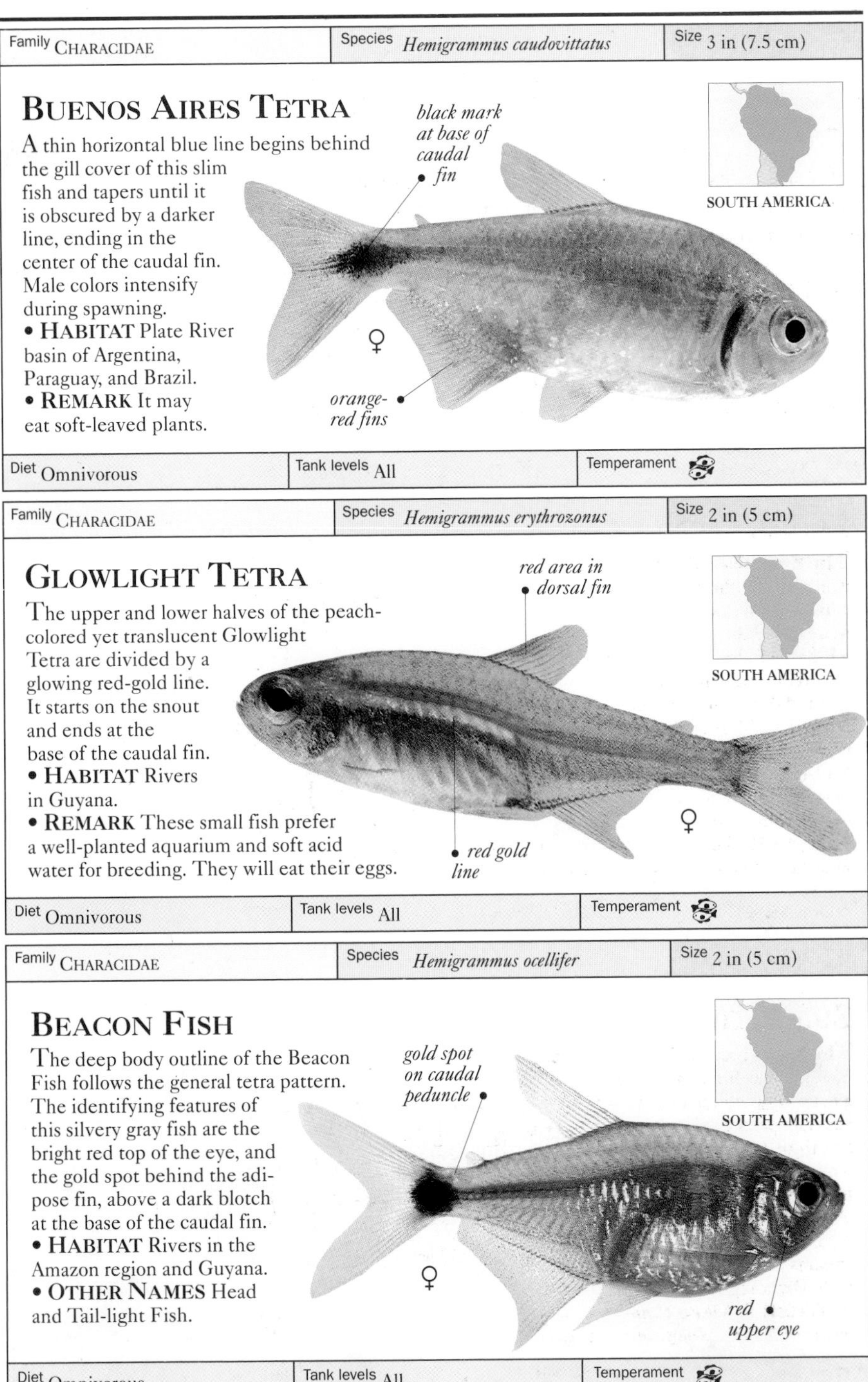

Family CHARACIDAE	Species *Hemigrammus caudovittatus*	Size 3 in (7.5 cm)

BUENOS AIRES TETRA

A thin horizontal blue line begins behind the gill cover of this slim fish and tapers until it is obscured by a darker line, ending in the center of the caudal fin. Male colors intensify during spawning.

• **HABITAT** Plate River basin of Argentina, Paraguay, and Brazil.

• **REMARK** It may eat soft-leaved plants.

Diet Omnivorous	Tank levels All	Temperament

Family CHARACIDAE	Species *Hemigrammus erythrozonus*	Size 2 in (5 cm)

GLOWLIGHT TETRA

The upper and lower halves of the peach-colored yet translucent Glowlight Tetra are divided by a glowing red-gold line. It starts on the snout and ends at the base of the caudal fin.

• **HABITAT** Rivers in Guyana.

• **REMARK** These small fish prefer a well-planted aquarium and soft acid water for breeding. They will eat their eggs.

Diet Omnivorous	Tank levels All	Temperament

Family CHARACIDAE	Species *Hemigrammus ocellifer*	Size 2 in (5 cm)

BEACON FISH

The deep body outline of the Beacon Fish follows the general tetra pattern. The identifying features of this silvery gray fish are the bright red top of the eye, and the gold spot behind the adipose fin, above a dark blotch at the base of the caudal fin.

• **HABITAT** Rivers in the Amazon region and Guyana.

• **OTHER NAMES** Head and Tail-light Fish.

Diet Omnivorous	Tank levels All	Temperament

Family CHARACIDAE	Species *Hemigrammus pulcher*	Size 2 in (5 cm)

PRETTY TETRA

The body of the Pretty Tetra is deep when compared with other members of this family. On mature specimens, the back and head are a dark gray-green color shading through to a purple-copper and down to a silver lower half. As with other silvery species, iridescences are seen according to lighting conditions. The scales are dark edged, and the eye is red above and pale bluish green below. The top of the caudal peduncle is marked with a gold line, beneath which a dark patch extends forward, terminating near the rear of the dorsal fin.

- **HABITAT** Peruvian section of the Amazon River.
- **REMARK** This popular fish will breed in captivity but may be reluctant to spawn unless full compatibility between the sexes is achieved. The female should be swollen with eggs before introducing her to the male. Use a heavily planted, 24 in (60 cm) tank for breeding.

Diet Omnivorous	Tank levels Middle and lower	Temperament

Family CHARACIDAE	Species *Hemigrammus rhodostomus*	Size 2 in (5 cm)

RUMMY-NOSE TETRA

The distinguishing feature of this slim-bodied tetra is the striking red head; the caudal fin is also patterned. The red area is confined to the head in the Rummy-nose Tetra but may extend as a streak on to the body in the similar False Rummy-nose (*Petitella georgiae*). The caudal fin is marked (faintly on this juvenile) by three horizontal black bars, and the lobe tips are colorless. A thin black, often indistinct line runs forward from the base of the caudal fin toward the base of the dorsal fin.

- **HABITAT** Lower stretches of the Amazon River.
- **REMARK** It is sensitive to water changes.

Diet Omnivorous	Tank levels Middle and lower	Temperament

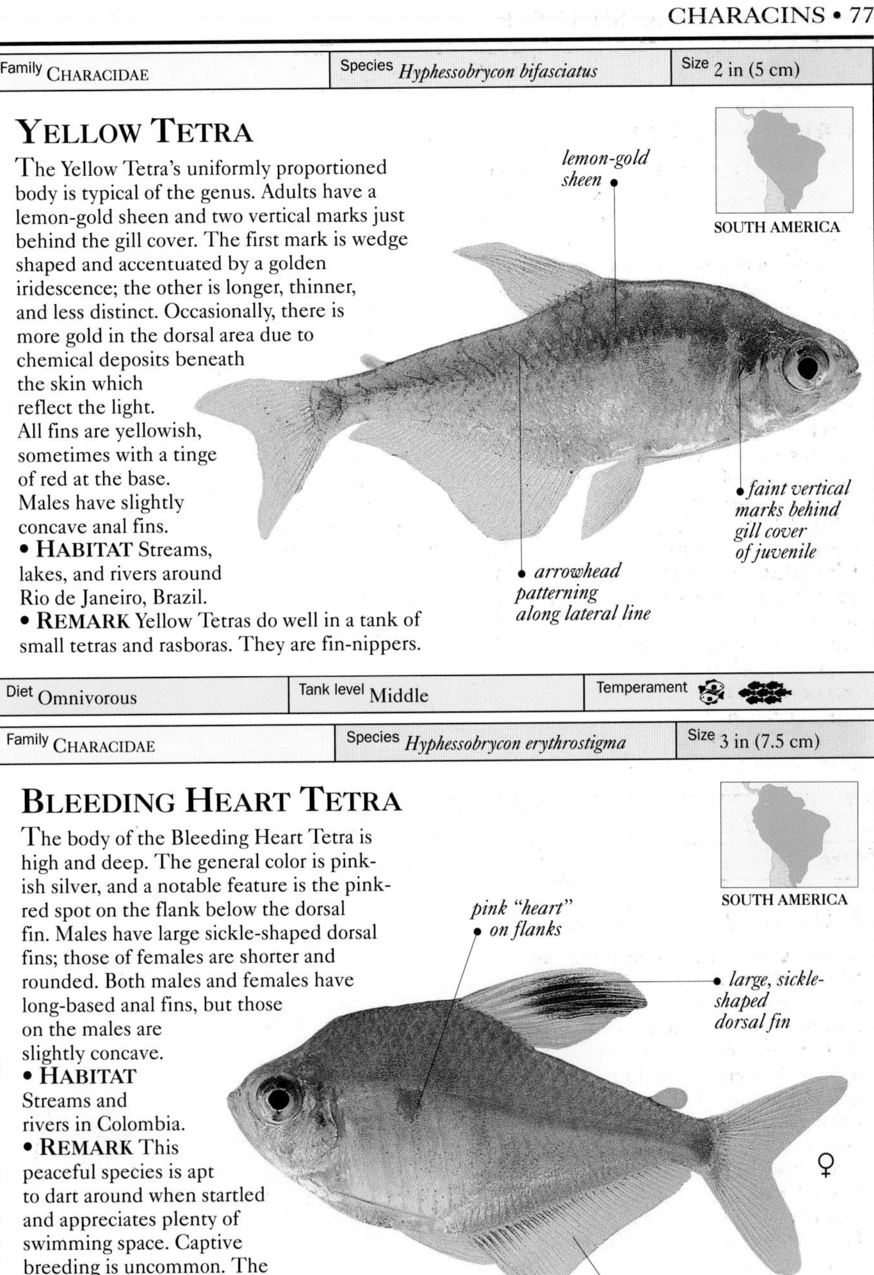

Family CHARACIDAE	Species *Hyphessobrycon bifasciatus*	Size 2 in (5 cm)

YELLOW TETRA

The Yellow Tetra's uniformly proportioned body is typical of the genus. Adults have a lemon-gold sheen and two vertical marks just behind the gill cover. The first mark is wedge shaped and accentuated by a golden iridescence; the other is longer, thinner, and less distinct. Occasionally, there is more gold in the dorsal area due to chemical deposits beneath the skin which reflect the light. All fins are yellowish, sometimes with a tinge of red at the base. Males have slightly concave anal fins.

• **HABITAT** Streams, lakes, and rivers around Rio de Janeiro, Brazil.

• **REMARK** Yellow Tetras do well in a tank of small tetras and rasboras. They are fin-nippers.

Diet Omnivorous	Tank level Middle	Temperament

Family CHARACIDAE	Species *Hyphessobrycon erythrostigma*	Size 3 in (7.5 cm)

BLEEDING HEART TETRA

The body of the Bleeding Heart Tetra is high and deep. The general color is pinkish silver, and a notable feature is the pink-red spot on the flank below the dorsal fin. Males have large sickle-shaped dorsal fins; those of females are shorter and rounded. Both males and females have long-based anal fins, but those on the males are slightly concave.

• **HABITAT** Streams and rivers in Colombia.

• **REMARK** This peaceful species is apt to dart around when startled and appreciates plenty of swimming space. Captive breeding is uncommon. The Lesser Bleeding Heart Tetra, a similar-looking species, has more rounded and less exaggerated finnage.

• **OTHER NAME** Formerly known as *Hyphessobrycon rubrostigma*.

Diet Omnivorous	Tank level Middle	Temperament

Family CHARACIDAE	Species *Hyphessobrycon flammeus*	Size 1¾ in (4.5 cm)

FLAME TETRA

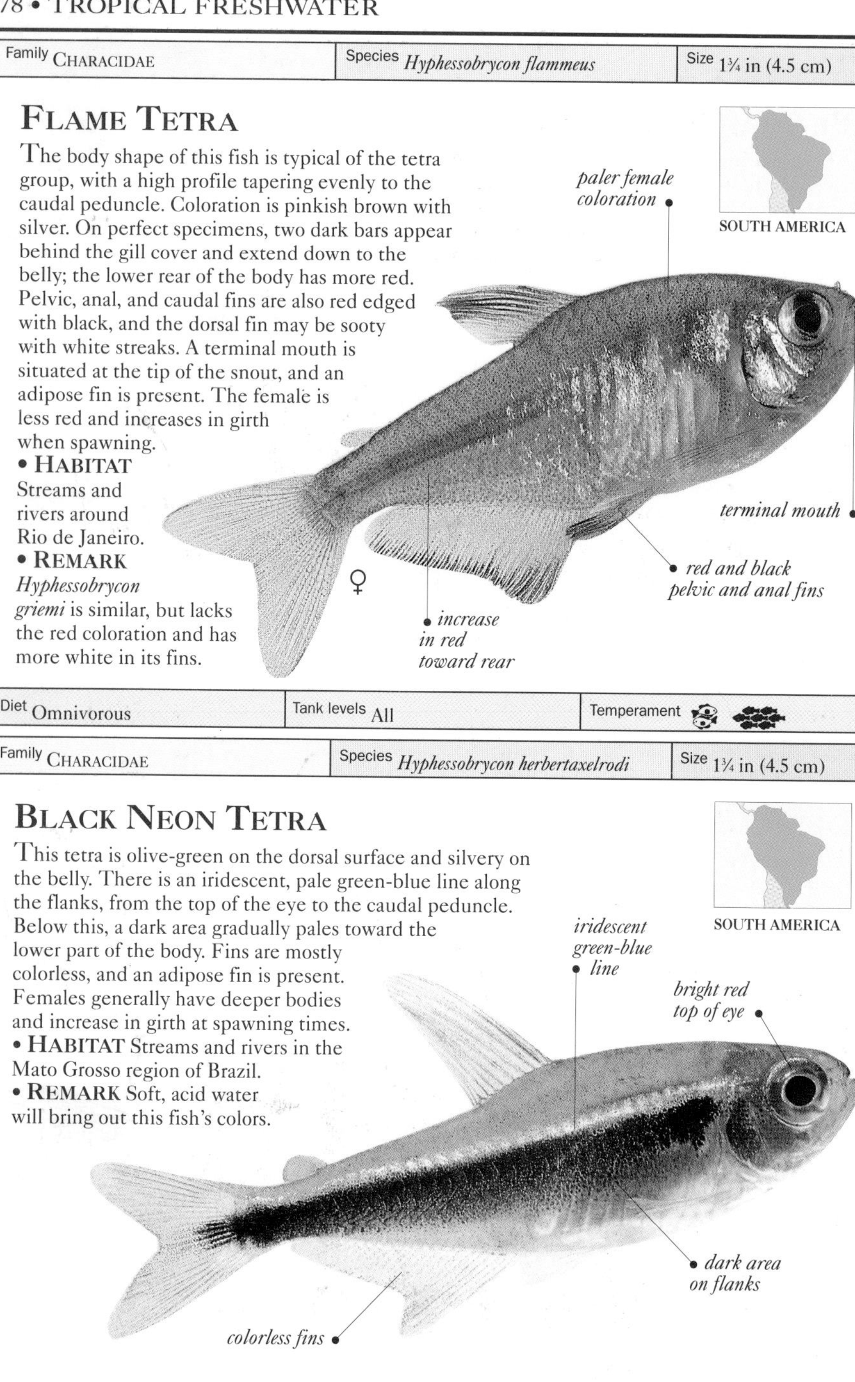

The body shape of this fish is typical of the tetra group, with a high profile tapering evenly to the caudal peduncle. Coloration is pinkish brown with silver. On perfect specimens, two dark bars appear behind the gill cover and extend down to the belly; the lower rear of the body has more red. Pelvic, anal, and caudal fins are also red edged with black, and the dorsal fin may be sooty with white streaks. A terminal mouth is situated at the tip of the snout, and an adipose fin is present. The female is less red and increases in girth when spawning.

• **HABITAT** Streams and rivers around Rio de Janeiro.

• **REMARK** *Hyphessobrycon griemi* is similar, but lacks the red coloration and has more white in its fins.

Diet Omnivorous	Tank levels All	Temperament

Family CHARACIDAE	Species *Hyphessobrycon herbertaxelrodi*	Size 1¾ in (4.5 cm)

BLACK NEON TETRA

This tetra is olive-green on the dorsal surface and silvery on the belly. There is an iridescent, pale green-blue line along the flanks, from the top of the eye to the caudal peduncle. Below this, a dark area gradually pales toward the lower part of the body. Fins are mostly colorless, and an adipose fin is present. Females generally have deeper bodies and increase in girth at spawning times.

• **HABITAT** Streams and rivers in the Mato Grosso region of Brazil.

• **REMARK** Soft, acid water will bring out this fish's colors.

Diet Omnivorous	Tank levels All	Temperament

Family CHARACIDAE	Species *Hyphessobrycon heterorhabdus*	Size 2 in (5 cm)

BELGIAN FLAG TETRA

The color of this tetra is pale grayish brown on the dorsal surface and silver on the flanks and ventral surface. There are three lines along the body; the uppermost is red, the middle faintly gold on this specimen, and the broader bottom line is black. The gill covers are silver. Females are much deeper in body shape.

• **HABITAT** Streams around and including the Tocantins River, lower Amazon.

• **REMARK** It resembles *Hemigrammus ulreyi*, a less commonly available species.

• **OTHER NAME** Flag Tetra.

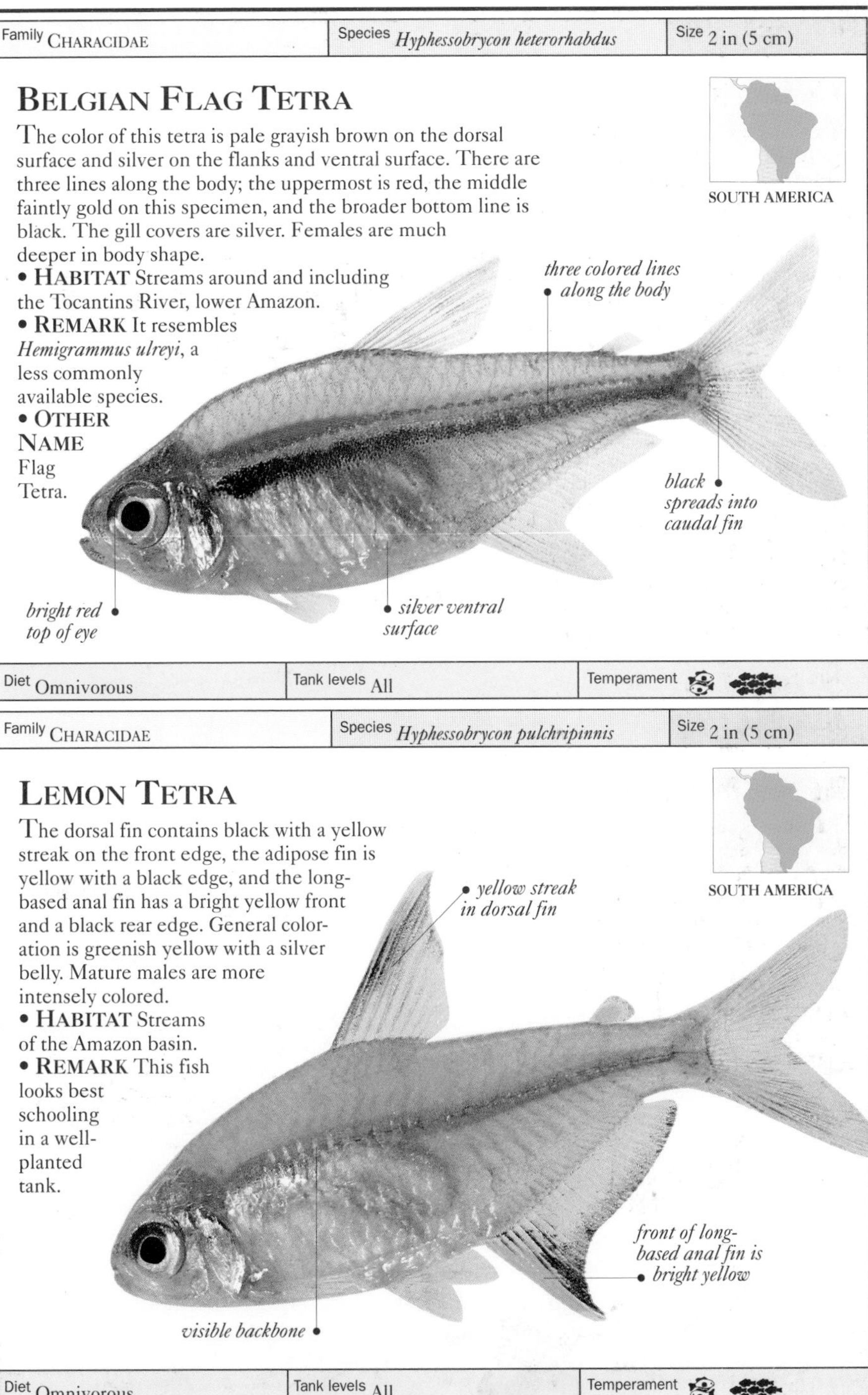

Diet Omnivorous	Tank levels All	Temperament

Family CHARACIDAE	Species *Hyphessobrycon pulchripinnis*	Size 2 in (5 cm)

LEMON TETRA

The dorsal fin contains black with a yellow streak on the front edge, the adipose fin is yellow with a black edge, and the long-based anal fin has a bright yellow front and a black rear edge. General coloration is greenish yellow with a silver belly. Mature males are more intensely colored.

• **HABITAT** Streams of the Amazon basin.

• **REMARK** This fish looks best schooling in a well-planted tank.

Diet Omnivorous	Tank levels All	Temperament

Family CHARACIDAE	Species *Hyphessobrycon rosaceus*	Size 2 in (5 cm)

ROSY TETRA

Tetra colors are enhanced in their natural setting

The coloring of this species is quite similar to the Bleeding Heart Tetra (see p.77). The body of the Rosy Tetra, however, is less deep and the spot on the flank is missing. The dorsal fin is marked with red and streaked with black; that of the male is sickle shaped, well produced, and reaches back over the adipose fin in mature specimens. The pelvic and anal fins are tinged with red and tipped with white. The caudal fin has red in each lobe and a gray margin.

• **HABITAT** Guyana and lower Amazon River.

• **REMARK** Similarly colored fishes are *Hyphessobrycon bentosi*, *H. erythrostigma*, and *H. ornatus*.

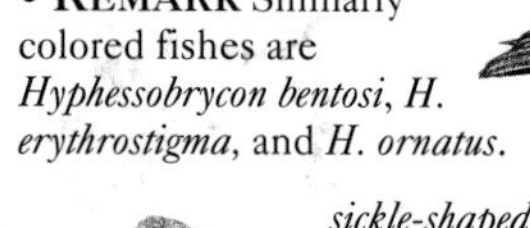

Diet Omnivorous	Tank level Middle	Temperament 

Family CHARACIDAE	Species *Hyphessobrycon serpae*	Size 2 in (5 cm)

SERPAE TETRA

The overall color is blood-red, fading to a paler shade below. A dark comma-shaped spot, just visible on this female, adorns the shoulder. Females are generally paler and plumper than males. Caudal, pelvic, adipose, and anal fins are red, the last having a black edge. A good proportion of the dorsal fin is black.

• **HABITAT** Guyana and the Amazon basin.

• **REMARK** This species is part of a group of similarly colored fishes (*Hyphessobrycon callistus*, *H. minor*, *H. haraldschultzei*, and *H. hasemani*). Confusion surrounds the existence, shape, and color of individual shoulder spots.

dorsal fin predominantly black

basic blood-red coloration

faint comma-shaped mark

♀

Diet Omnivorous	Tank level Middle	Temperament 

Family CHARACIDAE	Species *Megalamphodus megalopterus*	Size 2 in (5 cm)

BLACK PHANTOM TETRA

The Black Phantom Tetra is transparent gray-silver with a dark distinguishing mark on the shoulder. Its eye has a gold rim around the iris. Unusually, the female of this species has a more colorful red adipose fin.

- **HABITAT** Streams in Bolivia and Brazil.
- **REMARK** This species needs soft, acidic water for general well-being and breeding. Captive breeding can be problematic because the parents tend to eat the eggs, which are light-sensitive and prone to distintegration. A separate species tank for these tetras is advisable, although they will co-habit with smaller fishes.

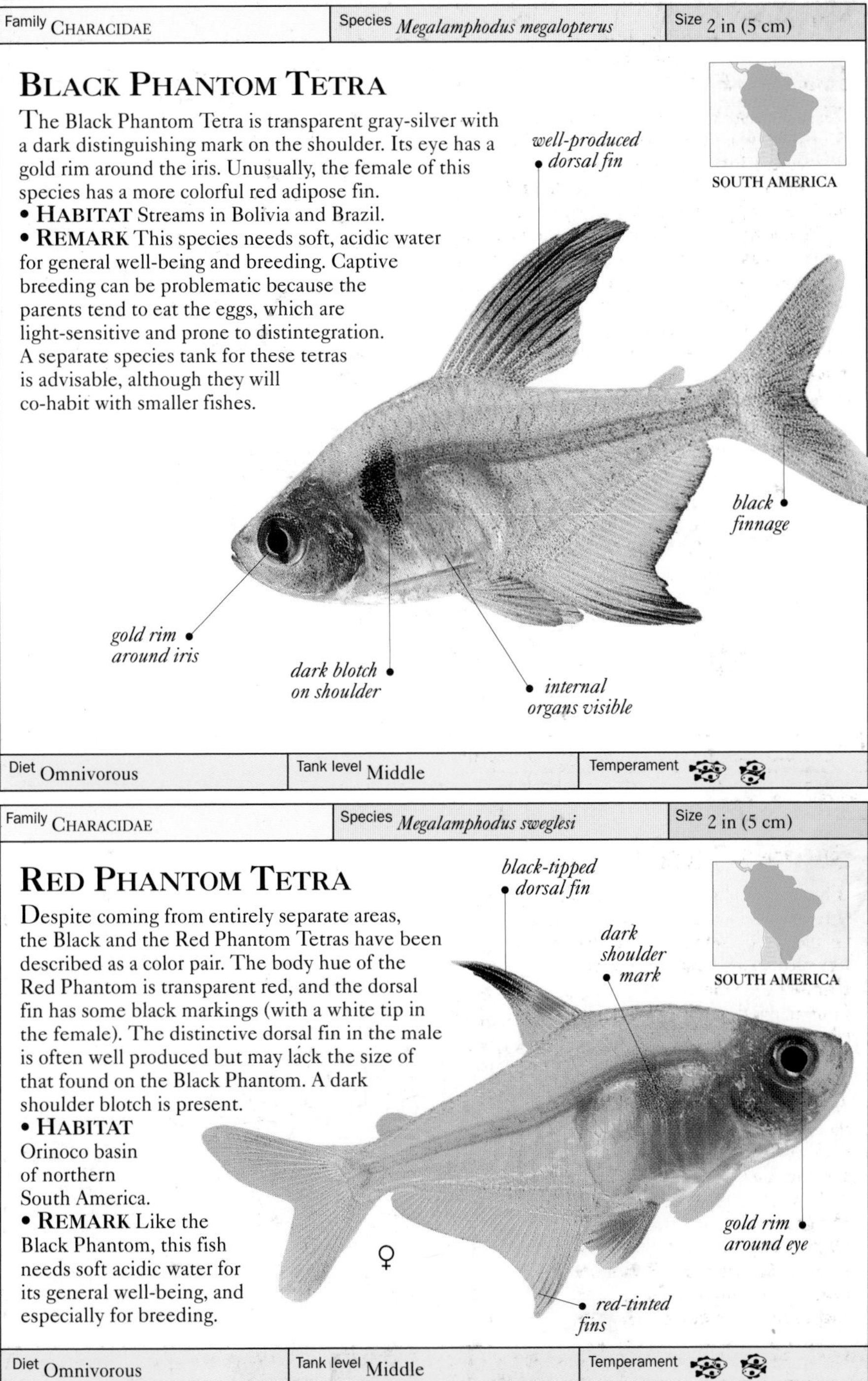

Diet Omnivorous	Tank level Middle	Temperament

Family CHARACIDAE	Species *Megalamphodus sweglesi*	Size 2 in (5 cm)

RED PHANTOM TETRA

Despite coming from entirely separate areas, the Black and the Red Phantom Tetras have been described as a color pair. The body hue of the Red Phantom is transparent red, and the dorsal fin has some black markings (with a white tip in the female). The distinctive dorsal fin in the male is often well produced but may lack the size of that found on the Black Phantom. A dark shoulder blotch is present.

- **HABITAT** Orinoco basin of northern South America.
- **REMARK** Like the Black Phantom, this fish needs soft acidic water for its general well-being, and especially for breeding.

Diet Omnivorous	Tank level Middle	Temperament

Family CHARACIDAE	Species *Nematobrycon palmeri*	Size 2½ in (6 cm)

EMPEROR TETRA

The dorsal surface of this peaceful tetra is pale brownish green, shading to a greenish violet. The lower half is black-blue, shading to cream-silver and giving the impression of a broad, dark band on the flanks. The long-based anal fin is yellowish. Above the "band," males may have a row of red-brown scales, and females show more creamy brown color.

• **HABITAT** Streams and rivers in Colombia.

• **REMARK** This peaceful fish looks best in a dark well-planted tank. Easily bred, a pair may spawn a few eggs daily over a long time.

Diet Omnivorous	Tank levels All	Temperament

Family CHARACIDAE	Species *Paracheirodon axelrodi*	Size 1¾ in (4.5 cm)

CARDINAL TETRA

A striking electric blue stripe adorns this fish, running from the snout, through the top half of the eye, to the adipose fin. The lower body is bright red, with a small, silver area along the front ventral surface. Females have deeper bodies.

• **HABITAT** Slow-flowing waters in Venezuela, Brazil, and Colombia.

• **REMARK** For best colors (and breeding conditions), provide soft, acidic water. This tetra is distinguished from similar fishes, *Paracheirodon innesi* and *P. simulans*, by the extent of the red band.

Diet Omnivorous	Tank levels All	Temperament

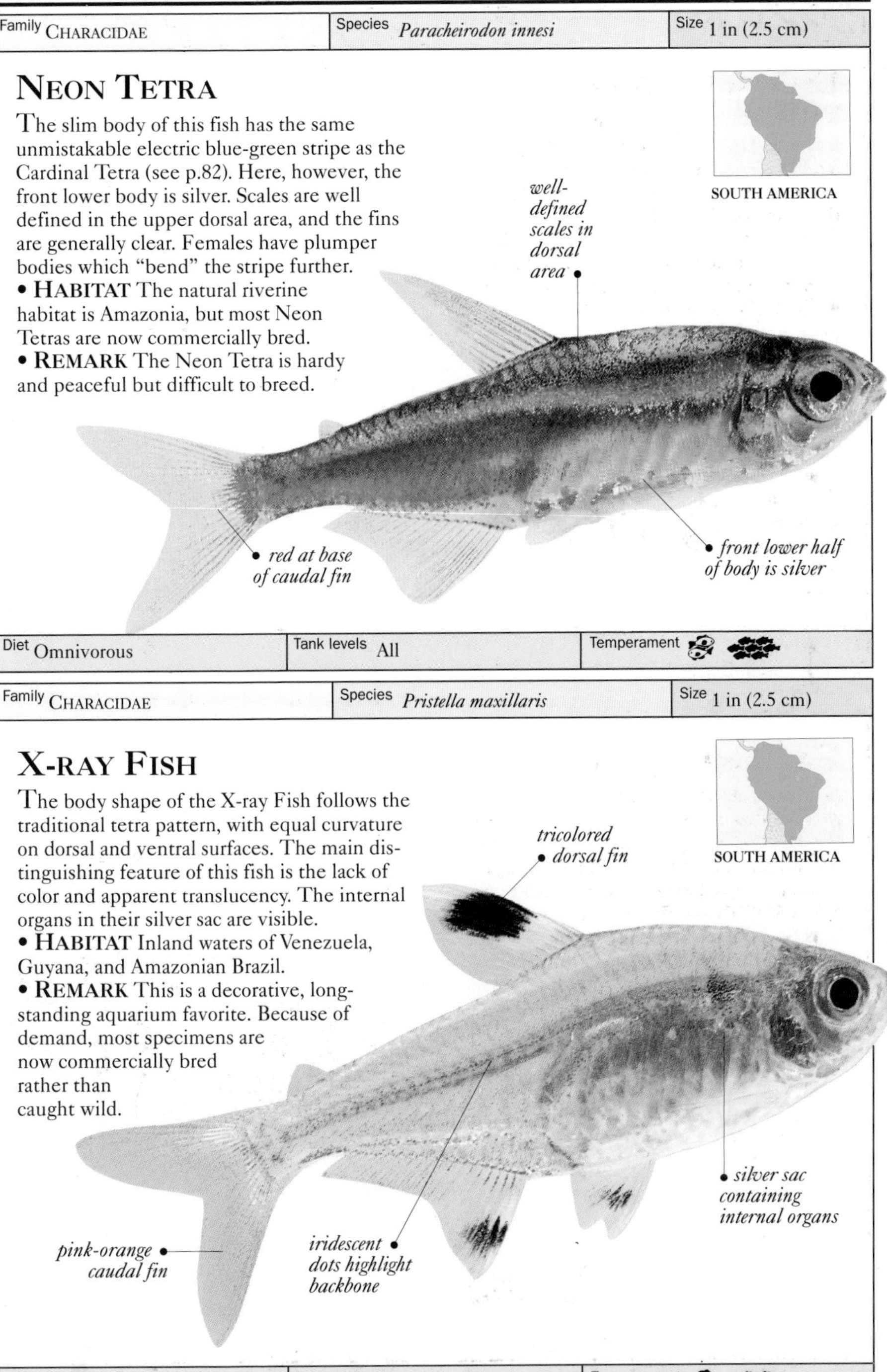

Family CHARACIDAE	Species *Paracheirodon innesi*	Size 1 in (2.5 cm)

NEON TETRA

The slim body of this fish has the same unmistakable electric blue-green stripe as the Cardinal Tetra (see p.82). Here, however, the front lower body is silver. Scales are well defined in the upper dorsal area, and the fins are generally clear. Females have plumper bodies which "bend" the stripe further.

• **HABITAT** The natural riverine habitat is Amazonia, but most Neon Tetras are now commercially bred.

• **REMARK** The Neon Tetra is hardy and peaceful but difficult to breed.

Diet Omnivorous	Tank levels All	Temperament

Family CHARACIDAE	Species *Pristella maxillaris*	Size 1 in (2.5 cm)

X-RAY FISH

The body shape of the X-ray Fish follows the traditional tetra pattern, with equal curvature on dorsal and ventral surfaces. The main distinguishing feature of this fish is the lack of color and apparent translucency. The internal organs in their silver sac are visible.

• **HABITAT** Inland waters of Venezuela, Guyana, and Amazonian Brazil.

• **REMARK** This is a decorative, long-standing aquarium favorite. Because of demand, most specimens are now commercially bred rather than caught wild.

Diet Omnivorous	Tank levels All	Temperament

OTHER CHARACINS

WHILE THE SMALLER species of the characin group (see pp.74–83) are more commonly kept in the aquarium, the species listed in this section, belonging to related family groups, have equally strong claims for aquarium consideration. Hatchetfishes (Gasteropelecidae), pencilfishes (Anostomidae), and piranhas (Serrasalmidae) are all equally interesting to keep.

Family ANOSTOMIDAE	Species *Abramites hypselonotus*	Size 5 in (13 cm)

MARBLED HEADSTANDER

Several broad, wavy, dark brown bands run diagonally over the pale yellowish body of this fish. A dark horizontal line runs from the tip of the snout back through the eye. Dorsal, pelvic, and adipose fins have brown markings, and the base of the caudal peduncle has a dark edge.

• **HABITAT** Streams and rivers of the Orinoco and Amazon river systems.

• **REMARK** This species swims and rests head down in the typical manner of the family Anostomidae. A diet with a high vegetable content is recommended: it will devour aquarium plants. It may also be slightly intolerant of its own kind.

• **OTHER NAMES** High-backed Headstander, Striped Headstander.

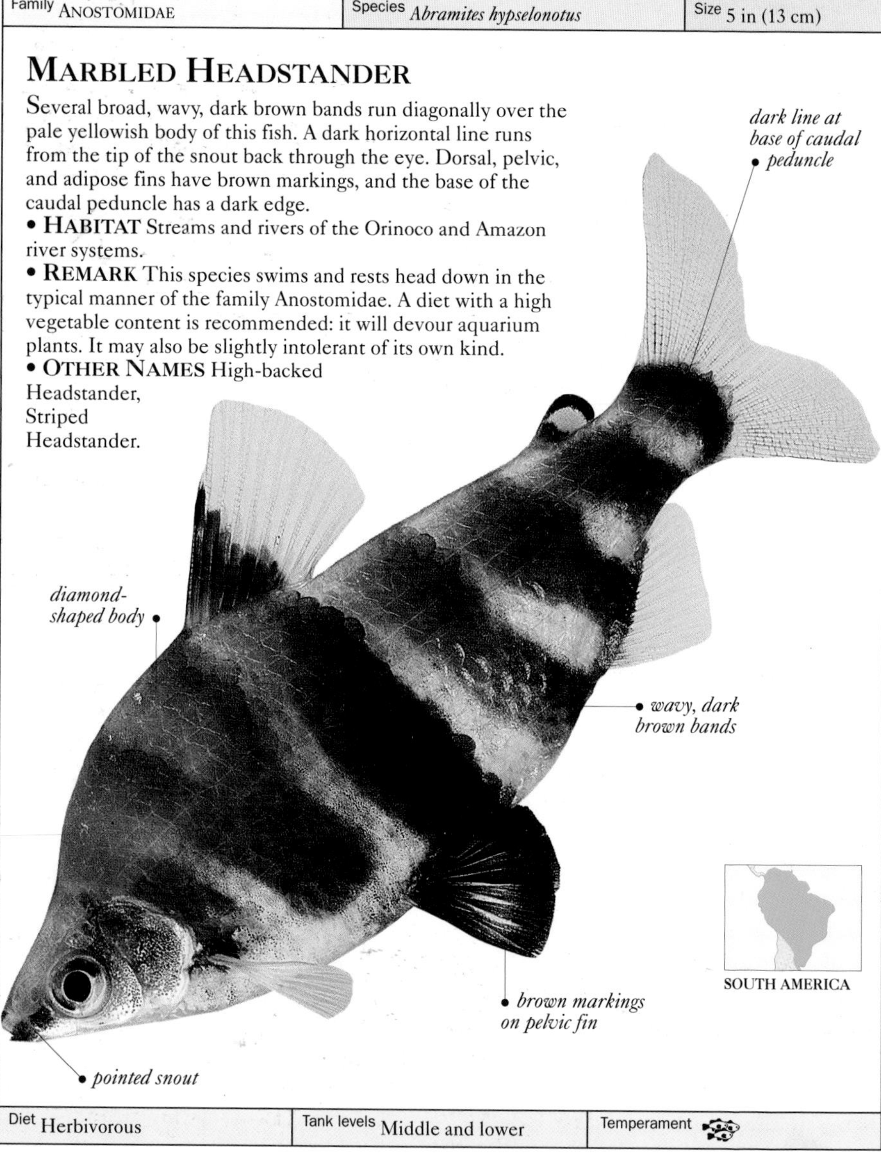

Diet Herbivorous	Tank levels Middle and lower	Temperament

Family ANOSTOMIDAE	Species *Anostomus anostomus*	Size 7 in (18 cm)

STRIPED ANOSTOMUS

The torpedo-shaped body of this species is yellow-gold with three broad, jagged-edged, dark bands the length of the body. The flattened head has a long, tapered snout and an acutely upturned mouth with a protruding lower jaw. The dorsal fin contains a red blotch, and the caudal fin has two bright red patches by the caudal peduncle.

• **HABITAT** Streams and rivers of the Orinoco and Amazon river systems in Guyana and Surinam.

• **REMARK** This handsome, hardy species appreciates underwater roots and stout-leaved plants among which it can feed in its characteristic head-down position. It needs some green food and lots of space. This fish rarely rests.

Anostomus feeds among nooks and crevices

lower jaw protrudes

dark horizontal bands

torpedo-shaped profile

SOUTH AMERICA

Diet Omnivorous	Tank levels All	Temperament

Family ANOSTOMIDAE	Species *Anostomus ternetzi*	Size 6¼in (6 cm)

TERNETZ'S ANOSTOMUS

SOUTH AMERICA

This fish's yellow-gold body is marked by three dark bands. The head is flattened, with a long, tapered snout, and the upturned mouth has a red tip. The caudal fin contains yellow and is red around the caudal peduncle. The small adipose fin may also contain red.

• **HABITAT** Streams and rivers of the Orinoco and Amazon systems.

• **REMARK** This fish requires green food and lots of space.

red tip on upturned mouth

red marks in caudal peduncle

broad, dark band along body

Diet Omnivorous	Tank levels All	Temperament 

Family CHARACIDAE	Species *Aphyocharax anisitsi*	Size 2¼ in (5.5 cm)

BLOODFIN

As the name suggests, red is normally present in the fins of this silvery-flanked species. The color is not, however, very apparent on this juvenile. The male anal fin carries tiny hooks to assist in spawning that may become entangled in an aquarium net.

- **HABITAT** Streams and rivers of Argentina and Paraguay.
- **REMARK** Bloodfins should be kept in schools. They breed freely but may eat their own eggs.
- **OTHER NAMES** Argentine Bloodfin, Red-finned Characin, Red-finned Tetra. Formerly classified as *Aphyocharax rubripinnis*.

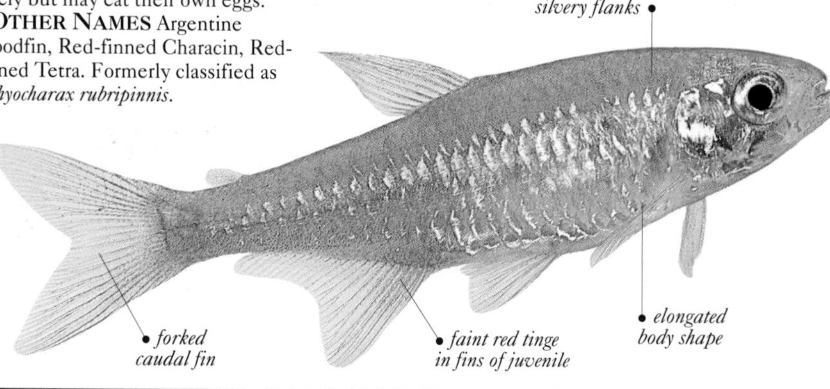

Diet Omnivorous	Tank levels All	Temperament 

Family CHARACIDAE	Species *Arnoldichthys spilopterus*	Size 3 in (7 cm)

BIG-SCALED AFRICAN CHARACIN

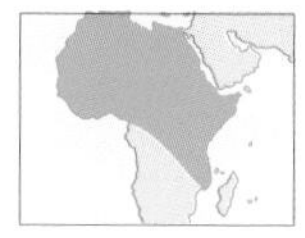

This characin has a brown dorsal surface with blue-green iridescences. Large scales with golden centers form a horizontal central line. The lower half of the body is silvery blue-green, shading to a pale belly. The dorsal fin has a white-edged dark blotch, and the caudal fin is grayish silver. Males have an orange and black anal fin and yellowish pelvic fins. Female anal fins have a dark blotch.

- **HABITAT** Streams in Nigeria.
- **REMARK** Needs plenty of swimming space and plants in which to hide.
- **OTHER NAMES** Spilopterus.

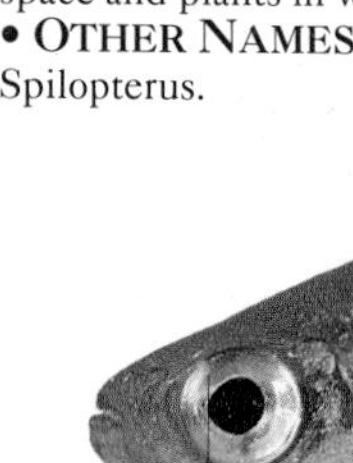
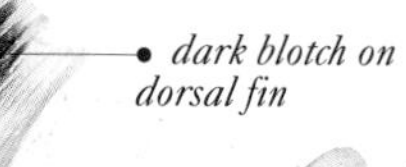

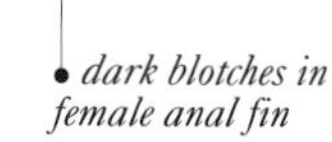

Diet Omnivorous	Tank levels All	Temperament 

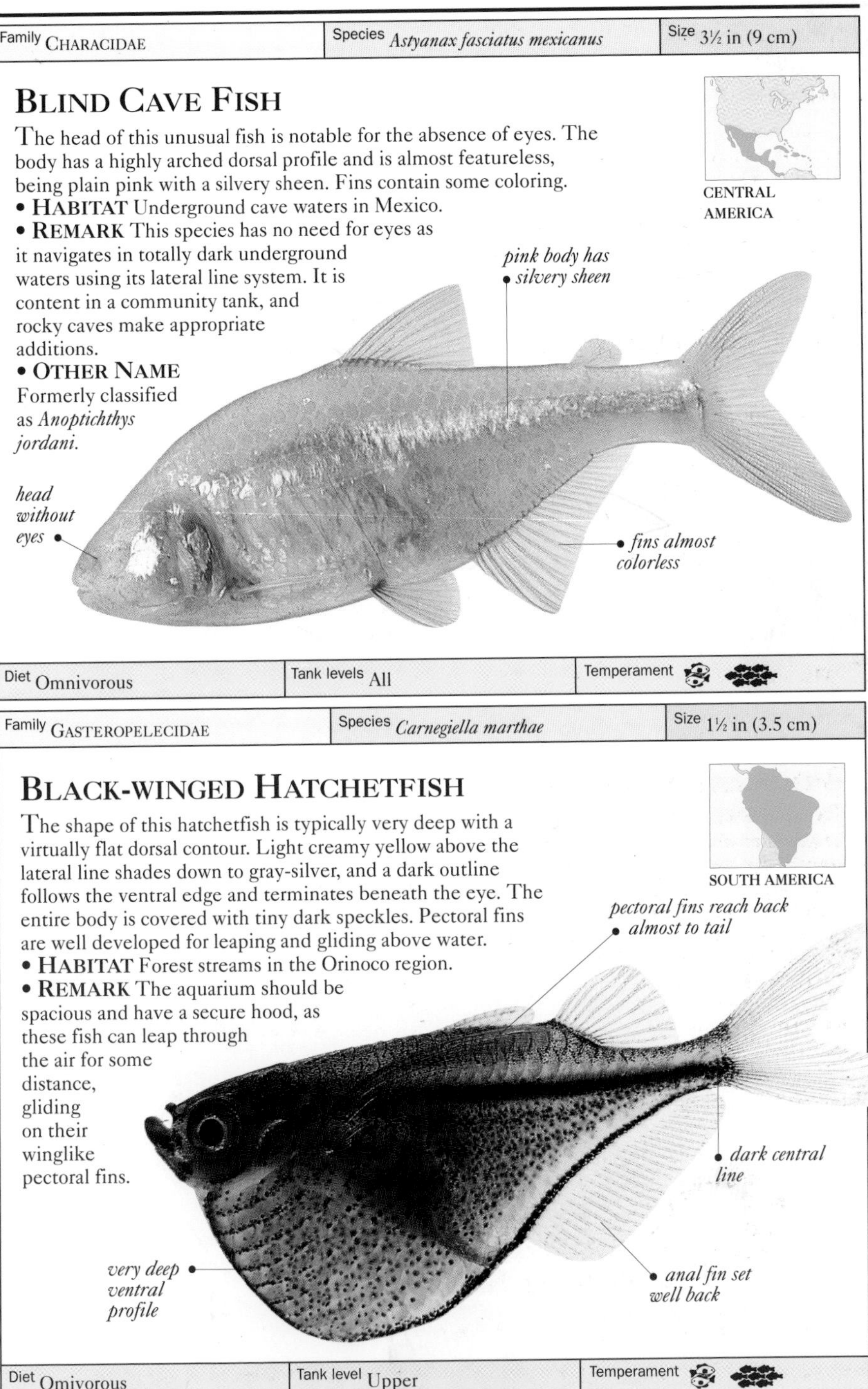

Family CHARACIDAE	Species *Astyanax fasciatus mexicanus*	Size 3½ in (9 cm)

BLIND CAVE FISH

The head of this unusual fish is notable for the absence of eyes. The body has a highly arched dorsal profile and is almost featureless, being plain pink with a silvery sheen. Fins contain some coloring.

- **HABITAT** Underground cave waters in Mexico.
- **REMARK** This species has no need for eyes as it navigates in totally dark underground waters using its lateral line system. It is content in a community tank, and rocky caves make appropriate additions.
- **OTHER NAME** Formerly classified as *Anoptichthys jordani.*

Diet Omnivorous	Tank levels All	Temperament

Family GASTEROPELECIDAE	Species *Carnegiella marthae*	Size 1½ in (3.5 cm)

BLACK-WINGED HATCHETFISH

The shape of this hatchetfish is typically very deep with a virtually flat dorsal contour. Light creamy yellow above the lateral line shades down to gray-silver, and a dark outline follows the ventral edge and terminates beneath the eye. The entire body is covered with tiny dark speckles. Pectoral fins are well developed for leaping and gliding above water.

- **HABITAT** Forest streams in the Orinoco region.
- **REMARK** The aquarium should be spacious and have a secure hood, as these fish can leap through the air for some distance, gliding on their winglike pectoral fins.

Diet Omivorous	Tank level Upper	Temperament

Family GASTEROPELECIDAE	Species *Carnegiella strigata strigata*	Size 2 in (5 cm)

MARBLED HATCHETFISH

SOUTH AMERICA

This fish is very deep-bodied with a flat dorsal contour. The color is normally silvery purple, but this specimen is showing green background colors. A dark line runs from the eye to the caudal peduncle, below which several dark, broken lines cross the lower body. Another dark line curves up along the front of the body. Pectoral fins are very well developed, whereas pelvic fins are hardly noticeable.

• **HABITAT** Streams and rivers throughout Amazonia and Guyana.

• **REMARK** Floating plants will provide the shade required for this subspecies. *Carnegiella strigata vesca* looks similar.

dorsal fin set well back

forked caudal fin

dark, broken lines

iridescence on body

Diet Omnivorous	Tank level Upper	Temperament

Family GASTEROPELECIDAE	Species *Carnegiella myersi*	Size 1 in (2.5 cm)

MYERS' HATCHETFISH

SOUTH AMERICA

The dorsal contour of this typically deep-bodied hatchetfish is almost flat. Body coloration is light greenish yellow above a dark line that runs from the eye to the caudal peduncle; below the line it is silver. The pectoral fins are well developed and reach back to the dorsal fin, which carries a dark spot. Pelvic fins are hardly noticeable.

• **HABITAT** Streams and rivers of Peru and Bolivia.

• **REMARK** This is the smallest hatchetfish.

very long pectoral fin

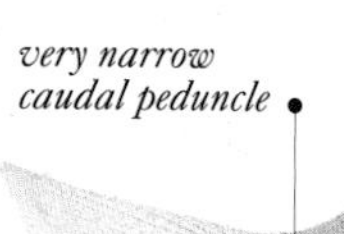

very narrow caudal peduncle

forked caudal fin

generally clear fins

deeply keeled ventral profile

Diet Omnivorous	Tank level Upper	Temperament 

Family CHALCEIDAE	Species *Chalceus macrolepidotus*	Size 10 in (25 cm)

PINK-TAILED CHALCEUS

This species takes its popular name from the bright pink caudal fin of prime specimens. Body coloration is golden olive-green on the dorsal surface, with silvery flanks. Scales are large and well defined, particularly above the level of the lateral line. The head is fairly short, and the mouth has a rather prominent upper lip.

• **HABITAT** Streams and rivers of Amazonia and Guyana.

• **REMARK** This large, active species needs plenty of room and food; it can become quite predatory towards smaller fishes.

large, well-defined scales

faintly pink tail on juvenile

cylindrical, elongated body

Diet Omnivorous	Tank levels Upper and middle	Temperament

Family CURIMATIDAE	Species *Chilodus punctatus*	Size 4 in (10 cm)

SPOTTED HEADSTANDER

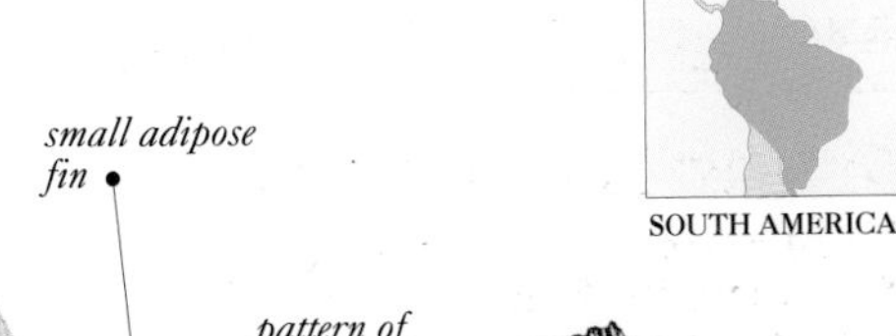

The elongated, silvery body of this maturing specimen is covered with a pattern of dark spots. A dark line runs from the snout through the eye to the gill cover. The blotches of this pattern may become larger during breeding. The head is pointed, with a steeply rising forehead. A squared-off dorsal fin is flecked with dark spots and has a dark top corner.

• **HABITAT** Streams and rivers of Amazonia and Guyana.

• **REMARK** Although omnivorous, this species appreciates green matter in its diet, and soft water. Flake foods can be crumbled, mixed with water, and painted onto rocks. When dry, the rocks can be placed in the aquarium for the fish to browse on. Provide roots or pieces of wood around which the fish can hide or rest. Ideally, the lighting should be subdued.

small adipose fin

pattern of spots on body

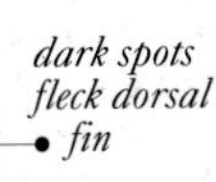

dark spots fleck dorsal fin

dark line

SOUTH AMERICA

Diet Omnivorous	Tank levels Middle and lower	Temperament

Family SERRASALMIDAE	Species *Colossoma bidens*	Size 16 in (40 cm)

PACU

The shape of this fish resembles that of the Piranha (see p.105). The chest area, the lower edge of the gill cover, and the pectoral, pelvic, and anal fins are red. The rest of the body is silver with faint dark spots above the lateral line. This fish has teeth, but its head is not as large as those of its carnivorous relatives. Anal and caudal fins have black edges.

- **HABITAT** Guapore River, on the borders of Bolivia and Brazil.
- **REMARK** The Pacu's diet consists of fruit and vegetable matter. This species can be confused with *Colossoma brachipomum*.

SOUTH AMERICA

dark blotch on caudal peduncle

large eye set well forward

Diet Herbivorous	Tank levels Upper and middle	Temperament

Family LEBIASINIDAE	Species *Copeina guttata*	Size 6 in (15 cm)

RED-SPOTTED COPEINA

The body of this species features a green-brown dorsal surface with darker flanks and a light yellowish ventral surface. Each large scale has a red marking at its forward apex, giving the fish the spotted appearance that is reflected in its common name.

- **HABITAT** Streams and rivers of central Amazonia.
- **REMARK** This species is relatively easy to keep and breeds readily. Eggs are laid in a hollow and guarded by the male.

SOUTH AMERICA

Diet Omnivorous	Tank levels Upper and middle	Temperament 

Family LEBIASINIDAE	Species *Copella arnoldi*	Size 3¼ in (8 cm)

SPLASHING TETRA

This creamy yellow young female has large, iridescent scales. A dark line runs from the snout through the eye to the gill cover. The caudal fin is distinctly forked. Fins of mature males are more extravagant and are yellowish with red marks.

• **HABITAT** Rivers and streams in Guyana and around the mouth of the Amazon River.

• **REMARK** This fish lays its eggs on the underside of overhanging plants, and the male splashes them to keep them moist.

SOUTH AMERICA

larger dark blotch in females

creamy yellow coloration

dark line through eye

♀

yellowish fins

Diet Omnivorous	Tank levels Upper and middle	Temperament

Family CHARACIDAE	Species *Tetragonopterus chalceus*	Size 5 in (12.5 cm)

FALSE SILVER TETRA

This tetra is very deep-bodied. It has a marked indentation in the dorsal profile above the eye. Coloration, as the name suggests, is silver with gold tones, and the scales are well defined. There are three blotches on the flanks: two less distinct ones behind the gill cover and one on the caudal peduncle. The female is often much stouter than the male when spawning.

• **HABITAT** Streams and rivers in Amazonia and Guyana.

• **REMARK** This active fish, whose generic name was shortened to create the popular name "tetra," needs plenty of swimming room. It is very similar in appearance to *Ctenobrycon spilurus*.

SOUTH AMERICA

indistinct band formed from blotches on body

polished metallic scales

Diet Omnivorous	Tank levels All	Temperament

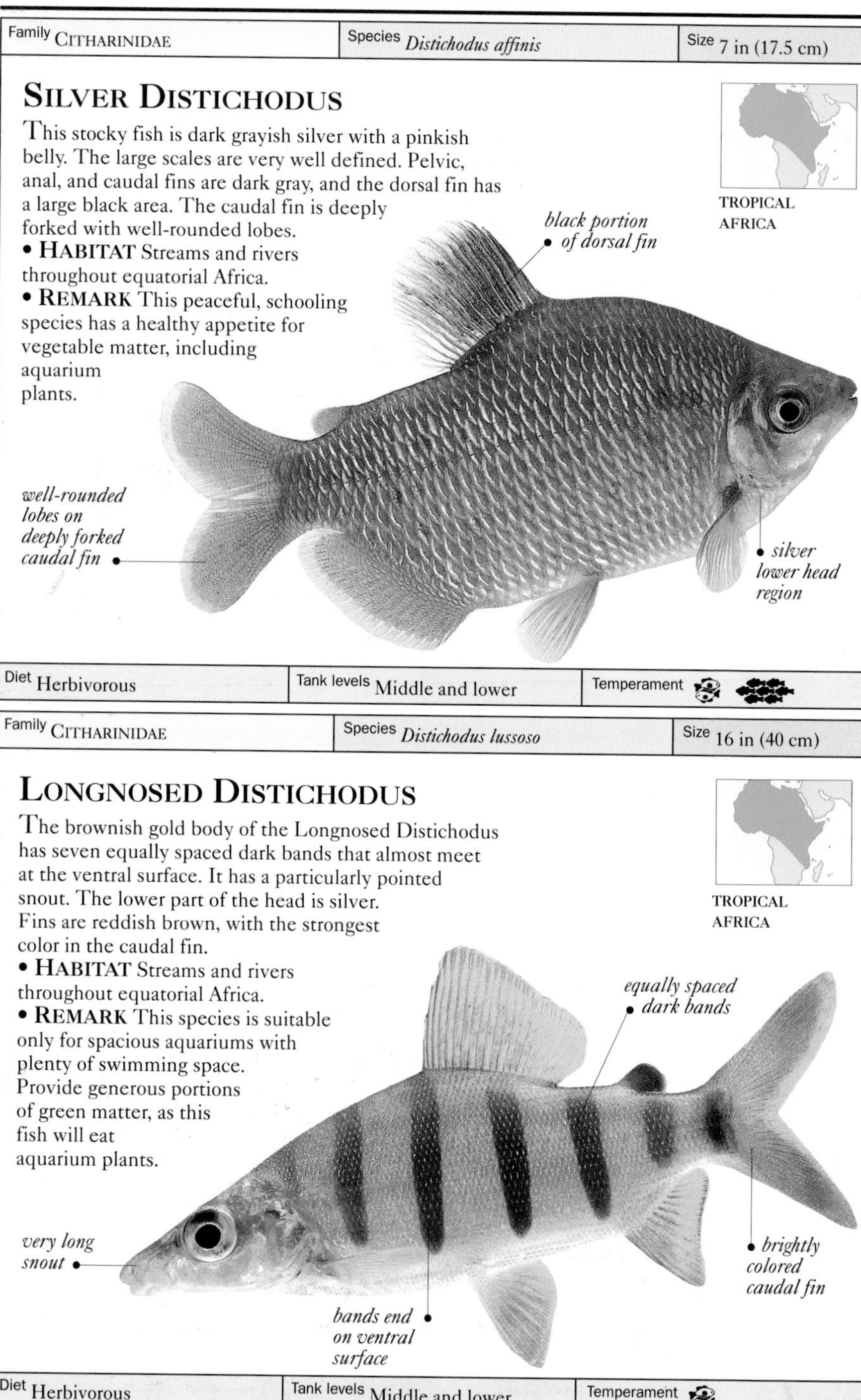

Family CITHARINIDAE | Species *Distichodus affinis* | Size 7 in (17.5 cm)

SILVER DISTICHODUS

This stocky fish is dark grayish silver with a pinkish belly. The large scales are very well defined. Pelvic, anal, and caudal fins are dark gray, and the dorsal fin has a large black area. The caudal fin is deeply forked with well-rounded lobes.

• **HABITAT** Streams and rivers throughout equatorial Africa.

• **REMARK** This peaceful, schooling species has a healthy appetite for vegetable matter, including aquarium plants.

Diet Herbivorous | Tank levels Middle and lower | Temperament

Family CITHARINIDAE | Species *Distichodus lussoso* | Size 16 in (40 cm)

LONGNOSED DISTICHODUS

The brownish gold body of the Longnosed Distichodus has seven equally spaced dark bands that almost meet at the ventral surface. It has a particularly pointed snout. The lower part of the head is silver. Fins are reddish brown, with the strongest color in the caudal fin.

• **HABITAT** Streams and rivers throughout equatorial Africa.

• **REMARK** This species is suitable only for spacious aquariums with plenty of swimming space. Provide generous portions of green matter, as this fish will eat aquarium plants.

Diet Herbivorous | Tank levels Middle and lower | Temperament

Family CITHARINIDAE	Species *Distichodus noboli*	Size 7 in (17 cm)

NOBOL'S DISTICHODUS

This grayish silver fish is decorated with large, well-defined, bright silver scales and randomly sprinkled silver iridescences. The lower part of the relatively small head is silver. Dorsal, anal, and caudal fins are gray, and the dorsal fin has a black and red front portion. A small adipose fin is present.

• **HABITAT** Streams and rivers of equatorial Africa.

• **REMARK** This species is one of the smallest in the *Distichodus* genus, which contains around 30 species. It is similar to *Distichodus notospilus*.

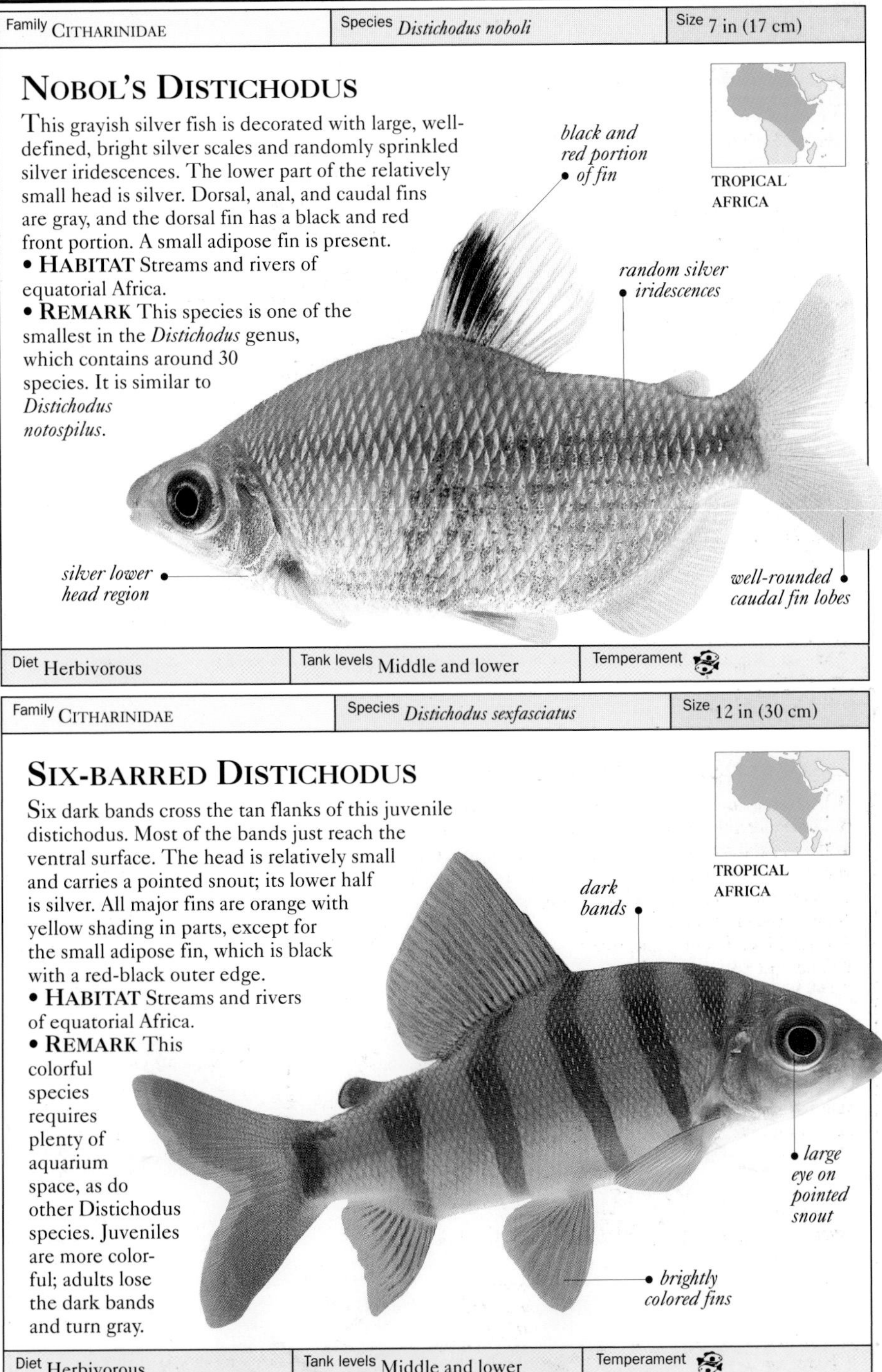

Diet Herbivorous	Tank levels Middle and lower	Temperament

Family CITHARINIDAE	Species *Distichodus sexfasciatus*	Size 12 in (30 cm)

SIX-BARRED DISTICHODUS

Six dark bands cross the tan flanks of this juvenile distichodus. Most of the bands just reach the ventral surface. The head is relatively small and carries a pointed snout; its lower half is silver. All major fins are orange with yellow shading in parts, except for the small adipose fin, which is black with a red-black outer edge.

• **HABITAT** Streams and rivers of equatorial Africa.

• **REMARK** This colorful species requires plenty of aquarium space, as do other Distichodus species. Juveniles are more colorful; adults lose the dark bands and turn gray.

Diet Herbivorous	Tank levels Middle and lower	Temperament

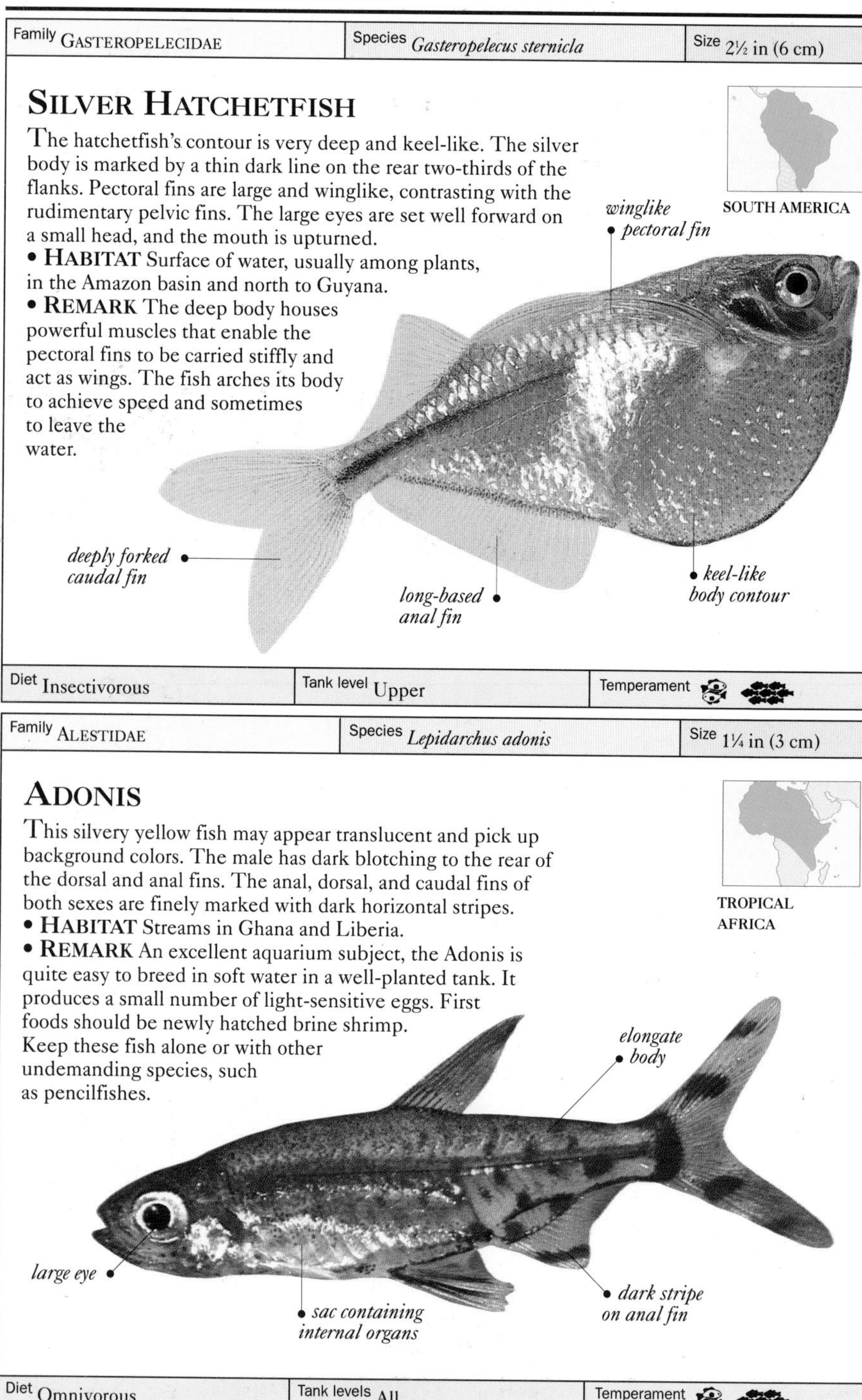

Family GASTEROPELECIDAE	Species *Gasteropelecus sternicla*	Size 2½ in (6 cm)

SILVER HATCHETFISH

The hatchetfish's contour is very deep and keel-like. The silver body is marked by a thin dark line on the rear two-thirds of the flanks. Pectoral fins are large and winglike, contrasting with the rudimentary pelvic fins. The large eyes are set well forward on a small head, and the mouth is upturned.

• **HABITAT** Surface of water, usually among plants, in the Amazon basin and north to Guyana.

• **REMARK** The deep body houses powerful muscles that enable the pectoral fins to be carried stiffly and act as wings. The fish arches its body to achieve speed and sometimes to leave the water.

Diet Insectivorous	Tank level Upper	Temperament

Family ALESTIDAE	Species *Lepidarchus adonis*	Size 1¼ in (3 cm)

ADONIS

This silvery yellow fish may appear translucent and pick up background colors. The male has dark blotching to the rear of the dorsal and anal fins. The anal, dorsal, and caudal fins of both sexes are finely marked with dark horizontal stripes.

• **HABITAT** Streams in Ghana and Liberia.

• **REMARK** An excellent aquarium subject, the Adonis is quite easy to breed in soft water in a well-planted tank. It produces a small number of light-sensitive eggs. First foods should be newly hatched brine shrimp. Keep these fish alone or with other undemanding species, such as pencilfishes.

Diet Omnivorous	Tank levels All	Temperament

Family ANOSTOMIDAE	Species *Leporinus desmotes*	Size 8¾ in (22 cm)

Black And Yellow Leporinus

SOUTH AMERICA

Several sooty black bands encircle the body at intervals, beginning at the tip of the snout and ending at the caudal peduncle. The background color is yellowish white. There is a faint amount of ground color on the center of the middle three bands. The terminal mouth resembles that of a hare, hence the name *Leporinus* (Latin for young hare).

• **HABITAT** Slow streams in the Amazon basin, from Guyana to the Plate River.

• **REMARK** The genus, although omnivorous, still requires plenty of vegetable matter. Plants are therefore at risk.

dorsal fin set far back

small adipose fin

harelike mouth

sooty black bands

Diet Omnivorous	Tank levels All	Temperament

Family ANOSTOMIDAE	Species *Leporinus frederici*	Size 14 in (35 cm)

Frederic's Leporinus

SOUTH AMERICA

Several dark-edged scales appear on this pale brown fish, and the general appearance is somewhat mottled. Three dark oval blotches mark the flanks, and smaller blotches may appear between the three major blotches according to the fish's mood. Indistinct vertical bands cross the body, and a further band occurs between the eye and the mouth.

• **HABITAT** Slow-moving streams in the Amazon basin, from Guyana to the Plate River.

• **REMARK** Juveniles adapt better than older fishes to aquarium conditions.

small adipose fin

yellow-red fins

dark oval blotches

Diet Omnivorous	Tank levels All	Temperament

Family ANOSTOMIDAE	Species *Leporinus octofasciatum*	Size 6 in (15 cm)

SOUTH AMERICA

EIGHT-BANDED LEPORINUS

The number of vertical bands on this characin appears to vary, with some ground color in the dark bands as in the Black and Yellow Leporinus (see p.95). Fins are mainly colorless, but the anal, pelvic, and dorsal fins carry some black, and the adipose fin has a black margin. Like many genus members, patterns may fade with age.

• **HABITAT** Slow-moving Amazonian streams, from Guyana to the Plate River.

vertical bands

large dark-rimmed eye

black margin in adipose fin

terminal mouth on small head

black tint in anal fins

Diet Omnivorous	Tank levels All	Temperament

Family ANOSTOMIDAE	Species *Leporinus arcus*	Size 15½ in (40 cm)

SOUTH AMERICA

LIPSTICK LEPORINUS

The pale yellow body of this streamlined fish is interrupted by a number of equally spaced, longitudinal stripes. They run the entire length of the body, from snout to caudal peduncle. The middle stripe is usually darker than those above or below it. The mouth is small with some red, and the eye is crossed by the middle body band.

• **HABITAT** Slow streams in Guyana, Venezuela, and the upper Amazon.

• **REMARK** These fish leap well, so secure the aquarium hood. The similar-looking Striped Leporinus (*Leporinus striatus*) lacks the dark crescent band around the tail base.

horizontal stripes

red mouth

small pelvic fin

Diet Omnivorous	Tank levels All	Temperament

Family SERRASALMIDAE	Species *Metynnis hypsauchen*	Size 5½ in (14 cm)

SCHREITMULLER'S METYNNIS

The ratio of height to length is very nearly equal on the body of this fish, which is similar in shape to a tilted parallelogram. The dorsal contour is pointed and the ventral contour is keel-shaped. Random dark spots appear on the flanks and indistinct vertical stripes may mark the smooth silver.

• **HABITAT** Rivers and streams of the Amazon basin, Guyana, and Paraguay.

• **REMARK** This species needs abundant vegetable matter.

• **OTHER NAME** Formerly known as *Metynnis schreitmulleri*.

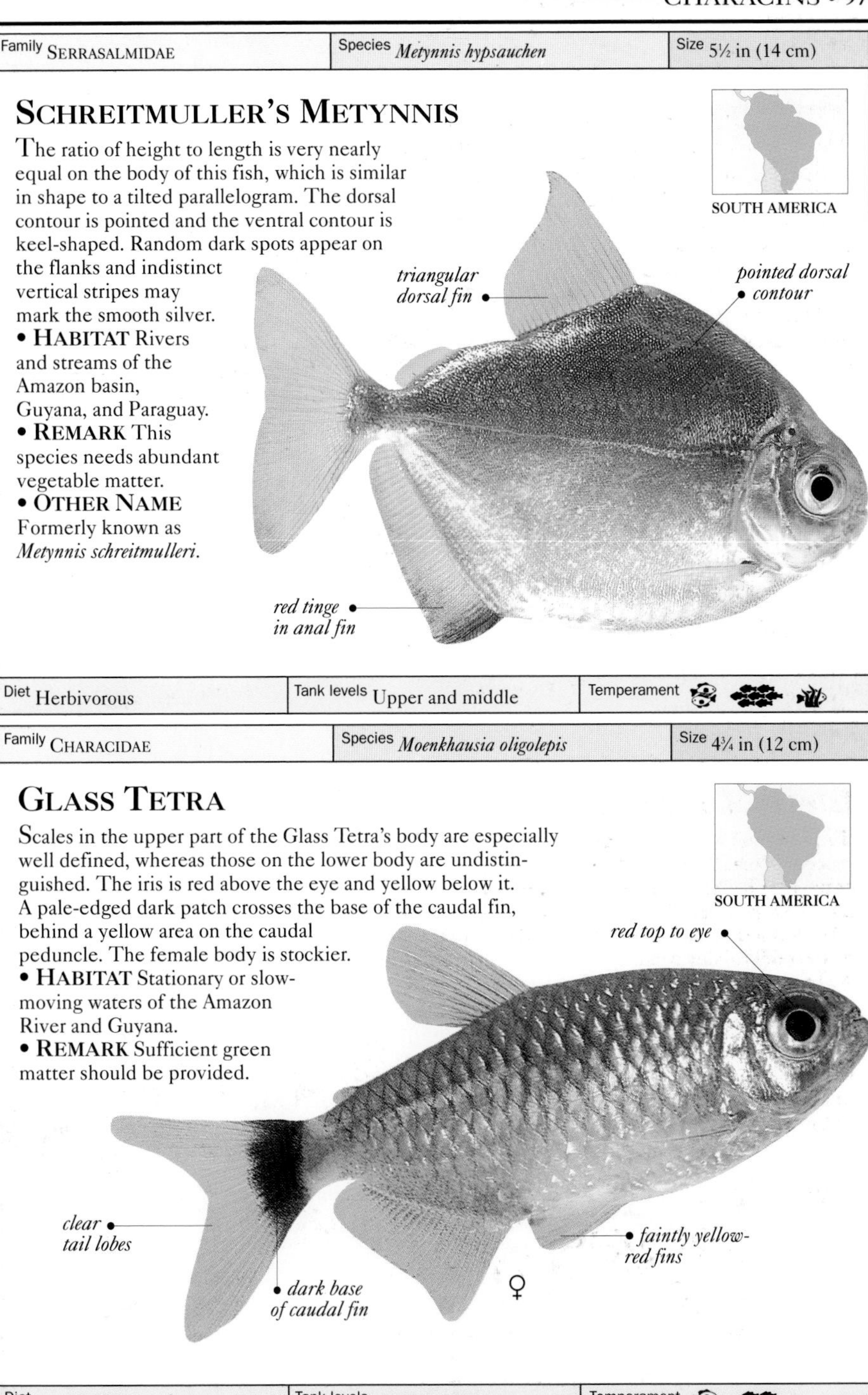

Diet Herbivorous	Tank levels Upper and middle	Temperament

Family CHARACIDAE	Species *Moenkhausia oligolepis*	Size 4¾ in (12 cm)

GLASS TETRA

Scales in the upper part of the Glass Tetra's body are especially well defined, whereas those on the lower body are undistinguished. The iris is red above the eye and yellow below it. A pale-edged dark patch crosses the base of the caudal fin, behind a yellow area on the caudal peduncle. The female body is stockier.

• **HABITAT** Stationary or slow-moving waters of the Amazon River and Guyana.

• **REMARK** Sufficient green matter should be provided.

Diet Omnivorous	Tank levels Middle and lower	Temperament

Family CHARACIDAE	Species *Moenkhausia pittieri*	Size 2½ in (6 cm)

DIAMOND TETRA

The coloration of the Diamond Tetra is greenish blue-gray on the dorsal surface and silver and white below. The iridescences are the fish's prime attraction; they are best in a tank that is lit from the side. This juvenile has a dark line that runs along the flanks to the caudal peduncle. Adult fins are bluish and edged with white; the dorsal fin of mature males is markedly sickle-shaped. Pelvic fins are long, and the caudal fin is deeply forked.The top of the eye is red.

• **HABITAT** Lake Valencia, Venezuela.

• **REMARK** The Diamond Tetra looks best in schools in a well-planted aquarium. An active swimmer, it needs plenty of space. It may be slow to mature.

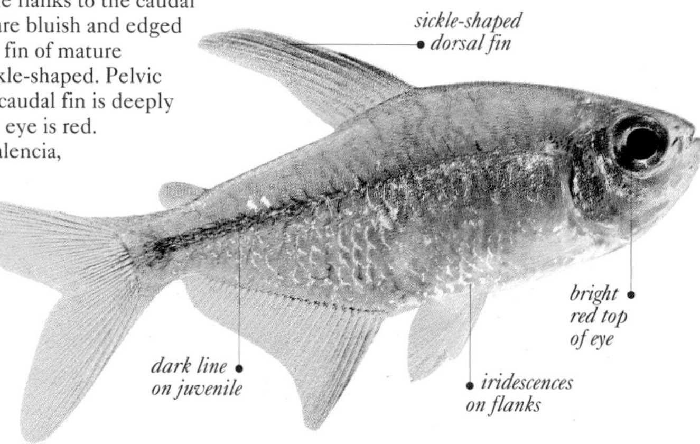

Diet Omnivorous	Tank level Middle	Temperament  

Family SERRASALMIDAE	Species *Mylossoma pluriventre*	Size 8 in (20 cm)

SILVER DOLLAR

The shape of this fish is deep, and the ventral region is especially keellike. Coloration is silvery, with small scales adding a polished effect. On the rear of the gill cover there is a small black blotch, and in juveniles, there may be dark vertical bands and a second dark blotch midway along the flanks. The broad anal fin and paddle-shaped caudal fin have red-orange edges.

• **HABITAT** Open waters in the southern Amazon, Paraguay, and the Plate River.

• **REMARK** The vegetarian habits of this fish mean that aquarium plants, especially softer-leaved species, are at risk.

• **OTHER NAME** Formerly known as *Mylossoma argenteum*.

Diet Herbivorous	Tank level Middle	Temperament  

Family CITHARINIDAE	Species *Nannaethiops unitaeniatus*	Size 2½ in (6.5 cm)

ONE-LINED AFRICAN TETRA

A dark line topped by a metallic gold streak runs from the snout to the end of the caudal fin of this elongated fish. The dorsal surface is greenish yellow-brown, and the ventral region is silvery gold. At spawning times the male develops red coloration in the square dorsal fin and in upper areas of the caudal fin.

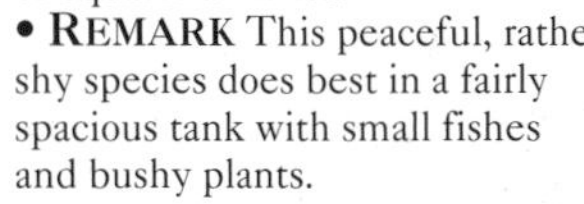

• **HABITAT** Streams and rivers of equatorial Africa.

• **REMARK** This peaceful, rather shy species does best in a fairly spacious tank with small fishes and bushy plants.

Diet Omnivorous	Tank levels Middle and lower	Temperament 

Family LEBIASINIDAE	Species *Nannostomus beckfordi aripirangensis*	Size 2½ in (6.5 cm)

GOLDEN PENCILFISH

As the name suggests, this fish is pencil-shaped. The dorsal surface is golden brown, which is intensified on mature specimens. The underside is silver below a wide, dark band running from the snout to the caudal fin and ending between two red patches. A gold band runs immediately above the black band. All fins except the pectorals have some some red color.

• **HABITAT** The island of Aripiranga in the lower Amazon region.

• **REMARK** The coloration of pencilfishes changes into blotchy patterns at night.

• **OTHER NAMES** Formerly classified in the *Nannobrycon* and *Poecilobrycon* genera.

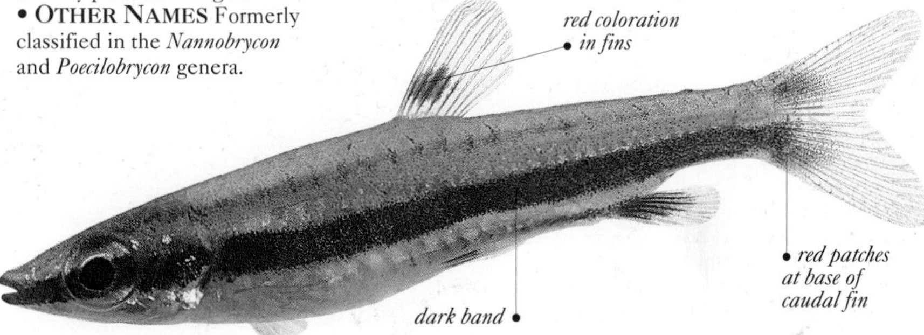

Diet Omnivorous	Tank level Middle	Temperament  

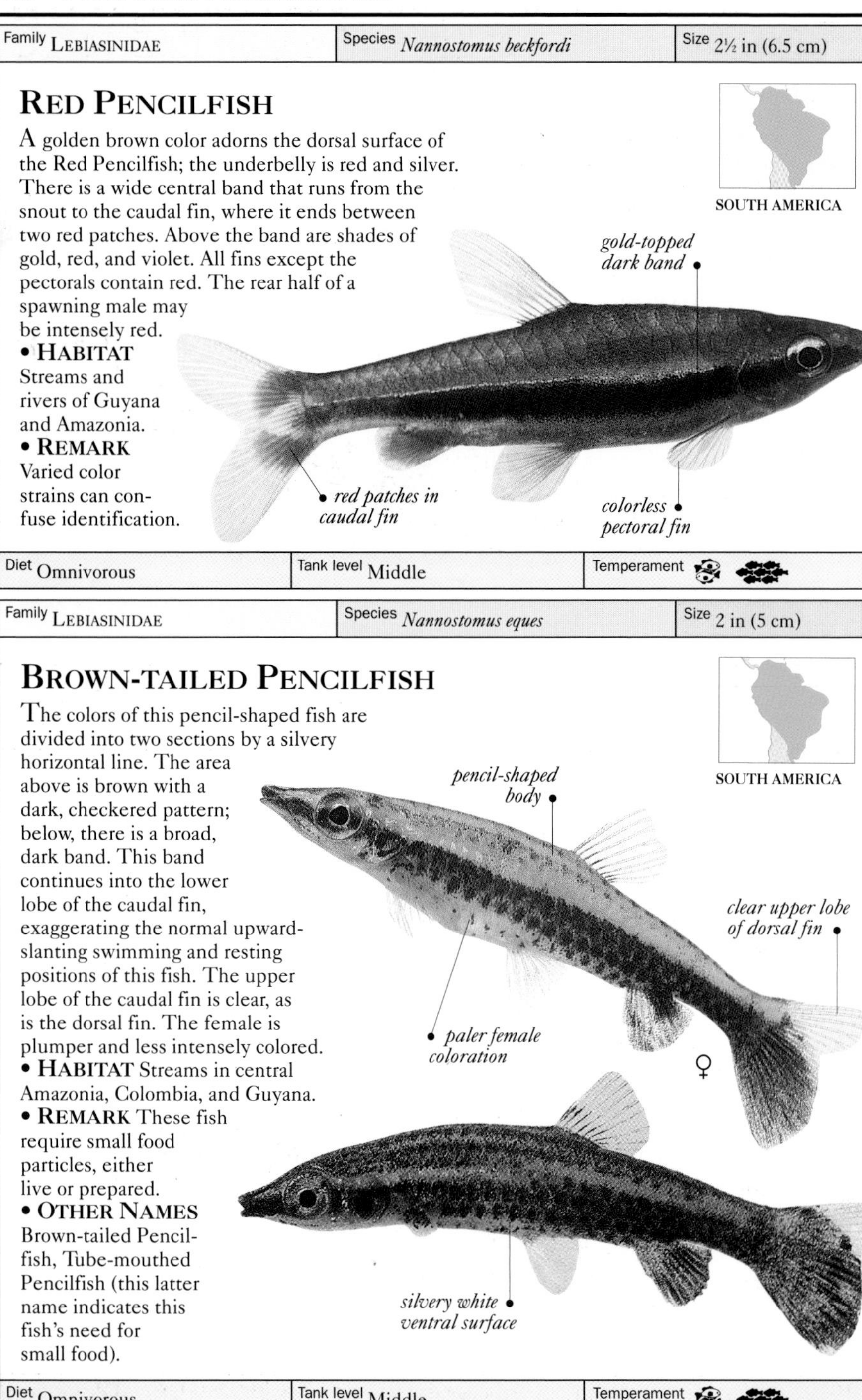

Family LEBIASINIDAE	Species *Nannostomus beckfordi*	Size 2½ in (6.5 cm)

RED PENCILFISH

A golden brown color adorns the dorsal surface of the Red Pencilfish; the underbelly is red and silver. There is a wide central band that runs from the snout to the caudal fin, where it ends between two red patches. Above the band are shades of gold, red, and violet. All fins except the pectorals contain red. The rear half of a spawning male may be intensely red.

• **HABITAT** Streams and rivers of Guyana and Amazonia.

• **REMARK** Varied color strains can confuse identification.

Diet Omnivorous	Tank level Middle	Temperament

Family LEBIASINIDAE	Species *Nannostomus eques*	Size 2 in (5 cm)

BROWN-TAILED PENCILFISH

The colors of this pencil-shaped fish are divided into two sections by a silvery horizontal line. The area above is brown with a dark, checkered pattern; below, there is a broad, dark band. This band continues into the lower lobe of the caudal fin, exaggerating the normal upward-slanting swimming and resting positions of this fish. The upper lobe of the caudal fin is clear, as is the dorsal fin. The female is plumper and less intensely colored.

• **HABITAT** Streams in central Amazonia, Colombia, and Guyana.

• **REMARK** These fish require small food particles, either live or prepared.

• **OTHER NAMES** Brown-tailed Pencilfish, Tube-mouthed Pencilfish (this latter name indicates this fish's need for small food).

Diet Omnivorous	Tank level Middle	Temperament

Family LEBIASINIDAE	Species *Nannostomus trifasciatus*	Size 2 in (5 cm)

THREE-LINED PENCILFISH

SOUTH AMERICA

Three dark bands run along the length of the body, which is a pale golden brown color. The central and upper bands are separated by a golden sheen, and each terminates in a bright red patch at the base of the caudal fin. Below the middle band the coloration is silvery white. The otherwise clear dorsal, anal, and pelvic fins have bright red areas.

- **HABITAT** Streams and rivers in Amazonia, especially the Negro River.
- **REMARK** During breeding, males in this species, like most in the genus, put on a prominent display to attract females and also to compete with and impress other males.

flattened head ends in pointed snout

red patch in dorsal fin

dark bands

twin red patches on caudal fin

Diet Omnivorous	Tank level Middle	Temperament

Family LEBIASINIDAE	Species *Nannostomus unifasciatus unifasciatus*	Size 3 in (7.5 cm)

ONE-LINED PENCILFISH

SOUTH AMERICA

The dorsal surface of this pencilfish is pale greenish brown, and the ventral surface and lower jaw are silvery white. A dark horizontal band runs from the snout through the eye to the base of the caudal fin, where it terminates in a dark blotch. This fish has a small, flattened head and a pointed snout. The lower part of the caudal fin is often dark with some red areas. All other fins are clear.

- **HABITAT** Streams and rivers of the Amazon and Guyana.
- **REMARK** Unfortunately, this species is not always in regular supply.

colorless fins

pale greenish brown dorsal surface

♀

dark band

Diet Omnivorous	Tank level Middle	Temperament

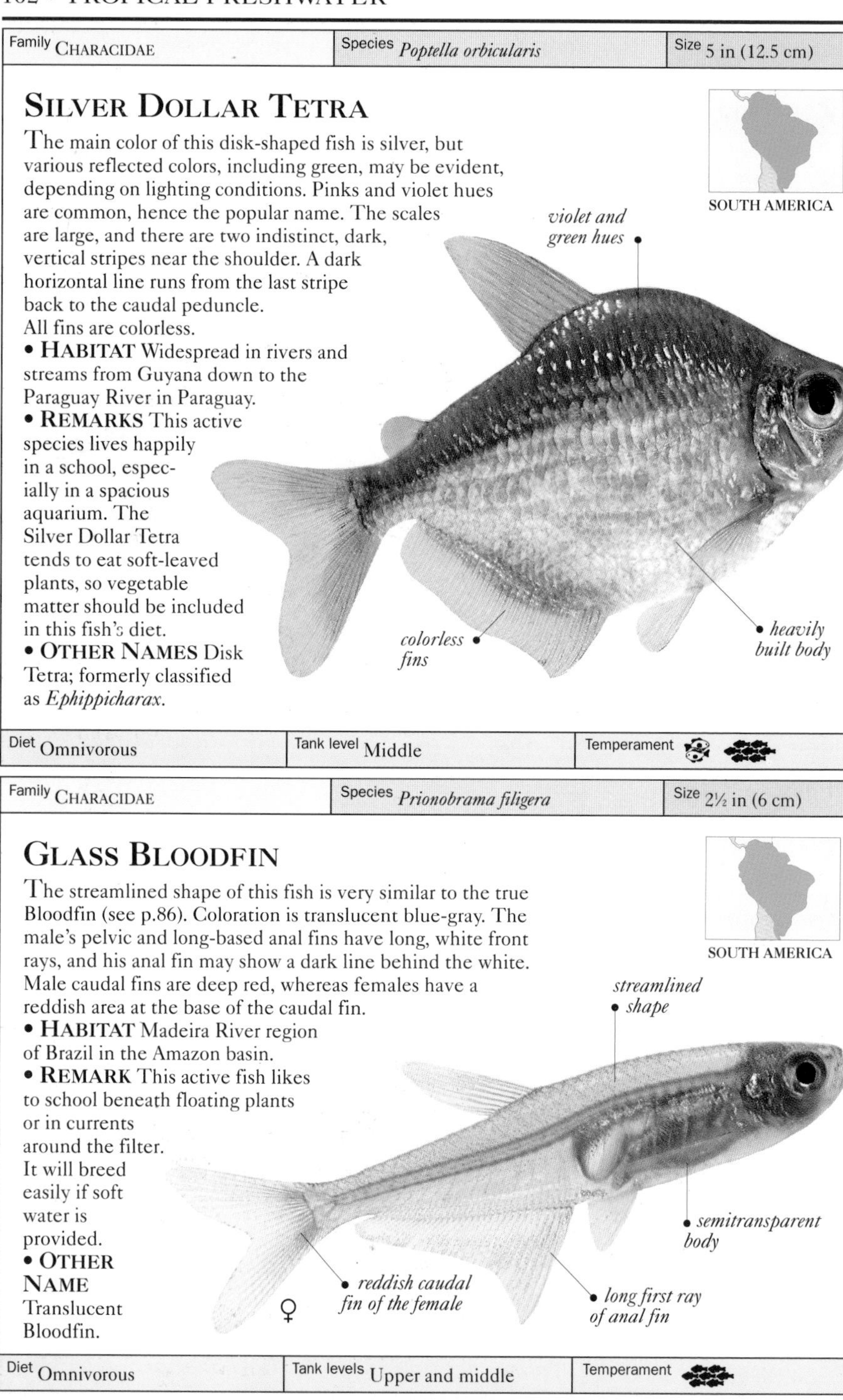

Family CHARACIDAE	Species *Poptella orbicularis*	Size 5 in (12.5 cm)

SILVER DOLLAR TETRA

The main color of this disk-shaped fish is silver, but various reflected colors, including green, may be evident, depending on lighting conditions. Pinks and violet hues are common, hence the popular name. The scales are large, and there are two indistinct, dark, vertical stripes near the shoulder. A dark horizontal line runs from the last stripe back to the caudal peduncle. All fins are colorless.

• **HABITAT** Widespread in rivers and streams from Guyana down to the Paraguay River in Paraguay.

• **REMARKS** This active species lives happily in a school, especially in a spacious aquarium. The Silver Dollar Tetra tends to eat soft-leaved plants, so vegetable matter should be included in this fish's diet.

• **OTHER NAMES** Disk Tetra; formerly classified as *Ephippicharax*.

Diet Omnivorous	Tank level Middle	Temperament

Family CHARACIDAE	Species *Prionobrama filigera*	Size 2½ in (6 cm)

GLASS BLOODFIN

The streamlined shape of this fish is very similar to the true Bloodfin (see p.86). Coloration is translucent blue-gray. The male's pelvic and long-based anal fins have long, white front rays, and his anal fin may show a dark line behind the white. Male caudal fins are deep red, whereas females have a reddish area at the base of the caudal fin.

• **HABITAT** Madeira River region of Brazil in the Amazon basin.

• **REMARK** This active fish likes to school beneath floating plants or in currents around the filter. It will breed easily if soft water is provided.

• **OTHER NAME** Translucent Bloodfin.

Diet Omnivorous	Tank levels Upper and middle	Temperament

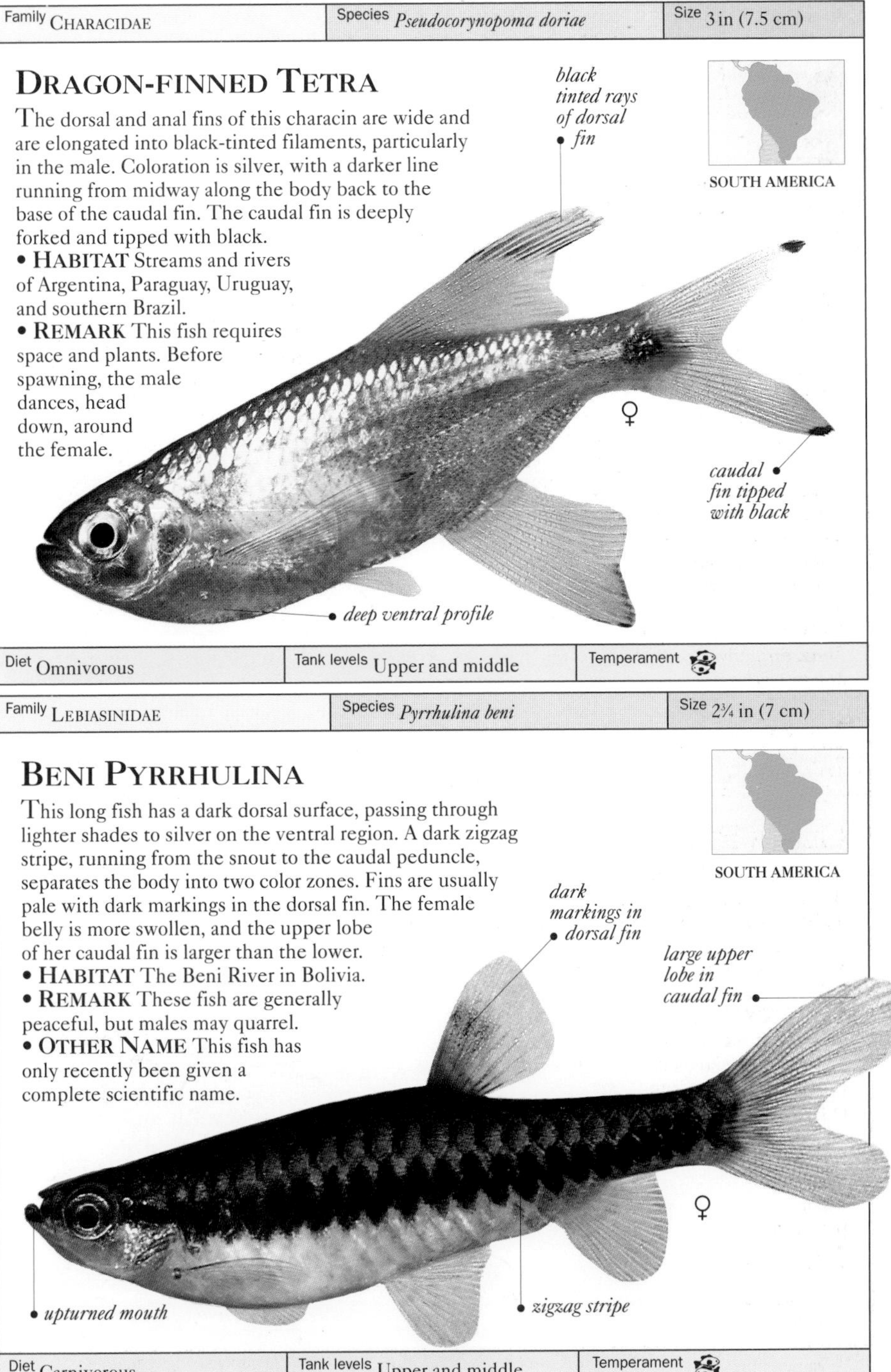

Family CHARACIDAE	Species *Pseudocorynopoma doriae*	Size 3 in (7.5 cm)

DRAGON-FINNED TETRA

The dorsal and anal fins of this characin are wide and are elongated into black-tinted filaments, particularly in the male. Coloration is silver, with a darker line running from midway along the body back to the base of the caudal fin. The caudal fin is deeply forked and tipped with black.

• **HABITAT** Streams and rivers of Argentina, Paraguay, Uruguay, and southern Brazil.

• **REMARK** This fish requires space and plants. Before spawning, the male dances, head down, around the female.

Diet Omnivorous	Tank levels Upper and middle	Temperament

Family LEBIASINIDAE	Species *Pyrrhulina beni*	Size 2¾ in (7 cm)

BENI PYRRHULINA

This long fish has a dark dorsal surface, passing through lighter shades to silver on the ventral region. A dark zigzag stripe, running from the snout to the caudal peduncle, separates the body into two color zones. Fins are usually pale with dark markings in the dorsal fin. The female belly is more swollen, and the upper lobe of her caudal fin is larger than the lower.

• **HABITAT** The Beni River in Bolivia.

• **REMARK** These fish are generally peaceful, but males may quarrel.

• **OTHER NAME** This fish has only recently been given a complete scientific name.

Diet Carnivorous	Tank levels Upper and middle	Temperament

Family LEBIASINIDAE	Species *Pyrrhulina filamentosa*	Size 2½ in (6 cm)

FILAMENTOUS PYRRHULINA

The forward ventral surface of this fish is significantly rounded. Coloration is reddish brown with a darker dorsal surface and a silver belly. A dark line runs from the snout to the caudal peduncle, below which there are three rows of bright red dots. Fins are yellowish, and the pelvic, anal, and caudal fins may be dark-edged. Females are plumper and slightly less colorful.

• **HABITAT** Streams and rivers in Guyana, Surinam, Venezuela, and the Amazon basin.

• **REMARK** This fish requires a tank well furnished with floating plants under which it can rest.

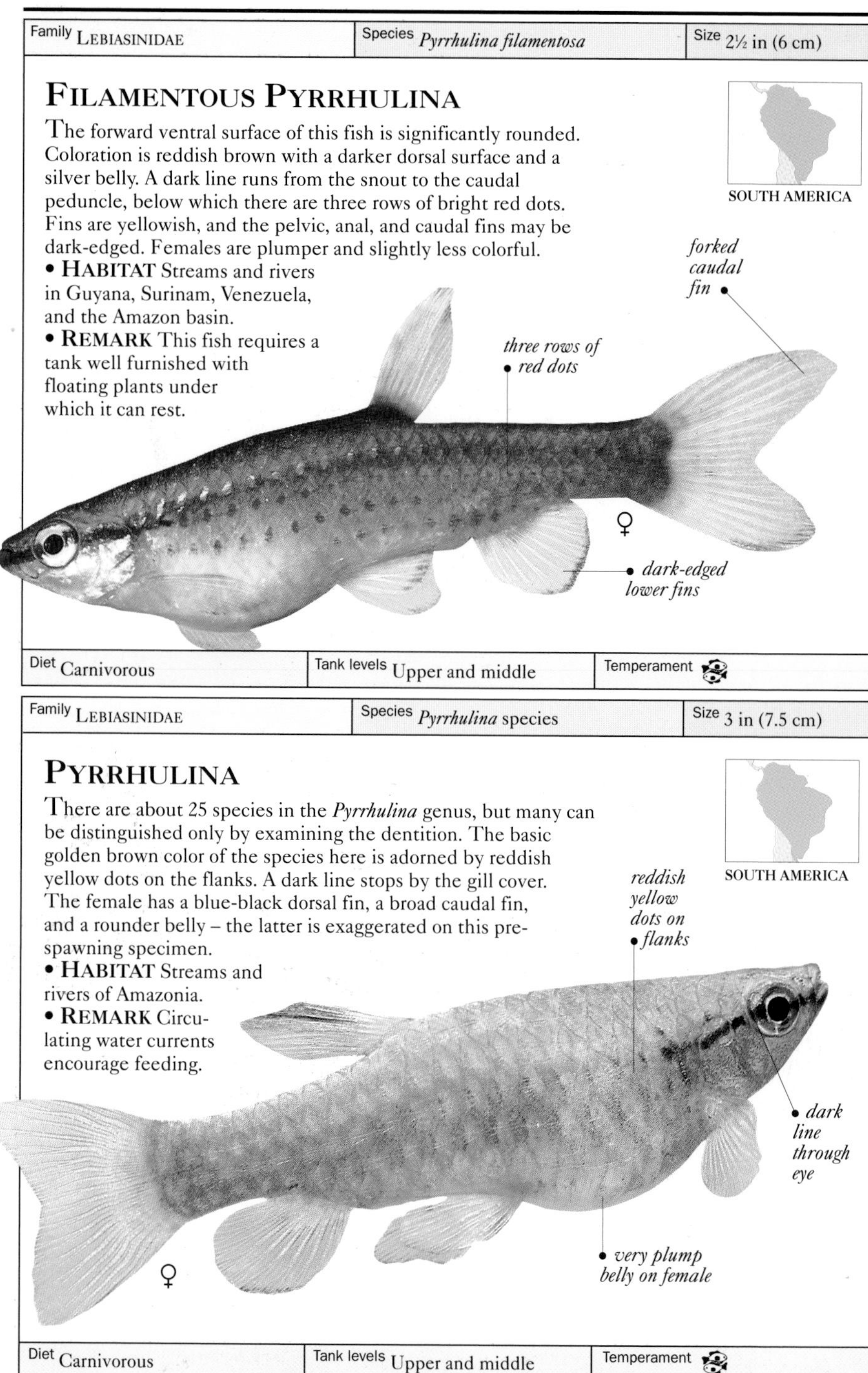

Diet Carnivorous	Tank levels Upper and middle	Temperament

Family LEBIASINIDAE	Species *Pyrrhulina* species	Size 3 in (7.5 cm)

PYRRHULINA

There are about 25 species in the *Pyrrhulina* genus, but many can be distinguished only by examining the dentition. The basic golden brown color of the species here is adorned by reddish yellow dots on the flanks. A dark line stops by the gill cover. The female has a blue-black dorsal fin, a broad caudal fin, and a rounder belly – the latter is exaggerated on this pre-spawning specimen.

• **HABITAT** Streams and rivers of Amazonia.

• **REMARK** Circulating water currents encourage feeding.

Diet Carnivorous	Tank levels Upper and middle	Temperament

Family SERRASALMIDAE	Species *Serrasalmus nattereri*	Size 12 in (30 cm)

RED-BELLIED PIRANHA

The body of this piranha is deeply oval and heavily built. Coloration is mainly steely gray, shading down through silvery gray flanks to a bright, orange-red chest and underbelly. Iridescences cover the flanks. Juveniles carry faint dark spots on the flanks that fade with age, and they lack the red and steely gray colorings. The adult is snub-nosed, and the lower jaw projects beyond the top jaw. Both jaws contain very sharp teeth.

- **HABITAT** Rivers from Guyana to the Plate River.
- **REMARK** These notoriously predatory fishes should be handled with extreme caution. It is illegal to import piranhas into the USA.

JUVENILE

ADULT

heavily built body

iridescences on flanks

projecting lower jaw filled with sharp teeth

orange-red underside

long-based, concave anal fin

Diet Carnivorous	Tank levels Middle and lower	Temperament

Family CHARACIDAE | Species *Thayeria boehlkei* | Size 3 in (7.5 cm)

PENGUIN FISH

The common name of this fish is due to its predominantly black-and-white coloring. Faint olive-green on the dorsal surface shades down to silver on the belly. A dark blurred band runs from the rear of the gill cover across the body and continuing into the lower lobe of the caudal fin, where it is bordered by white. Females share the markings but are plumper at spawning time.

• **HABITAT** Streams in Brazil.

• **REMARK** This fish swims with its head pointing upward.

Diet Omnivorous | Tank levels Upper and middle | Temperament

Family GASTEROPELECIDAE | Species *Thoracocharax stellatus* | Size 2¾ in (7 cm)

SILVER HATCHETFISH

The unusual body shape of this fish is very deep, with an almost flat dorsal contour. It is pale greenish yellow in color, shading down to gray-blue-silver. A faint, darker blue-gray line, starting behind the gill cover, ends as a small blotch on the rear of the caudal peduncle. The scales are larger than on other hatchetfishes. The dorsal fin carries a black blotch and is set well back.

• **HABITAT** Still waters from Brazil to Argentina.

• **REMARK** These fish require a spacious aquarium with a secure lid, for they can jump.

Diet Omnivorous | Tank level Upper | Temperament

CICHLIDS
SMALLER CICHLIDS

THE FAMILY CICHLIDAE comprises a large number of mostly heavy-bodied fishes that are widely distributed throughout Central and South America, tropical Africa, and, to a lesser extent, southern Asia. They generally live in still or slow-moving waters, sheltering among rocks and vegetation. As males vigorously defend their territory in the wild, a single pair is usually suitable for the average aquarium. Some cichlids dig to lay their eggs in the substrate, so rooted plants in the tank will be prone to damage. The smaller cichlids, or dwarf cichlids, include *Apistogramma* and *Pelvicachromis* species. They tend to be secretive spawners, often laying their eggs inside caves or in the aquarium equivalent – an overturned flowerpot.

Family CICHLIDAE	Species *Anomalachromis thomasi*	Size 3 in (7.5 cm)

AFRICAN BUTTERFLY CICHLID

The color of this stocky fish is golden brown with an overcast of violet and paler tones on the belly. Rows of iridescent scales decorate the flanks.

- **HABITAT** Streams in Liberia and Sierra Leone.
- **REMARK** This fish is territorial when spawning.
- **OTHER NAMES** *Hemichromis thomasi*, *Paratilapia thomasi*, *Pelmatochromis thomasi*, Thomas's Pelmatochromis.

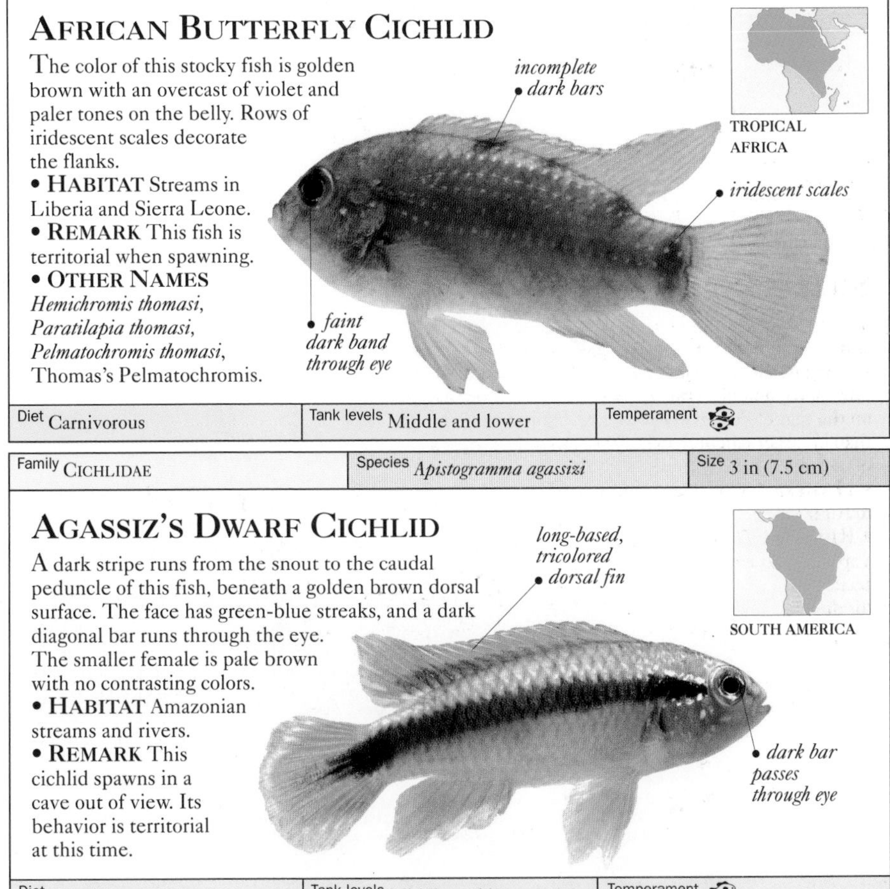

Diet Carnivorous	Tank levels Middle and lower	Temperament

Family CICHLIDAE	Species *Apistogramma agassizi*	Size 3 in (7.5 cm)

AGASSIZ'S DWARF CICHLID

A dark stripe runs from the snout to the caudal peduncle of this fish, beneath a golden brown dorsal surface. The face has green-blue streaks, and a dark diagonal bar runs through the eye. The smaller female is pale brown with no contrasting colors.

- **HABITAT** Amazonian streams and rivers.
- **REMARK** This cichlid spawns in a cave out of view. Its behavior is territorial at this time.

Diet Carnivorous	Tank levels Middle and lower	Temperament

Family CICHLIDAE	Species *Apistogramma cacatuoides*	Size 3 in (7.5 cm)

COCKATOO DWARF CICHLID

SOUTH AMERICA

The most distinctive characteristics of this species are the fins. The dorsal fin has extended rays like the crest of a cockatoo, and the caudal fin has red and black markings. Body coloration is grayish green. A wide, dark band runs horizontally along the flanks, and repeated broken lines run beneath this. Females have dark bars through the eyes and smaller fins.

- **HABITAT** Streams and rivers of the Peruvian Amazon.
- **REMARK** One male of this species is best kept with several females in a modestly sized aquarium.
- **OTHER NAME** Crested Dwarf Cichlid.

dorsal fin carries extended rays

grayish green body coloration

red and black marks on caudal fin

Diet Carnivorous	Tank level Lower	Temperament

Family CICHLIDAE	Species *Apistogramma macmasteri*	Size 3 in (7.5 cm)

MACMASTER'S DWARF CICHLID

The coloration on the dorsal surface of this fish is creamy gold, shading down through bluish flanks to pale yellow below. A dark horizontal line runs from the eye to the caudal peduncle, and the head carries pale blue markings. The front rays of the dorsal fin are black. The male has bright red top and bottom edges on a yellow caudal fin.

- **HABITAT** Streams and rivers in northern South America, especially the Rio Meta region of Colombia.
- **OTHER NAMES** *Apistogramma ornatipinnis*, *A. steindachneri* are similar.

dorsal fin has spiny rays

dark horizontal line

red edges on male tail

pale blue markings on head

Diet Carnivorous	Tank levels Middle and lower	Temperament 

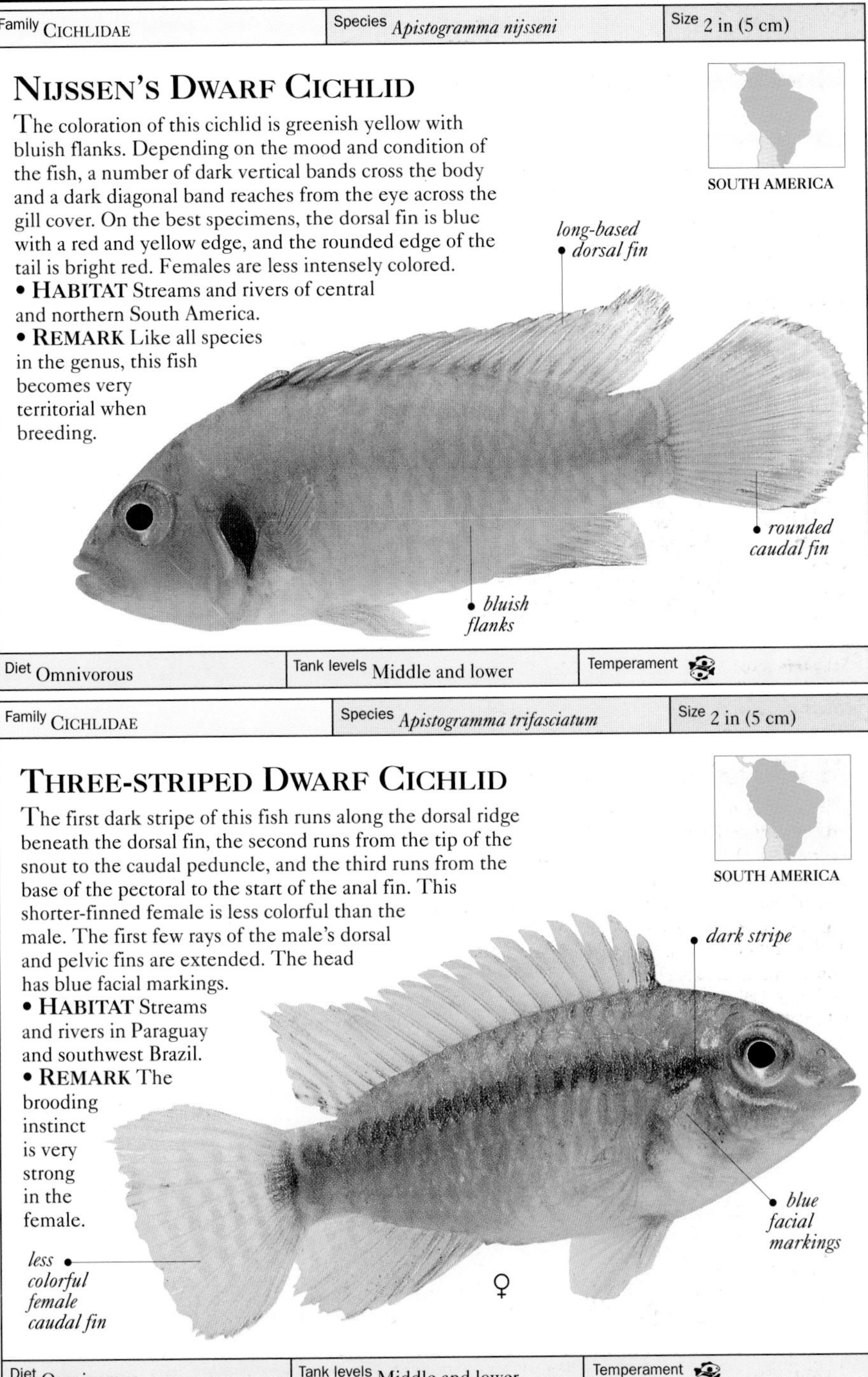

Family CICHLIDAE	Species *Apistogramma nijsseni*	Size 2 in (5 cm)

NIJSSEN'S DWARF CICHLID

The coloration of this cichlid is greenish yellow with bluish flanks. Depending on the mood and condition of the fish, a number of dark vertical bands cross the body and a dark diagonal band reaches from the eye across the gill cover. On the best specimens, the dorsal fin is blue with a red and yellow edge, and the rounded edge of the tail is bright red. Females are less intensely colored.

- **HABITAT** Streams and rivers of central and northern South America.
- **REMARK** Like all species in the genus, this fish becomes very territorial when breeding.

Diet Omnivorous	Tank levels Middle and lower	Temperament

Family CICHLIDAE	Species *Apistogramma trifasciatum*	Size 2 in (5 cm)

THREE-STRIPED DWARF CICHLID

The first dark stripe of this fish runs along the dorsal ridge beneath the dorsal fin, the second runs from the tip of the snout to the caudal peduncle, and the third runs from the base of the pectoral to the start of the anal fin. This shorter-finned female is less colorful than the male. The first few rays of the male's dorsal and pelvic fins are extended. The head has blue facial markings.

- **HABITAT** Streams and rivers in Paraguay and southwest Brazil.
- **REMARK** The brooding instinct is very strong in the female.

Diet Omnivorous	Tank levels Middle and lower	Temperament

Family CICHLIDAE	Species *Crenicara filamentosa*	Size 3 in (7.5 cm)

CHECKERBOARD CICHLID

SOUTH AMERICA

This fish gets its name from the horizontal pattern of dark blotches checkering its flanks. Greenish blue lines, more apparent under sidelighting, run on both sides of the blotches. The fins are speckled in red and edged in light blue, and terminate in extended filaments. Under the eye there is a red line and a dark band extending from the snout to the end of the gill cover.

- **HABITAT** Rivers in the Orinoco region.
- **REMARK** This shy species does best in soft, acid water, around rocks and at the plant bases. It prefers live foods.

extended filaments

red line under eye

equally spaced blotches

lyre-shaped caudal fin

Diet Carnivorous	Tank level Lower	Temperament

Family CICHLIDAE	Species *Nannacara anomala*	Size 3 in (7.5 cm)

GOLDEN-EYED DWARF CICHLID

SOUTH AMERICA

The color of this stocky fish is usually golden brown with greenish blue iridescent scales on the flanks. Darker markings may appear, depending on its mood. The head is rounded with a large golden eye and greenish blue facial markings. The female has a plainer yellow coloration.

- **HABITAT** Streams and rivers in Guyana, South America.
- **REMARK** The female often takes on a pattern of blotches when spawning.

rayed dorsal fin

arched dorsal surface

green-blue iridescent scales

plain yellow coloring in female

♀

Diet Carnivorous	Tank level Lower	Temperament

Family CICHLIDAE	Species *Nanochromis nudiceps*	Size 3 in (7.5 cm)

CONGO DWARF CICHLID

This subtly shaded, gray-brown fish has a bluish shoulder and pale purple areas on the belly. A pattern of dark and light horizontal bands is evident on the top of the caudal fin.

- **HABITAT** Congo River basin in central Africa.
- **REMARK** Spawning is similar to that of the Kribensis (see p.112), taking place in rocky caves or a conveniently placed flowerpot. Eggs hatch after about three days.
- **OTHER NAME** It has been suggested that *Nanochromis parilius* is the correct name of this popular aquarium species, and that the true *N. nudiceps* is rarely seen in the hobby.

TROPICAL AFRICA

eye is set high in flattened head

yellow and brown stripes in caudal fin

iridescent blue area under eye

purple shading on belly

♀

Diet Carnivorous	Tank level Lower	Temperament

Family CICHLIDAE	Species *Papiliochromis ramirezi*	Size 3 in (7.5 cm)

RAM

This wild fish is greenish brown with violet-blue iridescent scales. Many aquarium-bred varieties are commonly available. A dark bar runs from the bright red eye to the caudal peduncle. The anal, caudal, and dorsal fins have a pale red tinge and carry iridescent blue speckles.

- **HABITAT** Streams in Venezuela and Colombia.
- **OTHER NAMES** Dwarf Butterfly Cichlid. Previously placed in the genus *Apistogramma* and later in the genus *Microgeophagus*. *Papiliochromis* is the most recent classification.

SOUTH AMERICA

pale red tinge in dorsal fin

bright red eye markings

violet-blue iridescent speckles

red pelvic fin has dark front edge

Diet Carnivorous	Tank levels Middle and lower	Temperament

Family CICHLIDAE	Species *Pelvicachromis pulcher*	Size 4 in (10 cm)

KRIBENSIS

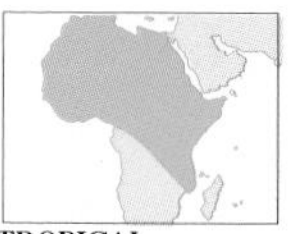

TROPICAL AFRICA

The dorsal and ventral body contours of this fish are equal in the male but are slightly heavier around the ventral region in the female. Colors are divided into two distinct halves by a dark band that runs from the snout, along the length of the body, and into the central rays of the caudal fin. The lower half of the body is silvery pink-violet in the male, whereas the belly of the female takes on a rich purple-plum color. The female has gold areas both above and below the eye, and both sexes have light bars across the forehead. The male dorsal fin is pointed, with some dark shading and a red-gold outer edging. The female dorsal fin is rounded and carries dark spots in the rear. Pelvic fins of the Kribensis are bluish red, except on a spawning female, whose fins are sooty black.

• **HABITAT** Niger River delta in West Africa.

• **REMARK** The Kribensis is a secretive yet prolific spawner. Water pH may have a bearing on proportion of sexes within a brood.

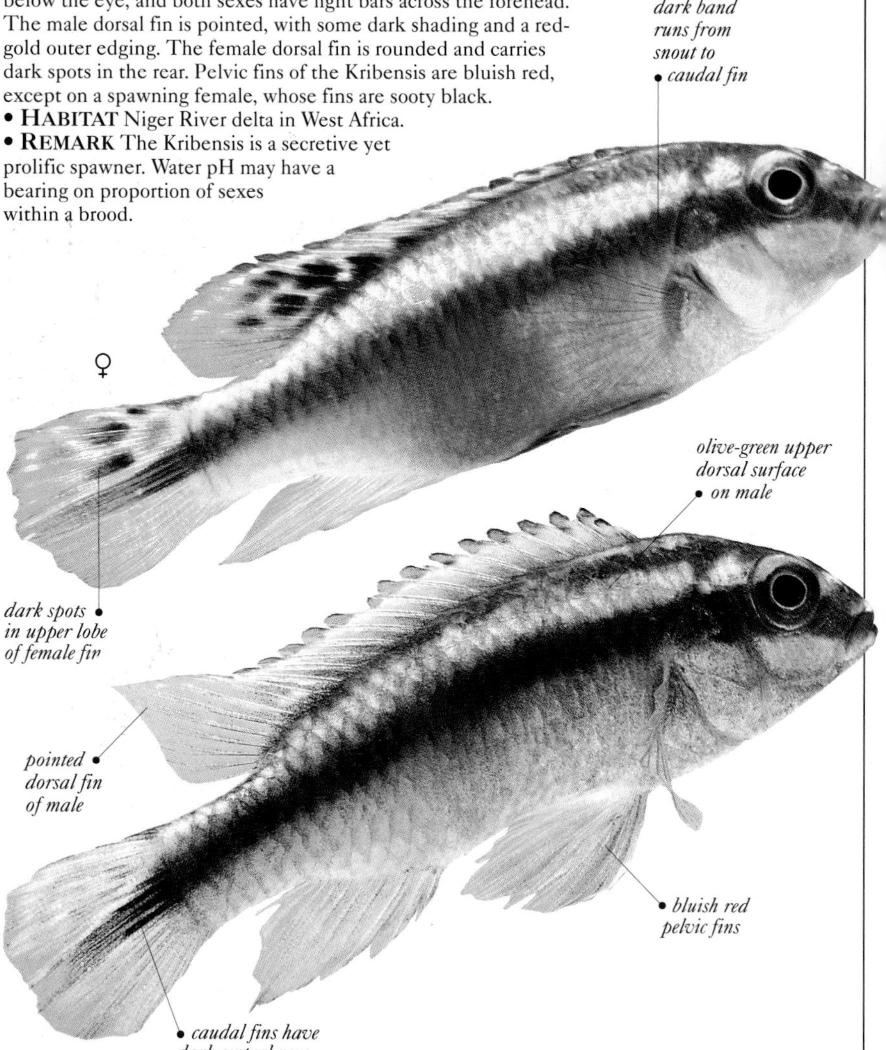

dark band runs from snout to caudal fin

♀

olive-green upper dorsal surface on male

dark spots in upper lobe of female fin

pointed dorsal fin of male

bluish red pelvic fins

caudal fins have dark central rays

Diet Omnivorous	Tank levels Middle and lower	Temperament 

CICHLIDS
LARGER CICHLIDS

THE LARGER STOCKY members of the family Cichlidae are chosen for both their interesting breeding habits and their majestic appearance. Many species, such as the angelfishes and discus fishes from South America, have attractive patterns and make excellent display specimens for large aquariums. A high level of parental care is involved in the breeding of all well-established cichlids, so they are often territorial at this time. Spawning sites are carefully chosen, cleaned, and guarded. As with many other large species, these fish have hearty appetites, so an efficient filtration system and frequent partial water changes are important. Water quality is not critical for most of these species, excluding the discus fish.

Family CICHLIDAE	Species *Aequidens maronii*	Size 4 in (10 cm)

KEYHOLE CICHLID

A dark curving bar passes through the eye of this stockily built fish, connecting the front of the dorsal fin with the lower edge of the gill cover. Background coloration is generally a creamy pale brown, but it may change to a mottled brown when the fish is disturbed. The dark blotch that gives the fish its common name appears on the flanks beneath the dorsal fin. It resembles the shape of a keyhole more closely on juvenile specimens.

- **HABITAT** Streams and rivers in Guyana.
- **REMARK** Unlike most cichlids, this fish is extremely peaceful, even shy. After spawning, which takes place on a flat rock in open water, the young may stay with the parents for several months.

Male adults have pointed dorsal and anal fins

Diet Omnivorous	Tank level Lower	Temperament

Family CICHLIDAE	Species *Aequidens pulcher*	Size 6¼ in (16 cm)

BLUE ACARA

Several dark bars vertically cross the stocky pale gray body of the Blue Acara. They are often connected by a horizontal bar running from behind the eye to the caudal peduncle. The metallic blue centers of each scale give an iridescent appearance, and there are additional blue lines on the head, especially below the eye and on the gill cover. Males have pointed dorsal and anal fins, which may extend past the caudal fin on some specimens.

• **HABITAT** Northern Venezuela; also Trinidad.

• **REMARK** It is territorial and aggressive when breeding.

Diet Omnivorous	Tank levels Middle and lower	Temperament

Family CICHLIDAE	Species *Aequidens rivulatus*	Size 9 in (23 cm)

GREEN TERROR

This color variety has a dark blotch midway along the flanks, and speckling on the sides. It is more elongate than the Blue Acara (above) and is distinctly green, with colored edges on the unpaired fins. Males may develop a lumpier head with increasing age.

• **HABITAT** Waterways in Ecuador and Peru.

• **REMARK** The Green Terror is very aggressive. The wild form of this species lacks anal and dorsal coloration.

Diet Omnivorous	Tank levels Middle and lower	Temperament

Family CICHLIDAE	Species *Astronotus ocellatus*	Size 11¼ in (28 cm)

RED OSCAR

This Red or Tiger Oscar is a domestic variety bred to increase the distribution of red pigment. The wild variety has irregular dark blotches and rust-colored markings. The head of this specimen is gray with less red coloration and a large, fleshy lipped mouth. The fins are functional rather than decorative; dorsal and anal fins are wider at the rear, and the caudal fin is rounded and paddle shaped.

• **HABITAT** Rivers in Amazonia and Guyana.

• **REMARK** A favorite pet despite its rapid rate of growth and large appetite, the Oscar needs regular thorough water changes. It spawns prolifically and is likely to produce around 3,000 fry. If fed from fingers, it readily becomes hand-tame.

• **OTHER NAME** Velvet Cichlid.

Marble-patterned juvenile Oscars

white edging on dorsal fin

narrow front of dorsal fin

fleshy lipped mouth

dark margin on anal fin

dark pelvic fins

eye has dark center and red rim

SOUTH AMERICA

Diet Carnivorous	Tank levels Middle and lower	Temperament

Family CICHLIDAE	Species *Cichlasoma citrinellum*	Size 12 in (30 cm)

MIDAS CICHLID

This cichlid's heavily built body is lemon-yellow and gold in color. The common name refers to the gold aspect, and the scientific name to the lemon shading. Mature males often develop a lump called the "nuchal hump" on the forehead. Juveniles are brown with black mottling.

• **HABITAT** Rivers and streams from southern Mexico to Nicaragua.

• **REMARK** These fish take part in jaw locking and other territorial displays before breeding.

• **OTHER NAMES** Red Devil Cichlid, Lemon Cichlid.

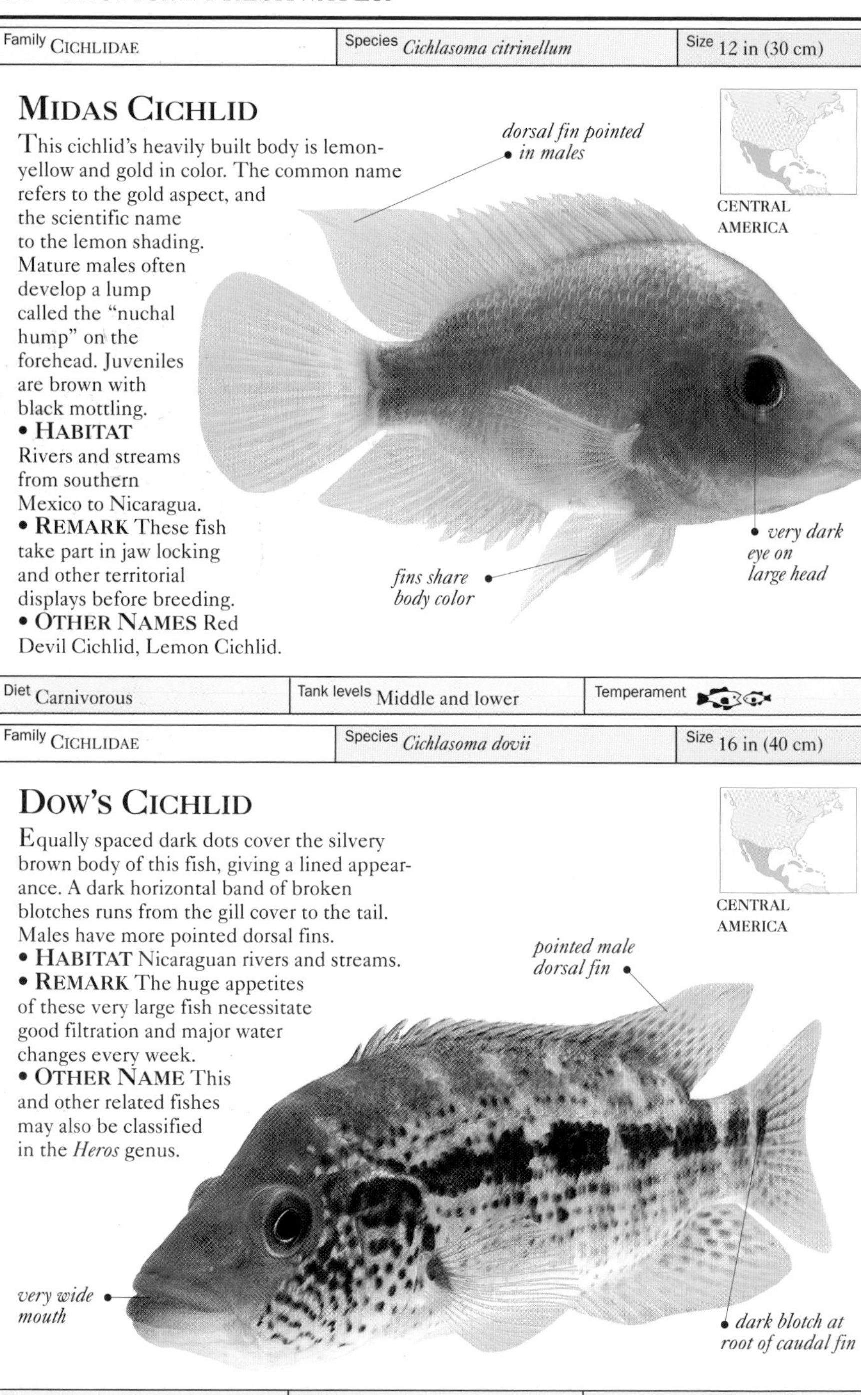

Diet Carnivorous	Tank levels Middle and lower	Temperament

Family CICHLIDAE	Species *Cichlasoma dovii*	Size 16 in (40 cm)

DOW'S CICHLID

Equally spaced dark dots cover the silvery brown body of this fish, giving a lined appearance. A dark horizontal band of broken blotches runs from the gill cover to the tail. Males have more pointed dorsal fins.

• **HABITAT** Nicaraguan rivers and streams.

• **REMARK** The huge appetites of these very large fish necessitate good filtration and major water changes every week.

• **OTHER NAME** This and other related fishes may also be classified in the *Heros* genus.

Diet Carnivorous	Tank levels Middle and lower	Temperament

Family CICHLIDAE	Species *Cichlasoma maculicauda*	Size 12 in (30 cm)

BLACK-BELT CICHLID

CENTRAL AMERICA

Dark speckles cluster sporadically on the silver-blue body of this cichlid, particularly on the midsection and on the caudal peduncle. The front part of the head and the base of the pectoral fin are marked with carmine-red, and speckles of this color appear above the gill cover. Dorsal and anal fins of the male are pointed.

• **HABITAT** Rivers and streams from southern Mexico to Panama.

dark vertical bar created by dots

red in caudal fin

carmine-red coloring

Diet Carnivorous	Tank levels All	Temperament

Family CICHLIDAE	Species *Crenicichla lepidota*	Size 8 in (20 cm)

TWO-SPOT PIKE CICHLID

SOUTH AMERICA

This torpedo-shaped fish varies in color, from silvery blue-gray to pearly green, or yellowish. A dark band runs from the snout to the base of the caudal fin. Iridescent speckles cover the upper half of the body, and narrow dark bands may be visible. Female Two-spot Pike Cichlids tend to be plumper around the midsection.

• **HABITAT** Weedbeds in streams and rivers in the Amazon basin of Brazil to northern Argentina.

• **REMARK** This predator needs space, and meaty or live foods.

long-based dorsal fin

wide mouth on flattened head

eyespot on base of caudal fin

short pelvic fin

Diet Carnivorous	Tank levels All	Temperament

Family CICHLIDAE	Species *Etroplus maculatus*	Size 3¼ in (8 cm)

ORANGE CHROMIDE

This golden yellow fish is covered with tiny red dots, which may spread into the fins. A central black blotch appears on the flanks. Anal and pelvic fins may be darker than shown. Males and females are alike.

- **HABITAT** Coastal brackish rivers of southern India and Sri Lanka.
- **REMARK** Eggs are laid on hard surfaces – flowerpots are ideal. Keep in a species tank or with similarly-sized fish.

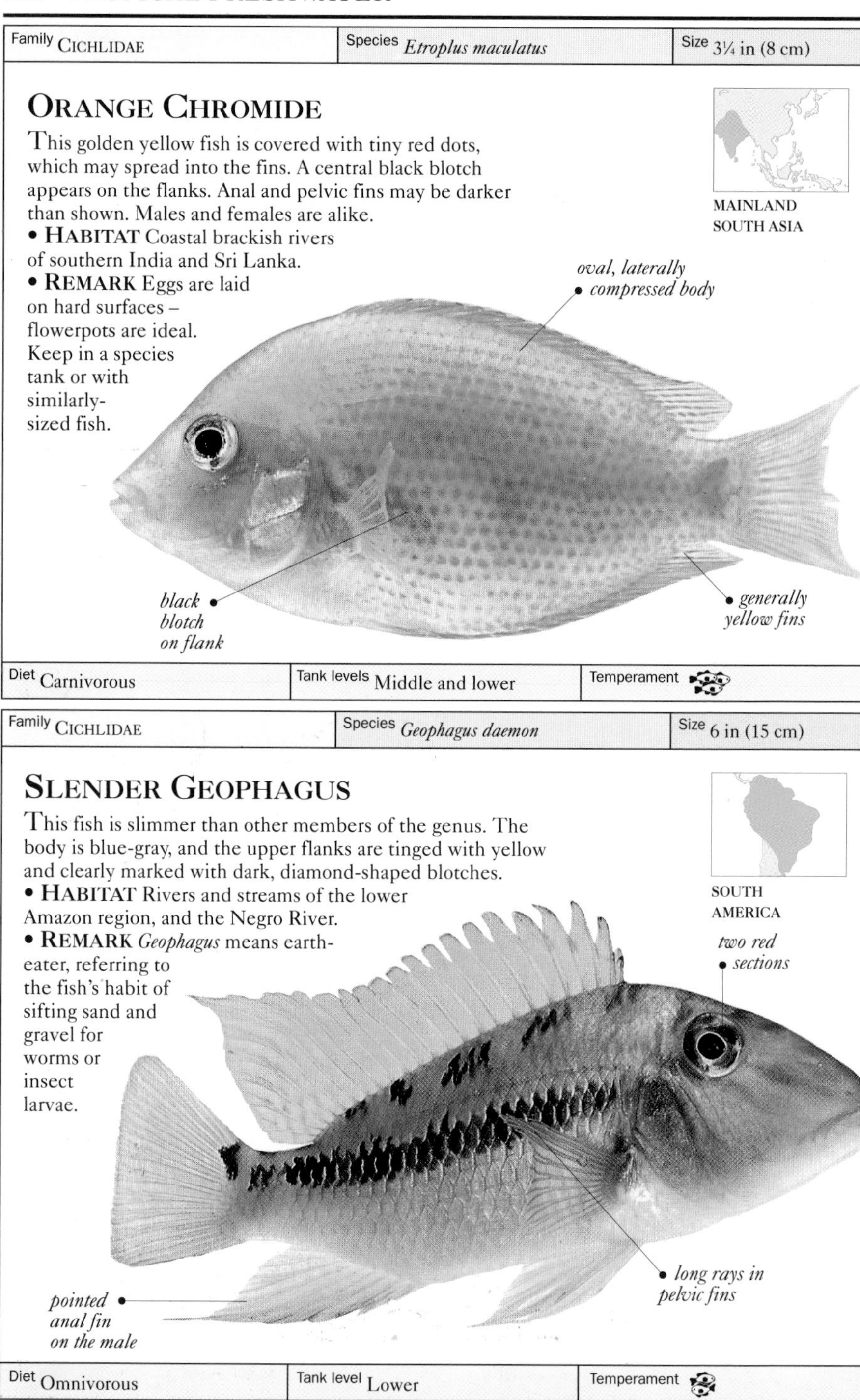

Diet Carnivorous	Tank levels Middle and lower	Temperament

Family CICHLIDAE	Species *Geophagus daemon*	Size 6 in (15 cm)

SLENDER GEOPHAGUS

This fish is slimmer than other members of the genus. The body is blue-gray, and the upper flanks are tinged with yellow and clearly marked with dark, diamond-shaped blotches.

- **HABITAT** Rivers and streams of the lower Amazon region, and the Negro River.
- **REMARK** *Geophagus* means earth-eater, referring to the fish's habit of sifting sand and gravel for worms or insect larvae.

Diet Omnivorous	Tank level Lower	Temperament

Family CICHLIDAE	Species *Hemichromis bimaculatus*	Size 4 in (10 cm)

JEWEL CICHLID

Metallic blue iridescent scales adorn the golden brown body of the Jewel Cichlid, and two dark spots occur on the flanks. These fish turn redder at spawning time. A strain that is permanently red is also available.

• **HABITAT** Forest streams from Ghana to Togoland.

• **OTHER NAME** *Hemichromis guttatus.*

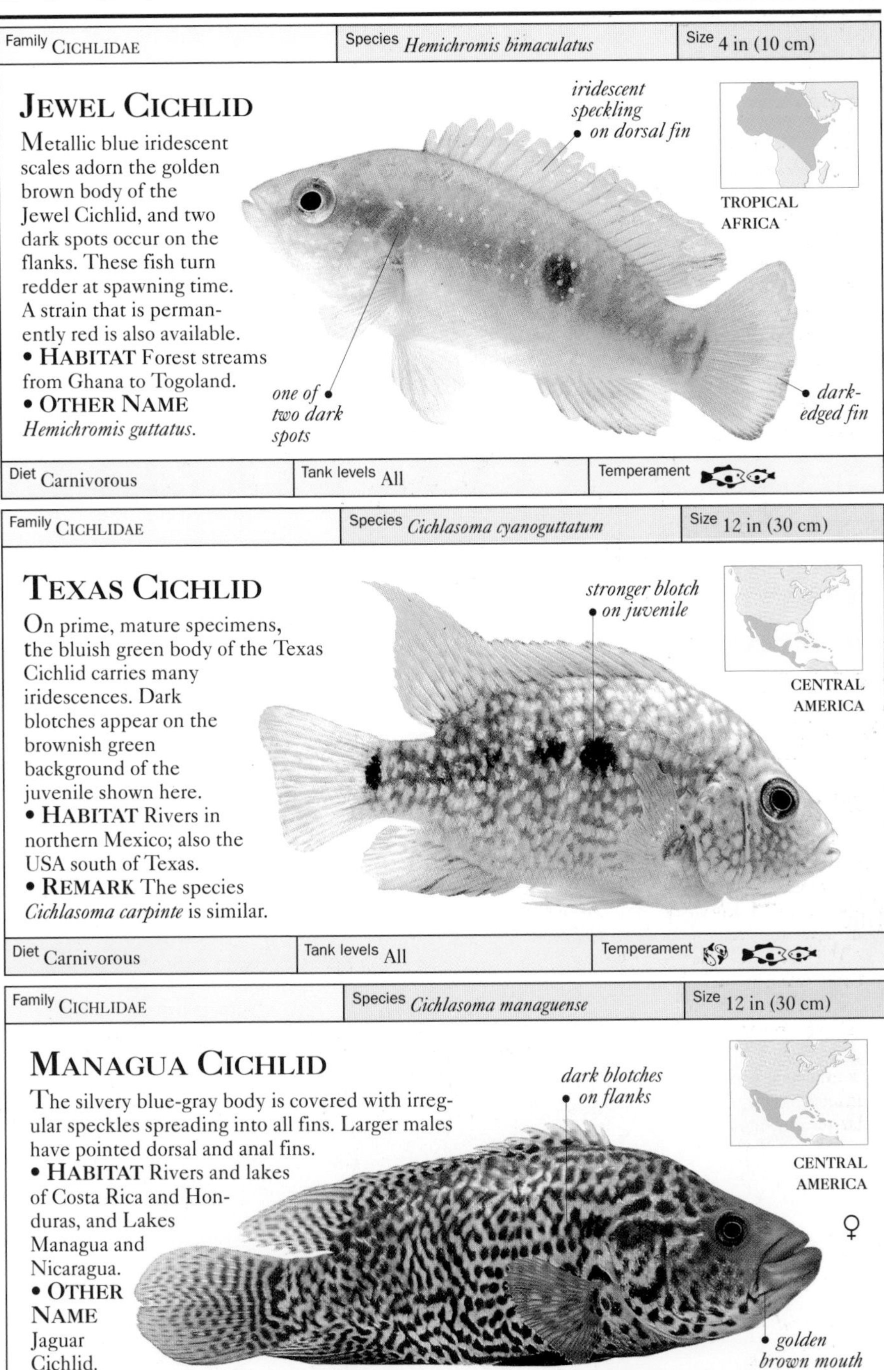

Diet Carnivorous	Tank levels All	Temperament

Family CICHLIDAE	Species *Cichlasoma cyanoguttatum*	Size 12 in (30 cm)

TEXAS CICHLID

On prime, mature specimens, the bluish green body of the Texas Cichlid carries many iridescences. Dark blotches appear on the brownish green background of the juvenile shown here.

• **HABITAT** Rivers in northern Mexico; also the USA south of Texas.

• **REMARK** The species *Cichlasoma carpinte* is similar.

Diet Carnivorous	Tank levels All	Temperament

Family CICHLIDAE	Species *Cichlasoma managuense*	Size 12 in (30 cm)

MANAGUA CICHLID

The silvery blue-gray body is covered with irregular speckles spreading into all fins. Larger males have pointed dorsal and anal fins.

• **HABITAT** Rivers and lakes of Costa Rica and Honduras, and Lakes Managua and Nicaragua.

• **OTHER NAME** Jaguar Cichlid.

Diet Carnivorous	Tank levels All	Temperament

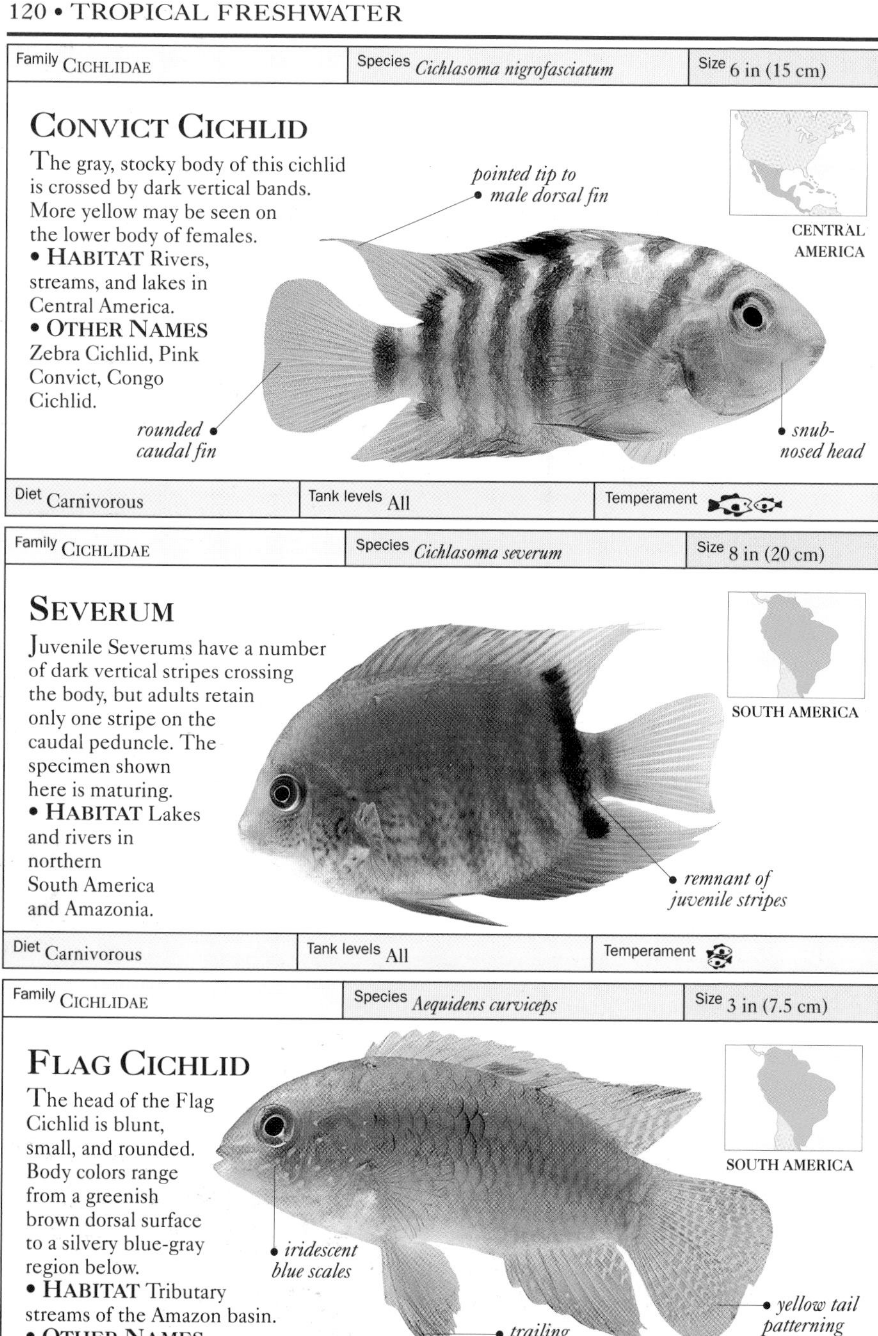

Family CICHLIDAE	Species *Cichlasoma nigrofasciatum*	Size 6 in (15 cm)

CONVICT CICHLID

The gray, stocky body of this cichlid is crossed by dark vertical bands. More yellow may be seen on the lower body of females.

• **HABITAT** Rivers, streams, and lakes in Central America.

• **OTHER NAMES** Zebra Cichlid, Pink Convict, Congo Cichlid.

Diet Carnivorous	Tank levels All	Temperament

Family CICHLIDAE	Species *Cichlasoma severum*	Size 8 in (20 cm)

SEVERUM

Juvenile Severums have a number of dark vertical stripes crossing the body, but adults retain only one stripe on the caudal peduncle. The specimen shown here is maturing.

• **HABITAT** Lakes and rivers in northern South America and Amazonia.

Diet Carnivorous	Tank levels All	Temperament

Family CICHLIDAE	Species *Aequidens curviceps*	Size 3 in (7.5 cm)

FLAG CICHLID

The head of the Flag Cichlid is blunt, small, and rounded. Body colors range from a greenish brown dorsal surface to a silvery blue-gray region below.

• **HABITAT** Tributary streams of the Amazon basin.

• **OTHER NAMES** Blunthead Cichlid, Sheepshead Acara.

Diet Carnivorous	Tank level Lower	Temperament

Family CICHLIDAE | Species *Cichlasoma festivum* | Size 6 in (15 cm)

FESTIVUM

A dark line runs from the snout of this fish, through the eye and on prime specimens to the rear of the dorsal fin. A greenish brown dorsal surface surmounts the silvery gray color below. The body is crossed with a number of indistinct dark bars, that may alter with the fish's mood. A dark blotch marks the caudal peduncle.

• **HABITAT** Densely vegetated areas of the Amazon basin to western Guyana.

Diet Carnivorous | Tank levels All | Temperament

Family CICHLIDAE | Species *Parapetenia festae* | Size 12 in (30 cm)

FESTAE CICHLID

Bluish green, iridescent vertical dark bands cross this fish's flanks between the gill covers and the caudal peduncle. The base color is golden green-yellow with red flushes that are more vivid in older fish. A bright-ringed dark spot appears at the base of the caudal fin. Male dorsal and anal fins are more pointed.

• **HABITAT** Rivers and streams in the Amazon basin.

Diet Carnivorous | Tank levels All | Temperament

FRESHWATER ANGELFISHES

THE BODY SHAPE of the freshwater angelfish is unlike that of other members of the cichlid family: it is disklike and laterally compressed, with long, trailing fins that add considerably to its height. There are two species of wild angelfishes: *Pterophyllum altum* (below), and *P. scalare* (opposite), from which color varieties have been developed (see pp.124–125). Angelfishes are popular because of their elegant outlines and graceful swimming action, and also for their intense parental care during breeding. Both parents guard and fan water over the eggs, which are laid on leaves and stems.

Family CICHLIDAE	Species *Pterophyllum altum*	Size 5 in (12.5 cm)

DEEP ANGELFISH

The natural coloration of this wild angelfish is brownish silver with several dark vertical bands that cross the body and enter the dorsal and anal fins. There may be some dark speckling between these bands. The distinguishing feature of this species is the distinct notch in the forehead outline above the snout. Dorsal and anal fins are long, and those of adults carry extended filaments. Pelvic fin rays extend well below the anal fin. Rays also extend from the top and bottom of the caudal fin.

• **HABITAT** Reed beds of the Orinoco River system, Venezuela.

• **REMARK** The shape of this species enables it to move deftly in and out of reed stems, while its coloration camouflages it perfectly when at rest among the plants. A deep tank is needed. It is rarely imported, and is not produced by commercial fish farms.

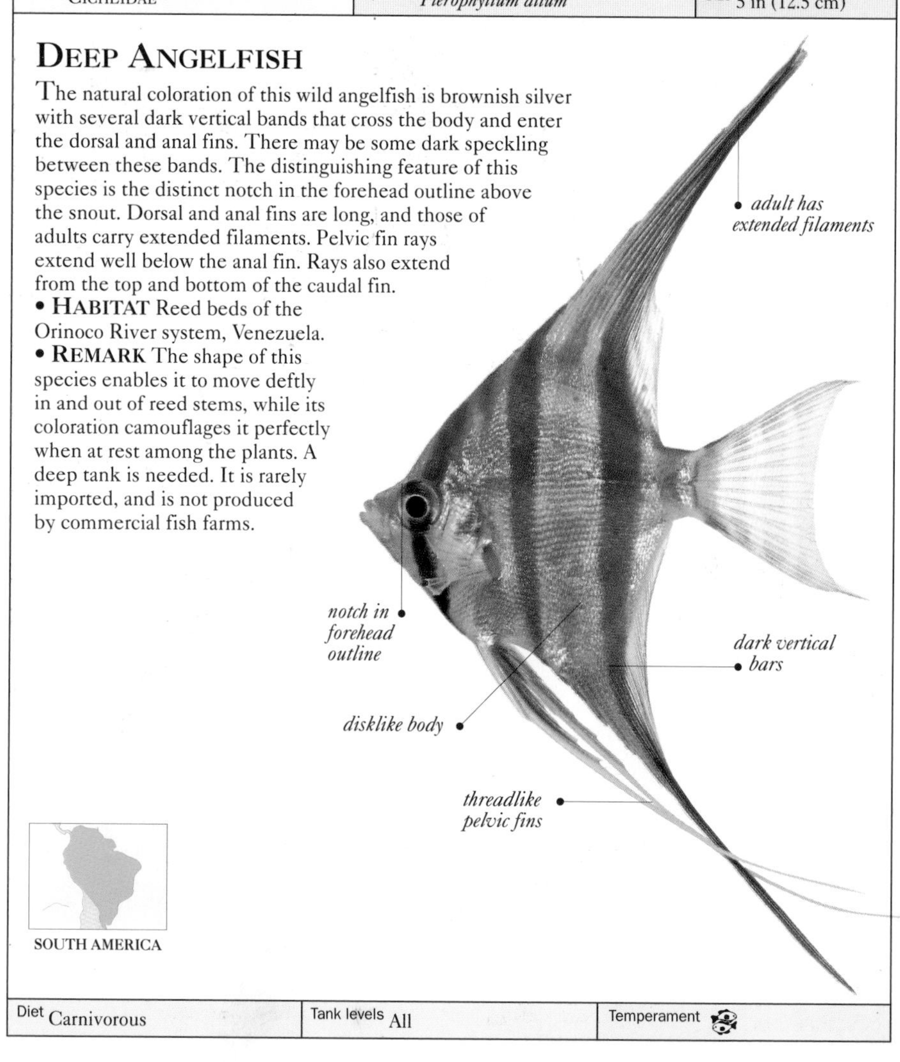

Diet Carnivorous	Tank levels All	Temperament

Family CICHLIDAE	Species *Pterophyllum scalare*	Size 5 in (12.5 cm)

ANGELFISH

The color of the wild form of this angelfish is silver with several dark vertical bands that enter the dorsal and anal fins. As with the Deep Angelfish (opposite), occasional dark speckling occurs between these bands. The fin structure is also similar: dorsal and anal fins are long, with filaments extending from the tips in mature adults. The juvenile wild fish is shown here. Selective breeding programs have resulted in many different color strains of this species, some of which are shown below and opposite. Sexual differences are not obvious.

• **HABITAT** Reed beds of the Amazon and Negro rivers.

• **REMARK** This species spawns readily and shows excellent parental care. A deep tank is required for these angelfish to develop fully.

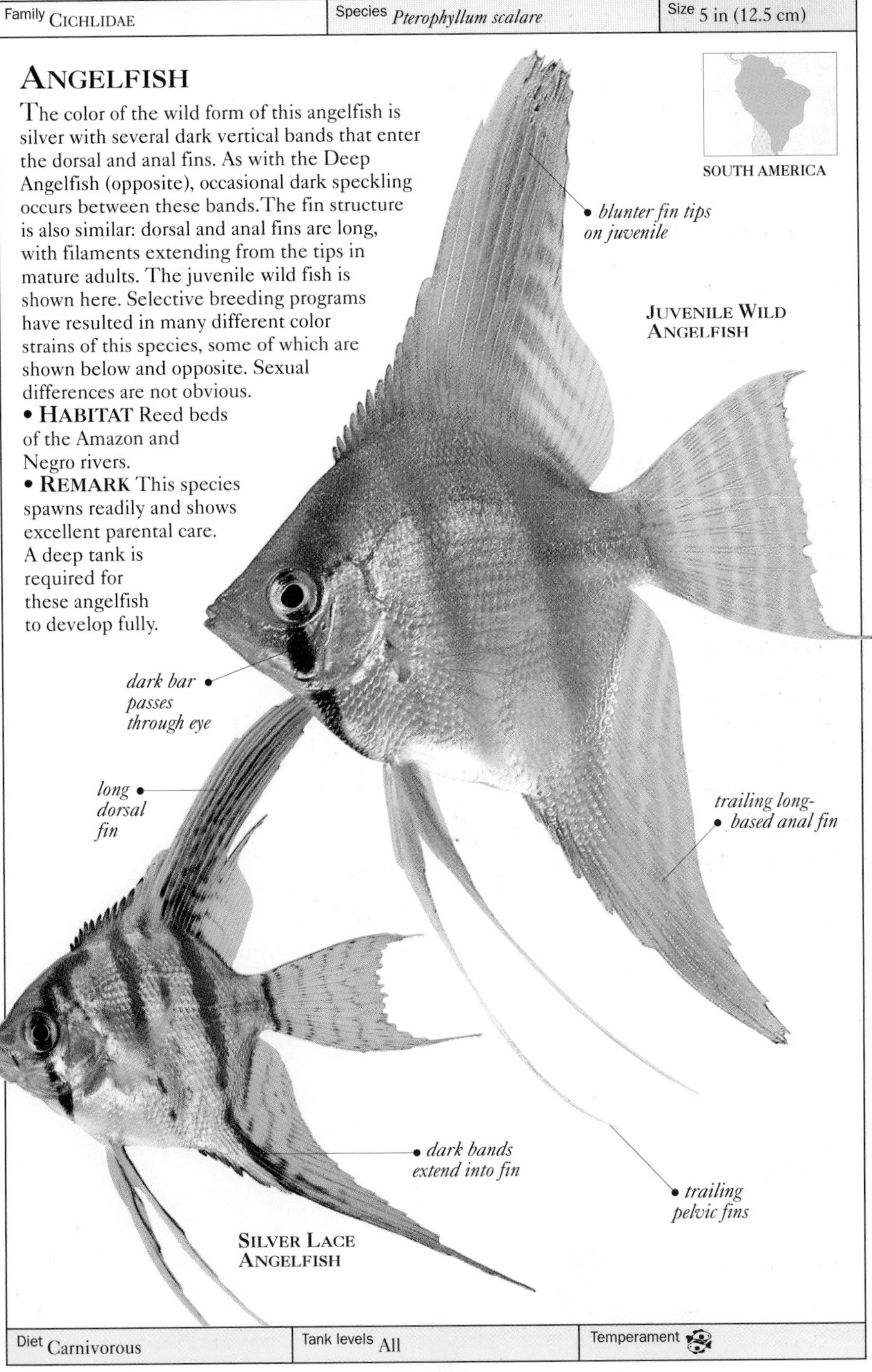

Diet Carnivorous	Tank levels All	Temperament

Family CICHLIDAE	Species *Pterophyllum scalare*	Size 4¼ in (11 cm)

ANGELFISH VARIETIES

These angelfishes are aquarium-bred strains of the wild angelfish species, *Pterophyllum scalare*. Various colorations and fin formations have been developed.

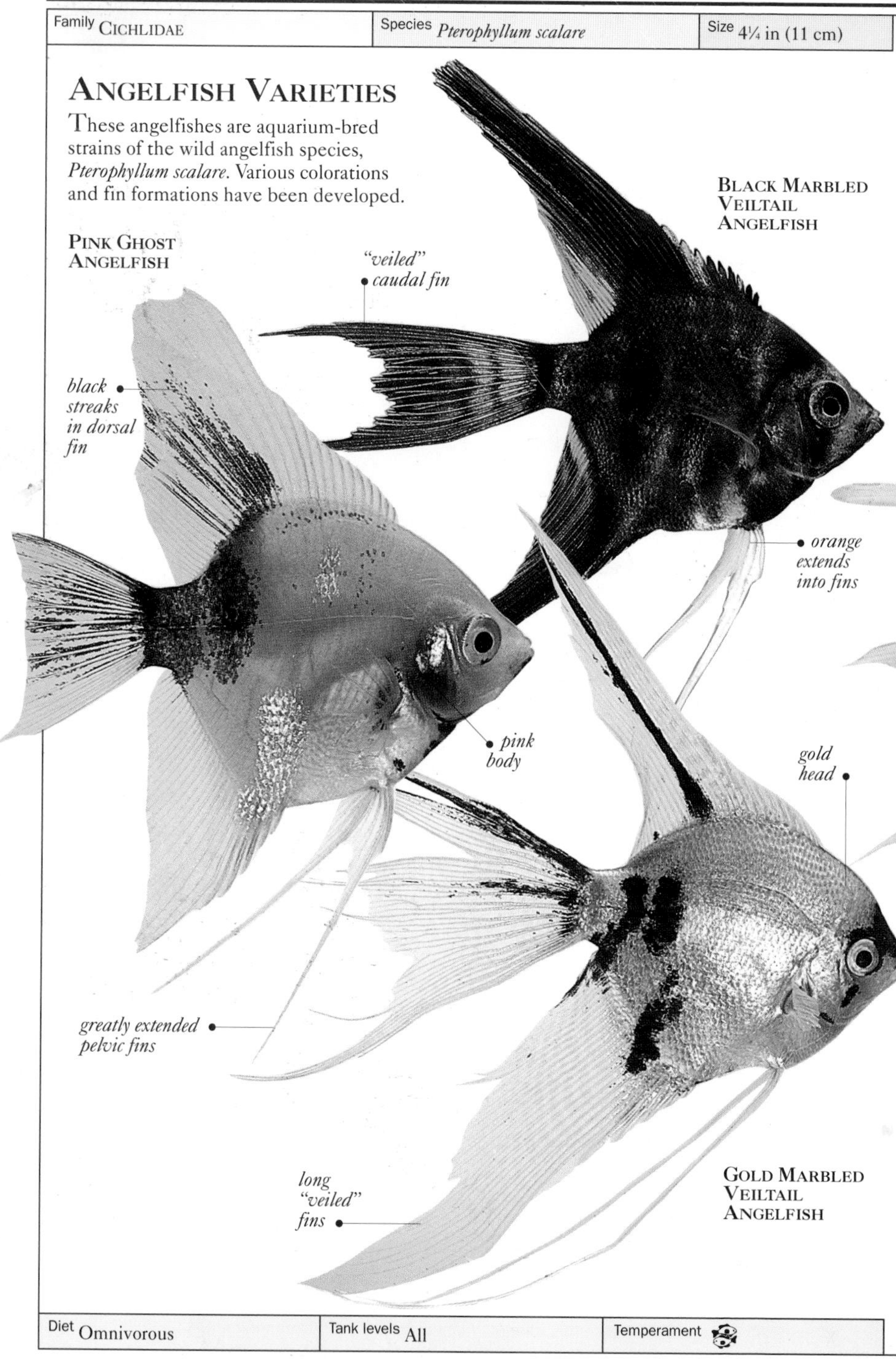

Diet Omnivorous	Tank levels All	Temperament

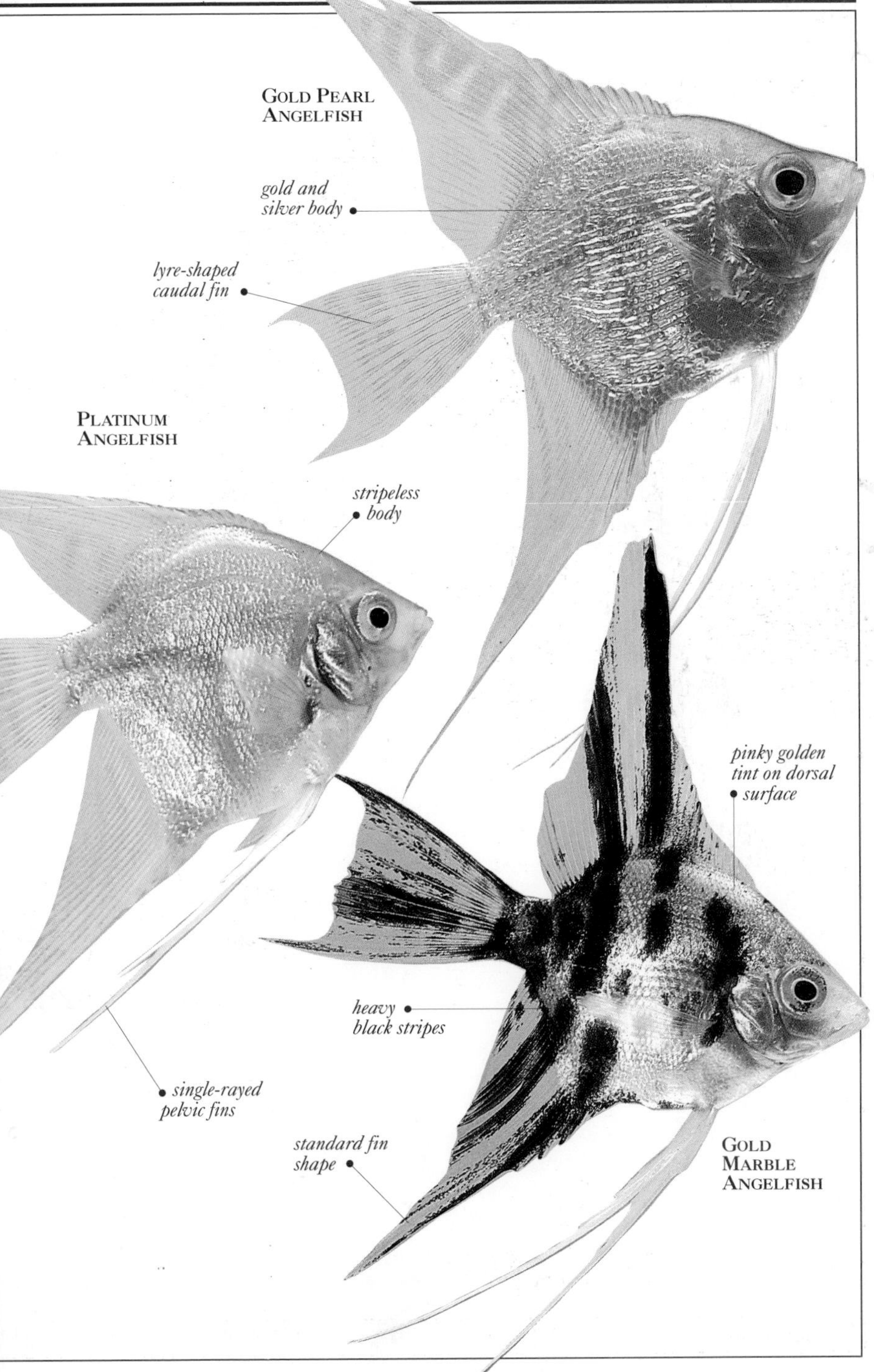
GOLD PEARL ANGELFISH
gold and silver body
lyre-shaped caudal fin
PLATINUM ANGELFISH
stripeless body
pinky golden tint on dorsal surface
heavy black stripes
single-rayed pelvic fins
standard fin shape
GOLD MARBLE ANGELFISH

DISCUS FISHES

LIKE THE FRESHWATER angelfishes (see p.122), the shape of discus fishes is uncharacteristic of the family Cichlidae, to which they belong. Discus fishes are for the specialist fishkeeper, as they require highly specific water conditions: water must be soft, slightly acidic, and filtered through peat. Several aquarium-bred subspecies of varying colors are available.

Family CICHLIDAE	Species *Symphysodon aequifasciata*	Size 8 in (20 cm)

BLUE DISCUS

The body of the discus fish is round, laterally compressed and, as the name suggests, disklike. Dorsal and anal fins are very long-based, almost reaching back to the caudal fin. The ovipositor of the female may be rounded. Many aquarium-developed strains have been bred from the wild *Symphysodon* genus, and their coloration varies, as can be seen here, opposite, and on p.128. On the Blue Discus, the variety shown here, dark vertical bars (seen more clearly on the adult) are overlaid with a pattern of blue wavy lines that extend into the dorsal and anal fins.

• **HABITAT** Rivers and lakes of Amazonia.

• **REMARK** This splendid fish requires high-quality water and a separate and secluded aquarium. Fry are best left with the parents for the first weeks, as they feed from the parents' skin secretions.

Discus fry feeding on skin secretions

wavy blue lines extend into dorsal fin

steeply rising forehead

dark inner margin in anal fin

SOUTH AMERICA

Diet Carnivorous	Tank levels Middle and lower	Temperament

Family CICHLIDAE	Species *Symphysodon* var.	Size 8 in (20 cm)

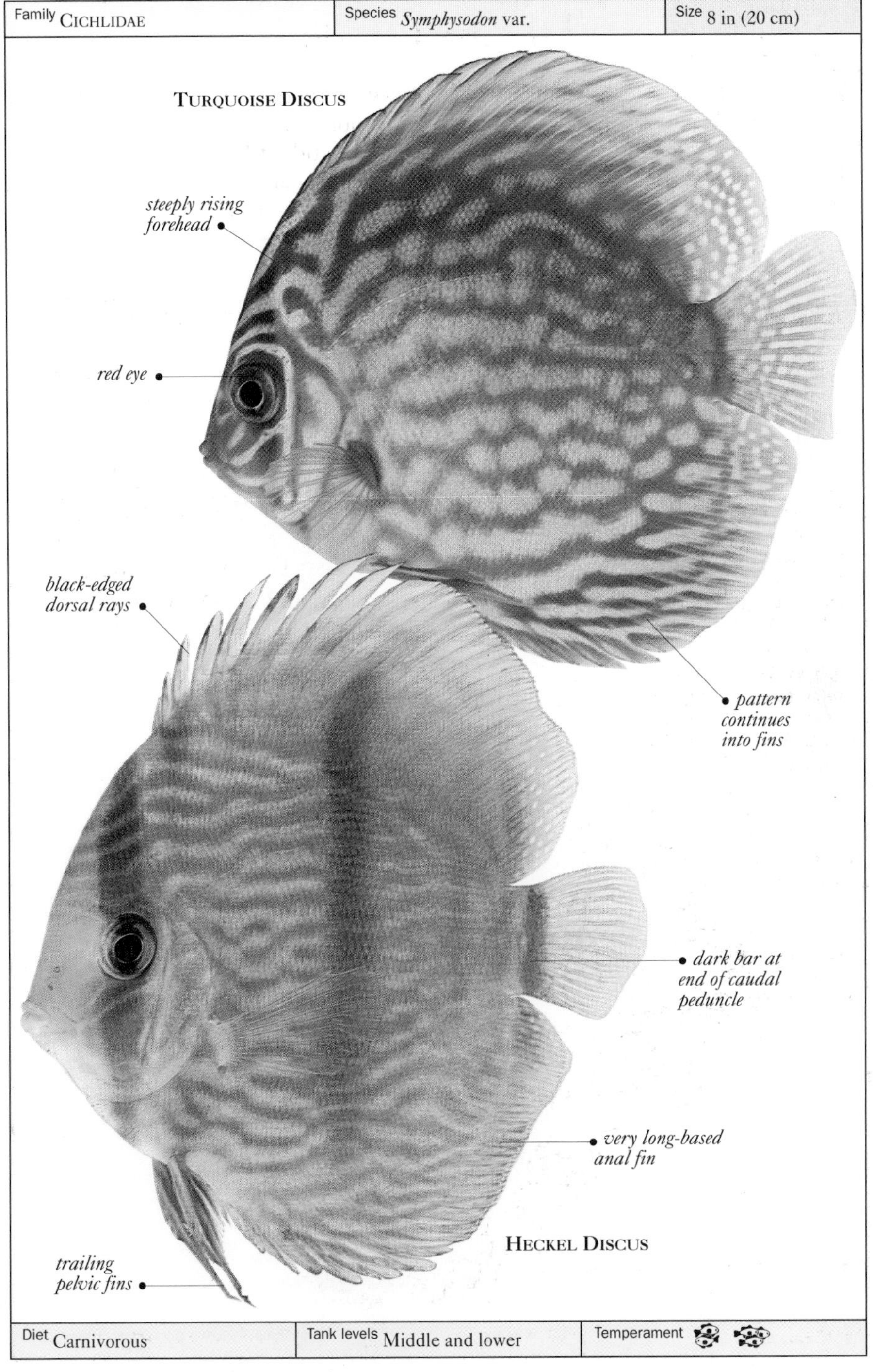

Diet Carnivorous	Tank levels Middle and lower	Temperament

Family CICHLIDAE	Species *Symphysodon aequifasciata*	Size 8 in (20 cm)

Vertical stripes match tall, reedy plants

Diet Carnivorous	Tank levels Middle and lower	Temperament

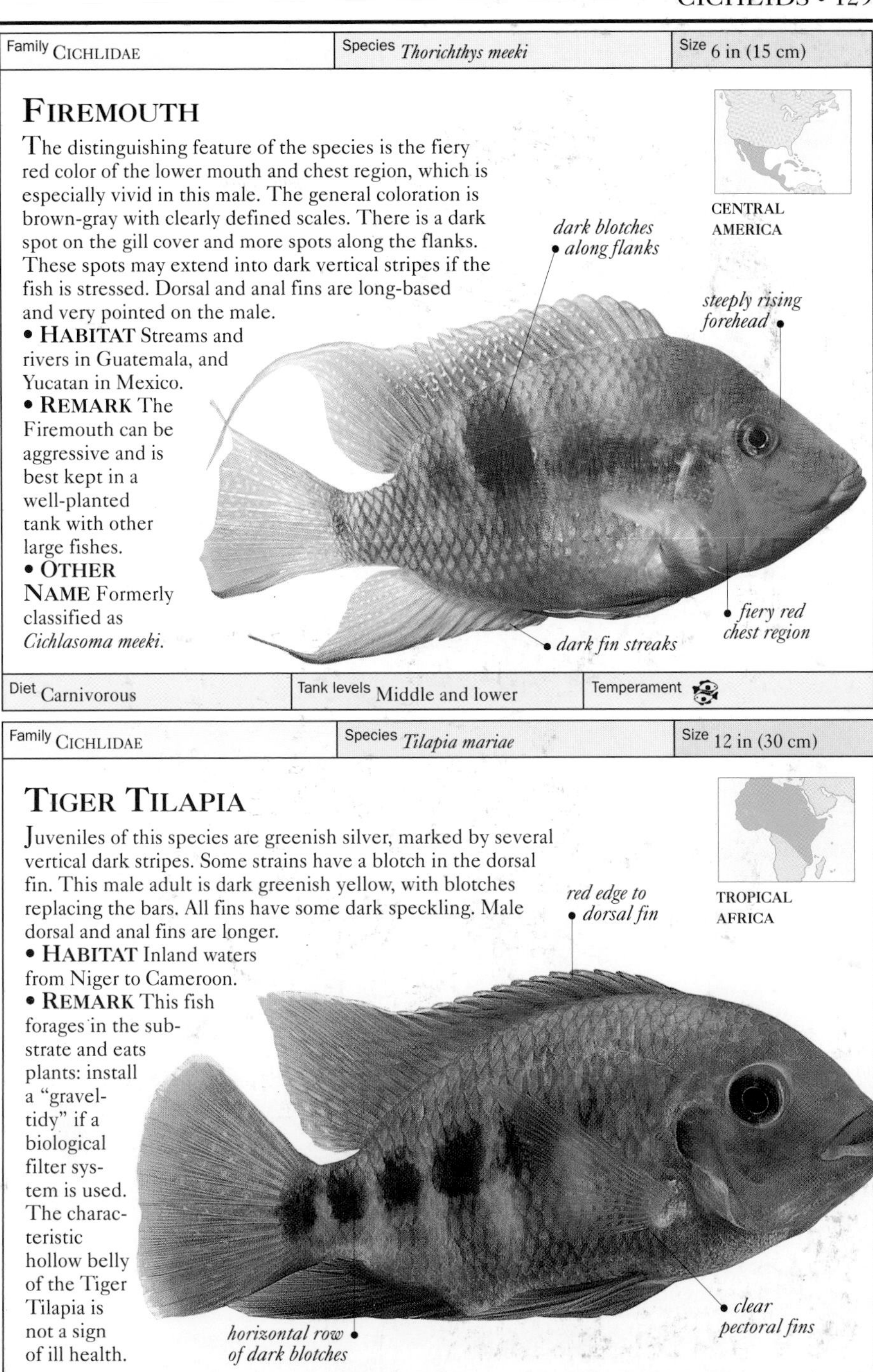

Family CICHLIDAE	Species *Thorichthys meeki*	Size 6 in (15 cm)

FIREMOUTH

The distinguishing feature of the species is the fiery red color of the lower mouth and chest region, which is especially vivid in this male. The general coloration is brown-gray with clearly defined scales. There is a dark spot on the gill cover and more spots along the flanks. These spots may extend into dark vertical stripes if the fish is stressed. Dorsal and anal fins are long-based and very pointed on the male.

• **HABITAT** Streams and rivers in Guatemala, and Yucatan in Mexico.

• **REMARK** The Firemouth can be aggressive and is best kept in a well-planted tank with other large fishes.

• **OTHER NAME** Formerly classified as *Cichlasoma meeki*.

Diet Carnivorous	Tank levels Middle and lower	Temperament

Family CICHLIDAE	Species *Tilapia mariae*	Size 12 in (30 cm)

TIGER TILAPIA

Juveniles of this species are greenish silver, marked by several vertical dark stripes. Some strains have a blotch in the dorsal fin. This male adult is dark greenish yellow, with blotches replacing the bars. All fins have some dark speckling. Male dorsal and anal fins are longer.

• **HABITAT** Inland waters from Niger to Cameroon.

• **REMARK** This fish forages in the substrate and eats plants: install a "gravel-tidy" if a biological filter system is used. The characteristic hollow belly of the Tiger Tilapia is not a sign of ill health.

Diet Omnivorous	Tank levels Middle and lower	Temperament

CICHLIDS
RIFT VALLEY CICHLIDS

FISHES FROM the Rift Valley lakes in Africa are popular for two reasons: they are brightly colored and, being members of the cichlid family, they show interesting breeding characteristics. While most are specific to their lake, different color specimens are found at different locations.

Family CICHLIDAE	Species *Aulonacara nyassae*	Size 6 in (15 cm)

PEACOCK CICHLID

This fish has many color variations, which are categorized by various, as yet unvalidated, scientific names. The basic color of *Aulonacara nyassae* is electric blue, covered with a pattern of dark vertical stripes. Females and young males are more subdued in color.

• **HABITAT** Endemic to rocky areas of Lake Malawi (formerly Lake Nyassa).

• **REMARK** These fish exist peacefully in a large aquarium. Their water should be alkaline; special "Malawi Salt Mixes" are commercially available.

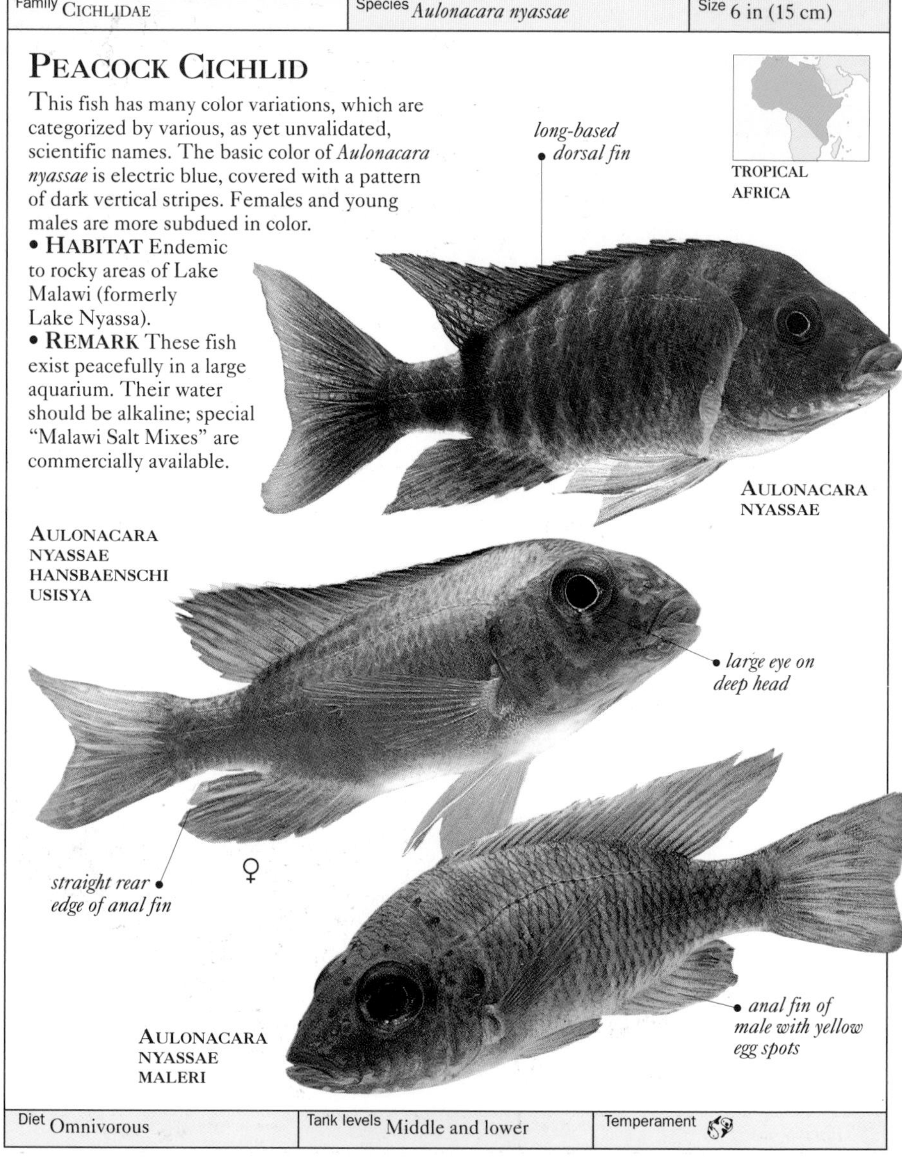

Diet Omnivorous	Tank levels Middle and lower	Temperament

Family CICHLIDAE	Species *Cyprichromis leptosoma*	Size 5 in (13 cm)

SLENDER CICHLID

The body is elongate, as the popular name suggests. The lower part of the head is pale yellow, and a small yellow saddle occurs on the upper part of the caudal peduncle. Dorsal and anal fins are blue-black with a pale inner edge.

• **HABITAT** Endemic to Lake Tanganyika, where it lives in schools high up in the water column.

• **REMARK** Males are intolerant of each other, but a large aquarium will support a number of specimens.

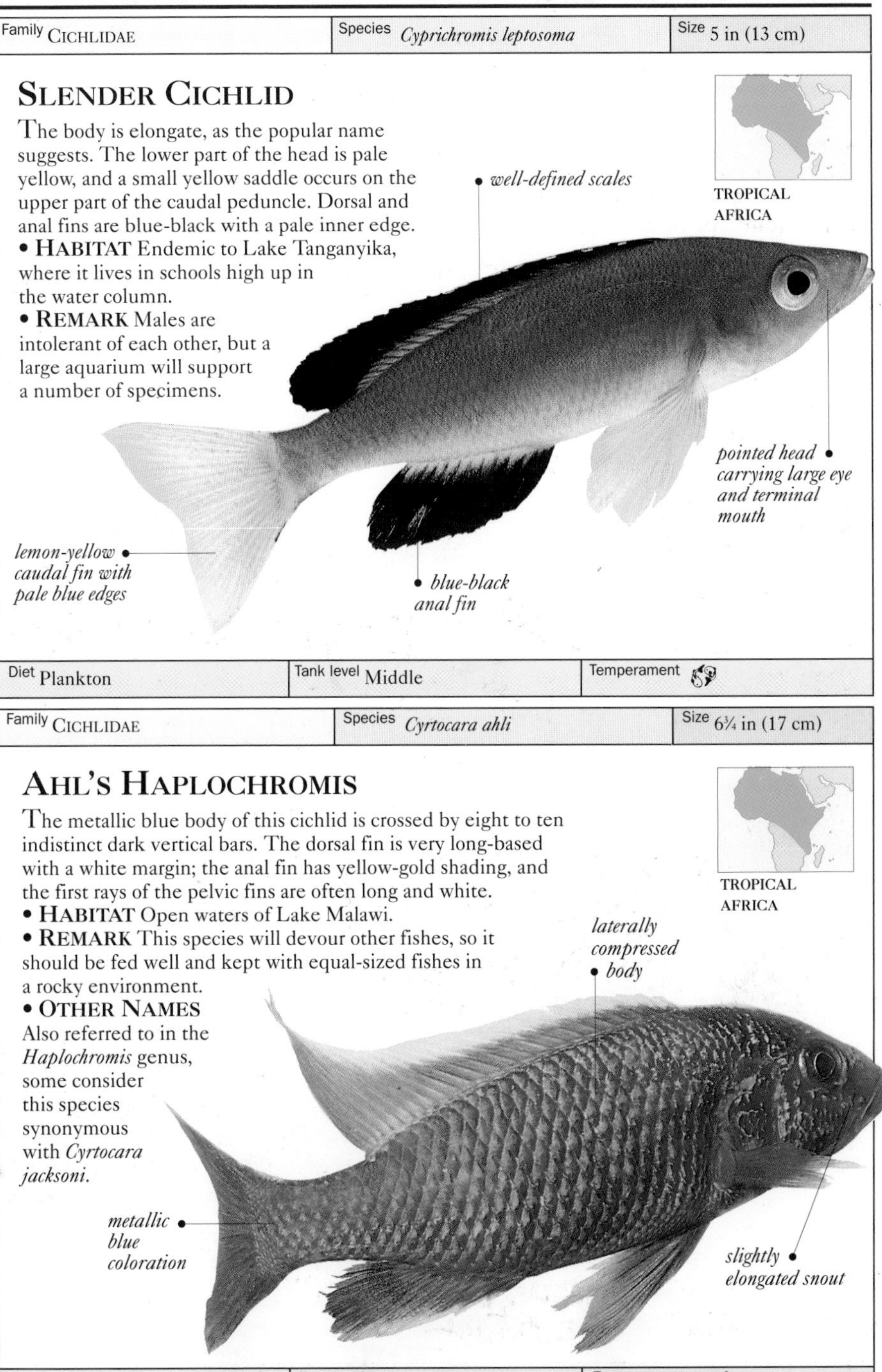

Diet Plankton	Tank level Middle	Temperament

Family CICHLIDAE	Species *Cyrtocara ahli*	Size 6¾ in (17 cm)

AHL'S HAPLOCHROMIS

The metallic blue body of this cichlid is crossed by eight to ten indistinct dark vertical bars. The dorsal fin is very long-based with a white margin; the anal fin has yellow-gold shading, and the first rays of the pelvic fins are often long and white.

• **HABITAT** Open waters of Lake Malawi.

• **REMARK** This species will devour other fishes, so it should be fed well and kept with equal-sized fishes in a rocky environment.

• **OTHER NAMES** Also referred to in the *Haplochromis* genus, some consider this species synonymous with *Cyrtocara jacksoni*.

Diet Piscivorous	Tank levels Middle and lower	Temperament

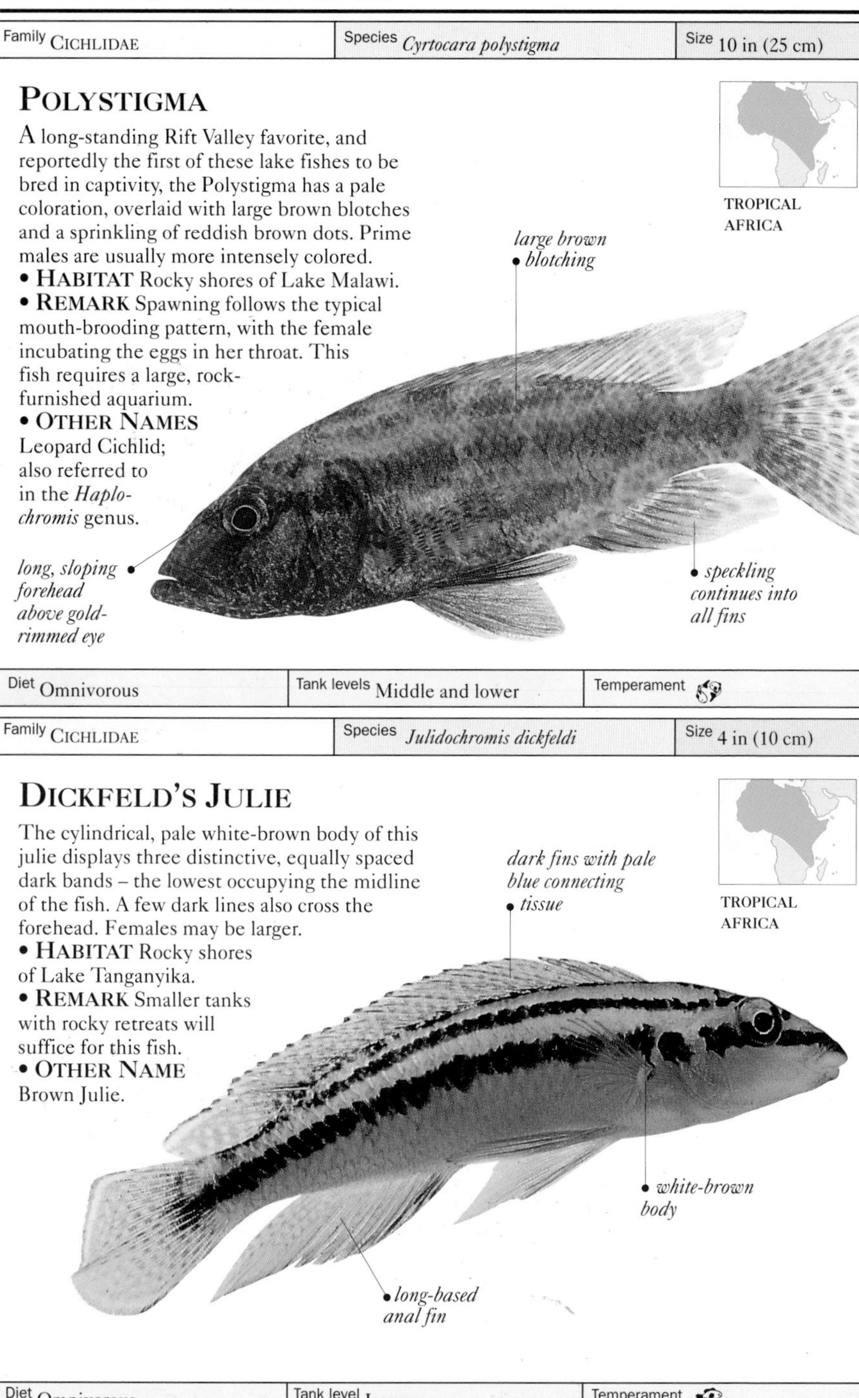

Family CICHLIDAE	Species *Cyrtocara polystigma*	Size 10 in (25 cm)

POLYSTIGMA

A long-standing Rift Valley favorite, and reportedly the first of these lake fishes to be bred in captivity, the Polystigma has a pale coloration, overlaid with large brown blotches and a sprinkling of reddish brown dots. Prime males are usually more intensely colored.

- **HABITAT** Rocky shores of Lake Malawi.
- **REMARK** Spawning follows the typical mouth-brooding pattern, with the female incubating the eggs in her throat. This fish requires a large, rock-furnished aquarium.
- **OTHER NAMES** Leopard Cichlid; also referred to in the *Haplochromis* genus.

Diet Omnivorous	Tank levels Middle and lower	Temperament

Family CICHLIDAE	Species *Julidochromis dickfeldi*	Size 4 in (10 cm)

DICKFELD'S JULIE

The cylindrical, pale white-brown body of this julie displays three distinctive, equally spaced dark bands – the lowest occupying the midline of the fish. A few dark lines also cross the forehead. Females may be larger.

- **HABITAT** Rocky shores of Lake Tanganyika.
- **REMARK** Smaller tanks with rocky retreats will suffice for this fish.
- **OTHER NAME** Brown Julie.

Diet Omnivorous	Tank level Lower	Temperament

Family CICHLIDAE	Species *Julidochromis marlieri*	Size 5 in (13 cm)

MARLIER'S JULIE

The cylindrical body of this fish is golden brown with three dark bands running along its length. The bands are crossed vertically at regular intervals by indistinct dark bars reaching almost to the ventral surface. Another dark bar runs from the corner of the mouth to the base of the pectoral fin.

- **HABITAT** Rocky shores of Lake Tanganyika.
- **REMARK** This species, together with *Julidochromis ornatus*, is the most colorful of the genus.

Diet Omnivorous	Tank level Lower	Temperament 

Family CICHLIDAE	Species *Julidochromis regani*	Size 5 in (13 cm)

REGAN'S JULIE

Four or five dark bands run the length of the body of this fish, covering the face and just falling short of the tail. The basic color is pale yellow-gold, although pale blue lines may appear around the mouth and lower head.

- **HABITAT** Rocky shores of Lake Tanganyika.
- **REMARK** A power filter and frequent partial water changes are beneficial.
- **OTHER NAME** Striped Julie.

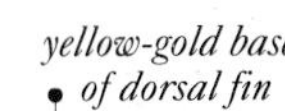

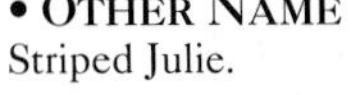

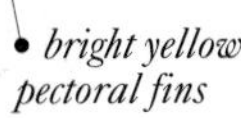

Diet Omnivorous	Tank level Lower	Temperament 

Family CICHLIDAE	Species *Labeotropheus fuelleborni*	Size 6¼ in (16 cm)

FUELLEBORN'S CICHLID

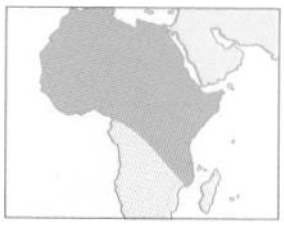

There are many color variations (or "morphs") of this species, particularly among females, which may show blotches of orange and black. The two morphs shown here share the same elongate and laterally compressed body shape, but the Red Top male is blue-gray with dark vertical bars. The Orange Blotch female, by contrast, is light gold-brown with small random speckles. Males also have egg spots on the anal fin. The distinguishing feature of the genus is the downturned upper lip, which has evolved to rasp algae from rocks.

- **HABITAT** Rocky shores of Lake Malawi.
- **REMARK** Fuelleborn's Cichlid is rather intolerant of its own kind and other similarly colored fishes.

long-based dorsal fin carries speckling

ORANGE BLOTCH MORPH

♀

down-turned top lip

RED TOP MORPH

TROPICAL AFRICA

Diet Herbivorous	Tank levels Middle and lower	Temperament

Family CICHLIDAE	Species *Lethrinops furcifer*	Size 7½ in (19 cm)

GREEN-FACED LETHRINOPS

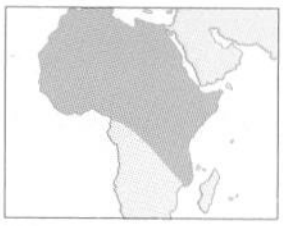

Indistinct dark blotches or poorly defined, dark vertical bars mark this silvery green fish. Pectoral, pelvic, and caudal fins may be tinted pink. The dorsal fin is pointed on the male, and the anal fin often reaches back to the caudal fin, carrying red or yellow egg spots. The triangular head is large, the mouth terminally situated, and the eyes are set very high.

- **HABITAT** Rocky shores of Lake Malawi.
- **REMARK** This fish is very similar in shape to the South American *Geophagus* genus and shares its characteristic of sifting mouthfuls of substratum for food.

high-set eyes with dark pupils

TROPICAL AFRICA

steep sloping snout carries terminal mouth

egg spots in male anal fin

faint red caudal coloring

Diet Omnivorous	Tank level Lower	Temperament 

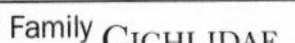

Family CICHLIDAE	Species *Melanochromis auratus*	Size 5 in (13 cm)

AURATUS

The basic coloration of male and female juveniles is bright yellow, with two white-edged black bars on the upper half of the body from the snout to the end of the caudal fin. A third, bordered dark line runs along the middle of the dorsal fin. Mature males have dark blue-black bodies marked by silvery blue horizontal lines. Females retain the yellow juvenile coloration.

• **HABITAT** Rocky shores of Lake Malawi.

• **REMARK** This mouth-brooder is typically intolerant of other fish. The male should be kept with a harem of females.

TROPICAL AFRICA

Diet Herbivorous	Tank levels Middle and lower	Temperament

Family CICHLIDAE	Species *Melanochromis chipokae*	Size 5 in (13 cm)

CHIPOKAE

The body of the Chipokae is laterally compressed and elongate. The mature male is dark blue-black with broad silvery blue lines along the center, ending at the base of the caudal fin. A second, fainter band runs beneath the dorsal fin. The female retains the bright yellow coloring and white-bordered black bands of the juvenile. Her pelvic and anal fins are yellow with dark front rays.

• **HABITAT** Rocky shores of Lake Malawi.

• **REMARK** This mouth-brooder is similar in appearance to the Auratus above, and the same remarks apply here.

TROPICAL AFRICA

female retains bright yellow juvenile color

♀

dark front pelvic fin rays

blue-black coloration of mature male

Diet Herbivorous	Tank levels Middle and lower	Temperament

Family CICHLIDAE	Species *Melanochromis johanni*	Size 5 in (13 cm)

JOHANNI

The coloration of mature males is a combination of blue, black, and brown, with one silvery, pale blue line running across the forehead, over the top of the eye, and along the body above the midline. A second line appears below the midline. The long-based dorsal fin is dark blue with a pale shade at the base. Females, like the specimen here, have a brownish yellow coloration and faint dark brown bands on the body.

• **HABITAT** Rocky shores of Lake Malawi.

• **REMARK** Colors of the genus vary from species to species, and from fish to fish within the species.

• **OTHER NAME** *Pseudotropheus daviesi.*

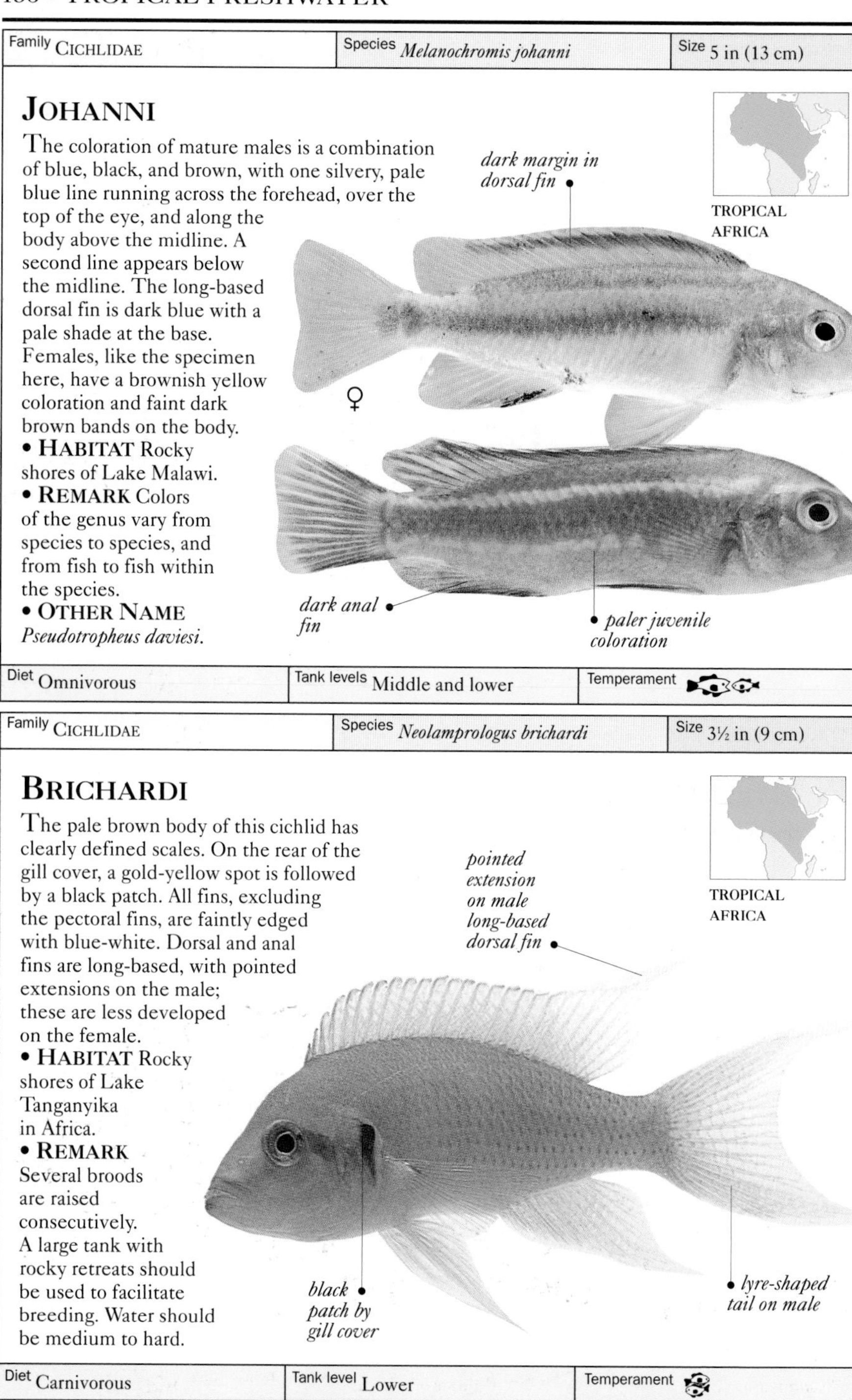

Diet Omnivorous	Tank levels Middle and lower	Temperament

Family CICHLIDAE	Species *Neolamprologus brichardi*	Size 3½ in (9 cm)

BRICHARDI

The pale brown body of this cichlid has clearly defined scales. On the rear of the gill cover, a gold-yellow spot is followed by a black patch. All fins, excluding the pectoral fins, are faintly edged with blue-white. Dorsal and anal fins are long-based, with pointed extensions on the male; these are less developed on the female.

• **HABITAT** Rocky shores of Lake Tanganyika in Africa.

• **REMARK** Several broods are raised consecutively. A large tank with rocky retreats should be used to facilitate breeding. Water should be medium to hard.

Diet Carnivorous	Tank level Lower	Temperament

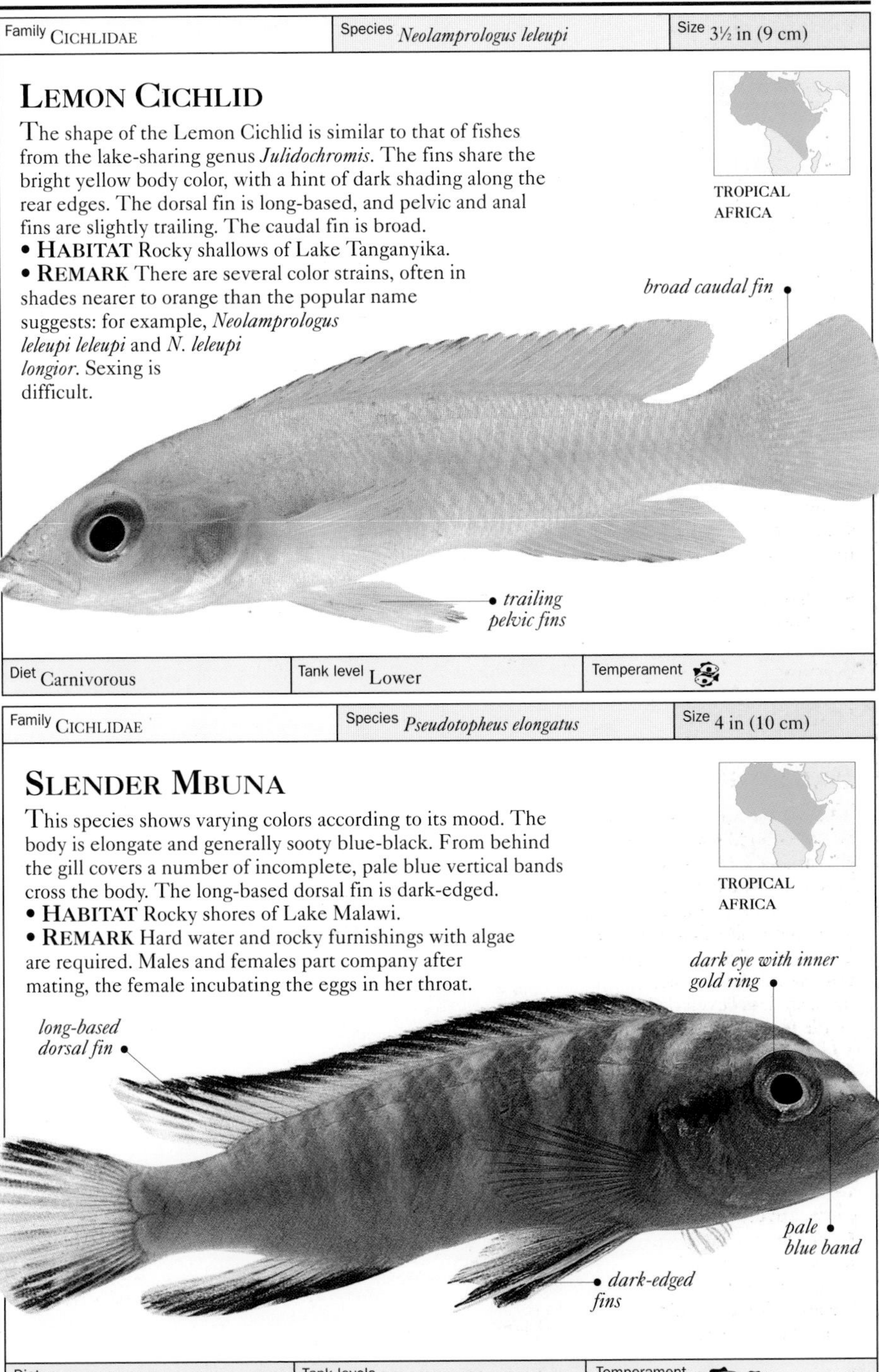

Family CICHLIDAE	Species *Neolamprologus leleupi*	Size 3½ in (9 cm)

LEMON CICHLID

The shape of the Lemon Cichlid is similar to that of fishes from the lake-sharing genus *Julidochromis*. The fins share the bright yellow body color, with a hint of dark shading along the rear edges. The dorsal fin is long-based, and pelvic and anal fins are slightly trailing. The caudal fin is broad.

- **HABITAT** Rocky shallows of Lake Tanganyika.
- **REMARK** There are several color strains, often in shades nearer to orange than the popular name suggests: for example, *Neolamprologus leleupi leleupi* and *N. leleupi longior*. Sexing is difficult.

Diet Carnivorous	Tank level Lower	Temperament

Family CICHLIDAE	Species *Pseudotopheus elongatus*	Size 4 in (10 cm)

SLENDER MBUNA

This species shows varying colors according to its mood. The body is elongate and generally sooty blue-black. From behind the gill covers a number of incomplete, pale blue vertical bands cross the body. The long-based dorsal fin is dark-edged.

- **HABITAT** Rocky shores of Lake Malawi.
- **REMARK** Hard water and rocky furnishings with algae are required. Males and females part company after mating, the female incubating the eggs in her throat.

Diet Omnivorous	Tank levels Middle and lower	Temperament

Family CICHLIDAE	Species *Pseudotropheus lombardoi*	Size 5 in (13 cm)

LOMBARDOI

The body shape of this species is deeper than other members of the genus, the dorsal contour being highly arched and the ventral surface flat in comparison. Males are bright yellow with faint brown bars crossing the body; fins are plain yellow with egg-spots on the anal fin. The female body is pale white-blue with several blue-black vertical bands extending into the dorsal fin.

• **HABITAT** Rocky shores of Lake Malawi.

• **REMARK** The Lombardoi requires a spacious, rocky aquarium. Free-swimming fry regain entry to the female's mouth by direct contact.

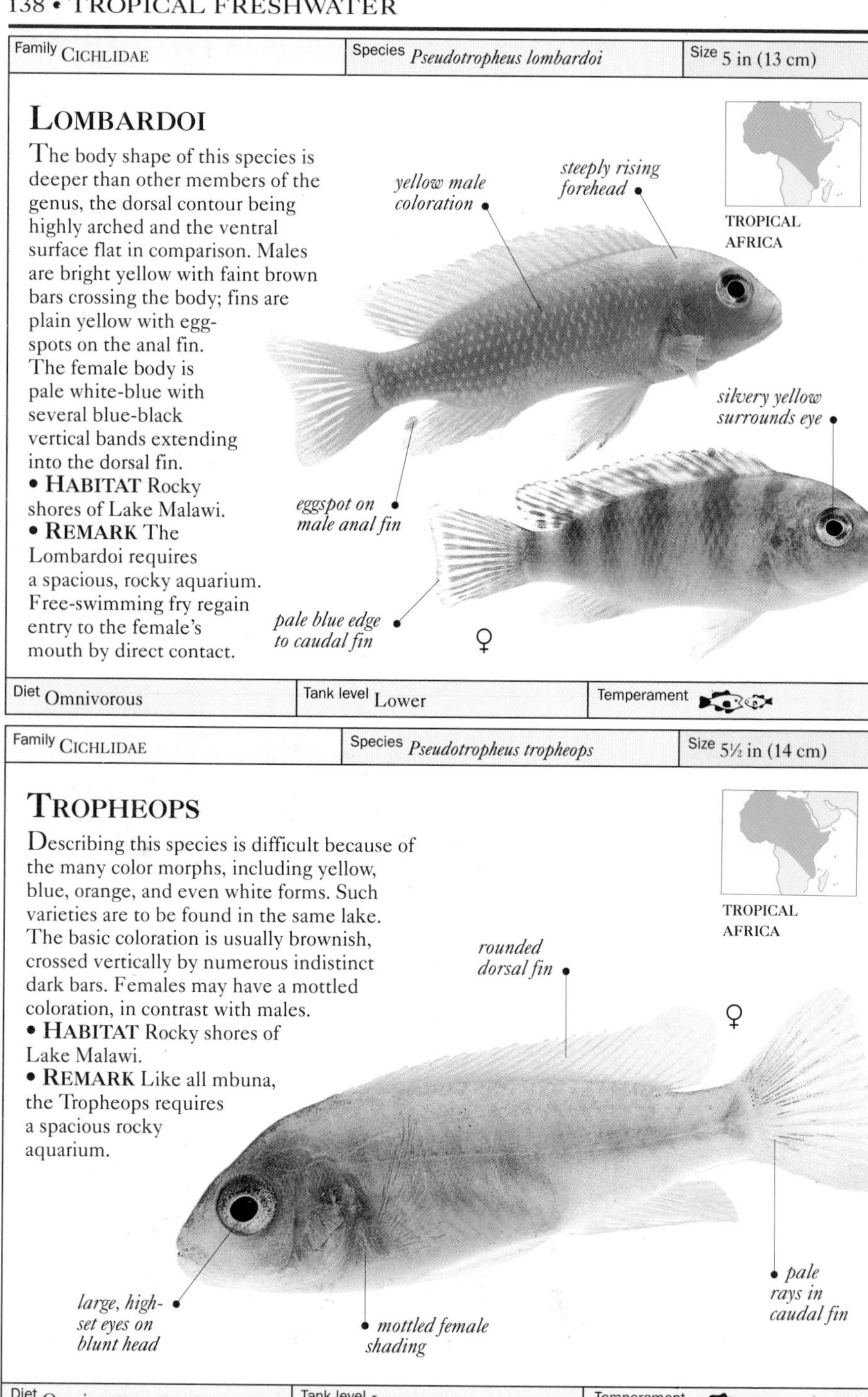

Diet Omnivorous	Tank level Lower	Temperament

Family CICHLIDAE	Species *Pseudotropheus tropheops*	Size 5½ in (14 cm)

TROPHEOPS

Describing this species is difficult because of the many color morphs, including yellow, blue, orange, and even white forms. Such varieties are to be found in the same lake. The basic coloration is usually brownish, crossed vertically by numerous indistinct dark bars. Females may have a mottled coloration, in contrast with males.

• **HABITAT** Rocky shores of Lake Malawi.

• **REMARK** Like all mbuna, the Tropheops requires a spacious rocky aquarium.

Diet Omnivorous	Tank level Lower	Temperament

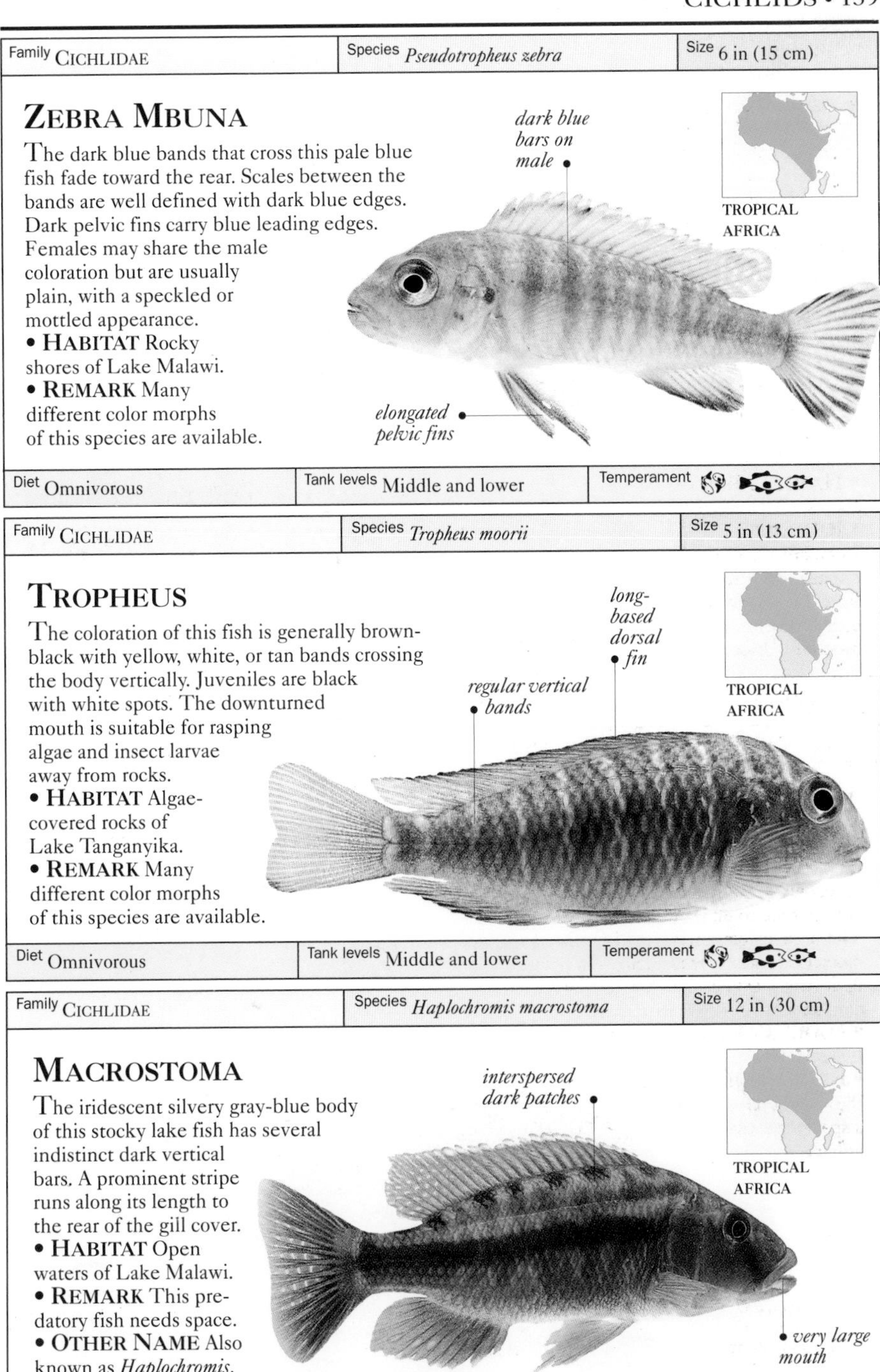

Family CICHLIDAE	Species *Pseudotropheus zebra*	Size 6 in (15 cm)

ZEBRA MBUNA

The dark blue bands that cross this pale blue fish fade toward the rear. Scales between the bands are well defined with dark blue edges. Dark pelvic fins carry blue leading edges. Females may share the male coloration but are usually plain, with a speckled or mottled appearance.

• **HABITAT** Rocky shores of Lake Malawi.

• **REMARK** Many different color morphs of this species are available.

Diet Omnivorous	Tank levels Middle and lower	Temperament

Family CICHLIDAE	Species *Tropheus moorii*	Size 5 in (13 cm)

TROPHEUS

The coloration of this fish is generally brown-black with yellow, white, or tan bands crossing the body vertically. Juveniles are black with white spots. The downturned mouth is suitable for rasping algae and insect larvae away from rocks.

• **HABITAT** Algae-covered rocks of Lake Tanganyika.

• **REMARK** Many different color morphs of this species are available.

Diet Omnivorous	Tank levels Middle and lower	Temperament

Family CICHLIDAE	Species *Haplochromis macrostoma*	Size 12 in (30 cm)

MACROSTOMA

The iridescent silvery gray-blue body of this stocky lake fish has several indistinct dark vertical bars. A prominent stripe runs along its length to the rear of the gill cover.

• **HABITAT** Open waters of Lake Malawi.

• **REMARK** This predatory fish needs space.

• **OTHER NAME** Also known as *Haplochromis*.

Diet Piscivorous	Tank level Middle	Temperament

ANABANTIDS

ANABANTIDS often inhabit oxygen-depleted waters of Africa and southeast Asia. To survive, they have developed an auxiliary breathing organ (the labyrinth organ), which is a folded mass of respiratory tissue situated near the gills. Air is gulped at the surface and stored in this organ, which then extracts the oxygen. This enables certain anabantids to travel overland to nearby waters. A well-known anabantid is the Siamese Fighting Fish, native to Thailand, the males of which will fight if put together.

Family ANABANTIDAE	Species *Anabas testudineus*	Size 10 in (25 cm)

CLIMBING PERCH

This fish is grayish silver with slightly paler flanks and a white belly. Random dark speckling occurs on the flanks, especially near the rear. There is a dark spot behind the gill cover, and a blotch on the caudal peduncle. The broad, flattened head has a wide, gaping mouth.

- **HABITAT** Widespread in fresh and brackish waters from southeast Asia to the Philippines; also southern China, India, and Sri Lanka.
- **REMARK** Keep this jumping fish in a species tank with a tight-fitting hood.

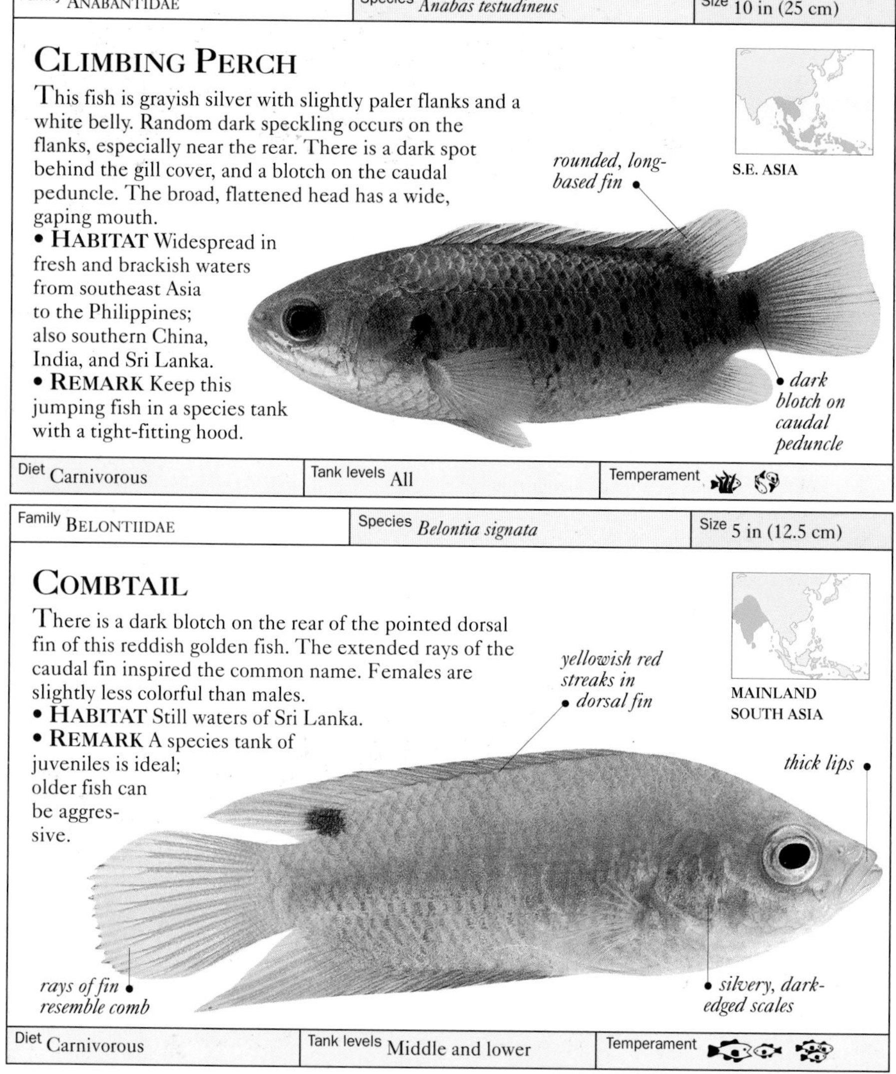

Diet Carnivorous	Tank levels All	Temperament

Family BELONTIIDAE	Species *Belontia signata*	Size 5 in (12.5 cm)

COMBTAIL

There is a dark blotch on the rear of the pointed dorsal fin of this reddish golden fish. The extended rays of the caudal fin inspired the common name. Females are slightly less colorful than males.

- **HABITAT** Still waters of Sri Lanka.
- **REMARK** A species tank of juveniles is ideal; older fish can be aggressive.

Diet Carnivorous	Tank levels Middle and lower	Temperament

Family BELONTIIDAE	Species *Betta bellica*	Size 4½ in (11 cm)

SLENDER BETTA

The Slender Betta is reddish brown with green or purple iridescent scales. The scales create a metallic sheen, especially under side-lighting. The head is pale with a marbled pattern and the eye is set forward.

- **HABITAT** Streams and still waters in southeast Asia.
- **REMARK** Males are likely to quarrel with each other.
- **OTHER NAME** Slim Fighting Fish.

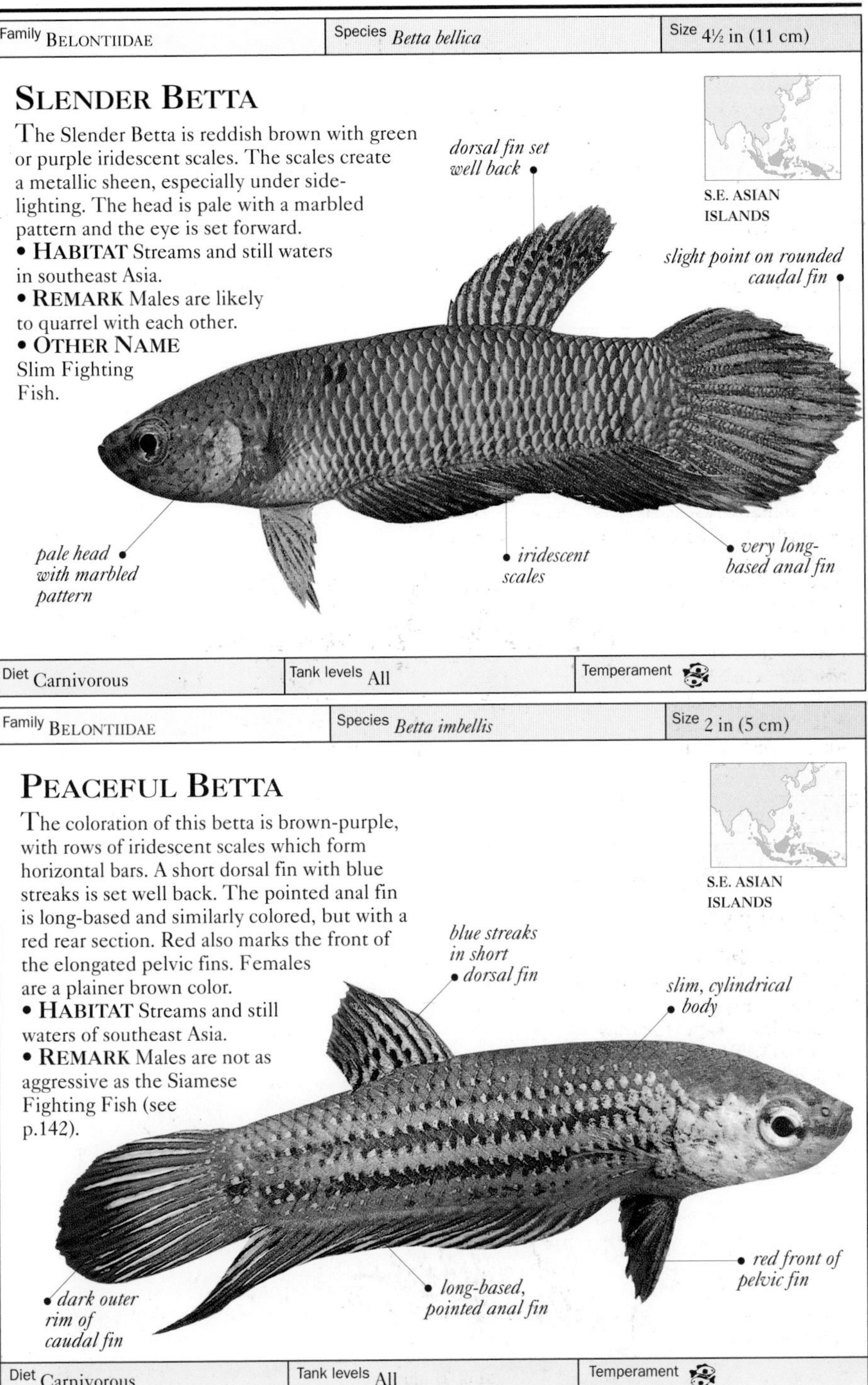

Diet Carnivorous	Tank levels All	Temperament

Family BELONTIIDAE	Species *Betta imbellis*	Size 2 in (5 cm)

PEACEFUL BETTA

The coloration of this betta is brown-purple, with rows of iridescent scales which form horizontal bars. A short dorsal fin with blue streaks is set well back. The pointed anal fin is long-based and similarly colored, but with a red rear section. Red also marks the front of the elongated pelvic fins. Females are a plainer brown color.

- **HABITAT** Streams and still waters of southeast Asia.
- **REMARK** Males are not as aggressive as the Siamese Fighting Fish (see p.142).

Diet Carnivorous	Tank levels All	Temperament

Family BELONTIIDAE	Species *Betta splendens*	Size 2½ in (6 cm)

SIAMESE FIGHTING FISH

When held erect in a show of aggression, the long flowing fins of the male would make a complete circle on a perfect specimen. The female has much shorter fins at all times. Colors and fin development differ greatly as most aquarium specimens have been selectively bred in captivity for years. Wild males and females are brown with red and green highlights and shorter fins.

- **HABITAT** Sluggish waters in Thailand.
- **REMARK** Males are aggressive, so keep only one per tank.

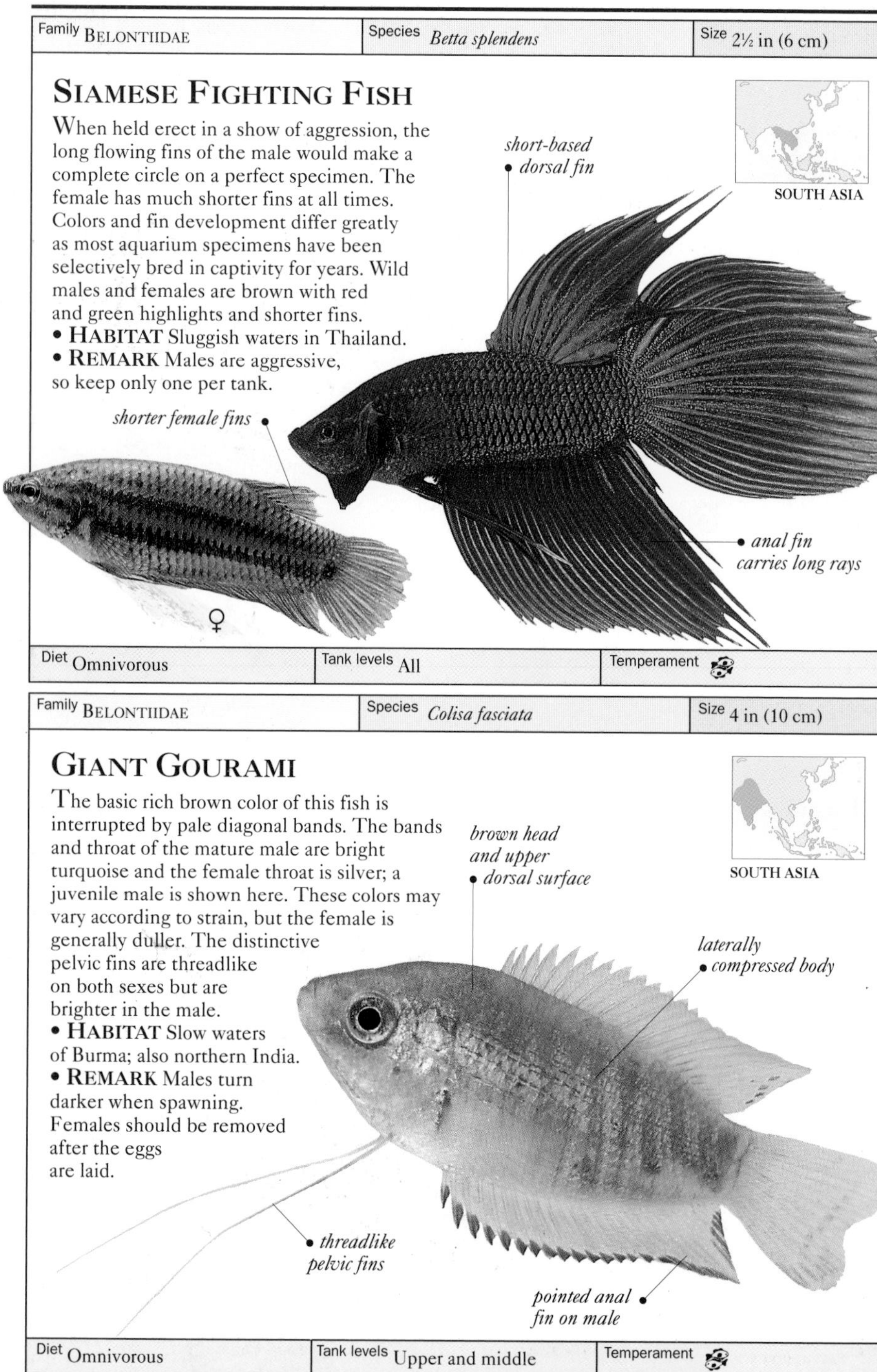

Diet Omnivorous	Tank levels All	Temperament

Family BELONTIIDAE	Species *Colisa fasciata*	Size 4 in (10 cm)

GIANT GOURAMI

The basic rich brown color of this fish is interrupted by pale diagonal bands. The bands and throat of the mature male are bright turquoise and the female throat is silver; a juvenile male is shown here. These colors may vary according to strain, but the female is generally duller. The distinctive pelvic fins are threadlike on both sexes but are brighter in the male.

- **HABITAT** Slow waters of Burma; also northern India.
- **REMARK** Males turn darker when spawning. Females should be removed after the eggs are laid.

Diet Omnivorous	Tank levels Upper and middle	Temperament

Family BELONTIIDAE	Species *Colisa labiosa*	Size 3¼ in (8 cm)

THICKLIPPED GOURAMI

Although similar to the Giant Gourami (see p.142), the bands on the body of this species are narrower and more numerous. There is a dark mark at the center of each band on adult specimens, creating the impression of a dark line along the flanks. The upturned mouth has well-formed lips, as the popular name suggests.

• **HABITAT** Sluggish backwaters of Burma; also found in northern India.

• **REMARK** During spawning, the male turns dark chocolate-brown. This fish is good for the community aquarium and a very prolific breeder; around 600 eggs are laid in a floating bubble nest.

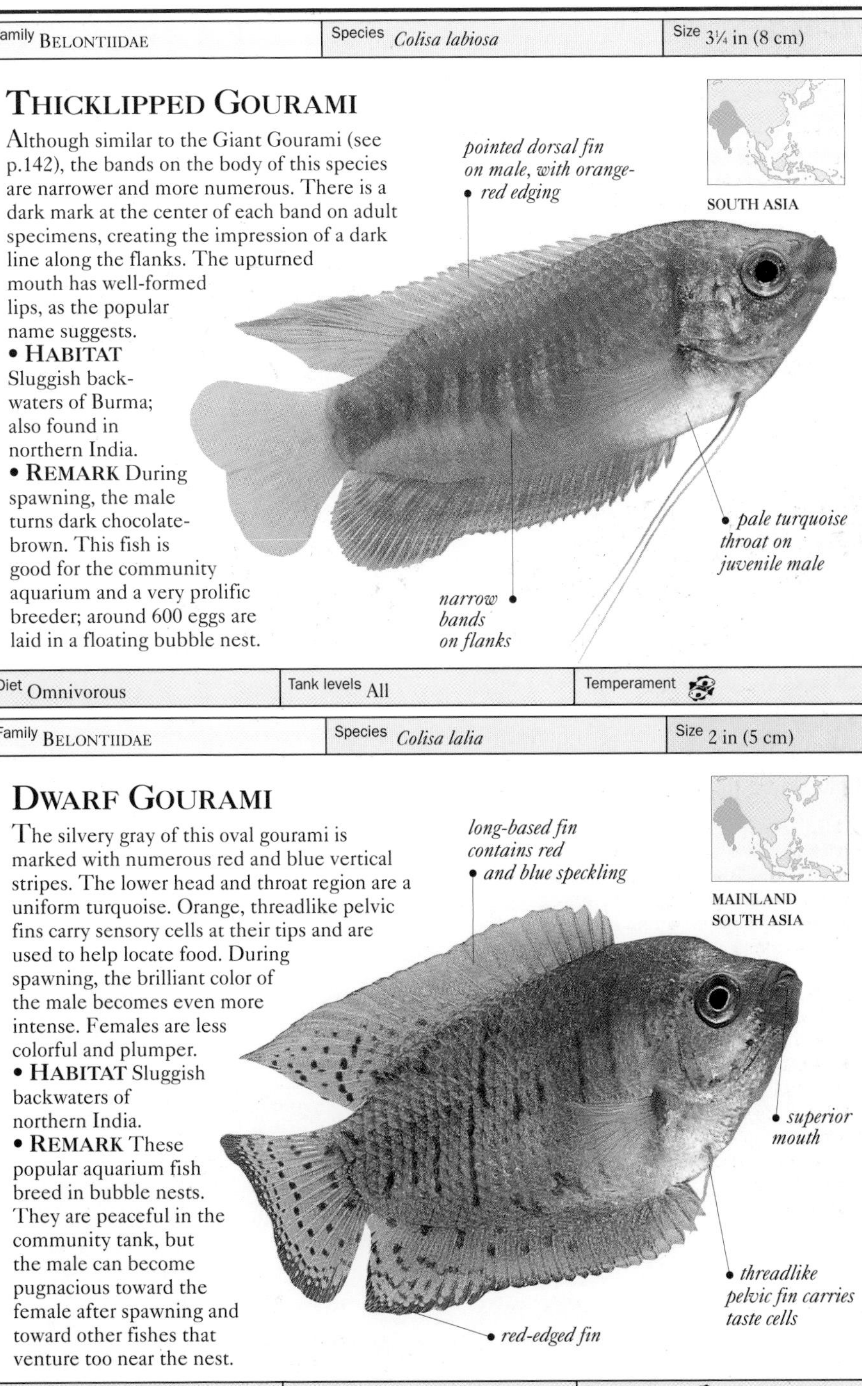

Diet Omnivorous	Tank levels All	Temperament

Family BELONTIIDAE	Species *Colisa lalia*	Size 2 in (5 cm)

DWARF GOURAMI

The silvery gray of this oval gourami is marked with numerous red and blue vertical stripes. The lower head and throat region are a uniform turquoise. Orange, threadlike pelvic fins carry sensory cells at their tips and are used to help locate food. During spawning, the brilliant color of the male becomes even more intense. Females are less colorful and plumper.

• **HABITAT** Sluggish backwaters of northern India.

• **REMARK** These popular aquarium fish breed in bubble nests. They are peaceful in the community tank, but the male can become pugnacious toward the female after spawning and toward other fishes that venture too near the nest.

Diet Omnivorous	Tank levels All	Temperament

Family ANABANTIDAE	Species *Ctenopoma acutirostre*	Size 6 in (15 cm)

SPOTTED CLIMBING PERCH

The greenish brown oval body of the Spotted Climbing Perch is covered with leopardlike spots, and a single dark spot marks the base of the caudal fin. The mouth can be exended to form a tube with which the fish engulfs prey. The head is sharply pointed, with a concave upper surface and a convex lower surface. Dorsal and anal fins are spiny and reach back almost to the caudal fin. The caudal peduncle is virtually absent.

• **HABITAT** Sluggish streams in Zaire, Central Africa.

• **REMARK** The Spotted Climbing Perch should not be kept with smaller species. It requires a large well-planted tank and should be fed live foods.

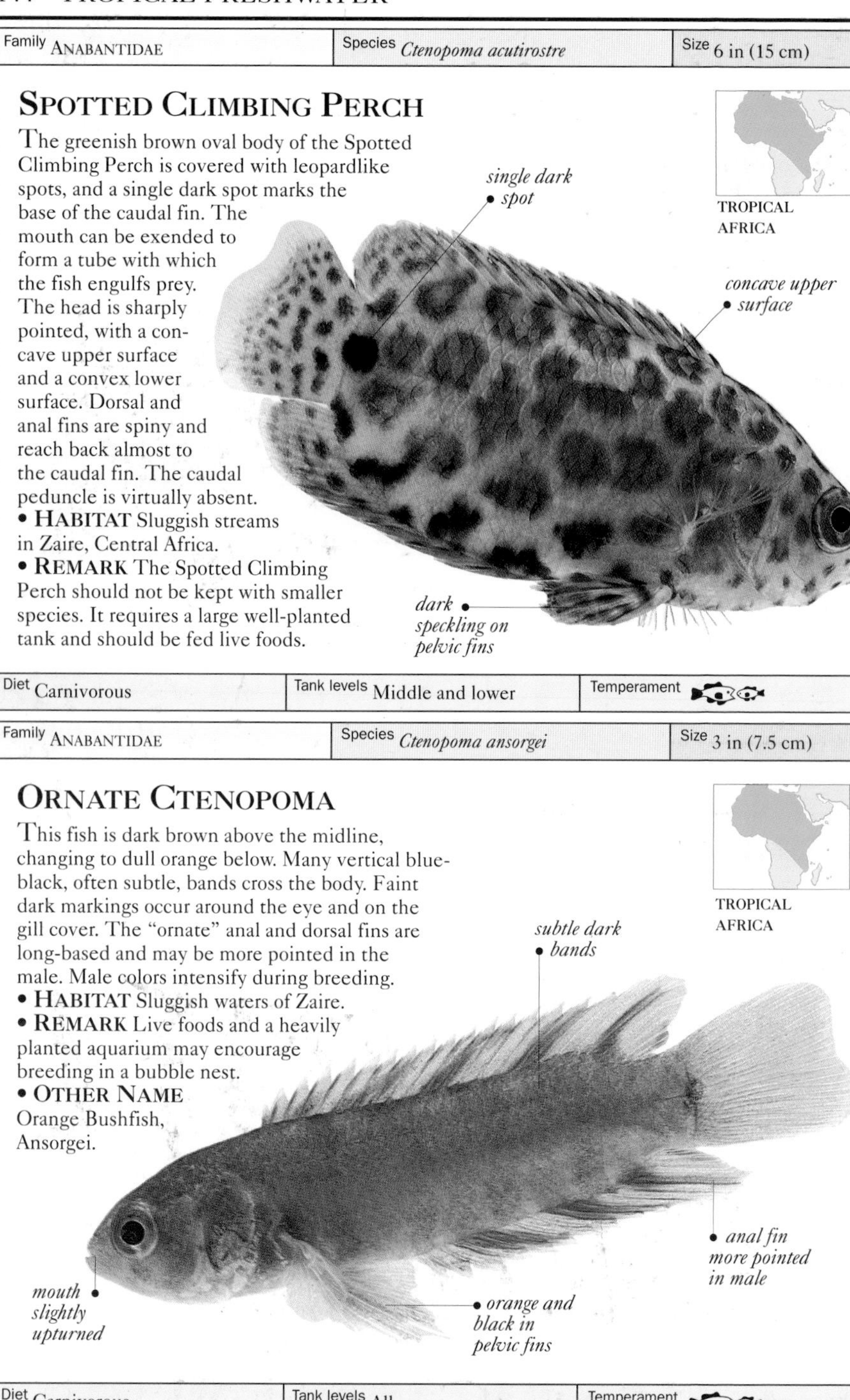

Diet Carnivorous	Tank levels Middle and lower	Temperament

Family ANABANTIDAE	Species *Ctenopoma ansorgei*	Size 3 in (7.5 cm)

ORNATE CTENOPOMA

This fish is dark brown above the midline, changing to dull orange below. Many vertical blue-black, often subtle, bands cross the body. Faint dark markings occur around the eye and on the gill cover. The "ornate" anal and dorsal fins are long-based and may be more pointed in the male. Male colors intensify during breeding.

• **HABITAT** Sluggish waters of Zaire.

• **REMARK** Live foods and a heavily planted aquarium may encourage breeding in a bubble nest.

• **OTHER NAME** Orange Bushfish, Ansorgei.

Diet Carnivorous	Tank levels All	Temperament

Family ANABANTIDAE	Species *Ctenopoma fasciolatum*	Size 3½ in (9 cm)

BANDED CLIMBING PERCH

The general shape and fin configuration of this fish are similar to those of the Paradisefish (*Macropodus opercularis*). The color may vary but it is usually brown. Scattered scales are pale metallic blue, giving an iridescent effect. They sometimes join up to give the impression of vertical bars. Further iridescences appear below the reddish gold-rimmed eye and on the gill cover. The fins share the body coloring and speckling. Male anal and dorsal fins are more pointed and extend toward the caudal fin. Males also have stronger body coloration when breeding.

- **HABITAT** Streams in Zaire.
- **REMARK** Males of these bubble nest breeders will guard the nest.

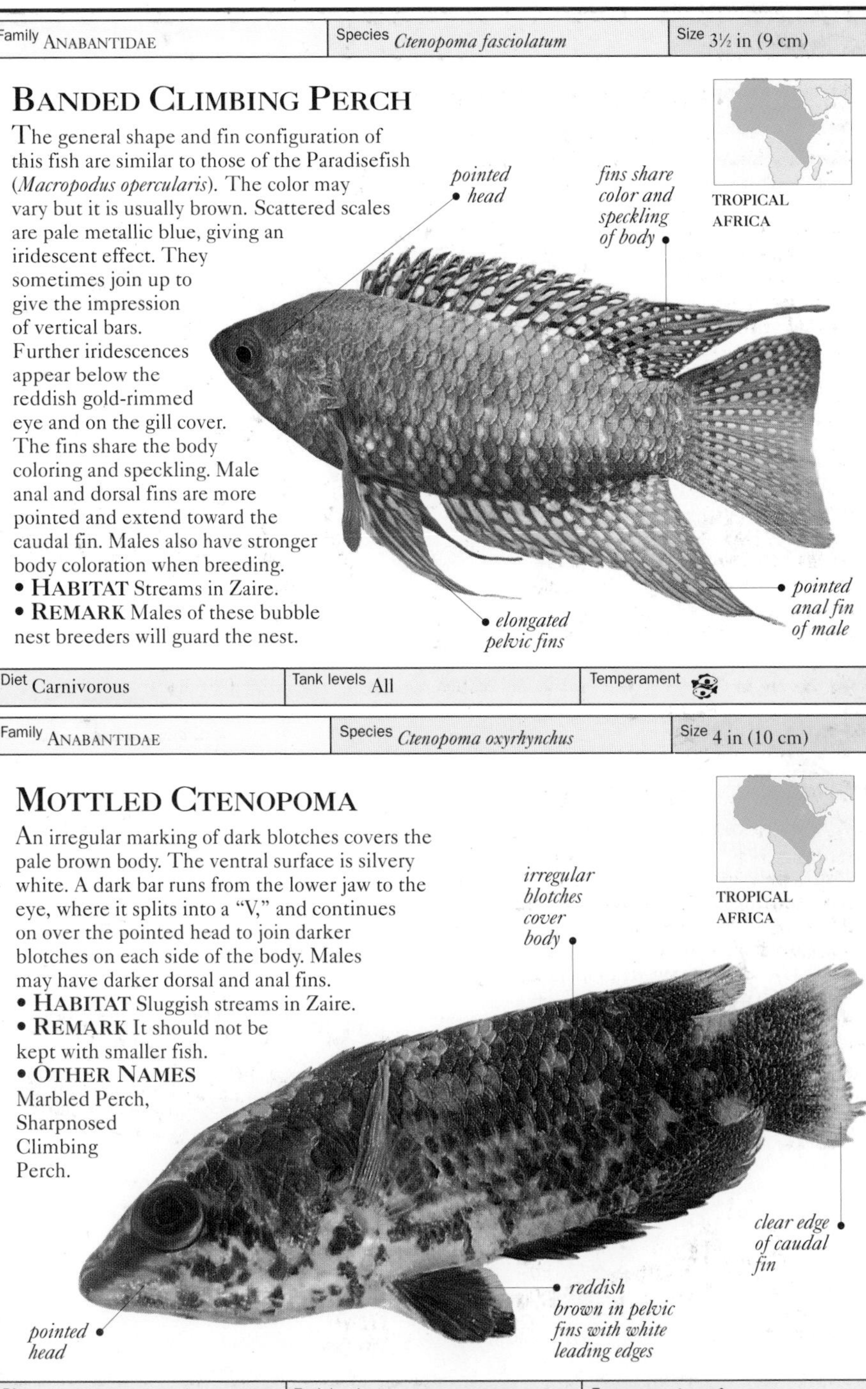

Diet Carnivorous	Tank levels All	Temperament

Family ANABANTIDAE	Species *Ctenopoma oxyrhynchus*	Size 4 in (10 cm)

MOTTLED CTENOPOMA

An irregular marking of dark blotches covers the pale brown body. The ventral surface is silvery white. A dark bar runs from the lower jaw to the eye, where it splits into a "V," and continues on over the pointed head to join darker blotches on each side of the body. Males may have darker dorsal and anal fins.

- **HABITAT** Sluggish streams in Zaire.
- **REMARK** It should not be kept with smaller fish.
- **OTHER NAMES** Marbled Perch, Sharpnosed Climbing Perch.

Diet Carnivorous	Tank levels All	Temperament

Family HELOSTOMATIDAE	Species *Helostoma temmincki*	Size 8 in (20 cm)

KISSING GOURAMI

The natural coloration of this oval species is silver-green with rows of tiny dark dots. More commonly available aquarium-bred varieties, as shown here, are a pale rose-pink. The pointed head carries a thick-lipped mouth, which is puckered to resemble a "kissing" posture. Dorsal and anal fins are long-based, equal in length, and have spines running two-thirds their length.

• **HABITAT** Streams and rivers in Thailand; also Borneo, Java, and Sumatra.

• **REMARK** The "kissing" behavior of adults occurs when the fish are grazing algae, or when two fish are contesting a territory.

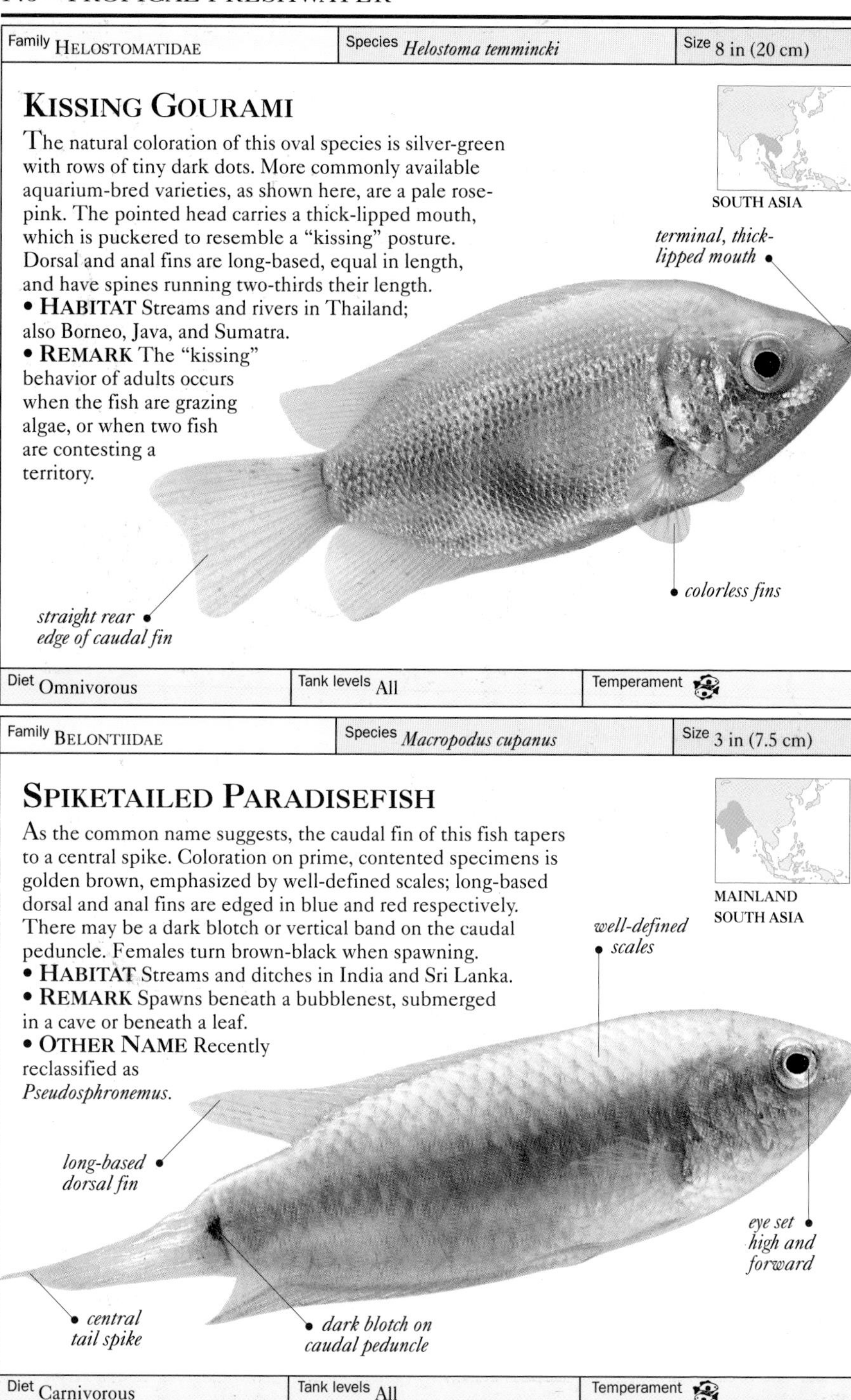

Diet Omnivorous	Tank levels All	Temperament

Family BELONTIIDAE	Species *Macropodus cupanus*	Size 3 in (7.5 cm)

SPIKETAILED PARADISEFISH

As the common name suggests, the caudal fin of this fish tapers to a central spike. Coloration on prime, contented specimens is golden brown, emphasized by well-defined scales; long-based dorsal and anal fins are edged in blue and red respectively. There may be a dark blotch or vertical band on the caudal peduncle. Females turn brown-black when spawning.

• **HABITAT** Streams and ditches in India and Sri Lanka.

• **REMARK** Spawns beneath a bubblenest, submerged in a cave or beneath a leaf.

• **OTHER NAME** Recently reclassified as *Pseudosphronemus*.

Diet Carnivorous	Tank levels All	Temperament

Family OSPHRONEMIDAE	Species *Osphronemus goramy*	Size 24 in (60 cm)

GOURAMI

The wild juvenile shown here has a silvery bronze-gray body crossed by dark vertical bars. The golden color variety beneath is also young. The heads of both are pointed and the eyes set well forward. The adult is gray with well-defined scales and has a pale gray area on the head above a relatively small eye. Its large, upturned mouth carries fleshy lips. The pelvic fins are filamentous.

• **HABITAT** Rivers and lakes of the Greater Sunda Islands.

• **REMARK** Like the Oscar (see p.115), this species is more attractive when young and soon outgrows the average aquarium. It is best kept with large fishes and provided with plenty of green food.

An adult Gourami will outgrow the average tank

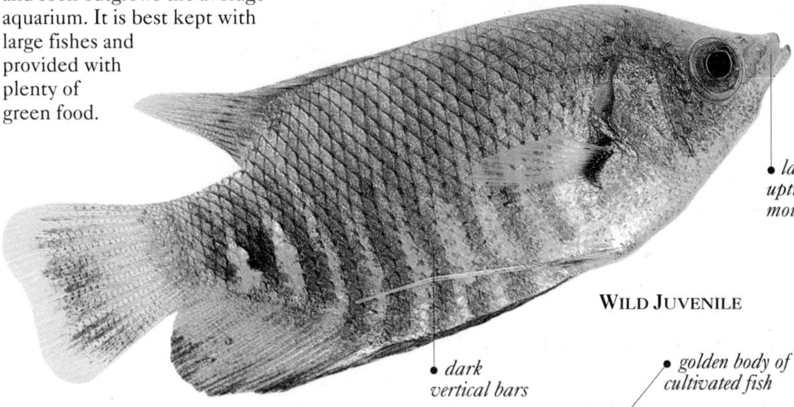

large, upturned mouth

WILD JUVENILE

dark vertical bars

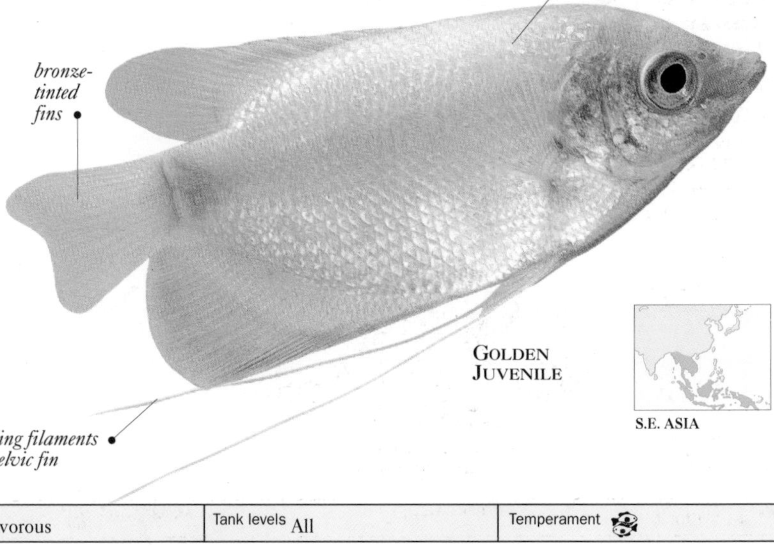

golden body of cultivated fish

bronze-tinted fins

GOLDEN JUVENILE

S.E. ASIA

trailing filaments on pelvic fin

Diet Herbivorous	Tank levels All	Temperament 

Family BELONTIIDAE	Species *Sphaerichthys osphromenoides*	Size 3¼ in (8 cm)

CHOCOLATE GOURAMI

The oval body of the Chocolate Gourami is pointed, curving to a long snout and a short tapering caudal peduncle. Pale-edged scales feature against a dark, chocolate brown body. Dorsal and anal fins run about half the length of the body. The head is marked with two distinct cream lines: one from the mouth to the bottom of the eye, the other above the eye and across the head. More cream vertical bands cross the body farther back.

• **HABITAT** Sluggish waters in Borneo, Malaysia, and Sumatra.

• **REMARK** This shy fish is a mouth-brooder. Live foods are required.

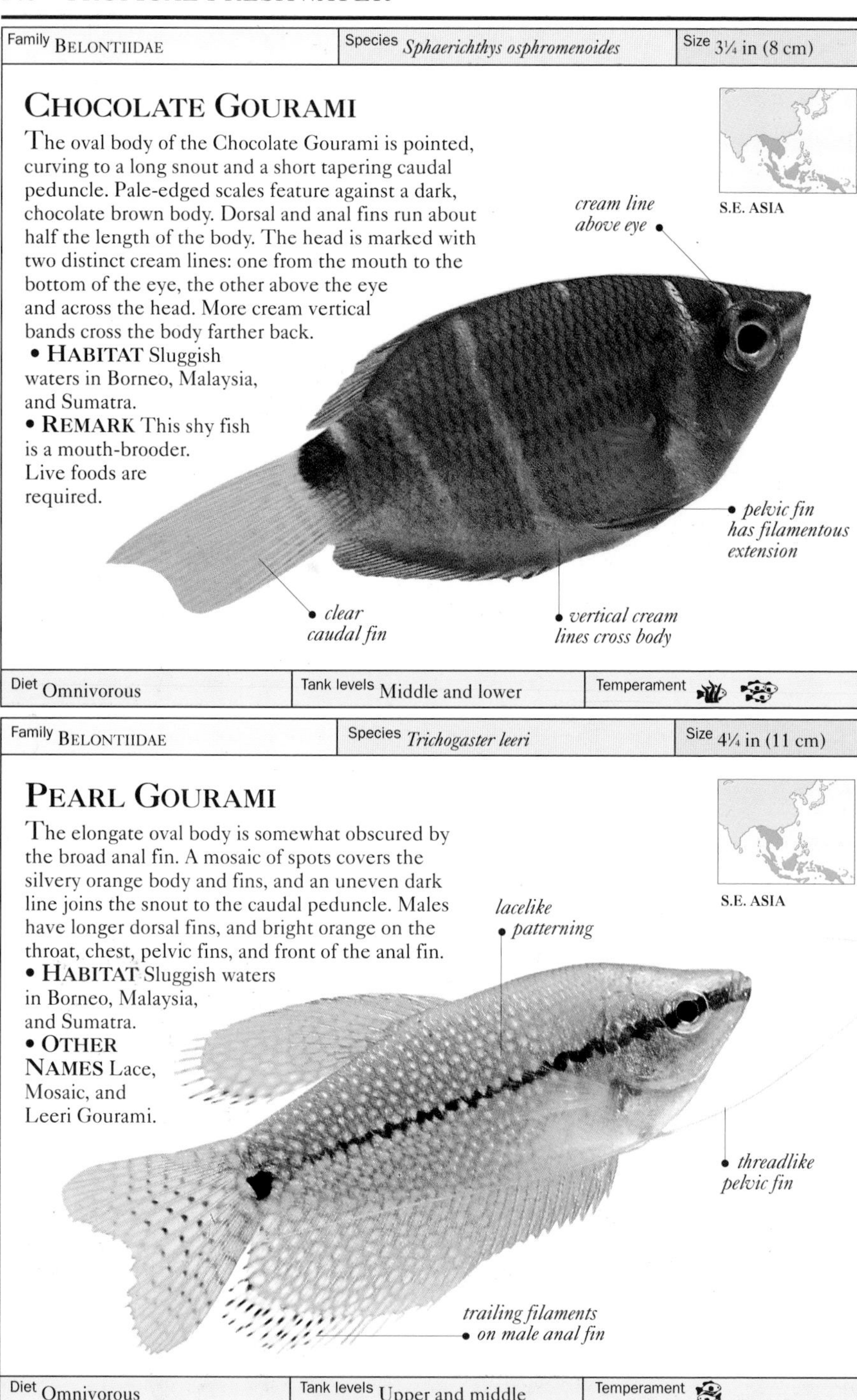

Diet Omnivorous	Tank levels Middle and lower	Temperament

Family BELONTIIDAE	Species *Trichogaster leeri*	Size 4¼ in (11 cm)

PEARL GOURAMI

The elongate oval body is somewhat obscured by the broad anal fin. A mosaic of spots covers the silvery orange body and fins, and an uneven dark line joins the snout to the caudal peduncle. Males have longer dorsal fins, and bright orange on the throat, chest, pelvic fins, and front of the anal fin.

• **HABITAT** Sluggish waters in Borneo, Malaysia, and Sumatra.

• **OTHER NAMES** Lace, Mosaic, and Leeri Gourami.

Diet Omnivorous	Tank levels Upper and middle	Temperament

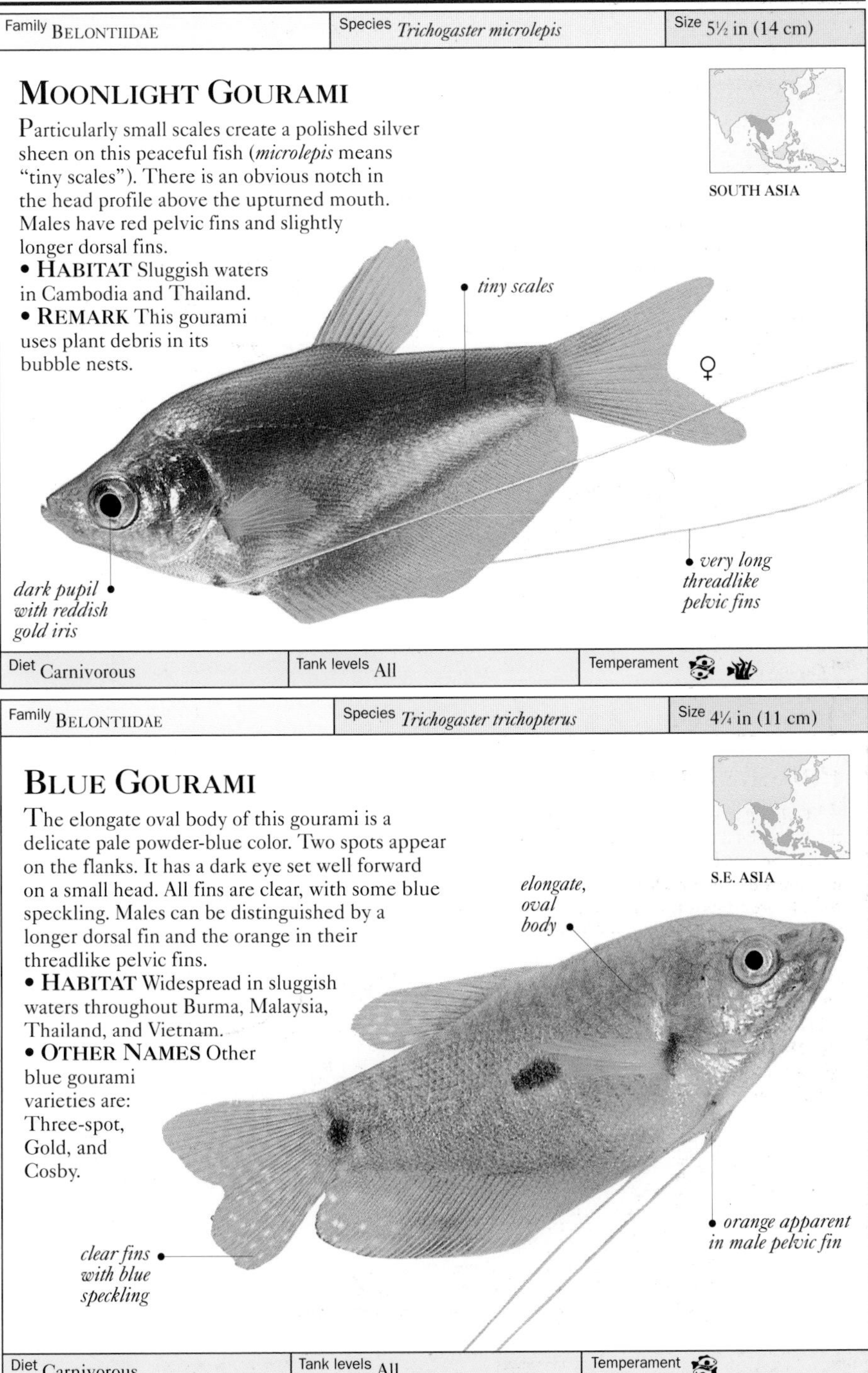

Family BELONTIIDAE	Species *Trichogaster microlepis*	Size 5½ in (14 cm)

MOONLIGHT GOURAMI

Particularly small scales create a polished silver sheen on this peaceful fish (*microlepis* means "tiny scales"). There is an obvious notch in the head profile above the upturned mouth. Males have red pelvic fins and slightly longer dorsal fins.

- **HABITAT** Sluggish waters in Cambodia and Thailand.
- **REMARK** This gourami uses plant debris in its bubble nests.

Diet Carnivorous	Tank levels All	Temperament

Family BELONTIIDAE	Species *Trichogaster trichopterus*	Size 4¼ in (11 cm)

BLUE GOURAMI

The elongate oval body of this gourami is a delicate pale powder-blue color. Two spots appear on the flanks. It has a dark eye set well forward on a small head. All fins are clear, with some blue speckling. Males can be distinguished by a longer dorsal fin and the orange in their threadlike pelvic fins.

- **HABITAT** Widespread in sluggish waters throughout Burma, Malaysia, Thailand, and Vietnam.
- **OTHER NAMES** Other blue gourami varieties are: Three-spot, Gold, and Cosby.

Diet Carnivorous	Tank levels All	Temperament

Family BELONTIIDAE	Species *Trichogaster trichopterus sumatranus*	Size 4½ in (11 cm)

GOLDEN OPALINE GOURAMI

This yellowish gold fish carries dark wavy markings across the dorsal surface. The ventral surface is yellow-silver. The long-based anal fin has red and yellow speckles and a clear edge. Other fins are clearer with some yellow specklings. Males have a longer dorsal fin and a stronger yellow-orange color in the pelvic fins.

• **HABITAT** Aquarium-developed.

• **REMARK** Like other color strains of *Trichogaster trichopterus*, this aquarium-bred subspecies is not naturally occurring.

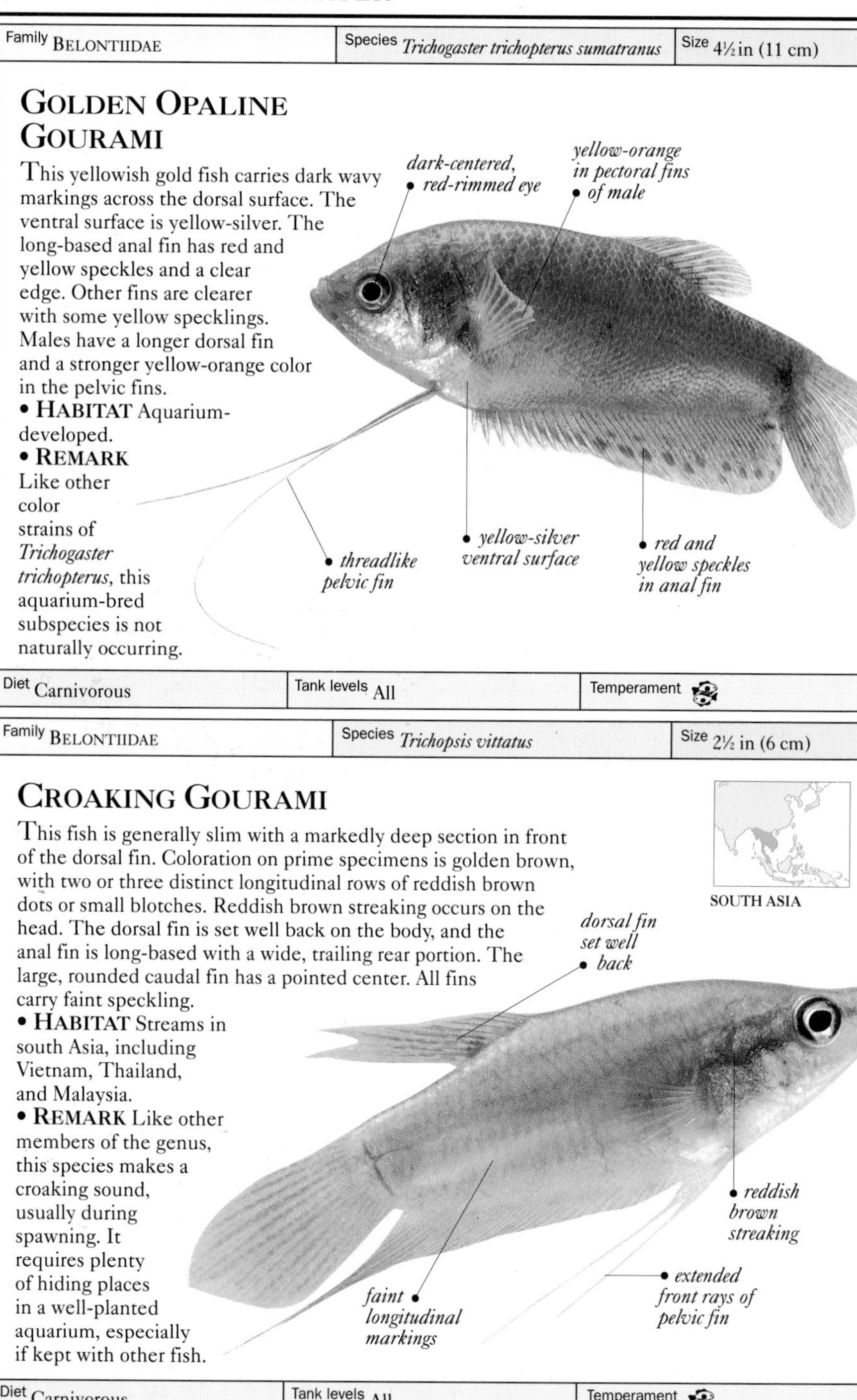

Diet Carnivorous	Tank levels All	Temperament

Family BELONTIIDAE	Species *Trichopsis vittatus*	Size 2½ in (6 cm)

CROAKING GOURAMI

This fish is generally slim with a markedly deep section in front of the dorsal fin. Coloration on prime specimens is golden brown, with two or three distinct longitudinal rows of reddish brown dots or small blotches. Reddish brown streaking occurs on the head. The dorsal fin is set well back on the body, and the anal fin is long-based with a wide, trailing rear portion. The large, rounded caudal fin has a pointed center. All fins carry faint speckling.

• **HABITAT** Streams in south Asia, including Vietnam, Thailand, and Malaysia.

• **REMARK** Like other members of the genus, this species makes a croaking sound, usually during spawning. It requires plenty of hiding places in a well-planted aquarium, especially if kept with other fish.

Diet Carnivorous	Tank levels All	Temperament

KILLIFISHES

KILLIFISHES BELONG TO the family Cyprinodontidae and are also known by the alternative common name of egg-laying tooth carps. They inhabit fresh waters of the tropical Americas, Africa, Asia, and south-western Europe. Some killifish species inhabit small bodies of water that dry up at certain times of the year; they lay eggs that can survive almost total dehydration. Adult males are usually larger, with longer fins, and are more brilliantly colored. All these fish will accept almost any food in captivity.

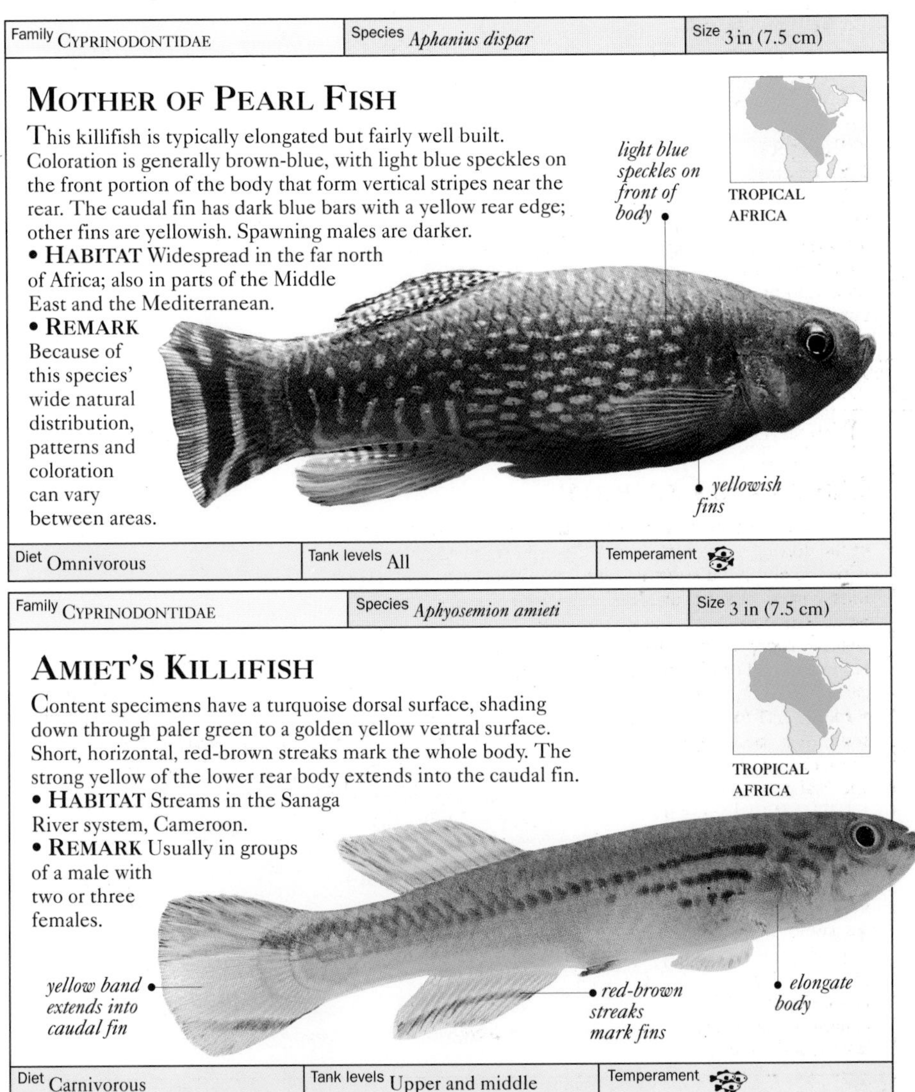

Family CYPRINODONTIDAE	Species *Aphanius dispar*	Size 3 in (7.5 cm)

MOTHER OF PEARL FISH

This killifish is typically elongated but fairly well built. Coloration is generally brown-blue, with light blue speckles on the front portion of the body that form vertical stripes near the rear. The caudal fin has dark blue bars with a yellow rear edge; other fins are yellowish. Spawning males are darker.

- **HABITAT** Widespread in the far north of Africa; also in parts of the Middle East and the Mediterranean.
- **REMARK** Because of this species' wide natural distribution, patterns and coloration can vary between areas.

Diet Omnivorous	Tank levels All	Temperament

Family CYPRINODONTIDAE	Species *Aphyosemion amieti*	Size 3 in (7.5 cm)

AMIET'S KILLIFISH

Content specimens have a turquoise dorsal surface, shading down through paler green to a golden yellow ventral surface. Short, horizontal, red-brown streaks mark the whole body. The strong yellow of the lower rear body extends into the caudal fin.

- **HABITAT** Streams in the Sanaga River system, Cameroon.
- **REMARK** Usually in groups of a male with two or three females.

Diet Carnivorous	Tank levels Upper and middle	Temperament

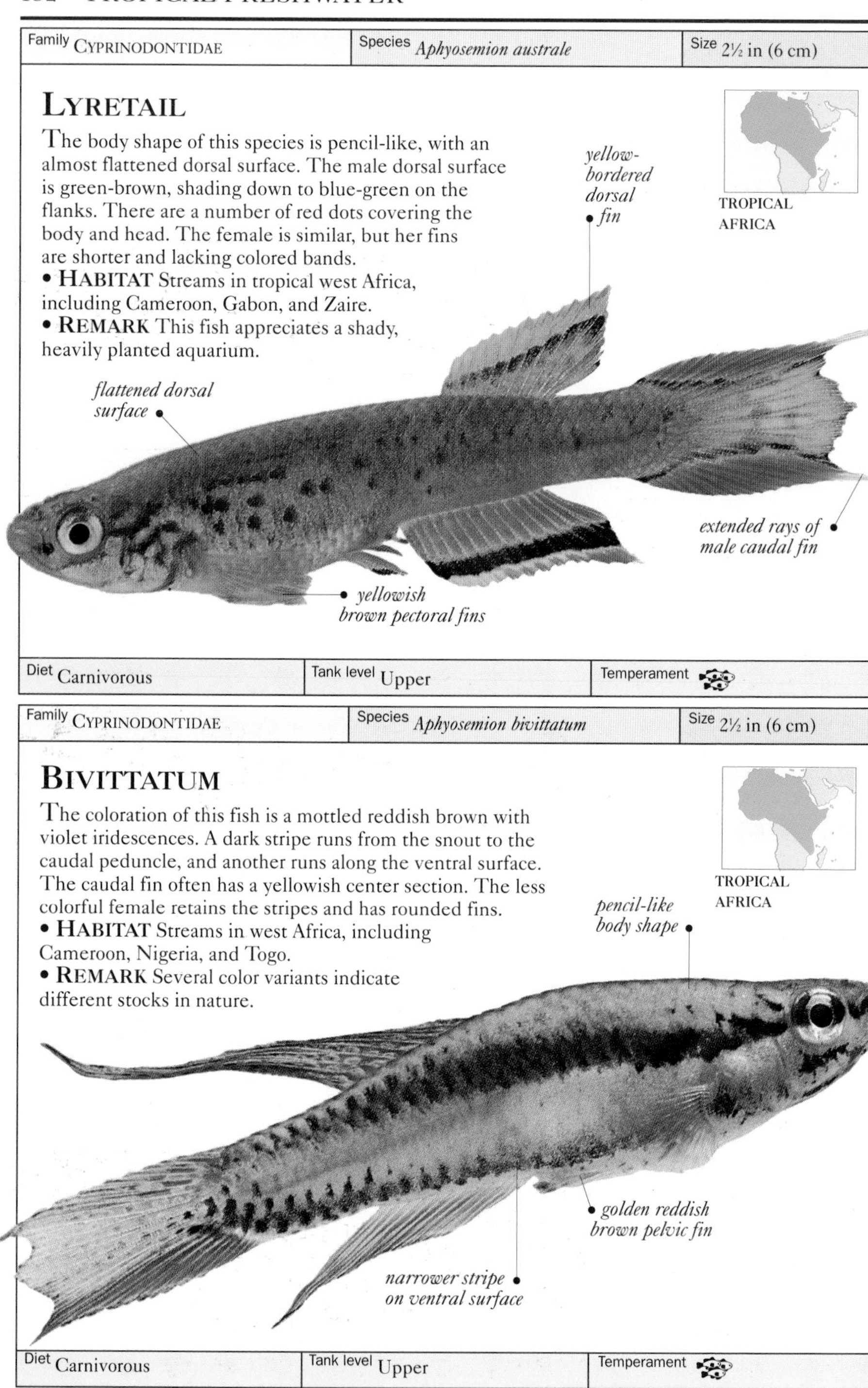

Family CYPRINODONTIDAE	Species *Aphyosemion australe*	Size 2½ in (6 cm)

LYRETAIL

The body shape of this species is pencil-like, with an almost flattened dorsal surface. The male dorsal surface is green-brown, shading down to blue-green on the flanks. There are a number of red dots covering the body and head. The female is similar, but her fins are shorter and lacking colored bands.

- **HABITAT** Streams in tropical west Africa, including Cameroon, Gabon, and Zaire.
- **REMARK** This fish appreciates a shady, heavily planted aquarium.

Diet Carnivorous	Tank level Upper	Temperament

Family CYPRINODONTIDAE	Species *Aphyosemion bivittatum*	Size 2½ in (6 cm)

BIVITTATUM

The coloration of this fish is a mottled reddish brown with violet iridescences. A dark stripe runs from the snout to the caudal peduncle, and another runs along the ventral surface. The caudal fin often has a yellowish center section. The less colorful female retains the stripes and has rounded fins.

- **HABITAT** Streams in west Africa, including Cameroon, Nigeria, and Togo.
- **REMARK** Several color variants indicate different stocks in nature.

Diet Carnivorous	Tank level Upper	Temperament

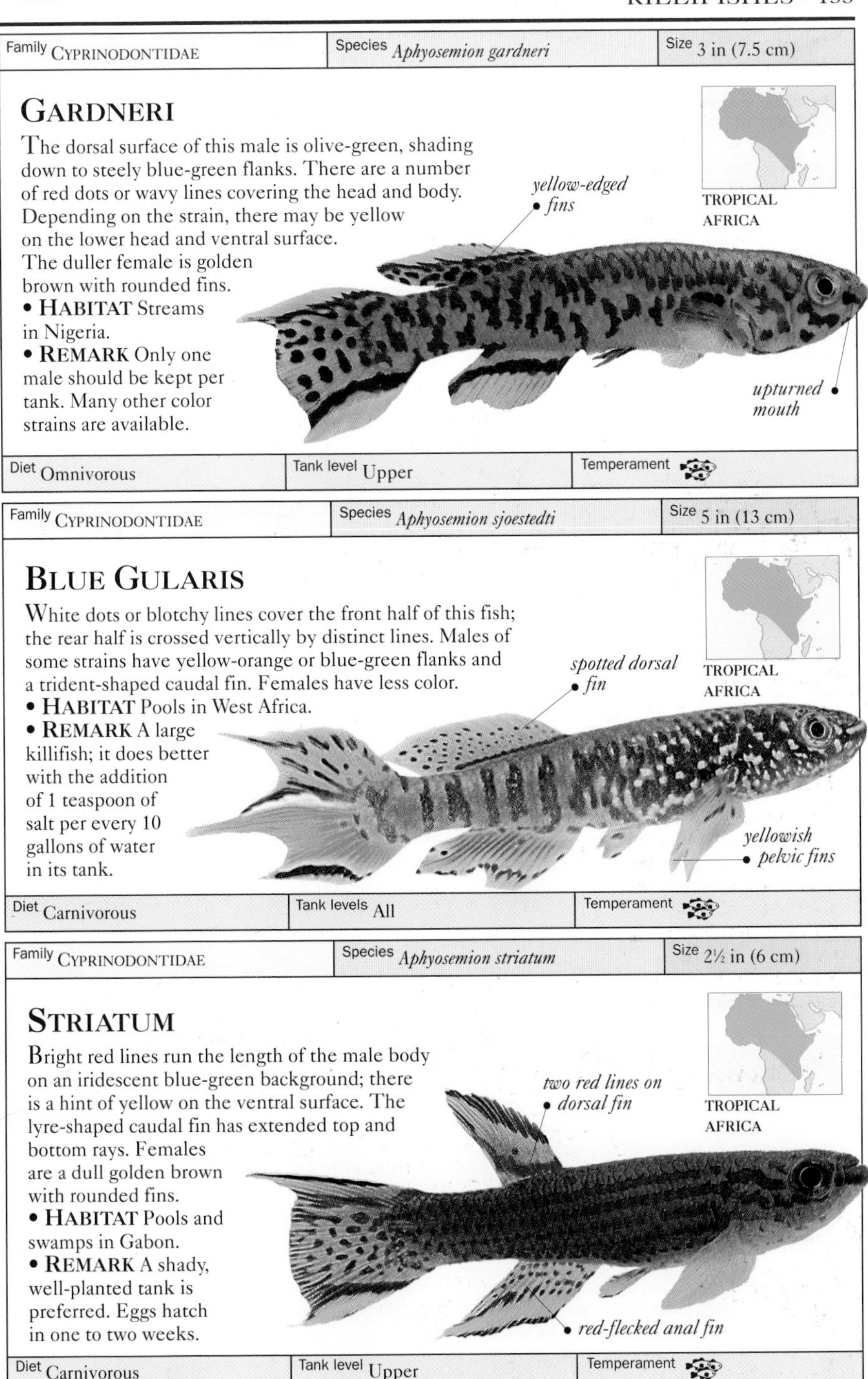

Family CYPRINODONTIDAE	Species *Aphyosemion gardneri*	Size 3 in (7.5 cm)

GARDNERI

The dorsal surface of this male is olive-green, shading down to steely blue-green flanks. There are a number of red dots or wavy lines covering the head and body. Depending on the strain, there may be yellow on the lower head and ventral surface. The duller female is golden brown with rounded fins.

- **HABITAT** Streams in Nigeria.
- **REMARK** Only one male should be kept per tank. Many other color strains are available.

Diet Omnivorous	Tank level Upper	Temperament

Family CYPRINODONTIDAE	Species *Aphyosemion sjoestedti*	Size 5 in (13 cm)

BLUE GULARIS

White dots or blotchy lines cover the front half of this fish; the rear half is crossed vertically by distinct lines. Males of some strains have yellow-orange or blue-green flanks and a trident-shaped caudal fin. Females have less color.

- **HABITAT** Pools in West Africa.
- **REMARK** A large killifish; it does better with the addition of 1 teaspoon of salt per every 10 gallons of water in its tank.

Diet Carnivorous	Tank levels All	Temperament

Family CYPRINODONTIDAE	Species *Aphyosemion striatum*	Size 2½ in (6 cm)

STRIATUM

Bright red lines run the length of the male body on an iridescent blue-green background; there is a hint of yellow on the ventral surface. The lyre-shaped caudal fin has extended top and bottom rays. Females are a dull golden brown with rounded fins.

- **HABITAT** Pools and swamps in Gabon.
- **REMARK** A shady, well-planted tank is preferred. Eggs hatch in one to two weeks.

Diet Carnivorous	Tank level Upper	Temperament

Family CYPRINODONTIDAE	Species *Aphyosemion walkeri*	Size 2½ in (6.5 cm)

WALKER'S APHYOSEMION

This fish is yellowish green with blue tones. A number of vertical red-brown streaks cover the body, and there are longitudinal streaks behind the gill cover and on the head. Dorsal and anal fins oppose each other and contain yellow or orange midsections and red-brown edges.

- **HABITAT** Forest streams of Ghana and the Ivory Coast.
- **REMARK** The eggs require about two months in damp peat moss before re-immersion activates hatching.

Diet Carnivorous	Tank levels All	Temperament

Family CYPRINODONTIDAE	Species *Aplocheilus dayi*	Size 2¾ in (7 cm)

CEYLON KILLIFISH

The Ceylon Killifish is golden yellow and is decorated with blue-green iridescences along the flanks that may form an occasional vertical streak. The head is flattened and the red-lipped mouth is wide. A small dorsal fin is set well back, and that of the female has a dark blotch at the base. The caudal fin is yellow with red markings. Males have more pointed dorsal and anal fins.

- **HABITAT** Streams and ditches in southern India and Sri Lanka.
- **REMARK** This surface dweller likes floating plants in which to rest. The eggs, laid over a period of days, hatch after about two weeks.

Diet Carnivorous	Tank level Upper	Temperament

Family CYPRINODONTIDAE	Species *Cynolebias bokermani*	Size 2 in (5 cm)

BOKERMAN'S CYNOLEBIAS

The deepest part of this fish lies in front of the dorsal and anal fins. A greenish golden brown coloring contrasts with a pale yellowish ventral surface. Several pale blue-green lines run vertically behind the metallic blue gill cover. There are a number of pale speckles along the top of the body that continue into the dorsal and caudal fins.

• **HABITAT** Isolated pools near the Brazilian coast.

• **REMARK** Eggs require about two months of storage in damp peat moss before re-immersion to hatch.

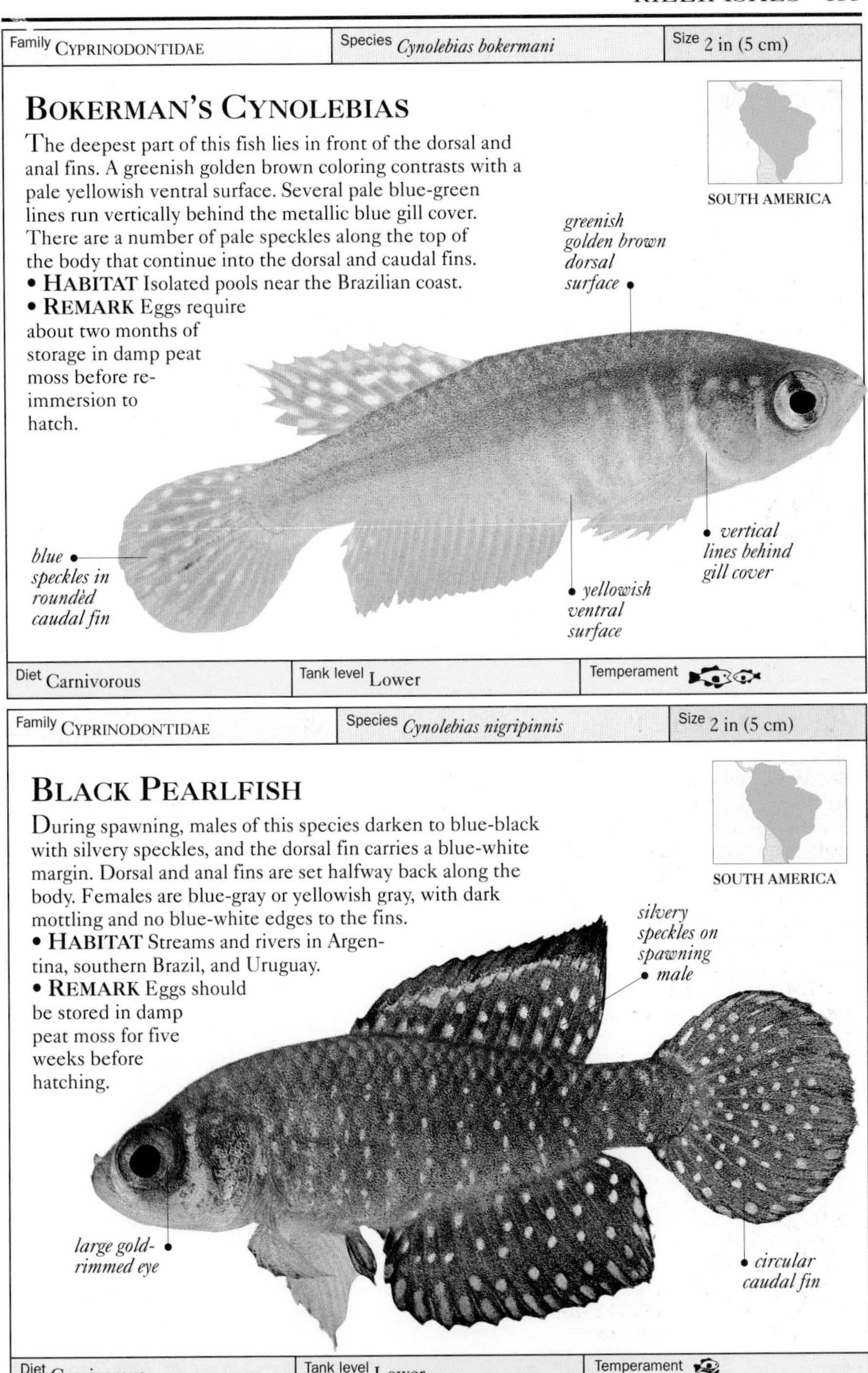

Diet Carnivorous	Tank level Lower	Temperament

Family CYPRINODONTIDAE	Species *Cynolebias nigripinnis*	Size 2 in (5 cm)

BLACK PEARLFISH

During spawning, males of this species darken to blue-black with silvery speckles, and the dorsal fin carries a blue-white margin. Dorsal and anal fins are set halfway back along the body. Females are blue-gray or yellowish gray, with dark mottling and no blue-white edges to the fins.

• **HABITAT** Streams and rivers in Argentina, southern Brazil, and Uruguay.

• **REMARK** Eggs should be stored in damp peat moss for five weeks before hatching.

Diet Carnivorous	Tank level Lower	Temperament

Family CYPRINODONTIDAE	Species *Epiplatys fasciolatus*	Size 3¼ in (8 cm)

BANDED EPIPLATYS

TROPICAL AFRICA

The male of this species is yellowish brown, shading to a pale ventral surface. The flanks may take on a bluish sheen in reflected light. A number of greenish golden dots cover the body, forming an oblique pattern, and the flanks may show red dots. In mature fish, fins are generally greenish yellow with red dots. The dorsal and anal fins are set well back, and the dorsal surface has a bluish tint. The female coloration is much more drab.

- **HABITAT** Streams in Liberia, Nigeria, and Sierra Leone.
- **REMARK** The Banded Epiplatys appreciates a shady, heavily planted aquarium. Although all killifish prefer live foods, they will accept flake foods. Eggs are laid in plants.

♀

dark-lipped mouth

well-defined scales

lighter ventral surface

rounded caudal fin

dorsal and anal fins set well back

bluish sheen on male flanks

Diet Carnivorous	Tank level Upper	Temperament

Family CYPRINODONTIDAE	Species *Jordanella floridae*	Size 3 in (7.5 cm)

AMERICAN FLAGFISH

UNITED STATES

The greenish blue body of this fish is covered with alternating rows of blue-green and red dots in a horizontal pattern reminiscent of the stripes in the American flag. A dark blotch often appears on the flanks below the dorsal fin but is more noticeable in the duller female. The female dorsal fin has a dark blotch at the rear.

- **HABITAT** Heavily vegetated ponds and lakes in Florida; also Mexico.
- **REMARK** The American Flagfish appreciates vegetable matter. There is only one close relative of this species which occurs in Yucatan, Mexico.

red in dorsal fin

clear pectoral fin

Diet Omnivorous	Tank levels All	Temperament

Family CYPRINODONTIDAE	Species *Pachypanchax playfairii*	Size 3 in (7.5 cm)

PLAYFAIR'S PANCHAX

The male is yellowish brown, shading to a paler belly. A number of equally spaced red dots cover the body and may be interspersed with iridescences. Fins are greenish yellow with red dots, but the pectoral and pelvic fins contain yellow tints. The female is less brightly colored and has a dark area at the base of the dorsal fin.

• **HABITAT** Streams in East Africa; also Madagascar, Zanzibar, and the Seychelles.

• **REMARK** It appreciates a shady, planted aquarium. Scales are raised, resembling the fish disease dropsy, but this is normal for the species.

Diet Carnivorous	Tank level Upper	Temperament

Family CYPRINODONTIDAE	Species *Pseudoepiplatys annulatus*	Size 1¾ in (4.5 cm)

CLOWN KILLIFISH

Four thick dark bands cross the spindle-shaped body of this pale yellowish brown fish. The male dorsal fin is yellow in front, while the anal fin has a dark front and a pale rear. The blue caudal fin carries a projecting center spike, marked with bright red horizontal lines. The body coloration of the female is similar, but she lacks the stronger fin colors.

• **HABITAT** Streams in Guinea, Liberia, Nigeria, and Sierra Leone.

• **REMARK** Densely vegetated aquariums are preferred.

Diet Carnivorous	Tank level Upper	Temperament

CATFISHES

THERE ARE AROUND 30 catfish families containing some 2,000 species. They are widely distributed, primarily in Africa, South America, and Southeast Asia. These bottom-dwellers are often nocturnal and have barbels on their downturned mouths that assist in detecting food. Many catfish are covered by bony plates, or scutes, and some can breathe atmospheric air.

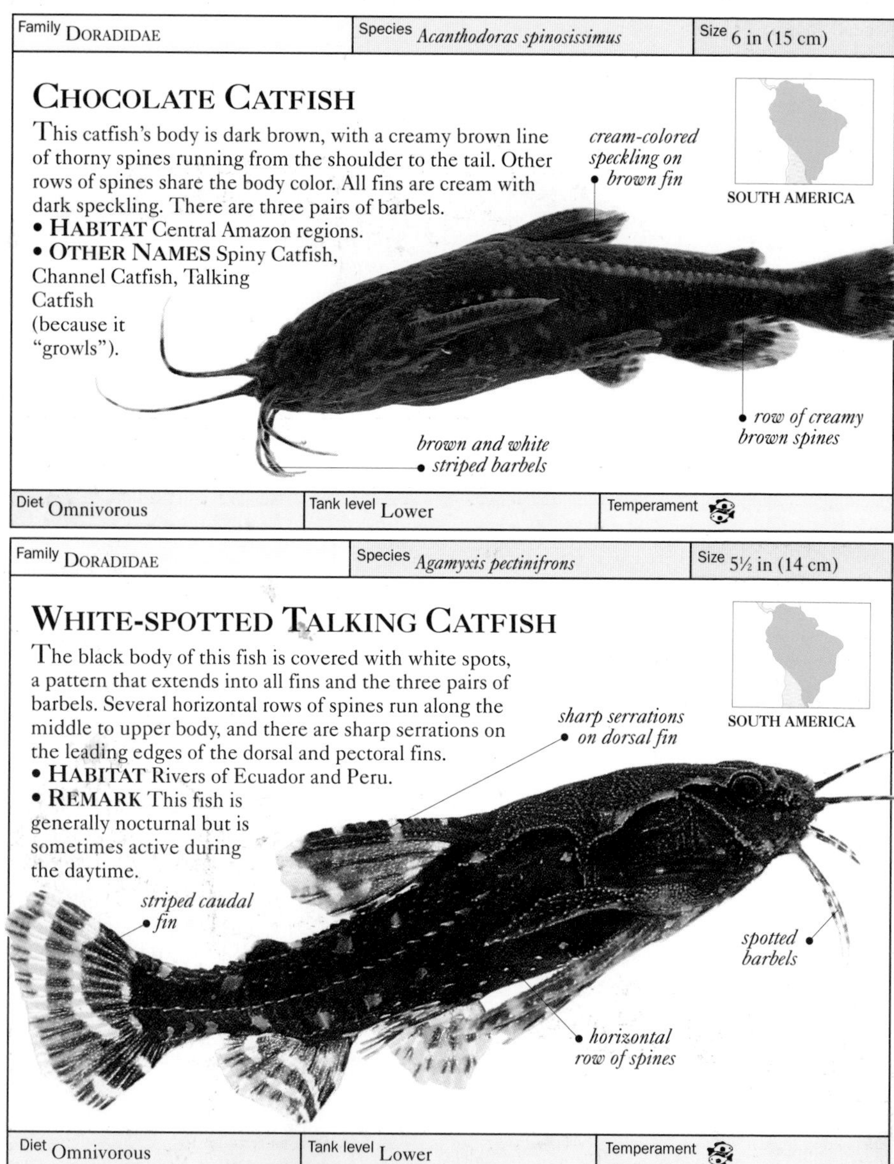

Family DORADIDAE	Species *Acanthodoras spinosissimus*	Size 6 in (15 cm)

CHOCOLATE CATFISH

This catfish's body is dark brown, with a creamy brown line of thorny spines running from the shoulder to the tail. Other rows of spines share the body color. All fins are cream with dark speckling. There are three pairs of barbels.

- **HABITAT** Central Amazon regions.
- **OTHER NAMES** Spiny Catfish, Channel Catfish, Talking Catfish (because it "growls").

Diet Omnivorous	Tank level Lower	Temperament

Family DORADIDAE	Species *Agamyxis pectinifrons*	Size 5½ in (14 cm)

WHITE-SPOTTED TALKING CATFISH

The black body of this fish is covered with white spots, a pattern that extends into all fins and the three pairs of barbels. Several horizontal rows of spines run along the middle to upper body, and there are sharp serrations on the leading edges of the dorsal and pectoral fins.

- **HABITAT** Rivers of Ecuador and Peru.
- **REMARK** This fish is generally nocturnal but is sometimes active during the daytime.

Diet Omnivorous	Tank level Lower	Temperament

Family DORADIDAE	Species *Amblydoras hancocki*	Size 5 in (13 cm)

HANCOCK'S AMBLYDORAS

The color of this fish can vary, but it is usually dark brown with darker, irregular blotches. A line of whitish spines runs along the lateral line, accentuated by a dark border beneath. The first one or two rays of the erect dorsal fin are dark. The whole body is covered with bony plates, and the head appears wrinkled. There are three pairs of long white and brown barbels.

- **HABITAT** Rivers of Brazil, Peru, and Guyana.
- **REMARK** A well-planted aquarium with a few rocks and other hiding places will suit this species.

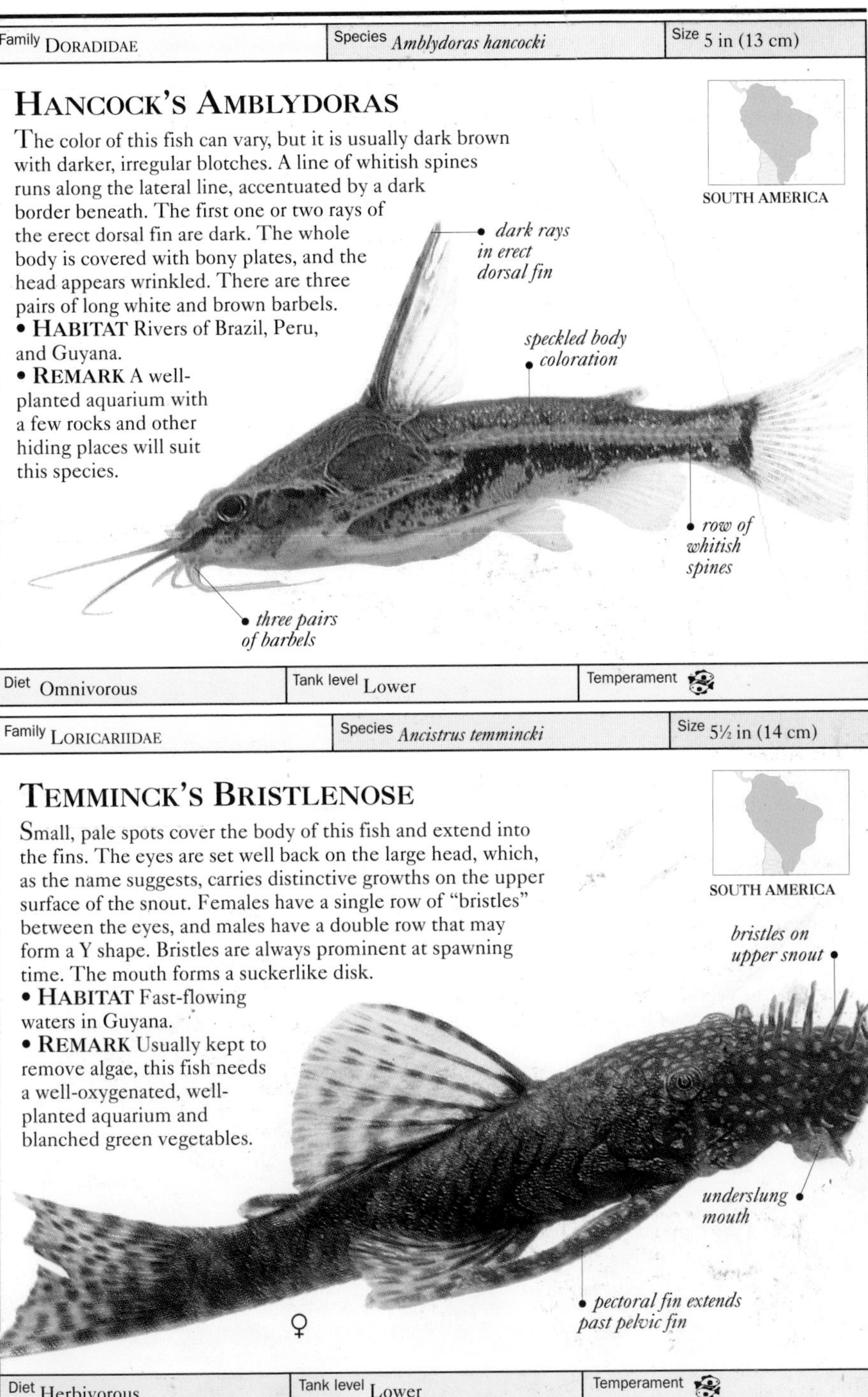

Diet Omnivorous	Tank level Lower	Temperament

Family LORICARIIDAE	Species *Ancistrus temmincki*	Size 5½ in (14 cm)

TEMMINCK'S BRISTLENOSE

Small, pale spots cover the body of this fish and extend into the fins. The eyes are set well back on the large head, which, as the name suggests, carries distinctive growths on the upper surface of the snout. Females have a single row of "bristles" between the eyes, and males have a double row that may form a Y shape. Bristles are always prominent at spawning time. The mouth forms a suckerlike disk.

- **HABITAT** Fast-flowing waters in Guyana.
- **REMARK** Usually kept to remove algae, this fish needs a well-oxygenated, well-planted aquarium and blanched green vegetables.

Diet Herbivorous	Tank level Lower	Temperament

Family AUCHENIPTERIDAE	Species *Auchenipterichthys thoracatus*	Size 5 in (13 cm)

MIDNIGHT CATFISH

Tiny, white, iridescent spots adorn the dark blue-gray body of this fish, prompting an association with the midnight sky. The ventral surface between the pectoral and pelvic fins is silvery white. The dorsal fin is set well forward on the body and is white with a black marking. A copulatory extension appears on the front of the pointed anal fin of the male. The male caudal fin has a longer top lobe.

• **HABITAT** Widespread in South America, from Panama down to the Plate River.

• **REMARK** This nocturnal fish has a retiring nature.

• **OTHER NAME** Zamora Woodcat.

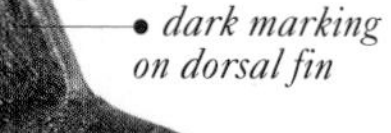

Diet Omnivorous	Tank level Lower	Temperament 

Family ASPREDINIDAE	Species *Bunocephalus kneri*	Size 5 in (13 cm)

BANJO CATFISH

SOUTH AMERICA

The shape of this fish is supposedly reminiscent of a banjo, with the flattened, broad outline tapering sharply at the dorsal fin into a very long caudal peduncle. Mottled, dark brown-black coloration covers the body. A sharply defined pair of ridges runs back from each eye, joining between the pectoral fins and continuing up to the dorsal fin. The skin is covered with rows of wartlike pimples that fall into two or three rows on the caudal peduncle. There are three pairs of barbels, the upper pair extending backwards. The high-set dorsal fin lies immediately above the pelvic fins, and the anal fin is set well back, about halfway along the caudal peduncle.

• **HABITAT** Streams and rivers in western Amazonia and Ecuador.

• **REMARK** The coloring makes this fish difficult to spot as it lies on the substrate, moving only occasionally. It has been known to spawn in the aquarium.

Diet Omnivorous	Tank level Lower	Temperament 

Family CALLICHTHYIDAE	Species *Callichthys callichthys*	Size 7 in (18 cm)

CALLICHTHYS

SOUTH AMERICA

The overlapping bony scutes of this catfish species are particularly prominent. They form two rows behind the gill cover, making a herringbone pattern. General body color is dull brown-gray. The head is broad and shallow, and the highly mobile eyes often move independently of each other.

- **HABITAT** Rivers in Brazil.
- **REMARK** Spawns differently from other catfishes: a bubble nest is built underneath vegetation to which the eggs are attached until hatching occurs. Males guard the nest.

armor plating covers head

two pairs of long barbels

two rows of bony scutes

Diet Omnivorous	Tank level Lower	Temperament

Family BAGRIDAE	Species *Chrysichthys ornatus*	Size 7½ in (19 cm)

ORNATE CATFISH

TROPICAL AFRICA

The golden brown body of this heavily built catfish is marked with areas of strong dark blotches, which are best seen on juveniles, as they fade with age. The ventral surface is silvery white. Two barbels are present on the upper snout, and six more barbels surround the wide mouth. The dorsal fin is held erect and, like the other fins, is speckled with dark dots. The pectoral fins have spines that are longer in the male.

- **HABITAT** Streams and rivers in the upper and middle regions of Zaire.
- **REMARK** This fish will prey on smaller species at night, so keep it with larger fish.

dark dots on erect dorsal fin

silvery white ventral surface

long barbels surround mouth

Diet Omnivorous	Tank level Lower	Temperament

Family CLARIIDAE	Species *Clarias batrachus*	Size 22 in (55 cm)

WALKING CATFISH

The wild form of this eel-shaped catfish is greenish brown with speckling. The piebald strain shown here, and a gold strain, have become increasingly popular with aquarists. The pectoral fins contain poisonous spines that are especially stout on the male. Pelvic fins remain small.

• **HABITAT** India and Sri Lanka; also Malaysia.

• **REMARK** This fish can exit the water and migrate by storing air in a special respiratory organ. Banned in several states as a threat to native fishes, it requires spacious quarters and a heavy hood. It grows very large.

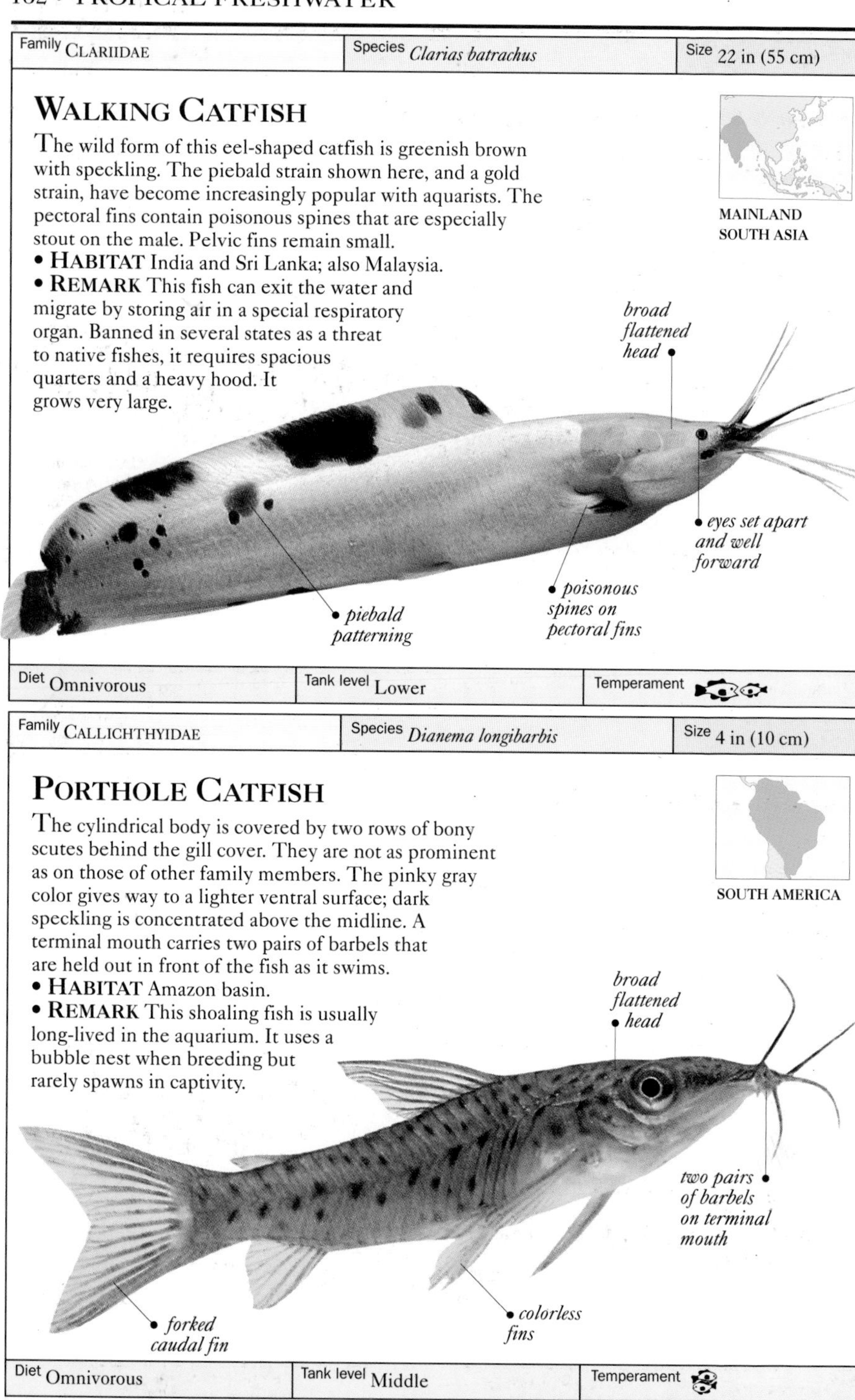

Diet Omnivorous	Tank level Lower	Temperament

Family CALLICHTHYIDAE	Species *Dianema longibarbis*	Size 4 in (10 cm)

PORTHOLE CATFISH

The cylindrical body is covered by two rows of bony scutes behind the gill cover. They are not as prominent as on those of other family members. The pinky gray color gives way to a lighter ventral surface; dark speckling is concentrated above the midline. A terminal mouth carries two pairs of barbels that are held out in front of the fish as it swims.

• **HABITAT** Amazon basin.

• **REMARK** This shoaling fish is usually long-lived in the aquarium. It uses a bubble nest when breeding but rarely spawns in captivity.

Diet Omnivorous	Tank level Middle	Temperament

Family CALLICHTHYIDAE	Species *Dianema urostriata*	Size 5 in (13 cm)

SOUTH AMERICA

FLAGTAIL PORTHOLE CATFISH

The fins of this fish are colorless, except for the caudal fin, which carries black and white stripes. Two rows of bony scutes cover the body. A creamy gray-brown shades to a lighter color on the belly and below the head. Speckling may be difficult to determine on the deep body tone.

• **HABITAT** Widespread in the Amazon basin.

• **REMARK** This is an active schooling fish, especially after dark. It may not be readily available.

• **OTHER NAME** Stripe-tailed Catfish.

elongate cylindrical body

black and white stripes on caudal fin

two rows of bony scutes

terminal mouth carrying two pairs of barbels

Diet Omnivorous	Tank level Middle	Temperament

Family SCHILBEIDAE	Species *Eutropiellus debauwi*	Size 3 in (7.5 cm)

TROPICAL AFRICA

AFRICAN GLASS CATFISH

This translucent creamy blue-gold fish has three horizontal black stripes crossing it. Two black marks in each lobe of the caudal fin continue from the upper and lower lines of the main body. The dorsal fin is set well forward, and the adipose fin looks more like a conventional rayed fin than the normal fatty adipose fins of some African catfish families.

• **HABITAT** Streams and rivers in Zaire.

• **REMARK** An active fish that should be kept in species groups. It resembles *Eutropiellus vanderweyeri*.

• **OTHER NAME** Three-striped Glass Catfish.

adipose fin set back on caudal peduncle

large eye on small head

narrow, long-based anal fin

Diet Omnivorous	Tank level Middle	Temperament

Family LORICARIIDAE	Species *Farlowella acus*	Size 8 in (20 cm)

TWIG CATFISH

This elongate catfish is brown with a dark line along the flanks, from the tip of the snout to the the caudal fin. Its underside is pale and its fin rays are speckled. Bony scutes cover the body. The snout develops bristles in the mature male.

• **HABITAT** Rivers in central and south Brazil.

• **REMARK** This catfish can be bred in the aquarium; eggs are laid on a firm clean surface and are guarded by the male. It requires extra green foods, as there is rarely sufficient algae in the aquarium.

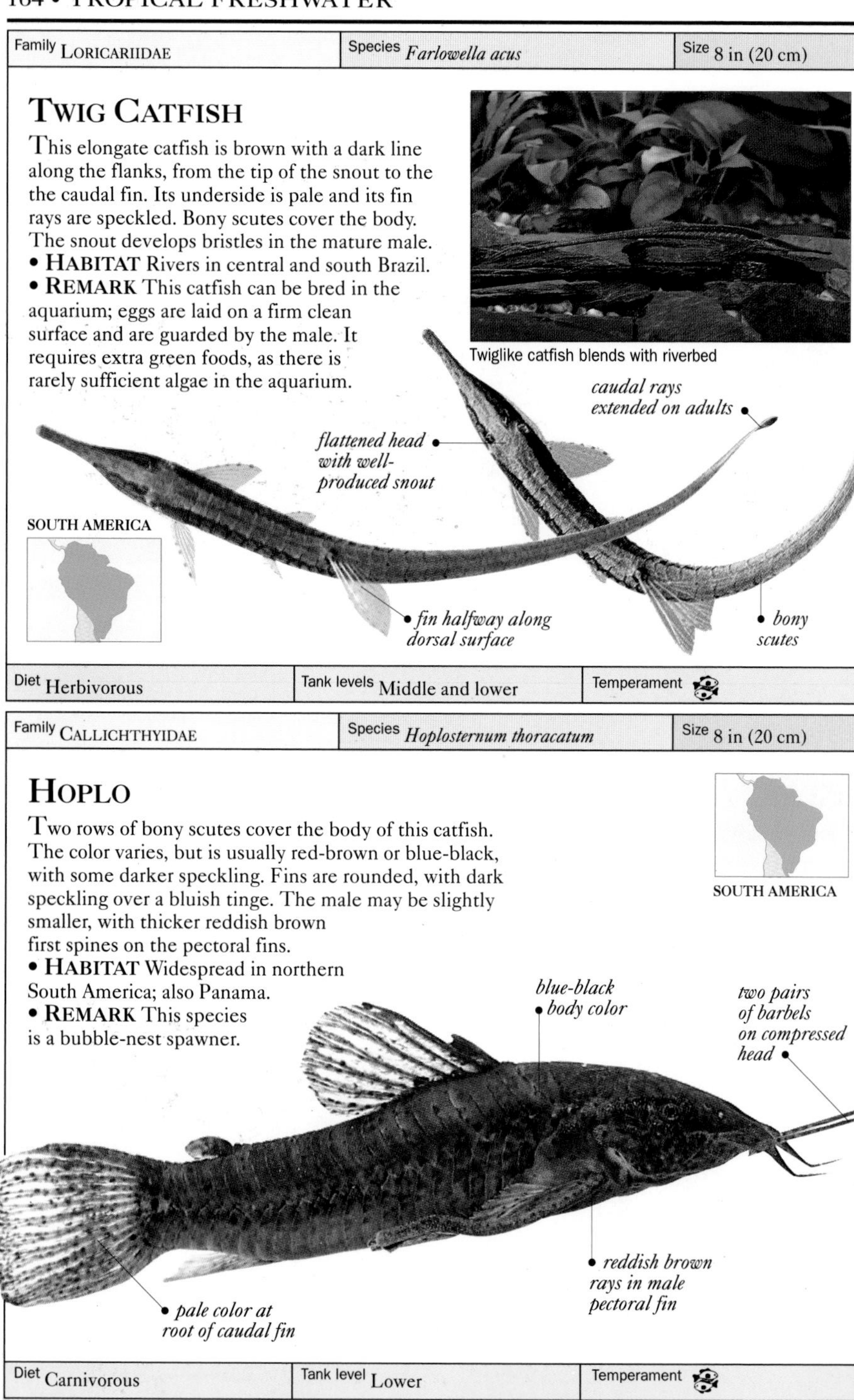

Twiglike catfish blends with riverbed

Diet Herbivorous	Tank levels Middle and lower	Temperament

Family CALLICHTHYIDAE	Species *Hoplosternum thoracatum*	Size 8 in (20 cm)

HOPLO

Two rows of bony scutes cover the body of this catfish. The color varies, but is usually red-brown or blue-black, with some darker speckling. Fins are rounded, with dark speckling over a bluish tinge. The male may be slightly smaller, with thicker reddish brown first spines on the pectoral fins.

• **HABITAT** Widespread in northern South America; also Panama.

• **REMARK** This species is a bubble-nest spawner.

Diet Carnivorous	Tank level Lower	Temperament

Family LORICARIIDAE	Species *Hypostomus multiradiatus*	Size 12 in (30 cm)

SUCKERMOUTH CATFISH

The greenish brown body of this catfish is covered with striking leopardlike spots which extend into the fins. The iris carries a lobe of skin that acts as a shade against bright light.

• **HABITAT** Flowing waters in South America; also Central America.

• **REMARK** Extra green foods should be supplied daily.

• **OTHER NAMES** Common Plecostomus; generic name formerly *Plecostomus*.

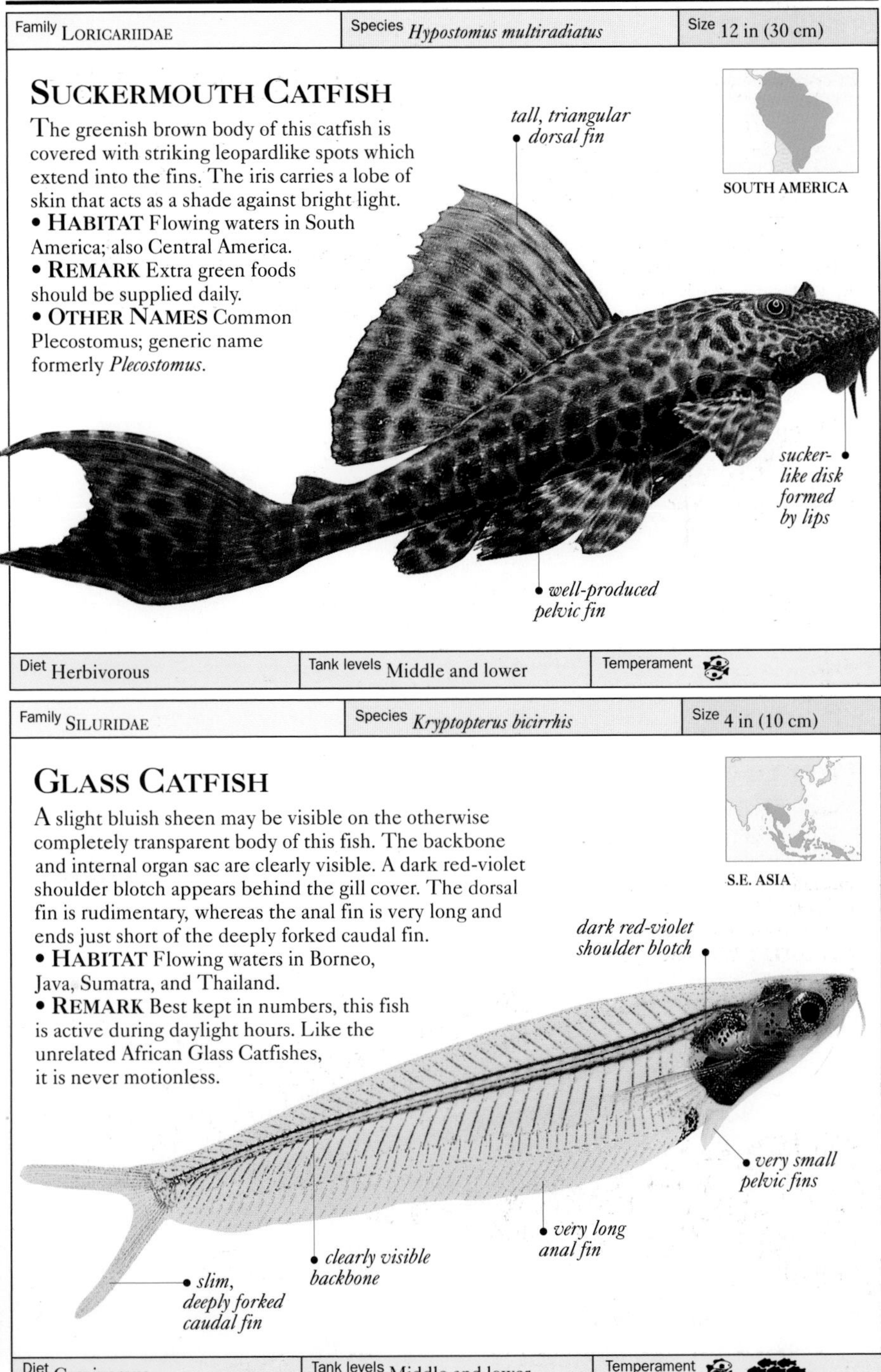

Diet Herbivorous	Tank levels Middle and lower	Temperament

Family SILURIDAE	Species *Kryptopterus bicirrhis*	Size 4 in (10 cm)

GLASS CATFISH

A slight bluish sheen may be visible on the otherwise completely transparent body of this fish. The backbone and internal organ sac are clearly visible. A dark red-violet shoulder blotch appears behind the gill cover. The dorsal fin is rudimentary, whereas the anal fin is very long and ends just short of the deeply forked caudal fin.

• **HABITAT** Flowing waters in Borneo, Java, Sumatra, and Thailand.

• **REMARK** Best kept in numbers, this fish is active during daylight hours. Like the unrelated African Glass Catfishes, it is never motionless.

Diet Carnivorous	Tank levels Middle and lower	Temperament

Family BAGRIDAE	Species *Leiocassis siamensis*	Size 5½ in (14 cm)

BUMBLEBEE CATFISH

This catfish's stocky body is dark brown with pale, irregular bars and patches. The pattern continues into the fins. An adipose fin is present, longer-based and fleshier than the dorsal fin. The dorsal fin carries a pale crescent shape in the center. There are four pairs of barbels.

• **HABITAT** Rivers and streams throughout Thailand.

• **REMARK** Nocturnal and normally peaceful, but it may devour smaller fishes.

• **OTHER NAME** Barred Siamese Catfish.

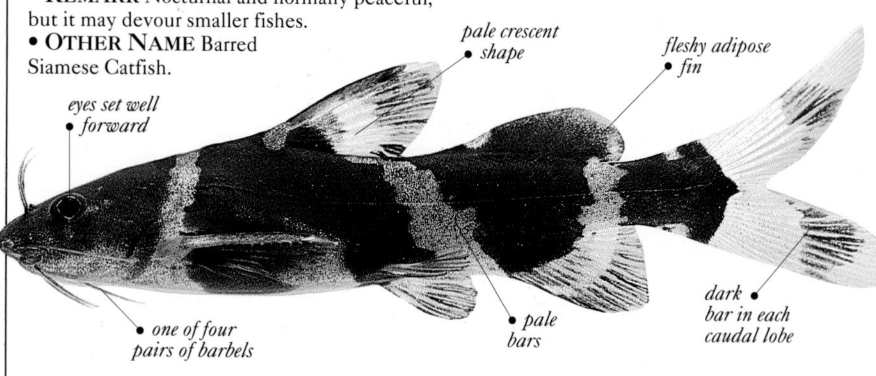

Diet Omnivorous	Tank level Lower	Temperament 

Family BAGRIDAE	Species *Mystus tengara*	Size 7 in (18 cm)

PEARL CATFISH

The general pearly blue color of this catfish contains a hint of pale brown on the dorsal surface and head. The ventral surface is silvery blue with some pink. Two thin, pale silver lines run from the shoulder to the end of the caudal peduncle, where they meet a dark, round spot. The long, triangular head has large eyes and four pairs of barbels. All fins are clear with a bluish tinge.

• **HABITAT** Streams and rivers in Burma; also India.

• **REMARK** This fish needs space, plantings, and hideaways.

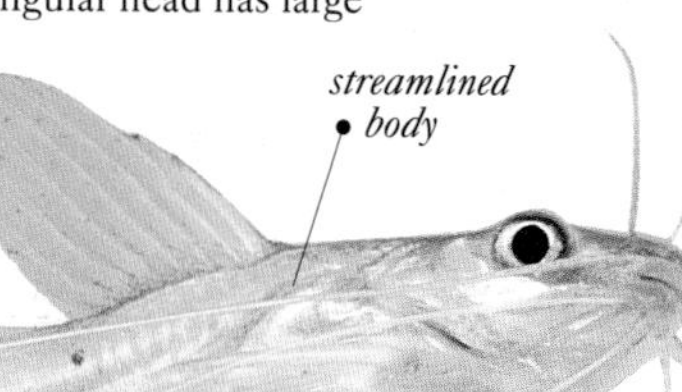

Diet Omnivorous	Tank level Lower	Temperament

Family LORICARIIDAE	Species *Otocinclus affinis*	Size 2 in (5 cm)

DWARF SUCKER CATFISH

This species has a long, almost tadpolelike shape. Its markings consist of dark mottled shades on the dorsal surface and a dark band that runs from the snout through the eye to the end of the caudal peduncle, where it terminates in a distinctive blotch. The lower half of the body is pale. The disk-shaped sucker, which gives this fish its common name, is carried underneath the long snout. Speckling appears in the dorsal, anal, and caudal fins.

- **HABITAT** Running waters in Brazil.
- **REMARK** The Dwarf Sucker Catfish spends much time rasping algae off all surfaces, including the tank sides, and it is often seen clinging to the glass. The sucker mouth also acts as an anchor in fast-flowing waters.

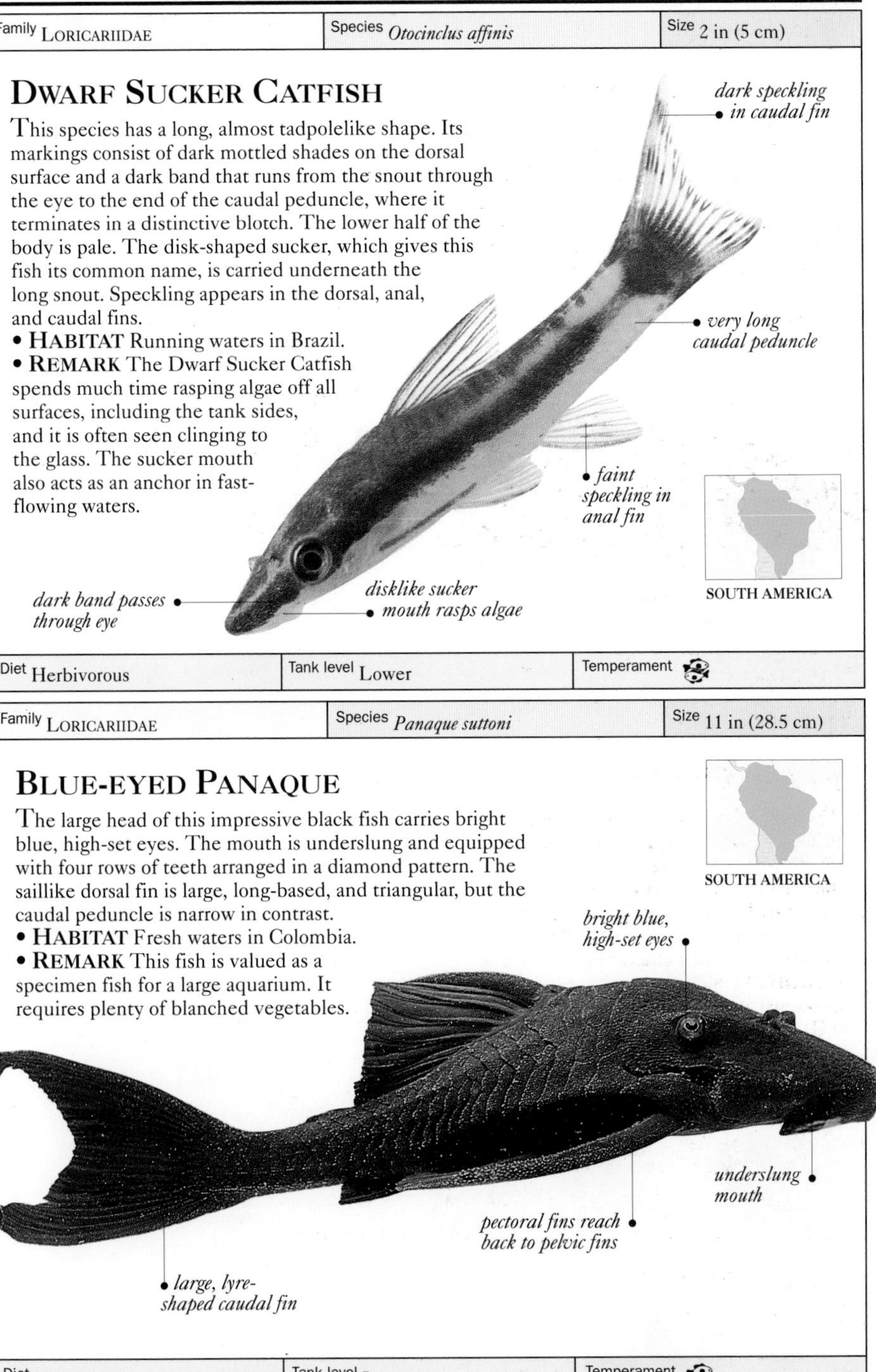

Diet Herbivorous	Tank level Lower	Temperament

Family LORICARIIDAE	Species *Panaque suttoni*	Size 11 in (28.5 cm)

BLUE-EYED PANAQUE

The large head of this impressive black fish carries bright blue, high-set eyes. The mouth is underslung and equipped with four rows of teeth arranged in a diamond pattern. The saillike dorsal fin is large, long-based, and triangular, but the caudal peduncle is narrow in contrast.

- **HABITAT** Fresh waters in Colombia.
- **REMARK** This fish is valued as a specimen fish for a large aquarium. It requires plenty of blanched vegetables.

Diet Herbivorous	Tank level Lower	Temperament

Family LORICARIIDAE	Species *Peckoltia pulcher*	Size 4 in (10 cm)

PRETTY PECKOLTIA

Narrow pale gray vertical bands cross the blue-black body of this species. The mottled coloration continues into all fins. The bony scutes, which replace scales, often carry bristles. When held erect, the dorsal fin is flaglike. Pectoral and pelvic fins are winglike, and the caudal fin is forked and terminates in sharp tips that make it almost lyre-shaped. The underslung mouth forms a sucker disk.

• **HABITAT** Negro River, Amazonia.

• **REMARK** This attractive species is a useful algae-eater and a good community fish, although it does require space.

Diet Herbivorous	Tank level Lower	Temperament 

Family PIMELODIDAE	Species *Phractocephalus hemiliopterus*	Size 47 in (120 cm)

RED-TAILED CATFISH

The upper part of this bulky fish, including the top lip, is gray-black with small, darker specklings. The lower body, including the lower lip and three pairs of long barbels, is white. The distinguishing orange-red caudal fin is spadelike and rounded. Juveniles, as seen here, may be more intensely colored.

• **HABITAT** Widespread throughout the Amazonian areas of Peru, Guyana, and Brazil.

• **REMARK** The adult form is more suitable for the public aquarium. It feeds heavily on live and dead fishes and other meat, and eventually outgrows even the largest home aquarium. Although it preys on smaller fish, it has a peaceful disposition.

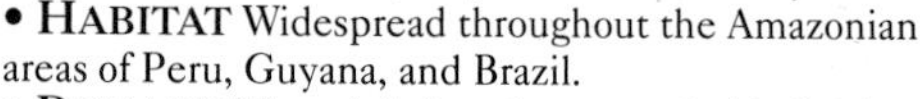

Diet Omnivorous	Tank levels Middle and lower	Temperament 

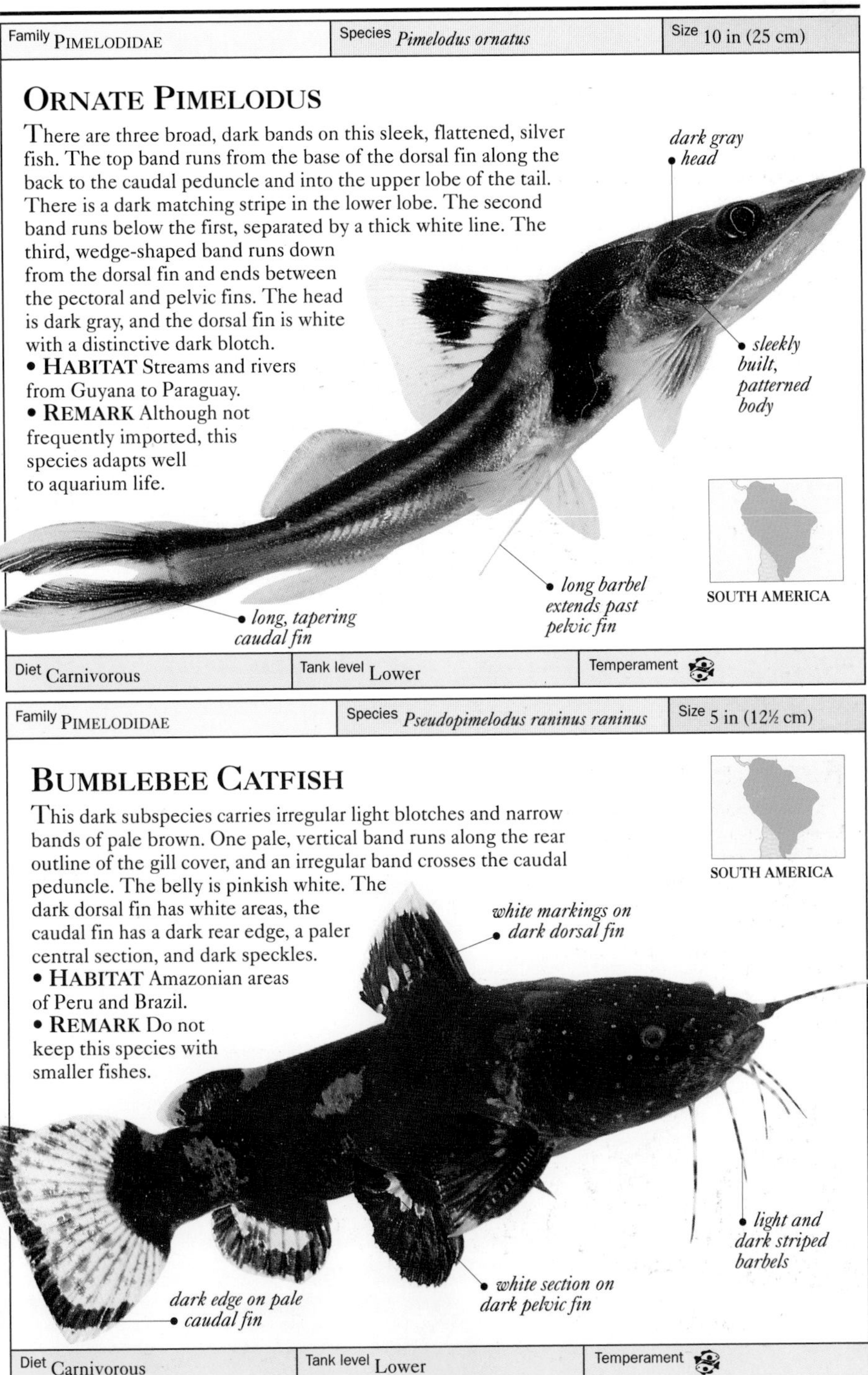

Family PIMELODIDAE	Species *Pimelodus ornatus*	Size 10 in (25 cm)

ORNATE PIMELODUS

There are three broad, dark bands on this sleek, flattened, silver fish. The top band runs from the base of the dorsal fin along the back to the caudal peduncle and into the upper lobe of the tail. There is a dark matching stripe in the lower lobe. The second band runs below the first, separated by a thick white line. The third, wedge-shaped band runs down from the dorsal fin and ends between the pectoral and pelvic fins. The head is dark gray, and the dorsal fin is white with a distinctive dark blotch.

- **HABITAT** Streams and rivers from Guyana to Paraguay.
- **REMARK** Although not frequently imported, this species adapts well to aquarium life.

Diet Carnivorous	Tank level Lower	Temperament

Family PIMELODIDAE	Species *Pseudopimelodus raninus raninus*	Size 5 in (12½ cm)

BUMBLEBEE CATFISH

This dark subspecies carries irregular light blotches and narrow bands of pale brown. One pale, vertical band runs along the rear outline of the gill cover, and an irregular band crosses the caudal peduncle. The belly is pinkish white. The dark dorsal fin has white areas, the caudal fin has a dark rear edge, a paler central section, and dark speckles.

- **HABITAT** Amazonian areas of Peru and Brazil.
- **REMARK** Do not keep this species with smaller fishes.

Diet Carnivorous	Tank level Lower	Temperament

Family PIMELODIDAE	Species *Pseudoplatystoma fasciata*	Size 35 in (90 cm)

TIGER SHOVELNOSE CATFISH

Dark gray on the dorsal surface of this catfish leads down to silvery white on the belly. Equally spaced dark bands encircle the body vertically, stopping at the ventral surface. The large head is broad and flattened, with a shallow sloping forehead. Speckled fins are surprisingly small. The deeply forked caudal fin is not used in locomotion; instead the body undulates to drive the fish forward at high speed. There are three pairs of highly extended barbels present.

• **HABITAT** Rivers of Venezuela and Peru.

• **REMARK** This nocturnal predatory fish is suitable only for large display aquariums.

Diet Carnivorous	Tank level Lower	Temperament 

Family LORICARIIDAE	Species *Rineloricaria species*	Size 5 in (13 cm)

WHIPTAIL CATFISH

The long filaments on the tail of this species have prompted the popular name. Coloration is brown with distinctive blotches; darker specimens are the most valued. Dark pigment on the first few rays of the dorsal fin separate this fish from its relatives. A sucker-disk formed by the underslung mouth, however, is a common family characteristic. Pectoral and anal fins are speckled. Adult males are slimmer and develop bristles on the head and pectoral fins.

• **HABITAT** Widespread in rivers throughout South America.

• **REMARK** Pieces of plastic pipe make good hiding places and spawning sites.

Catfish coloration merges with surroundings

Diet Herbivorous	Tank level Lower	Temperament 

Family MOCHOKIDAE	Species *Synodontis angelicus*	Size 8 in (20 cm)

ANGELICUS

Juveniles of this species are black and are covered with white spots. In adulthood the body turns dull gray with fewer spots. The adipose fin is typical of the family and carries spots only in the juvenile, as shown here. Sexual differences are apparent solely on the adult: the female has a more rounded body, and the male color may be intensified. A downturned mouth carries three pairs of barbels.

- **HABITAT** Slow-moving waters in Zaire.
- **REMARK** It cannot now be exported from Zaire and has become highly priced.
- **OTHER NAME** Polka-dot Synodontis.

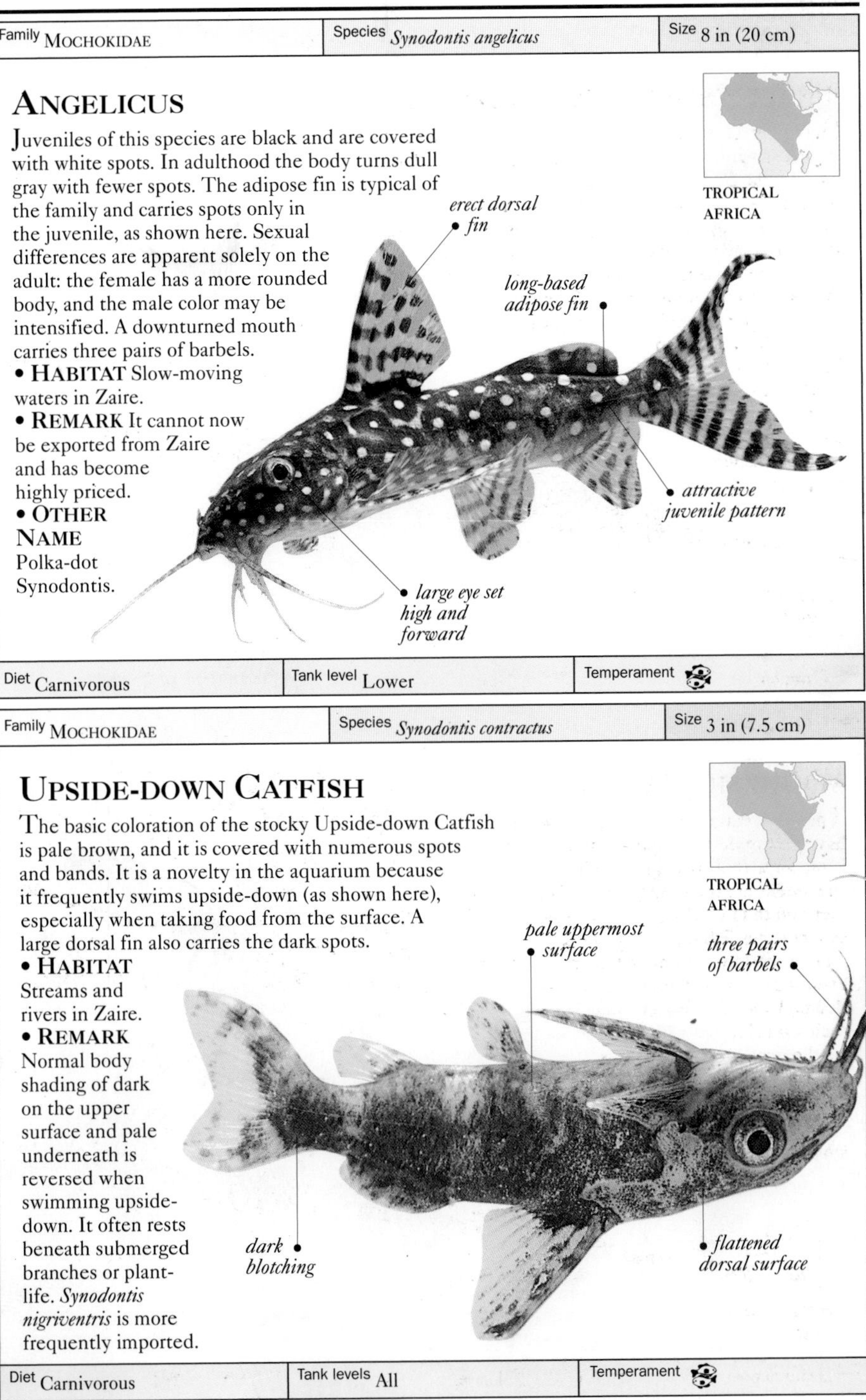

Diet Carnivorous	Tank level Lower	Temperament

Family MOCHOKIDAE	Species *Synodontis contractus*	Size 3 in (7.5 cm)

UPSIDE-DOWN CATFISH

The basic coloration of the stocky Upside-down Catfish is pale brown, and it is covered with numerous spots and bands. It is a novelty in the aquarium because it frequently swims upside-down (as shown here), especially when taking food from the surface. A large dorsal fin also carries the dark spots.

- **HABITAT** Streams and rivers in Zaire.
- **REMARK** Normal body shading of dark on the upper surface and pale underneath is reversed when swimming upside-down. It often rests beneath submerged branches or plant-life. *Synodontis nigriventris* is more frequently imported.

Diet Carnivorous	Tank levels All	Temperament

Family CALLICHTHYIDAE	Species *Brochis splendens*	Size 3¼ in (8 cm)

GREEN CATFISH

Fishes of the *Brochis* genus tend to have stockier bodies than those of the *Corydoras* genus. A more scientific difference between the genera is the number of soft dorsal fin rays – *Brochis* have more than *Corydoras*. Two rows of green-gray iridescent bony scutes are typical of both groups.

• **HABITAT** Sandy streams in the Amazonian basin of Brazil, Ecuador, and Peru.

• **REMARK** If water quality is bad, it may surface to swallow oxygen.

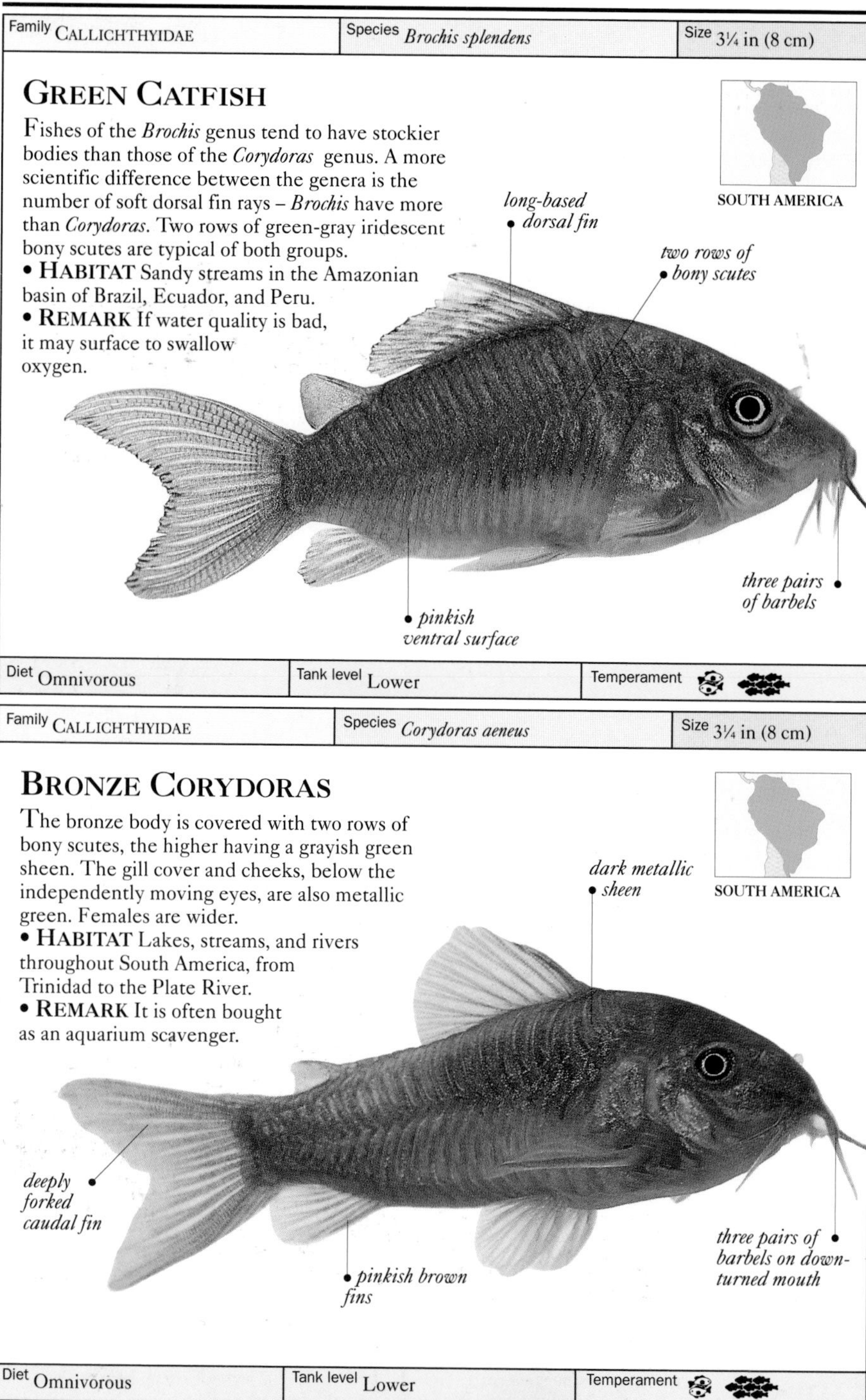

Diet Omnivorous	Tank level Lower	Temperament

Family CALLICHTHYIDAE	Species *Corydoras aeneus*	Size 3¼ in (8 cm)

BRONZE CORYDORAS

The bronze body is covered with two rows of bony scutes, the higher having a grayish green sheen. The gill cover and cheeks, below the independently moving eyes, are also metallic green. Females are wider.

• **HABITAT** Lakes, streams, and rivers throughout South America, from Trinidad to the Plate River.

• **REMARK** It is often bought as an aquarium scavenger.

Diet Omnivorous	Tank level Lower	Temperament

Family CALLICHTHYIDAE	Species *Corydoras barbatus*	Size 3½ in (9 cm)

BEARDED CORYDORAS

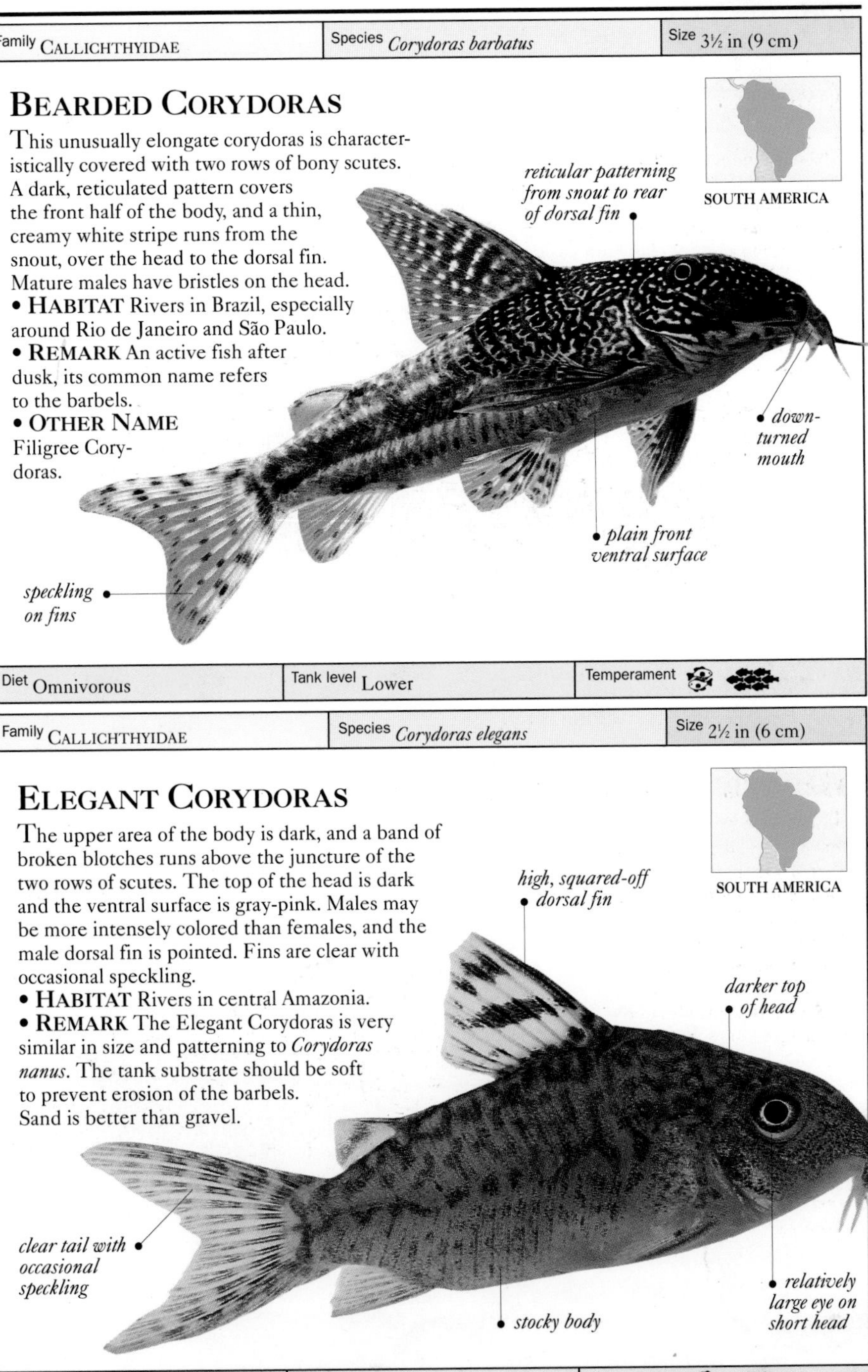

This unusually elongate corydoras is characteristically covered with two rows of bony scutes. A dark, reticulated pattern covers the front half of the body, and a thin, creamy white stripe runs from the snout, over the head to the dorsal fin. Mature males have bristles on the head.

- **HABITAT** Rivers in Brazil, especially around Rio de Janeiro and São Paulo.
- **REMARK** An active fish after dusk, its common name refers to the barbels.
- **OTHER NAME** Filigree Corydoras.

Diet Omnivorous	Tank level Lower	Temperament

Family CALLICHTHYIDAE	Species *Corydoras elegans*	Size 2½ in (6 cm)

ELEGANT CORYDORAS

The upper area of the body is dark, and a band of broken blotches runs above the juncture of the two rows of scutes. The top of the head is dark and the ventral surface is gray-pink. Males may be more intensely colored than females, and the male dorsal fin is pointed. Fins are clear with occasional speckling.

- **HABITAT** Rivers in central Amazonia.
- **REMARK** The Elegant Corydoras is very similar in size and patterning to *Corydoras nanus*. The tank substrate should be soft to prevent erosion of the barbels. Sand is better than gravel.

Diet Omnivorous	Tank level Lower	Temperament

Family CALLICHTHYIDAE	Species *Corydoras haraldshultzi*	Size 3 in (7.5 cm)

HARALD SHULTZ'S CORYDORAS

The rows of bony scutes on this species are masked by a dark reticular pattern. The rounded body is pinky blue-gray with a pale ventral surface. Along the rear flanks, the pattern forms parallel lines; on the head it forms separate dark spots. All fins, except the clear pelvic fins, carry the distinct pattern. Pectoral fins have white leading edges. The dots on the caudal fin give the impression of vertical stripes. There are three pairs of barbels on the downturned mouth.

• **HABITAT** Sandy-bottomed streams in the Amazon basin.

• **REMARK** This species is similar to *Corydoras sterbai*, although the latter fish appears to have more space between the horizontal lines on the flanks.

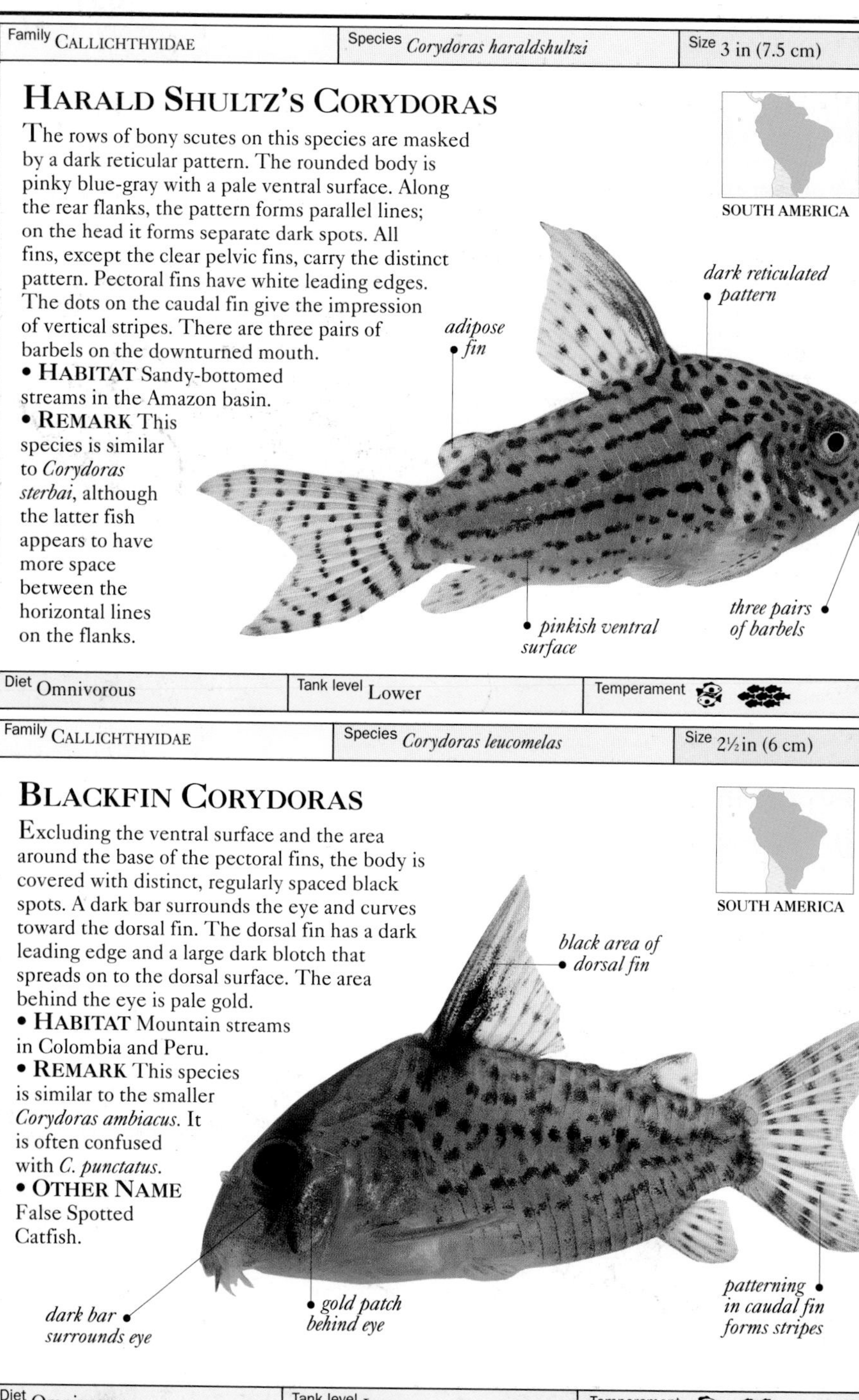

Diet Omnivorous	Tank level Lower	Temperament

Family CALLICHTHYIDAE	Species *Corydoras leucomelas*	Size 2½ in (6 cm)

BLACKFIN CORYDORAS

Excluding the ventral surface and the area around the base of the pectoral fins, the body is covered with distinct, regularly spaced black spots. A dark bar surrounds the eye and curves toward the dorsal fin. The dorsal fin has a dark leading edge and a large dark blotch that spreads on to the dorsal surface. The area behind the eye is pale gold.

• **HABITAT** Mountain streams in Colombia and Peru.

• **REMARK** This species is similar to the smaller *Corydoras ambiacus*. It is often confused with *C. punctatus*.

• **OTHER NAME** False Spotted Catfish.

Diet Omnivorous	Tank level Lower	Temperament

Family CALLICHTHYIDAE	Species *Corydoras napoensis*	Size 2½ in (6 cm)

Napo Corydoras

This golden yellow fish is covered by dark dots that connect to form three lines along the flanks. These lines mask the characteristic rows of bony scutes. Occasionally, gold "portholes" appear in the dark areas on the upper part of the body. There is a small gold area in front of the dorsal fin, and the head is covered with a dark, reticulated pattern. Gill covers have a metallic sheen and the throat region is white.

• **HABITAT** Napo River, a western tributary of the Amazon River.

• **REMARK** It is similar to *Corydoras nanus*, but there are slight differences in dorsal fin and body marks.

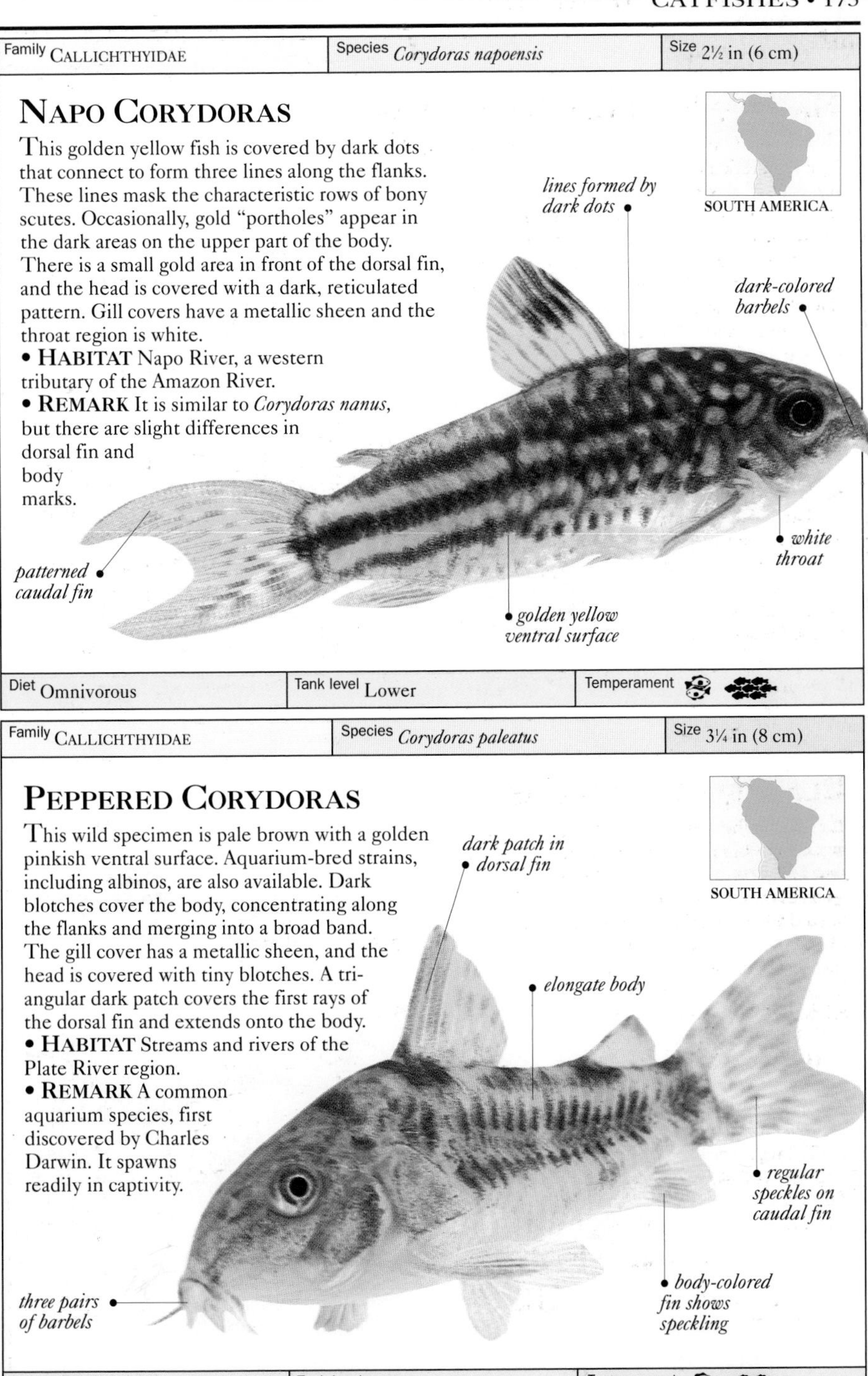

Diet Omnivorous	Tank level Lower	Temperament

Family CALLICHTHYIDAE	Species *Corydoras paleatus*	Size 3¼ in (8 cm)

Peppered Corydoras

This wild specimen is pale brown with a golden pinkish ventral surface. Aquarium-bred strains, including albinos, are also available. Dark blotches cover the body, concentrating along the flanks and merging into a broad band. The gill cover has a metallic sheen, and the head is covered with tiny blotches. A triangular dark patch covers the first rays of the dorsal fin and extends onto the body.

• **HABITAT** Streams and rivers of the Plate River region.

• **REMARK** A common aquarium species, first discovered by Charles Darwin. It spawns readily in captivity.

Diet Omnivorous	Tank level Lower	Temperament

LOACHES

MEMBERS OF THE family Cobitidae are distributed from North Africa to Eurasia and the Pacific Rim. Their mouths carry barbels, and some species have an erectile spine beneath each eye. The ventral surface is flattened as they are bottom-dwellers. Loaches are shy, nocturnal creatures, and they may need to be coaxed into view with their favorite worm-type live food.

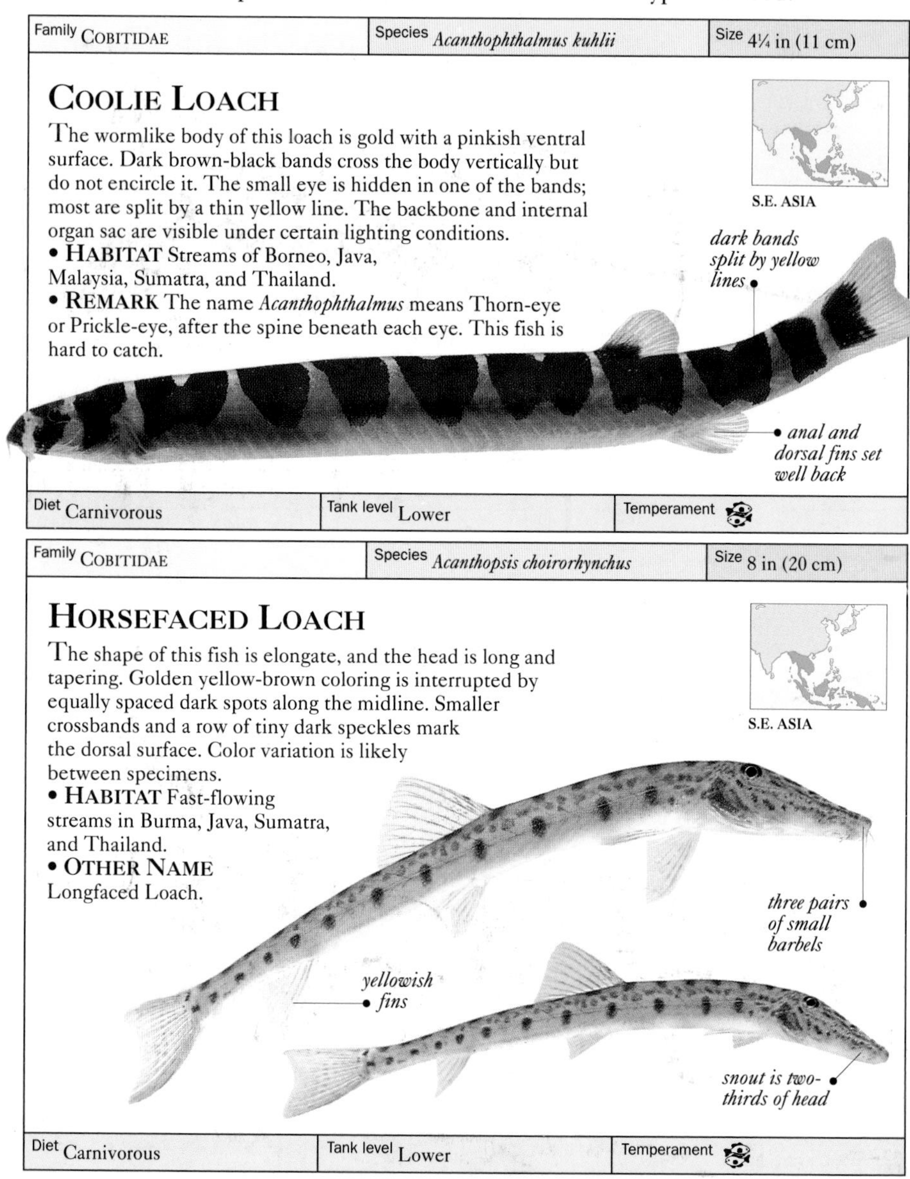

Family COBITIDAE	Species *Acanthophthalmus kuhlii*	Size 4¼ in (11 cm)

COOLIE LOACH

The wormlike body of this loach is gold with a pinkish ventral surface. Dark brown-black bands cross the body vertically but do not encircle it. The small eye is hidden in one of the bands; most are split by a thin yellow line. The backbone and internal organ sac are visible under certain lighting conditions.

- **HABITAT** Streams of Borneo, Java, Malaysia, Sumatra, and Thailand.
- **REMARK** The name *Acanthophthalmus* means Thorn-eye or Prickle-eye, after the spine beneath each eye. This fish is hard to catch.

Diet Carnivorous	Tank level Lower	Temperament

Family COBITIDAE	Species *Acanthopsis choirorhynchus*	Size 8 in (20 cm)

HORSEFACED LOACH

The shape of this fish is elongate, and the head is long and tapering. Golden yellow-brown coloring is interrupted by equally spaced dark spots along the midline. Smaller crossbands and a row of tiny dark speckles mark the dorsal surface. Color variation is likely between specimens.

- **HABITAT** Fast-flowing streams in Burma, Java, Sumatra, and Thailand.
- **OTHER NAME** Longfaced Loach.

Diet Carnivorous	Tank level Lower	Temperament

Family COBITIDAE	Species *Botia horae*	Size 4 in (10 cm)

SKUNK LOACH

The perfectly streamlined body of this loach is creamy gray, with a paler silvery color on the lower flanks and ventral surface. A dark stripe runs the length of the body along the dorsal surface, and a band encircles the caudal peduncle. Scales are very small, and the skin has a matte finish.

- **HABITAT** Streams and rivers in Thailand; also northern India.
- **REMARK** The Skunk Loach normally rests during the day among plants or retreats.
- **OTHER NAME** Hora's Loach; recently re-classified as *Botia morleti*.

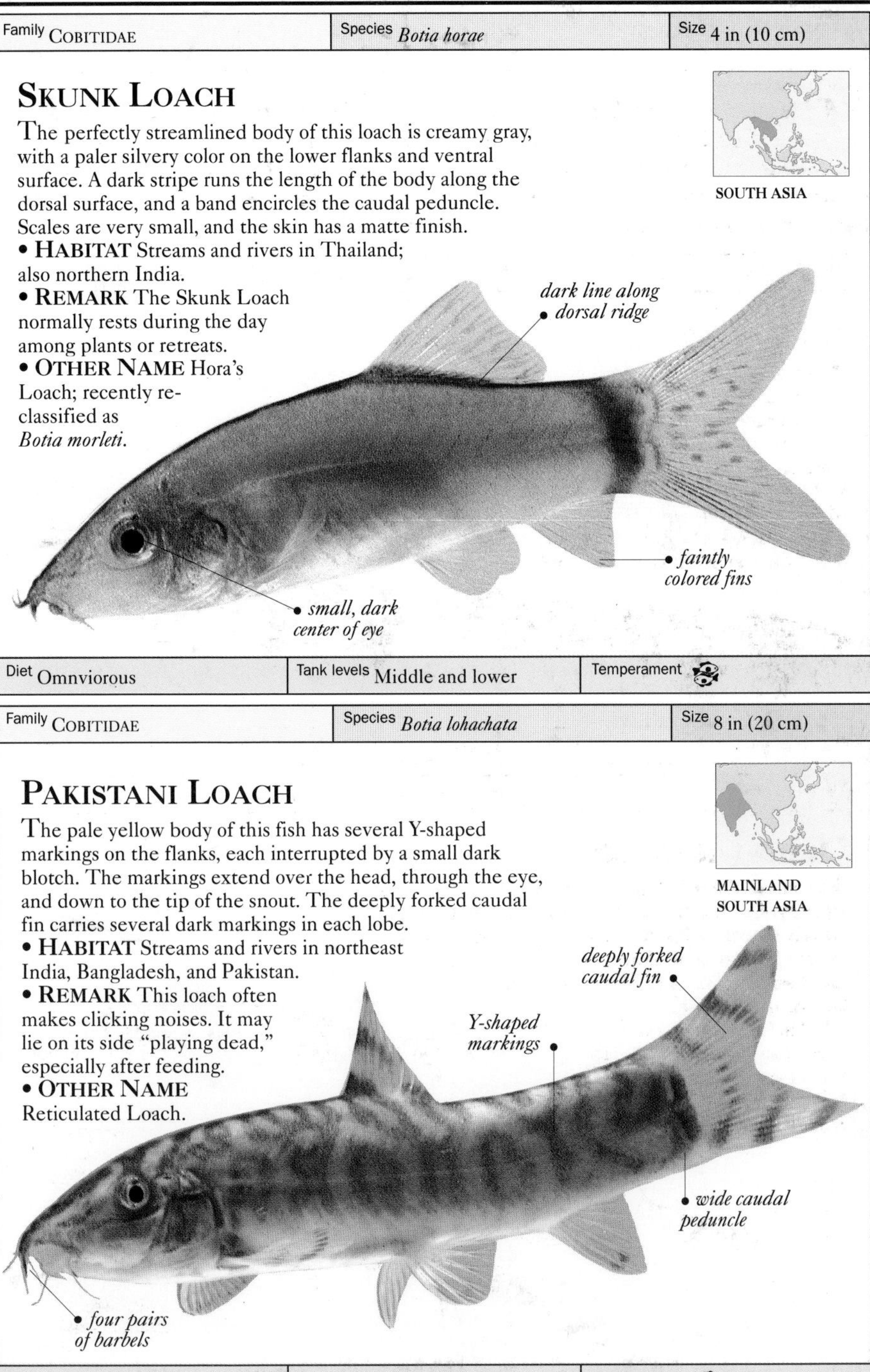

Diet Omnviorous	Tank levels Middle and lower	Temperament

Family COBITIDAE	Species *Botia lohachata*	Size 8 in (20 cm)

PAKISTANI LOACH

The pale yellow body of this fish has several Y-shaped markings on the flanks, each interrupted by a small dark blotch. The markings extend over the head, through the eye, and down to the tip of the snout. The deeply forked caudal fin carries several dark markings in each lobe.

- **HABITAT** Streams and rivers in northeast India, Bangladesh, and Pakistan.
- **REMARK** This loach often makes clicking noises. It may lie on its side "playing dead," especially after feeding.
- **OTHER NAME** Reticulated Loach.

Diet Omnivorous	Tank levels Middle and lower	Temperament

Family COBITIDAE	Species *Botia macracantha*	Size 12 in (30 cm)

CLOWN LOACH

Three black bands cross the orange arched body of this fish. Pectoral, pelvic, and caudal fins are red-orange; the dorsal and anal fins are black with paler edges. Small scales give the fish a very smooth, matte finish. There is an erectile spine in front of the eye, which may snag in an aquarium net.

• **HABITAT** Streams in Indonesia and Sumatra; also Borneo.

• **REMARK** This fish should be kept in numbers with hiding places such as rock caves.

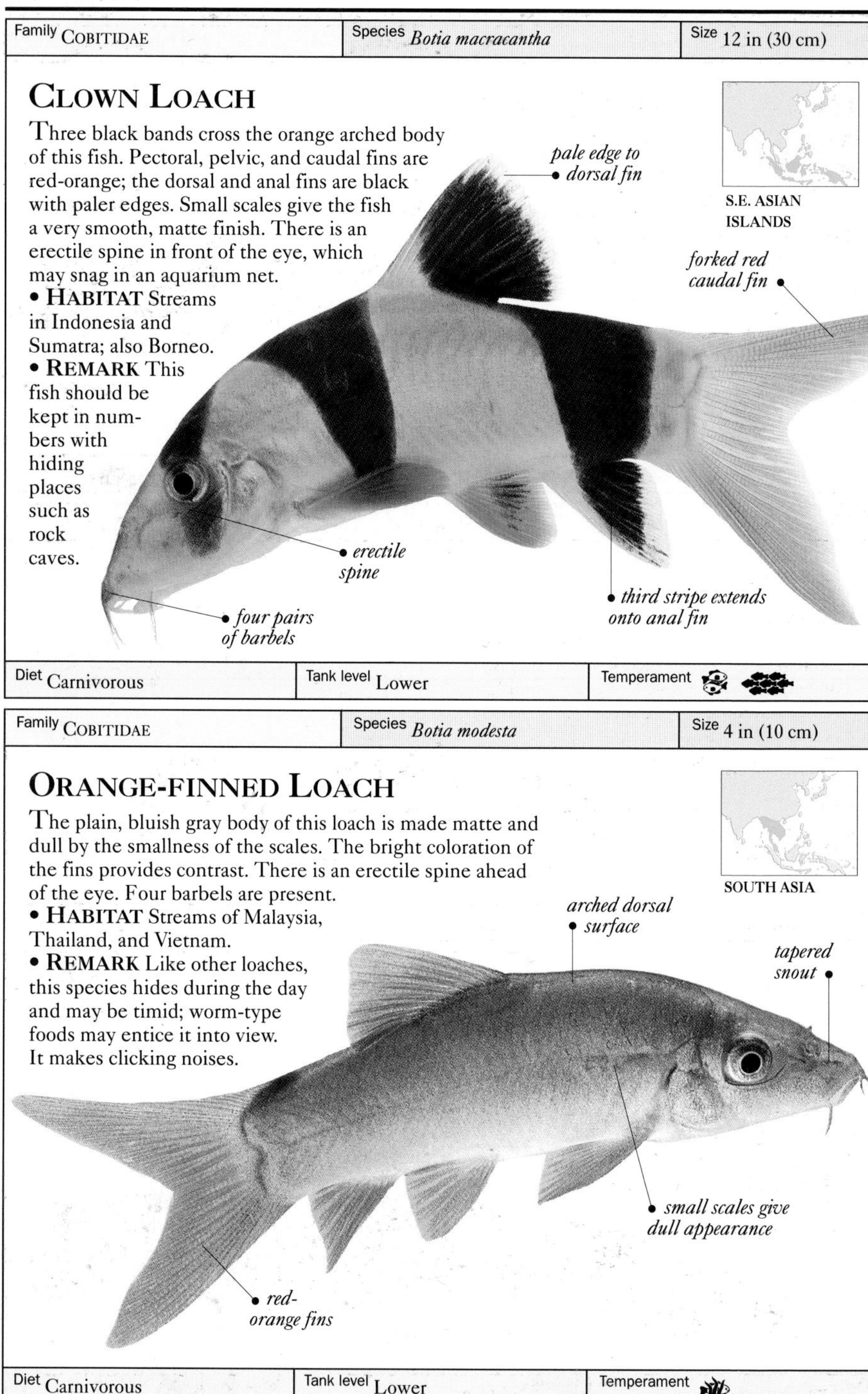

Diet Carnivorous	Tank level Lower	Temperament

Family COBITIDAE	Species *Botia modesta*	Size 4 in (10 cm)

ORANGE-FINNED LOACH

The plain, bluish gray body of this loach is made matte and dull by the smallness of the scales. The bright coloration of the fins provides contrast. There is an erectile spine ahead of the eye. Four barbels are present.

• **HABITAT** Streams of Malaysia, Thailand, and Vietnam.

• **REMARK** Like other loaches, this species hides during the day and may be timid; worm-type foods may entice it into view. It makes clicking noises.

Diet Carnivorous	Tank level Lower	Temperament

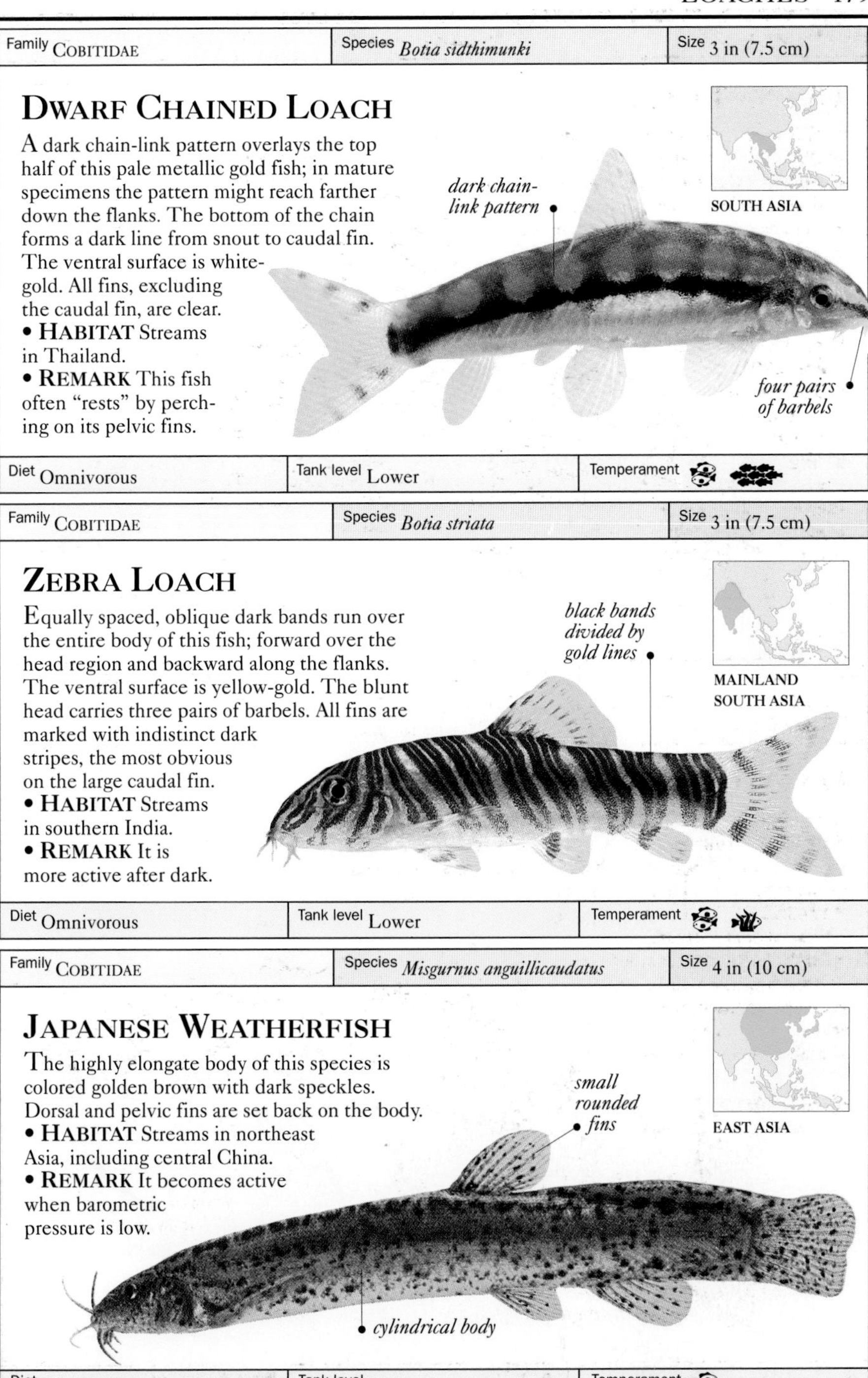

Family COBITIDAE	Species *Botia sidthimunki*	Size 3 in (7.5 cm)

DWARF CHAINED LOACH

A dark chain-link pattern overlays the top half of this pale metallic gold fish; in mature specimens the pattern might reach farther down the flanks. The bottom of the chain forms a dark line from snout to caudal fin. The ventral surface is white-gold. All fins, excluding the caudal fin, are clear.

• **HABITAT** Streams in Thailand.

• **REMARK** This fish often "rests" by perching on its pelvic fins.

Diet Omnivorous	Tank level Lower	Temperament

Family COBITIDAE	Species *Botia striata*	Size 3 in (7.5 cm)

ZEBRA LOACH

Equally spaced, oblique dark bands run over the entire body of this fish; forward over the head region and backward along the flanks. The ventral surface is yellow-gold. The blunt head carries three pairs of barbels. All fins are marked with indistinct dark stripes, the most obvious on the large caudal fin.

• **HABITAT** Streams in southern India.

• **REMARK** It is more active after dark.

Diet Omnivorous	Tank level Lower	Temperament

Family COBITIDAE	Species *Misgurnus anguillicaudatus*	Size 4 in (10 cm)

JAPANESE WEATHERFISH

The highly elongate body of this species is colored golden brown with dark speckles. Dorsal and pelvic fins are set back on the body.

• **HABITAT** Streams in northeast Asia, including central China.

• **REMARK** It becomes active when barometric pressure is low.

Diet Omnivorous	Tank level Lower	Temperament

OTHER TROPICAL EGG-LAYING FISHES

THERE ARE MANY tropical egg-laying fishes that are monotypic (meaning they are the sole species in a genus), and several genera that contain very few species. These smaller, diverse groups, which contain several more unusual fishes, including spiny eels, glassfish, and the rainbowfishes, with two dorsal fins, have been grouped together in the following section.

Family BADIDAE	Species *Badis badis*	Size 2½ in (6.5 cm)

BADIS

MAINLAND SOUTH ASIA

The coloration of this fish is highly variable, as it changes to suit its environment (an alternative popular name is the Dwarf Chameleon Fish). The basic color is brown, which changes to a red and blue speckled pattern on a contented specimen. Females are less brightly colored, especially at breeding times, when male colors intensify dramatically.

• **HABITAT** Still waters in India.

• **REMARK** These secretive spawners stick eggs to cave ceilings after male displays of strength. They prefer live food.

• **OTHER NAME** Formerly classified in the family Nandidae.

long-based dorsal fin contains soft and spiny rays

dark mark on caudal peduncle

anal fin set well back

♀

paler female colors

Diet Carnivorous	Tank level Lower	Temperament

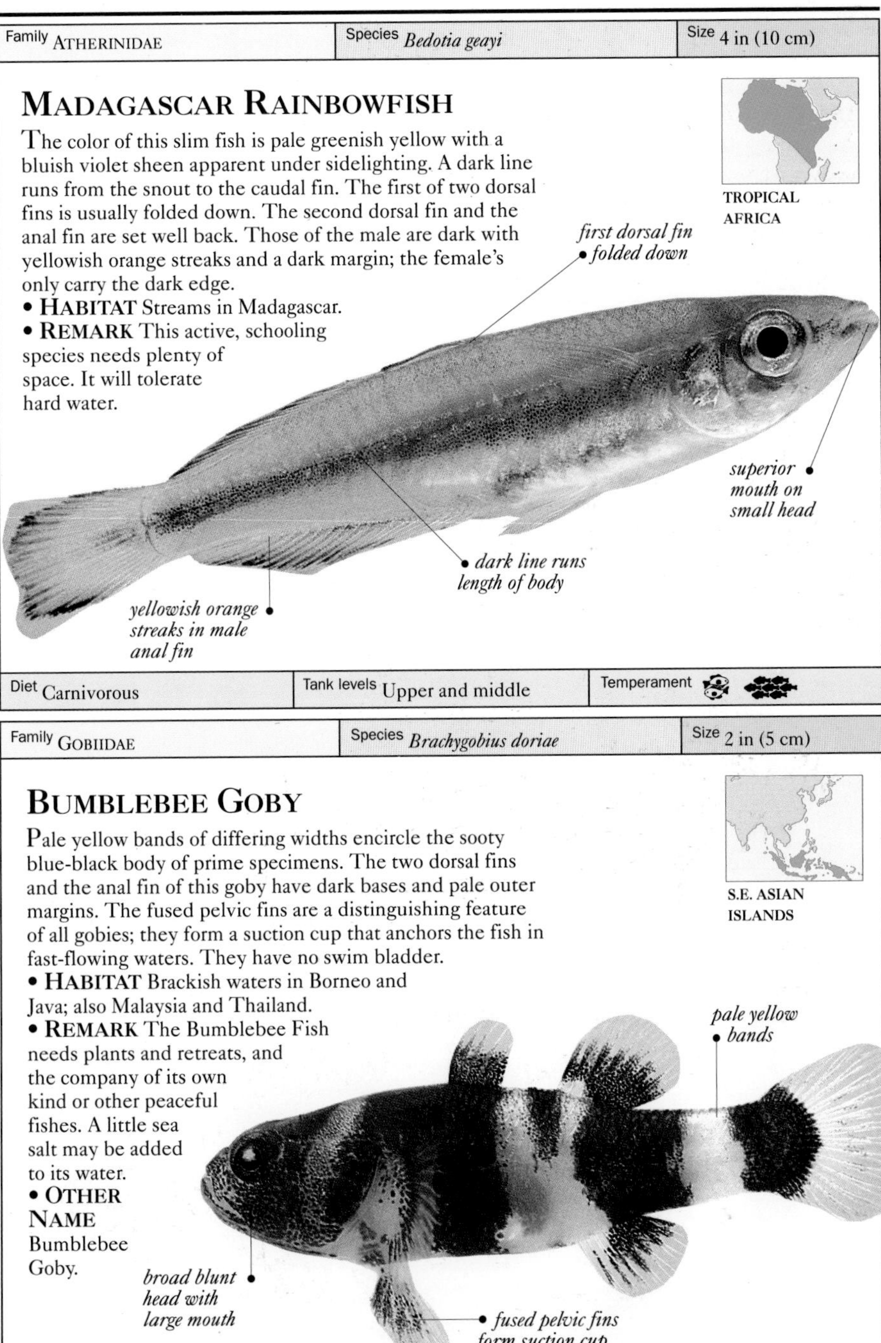

Family ATHERINIDAE	Species *Bedotia geayi*	Size 4 in (10 cm)

MADAGASCAR RAINBOWFISH

The color of this slim fish is pale greenish yellow with a bluish violet sheen apparent under sidelighting. A dark line runs from the snout to the caudal fin. The first of two dorsal fins is usually folded down. The second dorsal fin and the anal fin are set well back. Those of the male are dark with yellowish orange streaks and a dark margin; the female's only carry the dark edge.

• **HABITAT** Streams in Madagascar.

• **REMARK** This active, schooling species needs plenty of space. It will tolerate hard water.

Diet Carnivorous	Tank levels Upper and middle	Temperament

Family GOBIIDAE	Species *Brachygobius doriae*	Size 2 in (5 cm)

BUMBLEBEE GOBY

Pale yellow bands of differing widths encircle the sooty blue-black body of prime specimens. The two dorsal fins and the anal fin of this goby have dark bases and pale outer margins. The fused pelvic fins are a distinguishing feature of all gobies; they form a suction cup that anchors the fish in fast-flowing waters. They have no swim bladder.

• **HABITAT** Brackish waters in Borneo and Java; also Malaysia and Thailand.

• **REMARK** The Bumblebee Fish needs plants and retreats, and the company of its own kind or other peaceful fishes. A little sea salt may be added to its water.

• **OTHER NAME** Bumblebee Goby.

Diet Carnivorous	Tank level Lower	Temperament

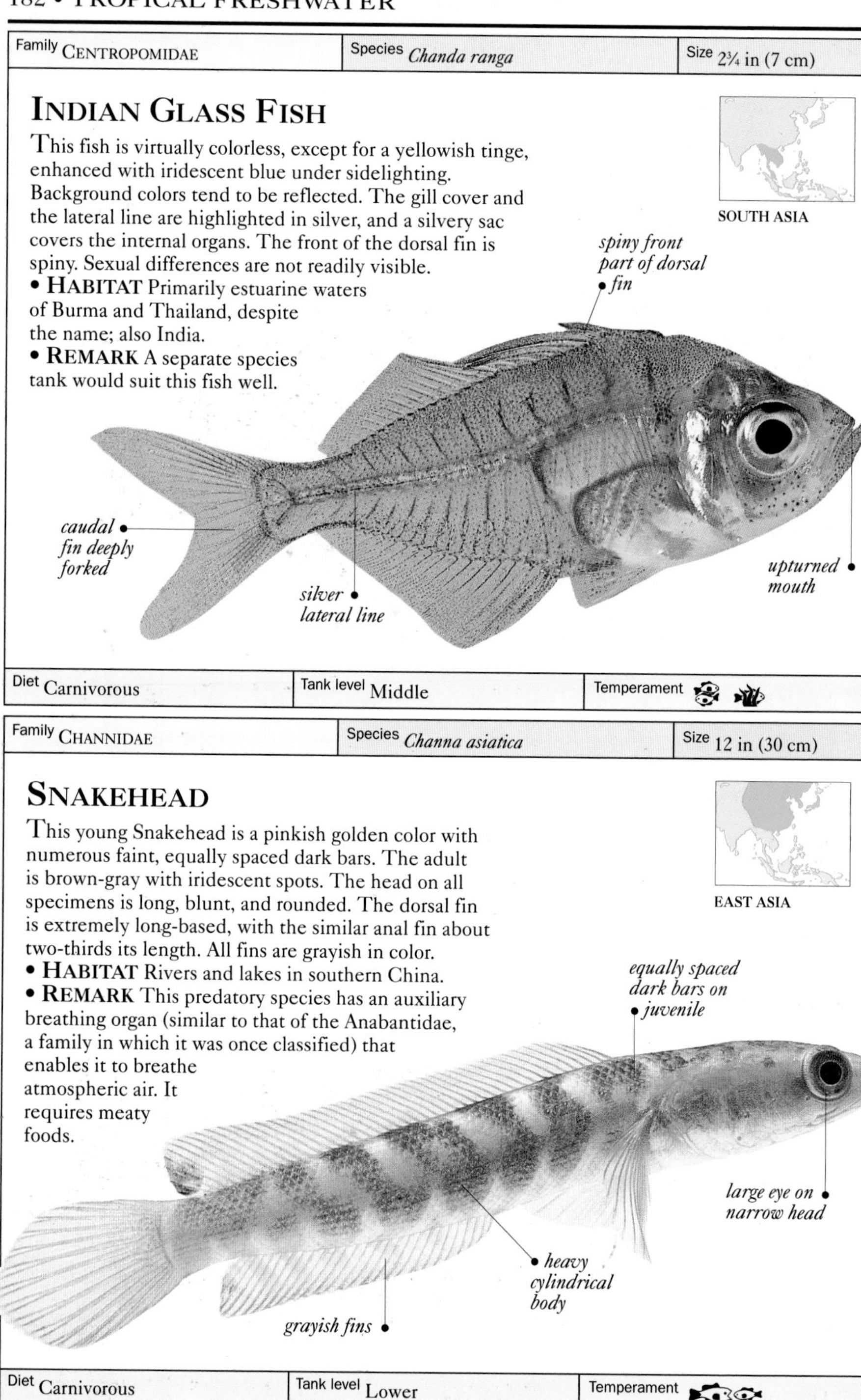

Family CENTROPOMIDAE	Species *Chanda ranga*	Size 2¾ in (7 cm)

INDIAN GLASS FISH

This fish is virtually colorless, except for a yellowish tinge, enhanced with iridescent blue under sidelighting. Background colors tend to be reflected. The gill cover and the lateral line are highlighted in silver, and a silvery sac covers the internal organs. The front of the dorsal fin is spiny. Sexual differences are not readily visible.

• **HABITAT** Primarily estuarine waters of Burma and Thailand, despite the name; also India.

• **REMARK** A separate species tank would suit this fish well.

Diet Carnivorous	Tank level Middle	Temperament

Family CHANNIDAE	Species *Channa asiatica*	Size 12 in (30 cm)

SNAKEHEAD

This young Snakehead is a pinkish golden color with numerous faint, equally spaced dark bars. The adult is brown-gray with iridescent spots. The head on all specimens is long, blunt, and rounded. The dorsal fin is extremely long-based, with the similar anal fin about two-thirds its length. All fins are grayish in color.

• **HABITAT** Rivers and lakes in southern China.

• **REMARK** This predatory species has an auxiliary breathing organ (similar to that of the Anabantidae, a family in which it was once classified) that enables it to breathe atmospheric air. It requires meaty foods.

Diet Carnivorous	Tank level Lower	Temperament

Family LOBOTIDAE	Species *Datnioides microlepis*	Size 16 in (40 cm)

SIAMESE TIGERFISH

SOUTH ASIA

This powerfully built, yellow-brown fish displays several dark vertical bars. A pale, dark-edged stripe runs from the tip of the snout along the forehead to the dorsal fin. The long-based dorsal fin carries continuations of the body bars and has a black edge to its spiny front section; the rear part is clear and soft-rayed. The dark pelvic fins have creamy front edges, and the caudal fin has a dark bar across its base.

• **HABITAT** Streams and rivers in Thailand; also Borneo and Sumatra.

• **REMARK** This predatory species is often found in brackish waters, so some sea salt may be added. It requires a heavily planted tank with retreats, and meaty foods. It eats smaller fishes.

dark vertical bars

anal fin crossed by dark bar

Diet Carnivorous	Tank levels Middle and lower	Temperament

Family MELANOTAENIIDAE	Species *Glossolepis incisus*	Size 6 in (15 cm)

RED RAINBOWFISH

S.E. ASIAN ISLANDS

The snout is notably pointed on this silver-orange species. Coloration on perfect male specimens is distinguished by unevenly distributed silver scales with bright red edges. Two dorsal fins are evident, the second one larger. The male has a more highly arched back, and the slimmer female, as shown here, is silver-green in color.

• **HABITAT** Lake Sentani in northern Papua New Guinea.

• **REMARK** This species is a schooling fish and should be kept with other rainbowfishes. It tolerates hard water.

larger second dorsal fin

♀

pale silver-green female coloration

pointed snout

long-based anal fin

Diet Omnivorous	Tank level Middle	Temperament

Family MORMYRIDAE	Species *Gnathonemus petersi*	Size 9 in (23 cm)

LONGNOSED ELEPHANT FISH

The head of this species is approximately a quarter of the body length. The fingerlike lower jaw is unusually extended, giving rise to the common name. The long head is balanced by a long, narrow caudal peduncle. Coloration is very dark gray, with two whitish, bracket-shaped marks on the flanks between the dorsal and anal fins, which are set very far back on the body. The narrow caudal fin is deeply forked. Pectoral fins are flipperlike, and the pelvic fins are small.

- **HABITAT** Rivers in Nigeria, Cameroon, and Zaire.
- **REMARK** This nocturnal species emits electrical impulses that enable it to navigate in the dark or in muddy waters. It is highly sensitive to water quality changes and has been used to monitor water quality in industrial contexts.
- **OTHER NAMES** Peter's Elephant-nose.

deeply forked caudal fin

long, narrow caudal peduncle

long-based anal fin is set well back

bracket-shaped whitish mark on flank

long, finger-like lower jaw

The jaw extension is used to plow for food in the substrate

TROPICAL AFRICA

Diet Carnivorous	Tank level Lower	Temperament

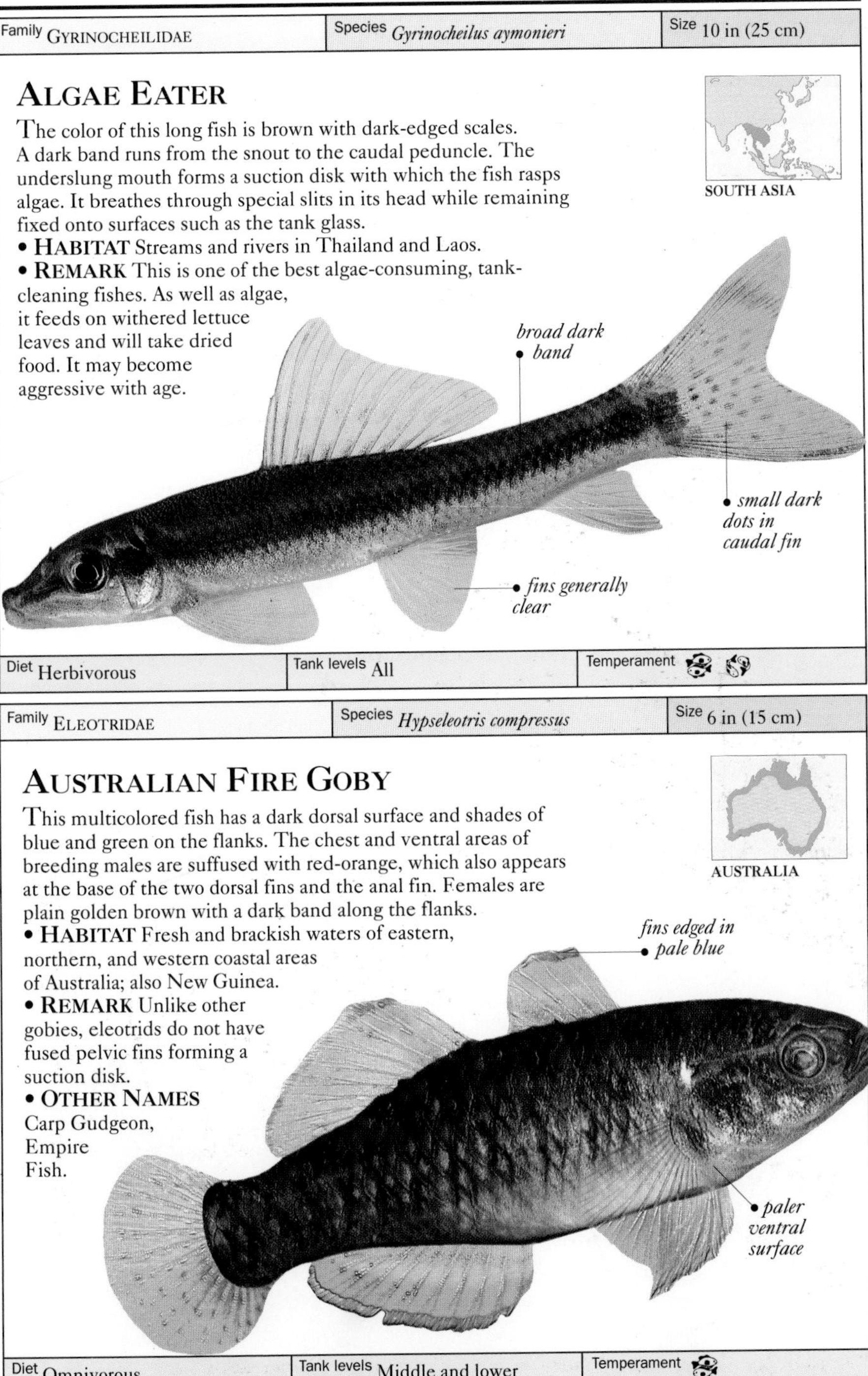

Family GYRINOCHEILIDAE	Species *Gyrinocheilus aymonieri*	Size 10 in (25 cm)

ALGAE EATER

The color of this long fish is brown with dark-edged scales. A dark band runs from the snout to the caudal peduncle. The underslung mouth forms a suction disk with which the fish rasps algae. It breathes through special slits in its head while remaining fixed onto surfaces such as the tank glass.

- **HABITAT** Streams and rivers in Thailand and Laos.
- **REMARK** This is one of the best algae-consuming, tank-cleaning fishes. As well as algae, it feeds on withered lettuce leaves and will take dried food. It may become aggressive with age.

Diet Herbivorous	Tank levels All	Temperament

Family ELEOTRIDAE	Species *Hypseleotris compressus*	Size 6 in (15 cm)

AUSTRALIAN FIRE GOBY

This multicolored fish has a dark dorsal surface and shades of blue and green on the flanks. The chest and ventral areas of breeding males are suffused with red-orange, which also appears at the base of the two dorsal fins and the anal fin. Females are plain golden brown with a dark band along the flanks.

- **HABITAT** Fresh and brackish waters of eastern, northern, and western coastal areas of Australia; also New Guinea.
- **REMARK** Unlike other gobies, eleotrids do not have fused pelvic fins forming a suction disk.
- **OTHER NAMES** Carp Gudgeon, Empire Fish.

Diet Omnivorous	Tank levels Middle and lower	Temperament

Family MELANOTAENIIDAE	Species *Iriatherina werneri*	Size 1½ in (4 cm)

THREADFIN RAINBOWFISH

S.E. ASIAN ISLANDS

The highly elongated fins are the most attractive feature of the Threadfin Rainbowfish. The round-tipped first dorsal fin is held high, and the second contains sooty black, threadlike rays. Pelvic fins are also black and threadlike, and the anal fin carries black extensions. The lyre-shaped caudal fin has rays trailing from the tips. The basic body coloration of mature specimens is golden brown-silver, with a bluish shine on the dorsal ridge. They also carry fine, reddish brown vertical lines.

• **HABITAT** Still waters in swamps and rivers in Papua New Guinea; also northern Australia.

• **REMARK** Should be kept in small groups in slightly soft, acid water, especially when breeding. Eggs can be laid in bushy plants or synthetic yarn mops, and should be hatched separately.

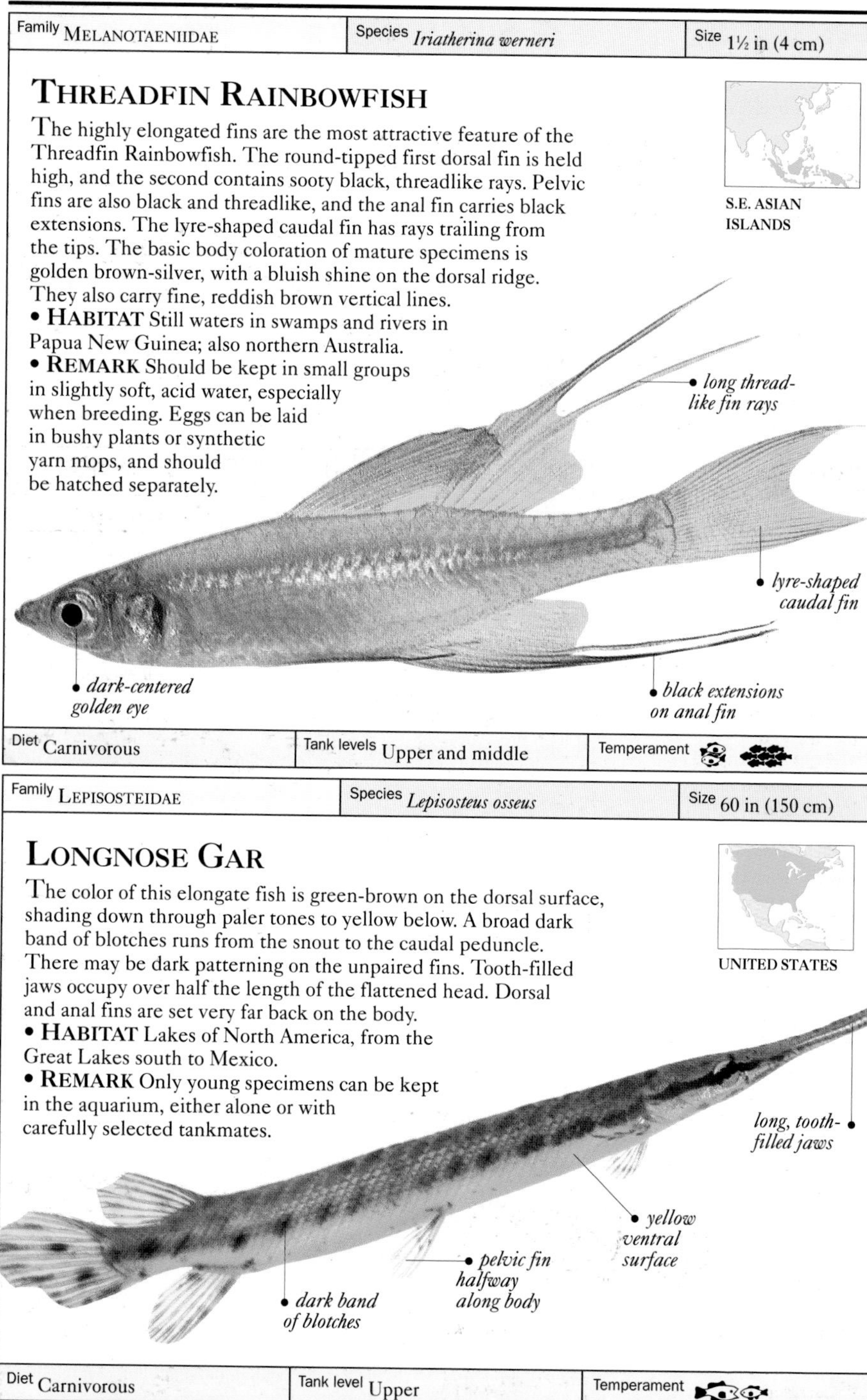

Diet Carnivorous	Tank levels Upper and middle	Temperament

Family LEPISOSTEIDAE	Species *Lepisosteus osseus*	Size 60 in (150 cm)

LONGNOSE GAR

UNITED STATES

The color of this elongate fish is green-brown on the dorsal surface, shading down through paler tones to yellow below. A broad dark band of blotches runs from the snout to the caudal peduncle. There may be dark patterning on the unpaired fins. Tooth-filled jaws occupy over half the length of the flattened head. Dorsal and anal fins are set very far back on the body.

• **HABITAT** Lakes of North America, from the Great Lakes south to Mexico.

• **REMARK** Only young specimens can be kept in the aquarium, either alone or with carefully selected tankmates.

Diet Carnivorous	Tank level Upper	Temperament

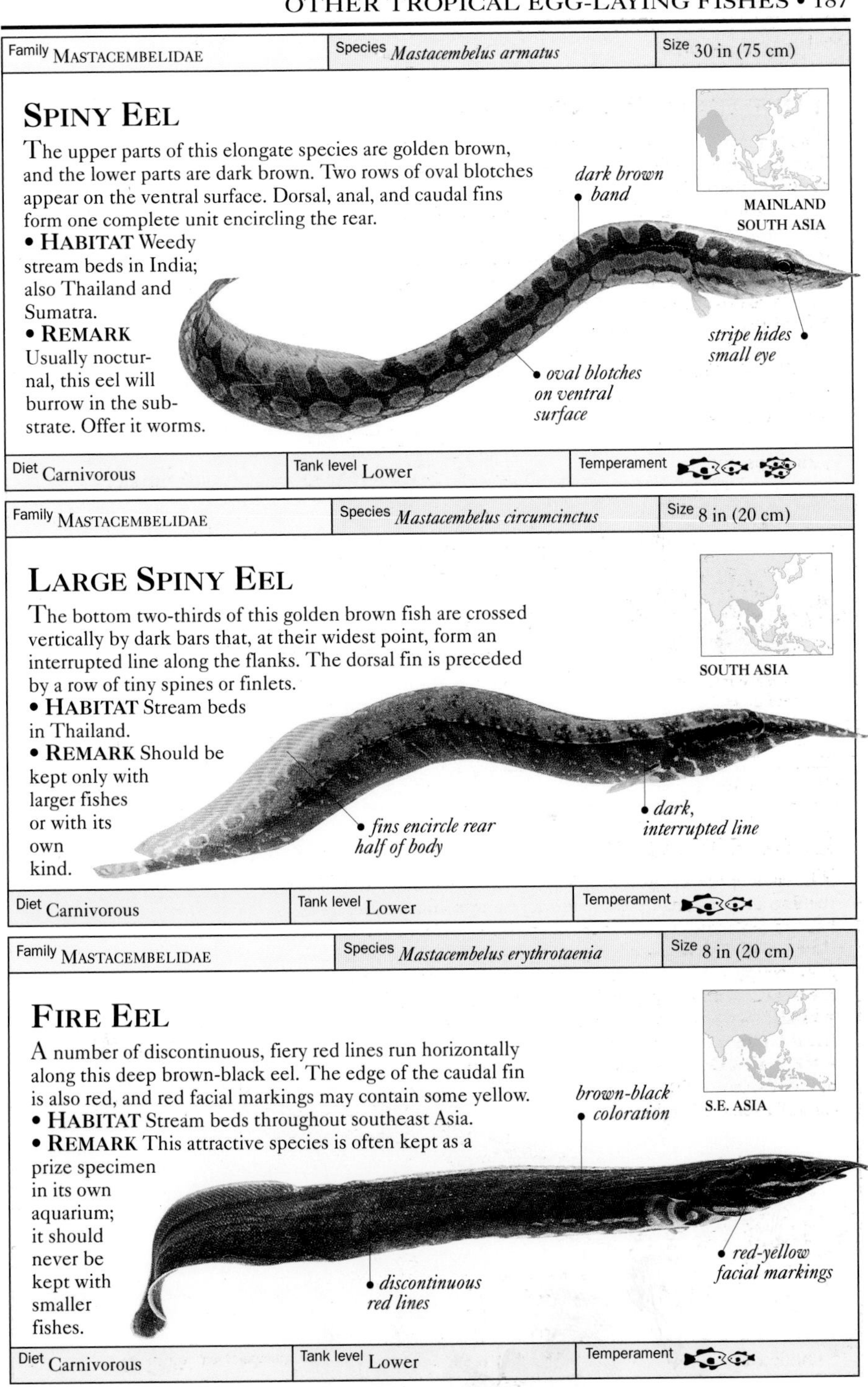

Family MASTACEMBELIDAE	Species *Mastacembelus armatus*	Size 30 in (75 cm)

SPINY EEL

The upper parts of this elongate species are golden brown, and the lower parts are dark brown. Two rows of oval blotches appear on the ventral surface. Dorsal, anal, and caudal fins form one complete unit encircling the rear.

• **HABITAT** Weedy stream beds in India; also Thailand and Sumatra.

• **REMARK** Usually nocturnal, this eel will burrow in the substrate. Offer it worms.

Diet Carnivorous	Tank level Lower	Temperament

Family MASTACEMBELIDAE	Species *Mastacembelus circumcinctus*	Size 8 in (20 cm)

LARGE SPINY EEL

The bottom two-thirds of this golden brown fish are crossed vertically by dark bars that, at their widest point, form an interrupted line along the flanks. The dorsal fin is preceded by a row of tiny spines or finlets.

• **HABITAT** Stream beds in Thailand.

• **REMARK** Should be kept only with larger fishes or with its own kind.

Diet Carnivorous	Tank level Lower	Temperament

Family MASTACEMBELIDAE	Species *Mastacembelus erythrotaenia*	Size 8 in (20 cm)

FIRE EEL

A number of discontinuous, fiery red lines run horizontally along this deep brown-black eel. The edge of the caudal fin is also red, and red facial markings may contain some yellow.

• **HABITAT** Stream beds throughout southeast Asia.

• **REMARK** This attractive species is often kept as a prize specimen in its own aquarium; it should never be kept with smaller fishes.

Diet Carnivorous	Tank level Lower	Temperament

Family MELANOTAENIIDAE	Species *Melanotaenia boesmani*	Size 4 in (10 cm)

BOESMAN'S RAINBOWFISH

The front part of the two-toned body is grayish blue, the rear plain yellow. Like most rainbowfishes, Boesman's has two separate dorsal fins. The rear dorsal fin and the anal fin are pale-edged and long-based, sharing the yellow coloration of the caudal fin. Males are generally more colorful.

- **HABITAT** Streams and lakes in Papua New Guinea.
- **REMARK** This fish prefers hard, fairly alkaline water.
- **OTHER NAME** Formerly classified in the family Atherinidae.

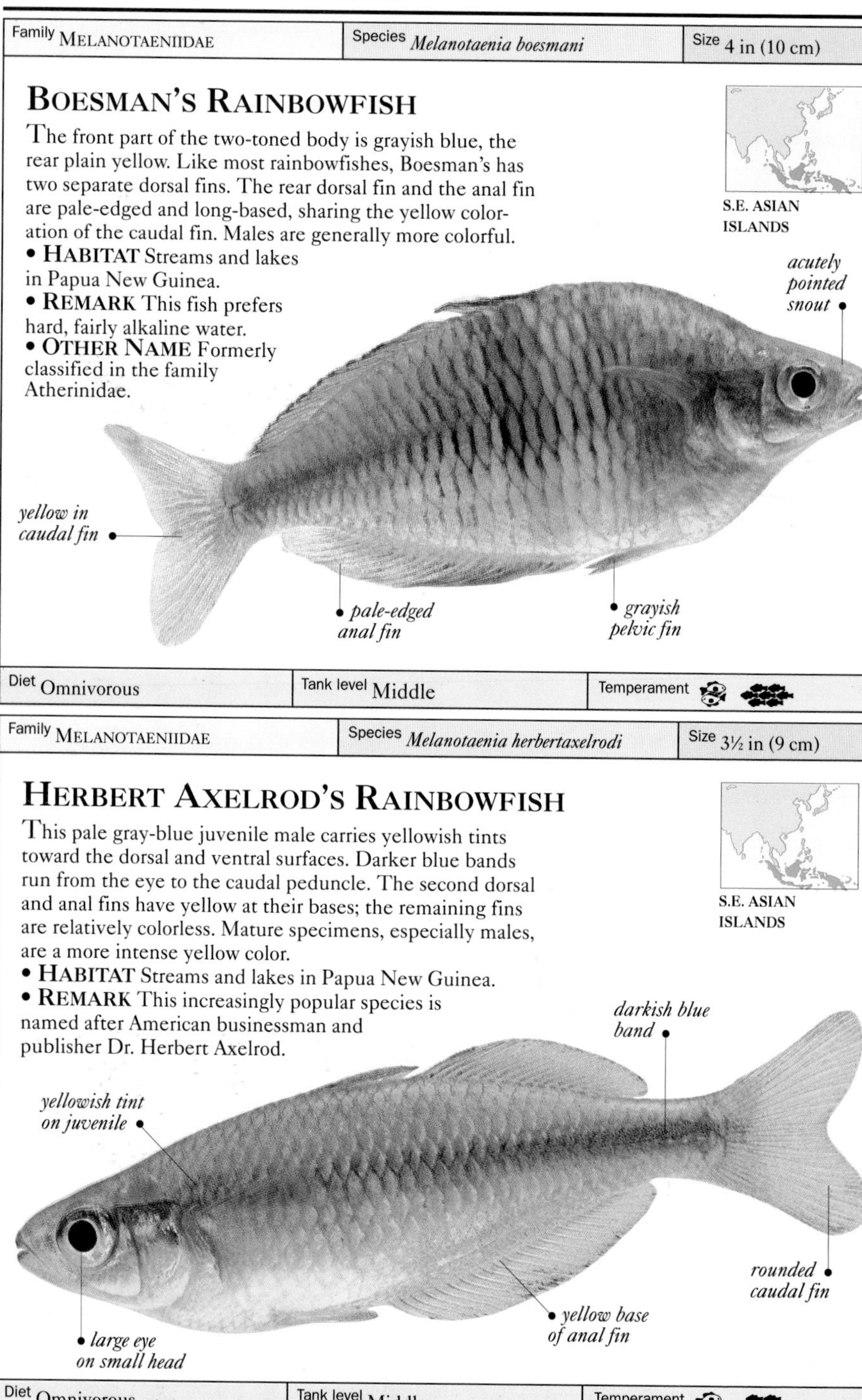

Diet Omnivorous	Tank level Middle	Temperament

Family MELANOTAENIIDAE	Species *Melanotaenia herbertaxelrodi*	Size 3½ in (9 cm)

HERBERT AXELROD'S RAINBOWFISH

This pale gray-blue juvenile male carries yellowish tints toward the dorsal and ventral surfaces. Darker blue bands run from the eye to the caudal peduncle. The second dorsal and anal fins have yellow at their bases; the remaining fins are relatively colorless. Mature specimens, especially males, are a more intense yellow color.

- **HABITAT** Streams and lakes in Papua New Guinea.
- **REMARK** This increasingly popular species is named after American businessman and publisher Dr. Herbert Axelrod.

Diet Omnivorous	Tank level Middle	Temperament

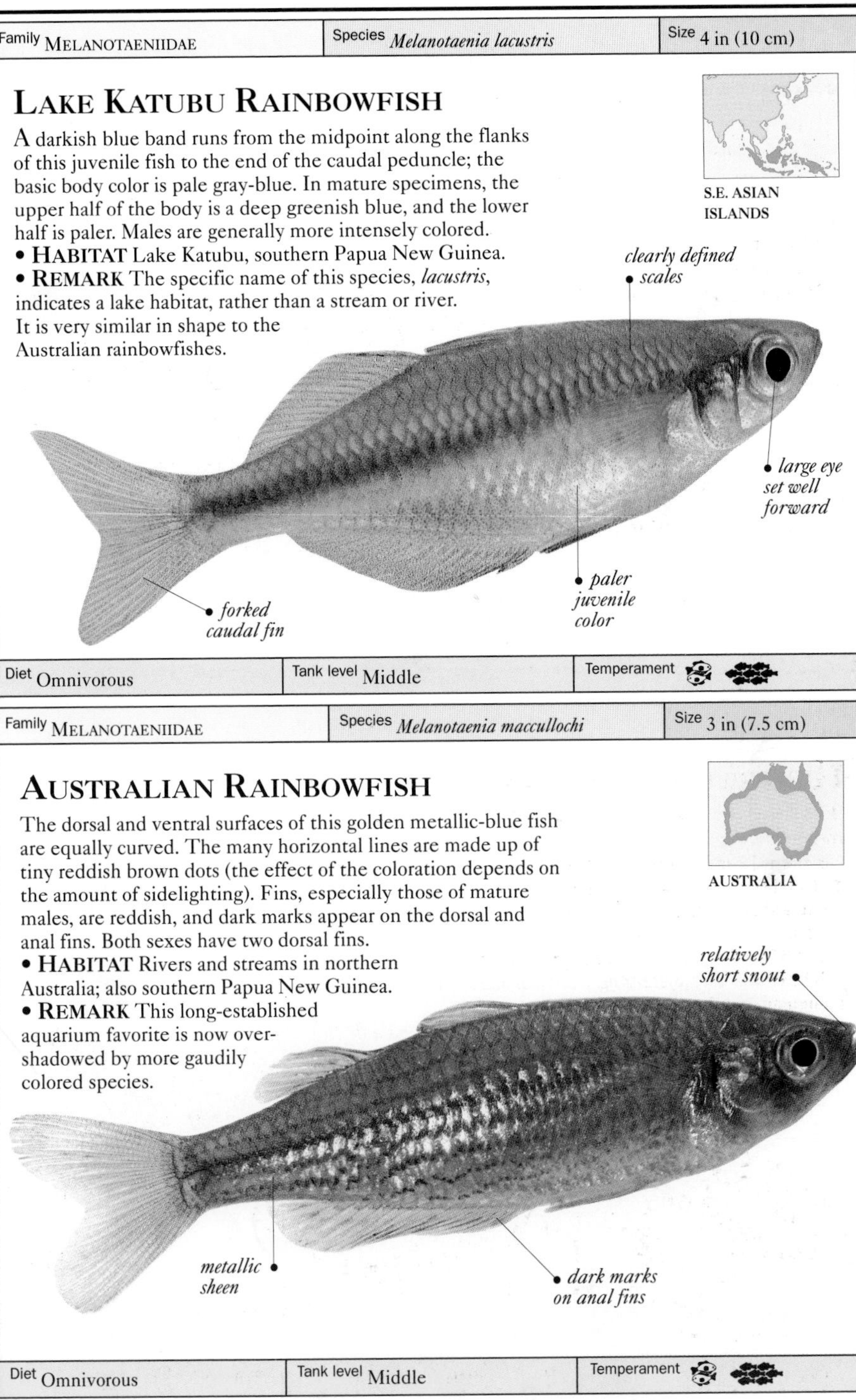

Family MELANOTAENIIDAE	Species *Melanotaenia lacustris*	Size 4 in (10 cm)

LAKE KATUBU RAINBOWFISH

A darkish blue band runs from the midpoint along the flanks of this juvenile fish to the end of the caudal peduncle; the basic body color is pale gray-blue. In mature specimens, the upper half of the body is a deep greenish blue, and the lower half is paler. Males are generally more intensely colored.

• **HABITAT** Lake Katubu, southern Papua New Guinea.

• **REMARK** The specific name of this species, *lacustris*, indicates a lake habitat, rather than a stream or river. It is very similar in shape to the Australian rainbowfishes.

Diet Omnivorous	Tank level Middle	Temperament

Family MELANOTAENIIDAE	Species *Melanotaenia maccullochi*	Size 3 in (7.5 cm)

AUSTRALIAN RAINBOWFISH

The dorsal and ventral surfaces of this golden metallic-blue fish are equally curved. The many horizontal lines are made up of tiny reddish brown dots (the effect of the coloration depends on the amount of sidelighting). Fins, especially those of mature males, are reddish, and dark marks appear on the dorsal and anal fins. Both sexes have two dorsal fins.

• **HABITAT** Rivers and streams in northern Australia; also southern Papua New Guinea.

• **REMARK** This long-established aquarium favorite is now overshadowed by more gaudily colored species.

Diet Omnivorous	Tank level Middle	Temperament

Family MELANOTAENIIDAE	Species *Melanotaenia splendida*	Size 5 in (12½ cm)

CHECKERED RAINBOWFISH

AUSTRALIA

This silvery violet fish has rows of thin, reddish brown stripes, which are formed by the darker-colored edges of the scales. Under sidelighting, colors may vary to include metallic blue-greens. The head is pointed, and the eye is set forward. There are two distinct dorsal fins. All fins are speckled with reddish brown dots. Males may have more red in the lower body.

- **HABITAT** Streams and rivers around the Gulf of Carpentaria, northern Australia.
- **REMARK** These active fish require plenty of space.

reddish brown stripes

silvery violet body coloration

reddish brown speckles on fins

♀

Diet Omnivorous	Tank levels Upper and middle	Temperament

Family MELANOTAENIIDAE	Species *Melanotaenia fluviatilis*	Size 5 in (12½ cm)

AUSTRALIAN RAINBOWFISH

AUSTRALIA

The silvery violet body of this rainbowfish may include yellow and blue hues. Rows of thin horizontal stripes are formed by the darker edges of the scales. The ventral surface is silvery. Dorsal, anal, and caudal fins are streaked with reddish brown, and other fins may have reddish brown speckles. The dorsal fin is in two sections.

- **HABITAT** Streams and rivers around the northeast coast of Australia.
- **REMARK** These active fish are good jumpers and require plenty of swimming space.

narrow caudal peduncle

marked indent in profile

long-based anal fin has reddish brown streaks

Diet Omnivorous	Tank levels Upper and middle	Temperament  

Family NANDIDAE	Species *Monocirrhus polyacanthus*	Size 4 in (10 cm)

SOUTH AMERICAN LEAF FISH

The color of this fish varies according to its surroundings. It is generally golden brown, with darker brown irregular blotches, which give the appearance of a decaying leaf. The mouth is very large and can be opened out to form a "funnel" for consuming food. A thin, dark horizontal line crosses the flanks, and there are two similar dark lines on the head that make a V shape, with the eye at their forward meeting point. The long-based dorsal fin is spiny, and the caudal fin is often held closed when swimming in the characteristic head-down position.

• **HABITAT** Streams and rivers of Amazonia and Guyana.

• **REMARK** This species drifts up to unsuspecting prey disguised as a dead leaf and then engulfs its victim using its protruding mouth. It requires many plants in which to lurk and plenty of fishes on which it can prey. Eggs are laid on flat surfaces, and the fry must be well fed on live foods.

Long chin growth resembles a leaf stem

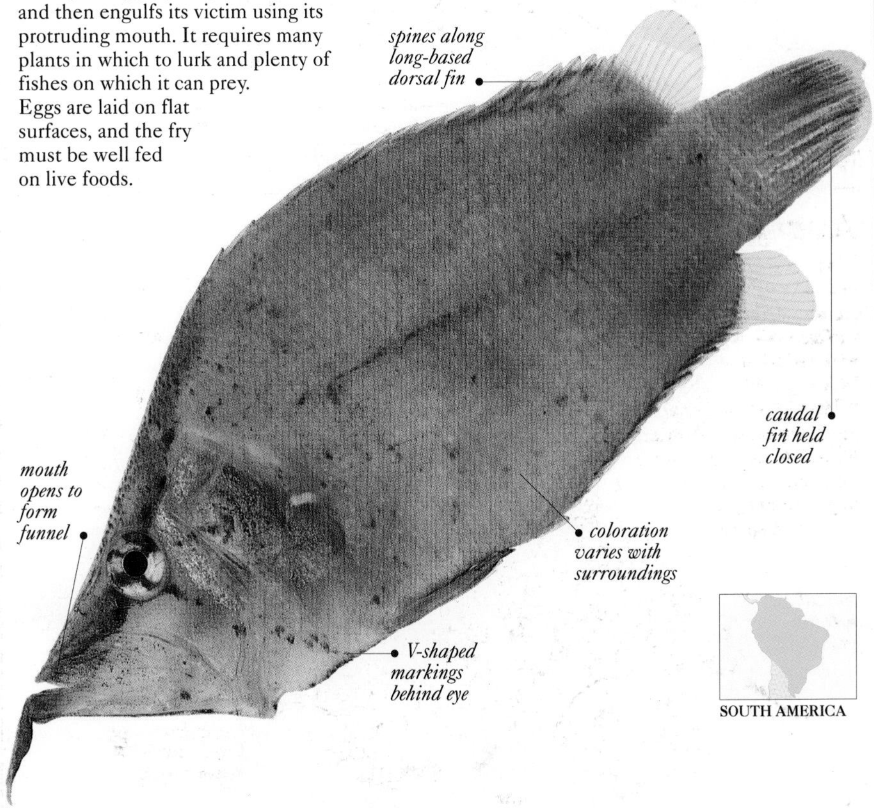

spines along long-based dorsal fin

caudal fin held closed

mouth opens to form funnel

coloration varies with surroundings

V-shaped markings behind eye

SOUTH AMERICA

Diet Carnivorous	Tank levels All	Temperament

Family MONODACTYLIDAE	Species *Monodactylus argenteus*	Size 9 in (23 cm)

MONO

The body of this disk-shaped fish is laterally compressed, like the freshwater angelfishes (see p.122). Very small scales cover a silver body. A dark bar passes through the large eye. Another slightly thinner bar runs down from the front of the dorsal fin. The highly arched lateral line is visible. Unpaired fins are yellowish orange, the dorsal and anal fins having black front edges.

- **HABITAT** Coastal waters, including harbors, from India to Tahiti, the Philippines, and Australia.
- **REMARK** Best kept in schools in a large, brackish water tank. It will eat tank plants.
- **OTHER NAMES** Fingerfish, Malayan Angelfish.

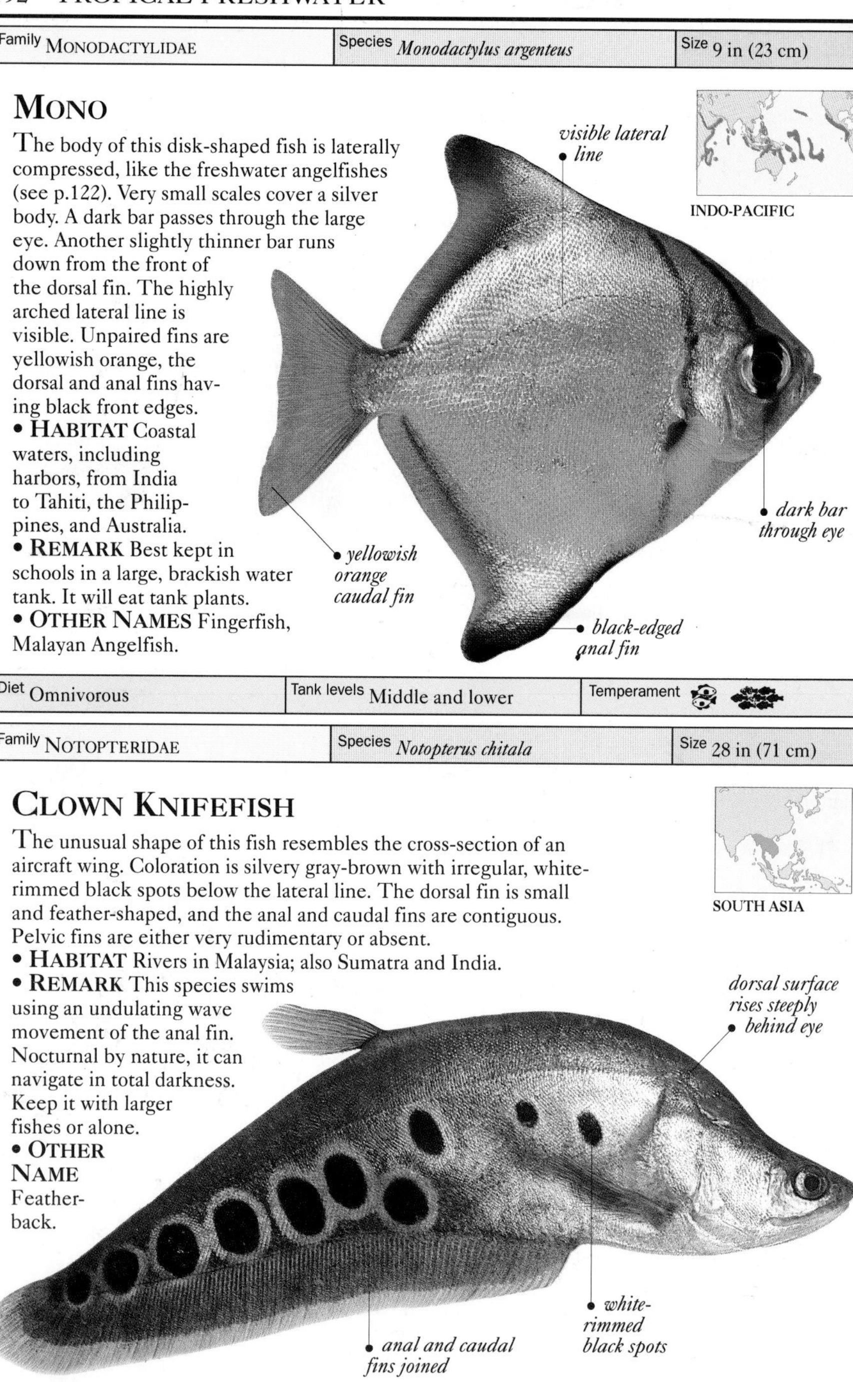

Diet Omnivorous	Tank levels Middle and lower	Temperament

Family NOTOPTERIDAE	Species *Notopterus chitala*	Size 28 in (71 cm)

CLOWN KNIFEFISH

The unusual shape of this fish resembles the cross-section of an aircraft wing. Coloration is silvery gray-brown with irregular, white-rimmed black spots below the lateral line. The dorsal fin is small and feather-shaped, and the anal and caudal fins are contiguous. Pelvic fins are either very rudimentary or absent.

- **HABITAT** Rivers in Malaysia; also Sumatra and India.
- **REMARK** This species swims using an undulating wave movement of the anal fin. Nocturnal by nature, it can navigate in total darkness. Keep it with larger fishes or alone.
- **OTHER NAME** Featherback.

Diet Carnivorous	Tank level Lower	Temperament

Family ORYZIATIDAE	Species *Oryzias melastigma*	Size 2 in (4.5 cm)

BLACK-SPOTTED MEDAKA

This fish is pale silver with a bluish iridescence that is enhanced under sidelighting. The backbone is visible, and the small dorsal fin is set very far back on the body.

• **HABITAT** Fresh and brackish waters of eastern India and Sri Lanka; also Myanmar (Burma), Indonesia, and Malaysia.

• **REMARK** Following spawning, fertilized eggs hang from the female's vent like a bunch of grapes, and brush off onto plants. Keep with non-aggressive fishes or in a species tank.

• **OTHER NAMES** Formerly classifed in the family Cyprinodontidae. Black-spotted Ricefish.

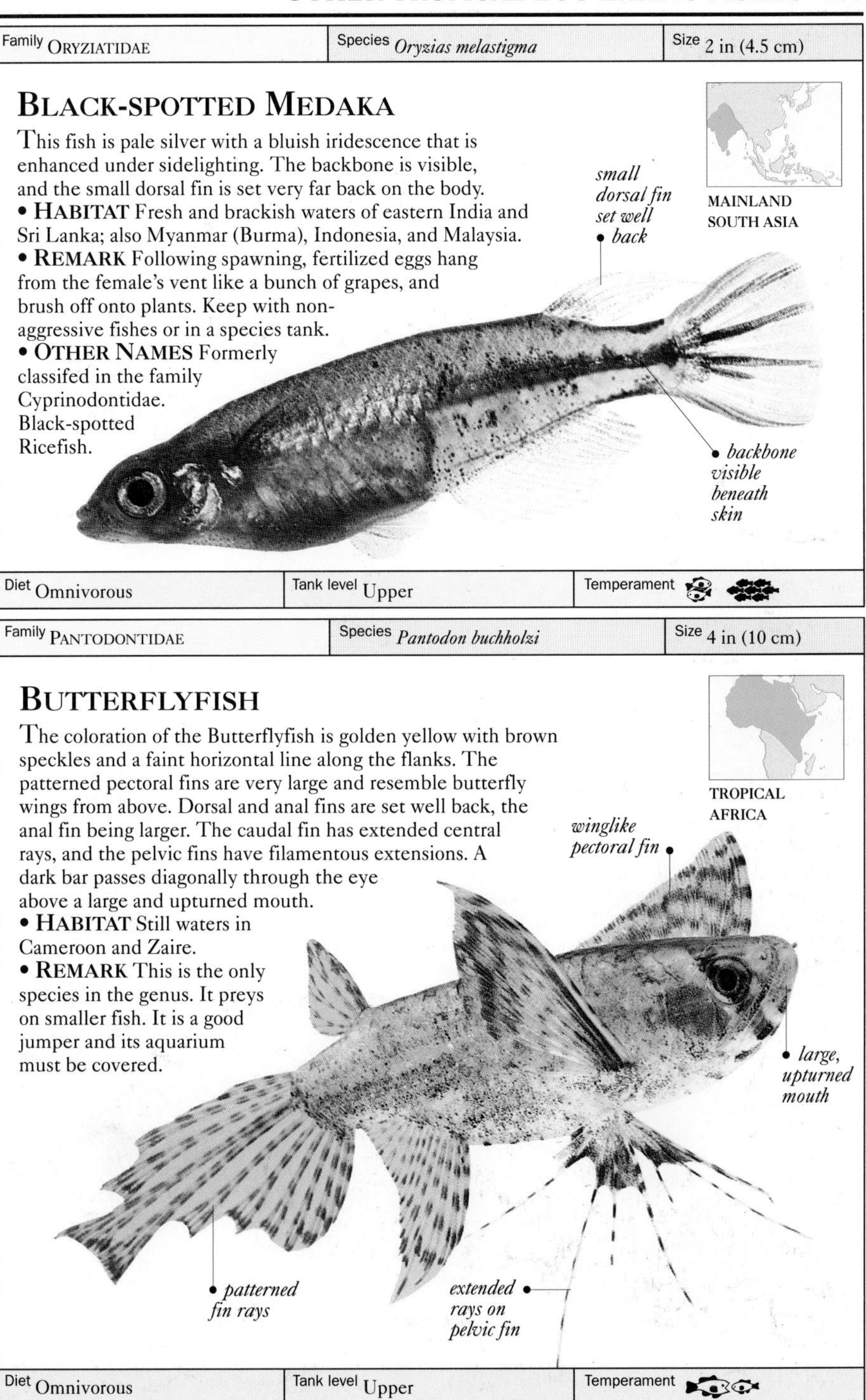

Diet Omnivorous	Tank level Upper	Temperament

Family PANTODONTIDAE	Species *Pantodon buchholzi*	Size 4 in (10 cm)

BUTTERFLYFISH

The coloration of the Butterflyfish is golden yellow with brown speckles and a faint horizontal line along the flanks. The patterned pectoral fins are very large and resemble butterfly wings from above. Dorsal and anal fins are set well back, the anal fin being larger. The caudal fin has extended central rays, and the pelvic fins have filamentous extensions. A dark bar passes diagonally through the eye above a large and upturned mouth.

• **HABITAT** Still waters in Cameroon and Zaire.

• **REMARK** This is the only species in the genus. It preys on smaller fish. It is a good jumper and its aquarium must be covered.

Diet Omnivorous	Tank level Upper	Temperament

Family SCATOPHAGIDAE	Species *Scatophagus argus*	Size 12 in (30 cm)

SCAT

The oblong shape of the Scat is emphasized by the position of the fins. Coloration is a mix of streaky brown and gold, with numerous dark, round spots. On adults (see inset), two dark vertical lines mark the forehead, and a golden streak runs behind the gill cover. Red markings appear on the dorsal surface. The long-based brown and gold dorsal fin has a spiny front section and a soft rear.

• **HABITAT** Coastal and estuarine waters from India to Tahiti and in the Philippines.

• **REMARK** The Scat is a true scavenger, readily eating aquarium plants. Vegetables and space are essential, and sea salt should be added to the water.

Adult Scat feeding on plant life

semi-clear caudal fin

spiny front of anal fin

INDO-PACIFIC

Diet Omnivorous	Tank levels Middle and lower	Temperament

Family OSTEOGLOSSIDAE	Species *Scleropages jardini*	Size 36 in (90 cm)

AUSTRALIAN AROWANA

The dull gray color of this heavily built fish is relieved by the gold-yellow rear edges of the scales. Yellow-gold markings also appear on the head and gill covers. A large, upturned mouth contains a bony tongue, and chin barbels are present. Sexual differences are indiscernible in juveniles, as here, and become apparent only at around five years of age.

• **HABITAT** Rivers in northern Australia.

• **REMARK** This mouthbreeder will hand-feed, but exercise caution. It needs a very large, covered species tank.

AUSTRALIA

gold-edged scales

upturned mouth contains bony tongue

very small pelvic fin

Diet Carnivorous	Tank levels All	Temperament 

Family GOBIIDAE	Species *Stigmatogobius sadanundio*	Size 3¼ in (8.5 cm)

KNIGHT GOBY

There are two dorsal fins on this gray-blue fish: the first consists of about six stiffly held rays (often with a black blotch); the second is equal in length to the long-based anal fin. Both carry dark spots. Females lack the longer fins and are yellowish in color.

• **HABITAT** Fresh and brackish waters in Borneo, Java, and Sumatra; also the Philippines.

• **REMARK** This fish may benefit from a teaspoonful of sea salt per one gallon (five liters) of tank water. Breeding is by secretive egg-depositing, often on the ceilings of caves, and plenty of retreats are required. It is peaceful but territorial.

• **OTHER NAME** Spotted Goby.

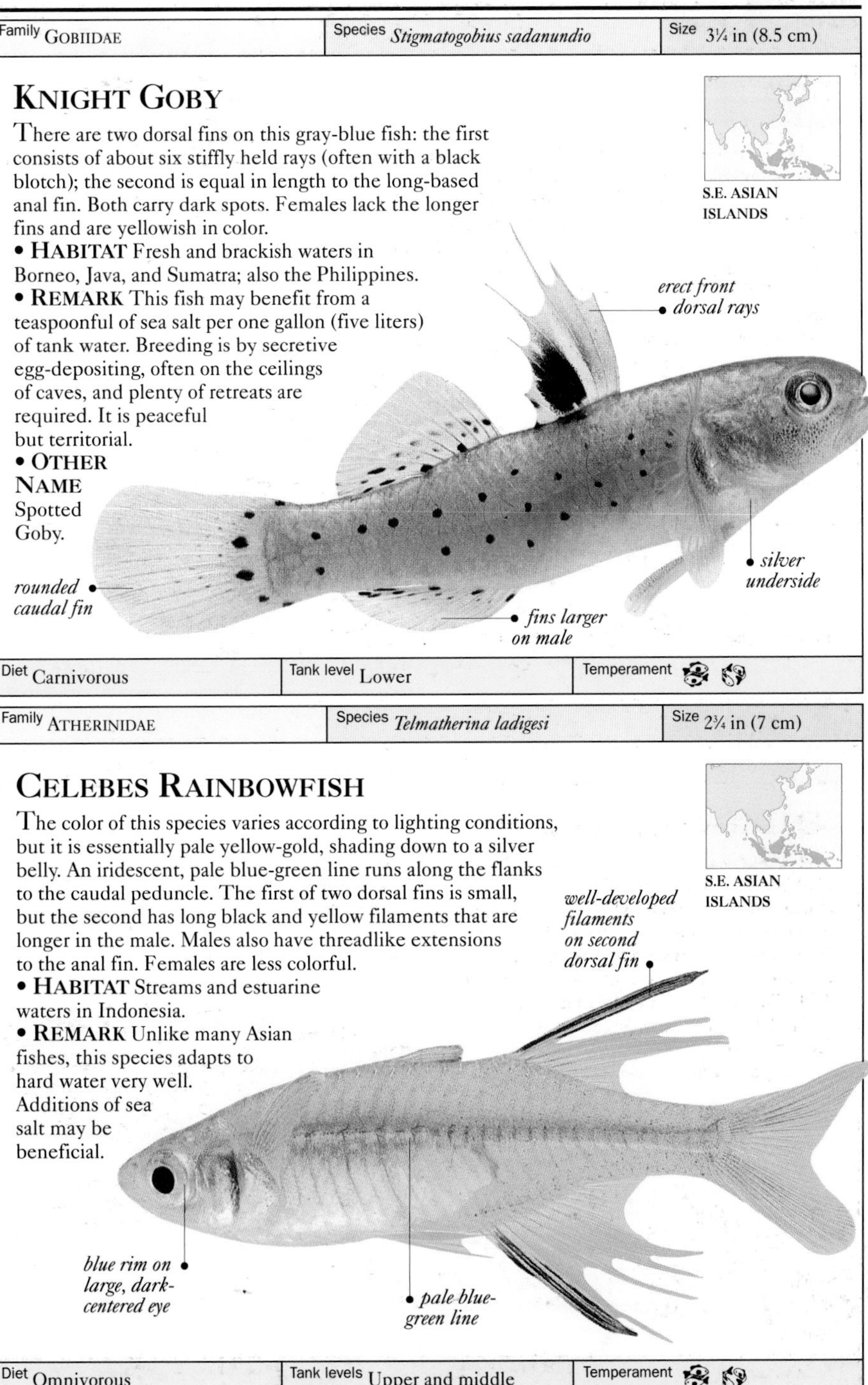

Diet Carnivorous	Tank level Lower	Temperament

Family ATHERINIDAE	Species *Telmatherina ladigesi*	Size 2¾ in (7 cm)

CELEBES RAINBOWFISH

The color of this species varies according to lighting conditions, but it is essentially pale yellow-gold, shading down to a silver belly. An iridescent, pale blue-green line runs along the flanks to the caudal peduncle. The first of two dorsal fins is small, but the second has long black and yellow filaments that are longer in the male. Males also have threadlike extensions to the anal fin. Females are less colorful.

• **HABITAT** Streams and estuarine waters in Indonesia.

• **REMARK** Unlike many Asian fishes, this species adapts to hard water very well. Additions of sea salt may be beneficial.

Diet Omnivorous	Tank levels Upper and middle	Temperament

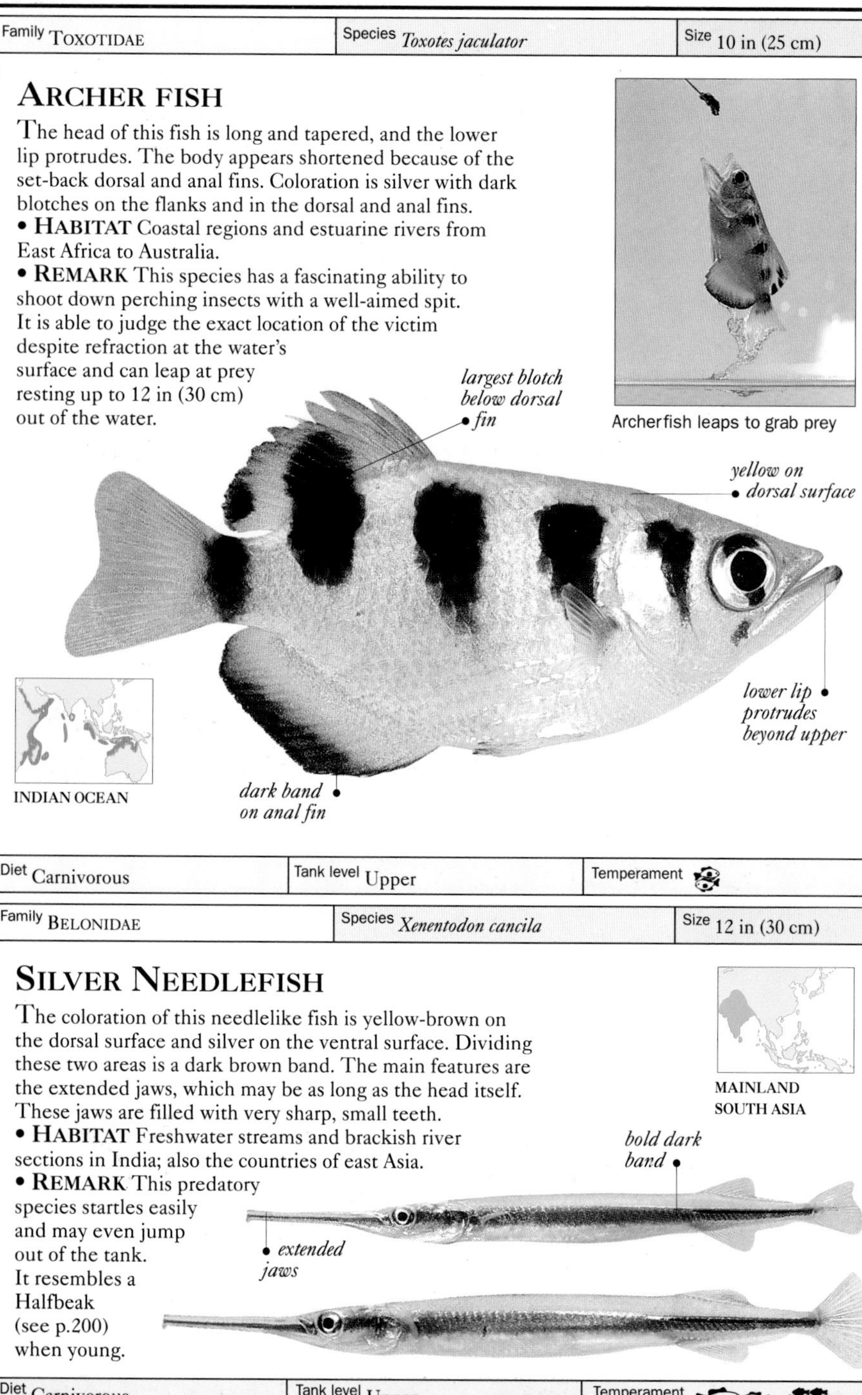

Family	Species	Size
TOXOTIDAE	*Toxotes jaculator*	10 in (25 cm)

ARCHER FISH

The head of this fish is long and tapered, and the lower lip protrudes. The body appears shortened because of the set-back dorsal and anal fins. Coloration is silver with dark blotches on the flanks and in the dorsal and anal fins.

• **HABITAT** Coastal regions and estuarine rivers from East Africa to Australia.

• **REMARK** This species has a fascinating ability to shoot down perching insects with a well-aimed spit. It is able to judge the exact location of the victim despite refraction at the water's surface and can leap at prey resting up to 12 in (30 cm) out of the water.

Archerfish leaps to grab prey

Diet	Tank level	Temperament
Carnivorous	Upper	

Family	Species	Size
BELONIDAE	*Xenentodon cancila*	12 in (30 cm)

SILVER NEEDLEFISH

The coloration of this needlelike fish is yellow-brown on the dorsal surface and silver on the ventral surface. Dividing these two areas is a dark brown band. The main features are the extended jaws, which may be as long as the head itself. These jaws are filled with very sharp, small teeth.

• **HABITAT** Freshwater streams and brackish river sections in India; also the countries of east Asia.

• **REMARK** This predatory species startles easily and may even jump out of the tank. It resembles a Halfbeak (see p.200) when young.

Diet	Tank level	Temperament
Carnivorous	Upper	

LIVEBEARERS

LIVEBEARERS ARE distinguished by their method of reproduction, in which eggs are fertilized and developed inside the female body. In the family Goodeidae, the developing young receive direct nourishment from the female. Most livebearers come from Central America; a few come from east Asia. They are hardy fish that adapt readily to changes in the water.

Family POECILIIDAE	Species *Alfaro cultratus*	Size 3½ in (9 cm)

KNIFE LIVEBEARER

CENTRAL AMERICA

The coloration of the Knife Livebearer is silvery yellow-brown with a metallic blue sheen under sidelighting. The dorsal surface is darker. A rounded dorsal fin is set halfway along the body and, as with other members of the family, anal fins differ between sexes. The anal fin of the slightly smaller male is modified to form a gonopodium, while the female anal fin is fan-shaped. All fins are yellowish, and the caudal fin may have a dark edge.

• **HABITAT** Streams in Costa Rica, Guatemala, Panama, and Nicaragua.

• **REMARK** This is a rather aggressive fish that appreciates a well-planted aquarium. Plants also provide refuge for the fry from their hungry parents.

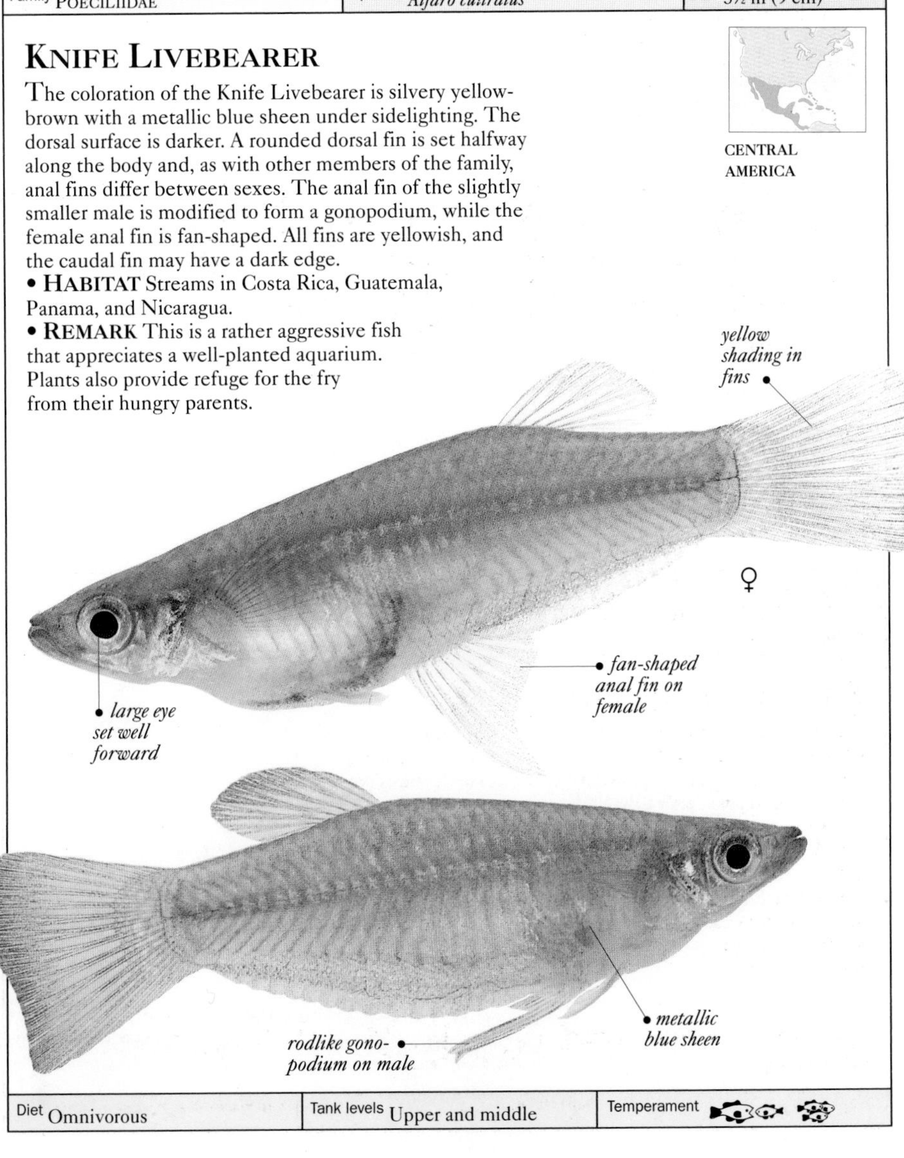

Diet Omnivorous	Tank levels Upper and middle	Temperament

Family GOODEIDAE	Species *Allotoca dugesi*	Size 2½ in (6 cm)

GOLDEN BUMBLEBEE GOODEID

This fish has a stocky, elongated body and a narrow caudal peduncle. The coloration on the lower flanks is golden yellow on the male and bluish, sometimes with dark bars, on the female. The male anal fin is not rodlike as with most other livebearers, but the female's is typically fan-shaped. A bluish band runs horizontally on both sexes, from behind the gill cover to the caudal peduncle.

• **HABITAT** Streams and rivers in the central highlands of Mexico.

• **REMARK** Females of the family Goodeidae cannot store sperm like Poeciliidae species, so mating is required for each brood.

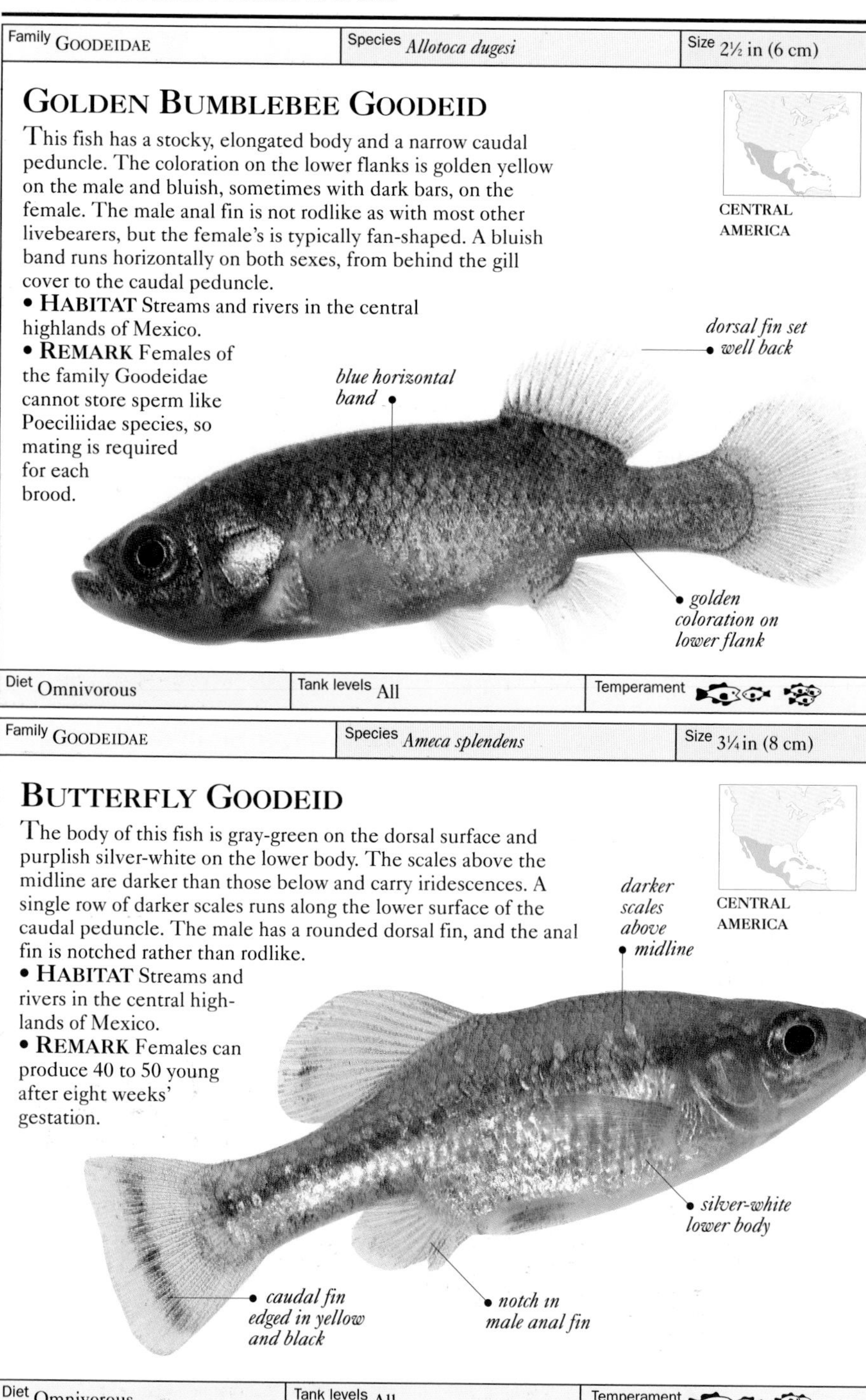

Diet Omnivorous	Tank levels All	Temperament

Family GOODEIDAE	Species *Ameca splendens*	Size 3¼ in (8 cm)

BUTTERFLY GOODEID

The body of this fish is gray-green on the dorsal surface and purplish silver-white on the lower body. The scales above the midline are darker than those below and carry iridescences. A single row of darker scales runs along the lower surface of the caudal peduncle. The male has a rounded dorsal fin, and the anal fin is notched rather than rodlike.

• **HABITAT** Streams and rivers in the central highlands of Mexico.

• **REMARK** Females can produce 40 to 50 young after eight weeks' gestation.

Diet Omnivorous	Tank levels All	Temperament

Family POECILIIDAE	Species *Brachyrhaphis roseni*	Size 2 in (5 cm)

CARDINAL BRACHY

On the best specimens, body coloration is greenish brown on the dorsal surface, with greenish yellow-gold flanks and a silver belly. Flanks are crossed by thin, equally spaced dark vertical bars that run the full depth of the body in front of the dorsal fin. The male dorsal fin is yellow and red with a dark outer edge, and his gonopodium is long and yellow. The female has a fan-shaped anal fin.

• **HABITAT** Streams in Costa Rica and Panama.

• **REMARK** This species was introduced to aquarists in 1988. A well-planted aquarium is necessary to protect the fry from their cannibalistic parents.

Diet Omnivorous	Tank levels All	Temperament

Family GOODEIDAE	Species *Characodon audax*	Size 2 in (5 cm)

BLACK PRINCE

All fins on this fish are rounded and jet black, as the name suggests. Body coloration is sooty gray on the dorsal surface with paler flanks below. There may be some pink around the throat and belly. Scales are slightly iridescent.

• **HABITAT** Streams and rivers in the central highlands of Mexico.

• **REMARK** Territorial males may be aggressive towards each other. The species requires green food, and prefers a tank with minimal water movement.

• **OTHER NAME** Bold Characodon.

Diet Omnivorous	Tank levels All	Temperament

Family HEMIRHAMPHIDAE	Species *Dermogenys pusillus*	Size 2½ in (6 cm)

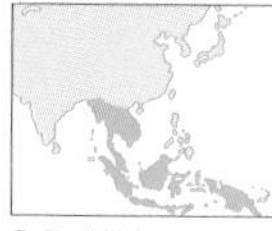

S. E. ASIA

WRESTLING HALFBEAK

The lower jaws of these two slender male fish are extended to approximately twice the length of the upper jaw, an adaptation for surface feeding. Coloration is greenish yellow-gold with patches of blue. The male anal fin appears to be folded, and that of the female is fan-shaped.

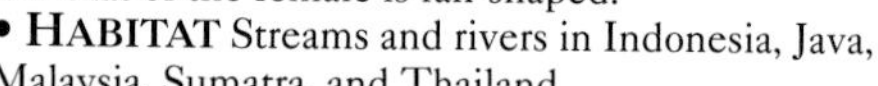

• **HABITAT** Streams and rivers in Indonesia, Java, Malaysia, Sumatra, and Thailand.

• **REMARK** Keep one male and two or three females in a group; males tend to fight by locking jaws with each other.

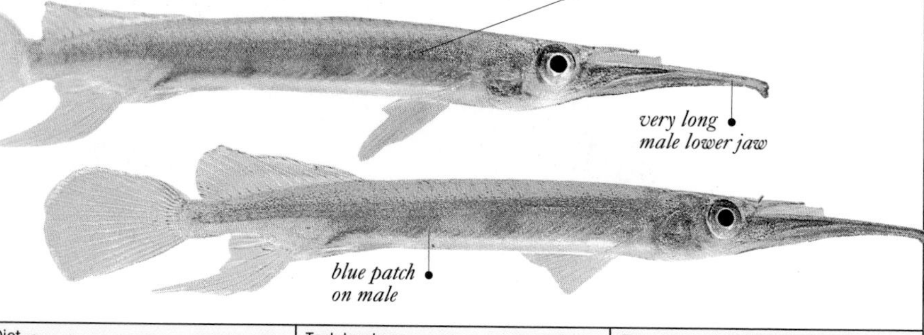

Diet Carnivorous	Tank levels Upper and middle	Temperament

Family POECILIIDAE	Species *Gambusia affinis*	Size 1½ in (4 cm)

UNITED STATES

MOSQUITO FISH

This fish resembles the female Guppy (see p.204). It is greenish gold with a distinctly swollen belly. The male has a long gonopodium, while the female anal fin is fan-shaped.

• **HABITAT** Streams and rivers of the eastern USA.

• **REMARK** This fish has been exported throughout the world to rid waters of mosquito larvae, and thus help in the eradication of yellow fever, encephalitis, malaria, and other mosquito-borne diseases.

Diet Omnivorous	Tank levels All	Temperament 

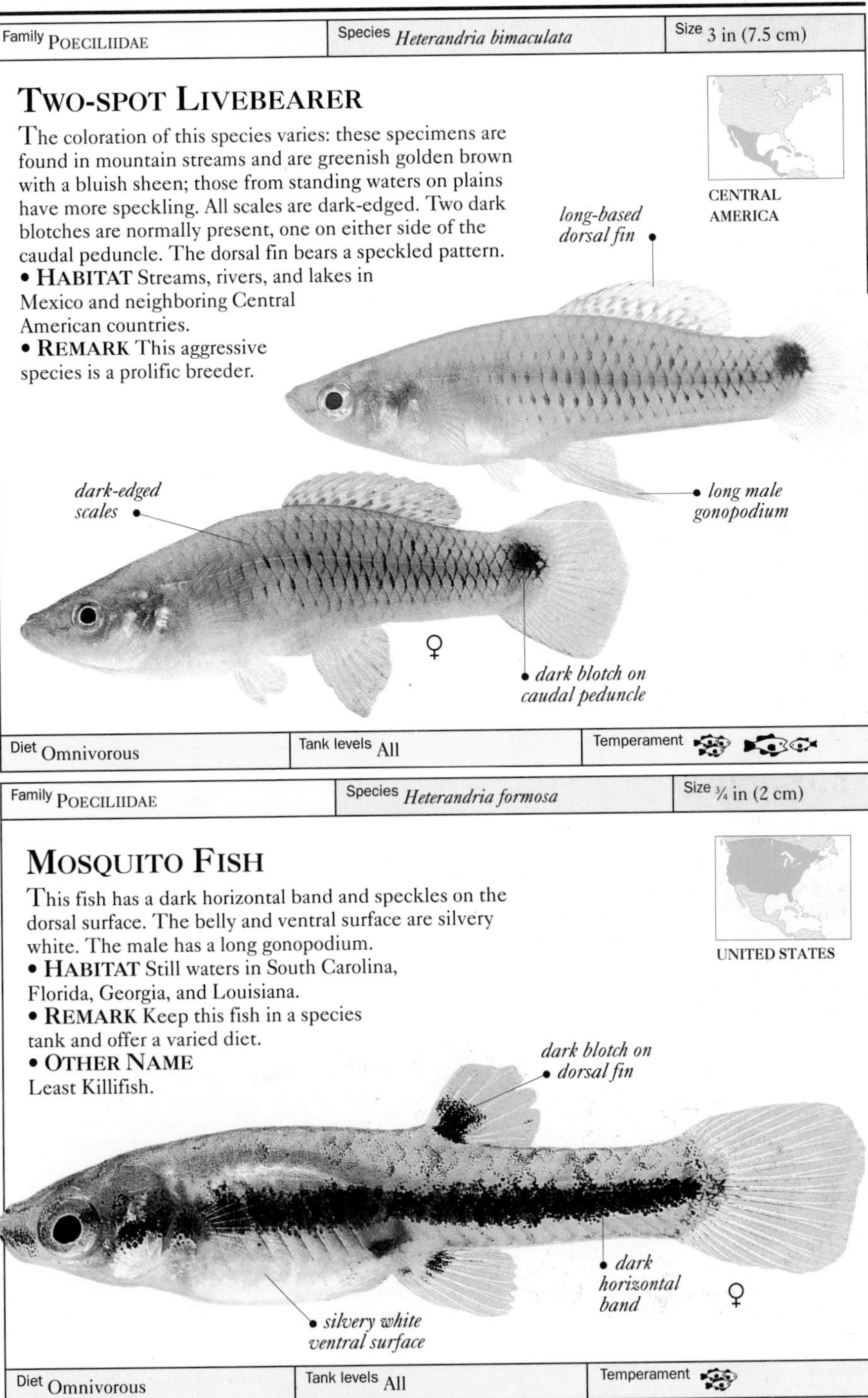

Family POECILIIDAE	Species *Heterandria bimaculata*	Size 3 in (7.5 cm)

TWO-SPOT LIVEBEARER

The coloration of this species varies: these specimens are found in mountain streams and are greenish golden brown with a bluish sheen; those from standing waters on plains have more speckling. All scales are dark-edged. Two dark blotches are normally present, one on either side of the caudal peduncle. The dorsal fin bears a speckled pattern.

• **HABITAT** Streams, rivers, and lakes in Mexico and neighboring Central American countries.

• **REMARK** This aggressive species is a prolific breeder.

Diet Omnivorous	Tank levels All	Temperament

Family POECILIIDAE	Species *Heterandria formosa*	Size ¾ in (2 cm)

MOSQUITO FISH

This fish has a dark horizontal band and speckles on the dorsal surface. The belly and ventral surface are silvery white. The male has a long gonopodium.

• **HABITAT** Still waters in South Carolina, Florida, Georgia, and Louisiana.

• **REMARK** Keep this fish in a species tank and offer a varied diet.

• **OTHER NAME** Least Killifish.

Diet Omnivorous	Tank levels All	Temperament

Family POECILIIDAE	Species *Poecilia nigrofasciata*	Size 2½ in (6 cm)

HUMPBACKED LIMIA

The humped back of this species is accentuated by the decorative dorsal fin. This fish has silvery blue flanks that are crossed vertically by dark bands. The "hump" is pronounced only on mature males, and the lower rear section of his body is keel-shaped. Females have deeper bellies, and their vertical bars are shorter and broader.

• **HABITAT** Streams and rivers on Haiti in the Caribbean Sea.

• **OTHER NAME** *Limia nigrofasciata.*

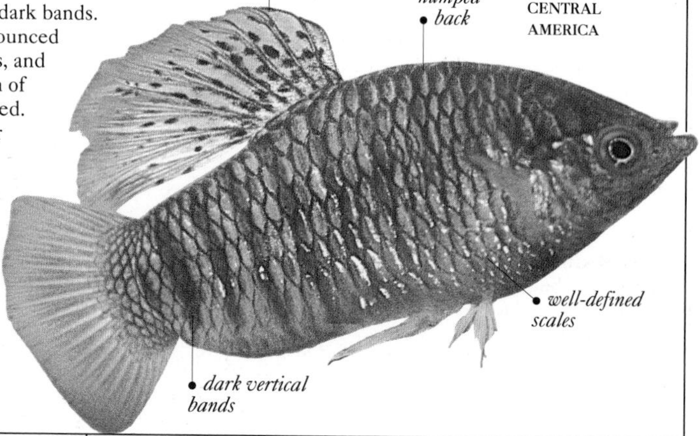

CENTRAL AMERICA

distinctive dorsal fin

humped back

well-defined scales

dark vertical bands

Diet Omnivorous	Tank levels All	Temperament

Family GOODEIDAE	Species *Skiffia francesae* x *multipunctatus*	Size 2 in (5 cm)

BLACK BEAUTY

The prominent black coloration of this hybrid species is tempered by a paler head region. The head is small and the eye set well forward. The dorsal fin is irregularly shaped with a ragged edge. The male anal fin is only partially modified for fertilization purposes, and the first few rays are slightly separated from the remainder of the fin. Anal, dorsal, and caudal fins all contain black.

• **HABITAT** Parental species originate in Central America.

• **REMARK** This fish is the offspring of *Skiffia francesae* and *S. multipunctatus.* Despite being a hybrid, its own offspring are fertile. It should be selectively bred in order to maintain the line. Its ragged dorsal fin is noted in the genus's common name of Sawfin Goodeid.

CENTRAL AMERICA

irregularly shaped dorsal fin

paler region on jet black body

♀

narrow caudal peduncle

clear edge of anal fin

Diet Omnivorous	Tank levels All	Temperament 

Family GOODEIDAE | Species *Xenotoca eiseni* | Size 2½ in (6 cm)

ORANGE-TAILED GOODEID

A bright orange to red patch appears on the caudal peduncle of this species, and is more intensely colored on the male. Coloration in front of the dorsal fin is yellowish brown; rearwards the color is metallic blue-green. A notch in the male anal fin is apparent, and his dorsal fin is often quite large and rounded. The lower jaw and throat regions may be pink.

• **HABITAT** Streams and rivers in the central highlands of Mexico.

• **REMARK** This species can be quarrelsome, and it has a reputation for fin-nipping. Medium-hard water is preferred.

• **OTHER NAME** Red-tailed Goodeid.

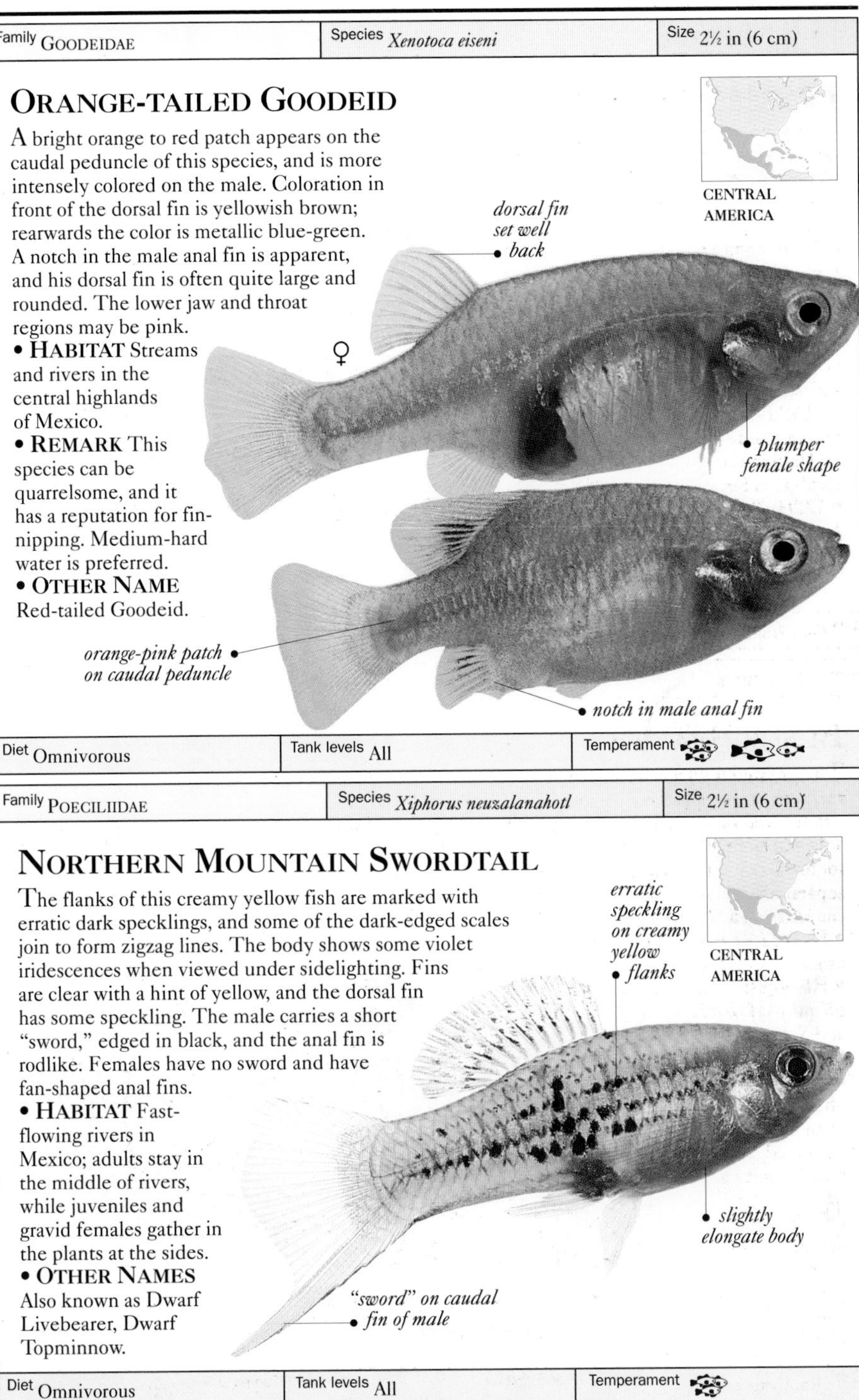

Diet Omnivorous | Tank levels All | Temperament

Family POECILIIDAE | Species *Xiphorus neuzalanahotl* | Size 2½ in (6 cm)

NORTHERN MOUNTAIN SWORDTAIL

The flanks of this creamy yellow fish are marked with erratic dark specklings, and some of the dark-edged scales join to form zigzag lines. The body shows some violet iridescences when viewed under sidelighting. Fins are clear with a hint of yellow, and the dorsal fin has some speckling. The male carries a short "sword," edged in black, and the anal fin is rodlike. Females have no sword and have fan-shaped anal fins.

• **HABITAT** Fast-flowing rivers in Mexico; adults stay in the middle of rivers, while juveniles and gravid females gather in the plants at the sides.

• **OTHER NAMES** Also known as Dwarf Livebearer, Dwarf Topminnow.

Diet Omnivorous | Tank levels All | Temperament

Family POECILIIDAE	Species *Poecilia reticulata*	Size 1¼ in (3 cm)

GUPPY

CENTRAL AMERICA

The wild Guppy is dark olive-green, shading to silver on the ventral surface. Aquarium-cultivated guppies conform to standards, but individual colors may differ greatly, as demonstrated by the selection shown here. Males are irregularly marked in red, orange, green, or black; no two males are exactly alike. Females are normally larger than males and lack the coloration and extravagant finnage, although some females are now appearing with colors in the single fins. When gravid, the females take on extra body depth, and a dark area appears around the vent. The male anal fin, or gonopodium, is rod-shaped and is used to fertilize the female internally.

• **HABITAT** Streams in Central America; also Trinidad and northern South America.

• **REMARK** To maintain color strains, interbreeding should be avoided. Females store sperm internally.

• **OTHER NAMES** Millions Fish. Formerly classified as *Lebistes*.

GOLD COBRA GUPPY

"snakeskin" markings

gonopodium on male

delta-shaped caudal fin

UNCOLORED GUPPY

less intense female coloration

♀

dark spot when gravid

smaller female fins

Diet Omnivorous	Tank levels All	Temperament

RED VARITAIL GUPPY
long dorsal fin
varying color pattern
RED-TAILED HALF-BLACK GUPPY
half-black body
well-developed caudal fin
BLOND GUPPY
flaglike dorsal fin
paler ventral surface
rounded caudal fin

Family POECILIIDAE	Species *Poecilia latipinna*	Size 4 in (10 cm)

SAILFIN MOLLY

All members of the family Poeciliidae, including the Sailfin Mollies, are stocky and fairly elongate. Many color strains of this species have been developed by selective breeding, samples of which are shown below and opposite. Wild-caught mollies are colored silvery green with some iridescences. The male dorsal fin is carried erect, like a sail, to impress females or challenge males. The male anal fin is adapted into a rodlike structure (the gonopodium) with which the female is internally fertilized; the female anal fin is fan shaped.

• **HABITAT** Coastal brackish and marine waters of Mexico, including the Gulf of Mexico; also the United States south of Carolina.

• **REMARK** Clear water and regular supplies of vegetables are required for optimum development. A separate well-planted tank is the best place for a female molly to give birth. Saline water can be tolerated.

CENTRAL AMERICA

GREEN MOLLY

rodlike anal fin

PLATINUM SAILFIN

pointed snout

plumper female body

♀

erect "sail-like" dorsal fin

clear fins

GREEN SAILFIN MOLLY

Diet Omnivorous	Tank levels All	Temperament

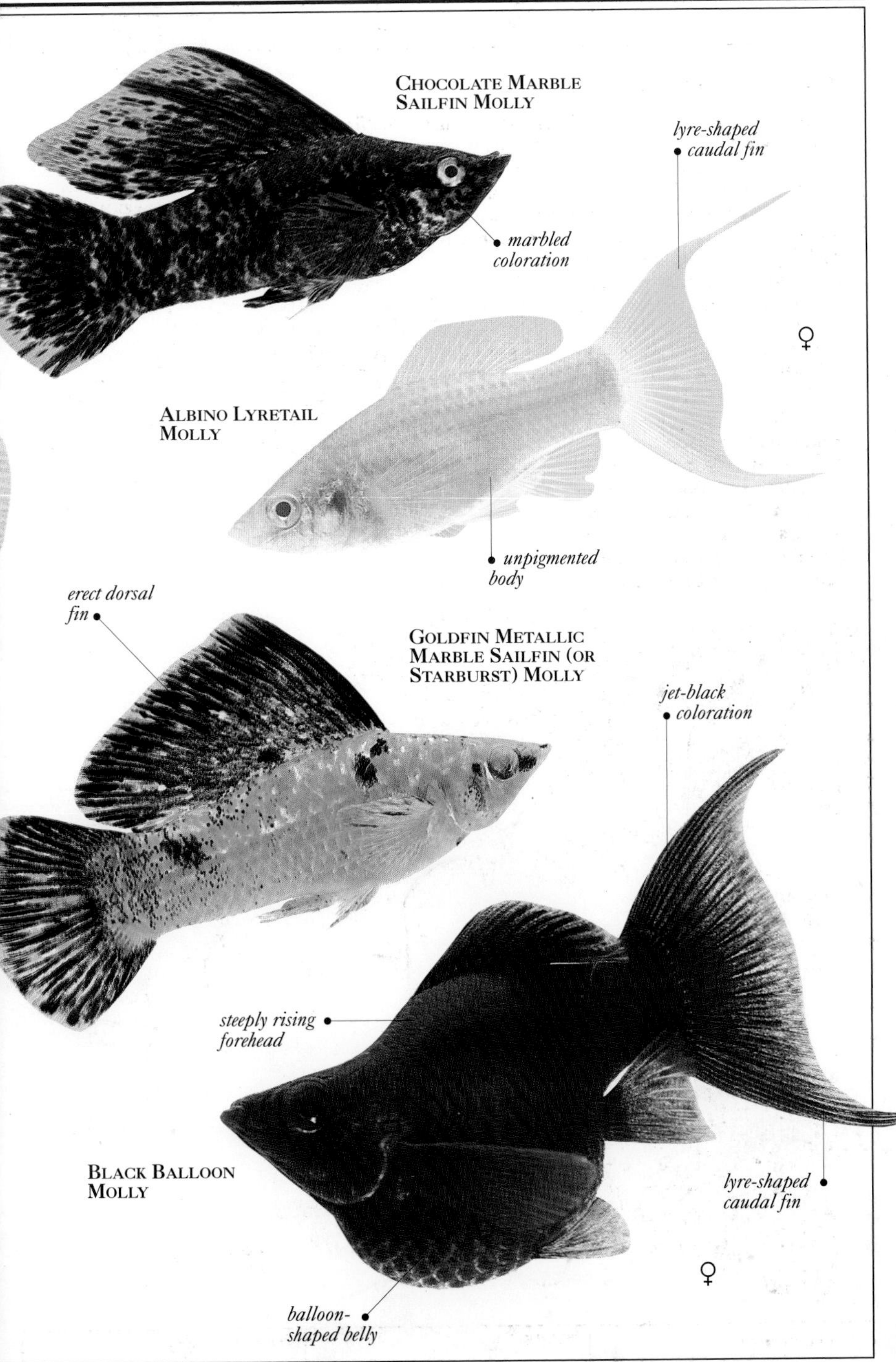

CHOCOLATE MARBLE SAILFIN MOLLY

ALBINO LYRETAIL MOLLY

GOLDFIN METALLIC MARBLE SAILFIN (OR STARBURST) MOLLY

BLACK BALLOON MOLLY

Family POECILIIDAE	Species *Xiphophorus helleri*	Size 4 in (10 cm)

SWORDTAIL

The wild male Swordtail is green with a purple stripe along the side and a yellow, swordlike caudal fin extension. The edges of the "sword" are black. Many different color strains and finnage variants have been selectively bred, examples of which are shown here. The female Green Swordtail, on this page, is closest to the original wild strain color. The male anal fin forms a gonopodium, while the female is without a "sword," and her body is slightly larger.

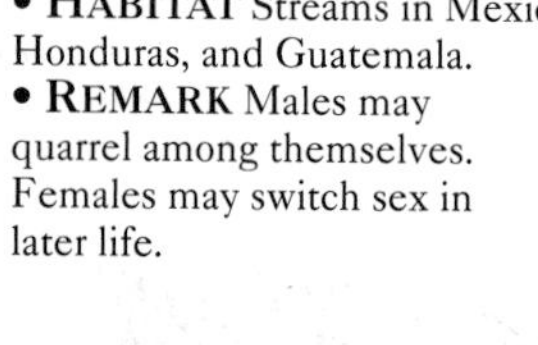

• **HABITAT** Streams in Mexico, Honduras, and Guatemala.
• **REMARK** Males may quarrel among themselves. Females may switch sex in later life.

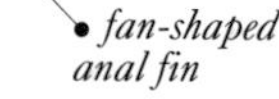

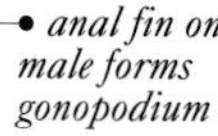

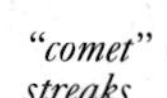

Diet Omnivorous	Tank levels All	Temperament 

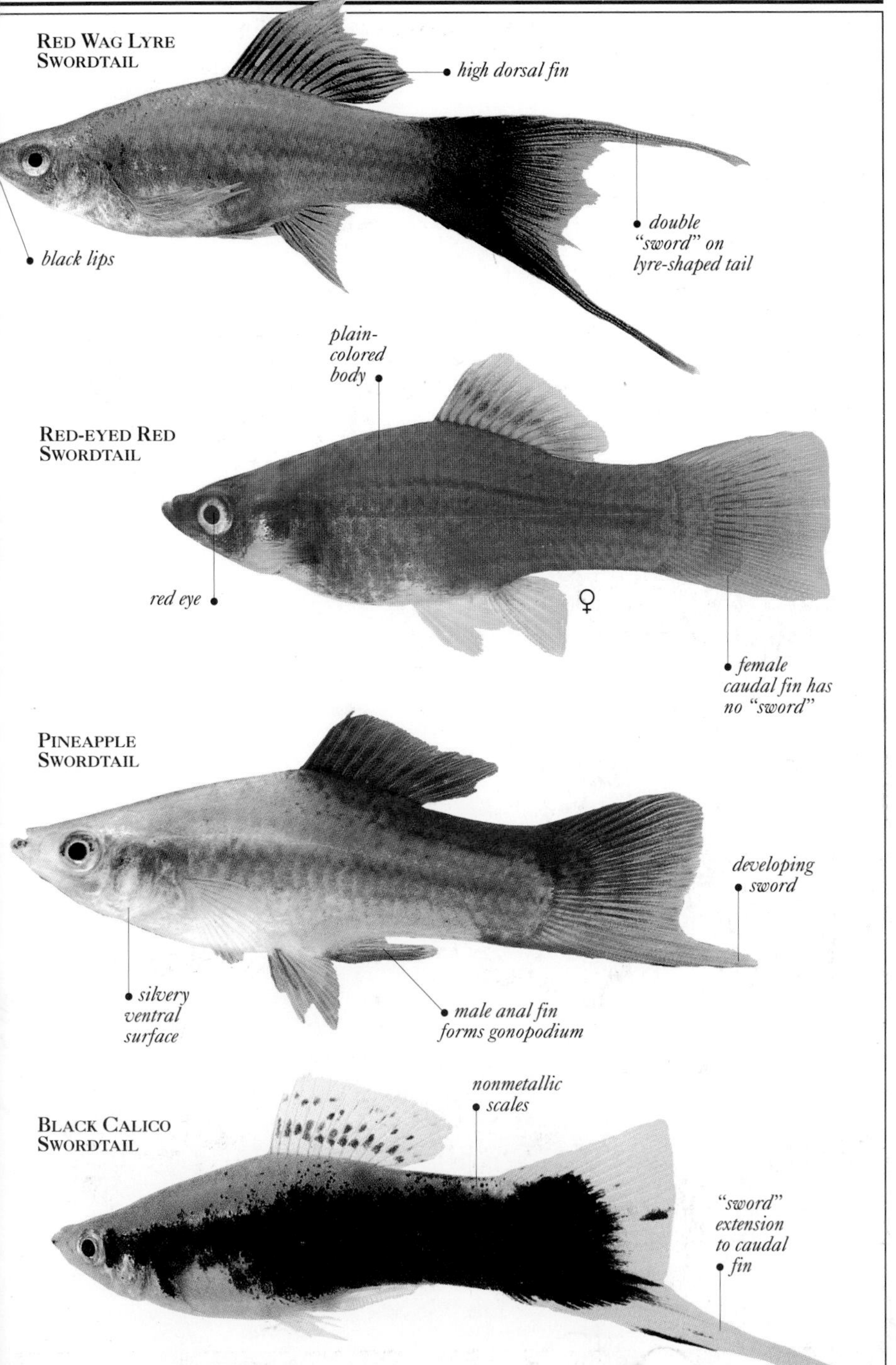
RED WAG LYRE SWORDTAIL
high dorsal fin
black lips
double "sword" on lyre-shaped tail
plain-colored body
RED-EYED RED SWORDTAIL
red eye
♀
female caudal fin has no "sword"
PINEAPPLE SWORDTAIL
developing sword
silvery ventral surface
male anal fin forms gonopodium
nonmetallic scales
BLACK CALICO SWORDTAIL
"sword" extension to caudal fin

Family POECILIIDAE	Species *Xiphophorus maculatus*	Size 1½ in (4 cm)

PLATY

CENTRAL AMERICA

The coloration of the wild Platy is gray with dark speckles and clear fins; there may be red in the dorsal fin. The Platy now appears in the aquarium in many cultivated variations, some of which are shown here. The "wagtail" is a very popular strain with a black mouth and black fins, and red or yellow body colors. The Red Wag Hi-fin Platy, shown opposite, is a fancy wagtail that has a tall dorsal fin. In all strains, the rodlike male anal fin is used to fertilize the female internally. She has a fan-shape anal fin and becomes much larger when gravid.

• **HABITAT** Originally from Mexico, Guatemala, and Honduras, the Platy is now bred commercially in Florida and the Pacific Rim.

• **REMARK** The colors of this good community collection fish will degenerate in later generations, unless breeding is strictly controlled.

GOLD COMET PLATY

BLUE CORAL PLATY

blue coral marking

male anal fin forms gonopodium

Diet Omnivorous	Tank levels All	Temperament 

high dorsal fin
RED WAG HI-FIN PLATY
♀
black fins
plain-colored body
RED HI-FIN PLATY
male anal fin forms gonopodium
highly developed dorsal fin
SUNSET MARIGOLD HI-FIN PLATY
darker rear of body

Family POECILIIDAE	Species *Xiphophorus variatus*	Size 2 in (5 cm)

VARIATUS PLATY

As with the related Swordtail and Platy (see pp.208–209 and pp.210–211), selective breeding has resulted in many color strains of this fish, often with exaggerated finnage. Of the three female strains shown below, the top one is probably the closest in color to the wild fish. The original wild form is greenish yellow with clearly defined dark-edged scales and possibly some dark flecks on the flanks. The body shape is more elongate than that of the Platy, but the male anal fins are similarly rodlike. Female fish are generally longer.

• **HABITAT** Originally found in streams in southern Mexico.

CENTRAL AMERICA

GREEN VARIATUS PLATY

clear edge of caudal fin

♀

greenish yellow body

CALICO PLATY

elongate caudal peduncle

♀

BLACK CALICO PLATY

colorless caudal fin

♀

fan-shaped anal fin

pale ventral surface

Diet Omnivorous	Tank levels All	Temperament

COLDWATER FRESHWATER FISHES

SINGLE-TAILED GOLDFISHES

GOLDFISHES HAVE BEEN kept in captivity longer than any other fishes, and many varieties developed from the one original species, *Carassius auratus*, remain popular. This section is devoted to single-tailed varieties – hardy fishes that can over-winter outdoors. Their cultivation is generally limited to developing exaggerated fins and various color strains.

Family CYPRINIDAE	Species *Carassius auratus*	Size Variable

COMMON GOLDFISH

Traditionally, the body color of the Goldfish is metallic red-orange with matching fins. Young fish may be greenish bronze, changing to adult coloration after about one year. Dorsal and anal fins are relatively long based, and the caudal fin is forked and stiffly held. The lateral line is visible. Females usually appear plumper when they are viewed from above. At spawning time the male develops small white spots (tubercles) on the gill covers and head.

• **REMARK** Goldfishes were first developed in 11th-century China from the occasional colorful or unusual specimen found among carp kept for food. Selective breeding established the distinguishing scale types: "metallic," "nacreous" (resembling mother-of-pearl), and "matte" (also known as calico).

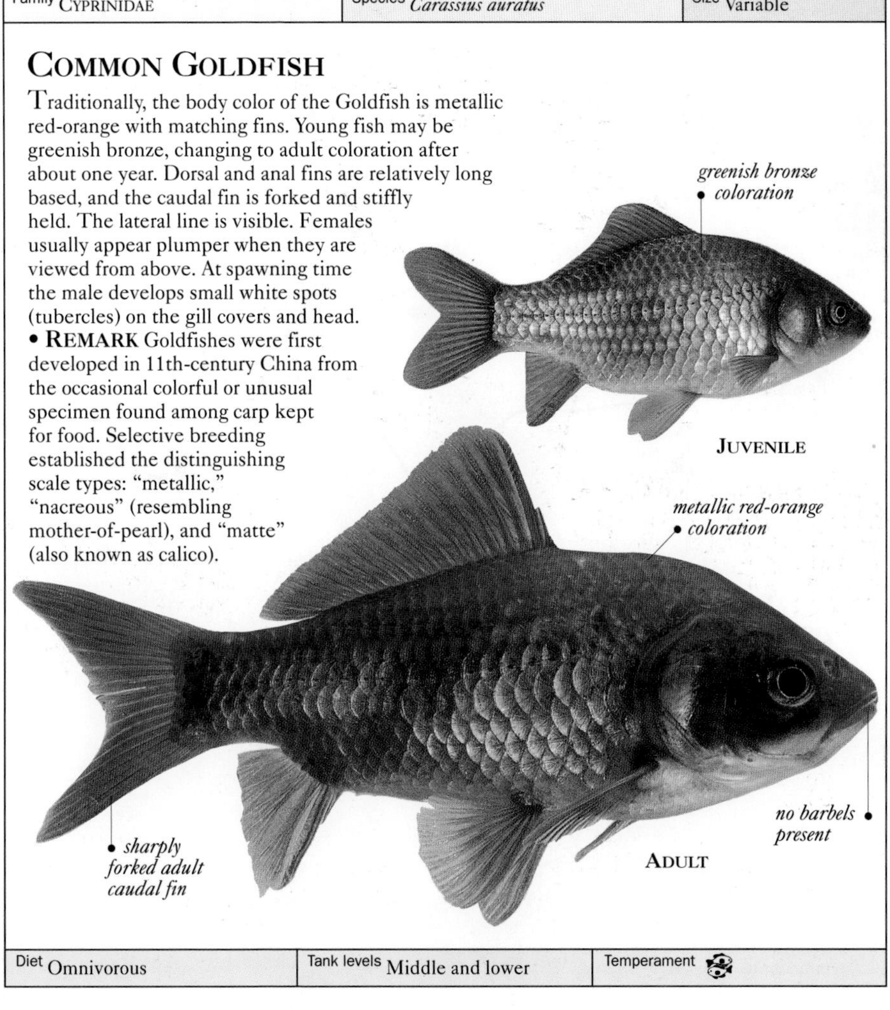

Diet Omnivorous	Tank levels Middle and lower	Temperament

Family CYPRINIDAE	Species *Carassius auratus*	Size Variable

COMET

The body shape of all Comets is elongate, with equally curved dorsal and ventral contours. It is not as deep as the Common Goldfish (see p.213). The colors of these fish depend on the strain, the most popular of which show red-orange and lemon-yellow colorations. The varieties shown here include an uncolored juvenile Comet, a Gold (or Metallic) Comet, and an extremely popular strain, the Sarasa (or Red Cap) Comet, which has a white or silver base color. A distinctive, cultivated feature of these varieties is the deeply forked caudal fin, which can be almost as long as the body.

• **REMARK** The Comet requires plenty of swimming room and is capable of swimming very fast over short distances. It is a hardy fish and benefits from being kept outdoors in a pond all year round.

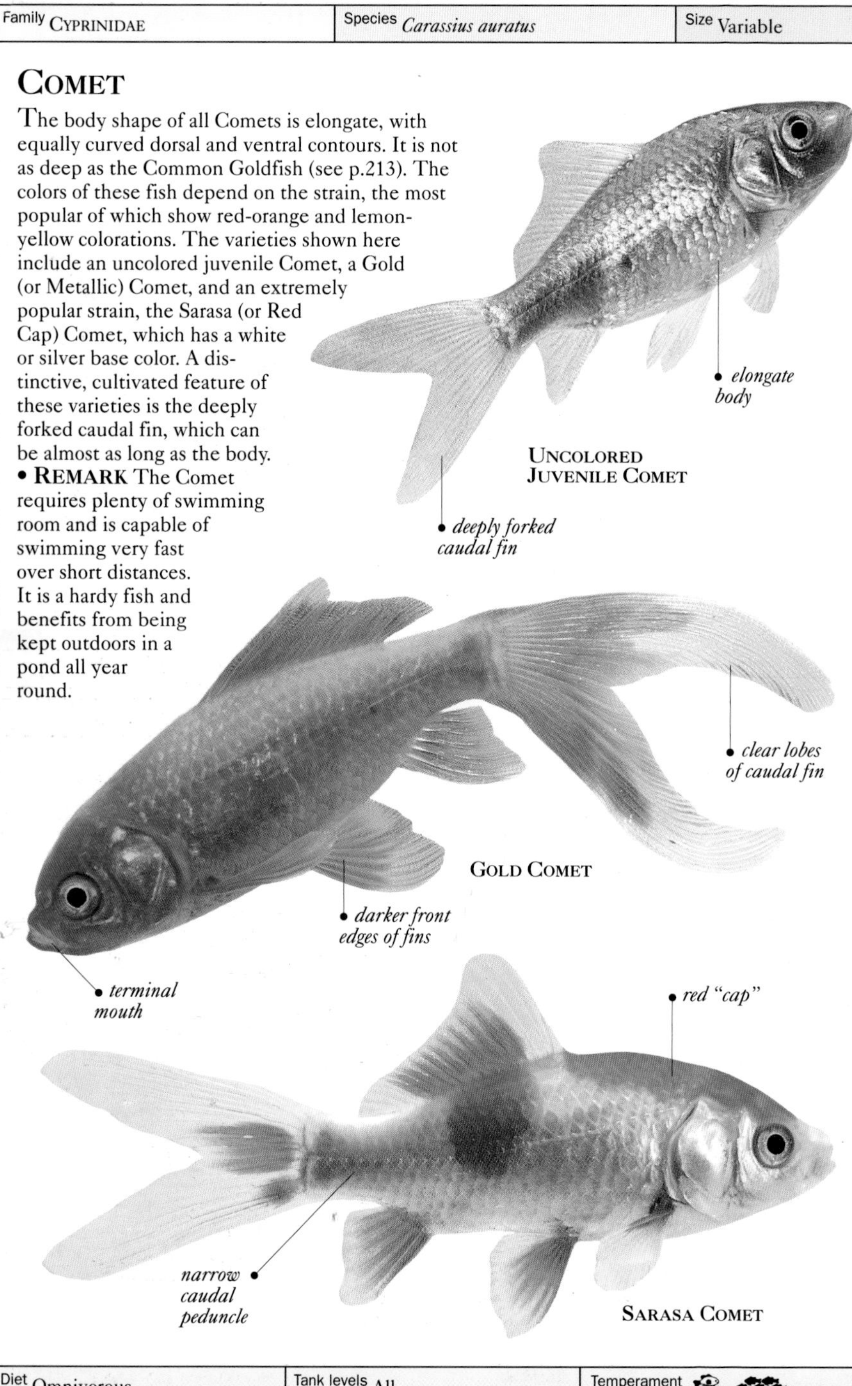

UNCOLORED JUVENILE COMET

GOLD COMET

SARASA COMET

Diet Omnivorous	Tank levels All	Temperament

Family CYPRINIDAE	Species *Carassius auratus*	Size Variable

NYMPH

The shape of the Nymph is like that of the Fantail or the Veiltail (see pp.217 and 220), but this fish has single anal and caudal fins, unlike the double fins of the latter two strains. The variety shown here is a metallic red strain.

• **REMARK** The Nymph is usually found among the offspring of a Fantail or a Veiltail. In breeding terms, this fish is known as a "recessive."

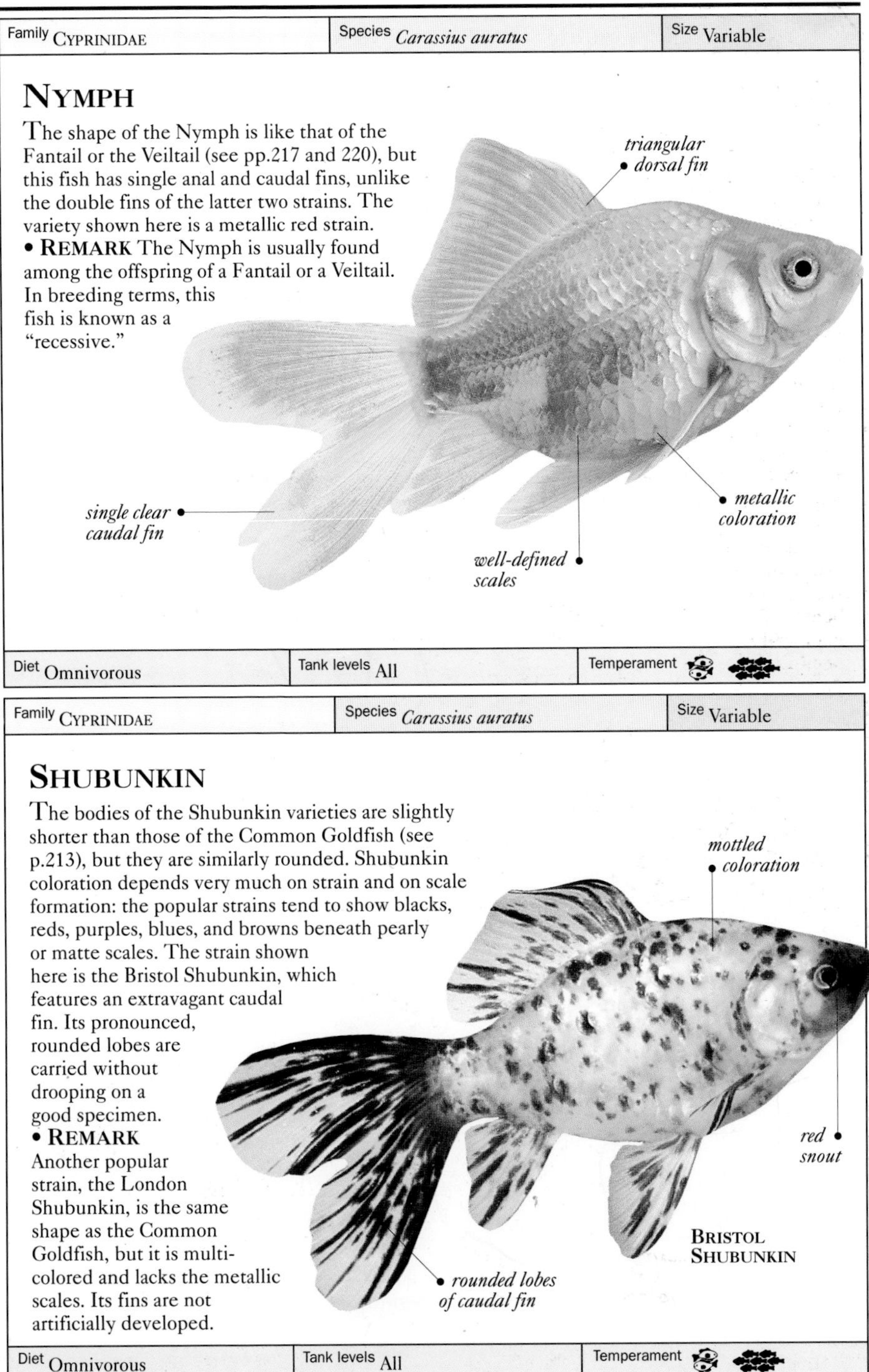

Diet Omnivorous	Tank levels All	Temperament

Family CYPRINIDAE	Species *Carassius auratus*	Size Variable

SHUBUNKIN

The bodies of the Shubunkin varieties are slightly shorter than those of the Common Goldfish (see p.213), but they are similarly rounded. Shubunkin coloration depends very much on strain and on scale formation: the popular strains tend to show blacks, reds, purples, blues, and browns beneath pearly or matte scales. The strain shown here is the Bristol Shubunkin, which features an extravagant caudal fin. Its pronounced, rounded lobes are carried without drooping on a good specimen.

• **REMARK** Another popular strain, the London Shubunkin, is the same shape as the Common Goldfish, but it is multi-colored and lacks the metallic scales. Its fins are not artificially developed.

Diet Omnivorous	Tank levels All	Temperament

TWIN-TAILED GOLDFISHES

THESE GOLDFISHES are termed "twintails" because their caudal and anal fins hang in double folds. Their aquarium-bred bodies become truncated and egg-shaped, and the ability to swim is gradually impaired as the form changes from the natural streamlined shape. These restrictions mean that twintails are not suited to outdoor ponds. They could not compete in the race for food, nor flee from predators. Their delicate fins may also become congested in inferior water conditions. The maximum size a twin-tailed goldfish attains depends on the size of the tank in which it is kept.

Family CYPRINIDAE	Species *Carassius auratus*	Size Variable

BUBBLE-EYE GOLDFISH

The enlarged fluid-filled sacs beneath the eyes of this variety of twintail are highly distinctive, and they sway as the fish swims. The rest of the body is roughly egg-shaped with a straight dorsal surface. The coloration varies but is usually metallic red-orange. The dorsal fin is absent and the anal and caudal fins are doubled, the extravagant caudal fin flowing from a down-turned caudal peduncle.

• **REMARK** The eye sacs are prone to damage, so it is best to keep this strain in its own aquarium, without sharp-edged furnishings.

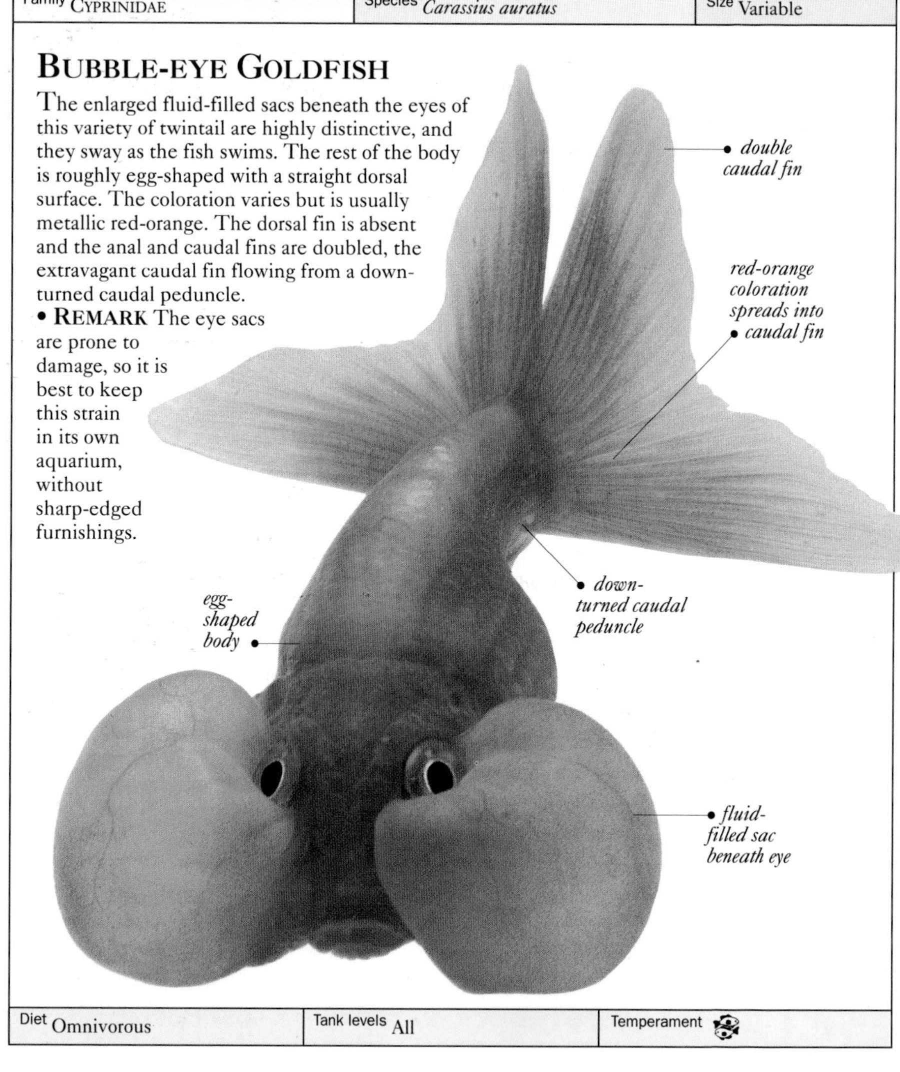

Diet Omnivorous	Tank levels All	Temperament

Family CYPRINIDAE	Species *Carassius auratus*	Size Variable

CELESTIAL GOLDFISH

The unusual eyes of this variety are directed permanently upward because of fleshy growths beneath them. Coloration is usually metallic red-orange, although it can vary according to scale formation. The dorsal fin is absent, and the anal and caudal fins are doubled. A stiffly held caudal fin flows from a continuation of the dorsal surface.

• **REMARK** The eyes take several months from birth to assume their "celestial" glance. This fish is not hardy and is therefore best kept in a separate indoor aquarium.

Diet Omnivorous	Tank levels All	Temperament

Family CYPRINIDAE	Species *Carassius auratus*	Size Variable

FANTAIL GOLDFISH

The coloration of the Fantail varies according to the scale formation and the relative differences in pigmentation. The dorsal fin is held high, and on good specimens it should measure half the body depth. Anal and caudal fins are doubled, and the caudal fin is carried above the horizontal line.

• **REMARK** This strain has no swimming difficulties, and it can therefore be kept outside in ponds.

Diet Omnivorous	Tank levels All	Temperament

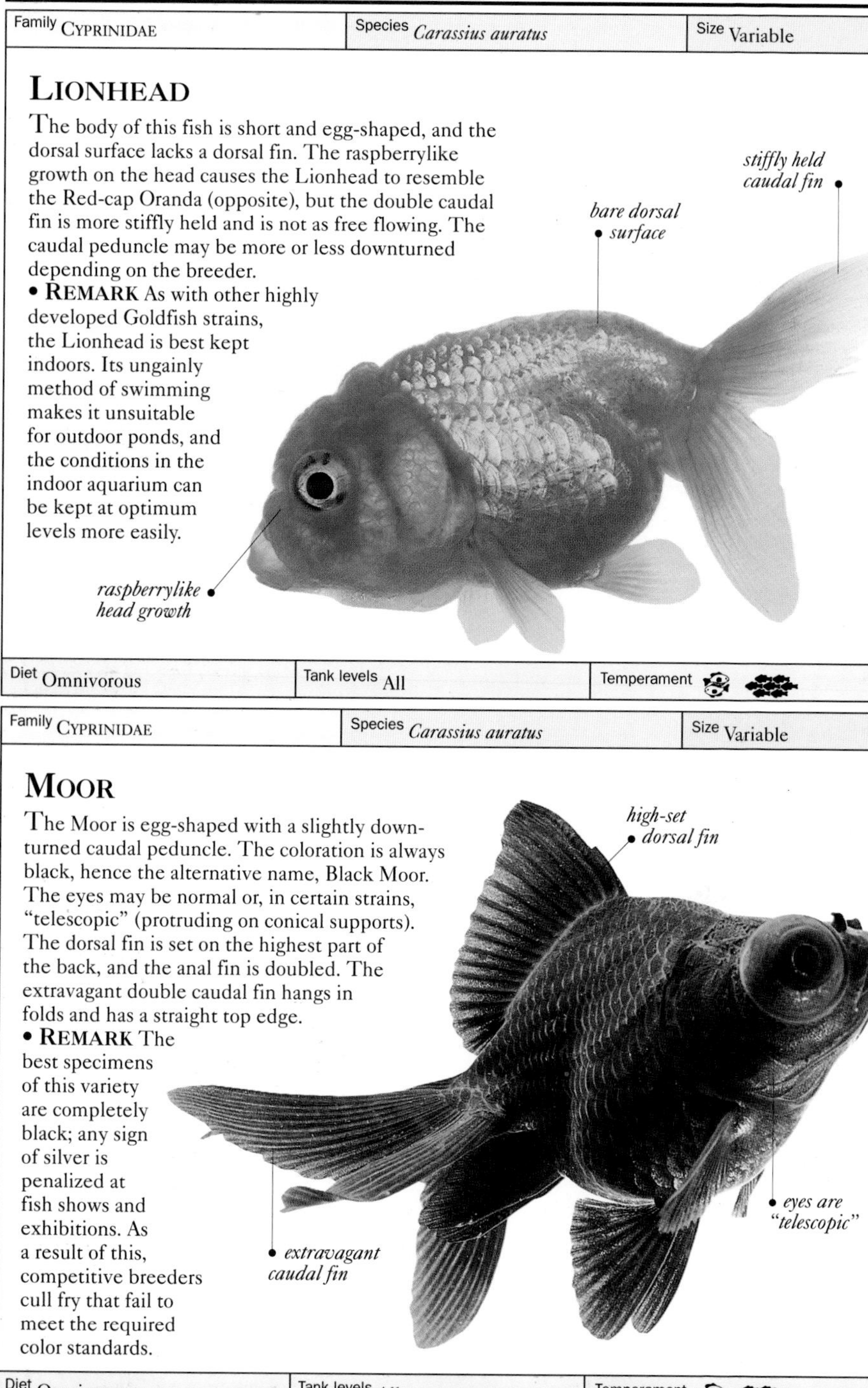

Family CYPRINIDAE	Species *Carassius auratus*	Size Variable

LIONHEAD

The body of this fish is short and egg-shaped, and the dorsal surface lacks a dorsal fin. The raspberrylike growth on the head causes the Lionhead to resemble the Red-cap Oranda (opposite), but the double caudal fin is more stiffly held and is not as free flowing. The caudal peduncle may be more or less downturned depending on the breeder.

• **REMARK** As with other highly developed Goldfish strains, the Lionhead is best kept indoors. Its ungainly method of swimming makes it unsuitable for outdoor ponds, and the conditions in the indoor aquarium can be kept at optimum levels more easily.

Diet Omnivorous	Tank levels All	Temperament

Family CYPRINIDAE	Species *Carassius auratus*	Size Variable

MOOR

The Moor is egg-shaped with a slightly down-turned caudal peduncle. The coloration is always black, hence the alternative name, Black Moor. The eyes may be normal or, in certain strains, "telescopic" (protruding on conical supports). The dorsal fin is set on the highest part of the back, and the anal fin is doubled. The extravagant double caudal fin hangs in folds and has a straight top edge.

• **REMARK** The best specimens of this variety are completely black; any sign of silver is penalized at fish shows and exhibitions. As a result of this, competitive breeders cull fry that fail to meet the required color standards.

Diet Omnivorous	Tank levels All	Temperament

Family CYPRINIDAE	Species *Carassius auratus*	Size Variable

RED-CAP ORANDA

The Oranda is short compared with other cultivated Goldfish, and has a slightly down-turned caudal peduncle. The color varies: this Oranda strain has a white body with a red cap on the head. The head growth is known as the "wen" and is peculiar to Orandas and to the Lionhead (opposite). The dorsal fin is high, and the anal and caudal fins are doubled and free flowing.

• **REMARK** Like other fancy strains, the Oranda needs a tank free of active or aggressive fishes, and it requires optimum water conditions to prevent fin damage and deterioration.

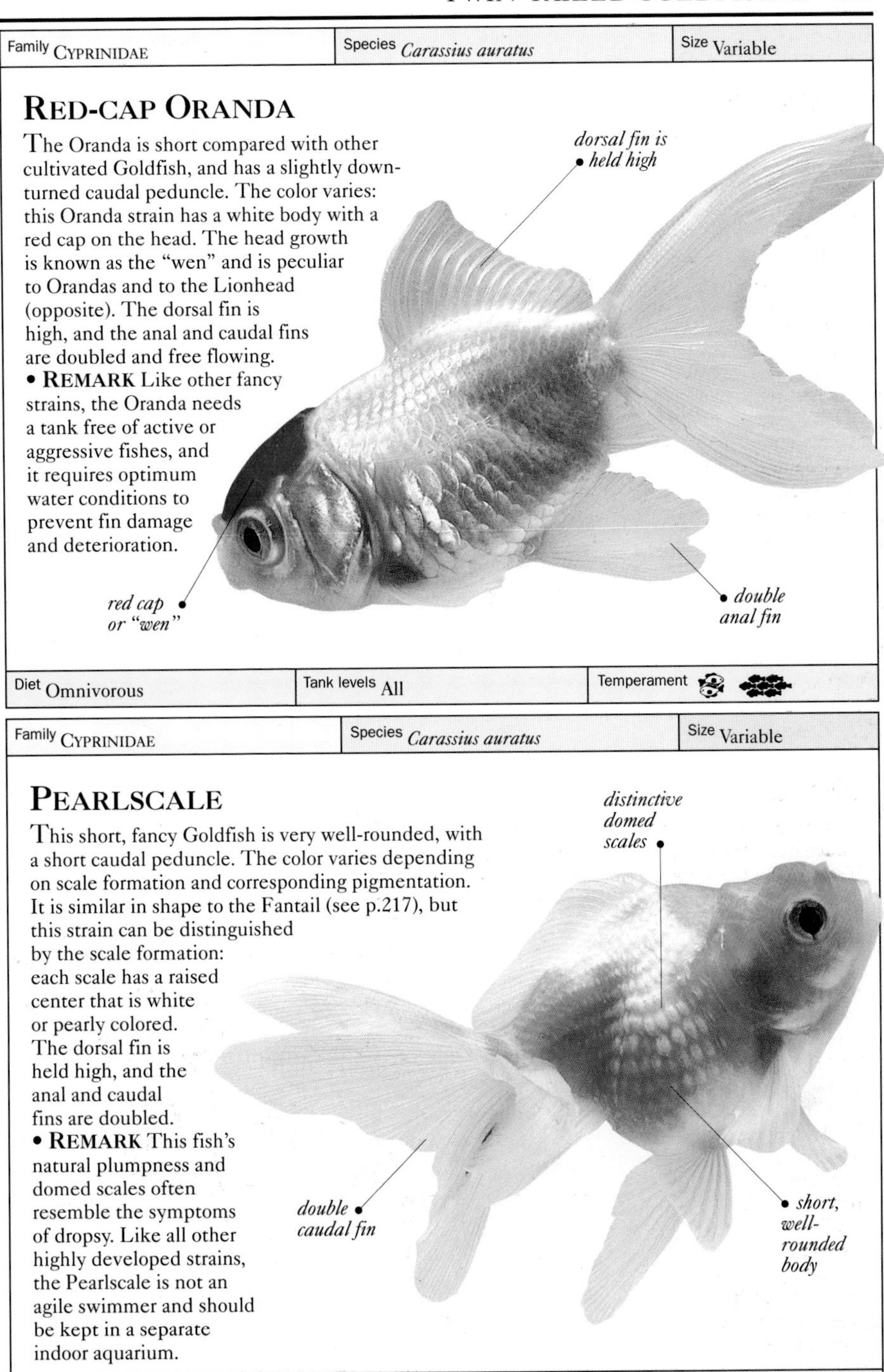

Diet Omnivorous	Tank levels All	Temperament

Family CYPRINIDAE	Species *Carassius auratus*	Size Variable

PEARLSCALE

This short, fancy Goldfish is very well-rounded, with a short caudal peduncle. The color varies depending on scale formation and corresponding pigmentation. It is similar in shape to the Fantail (see p.217), but this strain can be distinguished by the scale formation: each scale has a raised center that is white or pearly colored. The dorsal fin is held high, and the anal and caudal fins are doubled.

• **REMARK** This fish's natural plumpness and domed scales often resemble the symptoms of dropsy. Like all other highly developed strains, the Pearlscale is not an agile swimmer and should be kept in a separate indoor aquarium.

Diet Omnivorous	Tank levels All	Temperament

Family CYPRINIDAE	Species *Carassius auratus*	Size Variable

POM-POM

The scalation of this variety is usually metallic or nacreous, but it can vary. The Pom-pom is physically similar to the Lionhead (see p.218), but instead of a raspberrylike growth on the head, the nostril tissue has developed to form two distinct "pom-pons"; these hang down below the mouth on some varieties. On the original strain, the dorsal fin is absent. Recent strains have developed it.

• **REMARK** Special care is needed to maintain the delicate nasal growths in prime condition. Keep these fish in a separate aquarium with good quality water.

• **OTHER NAME** Also spelled Pom-pon.

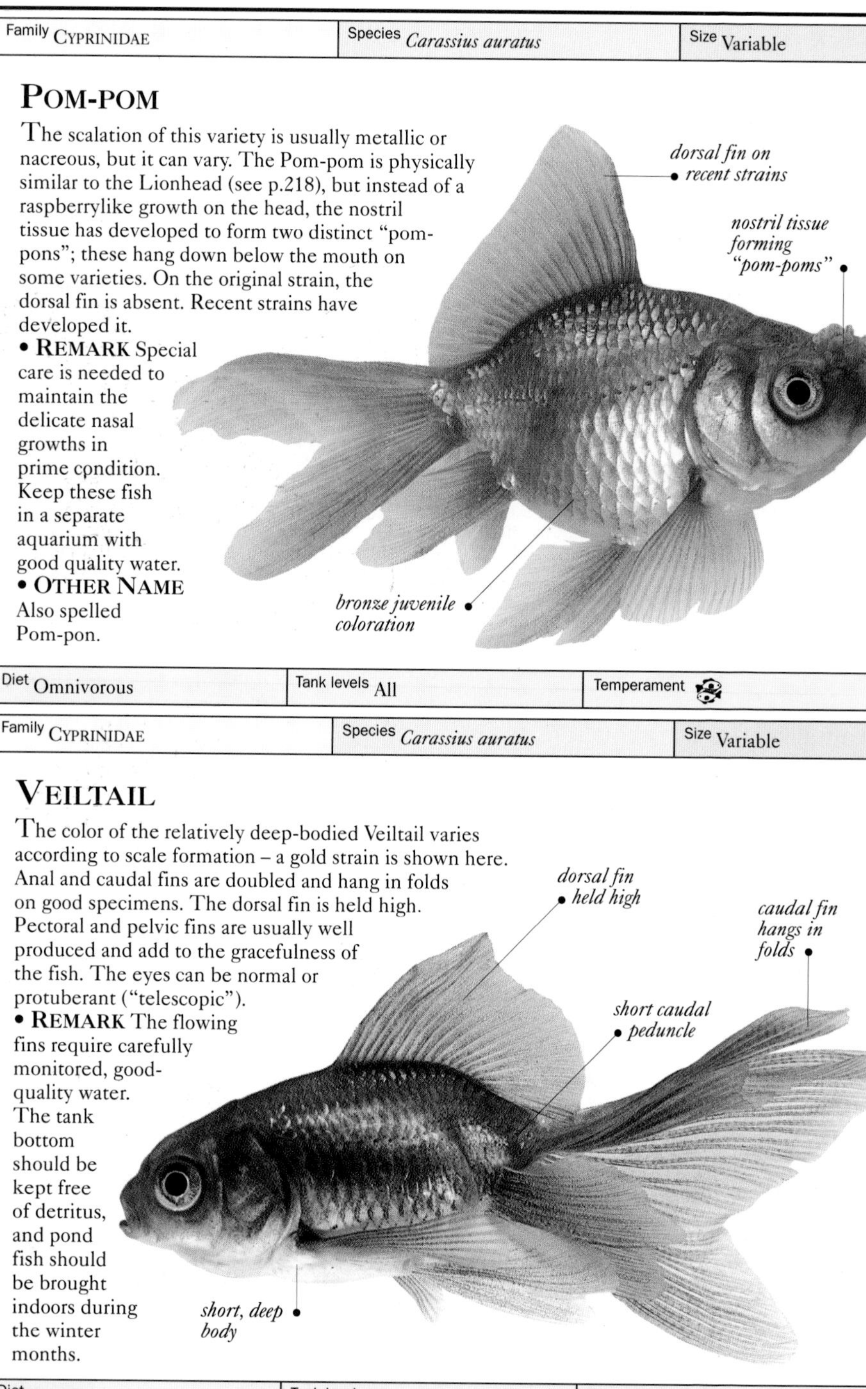

Diet Omnivorous	Tank levels All	Temperament

Family CYPRINIDAE	Species *Carassius auratus*	Size Variable

VEILTAIL

The color of the relatively deep-bodied Veiltail varies according to scale formation – a gold strain is shown here. Anal and caudal fins are doubled and hang in folds on good specimens. The dorsal fin is held high. Pectoral and pelvic fins are usually well produced and add to the gracefulness of the fish. The eyes can be normal or protuberant ("telescopic").

• **REMARK** The flowing fins require carefully monitored, good-quality water. The tank bottom should be kept free of detritus, and pond fish should be brought indoors during the winter months.

Diet Omnivorous	Tank levels All	Temperament

Family CYPRINIDAE	Species *Carassius auratus*	Size Variable

JAPANESE GOLDFISH STRAINS

A selection of twin-tailed strains cultivated in Japan are shown on the following two pages. Although there is no internationally accepted exhibiting standard for these twintails, they are becoming increasingly popular and readily available on the aquarium market.

• **REMARK** The names used to describe the shape of the "wen" – the fleshy head covering of the Lionhead (or Buffalohead, as it is called in Japan) – reflect the depth of Goldfish culture in Japan. "Tokin" is a Samurai helmet shape, "Bim-bari" denotes a side growth, and "Tatsugashira" means an overall head covering.

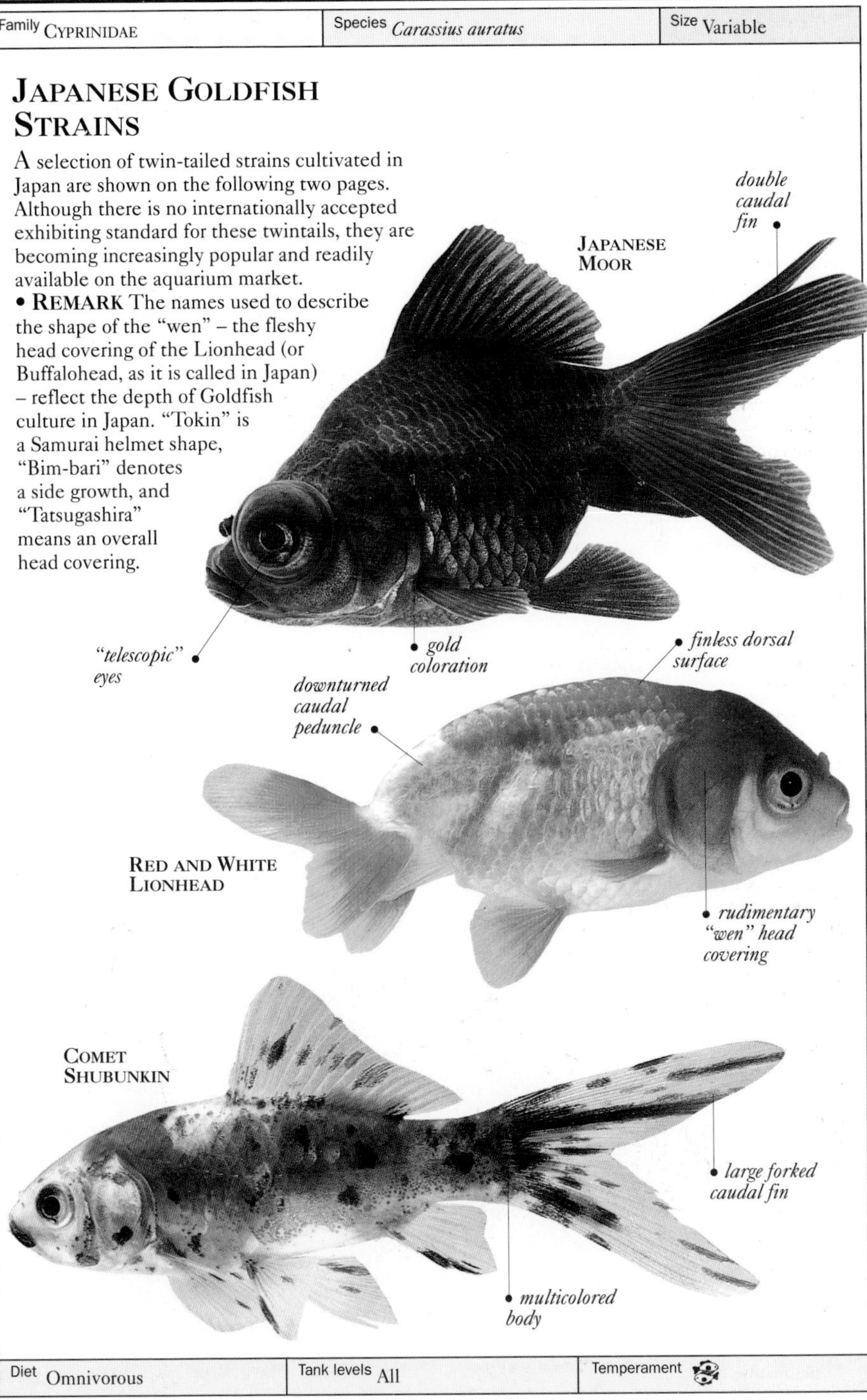

Diet Omnivorous	Tank levels All	Temperament

Family CYPRINIDAE	Species *Carassius auratus*	Size Variable

Diet Omnivorous	Tank levels All	Temperament

KOI

DESPITE THEIR long-term unsuitability for the indoor aquarium, there are many aquarium-bred strains of the ornamental Koi (*Cyprinus carpio*), and a selection is shown here. It is customary to view and judge these fish from above, and their colors and patterns have been developed accordingly. Koi originated in east Asia, but strains are now cultivated worldwide.

Family CYPRINIDAE	Species *Cyprinus carpio*	Size Variable

KOI

The shape of these classic ornamental fish is elongate, with moderately arched dorsal profiles in juveniles. The adults are more torpedo-shaped, rounded, and powerfully built. A wide mouth carries two pairs of barbels on a large head. Colors are extremely variable, as the Koi is a cultivated fish and not found in nature. The scalation of Koi also varies according to the strain. Strains with "doitsu" scalation, for example, carry only a few large scales, usually along the lateral line and on the dorsal surface. Strains with "matsuba" scalation have scales with a"pine-cone" effect; and those with "ginrin" covering feature metallic scales. The Asagi Koi shown here has a blue tone with matsuba scales; cheeks, fin bases, and chest areas are red. A selection of strains is shown on the following pages.

• **REMARK** Koi quickly outgrow the indoor aquarium, developing optimum size and best colors outdoors. Their bright colors stand out well against the darkness of the pond bottom. Koi are hearty consumers (especially of plants), and their environment should have an efficient filter system to deal with the waste. Attention to water quality is important.

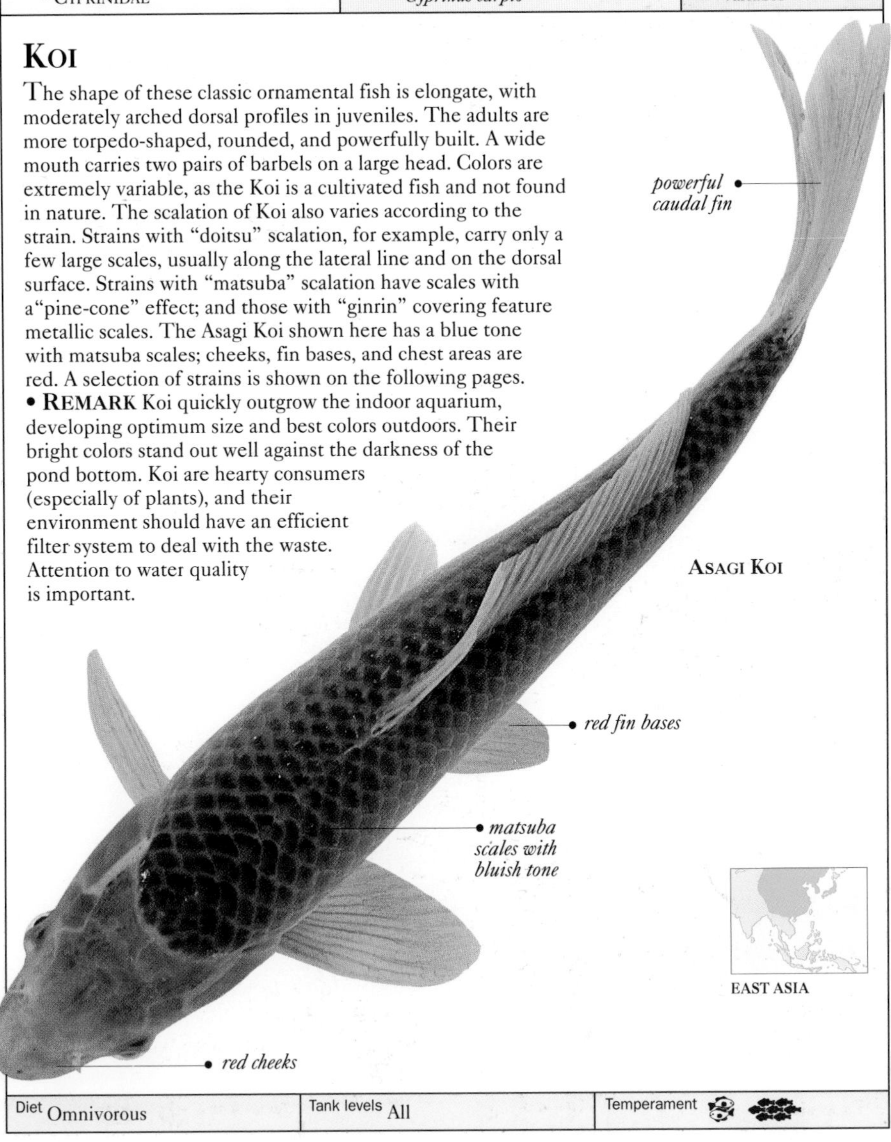

ASAGI KOI

Diet Omnivorous	Tank levels All	Temperament

Family CYPRINDAE	Species *Cyprinus carpio*	Size Variable

A colorful assortment of young Koi in an aquarium

Diet Omnivorous	Tank levels All	Temperament

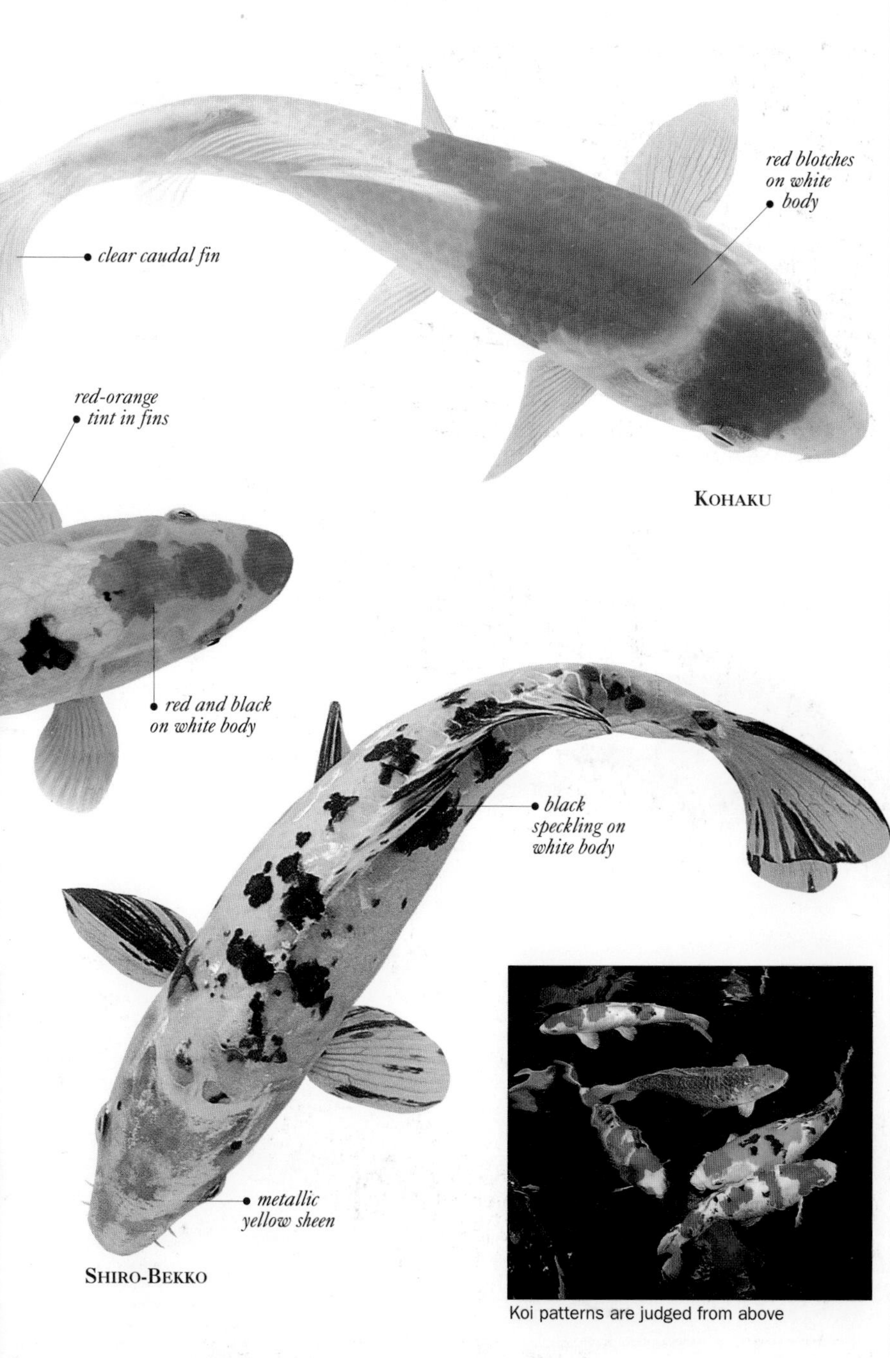

Koi patterns are judged from above

OTHER COLDWATER FRESHWATER FISHES

MANY FISH-KEEPERS' COLDWATER interests center around Goldfish and Koi, but there are other attractions in this field of the hobby. In spite of their relative obscurity, it is easy to keep different North American fishes, such as shiners and sunfish, as well as bitterlings and some species from Asia. Sunfish carry characteristic "ear flaps," which are extensions to the gill cover.

Family CYPRINIDAE	Species *Acanthorhodeus atranalis*	Size 3½ in (8 cm)

BITTERLING

The color of this fish is pinkish brown with a narrow, reddish caudal peduncle. An indistinct dark band runs vertically down the body and may spread at its midpoint toward a second band behind the gills. The broad, rounded dorsal and anal fins are slightly speckled with black.

• **HABITAT** Coastal regions in Japan.

• **REMARK** Bitterlings rival some of the tropical fish in color, and many new species are being exported from Japan.

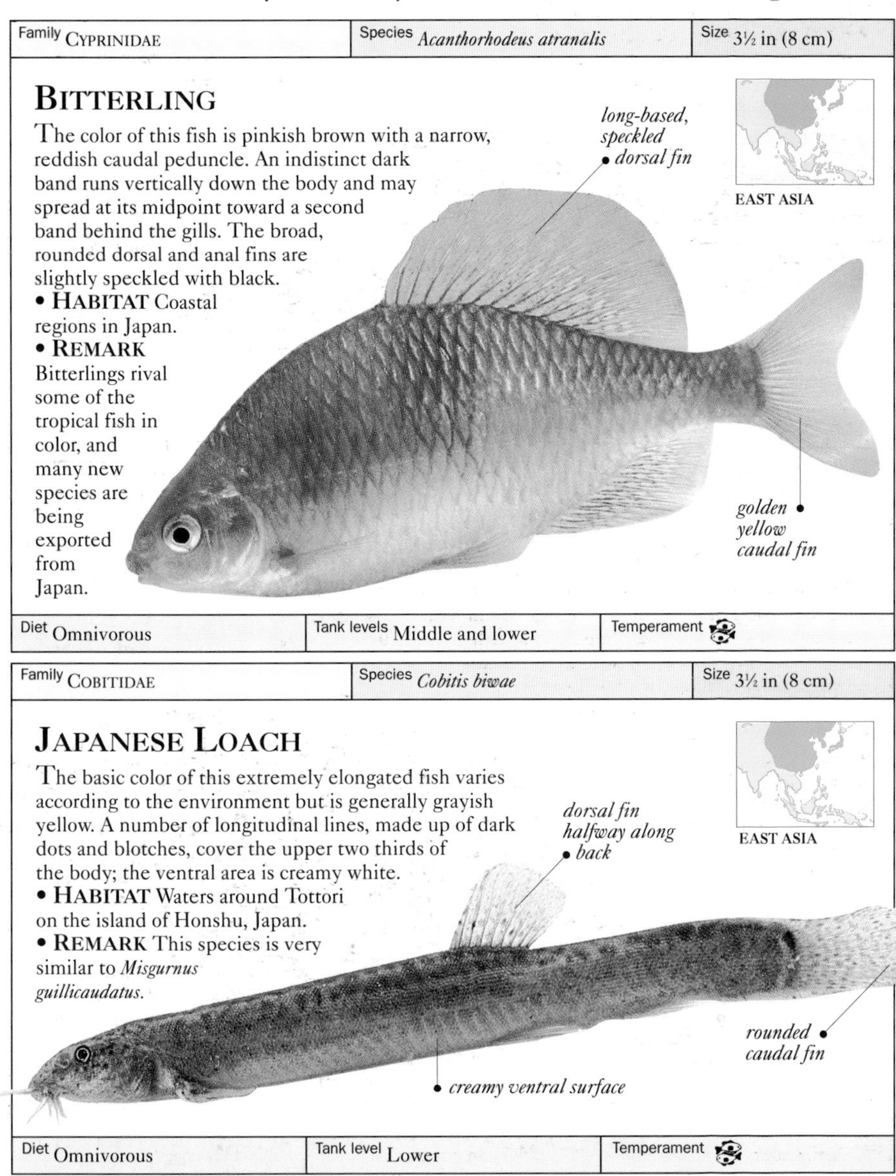

Diet Omnivorous	Tank levels Middle and lower	Temperament

Family COBITIDAE	Species *Cobitis biwae*	Size 3½ in (8 cm)

JAPANESE LOACH

The basic color of this extremely elongated fish varies according to the environment but is generally grayish yellow. A number of longitudinal lines, made up of dark dots and blotches, cover the upper two thirds of the body; the ventral area is creamy white.

• **HABITAT** Waters around Tottori on the island of Honshu, Japan.

• **REMARK** This species is very similar to *Misgurnus guillicaudatus.*

Diet Omnivorous	Tank level Lower	Temperament

Family GASTEROSTEIDAE	Species *Gasterosteus aculeatus*	Size 3½ in (8 cm)

THREE-SPINE STICKLEBACK

Brown mottling covers the silvery body of this fish. There are three erectile spines in front of the dorsal fin, and bony plates along the flanks. The lower parts of the male's head, throat, and ventral region turn bright red during spawning.

• **HABITAT** Inland coastal waters of Europe; also of North America, northern Asia, and Algeria.

• **REMARK** The female deposits eggs in a tunnel nest built by the male with plant matter. He fertilizes the eggs and guards them until they hatch. This fish requires live foods.

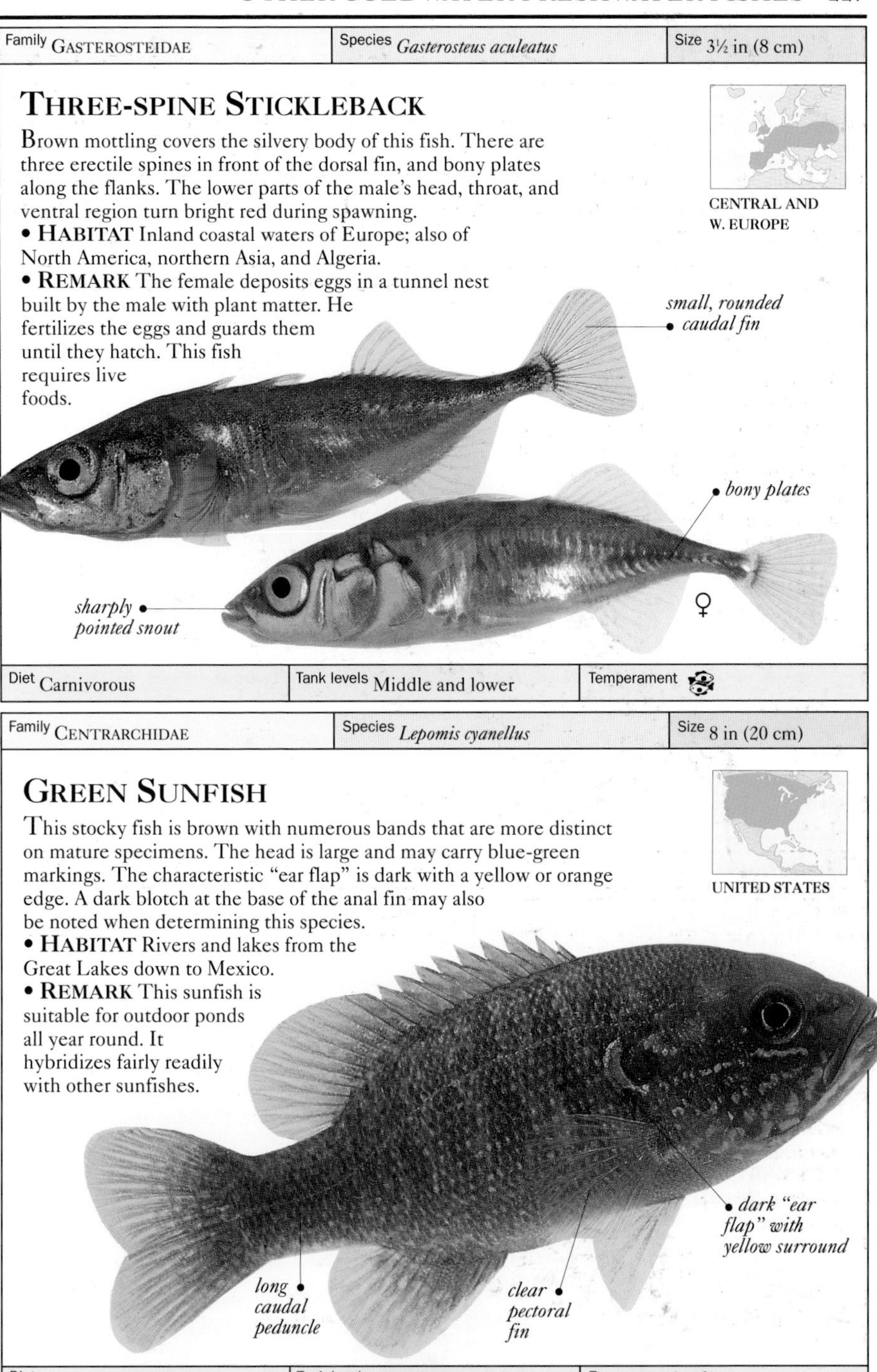

Diet Carnivorous	Tank levels Middle and lower	Temperament

Family CENTRARCHIDAE	Species *Lepomis cyanellus*	Size 8 in (20 cm)

GREEN SUNFISH

This stocky fish is brown with numerous bands that are more distinct on mature specimens. The head is large and may carry blue-green markings. The characteristic "ear flap" is dark with a yellow or orange edge. A dark blotch at the base of the anal fin may also be noted when determining this species.

• **HABITAT** Rivers and lakes from the Great Lakes down to Mexico.

• **REMARK** This sunfish is suitable for outdoor ponds all year round. It hybridizes fairly readily with other sunfishes.

Diet Carnivorous	Tank levels Middle and lower	Temperament

Family CENTRARCHIDAE	Species *Lepomis gibbosus*	Size 9 in (22.5 cm)

PUMPKINSEED

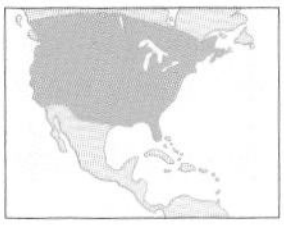

UNITED STATES

This oval fish is golden brown and covered with iridescent blue-green spots. The ventral region is yellow. Both head and gill covers are marked by blue-green wavy lines, and the "ear flap" is black with a reddish rear edge. These colors intensify during spawning.

• **HABITAT** Rivers and lakes of the USA from North Dakota down to South Carolina; also southern central Canada as far east as Quebec.

• **REMARK** The Pumpkinseed readily hybridizes with other sunfishes, notably *Lepomis cyanellus* and *L. macrochirus*. As with all family members, spawning occurs in pits dug by the male.

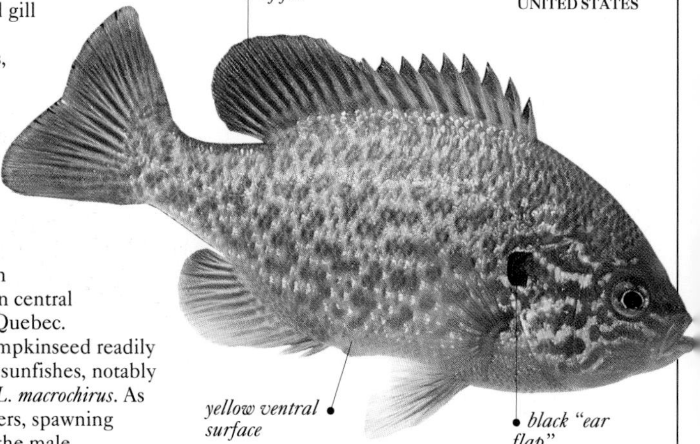

blue-green rear edge of fin

yellow ventral surface

black "ear flap"

Diet Carnivorous	Tank levels Middle and lower	Temperament

Family CENTRARCHIDAE	Species *Lepomis humilis*	Size 4 in (10 cm)

ORANGE-SPOTTED SUNFISH

UNITED STATES

The profile of this fish is much slimmer than other members of the genus. Coloration is pale greenish brown with scattered dots of red-orange on males and dark brown on females. A bluish sheen occurs on the gill cover and flanks, and the chest and ventral region of the male are yellowish. The characteristic dark "ear flap" has a white edge.

• **HABITAT** Rivers and lakes of the USA from North Dakota to Texas.

• **REMARK** The male emits a grunting sound during courtship. This fish hybridizes with other members of the sunfish family.

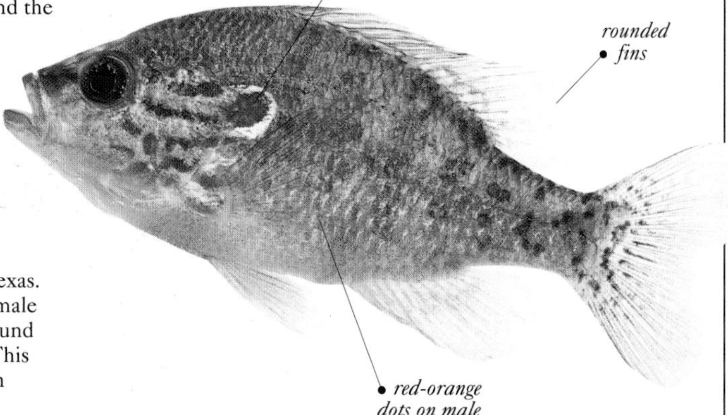

dark "ear flap"

rounded fins

red-orange dots on male

Diet Carnivorous	Tank levels Middle and lower	Temperament 

Family CENTRARCHIDAE	Species *Lepomis macrochirus*	Size 10 in (25 cm)

BLUEGILL

This greenish brown fish carries numerous vertical bars, some of which are divided by a pale line. The edge of the gill cover is pale blue, hence the popular name. The "ear flap" is plain black, and the ventral surface is paler between the pelvic fins and caudal peduncle. The throat region is yellow. Most fins are greenish yellow with a little dark patterning.

• **HABITAT** Rivers, streams, ponds, and lakes of the USA from Minnesota to Florida and Texas, including the East Coast.

• **REMARK** This rather aggressive fish regularly digs in the substrate. It hybridizes quite readily with other sunfishes.

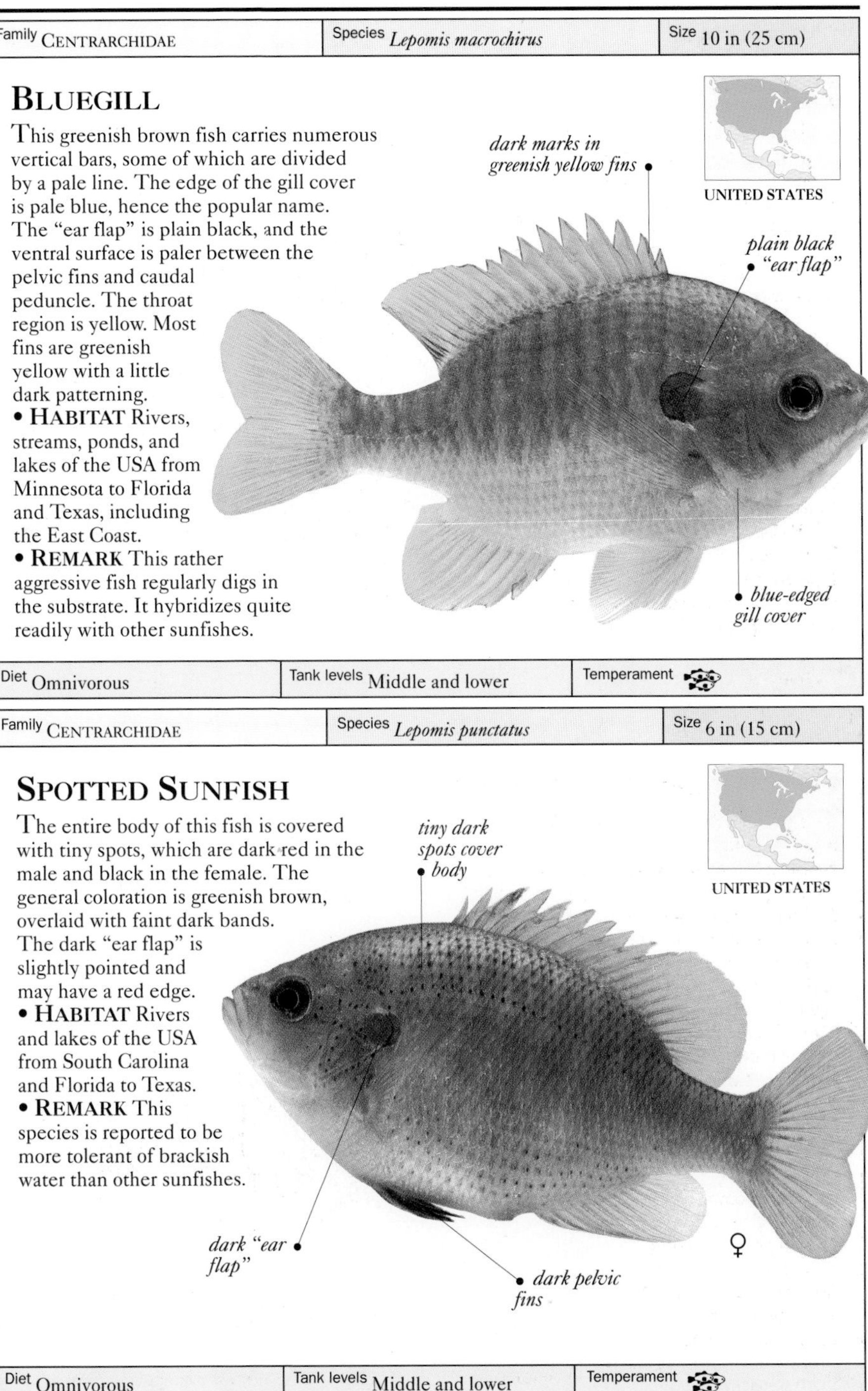

Diet Omnivorous	Tank levels Middle and lower	Temperament

Family CENTRARCHIDAE	Species *Lepomis punctatus*	Size 6 in (15 cm)

SPOTTED SUNFISH

The entire body of this fish is covered with tiny spots, which are dark red in the male and black in the female. The general coloration is greenish brown, overlaid with faint dark bands. The dark "ear flap" is slightly pointed and may have a red edge.

• **HABITAT** Rivers and lakes of the USA from South Carolina and Florida to Texas.

• **REMARK** This species is reported to be more tolerant of brackish water than other sunfishes.

Diet Omnivorous	Tank levels Middle and lower	Temperament

Family CATOSTOMIDAE	Species *Myxocyprinus asiatica sinensis*	Size 12 in (30 cm)

CHINESE SAILFIN SUCKER

The highly arched dorsal profile of this fish is exaggerated by the large, triangular dorsal fin and almost flat ventral surface. The basic color of the original species is golden brown; this subspecies is a pinkish rust color. Three broad, dark bands cross the body vertically, the last covering the short caudal peduncle and merging into the well-spread caudal fin. The head is small and appears to merge into the rest of the body.

• **HABITAT** Lakes in Japan; other subspecies are found in China.

• **REMARK** Although often sold with tropical fish, this subspecies does not require high temperatures. It appreciates vegetable matter in its diet.

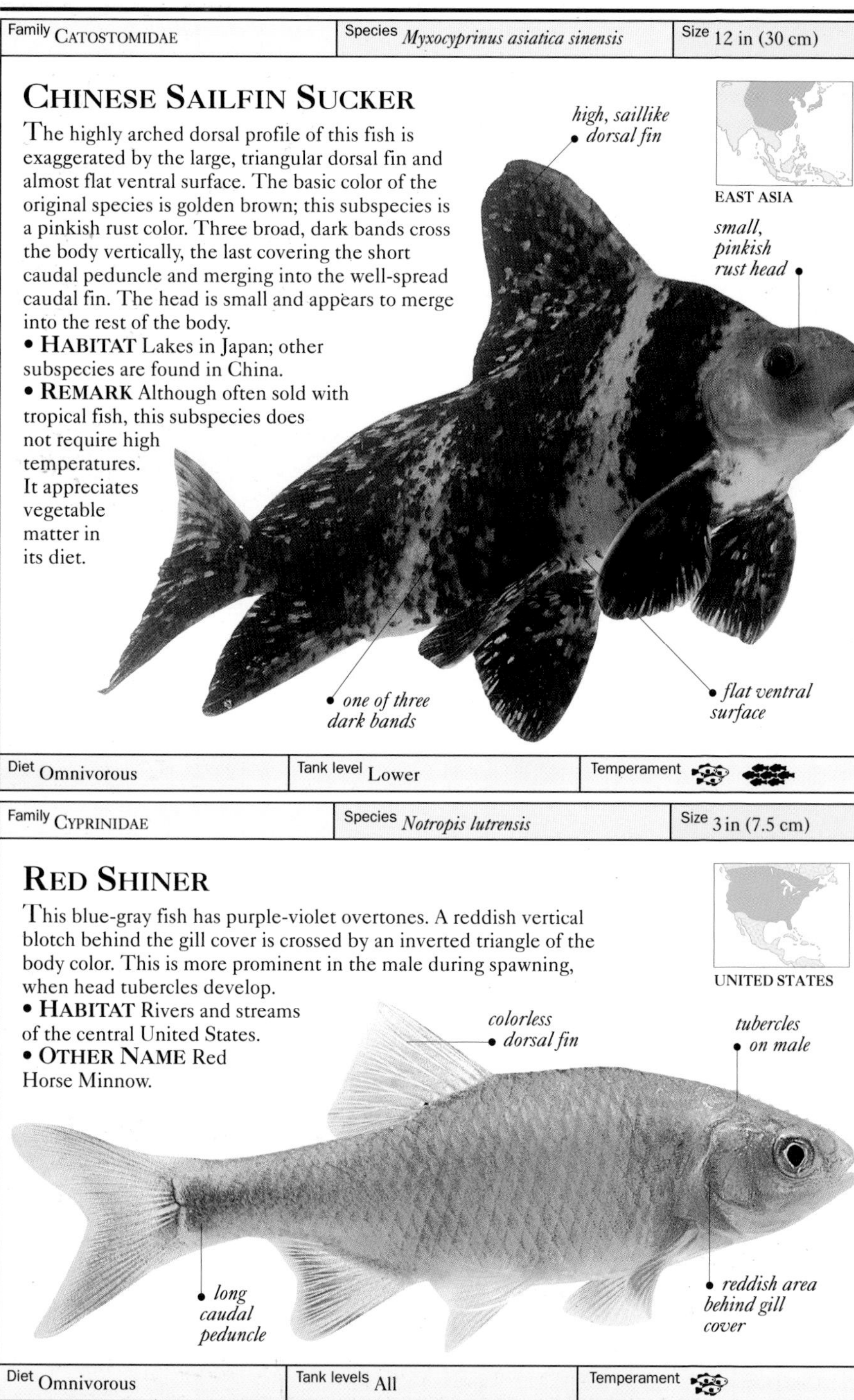

Diet Omnivorous	Tank level Lower	Temperament

Family CYPRINIDAE	Species *Notropis lutrensis*	Size 3 in (7.5 cm)

RED SHINER

This blue-gray fish has purple-violet overtones. A reddish vertical blotch behind the gill cover is crossed by an inverted triangle of the body color. This is more prominent in the male during spawning, when head tubercles develop.

• **HABITAT** Rivers and streams of the central United States.

• **OTHER NAME** Red Horse Minnow.

Diet Omnivorous	Tank levels All	Temperament

Family CYPRINIDAE	Species *Phoxinus phoxinus*	Size 5½ in (14 cm)

EUROPEAN MINNOW

This slim, silvery yellow fish has brown mottling on the upper body, and lower markings that may combine to form a regular horizontal pattern or a broad dark band. The ventral surface is silvery pink. Both sexes develop tubercles when breeding, and the male chest region may become redder while the female becomes fatter at this time.

- **HABITAT** Streams and rivers in Europe; also Asia.
- **REMARK** A long-established favorite in Europe, this minnow requires well-oxygenated water if it is to thrive in captivity; some owners even go so far as to simulate running water conditions for it.

A minnow feeding on a live worm

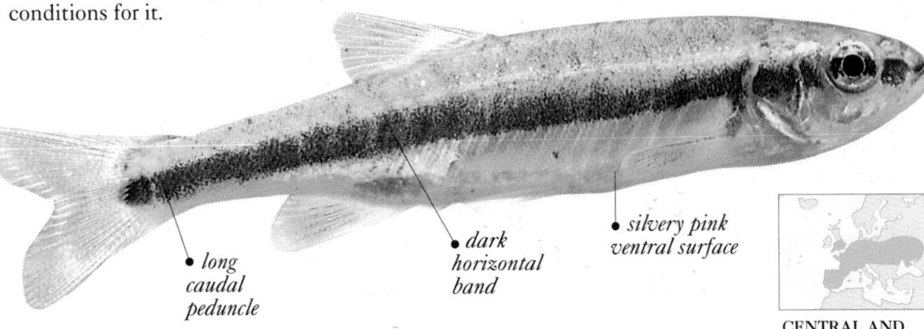

CENTRAL AND W. EUROPE

Diet Omnivorous	Tank level Upper	Temperament

Family CYPRINIDAE	Species *Pimephales promelas*	Size 4 in (10 cm)

FATHEAD MINNOW

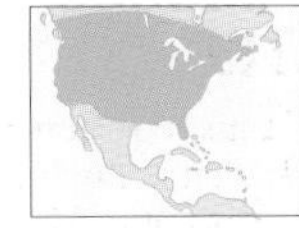

UNITED STATES

The coloration of this minnow is golden brown, with a paler ventral surface. There may be a dark line along the flanks with a small spot on the end of the caudal peduncle, as shown here. The male has a distinctly "fatter" head and develops tubercles during breeding; he also has a notch in the front of the dorsal fin formed by a shorter first ray.

- **HABITAT** Streams and rivers in central North America.
- **REMARK** A cultivated yellow-gold strain of a very similar species is available.

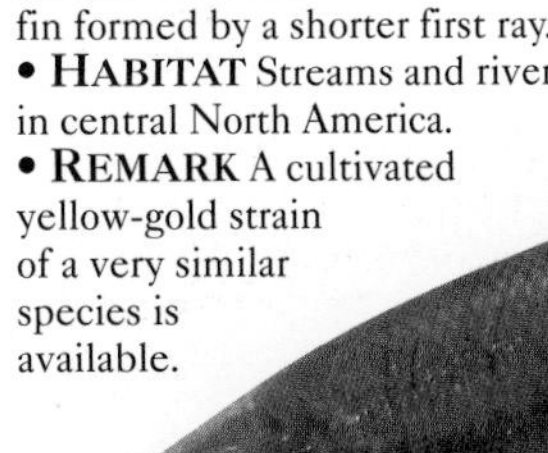
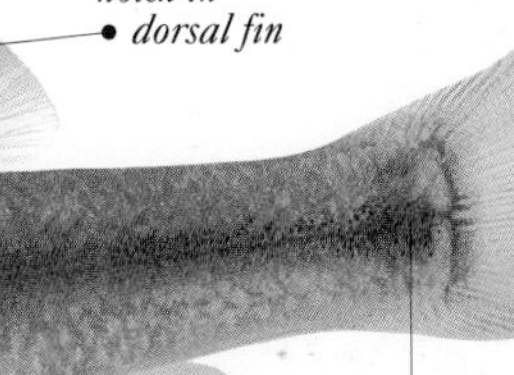

Diet Omnivorous	Tank levels Upper and middle	Temperament 

Family CYPRINIDAE	Species *Rhodeus ocellatus*	Size 3 in (7.5 cm)

JAPANESE ROSE BITTERLING

The shape of this species is similar to that of the barbs (see p.46). Coloration is pinkish violet on the flanks with a pink vertical stripe behind the gill cover. A blue line runs from the midpoint back to the caudal fin, where it ends in a blotch of red that bleeds into the caudal fin. Turquoise speckling may appear in the dorsal fin, and there is a notch in the dorsal profile above the red-topped eye. The female has a long ovipositor for egg laying.

• **HABITAT** Lakes and rivers in Japan.

• **REMARK** An increasing number of bitterlings have become available to the aquarist recently, and there is often confusion regarding the exact identity of individual species.

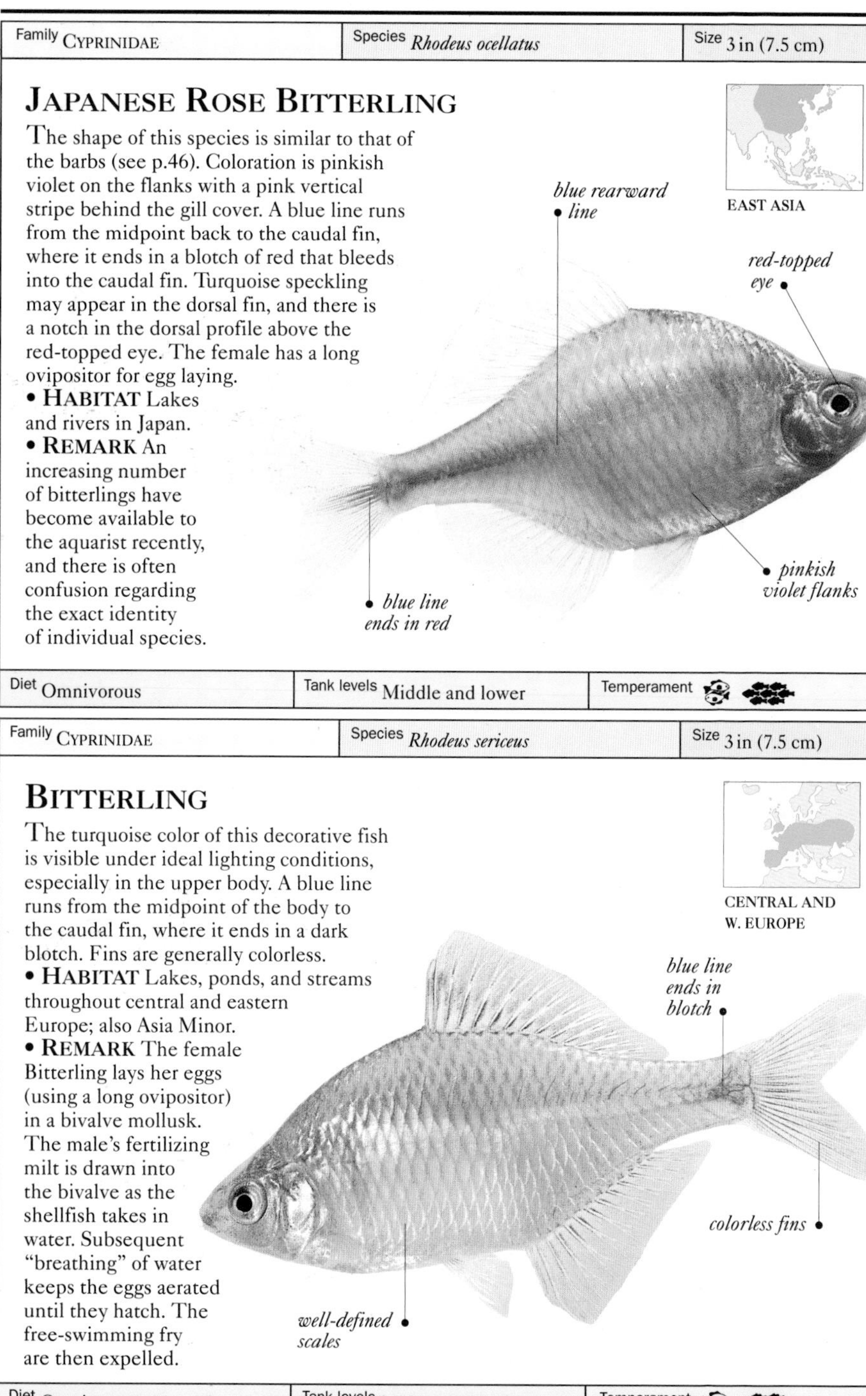

Diet Omnivorous	Tank levels Middle and lower	Temperament

Family CYPRINIDAE	Species *Rhodeus sericeus*	Size 3 in (7.5 cm)

BITTERLING

The turquoise color of this decorative fish is visible under ideal lighting conditions, especially in the upper body. A blue line runs from the midpoint of the body to the caudal fin, where it ends in a dark blotch. Fins are generally colorless.

• **HABITAT** Lakes, ponds, and streams throughout central and eastern Europe; also Asia Minor.

• **REMARK** The female Bitterling lays her eggs (using a long ovipositor) in a bivalve mollusk. The male's fertilizing milt is drawn into the bivalve as the shellfish takes in water. Subsequent "breathing" of water keeps the eggs aerated until they hatch. The free-swimming fry are then expelled.

Diet Omnivorous	Tank levels Middle and lower	Temperament

Family CYPRINIDAE	Species *Sarcocheilichthys sinensis*	Size 8 in (20 cm)

OILY GUDGEON

Four broad, dark brown bands cross the long, golden yellow body of this fish. The edge of each band is indistinct. The ventral profile is slightly flattened, as the Oily Gudgeon is a bottom-dweller. Fins are yellowish and heavily marked with dark brown or black. The male develops white tubercles on his snout during spawning. Females, like females of other genus members, have long ovipositors.

• **HABITAT** Flowing waters in China.

• **REMARK** An efficient filtration system is required, as this species constantly stirs up the substrate as it forages for food.

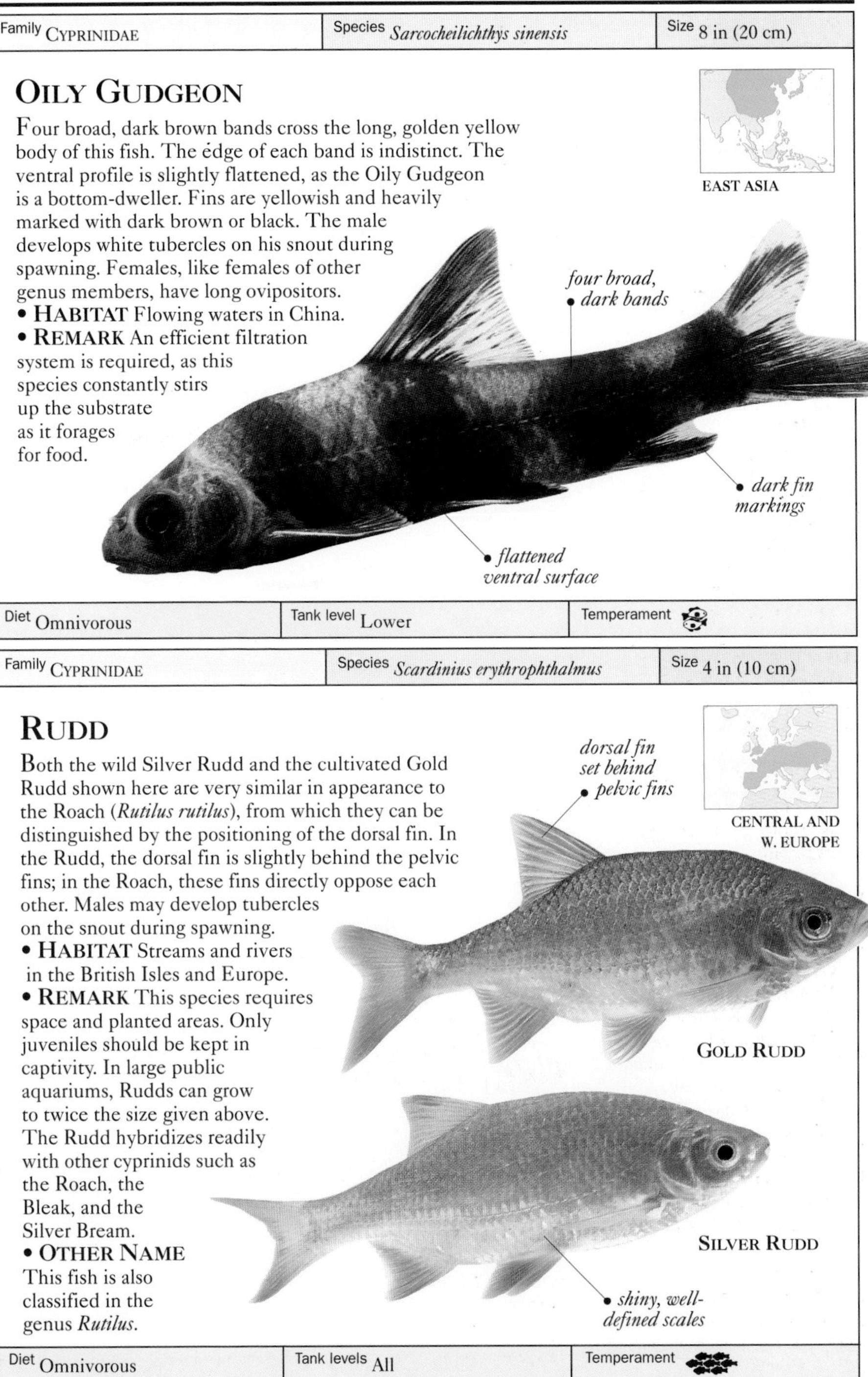

Diet Omnivorous	Tank level Lower	Temperament

Family CYPRINIDAE	Species *Scardinius erythrophthalmus*	Size 4 in (10 cm)

RUDD

Both the wild Silver Rudd and the cultivated Gold Rudd shown here are very similar in appearance to the Roach (*Rutilus rutilus*), from which they can be distinguished by the positioning of the dorsal fin. In the Rudd, the dorsal fin is slightly behind the pelvic fins; in the Roach, these fins directly oppose each other. Males may develop tubercles on the snout during spawning.

• **HABITAT** Streams and rivers in the British Isles and Europe.

• **REMARK** This species requires space and planted areas. Only juveniles should be kept in captivity. In large public aquariums, Rudds can grow to twice the size given above. The Rudd hybridizes readily with other cyprinids such as the Roach, the Bleak, and the Silver Bream.

• **OTHER NAME** This fish is also classified in the genus *Rutilus*.

Diet Omnivorous	Tank levels All	Temperament

TROPICAL MARINE FISHES

ANEMONEFISHES

THE FISHES in the family Pomacentridae that are referred to as "anemonefishes" derive the name from their relationship with sea anemones. The fish shelter within the tentacles of the anemones, protected from their poison by special skin mucus. Their ungainly swimming action has also earned them the name "clownfishes." These hardy fish are ideal starter fish.

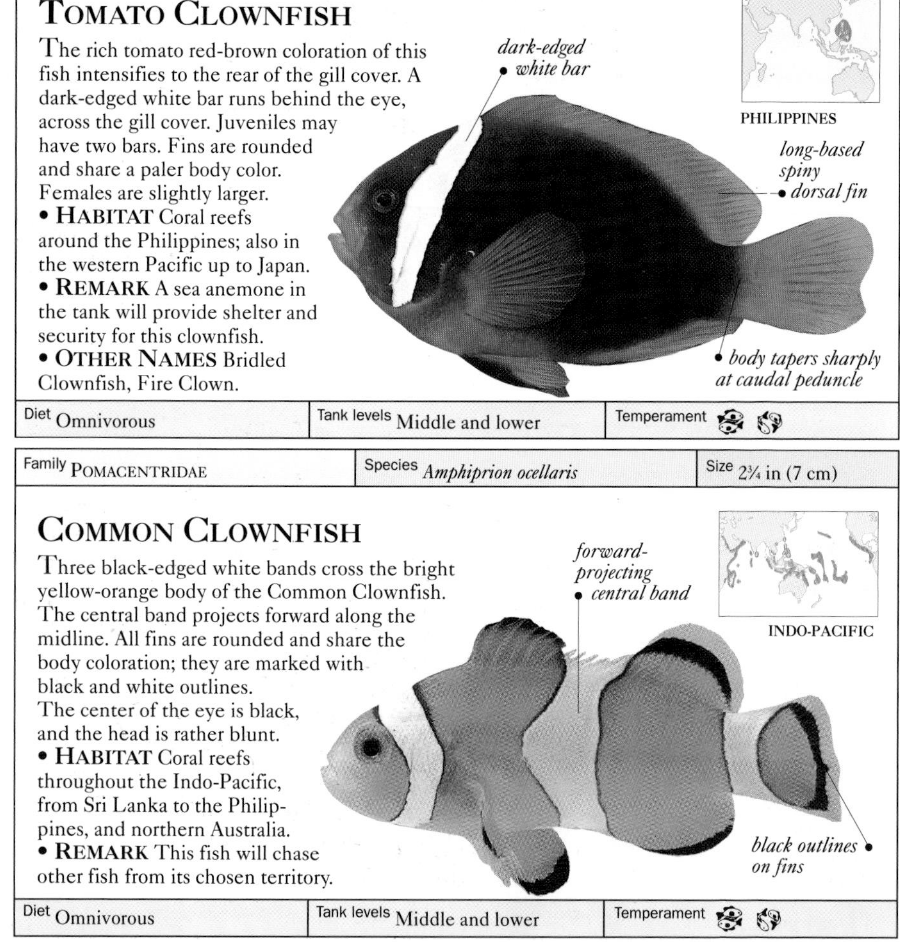

Family POMACENTRIDAE	Species *Amphiprion frenatus*	Size 3 in (7.5 cm)

TOMATO CLOWNFISH

The rich tomato red-brown coloration of this fish intensifies to the rear of the gill cover. A dark-edged white bar runs behind the eye, across the gill cover. Juveniles may have two bars. Fins are rounded and share a paler body color. Females are slightly larger.

- **HABITAT** Coral reefs around the Philippines; also in the western Pacific up to Japan.
- **REMARK** A sea anemone in the tank will provide shelter and security for this clownfish.
- **OTHER NAMES** Bridled Clownfish, Fire Clown.

Diet Omnivorous	Tank levels Middle and lower	Temperament

Family POMACENTRIDAE	Species *Amphiprion ocellaris*	Size 2¾ in (7 cm)

COMMON CLOWNFISH

Three black-edged white bands cross the bright yellow-orange body of the Common Clownfish. The central band projects forward along the midline. All fins are rounded and share the body coloration; they are marked with black and white outlines. The center of the eye is black, and the head is rather blunt.

- **HABITAT** Coral reefs throughout the Indo-Pacific, from Sri Lanka to the Philippines, and northern Australia.
- **REMARK** This fish will chase other fish from its chosen territory.

Diet Omnivorous	Tank levels Middle and lower	Temperament

Family POMACENTRIDAE	Species *Amphiprion perideraion*	Size 3 in (7.5 cm)

Pink Skunk Clownfish

A narrow white stripe runs from the tip of this fish's snout along the top of the delicate, golden pinkish body, to the end of the caudal peduncle. A narrow, dark-edged, white band crosses the body vertically, covering the gill cover. The dark eye has a gold rim around the pupil, and the rounded fins are a shade or two paler than the body. The dorsal and caudal fins of males have orange edges.

Sea anemones provide valued shelter

• **HABITAT** The Philippines; also coral reefs around Hong Kong, and from Thailand to northern Australia.

• **OTHER NAME** Salmon Clownfish.

PHILIPPINES

white band along dorsal surface

rounded fins

gold rim around eye

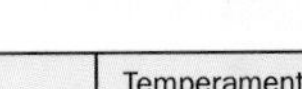

♀

Diet Omnivorous	Tank levels Middle and lower	Temperament 

Family POMACENTRIDAE	Species *Premnas biaculeatus*	Size 6 in (15 cm)

Maroon Clownfish

Significantly more heavily built than other species of anemonefish, the Maroon Clownfish has a very rich, dark brown-red color. The body is crossed vertically by three thin white stripes. A distinguishing feature of this species is the pair of large spines below the eye. (*Amphiprion* clownfishes lack these spines but have tiny spines at the rear of the gill cover and more scales on the head.)

• **HABITAT** Indo-Pacific reefs from Madagascar to the Solomon Islands, via the Philippines and Queensland, Australia.

• **REMARK** This fish is the only species in the genus. It is best kept with several variously sized specimens.

• **OTHER NAME** Spine-cheeked Clownfish.

INDO-PACIFIC

one of three thin white stripes

large spine below eye

Diet Omnivorous	Tank levels Middle and lower	Temperament

ANGELFISHES

THE ANGELFISHES (family Pomacanthidae) can be distinguished from their relatives, the butterflyfishes, by the presence of a sharp spine on the rear of the gill cover. There is also often a marked difference in coloration and patterning between juvenile and adult forms. Reproduction in angelfishes is by egg scattering, although it is unlikely to occur in an average-sized aquarium, where fishes may be immature or where there is a lack of space. Members of the angelfish family are polyp feeders, consuming living corals and sponges, for example. These special dietary requirements are likely to exclude the more exotic species from most collections, but commercial foods that include required natural ingredients are increasingly available.

Family POMACANTHIDAE	Species *Centropyge argi*	Size 3 in (7.5 cm)

CHERUBFISH

The rich dark blue body of this angelfish gives way to a yellow chest and head region. This region may vary from yellow to golden purple among subspecies from different locations. Long-based dorsal and anal fins share the body color and have black streaks radiating out toward dark margins bordered by electric blue.

- **HABITAT** Coral reefs in the Caribbean; also the western Atlantic.
- **REMARK** This hardy fish does not require a large aquarium. Cherubfish tend to pair, so look for two fish that appear inseparable when purchasing.
- **OTHER NAMES** Atlantic Pygmy Angelfish.

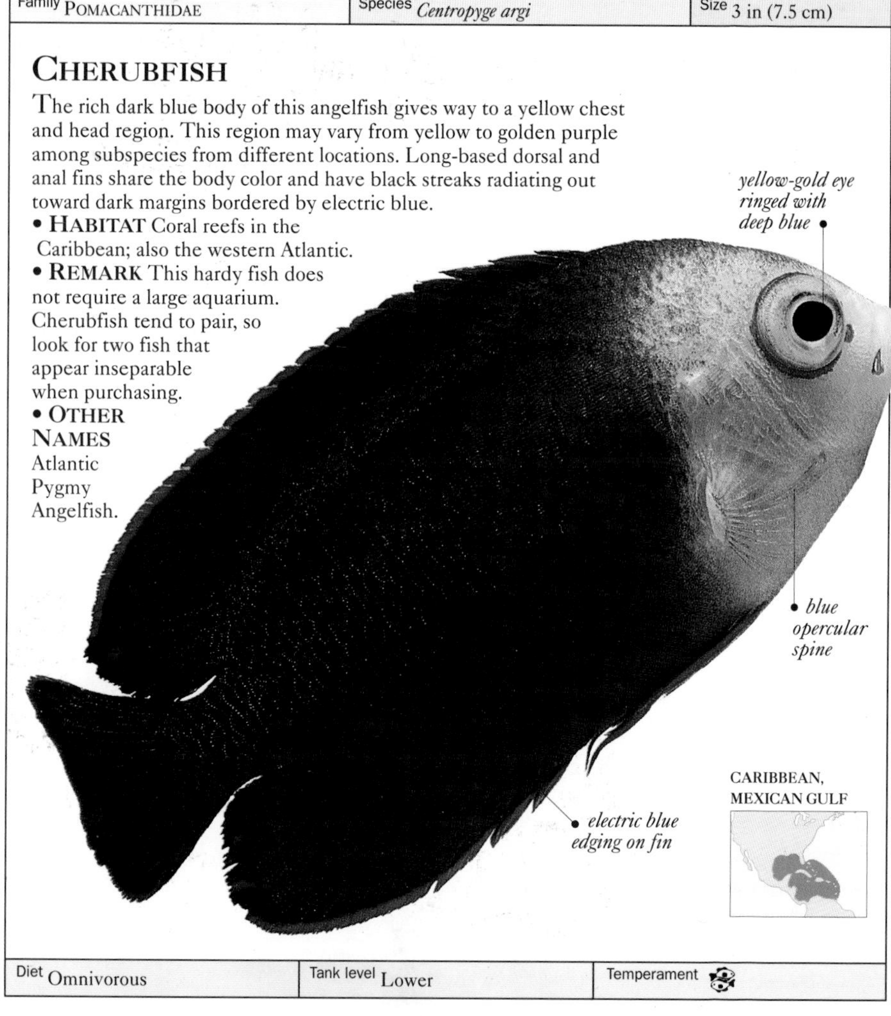

Diet Omnivorous	Tank level Lower	Temperament

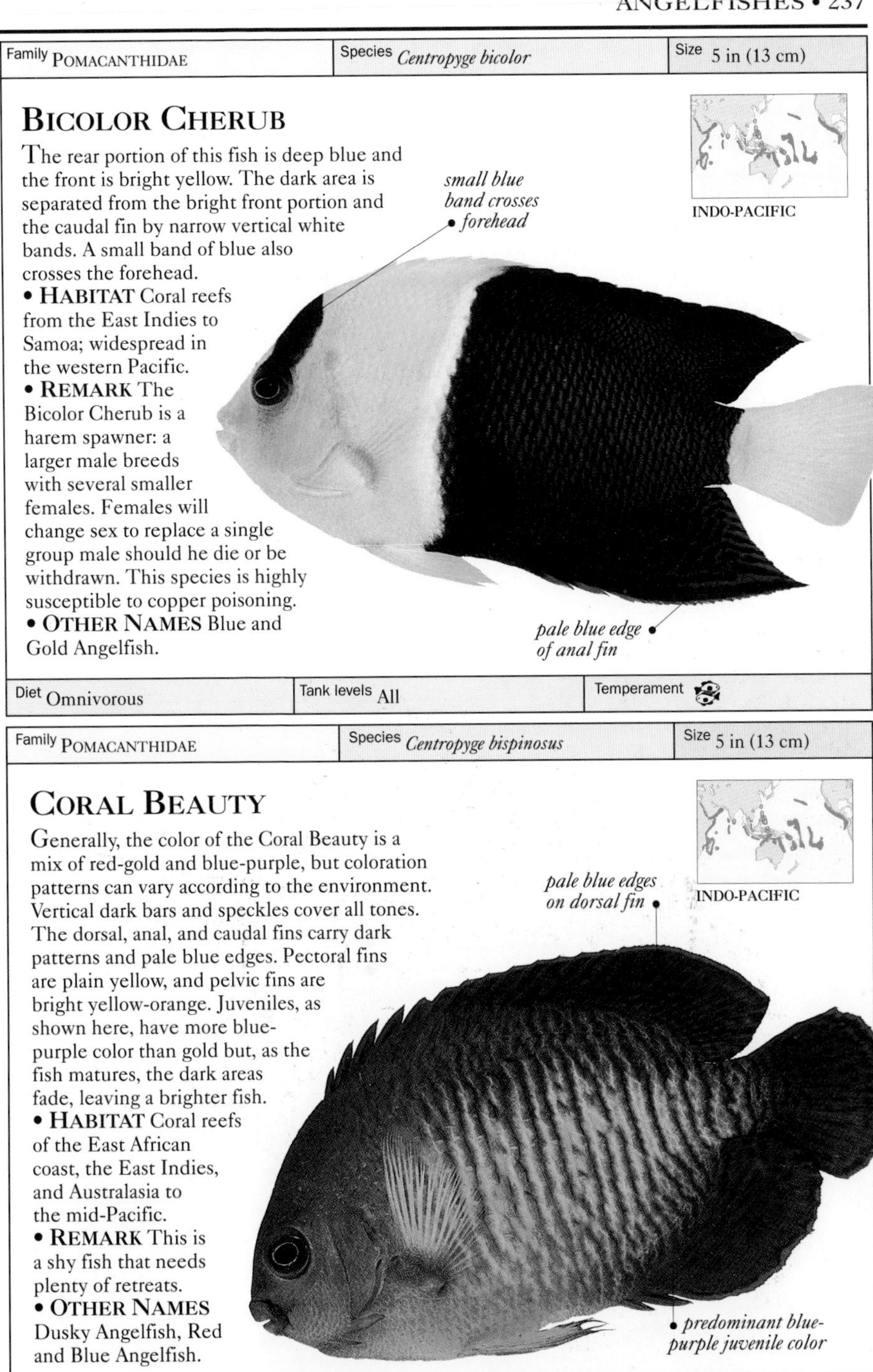

Family POMACANTHIDAE | Species *Centropyge bicolor* | Size 5 in (13 cm)

BICOLOR CHERUB

The rear portion of this fish is deep blue and the front is bright yellow. The dark area is separated from the bright front portion and the caudal fin by narrow vertical white bands. A small band of blue also crosses the forehead.

• **HABITAT** Coral reefs from the East Indies to Samoa; widespread in the western Pacific.

• **REMARK** The Bicolor Cherub is a harem spawner: a larger male breeds with several smaller females. Females will change sex to replace a single group male should he die or be withdrawn. This species is highly susceptible to copper poisoning.

• **OTHER NAMES** Blue and Gold Angelfish.

Diet Omnivorous | Tank levels All | Temperament

Family POMACANTHIDAE | Species *Centropyge bispinosus* | Size 5 in (13 cm)

CORAL BEAUTY

Generally, the color of the Coral Beauty is a mix of red-gold and blue-purple, but coloration patterns can vary according to the environment. Vertical dark bars and speckles cover all tones. The dorsal, anal, and caudal fins carry dark patterns and pale blue edges. Pectoral fins are plain yellow, and pelvic fins are bright yellow-orange. Juveniles, as shown here, have more blue-purple color than gold but, as the fish matures, the dark areas fade, leaving a brighter fish.

• **HABITAT** Coral reefs of the East African coast, the East Indies, and Australasia to the mid-Pacific.

• **REMARK** This is a shy fish that needs plenty of retreats.

• **OTHER NAMES** Dusky Angelfish, Red and Blue Angelfish.

Diet Omnivorous | Tank levels All | Temperament

Family POMACANTHIDAE	Species *Centropyge eibli*	Size 6 in (15 cm)

EIBL'S ANGELFISH

INDO-PACIFIC

The majority of the body of this species is gray-gold, patterned by vertical, evenly spaced wavy lines. These lines are red-gold at the front of the body, but change to gold-black to the rear, where they eventually match the black portions of the dorsal fin, caudal peduncle, and caudal fin. Dorsal, anal, and caudal fins may have gold or pale blue edgings, depending on geographical location. Some gold flecks appear on both anal and dorsal fins. The eye is ringed with gold and blue, then gold again; the opercular spine is light blue.

• **HABITAT** Deep waters from the Maldive Islands to Australia, Indonesia, and the mid-Pacific.

• **REMARK** The juvenile Orange-gilled Surgeonfish (*Acanthurus pyroferus*) mimics the appearance and behavior of this species.

wavy, vertical lines

gray-gold body coloration

yellow-edged anal fin

Diet Omnivorous	Tank level Lower	Temperament

Family POMACANTHIDAE	Species *Centropyge loriculus*	Size 4 in (10 cm)

FLAME ANGELFISH

PACIFIC OCEAN

The body of the Flame Angelfish, including most of the dorsal and anal fins, is an intense red-orange color, while the area from behind the gills to the caudal peduncle, and the caudal fin itself, is golden yellow. There are four to five dark vertical bars partially crossing the golden area. The outer edges of the dorsal and anal fins are violet; these broaden out and combine with black stripes on the rear areas of these two fins. Pectoral and pelvic fins and the opercular spine are red-orange.

• **HABITAT** Coral reefs of the western and central Pacific.

• **REMARK** This fish is hardy and easily managed, although it can be territorial. Keep it with larger fishes and provide plenty of retreats.

Diet Omnivorous	Tank level Lower	Temperament

Family POMACANTHIDAE	Species *Euxiphipops navarchus*	Size 10 in (25 cm)

BLUE-GIRDLED ANGELFISH

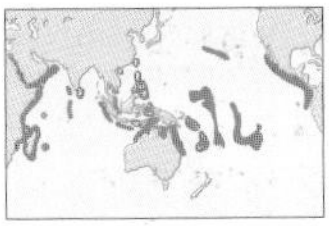

INDO-PACIFIC

A saddle of yellow, dotted with blue, extends down over the middle third of the body. At either end of the saddle, separated by pale blue bands, there are two dark blue areas with lighter blue speckles. The rearmost area covers the caudal peduncle and anal fin, as well as a portion of the yellow dorsal fin; the forward portion makes an inverted triangle up to the head region. The lower part of the head and the opercular spine are a pale creamy color, and all the fins, excluding the pectoral fins, are edged with pale blue. Juveniles are dark blue with white vertical stripes.

• **HABITAT** Coral reefs of the Indo-Pacific, often solitary or in pairs.

• **REMARK** A popular if expensive species, the Blue-girdled Angelfish requires plenty of space and hiding places.

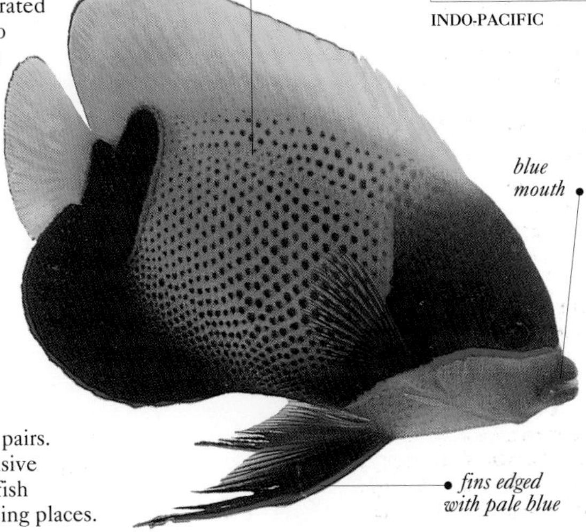

yellow saddle dotted with blue

blue mouth

fins edged with pale blue

Diet Omnivorous	Tank levels Middle and lower	Temperament

Family POMACANTHIDAE	Species *Holacanthus ciliaris*	Size 17½ in (45 cm)

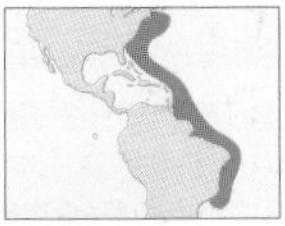

QUEEN ANGELFISH

WESTERN ATLANTIC

The whole of this fish, be it juvenile or adult, is outlined in bright blue, with the exception of the plain yellow caudal fin. The overall ground color can be changeable, depending on lighting conditions (and hybridization between similar species). This specimen is maturing. The adult fish has a golden brown to bright yellow-green body and well-defined scales. The rear edge of the gills and the base of the pectoral fins are bright blue. Small spines protect the gill cover. The anal and dorsal fins are extremely well produced and sweep back toward the caudal fin.

• **HABITAT** Western Atlantic and the Caribbean, often in pairs over coral reefs.

• **REMARK** Native waters are of a higher specific gravity, so acclimatize this fish to a large aquarium carefully.

opercular spine

well-defined scales

fins swept back

Diet Omnivorous	Tank levels Middle and lower	Temperament 

Family POMACANTHIDAE	Species *Holacanthus tricolor*	Size 24 in (60 cm)

ROCK BEAUTY

Juvenile Rock Beauties share the same coloration as the adult, but in different proportions: the juvenile is plain yellow, with a blue-edged dark spot on the flanks below the rear of the dorsal fin. In the adult, this spot covers three-quarters of the body; only the head, chest, and nape areas remain yellow. The dark dorsal and anal fins are outlined in yellow-red and the pectoral, pelvic, and caudal fins are yellow.

• **HABITAT** Coral reefs in the Caribbean and environs.

• **REMARK** This angelfish is aggressive toward its own kind in the aquarium and should not be kept as a pair or in a group. Offer foods with a high natural sponge content when possible.

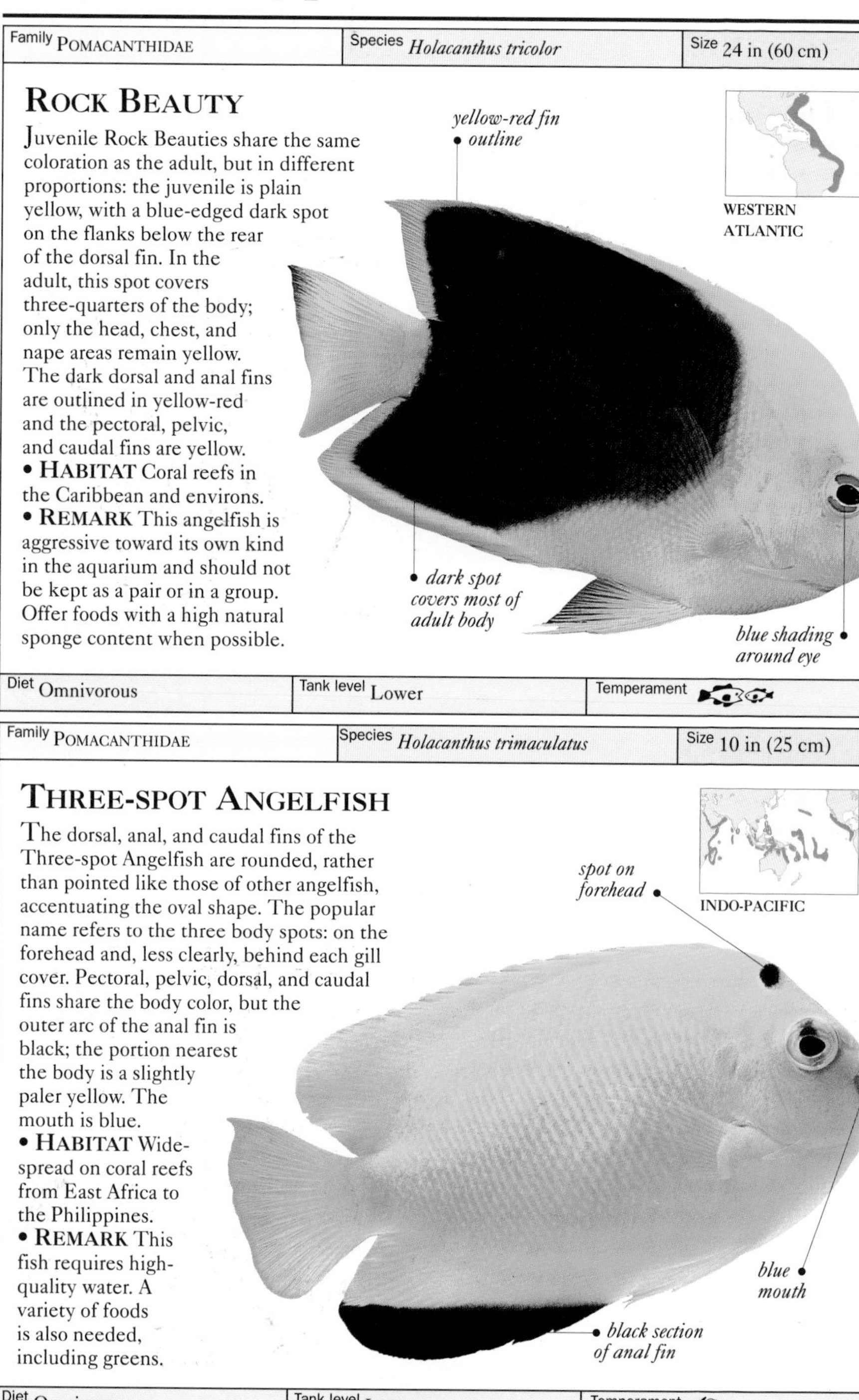

Diet Omnivorous	Tank level Lower	Temperament

Family POMACANTHIDAE	Species *Holacanthus trimaculatus*	Size 10 in (25 cm)

THREE-SPOT ANGELFISH

The dorsal, anal, and caudal fins of the Three-spot Angelfish are rounded, rather than pointed like those of other angelfish, accentuating the oval shape. The popular name refers to the three body spots: on the forehead and, less clearly, behind each gill cover. Pectoral, pelvic, dorsal, and caudal fins share the body color, but the outer arc of the anal fin is black; the portion nearest the body is a slightly paler yellow. The mouth is blue.

• **HABITAT** Widespread on coral reefs from East Africa to the Philippines.

• **REMARK** This fish requires high-quality water. A variety of foods is also needed, including greens.

Diet Omnivorous	Tank level Lower	Temperament

Family POMACANTHIDAE	Species *Pomacanthus annularis*	Size 16 in (40 cm)

BLUE RING ANGELFISH

Juveniles have a dark blue body with white, alternate, thick and thin vertical lines. The caudal fin is clear but may have pale spots. This coloring corresponds to that of the juvenile *Pomacanthus chrysurus*, except the latter has a yellow caudal fin. The adult is dark golden brown with royal blue lines; the common name describes the blue marking on the shoulder.

• **HABITAT** Sri Lanka to the Pacific Solomon Islands.

• **REMARK** Algae should be supplied.

Diet Mainly herbivorous	Tank level Lower	Temperament

Family POMACANTHIDAE	Species *Pomacanthus maculosus*	Size 16 in (40 cm)

HALF MOON ANGELFISH

The juveniles of this species carry the typical blue and white angelfish markings. They take on the yellow "half moon" crescent shape of the adult as the white lines fade with maturity. The adult is purple-gray with dark speckling, especially to the rear of the head and above the gill covers. The yellow crescent shape crosses the midpoint of the body. Dorsal and anal fins elongate with age and often have extreme filaments.

• **HABITAT** Coral reefs of the Red Sea and throughout the western Indian Ocean.

• **OTHER NAMES** Purple Moon Angelfish, Red Sea Halfmoon Angelfish, Sea-bride, Yellowbar Angelfish.

Diet Mainly herbivorous	Tank level Lower	Temperament

Family POMACANTHIDAE	Species *Pomacanthus imperator*	Size 12 in (30 cm)

EMPEROR ANGELFISH

The juvenile shown here is dark blue with concentric, slightly oval, white markings. In front of the gill cover the lines are almost vertical, with a slight backward sweep. Anal, dorsal, and caudal fins are marked with dark flecks. The adult Emperor Angel (below) has a plain yellow caudal fin and a yellow body crossed diagonally by pale blue-gray lines. These extend into the dorsal fin, which becomes pointed in mature fish. The anal fin, however, retains the dark blue of the juvenile. The mouth is pinky yellow, edged with pale blue (a color repeated in the opercular spine). The pelvic fins carry some red color among their basic blue.

• **HABITAT** Indo-Pacific from the East African coast (including the Red Sea) to Hawaii, and Australia.

• **REMARK** The relatively rare Emperor Angelfish can grow to an impressive size, so it requires a large aquarium. It prefers living with other large species.

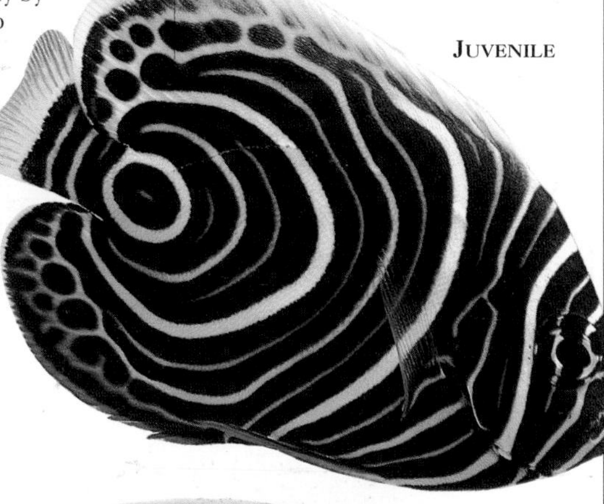

JUVENILE

ADULT

Diet Omnivorous	Tank levels Middle and lower	Temperament 

Family POMACANTHIDAE	Species *Pomacanthus paru*	Size 12 in (30 cm)

FRENCH ANGELFISH

Juveniles are black with four or five striking yellow vertical stripes. As these fish approach adulthood, the yellow bands fade and the fish turns dark gray. At the same time, the major part of the body to the rear of the gill covers becomes speckled. Limited speckling extends into the anal fin, but more appears on the dorsal fin (which often has a pale-colored tip).

• **HABITAT** Western Atlantic from Florida and the Caribbean to Brazil.

• **REMARK** Juveniles may quarrel among themselves in the aquarium. The adult is similar to the Gray Angelfish (*Pomacanthus arcuatus*), whose speckles are brighter and which has a yellow patch at the base of each pectoral fin.

WESTERN ATLANTIC

plain black body with bold yellow stripes

JUVENILE

adult extension to dorsal fin

pale yellow mouth

ADULT

dark gray body with bright speckling

Diet Omnivorous	Tank levels Middle and lower	Temperament

Family POMACANTHIDAE	Species *Pomacanthus semicirculatus*	Size 15 in (38 cm)

KORAN ANGELFISH

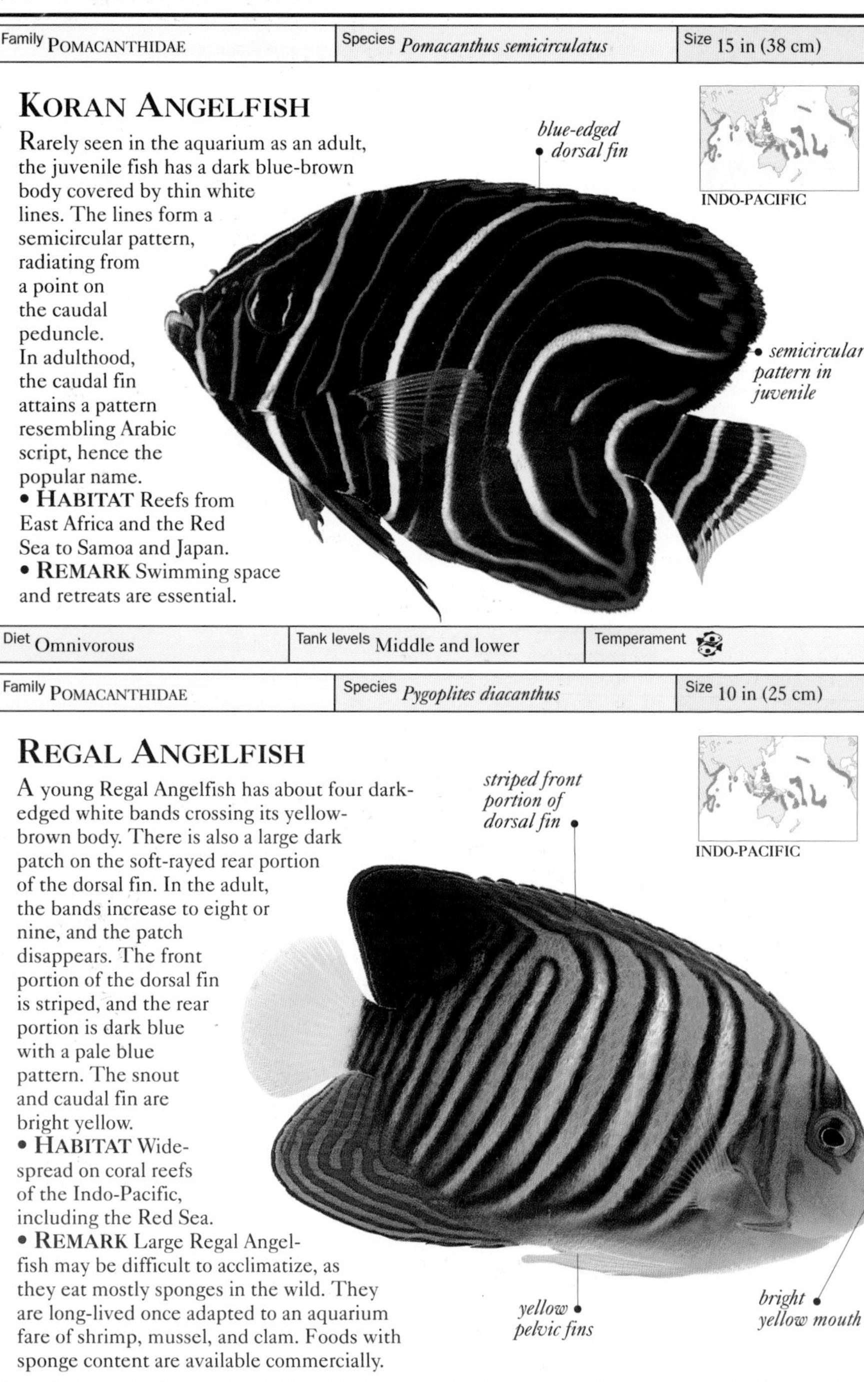

Rarely seen in the aquarium as an adult, the juvenile fish has a dark blue-brown body covered by thin white lines. The lines form a semicircular pattern, radiating from a point on the caudal peduncle. In adulthood, the caudal fin attains a pattern resembling Arabic script, hence the popular name.

• **HABITAT** Reefs from East Africa and the Red Sea to Samoa and Japan.

• **REMARK** Swimming space and retreats are essential.

Diet Omnivorous	Tank levels Middle and lower	Temperament

Family POMACANTHIDAE	Species *Pygoplites diacanthus*	Size 10 in (25 cm)

REGAL ANGELFISH

A young Regal Angelfish has about four dark-edged white bands crossing its yellow-brown body. There is also a large dark patch on the soft-rayed rear portion of the dorsal fin. In the adult, the bands increase to eight or nine, and the patch disappears. The front portion of the dorsal fin is striped, and the rear portion is dark blue with a pale blue pattern. The snout and caudal fin are bright yellow.

• **HABITAT** Widespread on coral reefs of the Indo-Pacific, including the Red Sea.

• **REMARK** Large Regal Angelfish may be difficult to acclimatize, as they eat mostly sponges in the wild. They are long-lived once adapted to an aquarium fare of shrimp, mussel, and clam. Foods with sponge content are available commercially.

Diet Omnivorous	Tank levels Middle and lower	Temperament

BUTTERFLYFISHES

MEMBERS OF THE butterflyfish family (Chaetodontidae) share the dazzling colors and patterns of the angelfish (see p.236). Unless they are comfortable in the aquarium, however, they may hide from suspected dangers. Unfortunately, it is the more colorful varieties that often adjust poorly to captivity, although retreats and hideaways will aid acclimatization. Butterflyfish prefer to retreat among coral at night, when they may change their patterns. They may also lose out to other species when feeding, so worms, dried foods, and algae should be carefully offered.

Family CHAETODONTIDAE	Species *Chaetodon auriga*	Size 8 in (20 cm)

THREADFIN BUTTERFLYFISH

Three-quarters of this fish is white, overlaid with two areas of opposing dark, diagonal lines. The rear uppermost part of the body is darker where the diagonal bands seem to merge together. A dark vertical bar crosses the head, passing through the eye, and yellow lines cross the snout. The background color of the spiky dorsal fin changes from white to yellow halfway back; the rear portion is plain yellow with an eyespot in the upper rear corner. Juveniles have the eyespot but paler coloring.

• **HABITAT** A very common species, widespread throughout reefs of the Indo-Pacific.

• **REMARK** This Butterflyfish is a popular choice and is readily obtainable.

INDO-PACIFIC

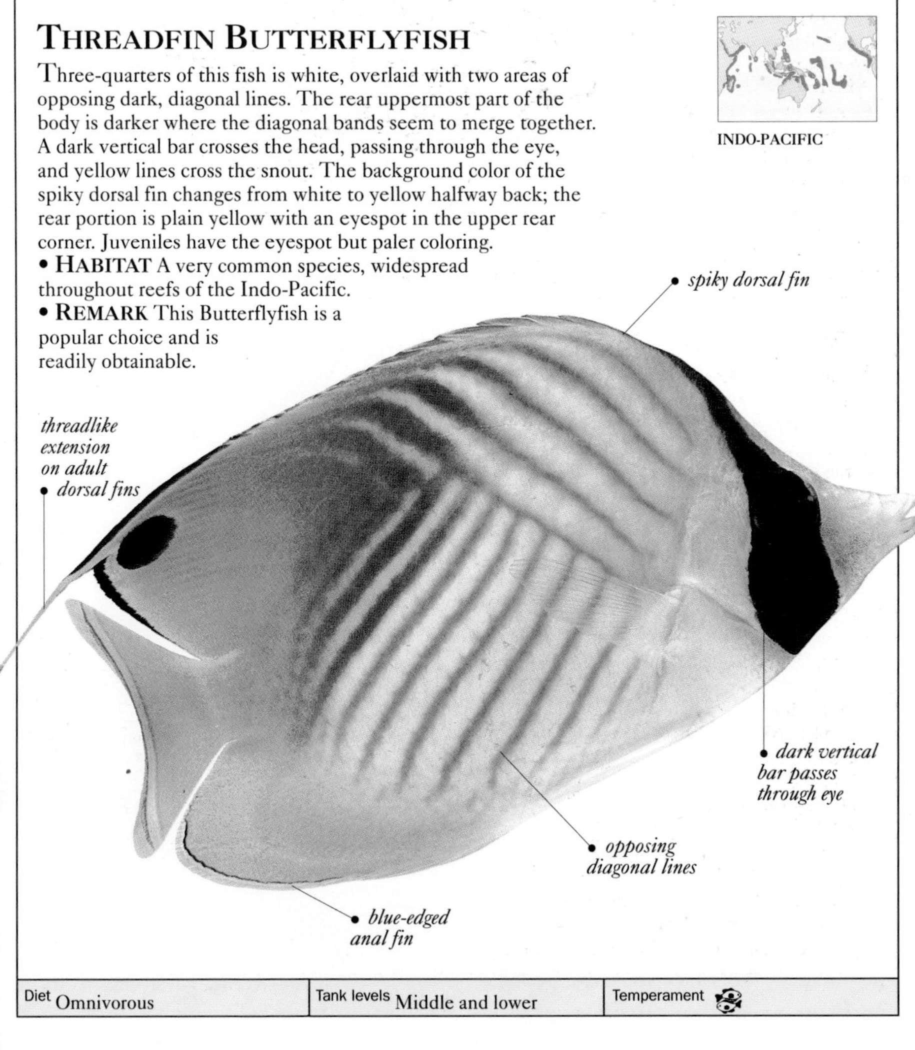

Diet Omnivorous	Tank levels Middle and lower	Temperament

Family CHAETODONTIDAE	Species *Chaetodon lunula*	Size 8 in (20 cm)

RACCOON BUTTERFLYFISH

INDO-PACIFIC

The color of this fish, including the fins, is yellow, with dark diagonal lines crossing the body upward from the pectoral fins. A dark saddle, bordered in front by a thin white line, and behind by a broad white band, crosses the forehead to mask each eye, giving the fish its raccoonlike appearance. There are distinct spines at the front of the dorsal and anal fins. Juveniles are paler ahead of the eye bar and have an eyespot on the dorsal fin. These characteristics change with adulthood; the eyespot fades while the pale area deepens to yellow.

• **HABITAT** Shallow waters from East Africa to Australia and Hawaii.

• **REMARK** *Chaetodon fasciatus*, a similar species, inhabits the Red Sea, but lacks the dark area on the caudal peduncle.

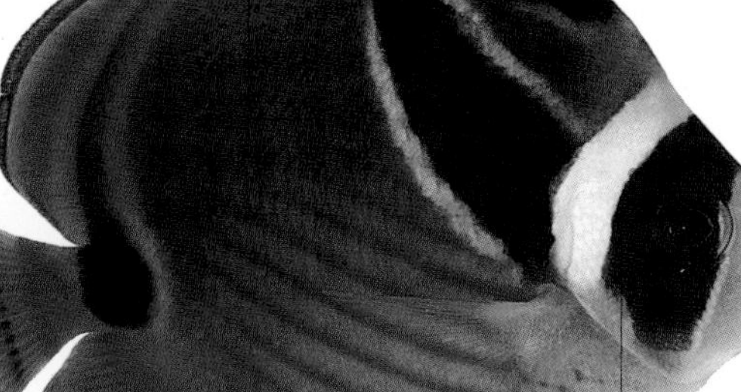

Diet Carnivorous	Tank levels Middle and lower	Temperament 

Family CHAETODONTIDAE	Species *Chaetodon quadrimaculatus*	Size 8 in (20 cm)

HAWAIIAN TEARDROP BUTTERFLYFISH

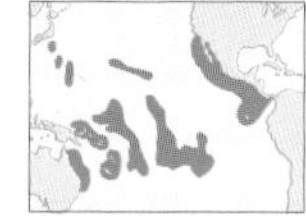
PACIFIC OCEAN

The coloration is distinctly divided in two: the dark brown dorsal area shades to golden yellow midway down the body. Two white patches appear within the brown area below the dorsal fin, which has a brown base. Like the anal fin, it has a blue line along its midsection. Fins are a golden reddish color. The caudal peduncle is brown, with red at the base of the caudal fin. The eye is crossed by a dark-bordered, orange-red bar with a white-yellow bar behind it.

• **HABITAT** Coral reefs around Hawaii.

• **REMARK** This fish is very similar in appearance to the Teardrop Butterflyfish (*Chaetodon unimaculatus*), but it is not as common. A limited natural range, such as that of the Hawaiian Teardrop, often indicates a specialist feeder which, in turn, means problems in aquarium acclimatization. This may well be one of those species which is best left in its natural reef habitat until suitable foods can be commercially produced.

one of two dorsal white patches

brown caudal peduncle

Diet Carnivorous	Tank levels Middle and lower	Temperament 

Family CHAETODONTIDAE	Species *Chaetodon unimaculatus*	Size 8 in (20 cm)

TEARDROP BUTTERFLYFISH

The body of this butterflyfish is yellow with a slightly paler area between the eye and the center of the flanks. Yellow obtuse-angled chevron patterning crosses the pale area. Midway along the body there is a large, dark "teardrop" marking. As the fish matures, the mark loses definition, and often becomes no more than a circular blob. A dark vertical bar passes through the eye; another crosses the caudal peduncle and the rear edges of the yellow anal and dorsal fins, bordered on each side by a narrow white margin. Juveniles are paler, with a clearer teardrop.

• **HABITAT** Widespread from the Red Sea to Hawaii.

• **REMARK** This species adapts well to captivity. Offer plenty of live, worm-type foods or good-quality frozen fish foods.

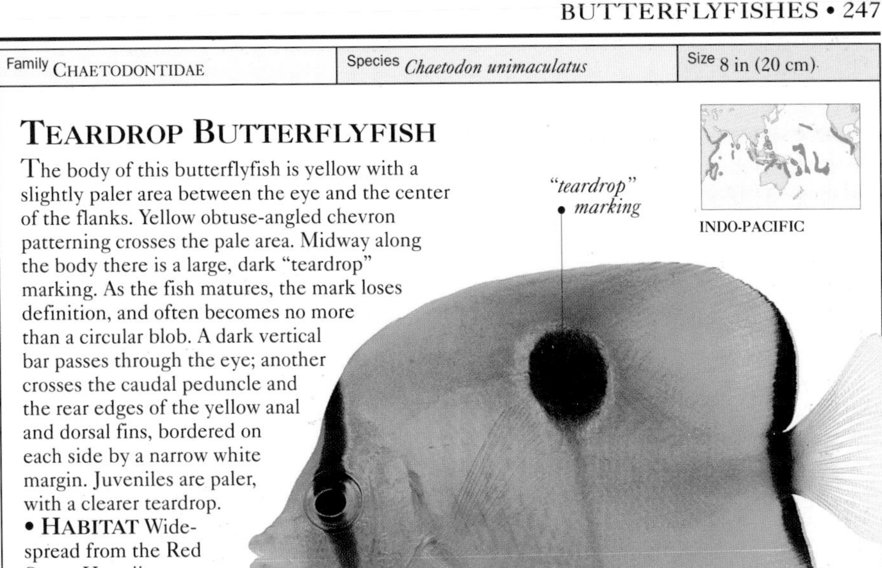

Diet Carnivorous	Tank levels Middle and lower	Temperament

Family CHAETODONTIDAE	Species *Chaetodon decussatus*	Size 8 in (20 cm)

BLACK-FINNED BUTTERFLYFISH

The pale cream body is overlaid in two areas with dark diagonal lines: one group rises from behind the head up to the dorsal region; the other runs from the first set of lines toward the rear of the anal fin. A dark vertical bar crosses the head and passes through the eye. The rear part of the body and the long-based anal and dorsal fins are mostly black. The yellow caudal fin has a black bar and a white edge. Pectoral fins are white.

• **HABITAT** A common species, widespread in the Indo-Pacific.

• **REMARK** This readily available fish is ideal for the beginner.

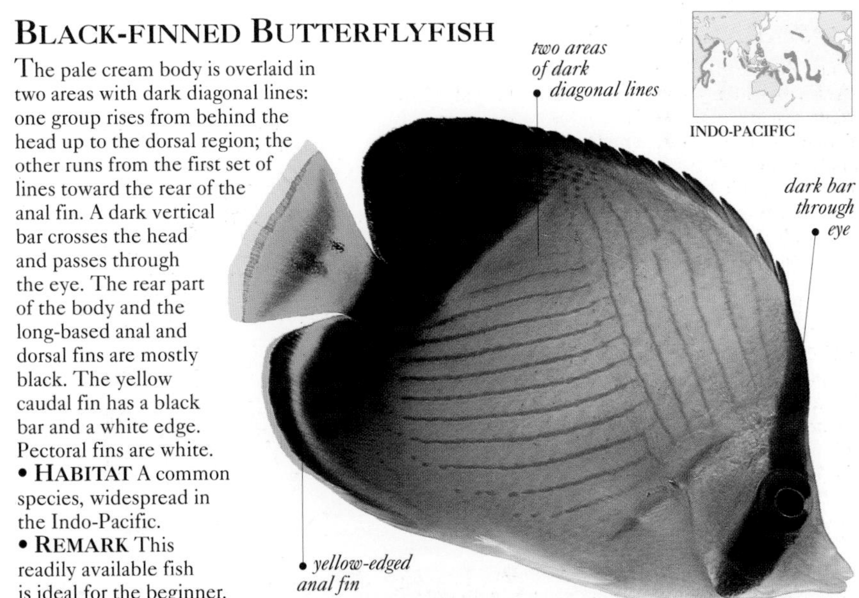

Diet Carnivorous	Tank levels Middle and lower	Temperament

Family CHAETODONTIDAE	Species *Chelmon rostratus*	Size 7 in (18 cm)

COPPERBANDED BUTTERFLYFISH

The plain silver background color of this species is unusual for the butterflyfish family, but this lack of deeper coloration is compensated for by the four black-edged, deep orange bands that cross the body vertically. The first band covers the eye, the fourth carries a white-ringed dark eyespot, (presenting any attacker with a false target). A fifth band crosses the rear of the dorsal and anal fins, where it precedes a white-edged black band. A further orange stripe runs down the forehead and along the snout. Pelvic fins are marked with orange and white. Juveniles are deeper orange.

• **HABITAT** Common throughout the Indo-Pacific and in shallow waters of the Red Sea.

• **REMARK** The long snout is used to pick out food from corals. Although popular, this is not a hardy or adaptable fish; retreats and hideaways will help it feel secure. Feed with plenty of worm foods.

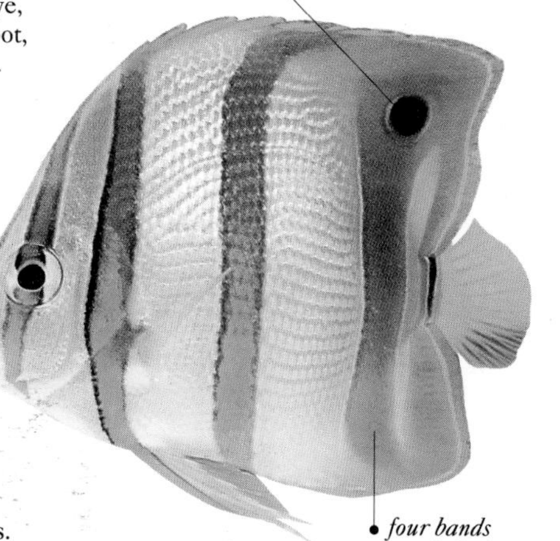

Diet Carnivorous	Tank levels Middle and lower	Temperament

Family CHAETODONTIDAE	Species *Forcipiger longirostris*	Size 10 in (25 cm)

FORCEPSFISH

Seen from a distance, the striking color of this fish camouflages its outline surprisingly well. The main body color is bright yellow, but the top half of the head, from the gill cover forward, is jet black; the lower jaw and throat region are silver. The rear edges of the dorsal and anal fins are pale blue and the anal fin carries a false eyespot.

• **HABITAT** Common among corals in shallow water, from the Red Sea and Indo-Pacific, to Central America and northward to Mexico.

• **REMARK** *Forcipiger flavissimus* is similar, but the number of dorsal fin spines and the snout dimensions differ.

long snout for easy food picking

spiky front rays of fin

false eyespot

Diet Carnivorous	Tank levels Middle and lower	Temperament 

Family CHAETODONTIDAE	Species *Heniochus acuminatus*	Size 7 in (18 cm)

INDO-PACIFIC

WIMPLEFISH

The dorsal and anal fins make this a "high" rather than an elongate fish, in contrast to other members of this group. The body is white with two black bands sloping rearward. The long trailing top section of the dorsal fin, which resembles a medieval wimple, is white, as is the corresponding section of the anal fin. The soft-rayed rear part of the dorsal fin is bright yellow, a color shared with the caudal fin. There may be small, horny protuberances above the eyes. Juveniles lack the long extension to the dorsal fin.

• **HABITAT** Red Sea and throughout the Indo-Pacific.

• **REMARK** A large aquarium is needed to keep several Wimplefish as one leader may bully the rest. Other species in the genus are seldom imported.

• **OTHER NAMES** Poor Man's Moorish Idol, Pennant Fish.

long trailing dorsal fin

black bands slope rearward across the body

black "saddle" crosses eyes

bright yellow caudal fin

Diet Omnivorous	Tank levels Middle and lower	Temperament

Damselfishes

The members of the family Pomacentridae in this section live in the same reef habitat as anemonefishes, but, not having the same immunity to sea anemones, most do not venture into the venomous tentacles. Quarrels may occur between damselfishes unless space and aquarium retreats are provided. There is often confusion over the scientific names of these fish, particularly among the bright blue species.

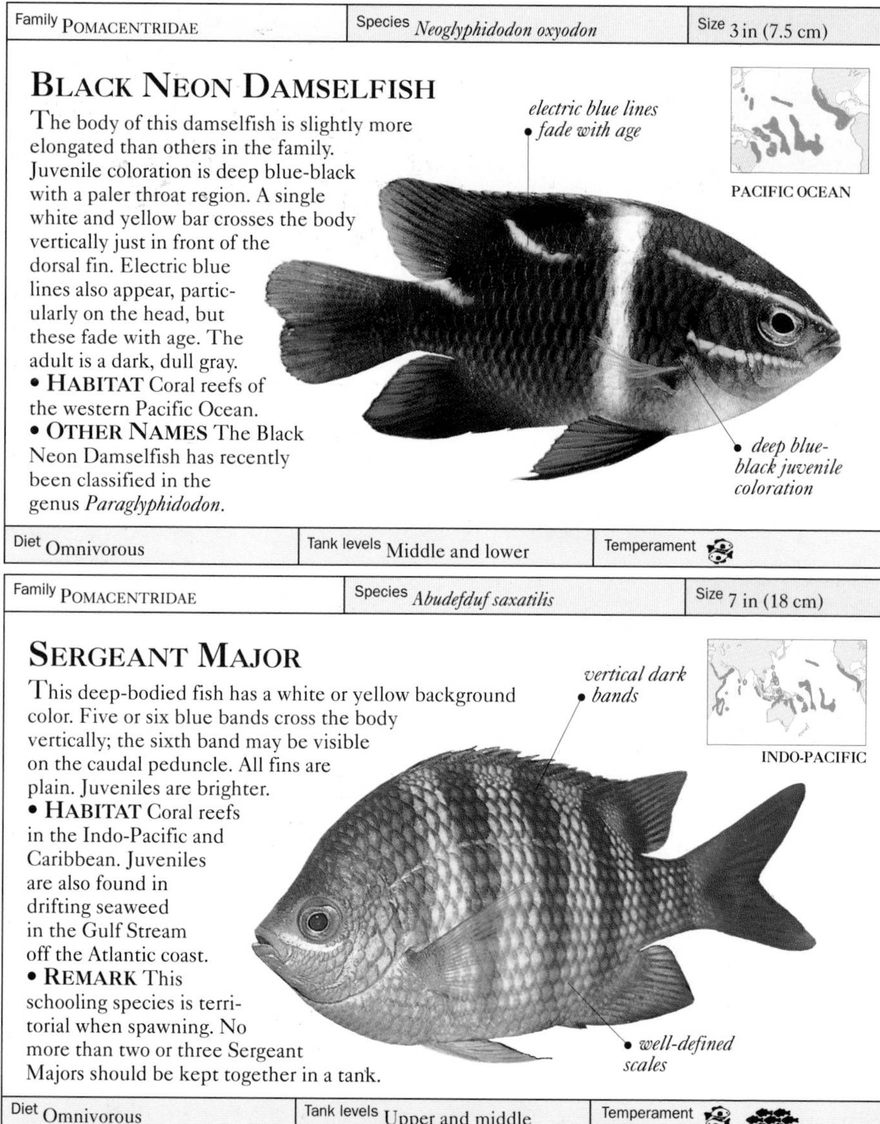

Family	Species	Size
POMACENTRIDAE	*Neoglyphidodon oxyodon*	3 in (7.5 cm)

Black Neon Damselfish

The body of this damselfish is slightly more elongated than others in the family. Juvenile coloration is deep blue-black with a paler throat region. A single white and yellow bar crosses the body vertically just in front of the dorsal fin. Electric blue lines also appear, particularly on the head, but these fade with age. The adult is a dark, dull gray.

- **HABITAT** Coral reefs of the western Pacific Ocean.
- **OTHER NAMES** The Black Neon Damselfish has recently been classified in the genus *Paraglyphidodon*.

Diet	Tank levels	Temperament
Omnivorous	Middle and lower	

Family	Species	Size
POMACENTRIDAE	*Abudefduf saxatilis*	7 in (18 cm)

Sergeant Major

This deep-bodied fish has a white or yellow background color. Five or six blue bands cross the body vertically; the sixth band may be visible on the caudal peduncle. All fins are plain. Juveniles are brighter.

- **HABITAT** Coral reefs in the Indo-Pacific and Caribbean. Juveniles are also found in drifting seaweed in the Gulf Stream off the Atlantic coast.
- **REMARK** This schooling species is territorial when spawning. No more than two or three Sergeant Majors should be kept together in a tank.

Diet	Tank levels	Temperament
Omnivorous	Upper and middle	

Family POMACENTRIDAE	Species *Chromis cyaneae*	Size 2 in (5 cm)

BLUE CHROMIS

The body of the Blue Chromis is elongated, with the dorsal contour slightly more rounded than the ventral. The central color is brilliant blue, with a darker top surface shading down to silvery blue below. Black-centered scales form speckled horizontal lines, particularly on the lower half of the body. The caudal fin is deeply forked.

- **HABITAT** Above reefs in the tropical western Atlantic.
- **REMARK** During breeding periods, an orange ovipositor (breeding tube) protrudes from the female through which the eggs are laid. In the wild it feeds on plankton.

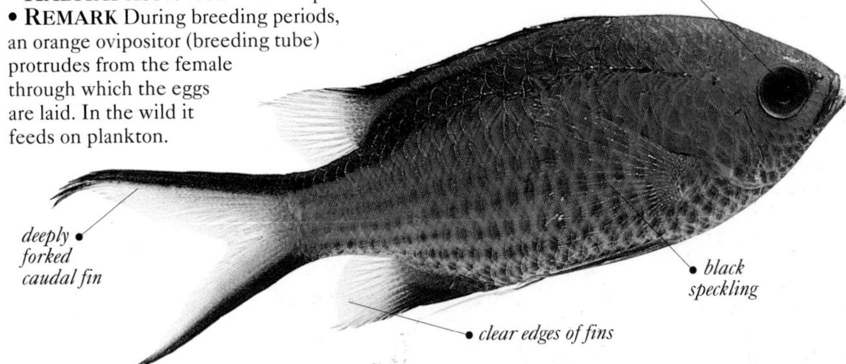

Diet Omnivorous	Tank level Lower	Temperament 

Family POMACENTRIDAE	Species *Chrysiptera parasema*	Size 4 in (10 cm)

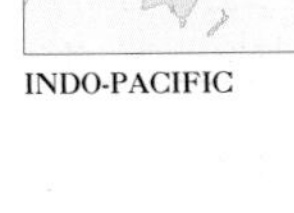

YELLOW-TAILED DAMSELFISH

The slightly arched dorsal profile of the Yellow-tailed Damselfish matches that of the ventral contour. The front three quarters of the body are bright blue, a color that extends into the spiny dorsal fin and the spines of the pelvic fins. The remainder of the body is yellow to orange, fading to clear outer margins on the unpaired fins.

- **HABITAT** Widespread throughout the Indo-Pacific, including the Red Sea.
- **OTHER NAME** Also known as *Abudefduf hemicyanea*.

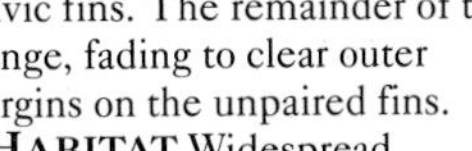

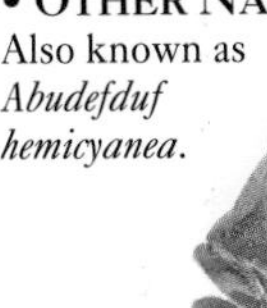

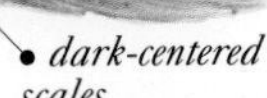

Diet Omnivorous	Tank levels All	Temperament  

Family POMACENTRIDAE	Species *Dascyllus aruanus*	Size 3¼ in (8 cm)

HUMBUG DAMSELFISH

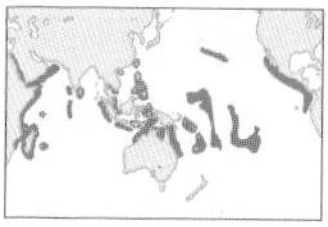

This damselfish is stocky, with a steeply rising forehead. Three black stripes cross the white body. The first stripe runs from the mouth into the rays of the dorsal fin; the next includes the pelvic fins and crosses the body at a slight angle. The clear tail distinguishes this fish from the Black-tailed Humbug (opposite), which has a black caudal fin.

- **HABITAT** Among corals in the Indo-Pacific, including the Red Sea but not Hawaii.
- **REMARK** A common, hardy species; ideal for the beginner.
- **OTHER NAMES** White-tailed Damselfish, Three-striped Damselfish.

one of three black stripes

white rear of caudal peduncle

INDO-PACIFIC

Diet Omnivorous	Tank levels All	Temperament

Family POMACENTRIDAE	Species *Dascyllus carneus*	Size 3¼ in (8 cm)

INDIAN DAMSELFISH

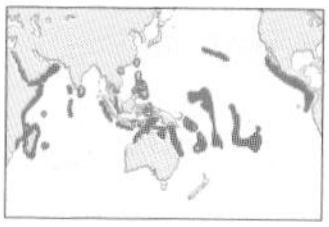

The shape of the Cloudy Damselfish is typical of the family, but its colors are not as strong as those of many other damselfishes. An indistinct black stripe separates the darker, brown head area from the paler, creamy main body. Both head and body are spotted with blue. On some specimens a white blotch may appear on the dorsal surface. The caudal fin and rear edge of the otherwise dark dorsal fin are clear; all other fins are black.

- **HABITAT** Among corals in the Indian Ocean and western Pacific Ocean.
- **REMARK** This fish is generally peaceful but may quarrel with its own kind.

indistinct dark stripe

clear caudal fin

blue spots over body

INDO-PACIFIC

Diet Carnivorous	Tank levels All	Temperament 

Family POMACENTRIDAE	Species *Dascyllus melanurus*	Size 3 in (7.5 cm)

BLACK-TAILED HUMBUG

PACIFIC OCEAN

The Black-tailed Humbug has the deep, stocky body and steeply rising forehead typical of the family. It is very similar in appearance to the Humbug Damselfish (opposite), with a white body covered by three equally spaced black stripes. The positive identifying feature, as the common name suggests, is the black area on the caudal fin that almost makes up a fourth stripe. By contrast, the Humbug Damselfish has a clear caudal fin.

• **HABITAT** Around corals throughout the western Pacific Ocean.

• **REMARK** Like most members of the genus, this fish is never far away from corals in the wild; the aquarium should therefore be furnished liberally with hiding places.

stripes extend into dorsal fin

distinctive black tail

Diet Carnivorous	Tank levels All	Temperament

Family POMACENTRIDAE	Species *Dascyllus trimaculatus*	Size 5 in (12.5 cm)

DOMINO DAMSELFISH

INDO-PACIFIC

Three white spots on a black body give this fish its dominolike appearance. One spot appears on each side of the body below the dorsal fin, and the third is centrally placed on the forehead. Two factors affect coloration: discontentment with tank conditions may make the blackness fade; and old age diminishes the white spots. If the colors fade, the dark-edged scales become more visible, giving the fish a netlike appearance.

• **HABITAT** Corals throughout the Indo-Pacific, including those in the Red Sea.

• **REMARK** Commonly available and popular with beginners, the Domino Damselfish presents relatively few problems in captivity. It usually leads the rush for food, sometimes at the expense of other fish. Provide plenty of rocky retreats.

Diet Omnivorous	Tank levels Middle and lower	Temperament

Family POMACENTRIDAE	Species *Microspathodon chrysurus*	Size 8 in (20 cm)

JEWEL FISH

The juvenile Jewel Fish is dark blue-black with bright blue spots. The dorsal, anal, and pelvic fins are dark with light blue edging, and the caudal fin is colorless. Adults lose the bright blue spots and develop a vivid yellow caudal fin.

• **HABITAT** Stands of fire coral in the Caribbean; also the tropical western Atlantic.

• **REMARK** Unaffected by the coral's stinging cells, inhabited away from predators.

• **OTHER NAME** Yellow-tailed Damsel.

A Jewel Fish patrols a bed of fire coral

CARIBBEAN, MEXICAN GULF

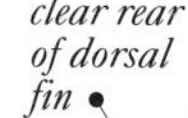

Diet Omnivorous	Tank level Lower	Temperament

Family POMACENTRIDAE	Species *Pomacentrus alleni*	Size 4 in (10 cm)

ALLEN'S DAMSELFISH

The upper half of the elongated body is electric blue-green with a deeper violet-blue below. The ventral surface and belly are yellow, and a black mark adorns the lower half of the caudal fin. The dorsal fin is black with a clear rear portion. Scales are clearly defined.

• **HABITAT** Among corals in the Indo-Pacific, particularly the Similian Islands, near Thailand.

• **REMARK** This fish is named after ichthyologist Gerald R. Allen.

INDO-PACIFIC

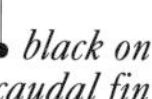

Diet Omnivorous	Tank levels All	Temperament

Family POMACENTRIDAE	Species *Pomacentrus caeruleus*	Size 4 in (10 cm)

Blue Devil

The elongated body of this striking species is brilliant blue with a black mark at the rear of the long-based dorsal fin. A black line passes from the snout through the eye. Each scale has a central yellow-white mark.

- **HABITAT** Widespread throughout the Indo-Pacific.
- **REMARK** Positive identification is often confused as the dark markings may vary, and some specimens develop more yellow in later life.

Diet Omnivorous	Tank levels All	Temperament

Family POMACENTRIDAE	Species *Stegastes planifrons*	Size 6 in (15 cm)

Yellow Damselfish

Three spots adorn the body of this juvenile Orange Damselfish: one at the base of the dorsal fin, one on the top of the caudal peduncle, and one at the base of the pectoral fin. This last, less distinct spot may vary in size with age. Adults are plain dark gray.

- **HABITAT** Coral and limestone rubble in the Caribbean; also the tropical western Atlantic.
- **REMARK** The adult Orange Damselfish is rather aggressive. It occurs in deeper waters.
- **OTHER NAMES** Formerly classified as *Eupomacentrus planifrons*; also known as the Orange Demoiselle and the Three Spot Damselfish.

Diet Omnivorous	Tank levels Upper and middle	Temperament

SURGEONS AND TANGS

SEVERAL MEMBERS of the family Acanthuridae are quarrelsome, and some carry sharp spines near the tail, hence the names "surgeon" and "tang." Long-based dorsal and anal fins and a sloping forehead are other distinctive features. They need green foods and spawn by egg scattering.

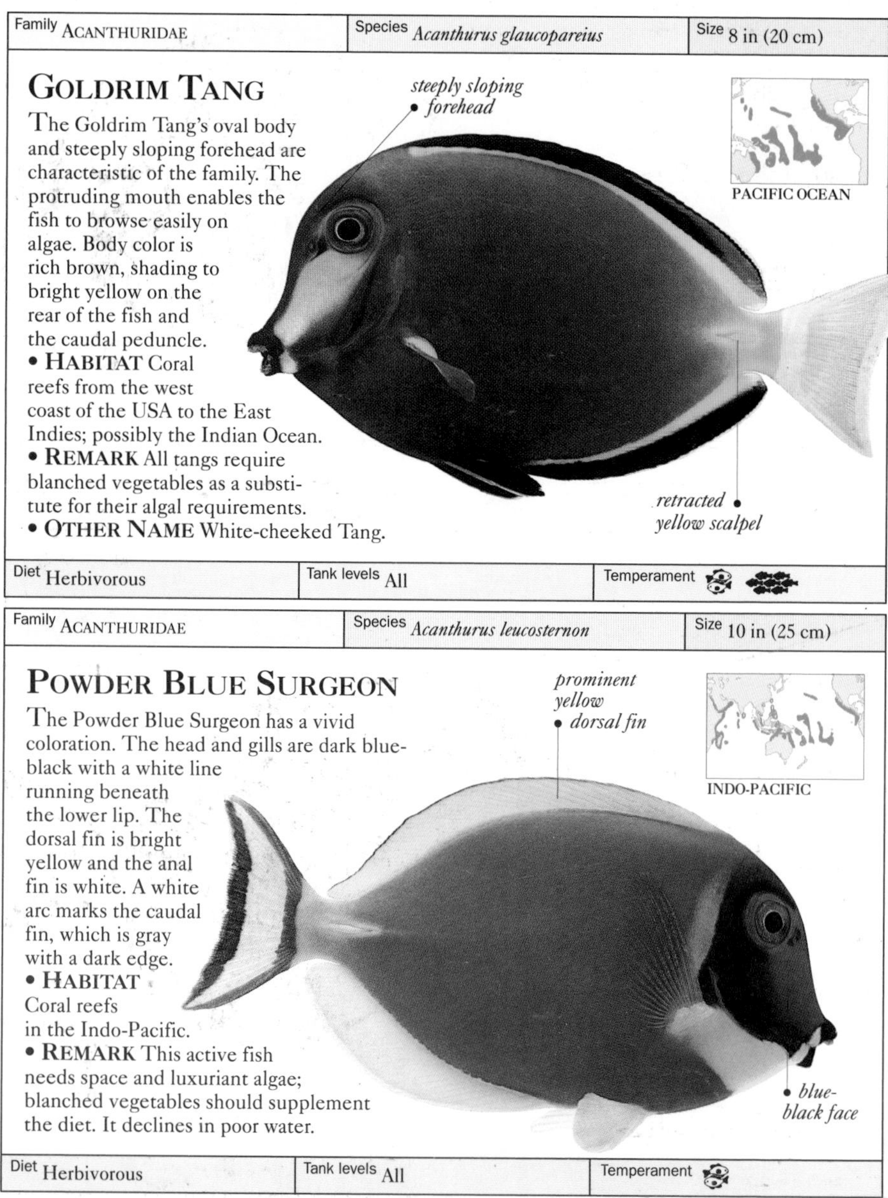

Family ACANTHURIDAE	Species *Acanthurus glaucopareius*	Size 8 in (20 cm)

GOLDRIM TANG

The Goldrim Tang's oval body and steeply sloping forehead are characteristic of the family. The protruding mouth enables the fish to browse easily on algae. Body color is rich brown, shading to bright yellow on the rear of the fish and the caudal peduncle.

• **HABITAT** Coral reefs from the west coast of the USA to the East Indies; possibly the Indian Ocean.

• **REMARK** All tangs require blanched vegetables as a substitute for their algal requirements.

• **OTHER NAME** White-cheeked Tang.

Diet Herbivorous	Tank levels All	Temperament

Family ACANTHURIDAE	Species *Acanthurus leucosternon*	Size 10 in (25 cm)

POWDER BLUE SURGEON

The Powder Blue Surgeon has a vivid coloration. The head and gills are dark blue-black with a white line running beneath the lower lip. The dorsal fin is bright yellow and the anal fin is white. A white arc marks the caudal fin, which is gray with a dark edge.

• **HABITAT** Coral reefs in the Indo-Pacific.

• **REMARK** This active fish needs space and luxuriant algae; blanched vegetables should supplement the diet. It declines in poor water.

Diet Herbivorous	Tank levels All	Temperament

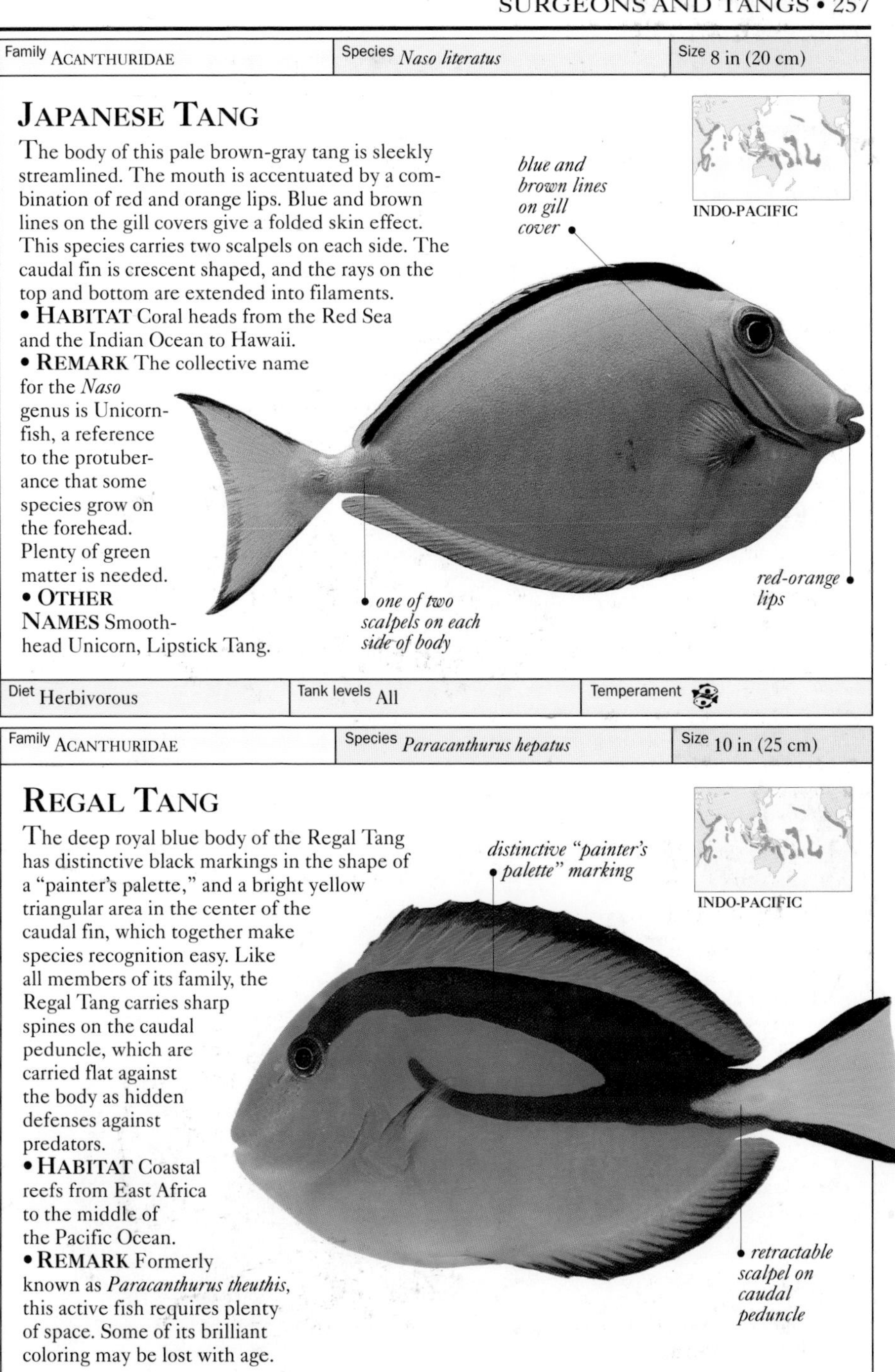

Family ACANTHURIDAE	Species *Naso literatus*	Size 8 in (20 cm)

JAPANESE TANG

The body of this pale brown-gray tang is sleekly streamlined. The mouth is accentuated by a combination of red and orange lips. Blue and brown lines on the gill covers give a folded skin effect. This species carries two scalpels on each side. The caudal fin is crescent shaped, and the rays on the top and bottom are extended into filaments.

• **HABITAT** Coral heads from the Red Sea and the Indian Ocean to Hawaii.

• **REMARK** The collective name for the *Naso* genus is Unicornfish, a reference to the protuberance that some species grow on the forehead. Plenty of green matter is needed.

• **OTHER NAMES** Smoothhead Unicorn, Lipstick Tang.

Diet Herbivorous	Tank levels All	Temperament

Family ACANTHURIDAE	Species *Paracanthurus hepatus*	Size 10 in (25 cm)

REGAL TANG

The deep royal blue body of the Regal Tang has distinctive black markings in the shape of a "painter's palette," and a bright yellow triangular area in the center of the caudal fin, which together make species recognition easy. Like all members of its family, the Regal Tang carries sharp spines on the caudal peduncle, which are carried flat against the body as hidden defenses against predators.

• **HABITAT** Coastal reefs from East Africa to the middle of the Pacific Ocean.

• **REMARK** Formerly known as *Paracanthurus theuthis*, this active fish requires plenty of space. Some of its brilliant coloring may be lost with age.

Diet Herbivorous	Tank levels All	Temperament

Family ACANTHURIDAE	Species *Zebrasoma flavescens*	Size 8 in (20 cm)

YELLOW TANG

The oval body of this fish is exaggerated by the surrounding fins to give a disclike appearance. The snout is relatively long, with a steeply-sloping forehead and high-set eyes. The overall body color is bright yellow, with paler coloration around the eyes, and white scalpels on the caudal peduncle. All fins are yellow, matching the body. Juveniles and adults share the same coloration, unlike some members of the family. Small scales give the body a velvety appearance.

• **HABITAT** Shallow waters, particularly around Hawaii.

• **REMARK** The Yellow Tang is similar to the juvenile Blue Tang (*Acanthurus caeruleus*).

• **OTHER NAME** Lau'i-pala.

uniformly yellow fins

steeply sloping forehead and long snout

very small scales

PACIFIC OCEAN

Diet Herbivorous	Tank levels All	Temperament

Family ACANTHURIDAE	Species *Zebrasoma xanthurum*	Size 8 in (20 cm)

PURPLE SAILFIN TANG

The body of the Purple Sailfin Tang is oval but looks disc shaped because of the stiffly held fins. The snout is fairly well extended, the forehead is steep, and the eyes are set high. This tang is deep blue-purple with darker, purple-red dots and lines concentrated on the head and front of the body. These markings peter out gradually behind the dorsal fin. The dorsal and anal fins are blue-purple, like the body, and marked with little speckles and streaks. Retractable scalpels on the caudal peduncle are somewhat obscured, as they blend with the body color. By contrast, the caudal fin is bright yellow.

• **HABITAT** Red Sea and Indian Ocean to the mid-Pacific.

• **REMARK** This fish is territorial and usually kept one to a tank, but some recommend keeping it in a school. It requires green foods, including blanched vegetables; algae-coated decorations provide an ideal grazing ground.

purple-red dots and lines

bright yellow caudal fin

INDO-PACIFIC

Diet Herbivorous	Tank levels All	Temperament 

TRIGGERFISHES

A PRINCIPAL FEATURE of the members of this family (Balistidae) is their ability to lock the first two dorsal fins in an upright position, providing a deterrent against being swallowed or dragged from crevices by predators. Swimming is achieved mainly by movements of the dorsal and anal fins. Triggerfishes spawn into pits dug in the sand. Some species guard their eggs.

Family BALISTIDAE	Species *Balistoides conspicillum*	Size 20 in (50 cm)

CLOWN TRIGGERFISH

The Clown Triggerfish has a slightly curved dorsal surface and a more pointed ventral surface, giving a nonsymmetrical appearance. The fish is dark brown-black and covered in white spots of varying sizes. The mouth is armed with sharp teeth and surrounded by a wide yellow "lipstick" band. The pectoral, anal, and second dorsal fins are colorless.

• **HABITAT** Widespread from East Africa, throughout the Indian Ocean, and to Fiji in the mid-Pacific.

• **REMARK** This is a popular fish, but juveniles can be difficult to acclimatize.

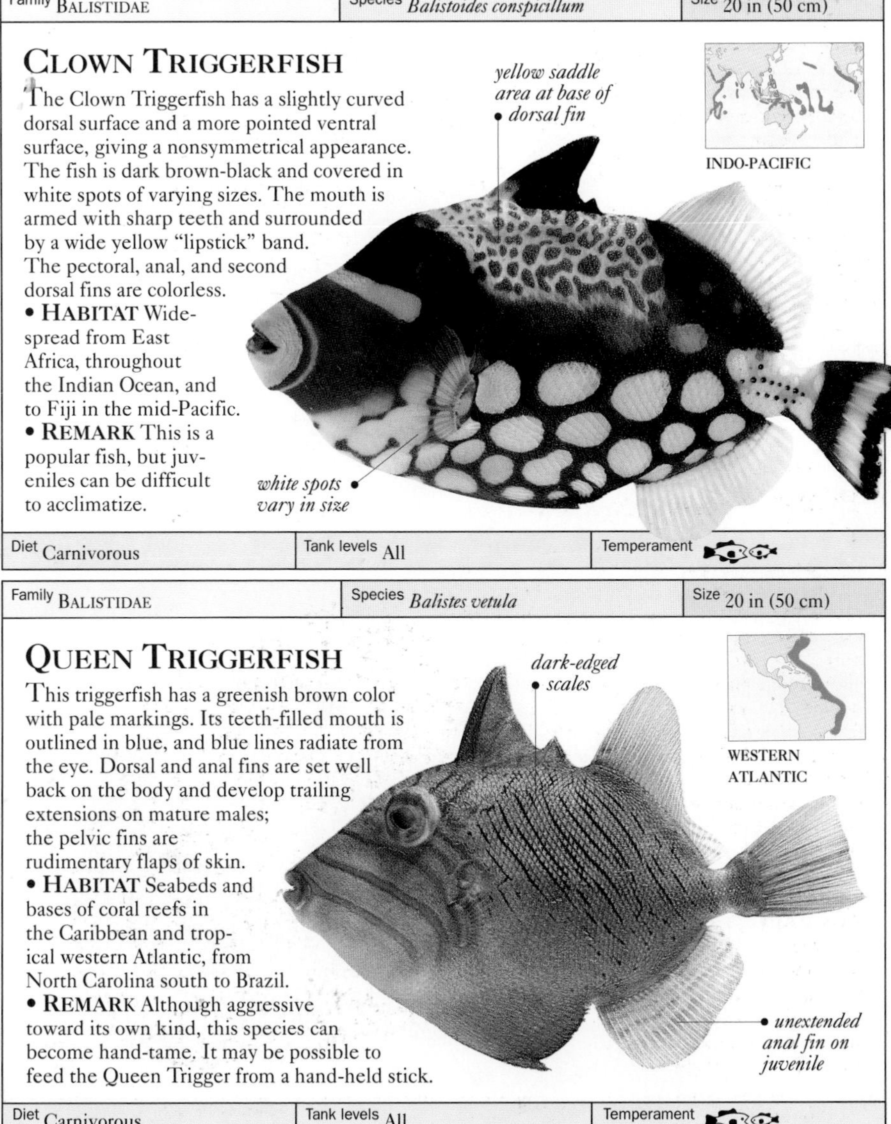

Diet Carnivorous	Tank levels All	Temperament

Family BALISTIDAE	Species *Balistes vetula*	Size 20 in (50 cm)

QUEEN TRIGGERFISH

This triggerfish has a greenish brown color with pale markings. Its teeth-filled mouth is outlined in blue, and blue lines radiate from the eye. Dorsal and anal fins are set well back on the body and develop trailing extensions on mature males; the pelvic fins are rudimentary flaps of skin.

• **HABITAT** Seabeds and bases of coral reefs in the Caribbean and tropical western Atlantic, from North Carolina south to Brazil.

• **REMARK** Although aggressive toward its own kind, this species can become hand-tame. It may be possible to feed the Queen Trigger from a hand-held stick.

Diet Carnivorous	Tank levels All	Temperament

Family BALISTIDAE	Species *Odonus niger*	Size 20 in (50 cm)

BLACK TRIGGERFISH

Despite its name, the body of this fish is not purely black; it may be a deep shade of brown, green, purple, or blue. The fish is not quite as angular in outline as other species in the family. Two dorsal fins are present, but the pelvic fins are reduced to stumps and perhaps a fold of skin. The large second dorsal fin and the anal fin provide the motive force for the fish, rather than the caudal fin, which is lyre shaped and has elongated outer rays.

• **HABITAT** Red Sea, through the Indian Ocean, and east to the central Pacific.

• **REMARK** Specimens have spawned in captivity; eggs are laid, fertilized, and guarded in nests or burrows in the substrate.

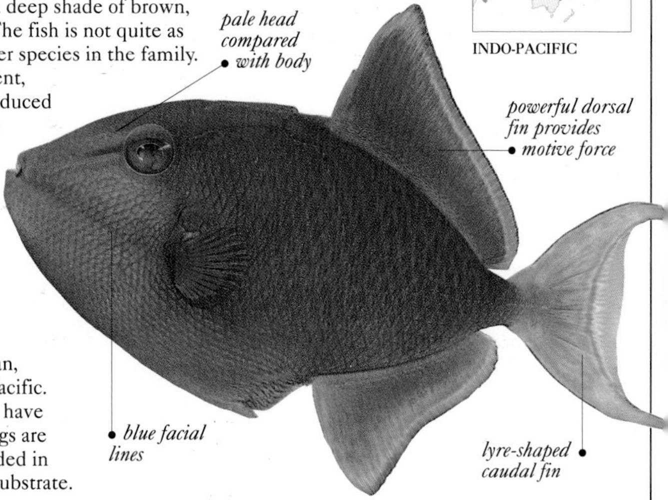

pale head compared with body

powerful dorsal fin provides motive force

blue facial lines

lyre-shaped caudal fin

INDO-PACIFIC

Diet Carnivorous	Tank levels All	Temperament

Family BALISTIDAE	Species *Pseudobalistes fuscus*	Size 20 in (50 cm)

BLUE-LINED TRIGGERFISH

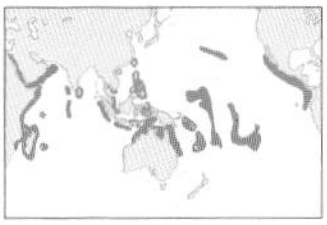

This diamond-shaped species has a slightly rounded dorsal surface and a pointed ventral surface. Other features typical of this family include a large head with high-set eyes; there are no pelvic fins. On this juvenile, a background hue of golden yellow-brown is overlaid by a pattern of interweaving blue lines. Juveniles may also have small patches of brown on the dorsal surface that fade with age, while adults can have greenish blue hues.

• **HABITAT** Red Sea and the Indian Ocean to the Pacific.

• **REMARK** The front dorsal fin is erected when threatened. This prevents enemies from swallowing this fish or withdrawing it from a crevice. It may become hand-tame but the teeth are capable of biting fingers.

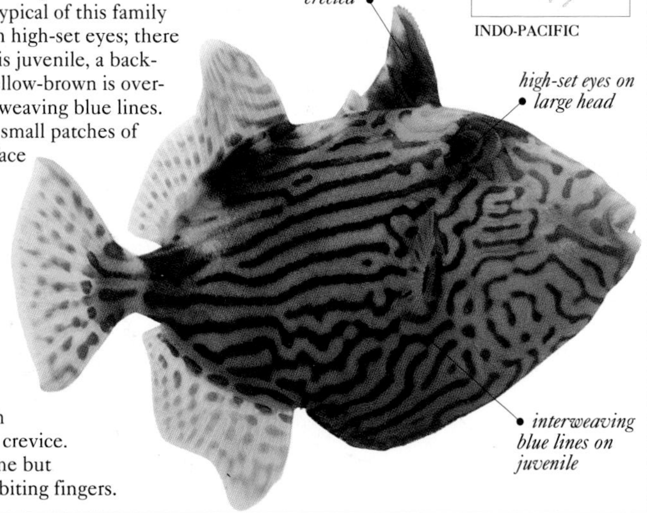

front dorsal fin can be erected

high-set eyes on large head

interweaving blue lines on juvenile

INDO-PACIFIC

Diet Carnivorous	Tank levels All	Temperament

Family BALISTIDAE	Species *Rhinecanthus aculeatus*	Size 12 in (30 cm)

PICASSO TRIGGERFISH

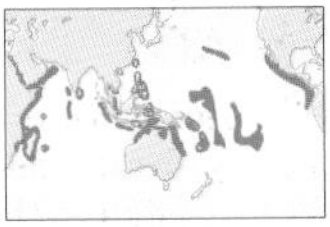

The body of this fish is more elongated than other triggerfish. Its popular name, Picasso, reflects its modernistic pattern. Yellow lines around the lips extend back past the gill cover to join up with a dark blue-lined patch which runs across the eyes. This coloration makes the mouth look deceptively larger, but it is no bigger than that of any other triggerfish.

• **HABITAT** Shallow waters in the Red Sea and the Indo-Pacific Oceans to Hawaii.

• **REMARK** Its drawn-out popular name in Hawaii, where it is the national fish, means "the fish which carries a needle, has a snout, and grunts like a pig."

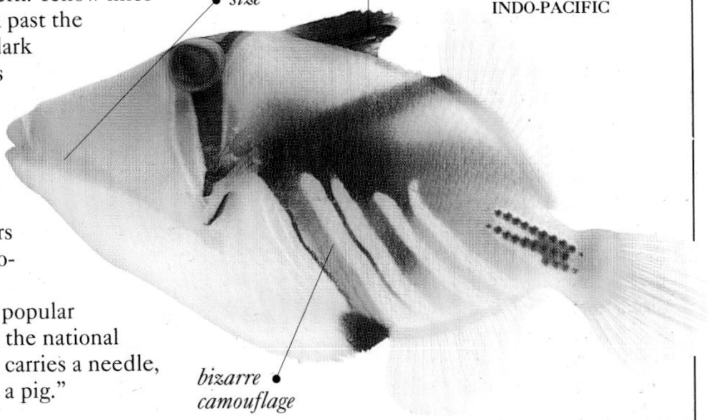

lines around mouth exaggerate size

one of two dorsal fins

bizarre camouflage

INDO-PACIFIC

Diet Carnivorous	Tank levels All	Temperament

WRASSES

WRASSES, MEMBERS OF the Labridae family, have distinct behavior patterns, including the removing of parasites or "cleaning" of other fishes, and the building of nighttime cocoon-like mucous structures. Sex reversal is common in single-sexed groups when required; spawning is by egg scattering.

Family LABRIDAE	Species *Bodianus rufus*	Size 24 in (60 cm)

SPANISH HOGFISH

The upper body section of this juvenile Spanish Hogfish is purple-blue, from the eye almost to the rear of the dorsal fin. Adults are largely red with yellow on the lower flanks. Most aquarium specimens are juveniles, however, with either purple-blue or blue-brown on the dorsal surface, and yellow on the ventral surface and tail.

• **HABITAT** Rocky outcrops of the Caribbean and tropical western Atlantic.

• **REMARK** Juveniles may act as "cleaners."

CARIBBEAN, MEXICAN GULF

Diet Omnivorous	Tank level Lower	Temperament

Family LABRIDAE	Species *Bodianus puchellus*	Size 10 in (25 cm)

CUBAN HOGFISH

Most of the body of the adult Cuban Hogfish is carmine-red, with some dark speckling. A tapering band of white runs from the bottom lip rearward. The last few rays of the dorsal fin and the upper caudal fin are yellow. Juveniles are mostly yellow.

• **HABITAT** Rocky outcrops of the Caribbean; also the Western Atlantic.

• **REMARK** Juveniles may act as "cleaners" to other fishes.

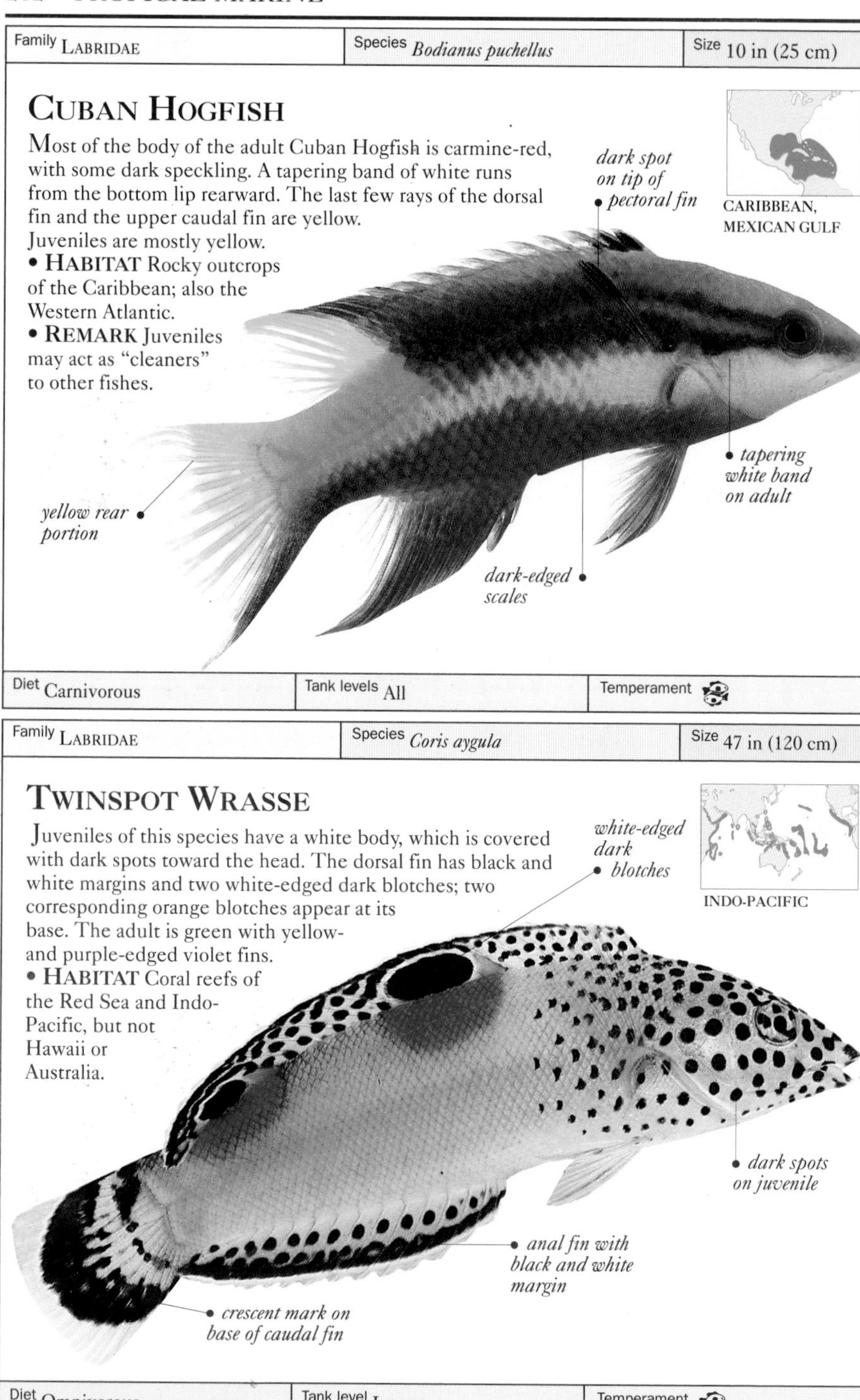

Diet Carnivorous	Tank levels All	Temperament

Family LABRIDAE	Species *Coris aygula*	Size 47 in (120 cm)

TWINSPOT WRASSE

Juveniles of this species have a white body, which is covered with dark spots toward the head. The dorsal fin has black and white margins and two white-edged dark blotches; two corresponding orange blotches appear at its base. The adult is green with yellow- and purple-edged violet fins.

• **HABITAT** Coral reefs of the Red Sea and Indo-Pacific, but not Hawaii or Australia.

Diet Omnivorous	Tank level Lower	Temperament

Family LABRIDAE	Species *Coris gaimardi*	Size 12 in (30 cm)

Clown Wrasse

The cylindrical body of this fish deepens with age; its color also varies from juvenile to adult. Juveniles have bright red or orange bodies and fins with white markings. Adults have a dark brown-red body with blue speckles and blue-green facial markings; dorsal and anal fins are red, edged with blue, and the caudal section is yellow.

• **HABITAT** Coral reefs from the central Indian Ocean to Hawaii, but not Australia.

• **REMARK** *Coris gaimardi africana* is similarly colored when adult and inhabits coral reefs of the East African coast.

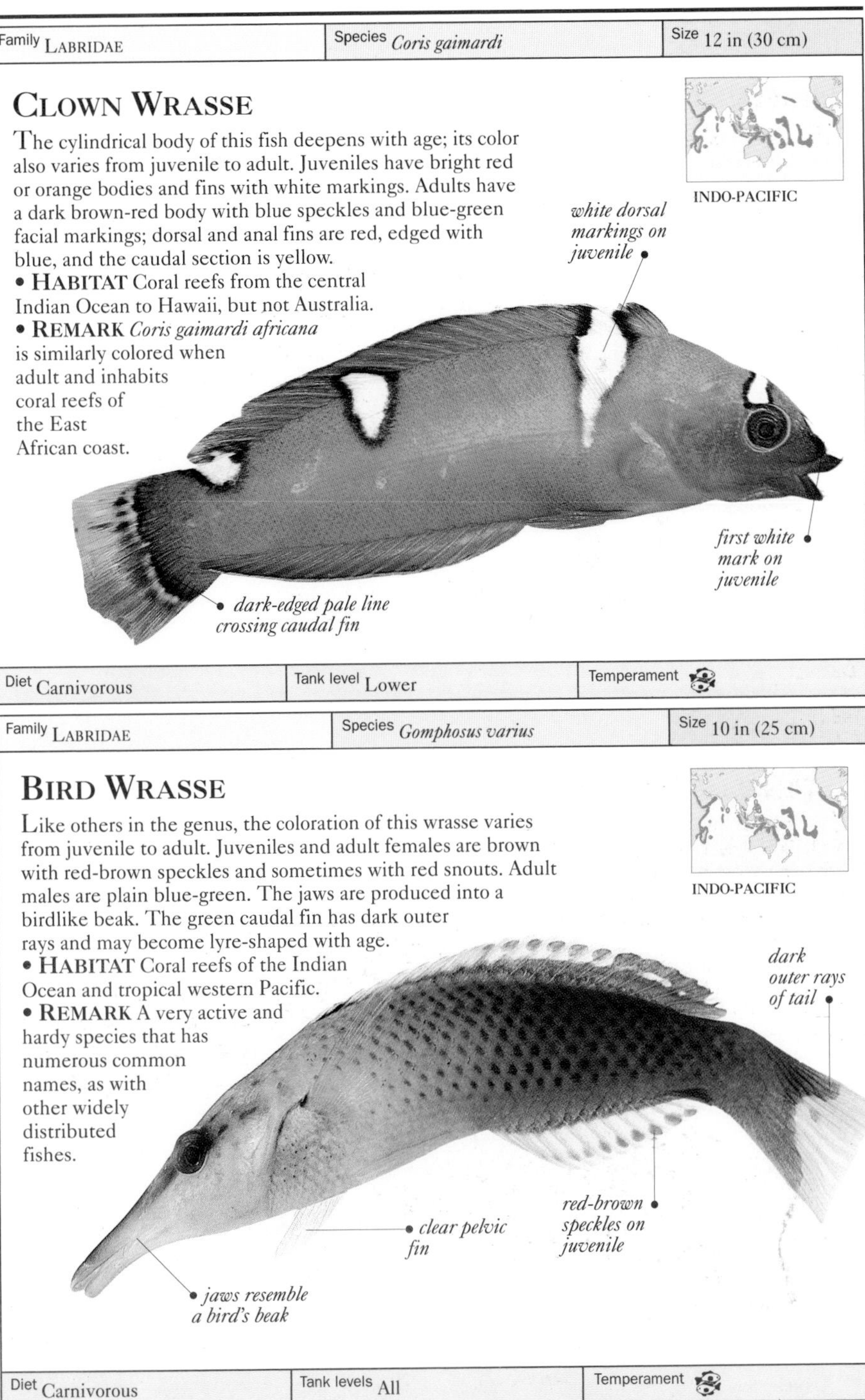

Diet Carnivorous	Tank level Lower	Temperament

Family LABRIDAE	Species *Gomphosus varius*	Size 10 in (25 cm)

Bird Wrasse

Like others in the genus, the coloration of this wrasse varies from juvenile to adult. Juveniles and adult females are brown with red-brown speckles and sometimes with red snouts. Adult males are plain blue-green. The jaws are produced into a birdlike beak. The green caudal fin has dark outer rays and may become lyre-shaped with age.

• **HABITAT** Coral reefs of the Indian Ocean and tropical western Pacific.

• **REMARK** A very active and hardy species that has numerous common names, as with other widely distributed fishes.

Diet Carnivorous	Tank levels All	Temperament

Family LABRIDAE	Species *Labroides phthirophagus*	Size 4 in (10 cm)

HAWAIIAN CLEANER WRASSE

This juvenile fish has a brightly colored body, the front half of which is yellow. A dark central stripe runs back from the snout and broadens toward the rear to include the center of the caudal fin. Dorsal and anal fins are blue, and the caudal fin has cerise on the top and bottom edges. Adults lose the brighter colors.

• **HABITAT** Establishes "cleaning stations" on coral reefs around Hawaii and the western Pacific.

• **REMARK** Offer "shellfish meat," or brine shrimp.

PACIFIC OCEAN

long-based dorsal fin

bright yellow front portion of juvenile

squared-off caudal fin

Diet Carnivorous	Tank levels All	Temperament

Family LABRIDAE	Species *Labroides dimidiatus*	Size 4 in (10 cm)

CLEANER WRASSE

The dorsal surface of this fish is pale brown, shading to creamy white on the flanks and ventral surface. An increasingly wide black stripe runs from the tip of the snout to the rear of the caudal fin. Pale blue areas highlight the sides of the stripes toward the rear.

• **HABITAT** Widely distributed on coral reefs and in rock pools of the Indo-Pacific, but not in Hawaii.

• **REMARK** The main attraction of this species is its cleaning activity: it picks parasites from the skin, or even inside of the mouths and gills, of other fish. Be sure that the mouth is set at the tip of the snout, as the similar-looking blenny, *Aspidontus taeniatus*, rips the flesh of other fish with its underslung mouth.

Cleaner Wrasse cleans a butterflyfish

INDO-PACIFIC

Diet Carnivorous	Tank levels All	Temperament 

Family LABRIDAE	Species *Lienardella fasciata*	Size 10 in (25 cm)

HARLEQUIN TUSKFISH

The heavy body of this fish is very similar to the large, freshwater, Central American cichlids. Body coloration is gray, crossed with red or orange, blue-edged vertical bands. Dorsal and anal fins are orange or red, and the pelvic and caudal fins have red edges. The mouth contains distinctive blue teeth.

• **HABITAT** Coral reefs in the western Pacific, including the New Hebrides, Taiwan, and the Great Barrier Reef.

• **REMARK** It requires plenty of room and a soft substrate for nighttime burrowing.

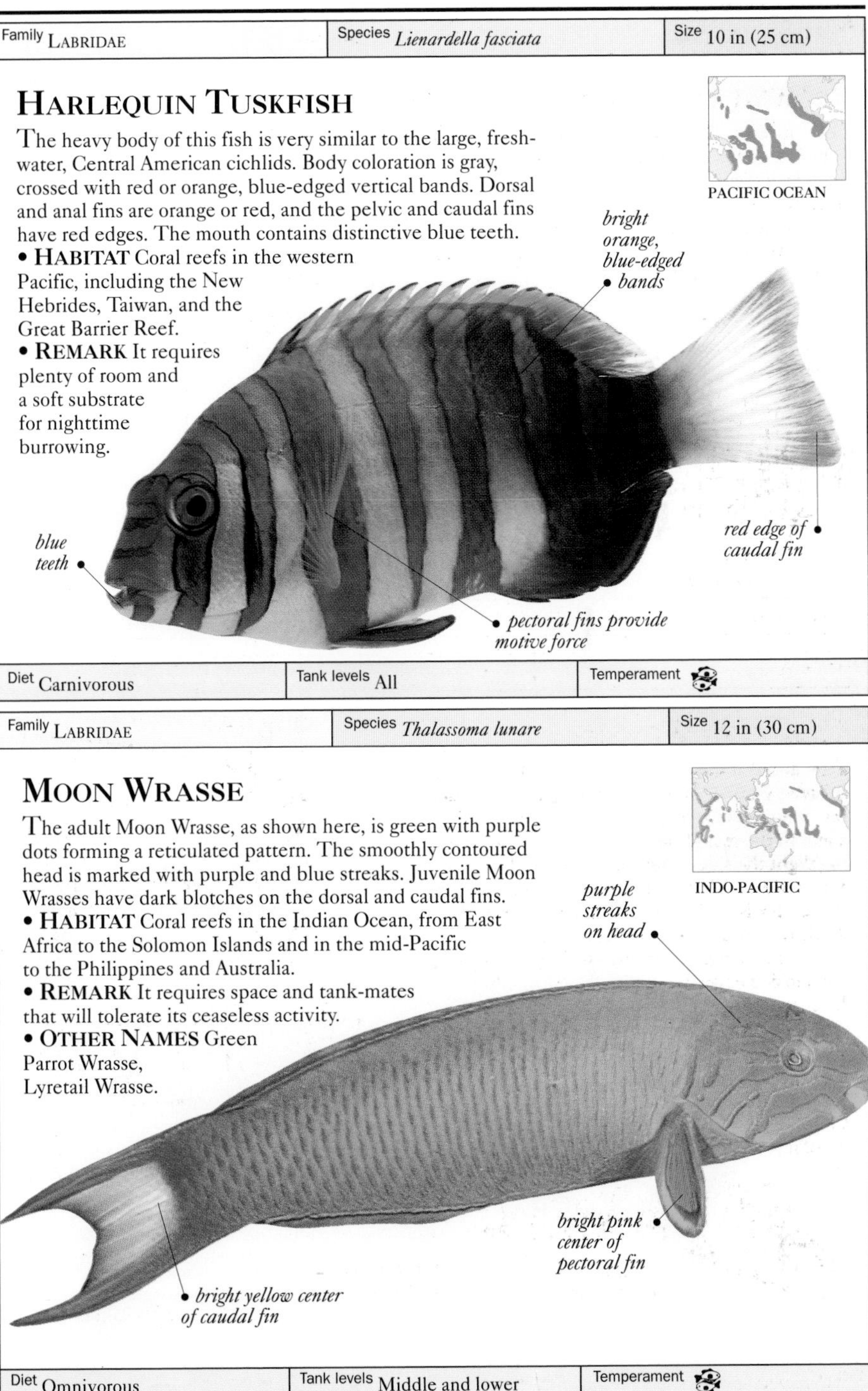

Diet Carnivorous	Tank levels All	Temperament

Family LABRIDAE	Species *Thalassoma lunare*	Size 12 in (30 cm)

MOON WRASSE

The adult Moon Wrasse, as shown here, is green with purple dots forming a reticulated pattern. The smoothly contoured head is marked with purple and blue streaks. Juvenile Moon Wrasses have dark blotches on the dorsal and caudal fins.

• **HABITAT** Coral reefs in the Indian Ocean, from East Africa to the Solomon Islands and in the mid-Pacific to the Philippines and Australia.

• **REMARK** It requires space and tank-mates that will tolerate its ceaseless activity.

• **OTHER NAMES** Green Parrot Wrasse, Lyretail Wrasse.

Diet Omnivorous	Tank levels Middle and lower	Temperament

SEA BASSES AND GROUPERS

MANY MEMBERS OF THE family Serranidae (the sea basses and groupers) are extremely attractive, but only small specimens of these natural predators are suitable for the average-sized aquarium. Fortunately, some of the smallest family species, including the basslets, are the most brilliantly colored. Sexing is difficult, as hermaphroditic changes occur during these fishes' lives: each fish has both male and female capabilities, but not simultaneously. Many species turn darker or paler or take on a bicolor pattern, when breeding, and females become obviously distended with eggs.

Family SERRANIDAE	Species *Anthias squamipinnis*	Size 4¾ in (12 cm)

WRECKFISH

The golden pink body of this fish is covered with well-defined scales. The head is pink to violet, and a thin orange-gold band runs across the top of the mouth, through the bottom of the eye, and to the base of the pectoral fin. The dorsal fin is long based and pink with gold speckles; that of the male has a long third ray. The caudal fin of both sexes is lyre shaped, and the female's may have a V-shaped pink blotch.

• **HABITAT** Very widespread, shoaling in great numbers around coral reefs from East Africa to the central Pacific.

• **REMARK** This fish may not accept dead food unless it can be fooled into thinking it is live (by introducing it in water currents or by jerking it on a thread). It does not thrive as a solitary specimen.

• **OTHER NAMES** Lyretail Coralfish, Pink Coralfish, Golden Jewelfish, Orange Sea Perch.

Wreckfish traverse the coral reef

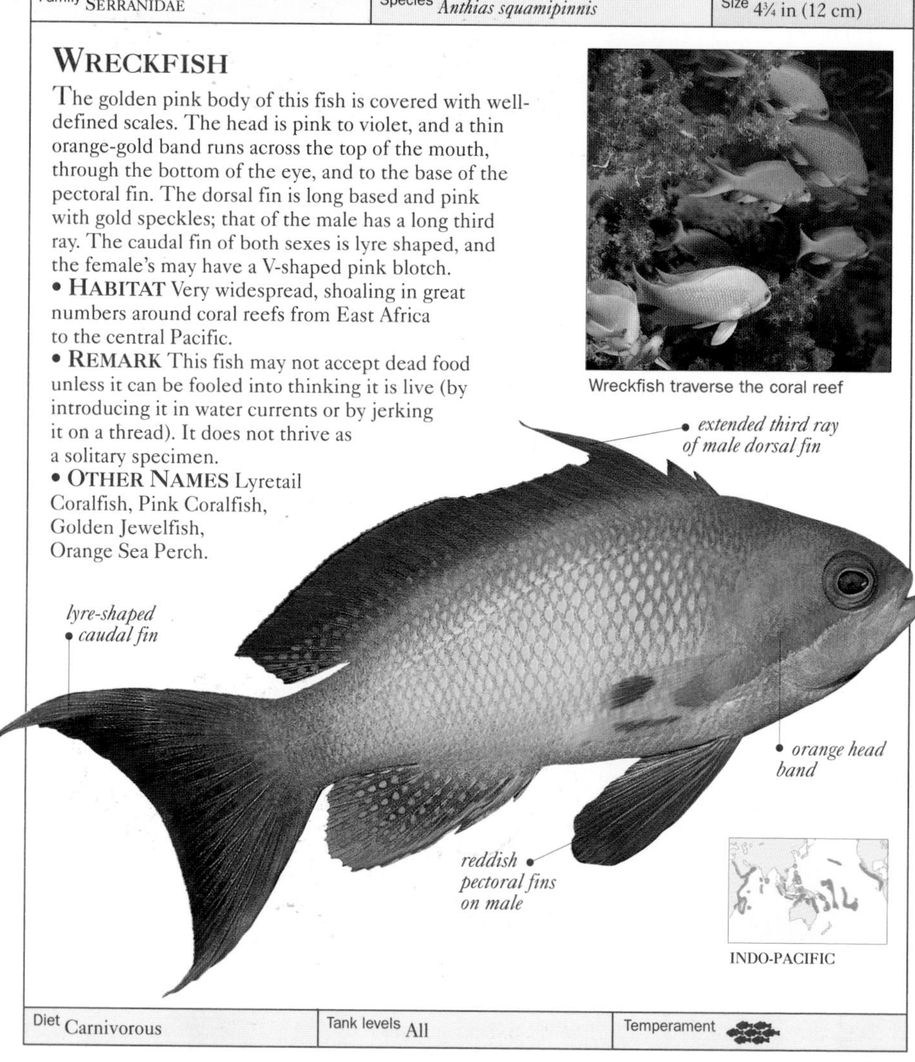

Diet Carnivorous	Tank levels All	Temperament

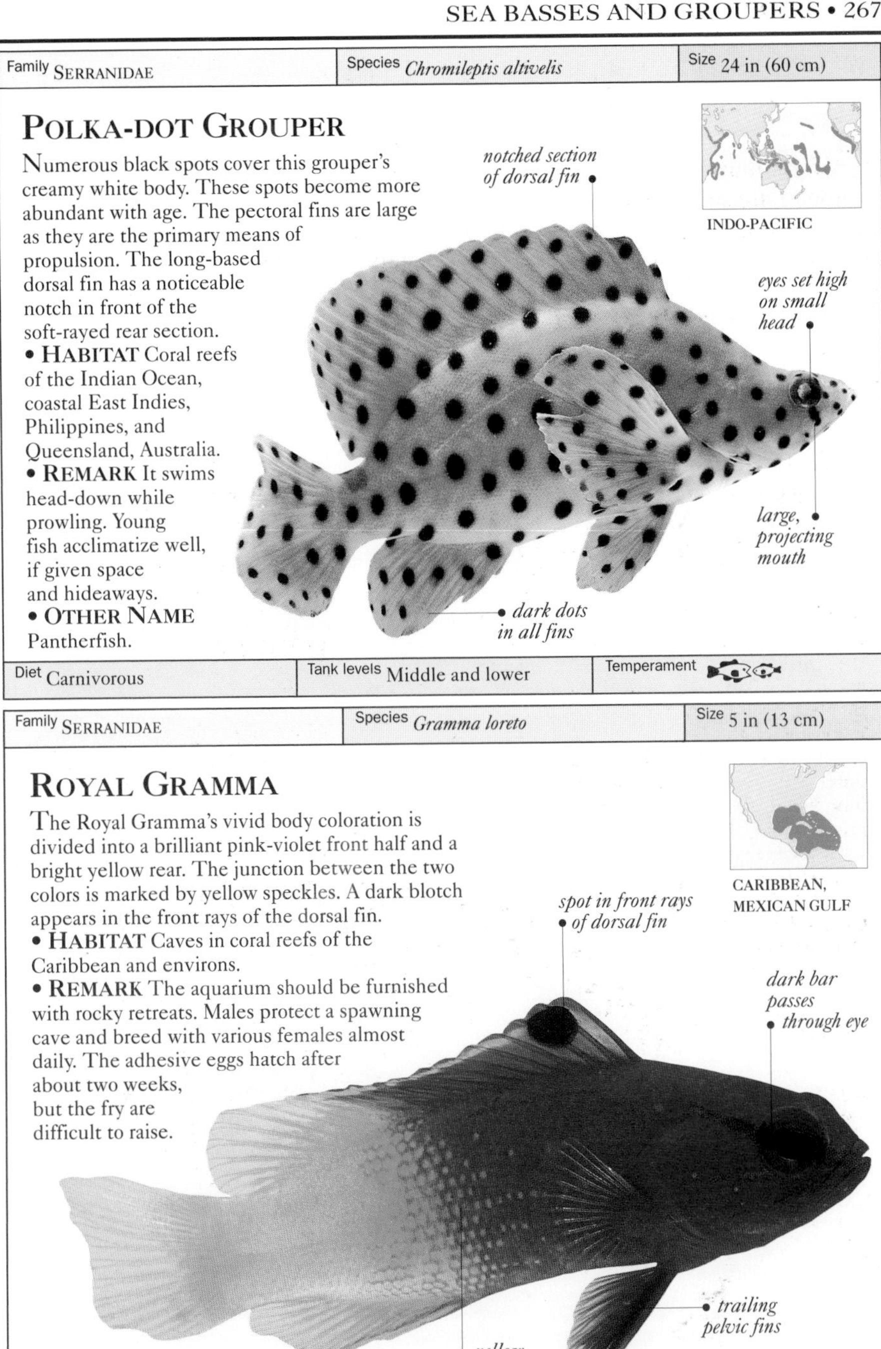

Family SERRANIDAE	Species *Chromileptis altivelis*	Size 24 in (60 cm)

POLKA-DOT GROUPER

Numerous black spots cover this grouper's creamy white body. These spots become more abundant with age. The pectoral fins are large as they are the primary means of propulsion. The long-based dorsal fin has a noticeable notch in front of the soft-rayed rear section.

• **HABITAT** Coral reefs of the Indian Ocean, coastal East Indies, Philippines, and Queensland, Australia.

• **REMARK** It swims head-down while prowling. Young fish acclimatize well, if given space and hideaways.

• **OTHER NAME** Pantherfish.

Diet Carnivorous	Tank levels Middle and lower	Temperament

Family SERRANIDAE	Species *Gramma loreto*	Size 5 in (13 cm)

ROYAL GRAMMA

The Royal Gramma's vivid body coloration is divided into a brilliant pink-violet front half and a bright yellow rear. The junction between the two colors is marked by yellow speckles. A dark blotch appears in the front rays of the dorsal fin.

• **HABITAT** Caves in coral reefs of the Caribbean and environs.

• **REMARK** The aquarium should be furnished with rocky retreats. Males protect a spawning cave and breed with various females almost daily. The adhesive eggs hatch after about two weeks, but the fry are difficult to raise.

Diet Plankton	Tank level Lower	Temperament

BATFISHES AND CARDINALFISHES

MEMBERS OF THE batfish family, (Platacidae) can be recognized by their winglike fins, but species identification is difficult. Adult coloration is more drab, and speculation surrounds the classification of the color forms. The cardinalfishes (Apogonidae) are mainly nocturnal. Mouthbreeding behavior and the presence of two erect dorsal fins are their chief characteristics.

Family PLATACIDAE	Species *Platax orbicularis*	Size 20 in (50 cm)

ORBICULATE BATFISH

These unusual fish are especially tall when young. They fill out to form disk shapes in adulthood. Colors are usually greenish brown, sometimes reddish, with a dark stripe or two toward the head (as in these juveniles), that fade with age. The dark dorsal and anal fins are very long-based and high, almost encircling the body.

• **HABITAT** Shallow coastal waters among mangroves in the Indo-Pacific, but not reaching Hawaii or the eastern Pacific.

• **REMARK** A constantly hungry species, the Orbiculate Batfish grows quickly in the aquarium and needs ample space. In the wild, it scavenges around pilings and piers.

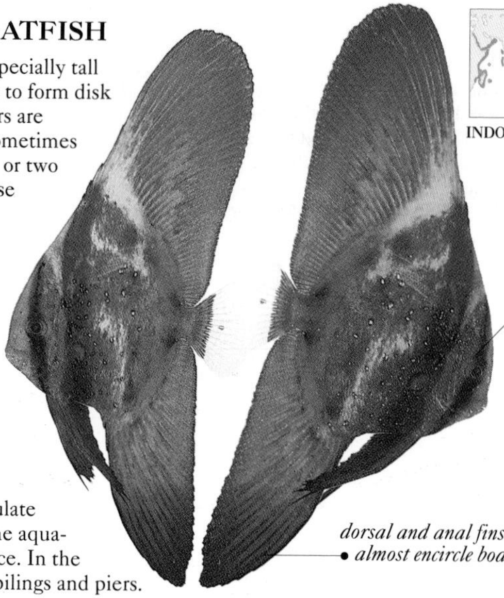

INDO-PACIFIC

forehead rises steeply from snout

dorsal and anal fins almost encircle body

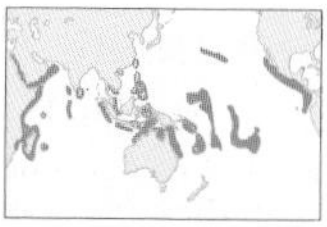

Diet Omnivorous	Tank levels Middle and lower	Temperament

Family APOGONIDAE	Species *Apogon notopterus*	Size 4 in (10 cm)

PAJAMA CARDINALFISH

The coloration and patterning of this Pajama Cardinalfish appears haphazard. Ground color is pinkish gray, and there are red-brown spots behind a dividing line.

• **HABITAT** Sheltered bays and lagoons among corals and in mangrove swamps of the Indo-Pacific.

• **REMARK** This shy species emerges at dusk to feed, assisted by its large eyes.

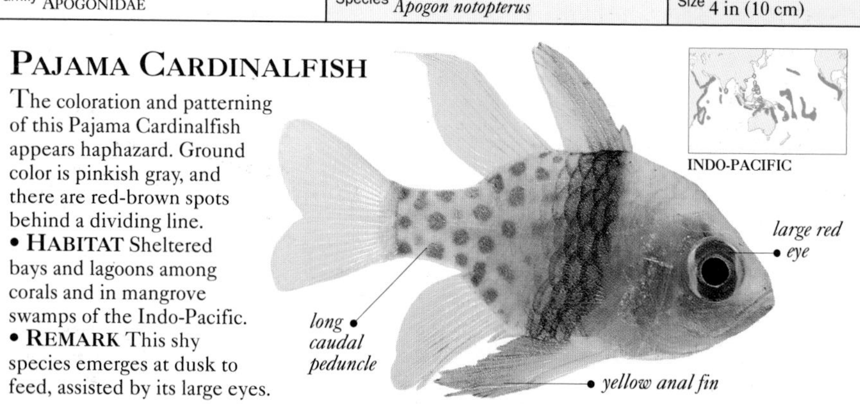

Diet Carnivorous	Tank levels Middle and lower	Temperament

BLENNIES

A COMMON FEATURE of the family Blennidae is their slimy skin – blennies are sometimes called slimefishes. Many are bottom-dwellers, living on the seabed at the base of reefs, or among corals in the shallow waters just below the tideline. The whiskerlike growths, or cirri, above the eyes are sensory, and are not found in all species of blenny.

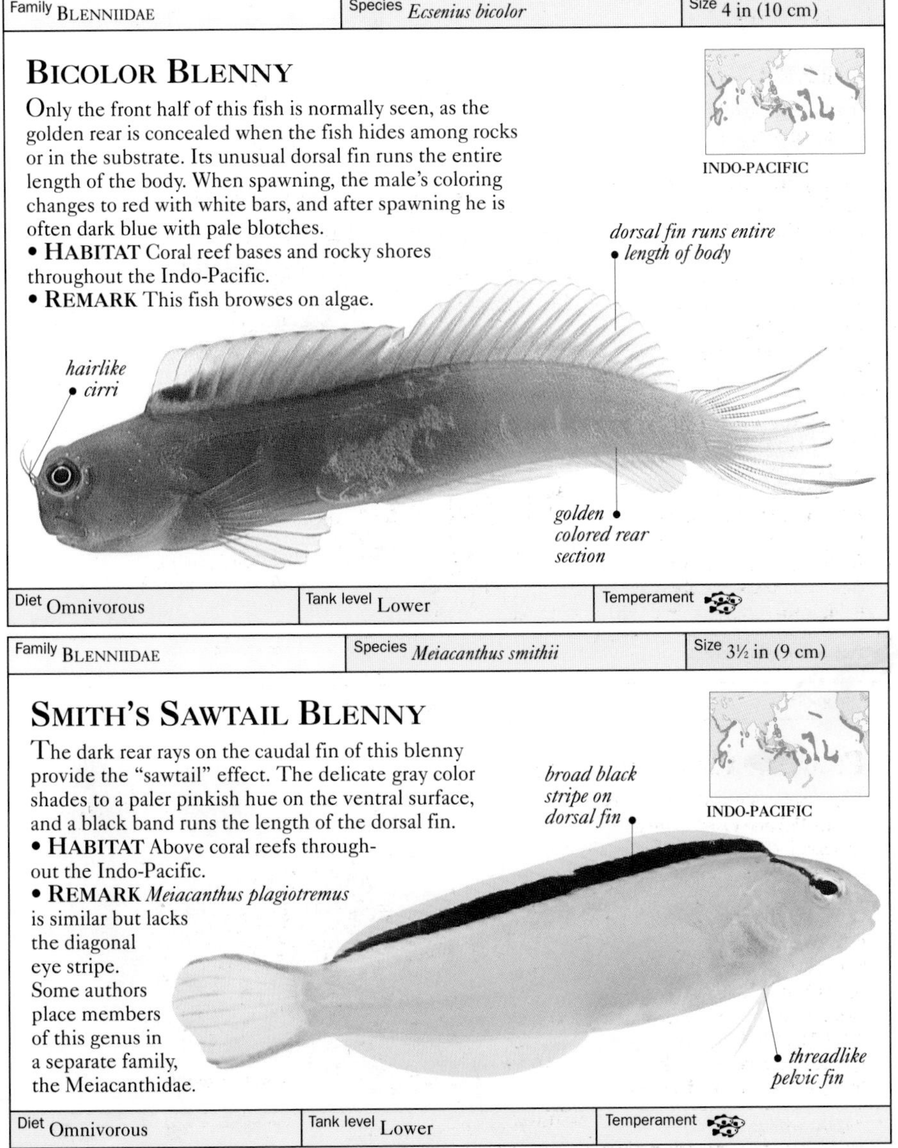

Family BLENNIIDAE	Species *Ecsenius bicolor*	Size 4 in (10 cm)

BICOLOR BLENNY

Only the front half of this fish is normally seen, as the golden rear is concealed when the fish hides among rocks or in the substrate. Its unusual dorsal fin runs the entire length of the body. When spawning, the male's coloring changes to red with white bars, and after spawning he is often dark blue with pale blotches.

- **HABITAT** Coral reef bases and rocky shores throughout the Indo-Pacific.
- **REMARK** This fish browses on algae.

Diet Omnivorous	Tank level Lower	Temperament

Family BLENNIIDAE	Species *Meiacanthus smithii*	Size 3½ in (9 cm)

SMITH'S SAWTAIL BLENNY

The dark rear rays on the caudal fin of this blenny provide the "sawtail" effect. The delicate gray color shades to a paler pinkish hue on the ventral surface, and a black band runs the length of the dorsal fin.

- **HABITAT** Above coral reefs throughout the Indo-Pacific.
- **REMARK** *Meiacanthus plagiotremus* is similar but lacks the diagonal eye stripe. Some authors place members of this genus in a separate family, the Meiacanthidae.

Diet Omnivorous	Tank level Lower	Temperament

BOXFISHES

THE BOX-SHAPED BODIES of members of the family Ostraciidae are covered with rigid plates. Pelvic fins are absent, and bony stumps may appear in their place on some species. All species are propelled slowly by movements of the dorsal, anal, and pectoral fins. When stressed, boxfishes excrete poison, and should be settled into a new aquarium first.

Family OSTRACIIDAE	Species *Lactoria cornuta*	Size 20 in (50 cm)

LONGHORNED COWFISH

The body of this fish is a tapering box shape. Bony plates have replaced scales, leaving the body largely inflexible. A yellow ground color is marked with blue dotting and facial lines. At each corner of the head there is a distinctive hornlike growth.

• **HABITAT** Seabeds throughout the Indo-Pacific.

• **REMARK** This fish rarely reaches full size in captivity.

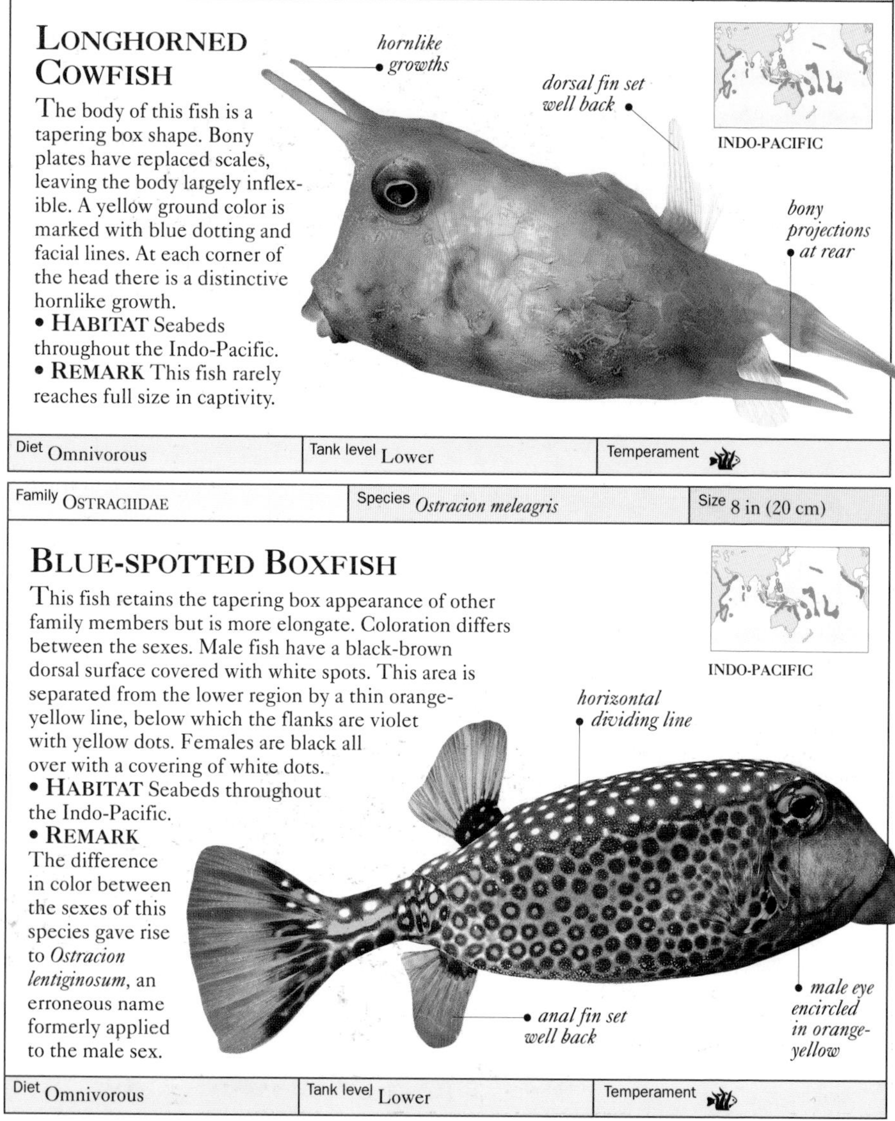

Diet Omnivorous	Tank level Lower	Temperament

Family OSTRACIIDAE	Species *Ostracion meleagris*	Size 8 in (20 cm)

BLUE-SPOTTED BOXFISH

This fish retains the tapering box appearance of other family members but is more elongate. Coloration differs between the sexes. Male fish have a black-brown dorsal surface covered with white spots. This area is separated from the lower region by a thin orange-yellow line, below which the flanks are violet with yellow dots. Females are black all over with a covering of white dots.

• **HABITAT** Seabeds throughout the Indo-Pacific.

• **REMARK** The difference in color between the sexes of this species gave rise to *Ostracion lentiginosum*, an erroneous name formerly applied to the male sex.

Diet Omnivorous	Tank level Lower	Temperament

FILEFISHES

THE ROUGH SKIN of the monacanthids accounts for the common name "filefishes," and for the alternative popular name of "leatherjackets." They are related to the triggerfishes, from whom they differ by being unable to lock the first dorsal spine into an upright position. Filefishes may swim head-down. In the wild they feed on polyps and algae.

Family MONACANTHIDAE	Species *Chaetoderma penicilligera*	Size 10 in (25 cm)

PRICKLY LEATHERJACKET

Gray-blue and yellow-gold tints color the rhomboid body of this fish. A number of thin dark horizontally wavy lines cross the entire body. The main features are the branched tentacles; they grow along the ventral and dorsal outlines and serve as camouflage.

• **HABITAT** Drifting seaweeds in the western Pacific, from the East Indies to Samoa.

• **REMARK** This fish is particularly hardy and sociable.

PACIFIC OCEAN

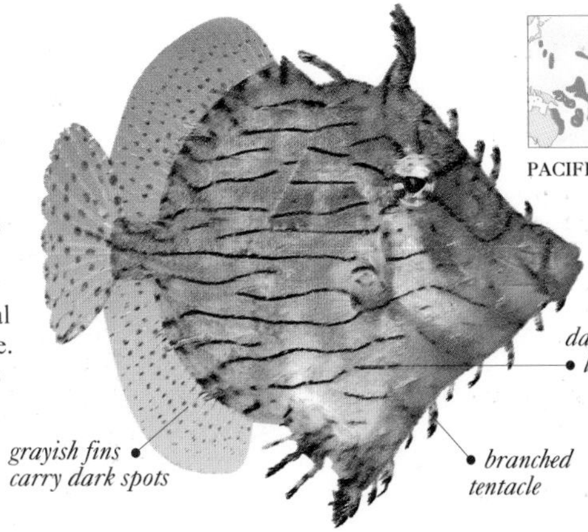

dark, wavy lines

grayish fins carry dark spots

branched tentacle

Diet Carnivorous	Tank levels Upper and middle	Temperament

Family MONACANTHIDAE	Species *Pervagor melanocephalus*	Size 5 in (13 cm)

LACE-FINNED LEATHERJACKET

The body color of this filefish is divided into two halves: the front half is purple, shading through brown to a bright yellow back at the caudal fin. Scales are very small. The first of the two dorsal fins comprises a single spine. The second dorsal fin is long-based and set above the similarly constructed anal fin. Pelvic fins are merely single spines.

• **HABITAT** Drifting seaweed throughout the Indo-Pacific Ocean, including the islands of Hawaii and Australia.

• **REMARK** Like other filefishes, this species is generally smaller and less active than the triggerfishes (see p.259).

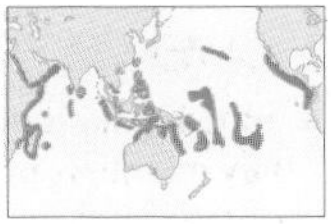

INDO-PACIFIC

single, upright spine

streaked fan-shaped caudal fin

pelvic spine

Diet Carnivorous	Tank levels Upper and middle	Temperament 

GOBIES

MEMBERS OF THE FAMILY Gobiidae are very similar in body shape to those of the family Blennidae (see p.269). Gobies can be distinguished by their pelvic fins, which grow together to form a suction disk used to anchor the fish to a rock or other resting place. Some gobies are brilliantly colored. They can be bred in the aquarium, but the tiny fry are difficult to raise.

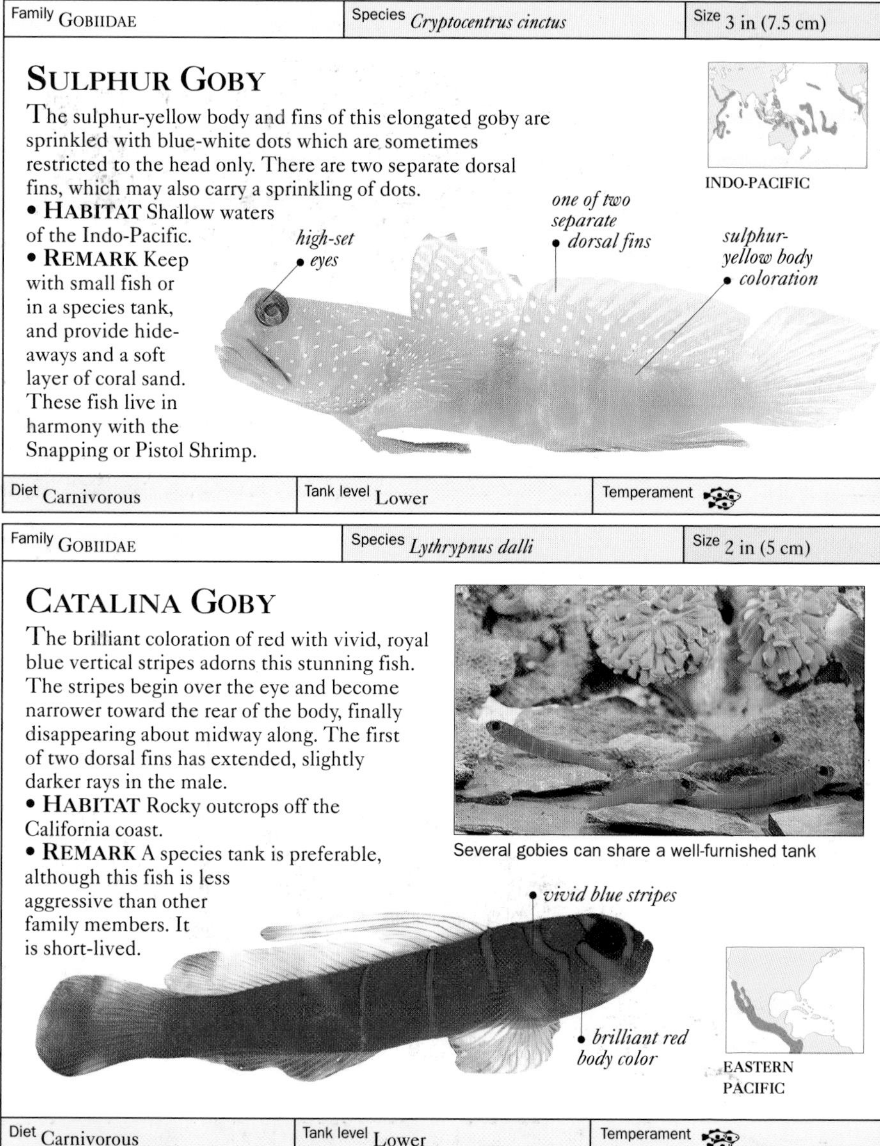

Family GOBIIDAE	Species *Cryptocentrus cinctus*	Size 3 in (7.5 cm)

SULPHUR GOBY

The sulphur-yellow body and fins of this elongated goby are sprinkled with blue-white dots which are sometimes restricted to the head only. There are two separate dorsal fins, which may also carry a sprinkling of dots.

• **HABITAT** Shallow waters of the Indo-Pacific.

• **REMARK** Keep with small fish or in a species tank, and provide hideaways and a soft layer of coral sand. These fish live in harmony with the Snapping or Pistol Shrimp.

Diet Carnivorous	Tank level Lower	Temperament

Family GOBIIDAE	Species *Lythrypnus dalli*	Size 2 in (5 cm)

CATALINA GOBY

The brilliant coloration of red with vivid, royal blue vertical stripes adorns this stunning fish. The stripes begin over the eye and become narrower toward the rear of the body, finally disappearing about midway along. The first of two dorsal fins has extended, slightly darker rays in the male.

• **HABITAT** Rocky outcrops off the California coast.

• **REMARK** A species tank is preferable, although this fish is less aggressive than other family members. It is short-lived.

Several gobies can share a well-furnished tank

Diet Carnivorous	Tank level Lower	Temperament

Family GOBIIDAE	Species *Nemateleotris decora*	Size 2½ in (6 cm)

PURPLE FIREFISH

INDO-PACIFIC

The coloration of this fish is divided: the front half of the body is golden yellow, with violet on top of the head and along the dorsal surface, while the rear half of the body is brownish gray. The first few rays of the front dorsal fin are elongated and colored black, violet, and red, as are the second dorsal fin, the anal fin, and the lyre-shaped caudal fin.

• **HABITAT** Caves in coral reefs from the central Indian Ocean to the central Pacific.

• **REMARK** As with related species, the pelvic fins are not fused but divided, as in the genus *Eleotris*. Retreats are essential.

violet-colored dorsal surface

striped colors on anal fin

long, violet-edged pelvic fin

Diet Carnivorous	Tank levels Middle and lower	Temperament

Family GOBIIDAE	Species *Nemateleotris magnifica*	Size 2½ in (6 cm)

FIREFISH

INDO-PACIFIC

As with the Purple Firefish (above), the coloration of this species is divided into two areas: the front half of the body is pinkish yellow, with a plain yellow area on the head, while the rear half is pinkish orange, shading through red to a dark brown-red. The first few rays of the front dorsal fin are elongated and yellow, with a pink front edge. The second dorsal fin and the anal fin are yellow with a brown-red outer edge.

• **HABITAT** Coral reef caves from the central Indian Ocean to the central Pacific.

• **REMARK** The pelvic fins are split in two, not fused together.

very long first ray of dorsal fin

bold speckling around head

long pelvic fin

pinkish yellow front section

Diet Carnivorous	Tank levels Middle and lower	Temperament

GRUNTS AND HAWKFISHES

LIKE THE BASSES and groupers, the grunts (family Pomadasyidae) usually grow too large for the average aquarium. Marked pattern changes occur between juvenile and adult stages. The hawkfishes (family Cirrhitidae), so named because they perch in wait for their prey like hawks, eat other fishes, but invertebrates are safe with them. They breed by egg depositing.

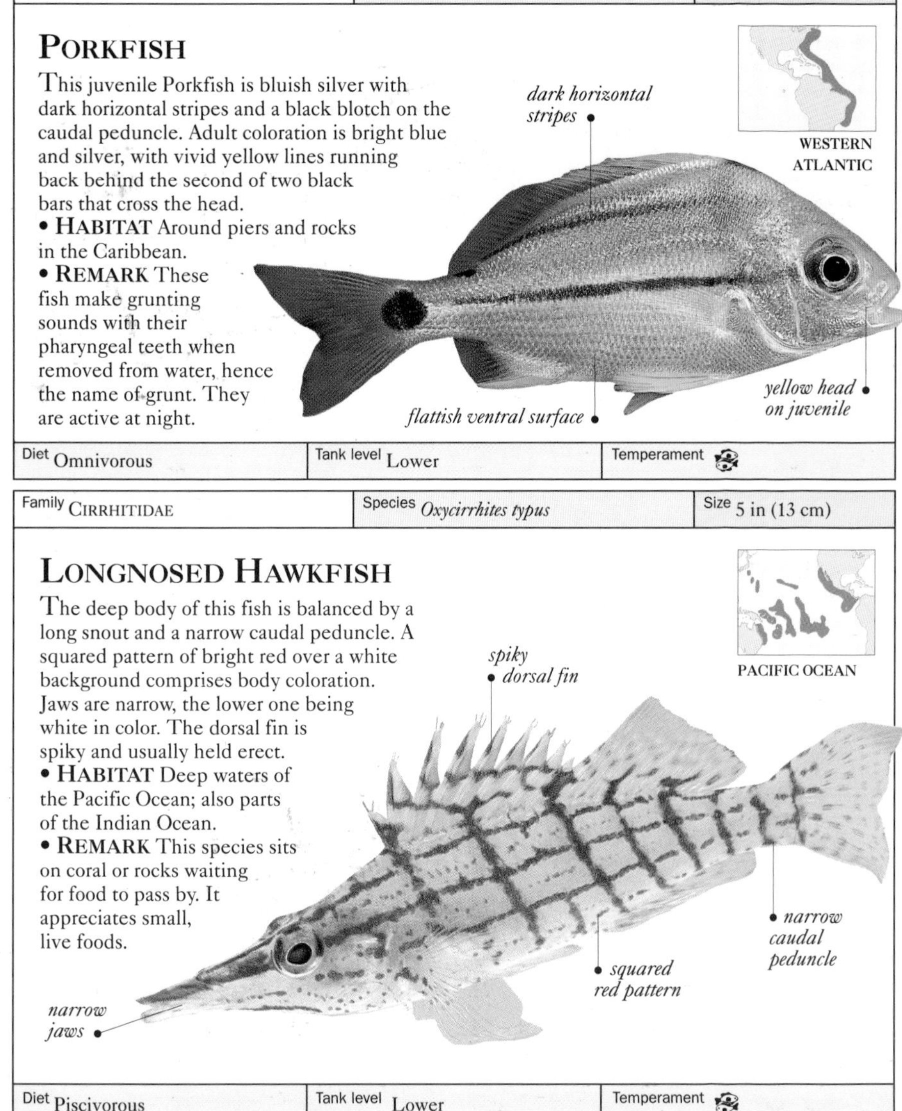

Family POMADASYIDAE	Species *Anisotremus virginicus*	Size 12 in (30 cm)

PORKFISH

This juvenile Porkfish is bluish silver with dark horizontal stripes and a black blotch on the caudal peduncle. Adult coloration is bright blue and silver, with vivid yellow lines running back behind the second of two black bars that cross the head.

• **HABITAT** Around piers and rocks in the Caribbean.

• **REMARK** These fish make grunting sounds with their pharyngeal teeth when removed from water, hence the name of grunt. They are active at night.

Diet Omnivorous	Tank level Lower	Temperament

Family CIRRHITIDAE	Species *Oxycirrhites typus*	Size 5 in (13 cm)

LONGNOSED HAWKFISH

The deep body of this fish is balanced by a long snout and a narrow caudal peduncle. A squared pattern of bright red over a white background comprises body coloration. Jaws are narrow, the lower one being white in color. The dorsal fin is spiky and usually held erect.

• **HABITAT** Deep waters of the Pacific Ocean; also parts of the Indian Ocean.

• **REMARK** This species sits on coral or rocks waiting for food to pass by. It appreciates small, live foods.

Diet Piscivorous	Tank level Lower	Temperament

JAWFISHES AND LIONFISHES

THE MOST NOTABLE characteristic of jawfishes (family Opisthognathidae) is their habit of building burrows in the substrate, into which they retreat tail-first. The graceful swimming action of the lionfishes (family Scorpaenidae) conceals a stealthy and predatory instinct. Their fins contain a powerful venom. Handle them only with extreme caution.

Family OPISTHOGNATHIDAE	Species *Opisthognathus aurifrons*	Size 4 in (10 cm)

YELLOW JAWFISH

The body of this fish is elongate, and the head is extremely broad. A pale creamy gray covers most of the body, but the head is bright yellow. A bluish cast appears toward the rear of the body. There are no obvious sexual differences.

• **HABITAT** Rubble and reefs of the tropical western Atlantic.

• **REMARK** This territorial but cautious species generally remains hovering above its burrow ready to snatch small, drifting animal fare. It may jump when startled, so secure the hood.

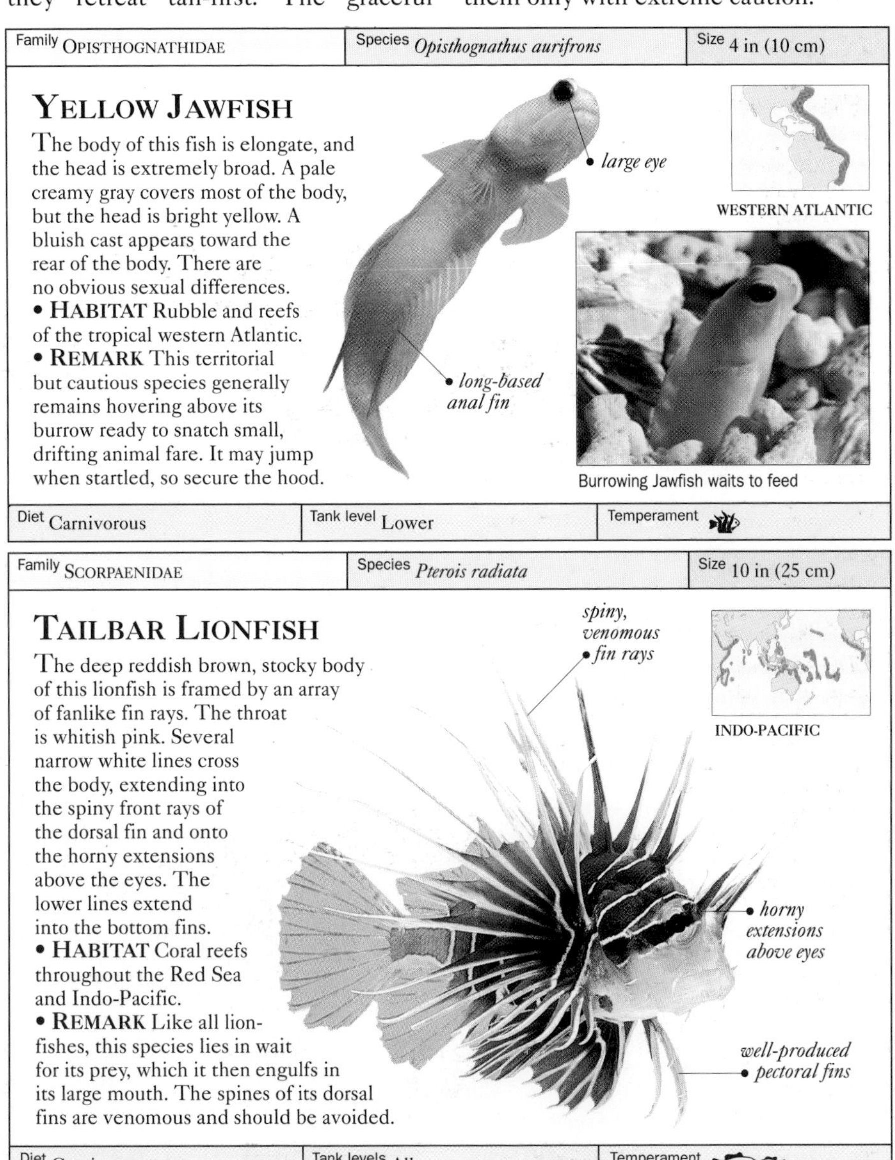

Burrowing Jawfish waits to feed

Diet Carnivorous	Tank level Lower	Temperament

Family SCORPAENIDAE	Species *Pterois radiata*	Size 10 in (25 cm)

TAILBAR LIONFISH

The deep reddish brown, stocky body of this lionfish is framed by an array of fanlike fin rays. The throat is whitish pink. Several narrow white lines cross the body, extending into the spiny front rays of the dorsal fin and onto the horny extensions above the eyes. The lower lines extend into the bottom fins.

• **HABITAT** Coral reefs throughout the Red Sea and Indo-Pacific.

• **REMARK** Like all lionfishes, this species lies in wait for its prey, which it then engulfs in its large mouth. The spines of its dorsal fins are venomous and should be avoided.

Diet Carnivorous	Tank levels All	Temperament

Family SCORPAENIDAE	Species *Pterois volitans*	Size 14 in (35 cm)

LIONFISH

The white body of this venomous fish is crossed vertically by light and dark brown-red bars. The eye is concealed by the pattern, beneath a pair of hornlike growths. The first spines of the dorsal fin are patterned with light and dark marks; they are spiny and very poisonous.

• **HABITAT** Red Sea and Indo-Pacific coral reefs.

• **REMARK** Handle with extreme caution, and feed with living or dead meaty foods, but not red meat.

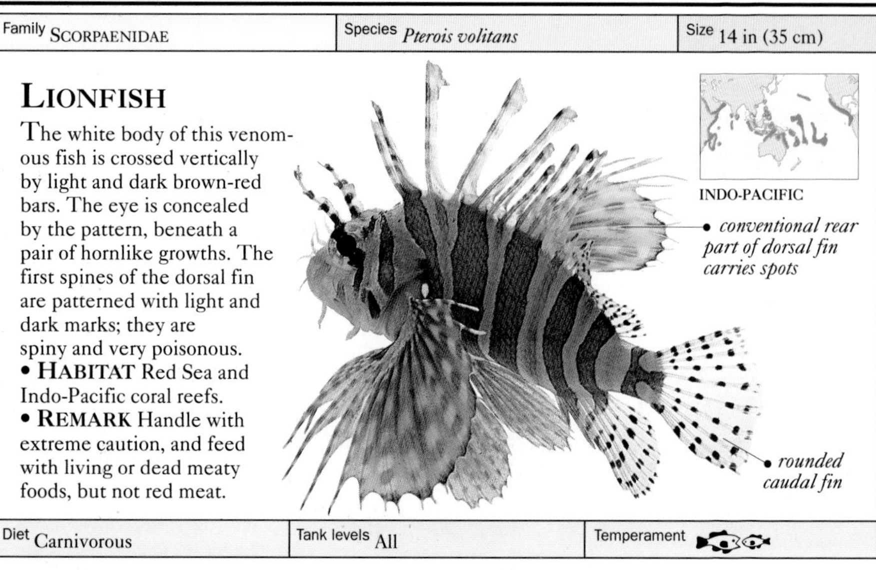

Diet Carnivorous	Tank levels All	Temperament

MANDARINFISHES

MANDARINFISHES and the related dragonets belong to the family Callionymidae, comprising attractive, but shy, bottom-dwelling species. *Synchiropus splendidus* (below) is the most colorful example. Males are brighter and have extensions to the dorsal and anal fins. Fertilization is internal, before the eggs are scattered. They feed on small marine animals.

Family CALLIONYMIDAE	Species *Synchiropus splendidus*	Size 3 in (7.5 cm)

MANDARINFISH

The body of this species is bluish green-gold, with a random pattern of wide, dark-edged blue lines extending on to the fins. The eyes are gold and black, and the lower head is pale beneath a dark line which runs from the snout to the gold-spotted gill cover.

• **HABITAT** Hideaways on reef bottoms in the Pacific, south to Australia.

• **REMARK** Keep the Mandarinfish in a quiet tank away from boisterous fishes.

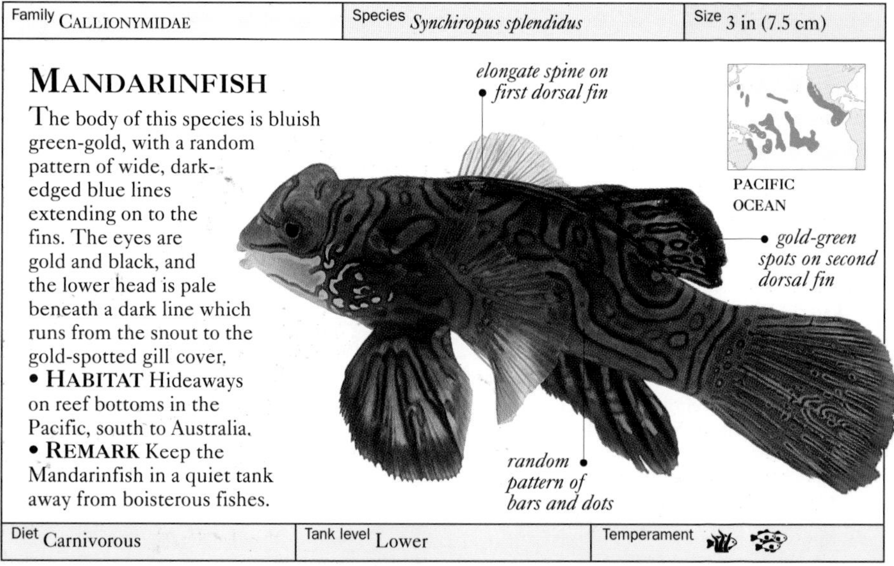

Diet Carnivorous	Tank level Lower	Temperament

MORAY EELS

MEMBERS OF THE family Muraenidae, moray eels are only suitable for the largest aquariums but make splendid attractions for those able to accommodate them. In the wild, they inhabit rocky caves and other retreats such as corals or shipwrecks. These fish must be handled with extreme care, as even the smallest bites can be painful. Only eels of large, unrestricted sizes are capable of breeding, and many moray eels need to migrate before spawning can occur. Never keep these predatory species with small fishes.

Family MURAENIDAE	Species *Echidna nebulosus*	Size 30 in (75 cm)

SNOWFLAKE MORAY EEL

The tubular flexible body of this eel is marked by two rows of evenly spaced dark blotches, each with a white "snowflake" mark. Scales are minute, giving the impression of a smooth skin. The dorsal fin begins behind the gill cover and runs the length of the body. Pectoral and pelvic fins are absent.

• **HABITAT** Widespread in reefs of the Red Sea and Indo-Pacific.

• **REMARK** Morays should be handled with care and provided with rocky lairs.

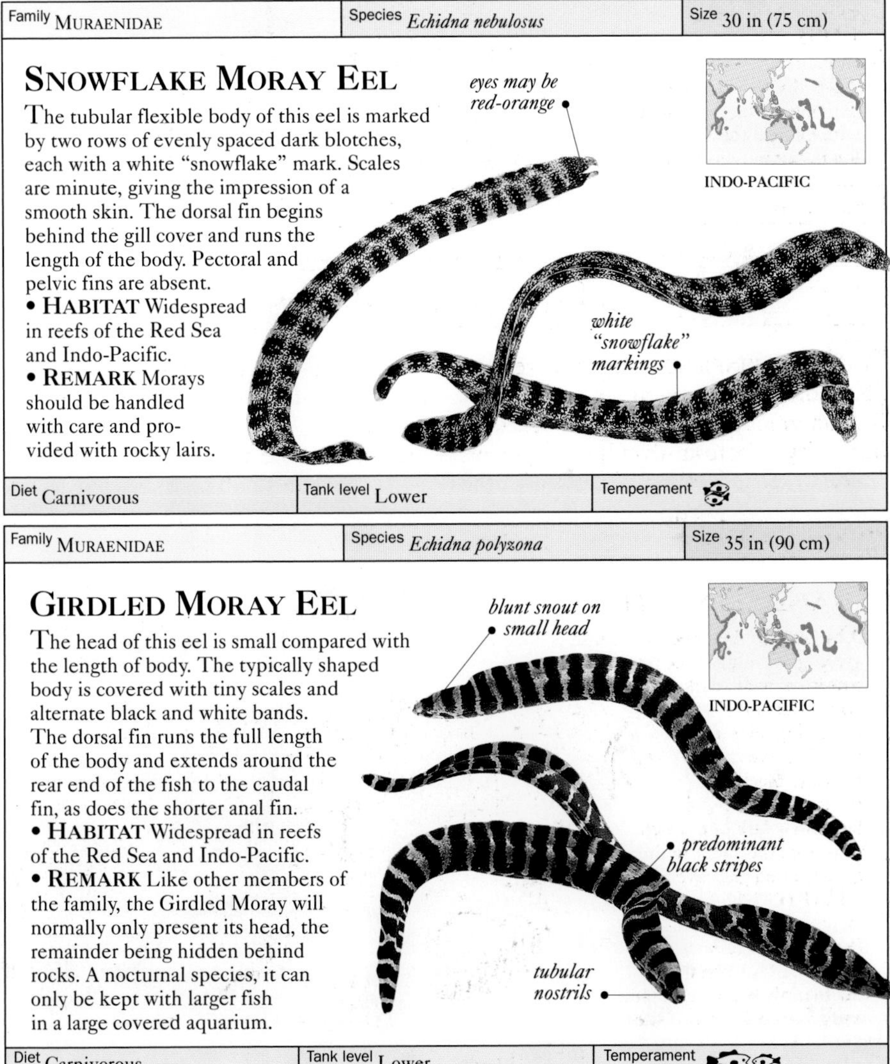

Diet Carnivorous	Tank level Lower	Temperament

Family MURAENIDAE	Species *Echidna polyzona*	Size 35 in (90 cm)

GIRDLED MORAY EEL

The head of this eel is small compared with the length of body. The typically shaped body is covered with tiny scales and alternate black and white bands. The dorsal fin runs the full length of the body and extends around the rear end of the fish to the caudal fin, as does the shorter anal fin.

• **HABITAT** Widespread in reefs of the Red Sea and Indo-Pacific.

• **REMARK** Like other members of the family, the Girdled Moray will normally only present its head, the remainder being hidden behind rocks. A nocturnal species, it can only be kept with larger fish in a large covered aquarium.

Diet Carnivorous	Tank level Lower	Temperament

Family MURAENIDAE	Species *Muraena lentiginosa*	Size 24 in (60 cm)

JEWEL MORAY EEL

This brown eel is covered with dark-edged yellowish "stars" that are arranged in rows and extend into the fins. The dorsal, anal, and caudal fins are contiguous. There are no scales, and the nostrils are characteristically tubular. The powerful jaws are filled with sharp teeth.

• **HABITAT** Sea caves and crevices from the Gulf of California south to Peru.

• **REMARK** A specimen fish for the large aquarium, the Jewel Moray Eel should be handled with care.

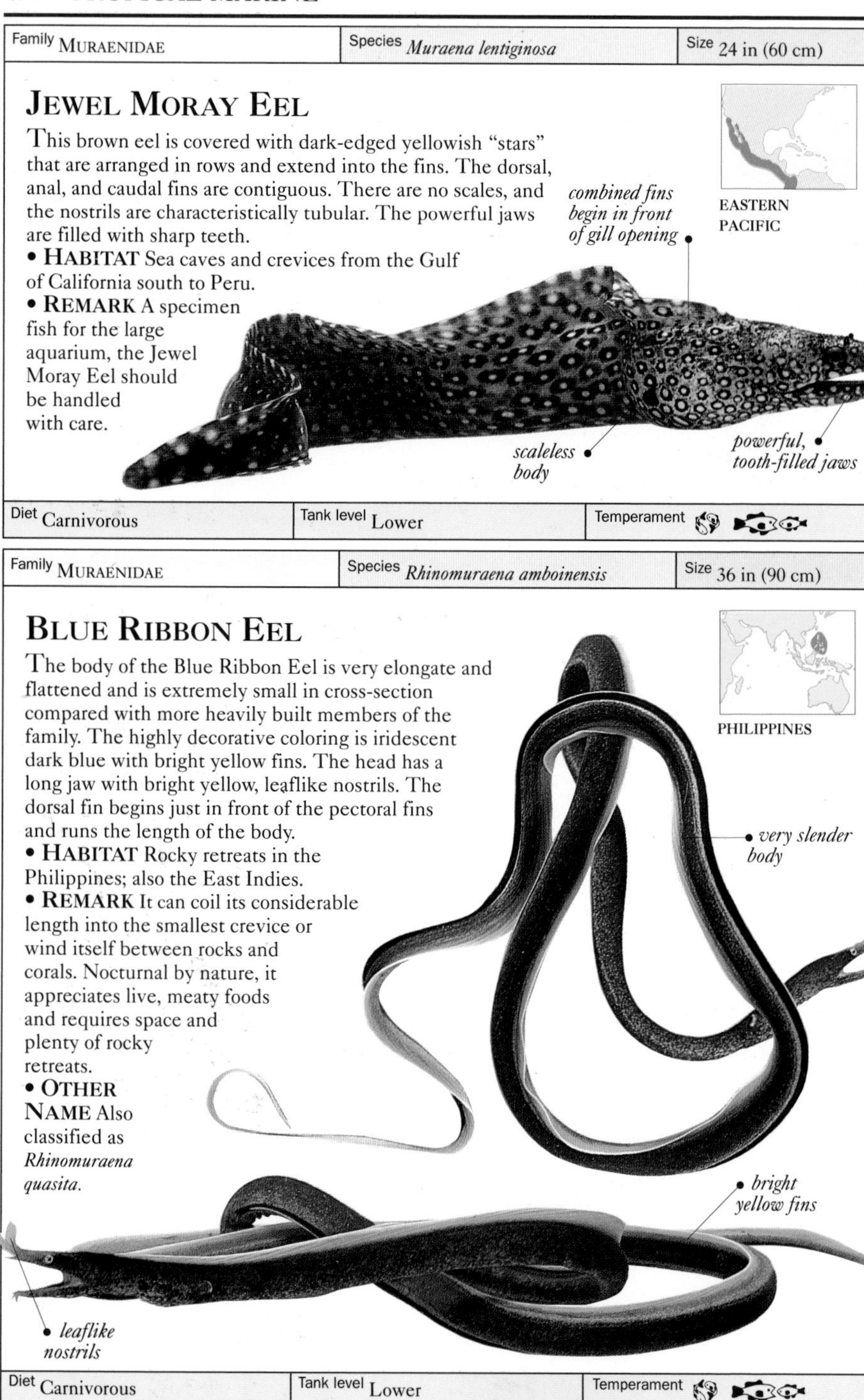

Diet Carnivorous	Tank level Lower	Temperament

Family MURAENIDAE	Species *Rhinomuraena amboinensis*	Size 36 in (90 cm)

BLUE RIBBON EEL

The body of the Blue Ribbon Eel is very elongate and flattened and is extremely small in cross-section compared with more heavily built members of the family. The highly decorative coloring is iridescent dark blue with bright yellow fins. The head has a long jaw with bright yellow, leaflike nostrils. The dorsal fin begins just in front of the pectoral fins and runs the length of the body.

• **HABITAT** Rocky retreats in the Philippines; also the East Indies.

• **REMARK** It can coil its considerable length into the smallest crevice or wind itself between rocks and corals. Nocturnal by nature, it appreciates live, meaty foods and requires space and plenty of rocky retreats.

• **OTHER NAME** Also classified as *Rhinomuraena quasita.*

Diet Carnivorous	Tank level Lower	Temperament

PIPEFISHES

THE COLORFUL MEMBERS of the pipefish and seahorse family (Syngnathidae) will live contentedly in reef-type aquariums in which invertebrates are present. Some pipefishes inhabit estuaries and are able to tolerate water of varying salt content. All these fishes have small mouths and require small types of live foods – brine shrimp and livebearer fry are ideal.

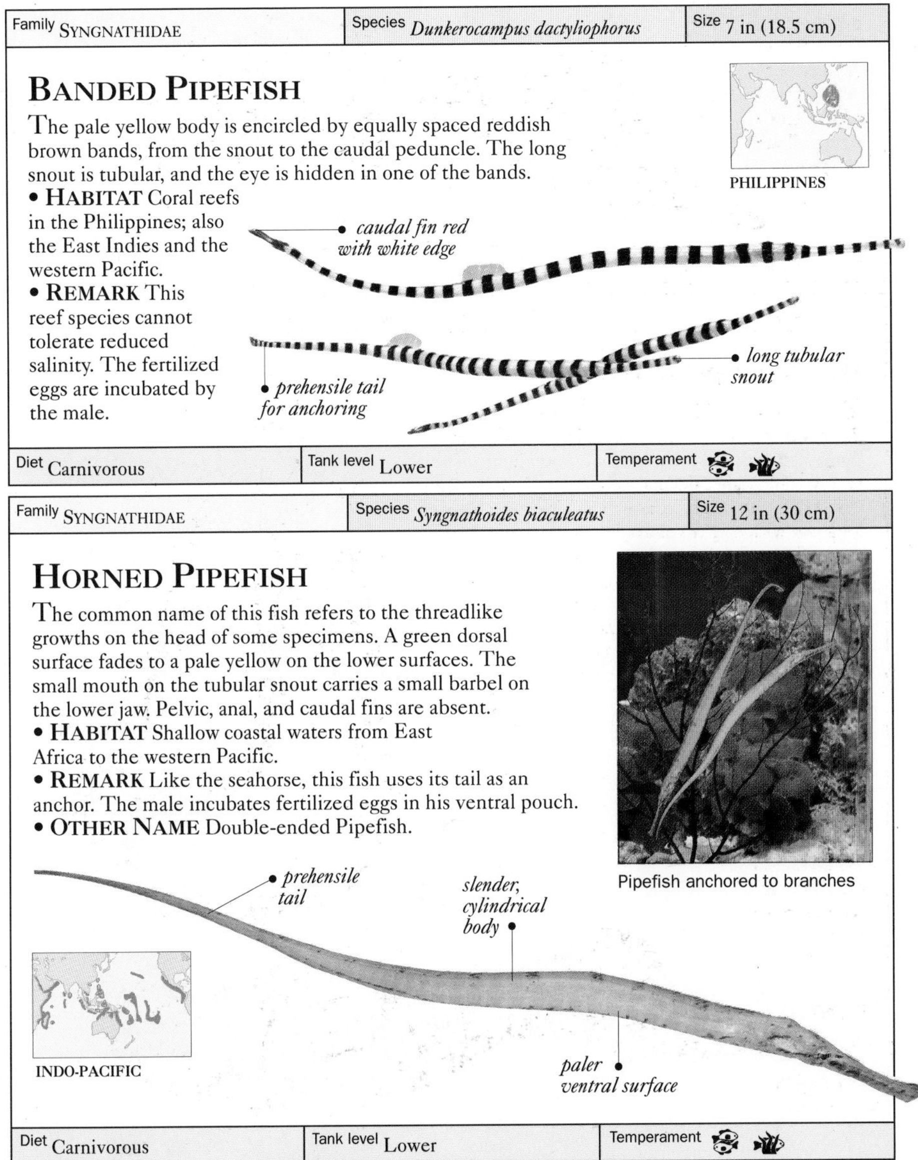

Family SYNGNATHIDAE	Species *Dunkerocampus dactyliophorus*	Size 7 in (18.5 cm)

BANDED PIPEFISH

The pale yellow body is encircled by equally spaced reddish brown bands, from the snout to the caudal peduncle. The long snout is tubular, and the eye is hidden in one of the bands.

• **HABITAT** Coral reefs in the Philippines; also the East Indies and the western Pacific.

• **REMARK** This reef species cannot tolerate reduced salinity. The fertilized eggs are incubated by the male.

Diet Carnivorous	Tank level Lower	Temperament

Family SYNGNATHIDAE	Species *Syngnathoides biaculeatus*	Size 12 in (30 cm)

HORNED PIPEFISH

The common name of this fish refers to the threadlike growths on the head of some specimens. A green dorsal surface fades to a pale yellow on the lower surfaces. The small mouth on the tubular snout carries a small barbel on the lower jaw. Pelvic, anal, and caudal fins are absent.

• **HABITAT** Shallow coastal waters from East Africa to the western Pacific.

• **REMARK** Like the seahorse, this fish uses its tail as an anchor. The male incubates fertilized eggs in his ventral pouch.

• **OTHER NAME** Double-ended Pipefish.

Pipefish anchored to branches

Diet Carnivorous	Tank level Lower	Temperament

Family SYNGNATHIDAE	Species *Hippocampus kuda*	Size 10 in (25 cm)

SEA HORSE

The Sea Horse's swimming position is vertical, with slight inclinations forward or backward, depending on direction of travel. The body is covered with armored plates. An equinelike head set at right angles to the body ends in a long tubular snout. A bony "coronet" may develop on the head.

• **HABITAT** Shallow coastal waters throughout the Indo-Pacific.

• **REMARK** *Hippocampus kuda* is unavailable in the USA, but *H. erectus,* or Northern Sea Horse, a dark sea horse with similar habits to *H. kuda*, is found in tropical and temperate waters of the western Atlantic. Females deposit eggs in the male's abdominal pouch from which fry emerge weeks later. Feed live foods such as small fishes or crustaceans.

INDO-PACIFIC

high-set eyes for good field of vision

bony "coronet"

long, tubular snout

ridges and rings of armored plates

prehensile tail acts as anchor

Diet Small, live foods	Tank levels Middle and lower	Temperament  

PORCUPINEFISHES AND PUFFERFISHES

THE LATIN FAMILY name of this group, Diodontidae, means "two teeth," as the front teeth of these fishes are fused together, giving the impression of a single top and bottom tooth. The scales are covered with sharp spines that create a formidable deterrent against predators when the fish is inflated. Pufferfishes (family Tetradontidae) have four teeth – two on each jaw. Both families enjoy small meaty foods.

Family DIODONTIDAE	Species *Diodon holocanthus*	Size 20 in (50 cm)

BALLOONFISH

The golden brown body of the Balloonfish has a pale underside, and dark dots are widely spaced over the body. The pectoral fins are large, but pelvic fins are absent. Dorsal and anal fins are set back on the body, and the caudal fin is rounded. This fish carries its spines folded against the body but will inflate itself when frightened.

- **HABITAT** Seaweed and near-shore rocky beds in the Indo-Pacific; also the Atlantic Ocean.
- **REMARK** Crustaceans, shellfish, and other invertebrate life will be eaten and should be excluded from the aquarium.

Diet Carnivorous	Tank level Lower	Temperament

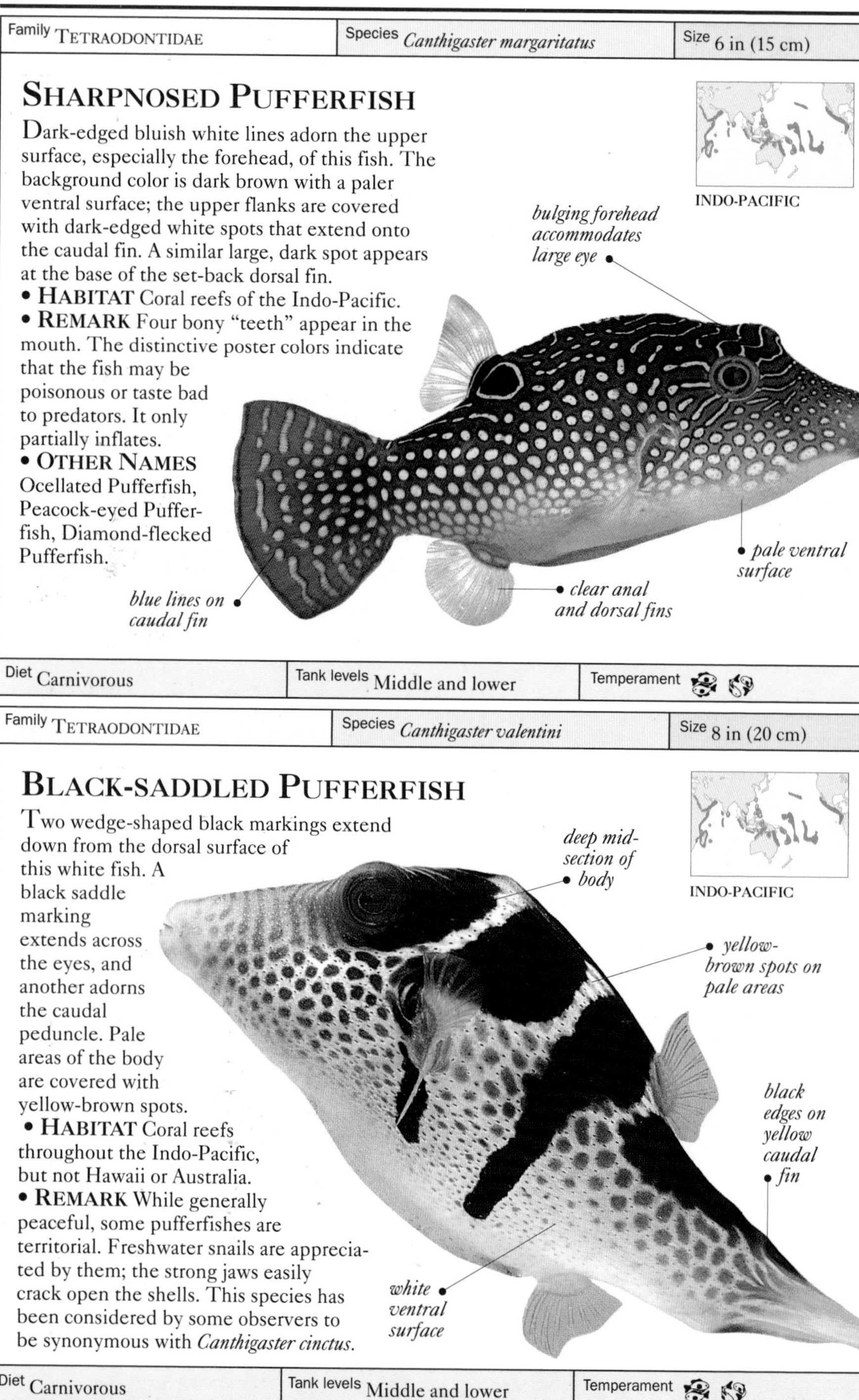

Family TETRAODONTIDAE	Species *Canthigaster margaritatus*	Size 6 in (15 cm)

SHARPNOSED PUFFERFISH

Dark-edged bluish white lines adorn the upper surface, especially the forehead, of this fish. The background color is dark brown with a paler ventral surface; the upper flanks are covered with dark-edged white spots that extend onto the caudal fin. A similar large, dark spot appears at the base of the set-back dorsal fin.

• **HABITAT** Coral reefs of the Indo-Pacific.

• **REMARK** Four bony "teeth" appear in the mouth. The distinctive poster colors indicate that the fish may be poisonous or taste bad to predators. It only partially inflates.

• **OTHER NAMES** Ocellated Pufferfish, Peacock-eyed Pufferfish, Diamond-flecked Pufferfish.

Diet Carnivorous	Tank levels Middle and lower	Temperament

Family TETRAODONTIDAE	Species *Canthigaster valentini*	Size 8 in (20 cm)

BLACK-SADDLED PUFFERFISH

Two wedge-shaped black markings extend down from the dorsal surface of this white fish. A black saddle marking extends across the eyes, and another adorns the caudal peduncle. Pale areas of the body are covered with yellow-brown spots.

• **HABITAT** Coral reefs throughout the Indo-Pacific, but not Hawaii or Australia.

• **REMARK** While generally peaceful, some pufferfishes are territorial. Freshwater snails are appreciated by them; the strong jaws easily crack open the shells. This species has been considered by some observers to be synonymous with *Canthigaster cinctus*.

Diet Carnivorous	Tank levels Middle and lower	Temperament

RABBITFISHES AND RAZORFISHES

THE RABBITFISHES (family Siganidae), carry poisonous spines on their dorsal and anal fins. Juveniles tend to be more colorful than adults, and all require space and vegetable foods. The razorfishes (family Centriscidae) are adapted for concealment among sea urchin spines. Dorsal, caudal, and anal fins are hidden by a bony back covering, the tip of which is spiny.

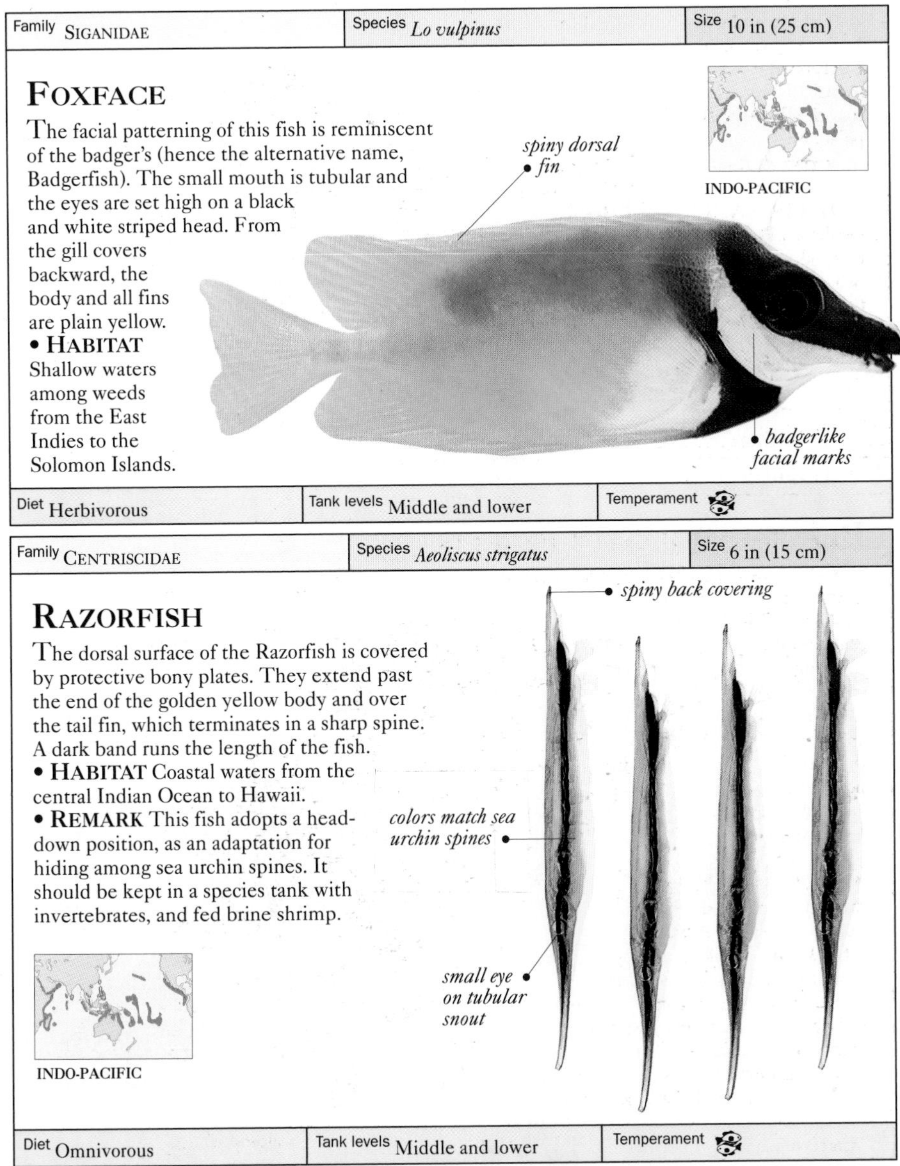

Family SIGANIDAE	Species *Lo vulpinus*	Size 10 in (25 cm)

FOXFACE

The facial patterning of this fish is reminiscent of the badger's (hence the alternative name, Badgerfish). The small mouth is tubular and the eyes are set high on a black and white striped head. From the gill covers backward, the body and all fins are plain yellow.

• **HABITAT** Shallow waters among weeds from the East Indies to the Solomon Islands.

Diet Herbivorous	Tank levels Middle and lower	Temperament

Family CENTRISCIDAE	Species *Aeoliscus strigatus*	Size 6 in (15 cm)

RAZORFISH

The dorsal surface of the Razorfish is covered by protective bony plates. They extend past the end of the golden yellow body and over the tail fin, which terminates in a sharp spine. A dark band runs the length of the fish.

• **HABITAT** Coastal waters from the central Indian Ocean to Hawaii.

• **REMARK** This fish adopts a head-down position, as an adaptation for hiding among sea urchin spines. It should be kept in a species tank with invertebrates, and fed brine shrimp.

Diet Omnivorous	Tank levels Middle and lower	Temperament

SQUIRRELFISHES

THE FAMILY HOLOCENTRIDAE is made up of several large-eyed schooling fishes. Its members are widely distributed in all warm seas. They patrol the aquarium in numbers at night but generally hide away from view among retreats during the daytime. Squirrelfishes are usually red, although each species is distinguished by variations in a white patterning.

Family HOLOCENTRIDAE	Species *Holocentrus diadema*	Size 12 in (30 cm)

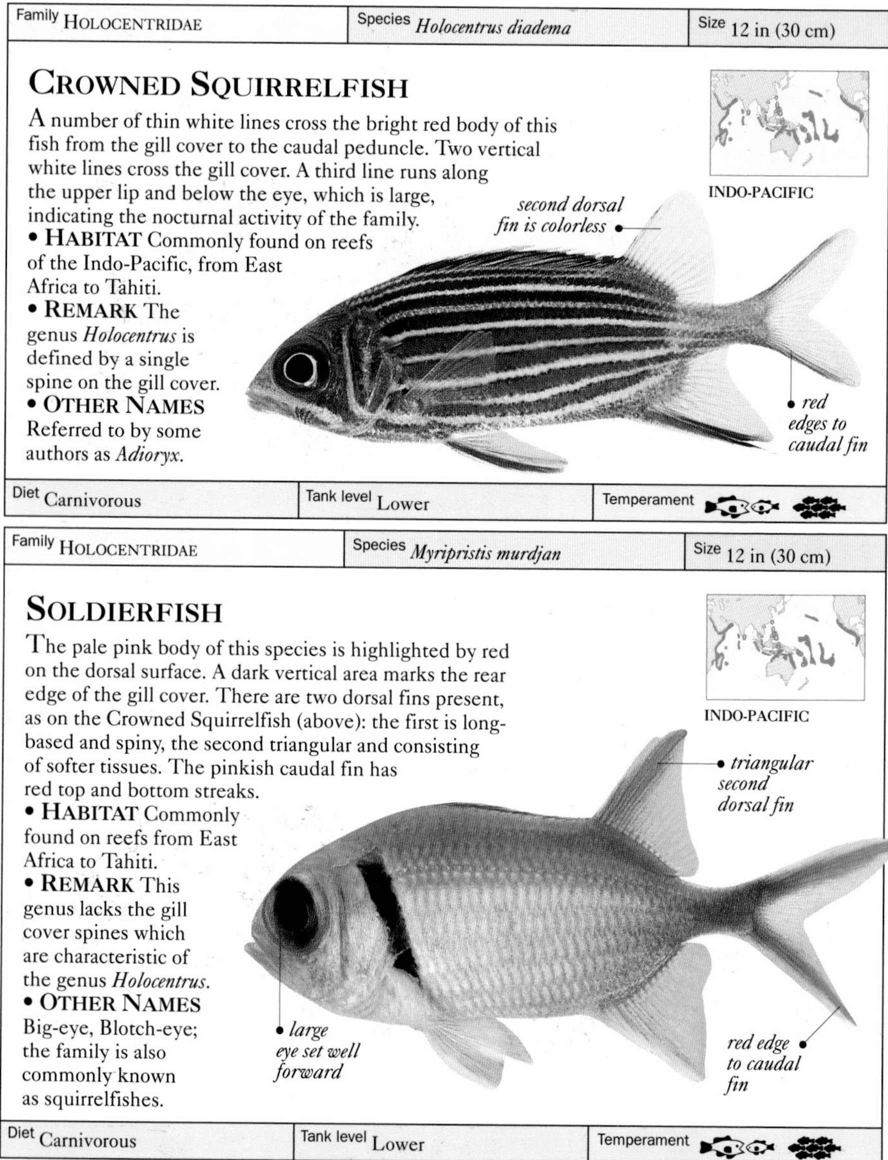

CROWNED SQUIRRELFISH

A number of thin white lines cross the bright red body of this fish from the gill cover to the caudal peduncle. Two vertical white lines cross the gill cover. A third line runs along the upper lip and below the eye, which is large, indicating the nocturnal activity of the family.

• **HABITAT** Commonly found on reefs of the Indo-Pacific, from East Africa to Tahiti.

• **REMARK** The genus *Holocentrus* is defined by a single spine on the gill cover.

• **OTHER NAMES** Referred to by some authors as *Adioryx*.

Diet Carnivorous	Tank level Lower	Temperament

Family HOLOCENTRIDAE	Species *Myripristis murdjan*	Size 12 in (30 cm)

SOLDIERFISH

The pale pink body of this species is highlighted by red on the dorsal surface. A dark vertical area marks the rear edge of the gill cover. There are two dorsal fins present, as on the Crowned Squirrelfish (above): the first is long-based and spiny, the second triangular and consisting of softer tissues. The pinkish caudal fin has red top and bottom streaks.

• **HABITAT** Commonly found on reefs from East Africa to Tahiti.

• **REMARK** This genus lacks the gill cover spines which are characteristic of the genus *Holocentrus*.

• **OTHER NAMES** Big-eye, Blotch-eye; the family is also commonly known as squirrelfishes.

Diet Carnivorous	Tank level Lower	Temperament

SWEETLIPS

JUVENILES OF THE family Haemulidae, commonly known as sweetlips, have an entirely different, less vivid, coloration from that of adults. Young sweetlips are excellent subjects for a large aquarium. All species originate in the Indo-Pacific. They are shy and require live foods. Sweetlips are considered by some to be a separate subfamily, Plectorhynchinae.

Family HAEMULIDAE	Species *Plectorhynchus chaetodonoides*	Size 17½ in (45 cm)

HARLEQUIN SWEETLIPS

The juvenile fish, as shown here, has a dark brown body with white patches, some with a brown central spot. The snout and mouth are covered by a white patch. The adult is gray and covered with small, dark red-brown spots. All fins are similarly colored.

• **HABITAT** Coral reefs from the East Indies and the Philippines to the central Pacific.

• **OTHER NAMES** Clown Sweetlips, Polka-dot Grunt.

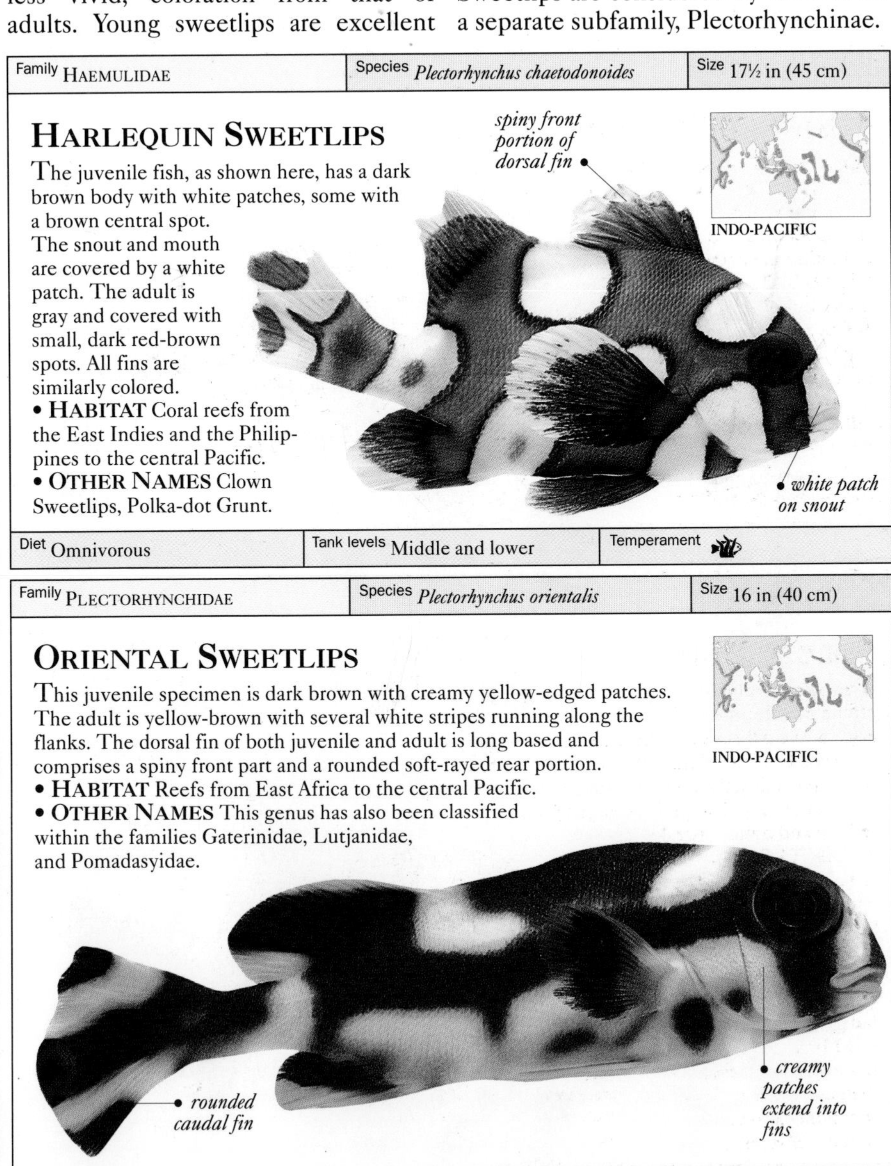

Diet Omnivorous	Tank levels Middle and lower	Temperament

Family PLECTORHYNCHIDAE	Species *Plectorhynchus orientalis*	Size 16 in (40 cm)

ORIENTAL SWEETLIPS

This juvenile specimen is dark brown with creamy yellow-edged patches. The adult is yellow-brown with several white stripes running along the flanks. The dorsal fin of both juvenile and adult is long based and comprises a spiny front part and a rounded soft-rayed rear portion.

• **HABITAT** Reefs from East Africa to the central Pacific.

• **OTHER NAMES** This genus has also been classified within the families Gaterinidae, Lutjanidae, and Pomadasyidae.

INDO-PACIFIC

Diet Omnivorous	Tank levels Middle and lower	Temperament

ZANCLIDAE

THE MOORISH IDOL shown below is the only species in the family Zanclidae. It is related to the family Acanthuridae, comprising surgeons and tangs, as can be seen in the physical similarity of the young. Juvenile Moorish Idols, however, lack scalpels on the caudal peduncle. Moorish Idols are schooling fishes, commonly found throughout the Indo-Pacific.

Family ZANCLIDAE	Species *Zanclus canescens*	Size 10 in (25 cm)

MOORISH IDOL

This monotypic species is very tall and laterally compressed. The pale yellow and white body is crossed vertically by dark bands that extend into the dorsal and anal fins. A yellow mark adorns the top of the extended snout beneath the steeply rising forehead. The bottom jaw is black. The dorsal fin has very long, extended rays and is white, black, and yellow. Mature adults carry tiny, distinctive, hornlike growths above the eye.

• **HABITAT** Coral reefs throughout the Indo-Pacific.

• **REMARK** This popular species is often difficult to acclimatize. It will not feed in aquariums if damage is caused by transportation in polluted shipping bags and may slowly decline from starvation.

• **OTHER NAME** Formerly classified as *Zanclus cornutus*.

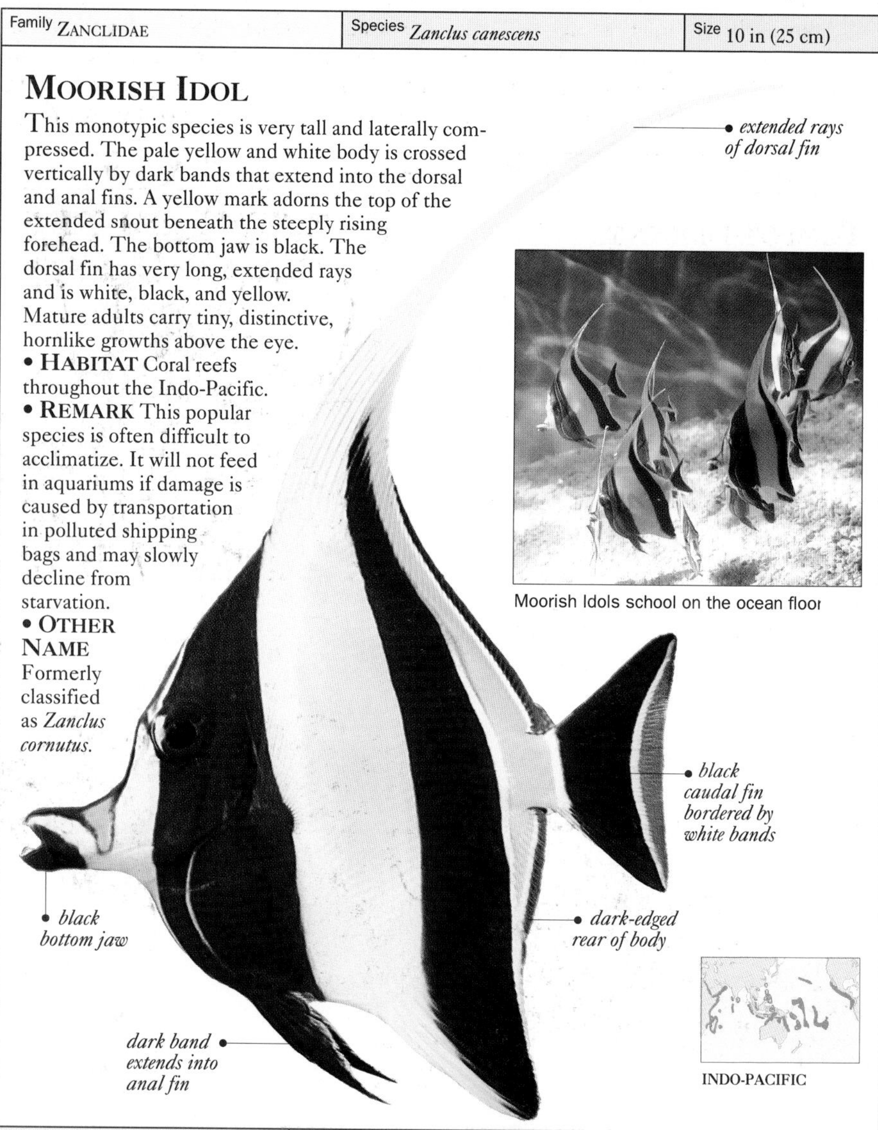

Moorish Idols school on the ocean floor

Diet Omnivorous	Tank levels Middle and lower	Temperament

COLDWATER MARINE FISHES

BLENNIES

COLDWATER MEMBERS of the family Blenniidae are active little fishes that scuttle around rocky crevices at the base of the aquarium. In nature, they are found in shallow coastal waters, often trapped in rock pools between tides. The characteristic growths (cirri) above the eye are one of the principal means of identification among these similarly colored species.

Family BLENNIIDAE	Species *Blennius gattorugine*	Size 8 in (20 cm)

TOMPOT BLENNY

The head is the deepest part of this fish's stocky body, which has reddish brown and white cross-banding on the flanks. The forehead rises steeply from a wide mouth. There are two branched, tentaclelike growths above the eyes known as cirri.

- **HABITAT** Shallow waters and rockpools of the eastern Atlantic Ocean, including the Mediterranean to the north of Scotland, but not the North Sea.
- **REMARK** Although territorial and likely to worry smaller fishes, the Tompot Blenny may itself be intimidated by larger fishes. A species aquarium would suit it well. This fish requires plenty of rocky retreats and feeds mainly on meaty foods. It can be hand-tamed.

Blennies hide in rocky retreats

MARITIME
W. EUROPE

Diet Omnivorous	Tank level Lower	Temperament 

Family LUMPENIDAE	Species *Chirolophis ascanii*	Size 10 in (25 cm)

YARRELL'S BLENNY

The pinkish brown body of this elongate fish is crossed by faint vertical bands. There are characteristic branched, reddish yellow tentacles above the eyes, plus smaller tentacles behind the nostrils. The dorsal fin has a few spiny rays at the front.

• **HABITAT** Shallow waters and rock pools of the eastern Atlantic around Britain and Norway; also Iceland.

• **REMARK** Requires suitable rocky furnishings, cold water, and good aeration.

• **OTHER NAME** It may also be classified in the family Sticheidae.

spiny rays at front of dorsal fin

branched tentacle above each eye

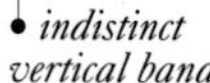

Diet Omnivorous	Tank level Lower	Temperament 

Family BLENNIIDAE	Species *Lipophrys pholis*	Size 6 in (15 cm)

SHANNY

A pattern of dark, blotchy bars is imposed on the stocky, creamy yellow body of the Shanny. Numerous tiny dark speckles appear between these bands. The long-based dorsal fin has a slight indentation halfway along its length. Pectoral fins are large and rounded, in contrast with the minimal pelvic fins.

• **HABITAT** Shallow waters and rock pools of the northeast Atlantic, as far south as Portugal and the Mediterranean.

• **REMARK** The male darkens during spawning. Eggs are laid under rocky overhangs or on cave ceilings and are guarded by the male. A Shanny needs rocky retreats and may continue to grow throughout its lifetime.

Empty shells provide a home

slight indentation along dorsal fin

white-lipped mouth

large, rounded pectoral fins

Diet Omnivorous	Tank level Lower	Temperament 

GOBIES AND CLINGFISHES

THE SCAVENGING MEMBERS of the goby family (Gobiidae) search constantly for food on rocky sea floors or in rock pools. Although similar in appearance to blennies, clingfishes (family Gobiesocidae) and gobies are easily recognized by their brighter coloration and by their pelvic fins, which combine to form suction disks. These disks prevent the fish from being dislodged by wave movements. Clingfishes spawn in the summer only.

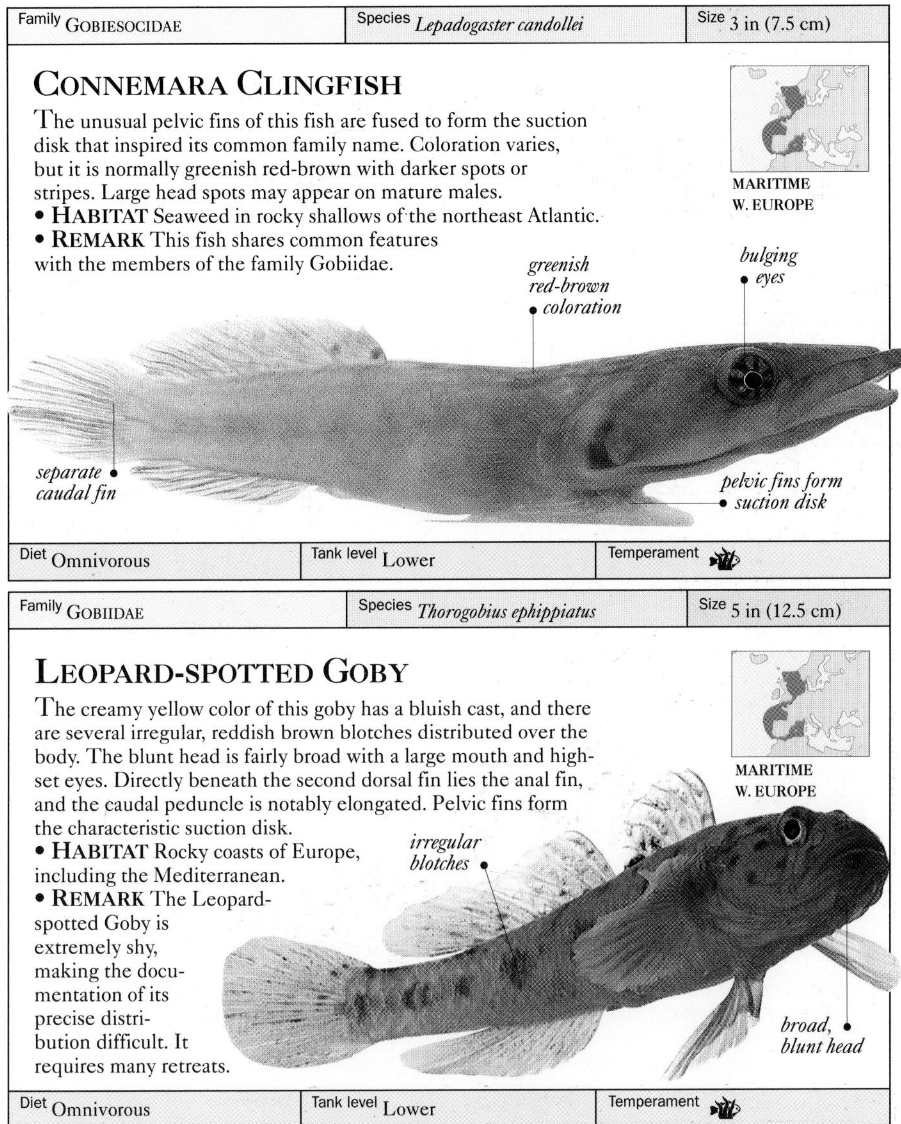

Family GOBIESOCIDAE	Species *Lepadogaster candollei*	Size 3 in (7.5 cm)

CONNEMARA CLINGFISH

The unusual pelvic fins of this fish are fused to form the suction disk that inspired its common family name. Coloration varies, but it is normally greenish red-brown with darker spots or stripes. Large head spots may appear on mature males.

- **HABITAT** Seaweed in rocky shallows of the northeast Atlantic.
- **REMARK** This fish shares common features with the members of the family Gobiidae.

Diet Omnivorous	Tank level Lower	Temperament

Family GOBIIDAE	Species *Thorogobius ephippiatus*	Size 5 in (12.5 cm)

LEOPARD-SPOTTED GOBY

The creamy yellow color of this goby has a bluish cast, and there are several irregular, reddish brown blotches distributed over the body. The blunt head is fairly broad with a large mouth and high-set eyes. Directly beneath the second dorsal fin lies the anal fin, and the caudal peduncle is notably elongated. Pelvic fins form the characteristic suction disk.

- **HABITAT** Rocky coasts of Europe, including the Mediterranean.
- **REMARK** The Leopard-spotted Goby is extremely shy, making the documentation of its precise distribution difficult. It requires many retreats.

Diet Omnivorous	Tank level Lower	Temperament

WRASSES

THE LARGE COLDWATER wrasse family (Labridae) offers a wide choice of species for aquarium culture, although in most cases only juveniles are suitable for captivity. A main attraction of the juveniles is the cleaning service they provide to other fish. Fortunately, the juvenile phase is often the most colorful period of the wrasses' lives. In adulthood, patterns and colors may change, and sometimes become much duller. Colors can vary between the sexes and sometimes alter with the fish's moods and the color of the substrate. Males may alter color at breeding times, and sex changes among these species are fairly common. Aquarium wrasses tend to be active during the day and bury themselves in the substrate at night.

Family LABRIDAE	Species *Centrolabrus exoletus*	Size 7 in (17.5 cm)

ROCK COCK

This deep-bodied fish is brown on the dorsal surface, yellow on the flank, and silvery white on the belly. There may be some speckling. The flanks become iridescent blue on a spawning male. The terminal mouth is especially small, and violet lines adorn the throat. The anal fin has several spines at its front, and a dark bar crosses the base of the caudal peduncle.

• **HABITAT** Seaweed in shallows from Norway to the Bay of Biscay, excluding the southern North Sea.

• **REMARK** The Rock Cock is usually active during the day but rests among rocks at night.

• **OTHER NAME** Small-mouthed Wrasse.

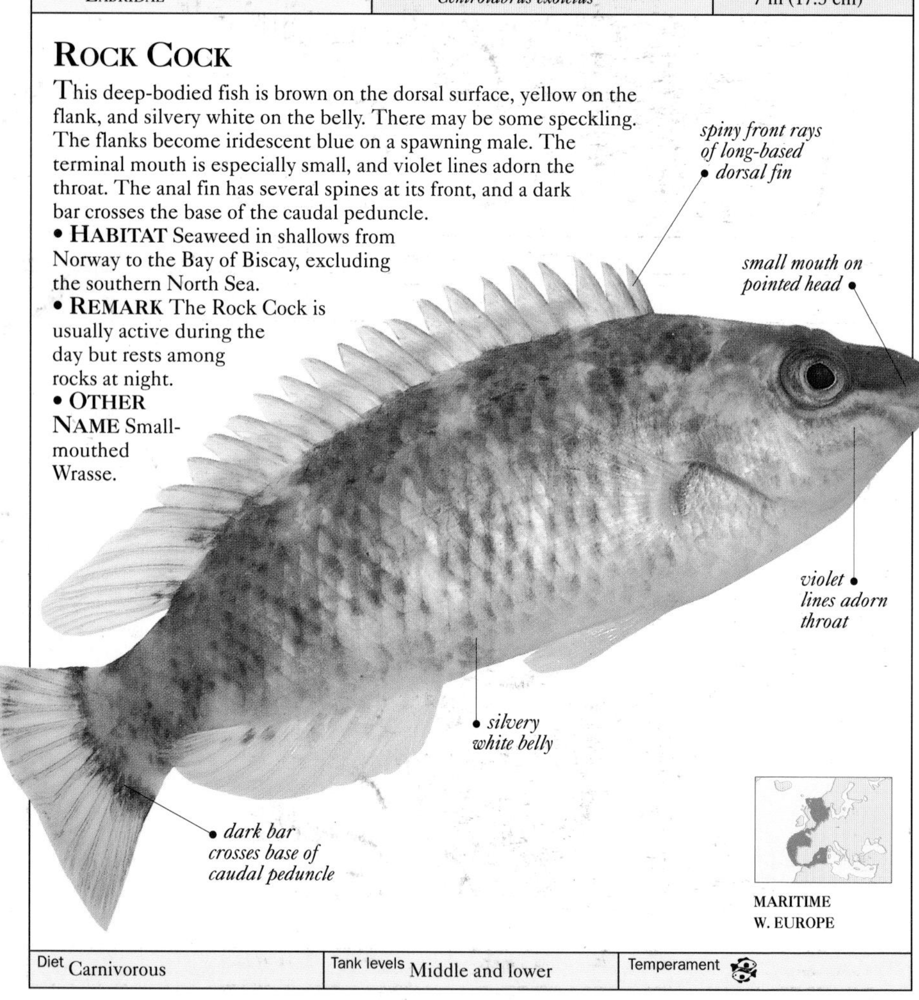

MARITIME W. EUROPE

Diet Carnivorous	Tank levels Middle and lower	Temperament

Family LABRIDAE	Species *Centrolabrus melops*	Size 10 in (25 cm)

CORKWING WRASSE

The Corkwing Wrasse's coloration is variable, depending on age and season. Males are usually creamy brown with reddish brown horizontal stripes, but when breeding they show blue iridescences on the flanks and blue facial markings. Females are generally much duller – usually a plain brown color.

• **HABITAT** Seaweed in shallow waters and rock pools in the English Channel and the Mediterranean; also from the Faroe Islands to the Azores in the eastern Atlantic.

• **REMARK** This is probably the most common wrasse in European waters. It builds a nest from algae in which it spawns.

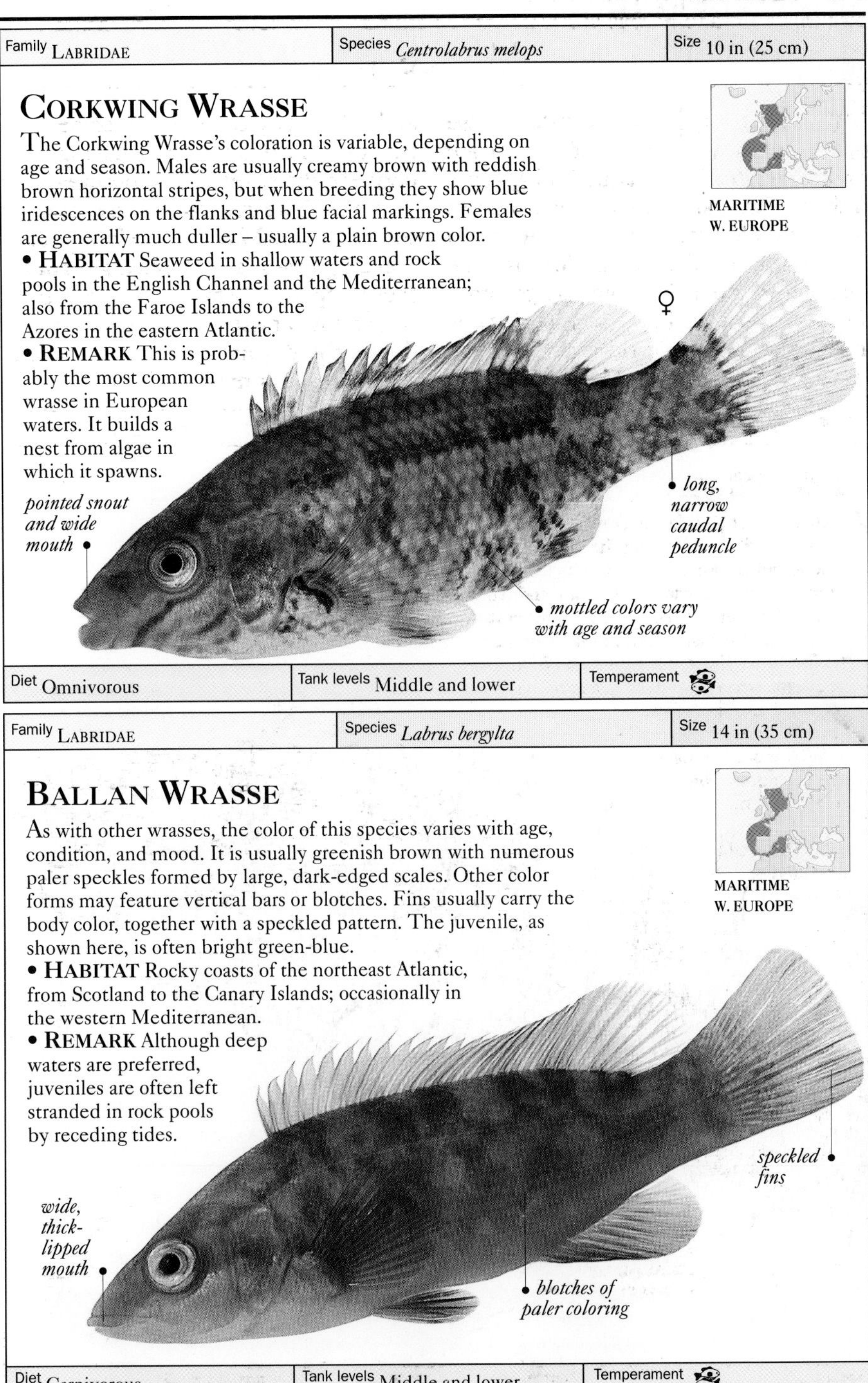

Diet Omnivorous	Tank levels Middle and lower	Temperament

Family LABRIDAE	Species *Labrus bergylta*	Size 14 in (35 cm)

BALLAN WRASSE

As with other wrasses, the color of this species varies with age, condition, and mood. It is usually greenish brown with numerous paler speckles formed by large, dark-edged scales. Other color forms may feature vertical bars or blotches. Fins usually carry the body color, together with a speckled pattern. The juvenile, as shown here, is often bright green-blue.

• **HABITAT** Rocky coasts of the northeast Atlantic, from Scotland to the Canary Islands; occasionally in the western Mediterranean.

• **REMARK** Although deep waters are preferred, juveniles are often left stranded in rock pools by receding tides.

Diet Carnivorous	Tank levels Middle and lower	Temperament

SCORPIONFISHES AND SEA SCORPIONS

THE FAMILIES SCORPAENIDAE and Triglidae consist of sedentary fishes that lie on the substrate waiting for prey, in the form of other fishes, to pass by. They are camouflaged with varying blotches and stripes. The decorative spines of Scorpionfishes are highly venomous and should be handled with caution. Sea scorpions are, on the other hand, harmless.

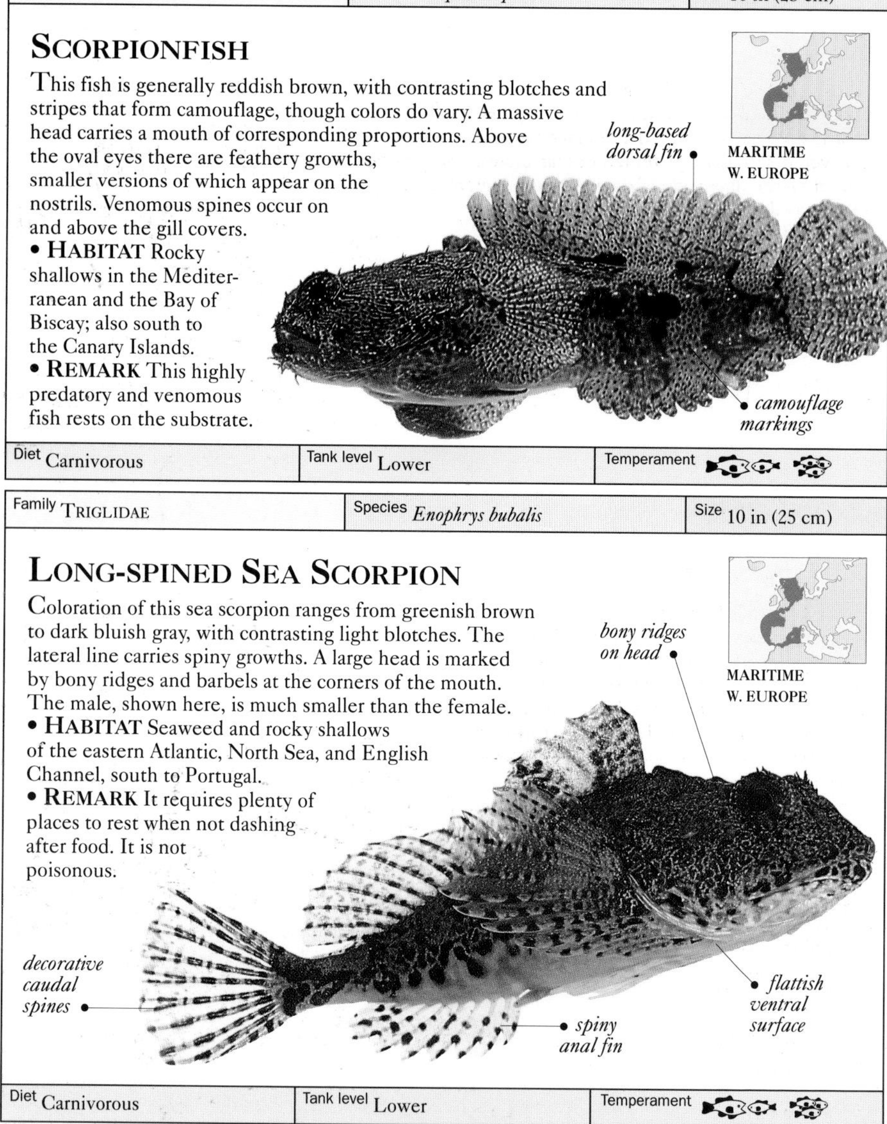

Family SCORPAENIDAE	Species *Scorpaena species*	Size 10 in (25 cm)

SCORPIONFISH

This fish is generally reddish brown, with contrasting blotches and stripes that form camouflage, though colors do vary. A massive head carries a mouth of corresponding proportions. Above the oval eyes there are feathery growths, smaller versions of which appear on the nostrils. Venomous spines occur on and above the gill covers.

- **HABITAT** Rocky shallows in the Mediterranean and the Bay of Biscay; also south to the Canary Islands.
- **REMARK** This highly predatory and venomous fish rests on the substrate.

Diet Carnivorous	Tank level Lower	Temperament

Family TRIGLIDAE	Species *Enophrys bubalis*	Size 10 in (25 cm)

LONG-SPINED SEA SCORPION

Coloration of this sea scorpion ranges from greenish brown to dark bluish gray, with contrasting light blotches. The lateral line carries spiny growths. A large head is marked by bony ridges and barbels at the corners of the mouth. The male, shown here, is much smaller than the female.

- **HABITAT** Seaweed and rocky shallows of the eastern Atlantic, North Sea, and English Channel, south to Portugal.
- **REMARK** It requires plenty of places to rest when not dashing after food. It is not poisonous.

Diet Carnivorous	Tank level Lower	Temperament

OTHER COLDWATER MARINE FISHES

THE FOLLOWING SELECTION includes fishes that may be found in temperate rock pools and coastal waters of Europe and its environs. It is presented as an inspirational token of the diverse and interesting species that can be found in similar waters of other geographical locations. When collecting from the wild, however, it is always vital to leave the habitat undisturbed.

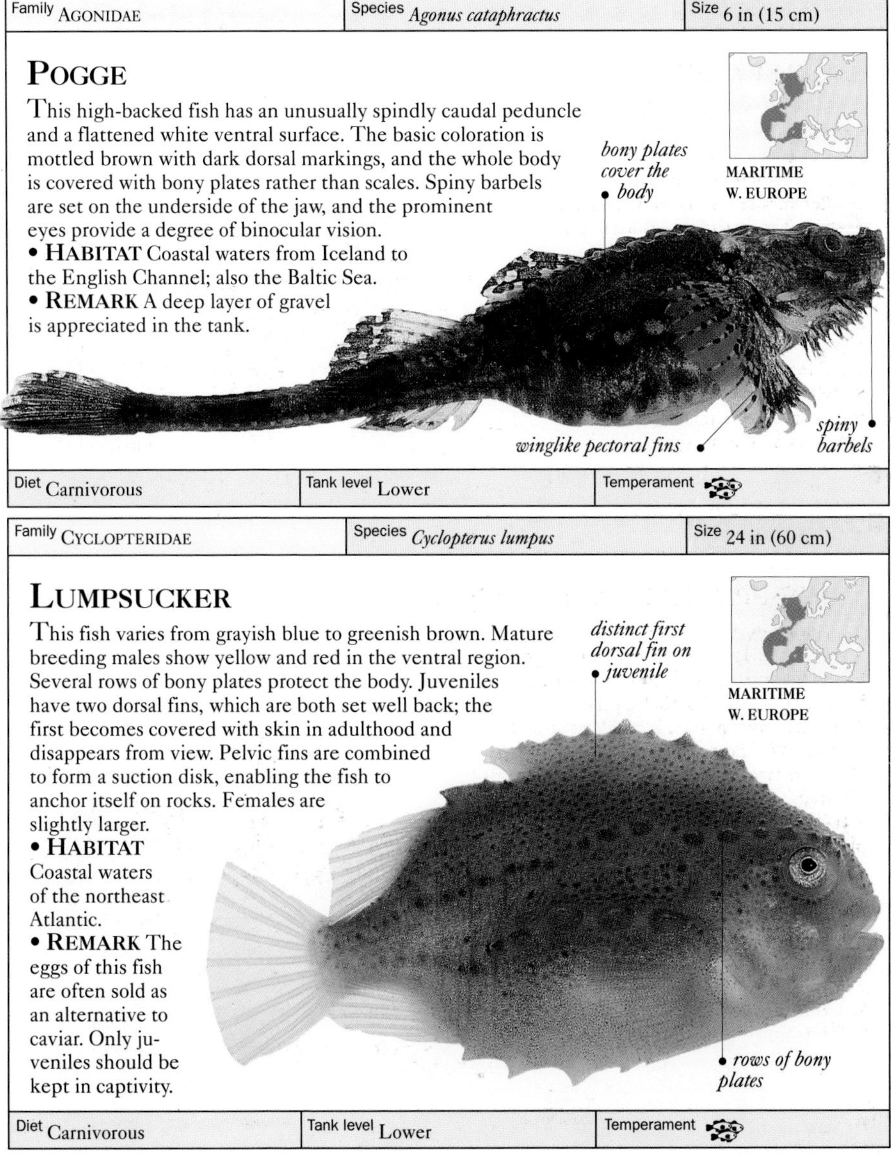

Family AGONIDAE	Species *Agonus cataphractus*	Size 6 in (15 cm)

POGGE

This high-backed fish has an unusually spindly caudal peduncle and a flattened white ventral surface. The basic coloration is mottled brown with dark dorsal markings, and the whole body is covered with bony plates rather than scales. Spiny barbels are set on the underside of the jaw, and the prominent eyes provide a degree of binocular vision.

- **HABITAT** Coastal waters from Iceland to the English Channel; also the Baltic Sea.
- **REMARK** A deep layer of gravel is appreciated in the tank.

Diet Carnivorous	Tank level Lower	Temperament

Family CYCLOPTERIDAE	Species *Cyclopterus lumpus*	Size 24 in (60 cm)

LUMPSUCKER

This fish varies from grayish blue to greenish brown. Mature breeding males show yellow and red in the ventral region. Several rows of bony plates protect the body. Juveniles have two dorsal fins, which are both set well back; the first becomes covered with skin in adulthood and disappears from view. Pelvic fins are combined to form a suction disk, enabling the fish to anchor itself on rocks. Females are slightly larger.

- **HABITAT** Coastal waters of the northeast Atlantic.
- **REMARK** The eggs of this fish are often sold as an alternative to caviar. Only juveniles should be kept in captivity.

Diet Carnivorous	Tank level Lower	Temperament

Family GASTEROSTEIDAE	Species *Spinachia spinachia*	Size 8 in (20 cm)

FIFTEEN-SPINED STICKLEBACK

The fifteen spines that gave this fish its common name are the remnants of the spiny front of the dorsal fin. The body is spindly with a flattened head and long caudal peduncle. Coloration is dark greenish brown, but males show a bluish sheen when spawning. Small dorsal and anal fins are set opposite each other, well back on the body, and the rudimentary pelvic fin is composed of only a single spine and ray. The caudal fin is small and rounded.

• **HABITAT** Seaweed in shallows of the northeast Atlantic, from the Bay of Biscay to Norway, including the North and Baltic Seas.

• **REMARK** It can tolerate brackish water. All sticklebacks require small live foods.

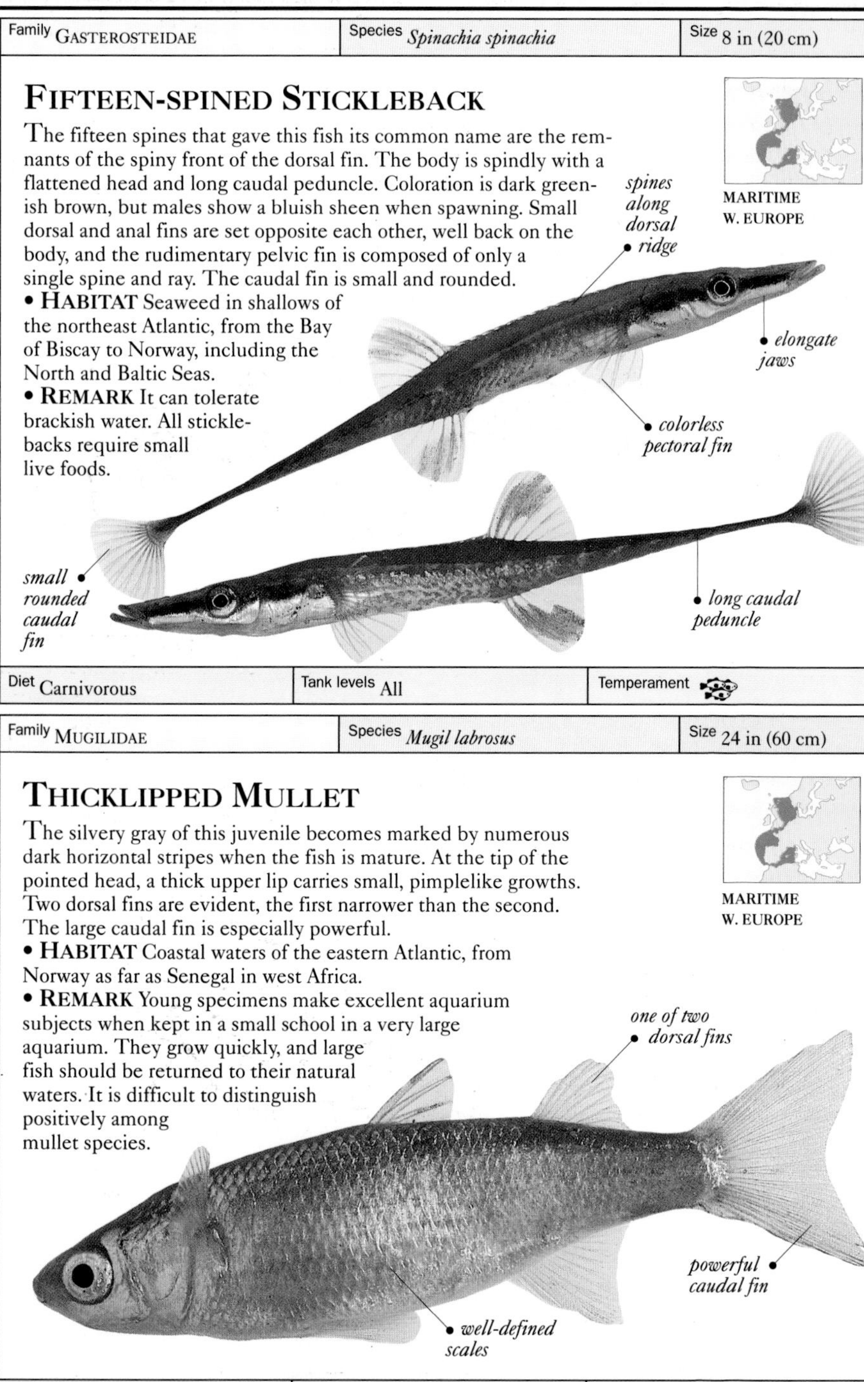

Diet Carnivorous	Tank levels All	Temperament

Family MUGILIDAE	Species *Mugil labrosus*	Size 24 in (60 cm)

THICKLIPPED MULLET

The silvery gray of this juvenile becomes marked by numerous dark horizontal stripes when the fish is mature. At the tip of the pointed head, a thick upper lip carries small, pimplelike growths. Two dorsal fins are evident, the first narrower than the second. The large caudal fin is especially powerful.

• **HABITAT** Coastal waters of the eastern Atlantic, from Norway as far as Senegal in west Africa.

• **REMARK** Young specimens make excellent aquarium subjects when kept in a small school in a very large aquarium. They grow quickly, and large fish should be returned to their natural waters. It is difficult to distinguish positively among mullet species.

Diet Omnivorous	Tank level Middle	Temperament

Family PHOLIDIDAE	Species *Pholis gunnellus*	Size 10 in (25 cm)

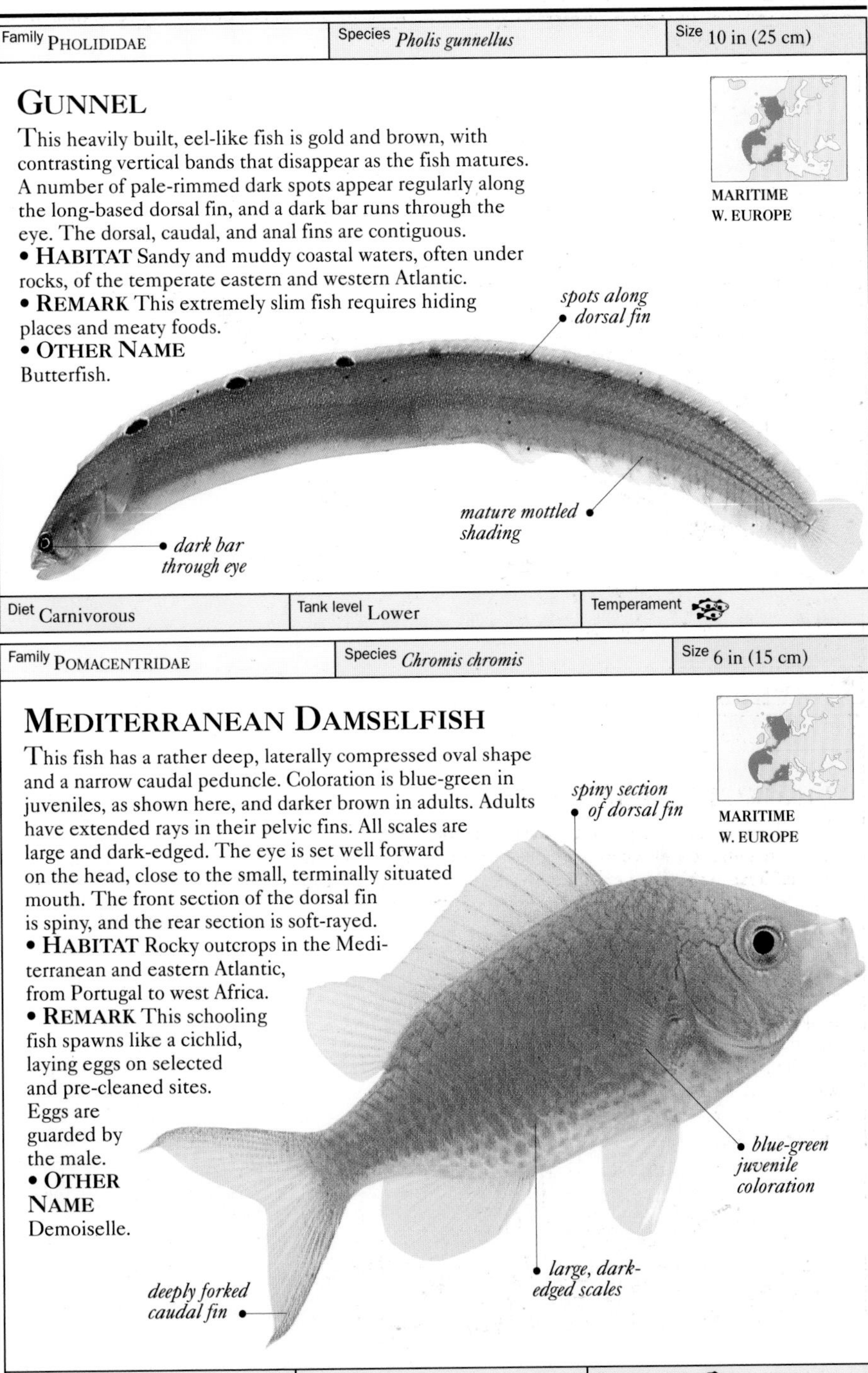

GUNNEL

This heavily built, eel-like fish is gold and brown, with contrasting vertical bands that disappear as the fish matures. A number of pale-rimmed dark spots appear regularly along the long-based dorsal fin, and a dark bar runs through the eye. The dorsal, caudal, and anal fins are contiguous.

• **HABITAT** Sandy and muddy coastal waters, often under rocks, of the temperate eastern and western Atlantic.

• **REMARK** This extremely slim fish requires hiding places and meaty foods.

• **OTHER NAME** Butterfish.

Diet Carnivorous	Tank level Lower	Temperament

Family POMACENTRIDAE	Species *Chromis chromis*	Size 6 in (15 cm)

MEDITERRANEAN DAMSELFISH

This fish has a rather deep, laterally compressed oval shape and a narrow caudal peduncle. Coloration is blue-green in juveniles, as shown here, and darker brown in adults. Adults have extended rays in their pelvic fins. All scales are large and dark-edged. The eye is set well forward on the head, close to the small, terminally situated mouth. The front section of the dorsal fin is spiny, and the rear section is soft-rayed.

• **HABITAT** Rocky outcrops in the Mediterranean and eastern Atlantic, from Portugal to west Africa.

• **REMARK** This schooling fish spawns like a cichlid, laying eggs on selected and pre-cleaned sites. Eggs are guarded by the male.

• **OTHER NAME** Demoiselle.

Diet Omnivorous	Tank level Lower	Temperament

GLOSSARY

WORDS PRINTED in bold type have their own definition elsewhere in the glossary.

• ACIDIC
Condition of water often due to decomposing vegetation or filtration through peat; pH balance is below 7. *See also* **Soft water**.

• ADIPOSE FIN
Small extra fin between **dorsal** and **caudal fins**.

• ADSORB
Collection of dissolved wastes by means of a suitable filter medium such as activated carbon.

• ALKALINE
Condition of water due to buildup of dissolved salts, usually calcium and magnesium; pH balance is above 7. *See also* **Hard water**.

• ANAL FIN
Single, vertical fin beneath the rear of the body.

• BARBEL
Whiskerlike growth around the mouth, used for locating food.

• BRACKISH
Mixture of fresh and salt water, found in estuaries.

• BRINE SHRIMP
Tiny saltwater crustaceans that make excellent first food for **fry**. Available live or frozen.

• BUBBLE NEST
Raft of bubbles that some fish use to protect eggs and **fry**.

• CAUDAL FIN
Tail fin, often divided into lobes.

• CAUDAL PEDUNCLE
Slender, muscular rear part of body, adjoining the tail.

• CIRRI
Branched, tentacle-like growths above the eyes of some **coldwater** marine fishes.

• COLDWATER FISH
Generally refers to fish kept under ambient temperatures, without additional heating.

• CULTIVATED
Aquarium-developed **strains** or **varieties** of fish, not found in nature. *See also* **Fancy**.

• DORSAL
Pertaining to top surface of a fish.

• DORSAL FIN
Single fin on the **dorsal** surface.

• EGG-LAYER
Fish whose eggs are fertilized and hatch externally.

• EGGSPOTS
Egg-shaped markings on the **anal fins** of male **mouth-brooders**.

• FAMILY
Group containing one or more **genera**. *See also* **Genus.**

• FANCY
Aquarium-developed **strains** or **varieties**. *See also* **Cultivated**.

• FRY
Newly hatched fish.

• GENUS (*pl.* GENERA)
Individual group within a **family**, containing one or more **species**.

• GILL
Respiratory organ used to extract dissolved oxygen from water.

• GILL COVER
See **Operculum.**

• GONOPODIUM
Modified **anal fin** of male **livebearing** fishes.

• GRAVID
Pregnant female **livebearer**, or female **egg-layer** full of ripe eggs.

• GUANIN
Crystals of urea deposited beneath the skin that bend and reflect light, causing iridescence.

• HARD WATER
Condition of water due to dissolved salts, usually of calcium and magnesium. *See also* **Alkaline**.

• LABYRINTH ORGAN
Auxiliary respiratory organ that allows some fish to "breathe" air.

• LATERAL LINE
Row of pores along the flanks, allowing the detection of vibrations, for navigation.

• LENGTH
Dimension of fish measured from snout to end of **caudal peduncle**; excludes **caudal fin.**

• LIVEBEARER
Fish that fertilizes and incubates eggs inside the female body.

• MILT
Fish sperm.

• MORPH
A natural color variant.

• MOUTH-BROODER
Species that incubates externally fertilized eggs and protects fry within the female throat cavity.

• NUCHAL HUMP
Pronounced forehead on mature male cichlids.

• OPERCULUM
Shiny bone covering gill opening; also called **gill cover**.

• PECTORAL FINS
Paired fins, one on each side of the head behind the **gill** opening.

• PELVIC FINS
Paired fins, ahead of the **anal fin**.

• PHARYNGEAL TEETH
Teeth in the throat of cyprinids.

• RAY
Tissue-supporting bone in fins.

• SALT
Usually refers to sodium chloride.

• SALT-MIX
Proprietary mixture of ingredients to make up artificial sea-water.

• SCALE
Small, protective platelet covering the fish's skin.

• SCALPEL
Sharp, retractable spine carried as a defense by surgeons and tangs.

• SCHOOL
Collection of fish swimming together, usually of one **species**.

• SCUTE
Overlapping bony plate (modified **scale**) covering the skin, found especially in catfishes.

• SOFT WATER
Condition of water due to lack of dissolved salts. *See also* **Acidic**.

• SPAWNING
Breeding.

• SPECIES
Group within a **genus**, the members of which share similar characteristics and that can breed successfully together.

• SPECIFIC GRAVITY (SG)
Density of a liquid containing dissolved minerals, compared with that of pure water.

• STRAIN
Aquarium-developed variant of a **species**. Same as **variety**.

• SUBSPECIES
Subgroup of a **species**, usually geographically separated.

• SUBSTRATE
Bottom material such as mud, gravel, rocks, or sand.

• SWIM BLADDER
Internal organ that automatically regulates neutral buoyancy.

• TUBERCLE
Small white pimple on the **gill covers** of many cyprinids, usually **spawning** males.

• VARIETY
See **Strain**.

• VENTRAL
Pertaining to underside of a fish.

Index

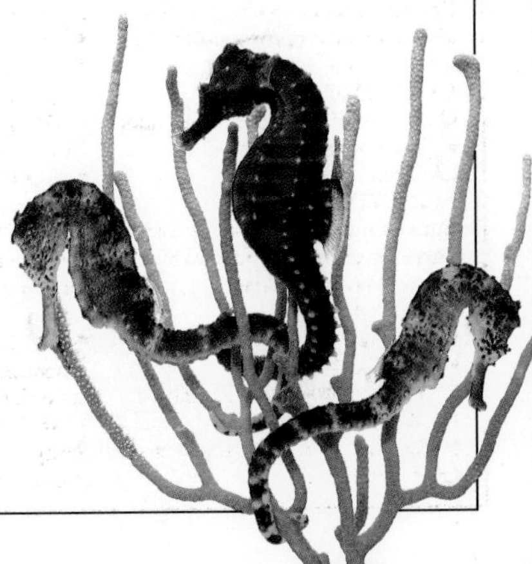

C

D

E

F

G

PQ

R

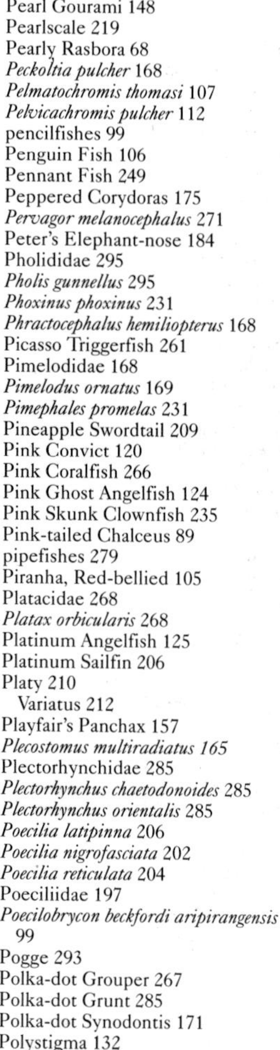

ACKNOWLEDGMENTS

The author would like to thank the following, without whom this book could not have been produced: Jane Cooke, Louise Bruce, Lesley Malkin, Spencer Holbrook, Jonathan Metcalf, Mary-Clare Jerram, and Gill Della Casa at Dorling Kindersley, Richmond; Jerry Young, our intrepid photographer; and Dr. Chris Andrews and Dr. Robert J. Goldstein for authentication.

Thanks also go to the following for providing fish for photographing and for offering invaluable advice: Keith Lambert of Wildwoods; Barry Jackson of Jackamoors; Max Gibbs of The Goldfish Bowl; Terry Jones of Wholesale Tropicals; Jimmy Croft & Paul Thomas of Waterworld; Dave & Mark Watkinson of Reef World; Simon Langdale of Iver Fishworld; Derek Lambert of Viviparous; Len Eldridge of the West London section of the British Killifish Association; fellow hobbyists within the Federation of British Aquatic Societies; South Park Aquatic Study Society; Isle of Wight Aquarist Society; Mike Quarm of the Sea Life Centre, Weymouth; Vernon Hunt of Portsmouth Aquarist Society; Oliver Crimmens of the Natural History Museum, London; and Andy Houghton. Finally, I could not have produced such a book without the full support and understanding of my wife, Janet.

Dorling Kindersley would like to thank: Michael Allaby for compiling the index; Charles Astwood for page makeup assistance; Caroline Church for the endpapers; Neal Cobourne for the jacket design; Julia Pashley for picture research; Alastair Wardle for DTP management, maps, and fonts; Angeles Gavira, Lucinda Hawksley, Constance Novis, Bella Pringle, and Helen Townsend for additional editorial assistance; Elaine Hewson, Chris Legee, Shaun Mc Nally, Sharon Moore, and Ann Thomson for extra design help.

All specially commissioned photography by Jerry Young, except for the following (a=all, i=inset, m=main): Derek Lambert 100t, 193t, 198t, 199, 200b, 202b, 203b; The Goldfish Bowl 10tl, 20tl, 54b, 66b, 87b, 99t, 190t, 218t, 228b, 232t, 252b, 254, 255b; Jane Burton/Kim Taylor 15, 20bl, 22br, 23cr, 24, 25(all food pics), 28a, 29a, 31rb, 32a, 33a, 34, 262t, 263b, 276t, 295t; Colin Keates 34tr; Dave King 3, 8bl, 14br, 15tr, 15tl, 25br, 30l, 40tc, 44tc, 106b, 121b, 122, 178t, 186b, 196i, 242b, 243b, 248b, 259t, 271b, 281t, 283b, 292t, 297, 302.

The publishers would also like to thank the following for permission to reproduce the photographs and illustrations indicated below: Ardea 18br, 264i (P. Morris), 235i (Ron & Valerie Taylor); Camera Press Ltd 8br; Bruce Coleman 231t (John Anthony), 26tl, 62i, 80i, 85i, 194i, 214c, 288i (Jane Burton), 225i (Eric Crichton), 31t (Adrian Davies), 30b (C.B. & D.W. Frith), 27t (Jennifer Fry), 26bl (M.P. Price), 85b, 103t, 147i, 191i, 231 (Hans Reinhard), 30t (Carl Roessler), 287i (John Taylor), 16t (Kim Taylor), 265b (Bill Wood); Mary Evans Picture Library 7a; The Goldfish Bowl 9m, 11tr, 20r, 27b, 34cl, 54i, 66i, 67b, 88t, 90t, 110t, 113i, 128i, 141, 154i, 164i, 170i, 184i, 194, 224i, 234t, 240t, 258b, 260t, 262b, 263t, 266m, 270b, 272i, 274t, 276t, 279b, 279i, 282t, 286m; Michael Holford 6b; Derek Lambert 16b, 27c, 36b, 42b; Dick Mills 9i, 18bc, 18bl, 19t, 73b, 129t, 145t, 202t, 215b, 228t, 272b, 275i, 286i; Oxford Scientific Films 115i (Max Gibbs); Planet Earth Pictures 250b (Ken Lucas), 126i (Paulo Oliviera), 266i (Peter Scoones); William Tomey 90b, 91b, 104b, 151t; A. van den Nieuwenhuizen 16a, 57t, 94b, 103b, 104t, 185b, 254i.

Illustrations by: King & King Design Associates 11, 12t, 12bl, 13t; Linden Artists Ltd 21a (Stewart Lafford).